Windows PowerShell Cookbook

SECOND EDITION

Windows PowerShell Cookbook

Lee Holmes

Beijing · Cambridge · Farnham · Köln · Sebastopol · Tokyo

Windows PowerShell Cookbook, Second Edition

by Lee Holmes

Copyright © 2010 Lee Holmes. All rights reserved.
Printed in the United States of America.

Published by O'Reilly Media, Inc., 1005 Gravenstein Highway North, Sebastopol, CA 95472.

O'Reilly books may be purchased for educational, business, or sales promotional use. Online editions are also available for most titles (*http://my.safaribooksonline.com*). For more information, contact our corporate/institutional sales department: (800) 998-9938 or *corporate@oreilly.com*.

Editor: Mike Hendrickson	**Indexer:** Newgen North America, Inc.
Production Editor: Teresa Elsey	**Cover Designer:** Karen Montgomery
Copyeditor: Genevieve d'Entremont	**Interior Designer:** David Futato
Proofreader: Teresa Elsey	**Illustrator:** Robert Romano

Printing History:

October 2007:	First Edition.
August 2010:	Second Edition.

ISBN: 978-0-596-80150-2

[LSI]   [2011-02-25]

1298459841

Table of Contents

Part I. Tour

Part II. Fundamentals

Part IV.   Administrator Tasks

Part V. References

Foreword

As someone who has written, or contributed to, more than a dozen books, I am well aware of the incredible amount of work and monumental commitment of time and resources involved with writing a book. That someone would choose to do this at essentially the same time one is burning the midnight oil while developing one of the most exciting products in Microsoft's history bespeaks a most committed person. However, more than simple commitment is involved. From my conversations with Lee, I can tell that he is passionate about Windows PowerShell. He sees the revolutionary changes introduced with the 2.0 release of the product. If Windows PowerShell 1.0 was the concept, Windows PowerShell 2.0 is the answer. If Windows PowerShell 1.0 was the vision, Windows PowerShell 2.0 is the reality. If Windows PowerShell 1.0 was for early adopters, Windows PowerShell 2.0 is moving into the mainstream.

With the inclusion of Windows PowerShell 2.0 in Windows 7 and Windows Server 2008 R2, we are beginning to see the commitment Microsoft is making to the product. That the SharePoint, SQL, Exchange, Active Directory Domain Services (AD DS), Internet Information Server (IIS) teams, and others have all made cmdlets should tell you that Windows PowerShell is not a passing fad. Windows PowerShell questions are already cropping up on Microsoft Certification Examinations, and as a network administrator or a consultant, you will need to learn Windows PowerShell.

Learning Windows PowerShell need not be tedious, boring, or exhausting. In fact, you will be joining a community that is at least as passionate about Windows PowerShell as Lee (or the rest of the Windows PowerShell team) or me (I write the *Hey, Scripting Guy!* blog seven days a week—the only Microsoft blog updated daily, by the way). What other product from Microsoft has inspired a half dozen songs to be written about it? Not by the marketing department, but by people who fell in love with Windows PowerShell, or, better yet, to use the community term: *became addicted*.

I attended a recent SQL Saturday in Charlotte, North Carolina, because I wanted to meet and interact with members of the Windows PowerShell community. That is right: there is a huge group of hardcore SQL administrators who are adopting Windows PowerShell because of its cool server management capabilities. In addition, a project known as the SQL Server PowerShell Extensions (SQLPSX) module (available from CodePlex) has wrapped much of the SQL Management Objects (SMO) into more than

130 useful functions. This provides ease of use for people who are not experts with SQL SMO and Windows PowerShell. By leveraging modules, the community is taking advantage of one of the great new features of Windows PowerShell 2.0. In fact, there are more than 200 Windows PowerShell projects on CodePlex. One person presenting at SQL Saturday declared that the active Windows PowerShell community was one of the great strengths of Windows PowerShell. You are not alone when it comes to learning and implementing Windows PowerShell.

I do not own every Windows PowerShell book ever written. I have probably looked at most Windows PowerShell books, but I found some of them redundant and some others confusing. However, a few of the Windows PowerShell books are essential. Lee's 1.0 version of this book fell into that category. I keep it within arm's length of my desk and grab it often. I have highlighted certain sections, dog-eared others, and placed sticky tabs on the more essential pages. Over the last couple years, Lee's *Windows PowerShell Cookbook* has grown to look more like a skinny porcupine on a bad hair day than a typical scripting book—and that is a good thing, because his book is not a typical scripting book; it is a cookbook. Just like a "real cookbook" that contains recipes for meals, this fascinating volume is what I find myself thumbing through when I am hungry to try something new with Windows PowerShell.

In reviewing Lee's upgraded *Windows PowerShell Cookbook*, I see that I will not be placed on a diet of "foo" and "bar"; instead, there are tasty morsels such as `Get-PageUrls`, a way-cool script that illustrates using regular expressions to extract URLs from a downloaded web page. It even fixes relative URLs so that they include the server from which they originated. All this happens faster than you can say "super useful" three times.

I found Chapter 14 on debugging to be well worth a careful read. Lee has a number of really good points, the premier one being: do not make the mistake in the first place. This echoes my own best practice. Of course, mistakes are made, errors are introduced, and that is when the debugger commands are called upon. Windows PowerShell 2.0 ships with some great debugging cmdlets, and Lee has some extremely cool scripts to simplify the process, or at least to reduce some of the tedium. I really like the `Watch-Expression` script because it automatically displays the values of expressions you wish to track.

If Chapter 14 is worth a careful read, Chapter 18 is worth a sticky tab because you will find yourself coming back to it often. Security and script signing is a subject of much debate in the Windows PowerShell community. You will want to hear about security from the horse's mouth. A common question I hear when giving presentations on Windows PowerShell is "How can I invoke a command as another user without switching contexts?" The genesis of this question is, of course, the Unix `sudo` command. Lee has a useful script named `Invoke-ElevatedCommand` that allows you to accomplish this task. Most excellent.

One other thing you need to read about is the Windows PowerShell Integrated Scripting Environment (ISE), in Chapter 19. A common request for years was for Microsoft to write a script editor. For years, I have been telling people we did write a script *editor*— Notepad. The Windows PowerShell ISE is much better than Notepad. Not only is the Windows PowerShell ISE a great script editor in its own right, but the Windows PowerShell team also exposed an object model that allows you to modify its behavior and to configure it to work in the way you wish to work. Lee has a whole section in Chapter 19 that talks about the ISE and how to modify it.

Working with files, directories, the registry, services, processes, WMI, remoting, transactions, and event handling—it is all in this book. I am not going to go over all that, because I do not want to spoil the plot. Suffice it to say that once this book sees print, it will rapidly join its dog-eared younger brother in that small collection of Windows PowerShell books that I consider essential.

—Ed Wilson
Microsoft Scripting Guy and author of *Windows PowerShell 2.0 Best Practices*

Foreword to the First Edition

When Lee asked me to write the foreword to his new book I was pleasantly surprised. I was under the impression that forewords were written by people who were respected and accomplished in their chosen field. Apparently, that isn't the case at all. My closest brush with accomplishment and respect came at a New Year's celebration long ago and involved hairspray and a butane lighter. I guess it doesn't matter too much—I mean, who reads the foreword to a scripting book anyway, right?

Lee wanted one of the Microsoft Scripting Guys to write the foreword. He wrote this book for the same hard-working admin scripters who frequent the TechNet Script Center. Lee thought it would make sense to have an original member of that team provide some perspective on where Windows admin scripting has been and where, with Windows PowerShell, it is going.

A lot has happened since Lee and I first spoke about this. I've left the Microsoft Scripting Guys team to work on the WMI SDK, and the Scripting Guys name has become a bit of a joke, given that the current driving force behind the team is a slight, half-sandwich-eating lady named Jean Ross. For now, Jean is keeping Greg around to do menial labor like packing up and shipping Dr. Scripto bobblehead dolls, but we'll just see what happens when he finally runs out of topics for his *Hey, Scripting Guy* column. The future of scripting could very well be The Scripting Girl.

Glue, Enablers, and a WSH

Whenever I think "perspective" and "scripting"—which is far too often—I think Bob Wells. Bob takes his scripting very seriously and has been promoting it inside and outside of Microsoft for years. When I joined the Scripting Guys team, Bob would preach to me about "glue" and "enablers." It took some time before I understood why he was talking about it so often and why finding just the right term for enablers was so important to him. I now know that it's because crisply defining these two concepts establishes a simple, useful framework in which to think about admin scripting. The glue part is the scripting language itself—the *foreach*s, *if*s, and *var*s.

It's what you use to orchestrate, or glue together, the set of subtasks you need to do to complete a larger task. The enablers (and, no, we never came up with a better term for them) are the instruments that actually accomplish each of the subtasks.

This table lists the glue and enablers that we, as Windows scripters, have had available to us over the years.

Glue	Enabler
Cmd.exe batch language	Command-line tools (OS, ResKit, Support Tools)
WSH	Command-line tools (OS, ResKit, Support Tools)
	Automation-enabled COM objects (WMI, ADSI)
Windows PowerShell	Command-line tools (OS, ResKit, Support Tools)
	Automation-enabled COM objects (WMI, ADSI)
	.NET Framework Class Library

Notice how each new environment lets you work with the enablers of the previous environment. This is important because it lets you carry forward your hard-earned knowledge. Objectively, we can say that WSH scripting is more powerful than batch scripting because it provides access to more enablers. You can automate more tasks because you have access to the additional functionality exposed by automatable COM objects. Less objectively, you could argue that even if you're only going to use command-line tools as enablers, WSH is a better choice than batch because it provides some really useful glue functionality; advances in available enablers make more things possible while advances in glue (sometimes) make things more convenient.

WSH scripting is a pretty capable environment. The WMI and ADSI COM libraries alone provide admins around the world with countless cycles of pain and elation. But there's always that pesky task that you just can't do with WSH, or that requires you to download a tool from some strangely named website at 2 a.m., when you really shouldn't be making decisions about what to install on your production servers. If only VBScript included the infamous Win32 API among its enablers, then, like those strange creatures known as developers, you could do *anything*.

Well, in developer land these days, the .NET Framework Class Library (FCL) is the new Win32 API. So, what we really need is a scripting environment that includes the FCL as an enabler. That's exactly what Windows PowerShell does. In fact, Windows PowerShell runs in the same environment as that library and, as a result, works seamlessly with it. I read a lot of press about the object-pipelining capabilities of Windows PowerShell. Those capabilities are very cool and represent an excellent advance in the glue department—an advance that certainly makes working with the FCL more natural. But the addition of the FCL as an enabler is the thing that makes Jeffrey et al.'s creation objectively more powerful than WSH. And even if you don't run into anything in the FCL that you need right away, it's comforting to know that when you make an investment and develop expertise in this latest environment, you gain access to all the enablers that your developer counterparts currently have or will have in the foreseeable future. It should also be comforting to know that if you spend the time to learn Windows PowerShell, that knowledge should last you as long as the .NET Framework lasts Microsoft.

Windows PowerShell follows in the tradition of WSH by improving on the glue aspect of its predecessor. One of the real pain points of working with COM objects in WSH was finding out what properties and methods were available. Unless you shelled out the bucks for a smart editor, you lost a lot of productivity context switching from writing a script and consulting documentation. Not so when working with objects in Windows PowerShell. Type this at a Windows PowerShell prompt:

```
$objShell = New-Object -com Shell.Application
$objShell | Get-Member
```

It does a scripter good, does it not?

That Lee Guy

Hopefully my rambling has convinced you that Windows PowerShell is a good thing and that it's worth your time to learn it. Now, why do I think you should learn it by buying and reading this book?

First off, I should tell you that the Windows PowerShell team is a bunch of odd ducks.* These folks are obsessed. From Jeffrey Snover on down, they are incredible teachers who love and believe in their technology so much that it's difficult to *stop* them from teaching you! Even among that bunch of quackers, Lee stands out. Have you ever heard the sound an Exchange server makes when it cringes? Well, ours cringe when Lee comes to work and starts answering questions on our internal Windows PowerShell mailing list. Lee has amassed unique knowledge about how to leverage Windows PowerShell to address problems that arise in the real world. And he and O'Reilly have done us a great service by capturing and sharing some of that knowledge in this book.

Windows system admin scripters are the coolest people on the planet. It continues to be a pleasure to work for you, and I sincerely hope you enjoy the book.

—Dean Tsaltas
Microsoft Scripting Guy Emeritus

---

* Canadian ducks (Canuck ducks) in many cases.

Preface

In late 2002, Slashdot posted a story about a "next-generation shell" rumored to be in development at Microsoft. As a longtime fan of the power unlocked by shells and their scripting language, the post immediately captured my interest. Could this shell provide the command-line power and productivity I'd long loved on Unix systems?

Since I had just joined Microsoft six months earlier, I jumped at the chance to finally get to the bottom of a Slashdot-sourced Microsoft Mystery. The post talked about strong integration with the .NET Framework, so I posted a query to an internal C# mailing list. I got a response that the project was called "Monad," which I then used to track down an internal prototype build.

Prototype was a generous term. In its early stages, the build was primarily a proof of concept. Want to clear the screen? No problem! Just lean on the Enter key until your previous commands and output scroll out of view! But even at these early stages, it was immediately clear that Monad marked a revolution in command-line shells. As with many things of this magnitude, its beauty was self-evident. Monad passed full-fidelity .NET objects between its commands. For even the most complex commands, Monad abolished the (until now, standard) need for fragile text-based parsing. Simple and powerful data manipulation tools supported this new model, creating a shell both powerful and easy to use.

I joined the Monad development team shortly after that to help do my part to bring this masterpiece of technology to the rest of the world. Since then, Monad has grown to become a real, tangible product—now called Windows PowerShell.

So why write a book about it? And why *this* book?

Many users have picked up PowerShell for the sake of learning PowerShell. Any tangible benefits come by way of side effect. Others, though, might prefer to opportunistically learn a new technology as it solves their needs. How do you use PowerShell to navigate the filesystem? How can you manage files and folders? Retrieve a web page?

This book focuses squarely on helping you learn PowerShell through task-based solutions to your most pressing problems. Read a recipe, read a chapter, or read the entire book—regardless, you're bound to learn something.

Who This Book Is For

This book helps you use PowerShell to *get things done*. It contains hundreds of solutions to specific, real-world problems. For systems management, you'll find plenty of examples that show how to manage the filesystem, the Windows Registry, event logs, processes, and more. For enterprise administration, you'll find two entire chapters devoted to WMI, Active Directory, and other enterprise-focused tasks.

Along the way, you'll also learn an enormous amount about PowerShell: its features, its commands, and its scripting language—but you'll most importantly solve problems.

How This Book Is Organized

This book consists of five main sections: a guided tour of PowerShell, PowerShell fundamentals, common tasks, administrator tasks, and a detailed reference.

Part I: Tour

A Guided Tour of Windows PowerShell breezes through PowerShell at a high level. It introduces PowerShell's core features:

- An interactive shell
- A new command model
- An object-based pipeline
- A razor-sharp focus on administrators
- A consistent model for learning and discovery
- Ubiquitous scripting
- Integration with critical management technologies
- A consistent model for interacting with data stores

The tour lets you become familiar with PowerShell as a whole. This familiarity will create a mental framework for you to understand the solutions from the rest of the book.

Part II: Fundamentals

Chapters 1 through 8 cover the fundamentals that underpin the solutions in this book. This section introduces you to the PowerShell interactive shell, fundamental pipeline and object concepts, and many features of the PowerShell scripting language.

Part III: Common Tasks

Chapters 9 through 19 cover the tasks you will run into most commonly when starting to tackle more complex problems in PowerShell. This includes working with simple and structured files, Internet-connected scripts, code reuse, user interaction, and more.

Part IV: Administrator Tasks

Chapters 20 through 31 focus on the most common tasks in systems and enterprise management. Chapters 20 through 25 focus on individual systems: the filesystem, the registry, event logs, processes, services, and more. Chapters 26 and 27 focus on Active Directory, as well as the typical tasks most common in managing networked or domain-joined systems.

Part V: References

Many books belch useless information into their appendixes simply to increase page count. In this book, however, the detailed references underpin an integral and essential resource for learning and using PowerShell. The appendixes cover:

- The PowerShell language and environment
- Regular expression syntax and PowerShell-focused examples
- XPath quick reference
- .NET string formatting syntax and PowerShell-focused examples
- .NET DateTime formatting syntax and PowerShell-focused examples
- Administrator-friendly .NET classes and their uses
- Administrator-friendly WMI classes and their uses
- Administrator-friendly COM objects and their uses
- Selected events and their uses
- PowerShell's standard verbs

What You Need to Use This Book

The majority of this book requires only a working installation of Windows PowerShell. Windows 7 and Windows Server 2008 R2 include Windows PowerShell by default. If you do not yet have PowerShell installed, you may obtain it by following the download link at *http://www.microsoft.com/PowerShell*. This link provides download instructions for PowerShell on Windows XP, Windows Server 2003, and Windows Vista. For Windows Server 2008, PowerShell comes installed as an optional component that you can enable through the Control Panel like other optional components.

The Active Directory scripts given in Chapter 26 are most useful when applied to an enterprise environment, but Recipe 26.1 shows how to install additional software (Active Directory Lightweight Directory Services, or Active Directory Application Mode) that lets you run these scripts against a local installation.

Conventions Used in This Book

The following typographical conventions are used in this book:

Plain text
: Indicates menu titles, menu options, menu buttons, and keyboard accelerators

Italic
: Indicates new terms, URLs, email addresses, filenames, file extensions, pathnames, directories, and Unix utilities

`Constant width`
: Indicates commands, options, switches, variables, attributes, keys, functions, types, classes, namespaces, methods, modules, properties, parameters, values, objects, events, event handlers, tags, macros, or the output from commands

`Constant width bold`
: Shows commands or other text that should be typed literally by the user

`Constant width italic`
: Shows text that should be replaced with user-supplied values

 This icon signifies a tip, suggestion, or general note.

 This icon indicates a warning or caution.

Code Examples

Obtaining Code Examples

To obtain electronic versions of the programs and examples given in this book, visit the *Examples* link at:

> *http://www.oreilly.com/catalog/9780596801519*

Using Code Examples

This book is here to help you get your job done. In general, you may use the code in this book in your programs and documentation. You do not need to contact us for permission unless you're reproducing a significant portion of the code. For example, writing a program that uses several chunks of code from this book does not require permission. Selling or distributing a CD-ROM of examples from O'Reilly books *does* require permission. Answering a question by citing this book and quoting example code does not require permission. Incorporating a significant amount of example code from this book into your product's documentation *does* require permission.

We appreciate, but do not require, attribution. An attribution usually includes the title, author, publisher, and ISBN. For example: "*Windows PowerShell Cookbook* by Lee Holmes. Copyright 2010 Lee Holmes, 978-0-596-80150-2."

If you feel your use of code examples falls outside fair use or the permission given, feel free to contact us at *permissions@oreilly.com*.

Comments and Questions

Please address comments and questions concerning this book to the publisher:

O'Reilly Media, Inc.
1005 Gravenstein Highway North
Sebastopol, CA 95472
800-998-9938 (in the United States or Canada)
707-829-0515 (international or local)

We have a web page for this book, where we list errata, examples, and any additional information. You can access this page at:

http://www.oreilly.com/catalog/9780596801502

To comment or ask technical questions about this book, send email to:

bookquestions@oreilly.com

For more information about our books, conferences, Resource Centers, and the O'Reilly Network, see our website at:

http://www.oreilly.com

Safari® Books Online

Safari Safari Books Online is an on-demand digital library that lets you easily search over 7,500 technology and creative reference books and videos to find the answers you need quickly.

With a subscription, you can read any page and watch any video from our library online. Read books on your cell phone and mobile devices. Access new titles before they are available for print, and get exclusive access to manuscripts in development and post feedback for the authors. Copy and paste code samples, download chapters, bookmark key sections, and benefit from tons of other time-saving features.

O'Reilly Media has uploaded this book to the Safari Books Online service. To have full digital access to this book and others on similar topics from O'Reilly and other publishers, sign up for free at *http://my.safaribooksonline.com*.

Acknowledgments

Writing is the task of crafting icebergs. The heft of the book you hold in your hands is just a hint of the multiyear, multirelease effort it took to get it there. And by a cast much larger than me.

The groundwork started decades ago. My parents nurtured my interest in computers and software, supported an evening-only bulletin board service, put up with "viruses" that told them to buy a new computer for Christmas, and even listened to me blather about batch files or how PowerShell compares to Excel. Without their support, who knows where I'd be.

My family and friends have helped keep me sane for two editions of the book now. Ariel: you are the light of my life. Robin: thinking of you reminds me each day that serendipity is still alive and well in this busy world. Thank you to all of my friends and family for being there for me. You can have me back now. :)

I would not have written either edition of this book without the tremendous influence of Guy Allen, visionary of the University of Toronto's Professional Writing program. Guy: your mentoring forever changed me, just as it molds thousands of others from English hackers into writers.

Of course, members of the PowerShell team (both new and old) are the ones that made this a book about PowerShell. Building this product with you has been a unique challenge and experience—but most of all, a distinct pleasure. In addition to the PowerShell team, the entire PowerShell community defined this book's focus. From MVPs, to early adopters, to newsgroup lurkers: your support, questions, and feedback have been the inspiration behind each page.

Converting thoughts into print always involves a cast of unsung heroes, even though each author tries his best to convince the world how important these heroes are.

Thank you to the many technical reviewers who participated in O'Reilly's Open Feedback Publishing System, especially Johannes Rössel, Aleksandar Nikolic, Jerome L. Cruz, David Moravec, Richard Siddaway, and Andrew Tearle. I truly appreciate you donating your nights and weekends to help craft something of which we can all be proud.

To the awesome staff at O'Reilly—Mike Hendrickson, Genevieve d'Entremont, Teresa Elsey, Laurel Ruma, the O'Reilly Tools Monks, and the production team—your patience and persistence helped craft a book that holds true to its original vision. You also ensured that the book didn't just knock around in my head but actually got out the door.

This book would not have been possible without the support from each and every one of you.

## PART I

Tour

A Guided Tour of Windows PowerShell

Introduction

Windows PowerShell promises to revolutionize the world of system management and command-line shells. From its object-based pipelines, to its administrator focus, to its enormous reach into other Microsoft management technologies, PowerShell drastically improves the productivity of administrators and power users alike.

When learning a new technology, it is natural to feel bewildered at first by all the unfamiliar features and functionality. This perhaps rings especially true for users new to Windows PowerShell because it may be their first experience with a fully featured command-line shell. Or worse, they've heard stories of PowerShell's fantastic integrated scripting capabilities and fear being forced into a world of programming that they've actively avoided until now.

Fortunately, these fears are entirely misguided; PowerShell is a shell that both grows with you and grows on you. Let's take a tour to see what it is capable of:

- PowerShell works with standard Windows commands and applications. You don't have to throw away what you already know and use.

- PowerShell introduces a powerful new type of command. PowerShell commands (called *cmdlets*) share a common *Verb-Noun* syntax and offer many usability improvements over standard commands.

- PowerShell understands objects. Working directly with richly structured objects makes working with (and combining) PowerShell commands immensely easier than working in the plain-text world of traditional shells.

- PowerShell caters to administrators. Even with all its advances, PowerShell focuses strongly on its use as an interactive shell: the experience of entering commands in a running PowerShell application.

- PowerShell supports discovery. Using three simple commands, you can learn and discover almost anything PowerShell has to offer.

- PowerShell enables ubiquitous scripting. With a fully fledged scripting language that works directly from the command line, PowerShell lets you automate tasks with ease.

- PowerShell bridges many technologies. By letting you work with .NET, COM, WMI, XML, and Active Directory, PowerShell makes working with these previously isolated technologies easier than ever before.

- PowerShell simplifies management of data stores. Through its provider model, PowerShell lets you manage data stores using the same techniques you already use to manage files and folders.

We'll explore each of these pillars in this introductory tour of PowerShell. If you are running Windows 7 or Windows 2008 R2, version two of PowerShell is already installed. If not, visit the download link at *http://www.microsoft.com/PowerShell* to install it. PowerShell and its supporting technologies are together referred to as the *Windows Management Framework*.

An Interactive Shell

At its core, PowerShell is first and foremost an interactive shell. While it supports scripting and other powerful features, its focus as a shell underpins everything.

Getting started in PowerShell is a simple matter of launching *PowerShell.exe* rather than *cmd.exe*—the shells begin to diverge as you explore the intermediate and advanced functionality, but you can be productive in PowerShell immediately.

To launch Windows PowerShell, do one of the following:

- Click Start→All Programs→Accessories→Windows PowerShell
- Click Start→Run, and then type "PowerShell"

A PowerShell prompt window opens that's nearly identical to the traditional command prompt window of Windows XP, Windows Server 2003, and their many ancestors. The PS C:\Documents and Settings\Lee> prompt indicates that PowerShell is ready for input, as shown in Figure T-1.

Once you've launched your PowerShell prompt, you can enter DOS-style and Unix-style commands to navigate around the filesystem just as you would with any Windows or Unix command prompt—as in the interactive session shown in Example T-1. In this example, we use the pushd, cd, dir, pwd, and popd commands to store the current location, navigate around the filesystem, list items in the current directory, and then return to the original location. Try it!

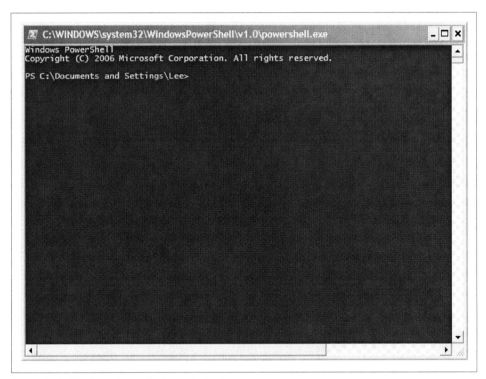

Figure T-1. Windows PowerShell, ready for input

Example T-1. Entering many standard DOS- and Unix-style file manipulation commands produces the same results you get when you use them with any other Windows shell

```
PS C:\Documents and Settings\Lee> function Prompt { "PS > " }
PS > pushd .
PS > cd \
PS > dir


    Directory: C:\


Mode                LastWriteTime     Length Name
----                -------------     ------ ----
d----         11/2/2006    4:36 AM            $WINDOWS.~BT
d----          5/8/2007    8:37 PM            Blurpark
d----         11/29/2006   2:47 PM            Boot
d----         11/28/2006   2:10 PM            DECCHECK
d----         10/7/2006    4:30 PM            Documents and Settings
d----          5/21/2007   6:02 PM            F&SC-demo
d----          4/2/2007    7:21 PM            Inetpub
d----          5/20/2007   4:59 PM            Program Files
d----          5/21/2007   7:26 PM            temp
d----          5/21/2007   8:55 PM            Windows
-a---          1/7/2006   10:37 PM          0 autoexec.bat
```

```
-ar-s          11/29/2006   1:39 PM         8192  BOOTSECT.BAK
-a---           1/7/2006   10:37 PM            0  config.sys
-a---           5/1/2007    8:43 PM        33057  RUU.log
-a---           4/2/2007    7:46 PM         2487  secedit.INTEG.RAW


PS > popd
PS > pwd

Path
----
C:\Documents and Settings\Lee
```

In this example, our first command customizes the prompt. In *cmd.exe*, customizing the prompt looks like `prompt $P$G`. In bash, it looks like `PS1="[\h] \w> "`. In PowerShell, you define a function that returns whatever you want displayed. Recipe 11.2 introduces functions and how to write them.

The `pushd` command is an alternative name (alias) to the much more descriptively named PowerShell command `Push-Location`. Likewise, the `cd`, `dir`, `popd`, and `pwd` commands all have more memorable counterparts.

Although navigating around the filesystem is helpful, so is running the tools you know and love, such as `ipconfig` and `notepad`. Type the command name and you'll see results like those shown in Example T-2.

Example T-2. Windows tools and applications such as ipconfig run in PowerShell just as they do in cmd.exe

```
PS > ipconfig

Windows IP Configuration


Ethernet adapter Wireless Network Connection 4:

        Connection-specific DNS Suffix . : hsd1.wa.comcast.net.
        IP Address. . . . . . . . . . . : 192.168.1.100
        Subnet Mask . . . . . . . . . . : 255.255.255.0
        Default Gateway . . . . . . . . : 192.168.1.1
PS > notepad
(notepad launches)
```

Entering `ipconfig` displays the IP addresses of your current network connections. Entering `notepad` runs—as you'd expect—the Notepad editor that ships with Windows. Try them both on your own machine.

Structured Commands (Cmdlets)

In addition to supporting traditional Windows executables, PowerShell introduces a powerful new type of command called a *cmdlet* (pronounced *command-let*). All cmdlets are named in a *Verb-Noun* pattern, such as Get-Process, Get-Content, and Stop-Process.

```
PS > Get-Process -Name lsass

Handles  NPM(K)    PM(K)    WS(K) VM(M)   CPU(s)     Id ProcessName
-------  ------    -----    ----- -----   ------     -- -----------
    668      13     6228     1660    46            932 lsass
```

In this example, you provide a value to the ProcessName parameter to get a specific process by name.

 Once you know the handful of common verbs in PowerShell, learning how to work with new nouns becomes much easier. While you may never have worked with a certain object before (such as a Service), the standard Get, Set, Start, and Stop actions still apply. For a list of these common verbs, see Table J-1 in Appendix J.

You don't always have to type these full cmdlet names, however. PowerShell lets you use the Tab key to auto-complete cmdlet names and parameter names:

```
PS > Get-Pr<TAB> -N<TAB> lsass
```

For quick interactive use, even that may be too much typing. To help improve your efficiency, PowerShell defines aliases for all common commands and lets you define your own. In addition to alias names, PowerShell only requires that you type enough of the parameter name to disambiguate it from the rest of the parameters in that cmdlet. PowerShell is also case-insensitive. Using the built-in gps alias (which represents the Get-Process cmdlet) along with parameter shortening, you can instead type:

```
PS > gps -n lsass
```

Going even further, PowerShell supports *positional parameters* on cmdlets. Positional parameters let you provide parameter values in a certain position on the command line, rather than having to specify them by name. The Get-Process cmdlet takes a process name as its first positional parameter. This parameter even supports wildcards:

```
PS > gps l*s
```

Deep Integration of Objects

PowerShell begins to flex more of its muscle as you explore the way it handles structured data and richly functional objects. For example, the following command generates a simple text string. Since nothing captures that output, PowerShell displays it to you:

```
PS > "Hello World"
Hello World
```

The string you just generated is, in fact, a fully functional object from the .NET Framework. For example, you can access its Length property, which tells you how many characters are in the string. To access a property, you place a dot between the object and its property name:

```
PS > "Hello World".Length
11
```

All PowerShell commands that produce output generate that output as objects as well. For example, the Get-Process cmdlet generates a System.Diagnostics.Process object, which you can store in a variable. In PowerShell, variable names start with a $ character. If you have an instance of Notepad running, the following command stores a reference to it:

```
$process = Get-Process notepad
```

Since this is a fully functional Process object from the .NET Framework, you can call methods on that object to perform actions on it. This command calls the Kill() method, which stops a process. To access a method, you place a dot between the object and its method name:

```
$process.Kill()
```

PowerShell supports this functionality more directly through the Stop-Process cmdlet, but this example demonstrates an important point about your ability to interact with these rich objects.

Administrators as First-Class Users

While PowerShell's support for objects from the .NET Framework quickens the pulse of most users, PowerShell continues to focus strongly on administrative tasks. For example, PowerShell supports MB (for megabyte) and GB (for gigabyte) as some of its standard administrative constants. For example, how many disks will it take to back up a 40 GB hard drive to CD-ROM?

```
PS > 40GB / 650MB
63.0153846153846
```

Although the .NET Framework is traditionally a development platform, it contains a wealth of functionality useful for administrators too! In fact, it makes PowerShell a great calendar. For example, is 2008 a leap year? PowerShell can tell you:

```
PS > [DateTime]::IsLeapYear(2008)
True
```

Going further, how might you determine how much time remains until summer? The following command converts "06/21/2011" (the start of summer) to a date, and then subtracts the current date from that. It stores the result in the $result variable, and then accesses the TotalDays property.

```
PS > $result = [DateTime] "06/21/2011" - [DateTime]::Now
PS > $result.TotalDays
283.0549285662616
```

Composable Commands

Whenever a command generates output, you can use a *pipeline character* (|) to pass that output directly to another command as input. If the second command understands the objects produced by the first command, it can operate on the results. You can chain together many commands this way, creating powerful compositions out of a few simple operations. For example, the following command gets all items in the *Path1* directory and moves them to the *Path2* directory:

```
Get-Item Path1\* | Move-Item -Destination Path2
```

You can create even more complex commands by adding additional cmdlets to the pipeline. In Example T-3, the first command gets all processes running on the system. It passes those to the Where-Object cmdlet, which runs a comparison against each incoming item. In this case, the comparison is $_.Handles -ge 500, which checks whether the Handles property of the current object (represented by the $_ variable) is greater than or equal to 500. For each object in which this comparison holds true, you pass the results to the Sort-Object cmdlet, asking it to sort items by their Handles property. Finally, you pass the objects to the Format-Table cmdlet to generate a table that contains the Handles, Name, and Description of the process.

Example T-3. You can build more complex PowerShell commands by using pipelines to link cmdlets, as shown in this example with Get-Process, Where-Object, Sort-Object, and Format-Table

```
PS > Get-Process |
   Where-Object { $_.Handles -ge 500 } |
   Sort-Object Handles |
   Format-Table Handles,Name,Description -Auto


Handles Name       Description
------- ----       -----------
    588 winlogon
    592 svchost
```

```
 667 lsass
 725 csrss
 742 System
 964 WINWORD  Microsoft Office Word
1112 OUTLOOK  Microsoft Office Outlook
2063 svchost
```

Techniques to Protect You from Yourself

While aliases, wildcards, and composable pipelines are powerful, their use in commands that modify system information can easily be nerve-wracking. After all, what does this command do? Think about it, but don't try it just yet:

```
PS > gps [b-t]*[c-r] | Stop-Process
```

It appears to stop all processes that begin with the letters b through t and end with the letters c through r. How can you be sure? Let PowerShell tell you. For commands that modify data, PowerShell supports -WhatIf and -Confirm parameters that let you see what a command *would* do:

```
PS > gps [b-t]*[c-r] | Stop-Process -whatif
What if: Performing operation "Stop-Process" on Target "ctfmon (812)".
What if: Performing operation "Stop-Process" on Target "Ditto (1916)".
What if: Performing operation "Stop-Process" on Target "dsamain (316)".
What if: Performing operation "Stop-Process" on Target "ehrecvr (1832)".
What if: Performing operation "Stop-Process" on Target "ehSched (1852)".
What if: Performing operation "Stop-Process" on Target "EXCEL (2092)".
What if: Performing operation "Stop-Process" on Target "explorer (1900)".
(...)
```

In this interaction, using the -WhatIf parameter with the Stop-Process pipelined command lets you preview which processes on your system will be stopped before you actually carry out the operation.

Note that this example is not a dare! In the words of one reviewer:

> Not only did it stop everything, but on Vista, it forced a shutdown with only one minute warning!
>
> It was very funny though ... At least I had enough time to save everything first!

Common Discovery Commands

While reading through a guided tour is helpful, I find that most learning happens in an ad hoc fashion. To find all commands that match a given wildcard, use the Get-Command cmdlet. For example, by entering the following, you can find out which PowerShell commands (and Windows applications) contain the word *process*.

```
PS > Get-Command *process*

CommandType     Name            Definition
-----------     ----            ----------
Cmdlet          Get-Process     Get-Process [[-Name] <Str...
Application     qprocess.exe    c:\windows\system32\qproc...
Cmdlet          Stop-Process    Stop-Process [-Id] <Int32...
```

To see what a command such as Get-Process does, use the Get-Help cmdlet, like this:

```
PS > Get-Help Get-Process
```

Since PowerShell lets you work with objects from the .NET Framework, it provides the Get-Member cmdlet to retrieve information about the properties and methods that an object, such as a .NET System.String, supports. Piping a string to the Get-Member command displays its type name and its members:

```
PS > "Hello World" | Get-Member


    TypeName: System.String

Name               MemberType            Definition
----               ----------            ----------
(...)
PadLeft            Method                System.String PadLeft(Int32 tota...
PadRight           Method                System.String PadRight(Int32 tot...
Remove             Method                System.String Remove(Int32 start...
Replace            Method                System.String Replace(Char oldCh...
Split              Method                System.String[] Split(Params Cha...
StartsWith         Method                System.Boolean StartsWith(String...
Substring          Method                System.String Substring(Int32 st...
ToCharArray        Method                System.Char[] ToCharArray(), Sys...
ToLower            Method                System.String ToLower(), System....
ToLowerInvariant   Method                System.String ToLowerInvariant()
ToString           Method                System.String ToString(), System...
ToUpper            Method                System.String ToUpper(), System....
ToUpperInvariant   Method                System.String ToUpperInvariant()
Trim               Method                System.String Trim(Params Char[]...
TrimEnd            Method                System.String TrimEnd(Params Cha...
TrimStart          Method                System.String TrimStart(Params C...
Chars              ParameterizedProperty System.Char Chars(Int32 index) {...
Length             Property              System.Int32 Length {get;}
```

Ubiquitous Scripting

PowerShell makes no distinction between the commands typed at the command line and the commands written in a script. Your favorite cmdlets work in scripts and your favorite scripting techniques (e.g., the foreach statement) work directly on the command line. For example, to add up the handle count for all running processes:

```
PS > $handleCount = 0
PS > foreach($process in Get-Process) { $handleCount += $process.Handles }
PS > $handleCount
19403
```

While PowerShell provides a command (`Measure-Object`) to measure statistics about collections, this short example shows how PowerShell lets you apply techniques that normally require a separate scripting or programming language.

In addition to using PowerShell scripting keywords, you can also create and work directly with objects from the .NET Framework that you may be familiar with. PowerShell becomes almost like the C# immediate mode in Visual Studio. Example T-4 shows how PowerShell lets you easily interact with the .NET Framework.

Example T-4. Using objects from the .NET Framework to retrieve a web page and process its content

```
PS > $webClient = New-Object System.Net.WebClient
PS > $content = $webClient.DownloadString("http://blogs.msdn.com/PowerShell/rss.aspx")
PS > $content.Substring(0,1000)
<?xml version="1.0" encoding="UTF-8" ?>
<?xml-stylesheet type="text/xsl" href="http://blogs.msdn.com/utility/FeedS
tylesheets/rss.xsl" media="screen"?><rss version="2.0" xmlns:dc="http://pu
rl.org/dc/elements/1.1/" xmlns:slash="http://purl.org/rss/1.0/modules/slas
h/" xmlns:wfw="http://wellformedweb.org/CommentAPI/"><channel><title>Windo
(...)
```

Ad Hoc Development

By blurring the lines between interactive administration and writing scripts, the history buffers of PowerShell sessions quickly become the basis for ad hoc script development. In this example, you call the `Get-History` cmdlet to retrieve the history of your session. For each item, you get its `CommandLine` property (the thing you typed) and send the output to a new script file.

```
PS > Get-History | Foreach-Object { $_.CommandLine } > c:\temp\script.ps1
PS > notepad c:\temp\script.ps1
(save the content you want to keep)
PS > c:\temp\script.ps1
```

 If this is the first time you've run a script in PowerShell, you will need to configure your Execution Policy. For more information about selecting an execution policy, see Recipe 18.1.

For more detail about saving your session history into a script, see Recipe 1.17.

Bridging Technologies

We've seen how PowerShell lets you fully leverage the .NET Framework in your tasks, but its support for common technologies stretches even further. As Example T-5 (continued from Example T-4) shows, PowerShell supports XML.

Example T-5. Working with XML content in PowerShell

```
PS > $xmlContent = [xml] $content
PS > $xmlContent

xml                      xml-stylesheet            rss
---                      --------------            ---
version="1.0" encoding... type="text/xsl" href="... rss


PS > $xmlContent.rss

version : 2.0
dc      : http://purl.org/dc/elements/1.1/
slash   : http://purl.org/rss/1.0/modules/slash/
wfw     : http://wellformedweb.org/CommentAPI/
channel : channel



PS > $xmlContent.rss.channel.item | select Title

title
-----
CMD.exe compatibility
Time Stamping Log Files
Microsoft Compute Cluster now has a PowerShell Provider and Cmdlets
The Virtuous Cycle: .NET Developers using PowerShell
(...)
```

PowerShell also lets you work with Windows Management Instrumentation (WMI):

```
PS > Get-WmiObject Win32_Bios


SMBIOSBIOSVersion : ASUS A7N8X Deluxe ACPI BIOS Rev 1009
Manufacturer      : Phoenix Technologies, LTD
Name              : Phoenix - AwardBIOS v6.00PG
SerialNumber      : xxxxxxxxxxx
Version           : Nvidia - 42302e31
```

Or, as Example T-6 shows, Active Directory Service Interfaces (ADSI).

Example T-6. Working with Active Directory in PowerShell

```
PS > [ADSI] "WinNT://./Administrator" | Format-List *


UserFlags       : {66113}
MaxStorage      : {-1}
PasswordAge     : {19550795}
PasswordExpired : {0}
LoginHours      : {255 255 255 255 255 255 255 255 255 255 255
                  255 255 255 255 255 255 255 255 255 255}
FullName        : {}
Description     : {Built-in account for administering the compu
                  ter/domain}
```

```
BadPasswordAttempts      : {0}
LastLogin                : {5/21/2007 3:00:00 AM}
HomeDirectory            : {}
LoginScript              : {}
Profile                  : {}
HomeDirDrive             : {}
Parameters               : {}
PrimaryGroupID           : {513}
Name                     : {Administrator}
MinPasswordLength        : {0}
MaxPasswordAge           : {3710851}
MinPasswordAge           : {0}
PasswordHistoryLength    : {0}
AutoUnlockInterval       : {1800}
LockoutObservationInterval : {1800}
MaxBadPasswordsAllowed   : {0}
RasPermissions           : {1}
objectSid                : {1 5 0 0 0 0 5 21 0 0 0 121 227 252 83 122
                           130 50 34 67 23 10 50 244 1 0 0}
```

Or, as Example T-7 shows, even scripting traditional COM objects.

Example T-7. Working with COM objects in PowerShell

```
PS > $firewall = New-Object -com HNetCfg.FwMgr
PS > $firewall.LocalPolicy.CurrentProfile


Type                                             : 1
FirewallEnabled                                  : True
ExceptionsNotAllowed                             : False
NotificationsDisabled                            : False
UnicastResponsesToMulticastBroadcastDisabled     : False
RemoteAdminSettings                              : System.__ComObject
IcmpSettings                                     : System.__ComObject
GloballyOpenPorts                                : {Media Center Extender Serv
                                                   ice, Remote Media Center Ex
                                                   perience, Adam Test Instanc
                                                   e, QWAVE...}
Services                                         : {File and Printer Sharing,
                                                   UPnP Framework, Remote Desk
                                                   top}
AuthorizedApplications                           : {Remote Assistance, Windows
                                                   Messenger, Media Center, T
                                                   rillian...}
```

Namespace Navigation Through Providers

Another avenue PowerShell offers for working with the system is *providers*. PowerShell providers let you navigate and manage data stores using the same techniques you already use to work with the filesystem, as illustrated in Example T-8.

Example T-8. Navigating the filesystem

```
PS > Set-Location c:\
PS > Get-ChildItem


    Directory: C:\
Mode              LastWriteTime    Length Name
----              -------------    ------ ----
d----        11/2/2006    4:36 AM         $WINDOWS.~BT
d----         5/8/2007    8:37 PM         Blurpark
d----        11/29/2006    2:47 PM        Boot
d----        11/28/2006    2:10 PM        DECCHECK
d----        10/7/2006    4:30 PM         Documents and Settings
d----         5/21/2007    6:02 PM        F&SC-demo
d----         4/2/2007    7:21 PM         Inetpub
d----         5/20/2007    4:59 PM        Program Files
d----         5/21/2007   11:47 PM        temp
d----         5/21/2007    8:55 PM        Windows
-a---         1/7/2006   10:37 PM       0 autoexec.bat
-ar-s        11/29/2006    1:39 PM    8192 BOOTSECT.BAK
-a---         1/7/2006   10:37 PM       0 config.sys
-a---         5/1/2007    8:43 PM   33057 RUU.log
-a---         4/2/2007    7:46 PM    2487 secedit.INTEG.RAW
```

This also works on the registry, as shown in Example T-9.

Example T-9. Navigating the registry

```
PS > Set-Location HKCU:\Software\Microsoft\Windows\
PS > Get-ChildItem


    Hive: HKEY_CURRENT_USER\Software\Microsoft\Windows

SKC VC Name                          Property
--- -- ----                          --------
 30  1 CurrentVersion                {ISC}
  3  1 Shell                         {BagMRU Size}
  4  2 ShellNoRoam                   {(default), BagMRU Size}


PS > Set-Location CurrentVersion\Run
PS > Get-ItemProperty .


(...)
FolderShare          : "C:\Program Files\FolderShare\FolderShare.exe" /
                       background
TaskSwitchXP         : d:\lee\tools\TaskSwitchXP.exe
ctfmon.exe           : C:\WINDOWS\system32\ctfmon.exe
Ditto                : C:\Program Files\Ditto\Ditto.exe
(...)
```

Or even the machine's certificate store, as Example T-10 illustrates.

Example T-10. Navigating the certificate store

```
PS > Set-Location cert:\CurrentUser\Root
PS > Get-ChildItem


    Directory: Microsoft.PowerShell.Security\Certificate::CurrentUser\Root


Thumbprint                                Subject
----------                                -------
CDD4EEAE6000AC7F40C3802C171E30148030C072  CN=Microsoft Root Certificate...
BE36A4562FB2EE05DBB3D32323ADF445084ED656  CN=Thawte Timestamping CA, OU...
A43489159A520F0D93D032CCAF37E7FE20A8B419  CN=Microsoft Root Authority, ...
9FE47B4D05D46E8066BAB1D1BFC9E48F1DBE6B26  CN=PowerShell Local Certifica...
7F88CD7223F3C813818C994614A89C99FA3B5247  CN=Microsoft Authenticode(tm)...
245C97DF7514E7CF2DF8BE72AE957B9E04741E85  OU=Copyright (c) 1997 Microso...
(...)
```

Much, Much More

As exciting as this guided tour was, it barely scratches the surface of how you can use PowerShell to improve your productivity and systems management skills. For more information about getting started in PowerShell, see Chapter 1.

Fundamentals

The Windows PowerShell Interactive Shell

1.0 Introduction

Above all else, the design of Windows PowerShell places priority on its use as an efficient and powerful interactive shell. Even its scripting language plays a critical role in this effort, as it too heavily favors interactive use.

What surprises most people when they first launch PowerShell is its similarity to the command prompt that has long existed as part of Windows. Familiar tools continue to run. Familiar commands continue to run. Even familiar hotkeys are the same. Supporting this familiar user interface, though, is a powerful engine that lets you accomplish once cumbersome administrative and scripting tasks with ease.

This chapter introduces PowerShell from the perspective of its interactive shell.

1.1 Run Programs, Scripts, and Existing Tools

Problem

You rely on a lot of effort invested in your current tools. You have traditional executables, Perl scripts, VBScript, and of course, a legacy build system that has organically grown into a tangled mess of batch files. You want to use PowerShell, but you don't want to give up everything you already have.

Solution

To run a program, script, batch file, or other executable command in the system's path, enter its filename. For these executable types, the extension is optional:

```
Program.exe arguments
ScriptName.ps1 arguments
BatchFile.cmd arguments
```

To run a command that contains a space in its name, enclose its filename in single-quotes (') and precede the command with an ampersand (&), known in PowerShell as the *invoke operator*:

```
& 'C:\Program Files\Program\Program.exe' arguments
```

To run a command in the current directory, place .\ in front of its filename:

```
.\Program.exe arguments
```

To run a command with spaces in its name from the current directory, precede it with both an ampersand and .\:

```
& '.\Program With Spaces.exe' arguments
```

Discussion

In this case, the solution is mainly to use your current tools as you always have. The only difference is that you run them in the PowerShell interactive shell, rather than *cmd.exe*.

The final three tips in the solution merit special attention. They are the features of PowerShell that many new users stumble on when it comes to running programs. The first is running commands that contain spaces. In *cmd.exe*, the way to run a command that contains spaces is to surround it with quotes:

```
"C:\Program Files\Program\Program.exe"
```

In PowerShell, though, placing text inside quotes is part of a feature that lets you evaluate complex expressions at the prompt, as shown in Example 1-1.

Example 1-1. Evaluating expressions at the PowerShell prompt

```
PS > 1 + 1
2
PS > 26 * 1.15
29.9
PS > "Hello" + " World"
Hello World
PS > "Hello World"
Hello World
PS > "C:\Program Files\Program\Program.exe"
C:\Program Files\Program\Program.exe
PS >
```

So, a program name in quotes is no different from any other string in quotes. It's just an expression. As shown previously, the way to run a command in a string is to precede that string with the *invoke operator* (&). If the command you want to run is a batch file that modifies its environment, see Recipe 3.5.

By default, PowerShell's security policies prevent scripts from running. Once you begin writing or using scripts, though, you should configure this policy to something less restrictive. For information on how to configure your execution policy, see Recipe 18.1.

The second command that new users (and seasoned veterans before coffee!) sometimes stumble on is running commands from the current directory. In *cmd.exe*, the current directory is considered part of the *path*: the list of directories that Windows searches to find the program name you typed. If you are in the *C:\Programs* directory, cmd.exe looks in *C:\Programs* (among other places) for applications to run.

PowerShell, like most Unix shells, requires that you explicitly state your desire to run a program from the current directory. To do that, you use the `.\Program.exe` syntax, as shown previously. This prevents malicious users on your system from littering your hard drive with evil programs that have names similar to (or the same as) commands you might run while visiting that directory.

To save themselves from having to type the location of commonly used scripts and programs, many users put these utilities along with their PowerShell scripts in a "tools" directory, which they add to their system's path. If PowerShell can find a script or utility in your system's path, you do not need to explicitly specify its location.

Scripts and examples from this book are available at *http://www.oreilly .com/catalog/9780596801519*.

To learn how to write a PowerShell script, see Recipe 11.1.

See Also

Recipe 3.5, "Program: Retain Changes to Environment Variables Set by a Batch File"

Recipe 11.1, "Write a Script"

Recipe 18.1, "Enable Scripting Through an Execution Policy"

1.2 Resolve Errors Calling Native Executables

Problem

You have a command line that works from *cmd.exe*, and want to resolve errors that occur from running that command in PowerShell.

Solution

Enclose any affected command arguments in single quotes to prevent them from being interpreted by PowerShell, and replace any single quotes in the command with two single quotes.

```
PS > cmd /c echo '!"#$%&''()*+,-./09:;<=>?@AZ[\]^_`az{|}~'
!"#$%&'()*+,-./09:;<=>?@AZ[\]^_`az{|}~
```

Discussion

One of PowerShell's primary goals has always been command consistency. Because of this, cmdlets are very regular in the way that they accept parameters. Native executables write their own parameter parsing, so you never know what to expect when working with them. In addition, PowerShell offers many features that make you more efficient at the command line: command substitution, variable expansion, and more. Since many native executables were written before PowerShell was developed, they may use special characters that conflict with these features.

 Unlike it does with cmdlets, PowerShell doesn't apply special parameter processing to native executables. However, version one of PowerShell did incorrectly process some arguments that contained the colon character if the argument looked like parameters for a cmdlet. If you've experienced this (or perhaps formed a superstition that "calling native executables doesn't work properly"), try again.

As an example, the command given in the Solution uses all the special characters available on a typical keyboard. Without the quotes, PowerShell treats some of them as language features, as shown in Table 1-1.

Table 1-1. Sample of special characters

Special character	Meaning
"	The beginning (or end) of quoted text
#	The beginning of a comment
$	The beginning of a variable
&	Reserved for future use
( )	Parentheses used for subexpressions
;	Statement separator
{ }	Script block
|	Pipeline separator
`	Escape character

When surrounded by single quotes, PowerShell accepts these characters as written, without the special meaning.

Despite these precautions, you may still sometimes run into a command that doesn't seem to work when called from PowerShell. To see *exactly* what PowerShell passes to that command, you can view the output of the trace source called `NativeCommandPara meterBinder`:

```
PS > Trace-Command NativeCommandParameterBinder {
    cmd /c echo '!"#$%&''()*+,-./09:;<=>?@AZ[\]^_`az{|}~'
} -PsHost

DEBUG: NativeCommandParameterBinder Information: 0 :  WriteLine
Argument 0: /c
DEBUG: NativeCommandParameterBinder Information: 0 :  WriteLine
Argument 1: echo
DEBUG: NativeCommandParameterBinder Information: 0 :  WriteLine
Argument 2: !#$%&'()*+,-./09:;<=>?@AZ[\]^_`az{|}~
!"#$%&'()*+,-./09:;<=>?@AZ[\]^_`az{|}~
```

If the command arguments shown in this output don't match the arguments you expect, they have special meaning to PowerShell and should be escaped.

See Also

Get-Help Trace-Command

Appendix A, *PowerShell Language and Environment*

1.3 Run a PowerShell Command

Problem

You want to run a PowerShell command.

Solution

To run a PowerShell command, type its name at the command prompt. For example:

```
PS > Get-Process

Handles  NPM(K)    PM(K)    WS(K) VM(M)  CPU(s)    Id ProcessName
-------  ------    -----    ----- -----  ------    -- -----------
    133       5    11760     7668    46          1112 audiodg
    184       5    33248      508    93          1692 avgamsvr
    143       7    31852      984    97          1788 avgemc
```

Discussion

The `Get-Process` command is an example of a native PowerShell command, called a *cmdlet*. As compared to traditional commands, cmdlets provide significant benefits to both administrators and developers:

- They share a common and regular command-line syntax.
- They support rich pipeline scenarios (using the output of one command as the input of another).
- They produce easily manageable object-based output, rather than error-prone plain text output.

Because the `Get-Process` cmdlet generates rich object-based output, you can use its output for many process-related tasks.

The `Get-Process` cmdlet is just one of the many that PowerShell supports. See Recipe 1.7 to learn techniques for finding additional commands that PowerShell supports.

For more information about working with classes from the .NET Framework, see Recipe 3.8.

See Also

Recipe 1.7, "Find a Command to Accomplish a Task"

Recipe 3.8, "Work with .NET Objects"

1.4 Invoke a Long-Running or Background Command

Problem

You want to invoke a long-running command on a local or remote computer.

Solution

Invoke the command as a `Job` to have PowerShell run it in the background:

```
PS > Start-Job { while($true) { Get-Random; Start-Sleep 5 } } -Name Sleeper

Id          Name          State      HasMoreData    Location
--          ----          -----      -----------    --------
1           Sleeper       Running    True           localhost

PS > Receive-Job Sleeper
671032665
1862308704
PS > Stop-Job Sleeper
```

Discussion

PowerShell's job cmdlets provide a consistent way to create and interact with background tasks. In the Solution, we use the `Start-Job` cmdlet to launch a background job on the local computer. We give it the name of `Sleeper`, but otherwise we don't customize much of its execution environment.

In addition to allowing you to customize the job name, the `Start-Job` cmdlet also lets you launch the job under alternate user credentials or as a 32-bit process (if run originally from a 64-bit process).

Once you have launched a job, you can use the other `Job` cmdlets to interact with it:

`Get-Job`
> Gets all jobs associated with the current session.

`Wait-Job`
> Waits for a job until it has output ready to be retrieved.

`Receive-Job`
> Retrieves any output the job has generated since the last call to `Receive-Job`.

`Stop-Job`
> Stops a job.

`Remove-Job`
> Removes a job from the list of active jobs.

 In addition to the `Start-Job` cmdlet, you can also use the `-AsJob` parameter in many cmdlets to have them perform their tasks in the background. Two of the most useful examples are the `Invoke-Command` cmdlet (when operating against remote computers) and the set of WMI-related cmdlets.

If your job generates an error, the `Receive-Job` cmdlet will display it to you when you receive the results, as shown in Example 1-2. If you want to investigate these errors further, the object returned by `Get-Job` exposes them through the `Error` property.

Example 1-2. Retrieving errors from a Job

```
PS > Start-Job -Name ErrorJob { Write-Error Error! }

WARNING: column "Command" does not fit into the display and was removed.

Id          Name          State     HasMoreData     Location
--          ----          -----     -----------     --------
1           ErrorJob      Running   True            localhost


PS > Receive-Job ErrorJob
Error!
```

```
    + CategoryInfo          : NotSpecified: (:) [Write-Error], WriteError
   Exception
    + FullyQualifiedErrorId : Microsoft.PowerShell.Commands.WriteErrorExc
   eption,Microsoft.PowerShell.Commands.WriteErrorCommand

PS > $job = Get-Job ErrorJob
PS > $job | Format-List *


State        : Completed
HasMoreData  : False
StatusMessage :
Location     : localhost
Command      :  Write-Error Error!
JobStateInfo : Completed
Finished     : System.Threading.ManualResetEvent
InstanceId   : 801e932c-5580-4c8b-af06-ddd1024840b7
Id           : 1
Name         : ErrorJob
ChildJobs    : {Job2}
Output       : {}
Error        : {}
Progress     : {}
Verbose      : {}
Debug        : {}
Warning      : {}



PS > $job.ChildJobs[0] | Format-List *


State        : Completed
StatusMessage :
HasMoreData  : False
Location     : localhost
Runspace     : System.Management.Automation.RemoteRunspace
Command      :  Write-Error Error!
JobStateInfo : Completed
Finished     : System.Threading.ManualResetEvent
InstanceId   : 60fa85da-448b-49ff-8116-6eae6c3f5006
Id           : 2
Name         : Job2
ChildJobs    : {}
Output       : {}
Error        : {Microsoft.PowerShell.Commands.WriteErrorException,Microso
               ft.PowerShell.Commands.WriteErrorCommand}
Progress     : {}
Verbose      : {}
Debug        : {}
Warning      : {}



PS > $job.ChildJobs[0].Error
```

```
Error!
    + CategoryInfo          : NotSpecified: (:) [Write-Error], WriteError
    Exception
    + FullyQualifiedErrorId : Microsoft.PowerShell.Commands.WriteErrorExc
    eption,Microsoft.PowerShell.Commands.WriteErrorCommand

PS >
```

As this example shows, jobs are sometimes containers for other jobs, called *child jobs*. Jobs created through the `Start-Job` cmdlet will always be child jobs attached to a generic container. To access the errors returned by these jobs, you instead access the errors in its first child job (called child job number zero).

See Also

Recipe 28.7, "Improve the Performance of Large-Scale WMI Operations"

Recipe 29.11, "Invoke a Command on a Remote Computer"

1.5 Notify Yourself of Job Completion

Problem

You want to notify yourself when a long-running job completes.

Solution

Use the `Register-TemporaryEvent` command given in Recipe 31.3 to register for the event's `StateChanged` event:

```
PS > $job = Start-Job -Name TenSecondSleep { Start-Sleep 10 }
PS > Register-TemporaryEvent $job StateChanged -Action {
    [Console]::Beep(100,100)
    Write-Host "Job #$($sender.Id) ($($sender.Name)) complete."
}

PS > Job #6 (TenSecondSleep) complete.
PS >
```

Discussion

When a job completes, it raises a `StateChanged` event to notify subscribers that its state has changed. We can use PowerShell's event handling cmdlets to register for notifications about this event, but they are not geared toward this type of one-time event handling. To solve that, we use the `Register-TemporaryEvent` command given in Recipe 31.3.

In our example action block in that solution, we simply emit a beep and write a message saying that the job is complete.

As another option, you can also update your prompt function to highlight jobs that are complete but still have output you haven't processed:

```
$psJobs = @(Get-Job -State Completed | ? { $_.HasMoreData })
if($psJobs.Count -gt 0) { ($psJobs | Out-String).Trim() | Write-Host -Fore Yellow }
```

For more information about events and this type of automatic event handling, see Chapter 31.

See Also

Recipe 1.1, "Run Programs, Scripts, and Existing Tools"

Chapter 31, *Event Handling*

1.6 Customize Your Shell, Profile, and Prompt

Problem

You want to customize PowerShell's interactive experience with a personalized prompt, aliases, and more.

Solution

When you want to customize aspects of PowerShell, place those customizations in your personal profile script. PowerShell provides easy access to this profile script by storing its location in the $profile variable.

 By default, PowerShell's security policies prevent scripts (including your profile) from running. Once you begin writing scripts, though, you should configure this policy to something less restrictive. For information on how to configure your execution policy, see Recipe 18.1.

To create a new profile (and overwrite one if it already exists):

```
New-Item -type file -force $profile
```

To edit your profile:

```
notepad $profile
```

To see your profile file:

```
Get-ChildItem $profile
```

Once you create a profile script, you can add a function called Prompt that returns a string. PowerShell displays the output of this function as your command-line prompt.

```
function Prompt
{
```

```
    "PS [$env:COMPUTERNAME] >"
}
```

This example prompt displays your computer name, and looks like PS [LEE-DESK]>.

You may also find it helpful to add aliases to your profile. Aliases let you refer to common commands by a name that you choose. Personal profile scripts let you automatically define aliases, functions, variables, or any other customizations that you might set interactively from the PowerShell prompt. Aliases are among the most common customizations, as they let you refer to PowerShell commands (and your own scripts) by a name that is easier to type.

 If you want to define an alias for a command but also need to modify the parameters to that command, then define a function instead.

For example:

```
Set-Alias new New-Object
Set-Alias iexplore 'C:\Program Files\Internet Explorer\iexplore.exe'
```

Your changes will become effective once you save your profile and restart PowerShell. To reload your profile immediately, run this command:

```
. $profile
```

Functions are also very common customizations, with the most popular being the Prompt function.

Discussion

The Solution discusses three techniques to make useful customizations to your PowerShell environment: aliases, functions, and a hand-tailored prompt. You can (and will often) apply these techniques at any time during your PowerShell session, but your profile script is the standard place to put customizations that you want to apply to every session.

 To remove an alias or function, use the Remove-Item cmdlet:

```
Remove-Item function:\MyCustomFunction
Remove-Item alias:\new
```

Although the Prompt function returns a simple string, you can also use the function for more complex tasks. For example, many users update their console window title (by changing the $host.UI.RawUI.WindowTitle variable) or use the Write-Host cmdlet to output the prompt in color. If your prompt function handles the screen output itself, it still needs to return a string (for example, a single space) to prevent PowerShell from using its default. If you don't want this extra space to appear in your prompt, add an extra space at the end of your Write-Host command and return the backspace ("`b") character, as shown in Example 1-3.

Example 1-3. An example PowerShell prompt

```
##############################################################################
##
## From Windows PowerShell Cookbook (O'Reilly)
## by Lee Holmes (http://www.leeholmes.com/guide)
##
##############################################################################

Set-StrictMode -Version Latest

function Prompt
{
    $id = 1
    $historyItem = Get-History -Count 1
    if($historyItem)
    {
        $id = $historyItem.Id + 1
    }

    Write-Host -ForegroundColor DarkGray "`n[$(Get-Location)]"
    Write-Host -NoNewLine "PS:$id > "
    $host.UI.RawUI.WindowTitle = "$(Get-Location)"

    "`b"
}
```

In addition to showing the current location, this prompt also shows the ID for that command in your history. This lets you locate and invoke past commands with relative ease:

```
[C:\]
PS:73 >5 * 5
25

[C:\]
PS:74 >1 + 1
2

[C:\]
PS:75 >Invoke-History 73
5 * 5
25

[C:\]
PS:76 >
```

Although the profile referenced by $profile is the one you will almost always want to use, PowerShell actually supports four separate profile scripts. For further details on these scripts (along with other shell customization options), see "Common Customization Points" on page 761.

See Also

Recipe 18.1, "Enable Scripting Through an Execution Policy"

"Common Customization Points" on page 761

1.7 Find a Command to Accomplish a Task

Problem

You want to accomplish a task in PowerShell but don't know the command or cmdlet to accomplish that task.

Solution

Use the Get-Command cmdlet to search for and investigate commands.

To get the summary information about a specific command, specify the command name as an argument:

```
Get-Command CommandName
```

To get the detailed information about a specific command, pipe the output of Get-Command to the Format-List cmdlet:

```
Get-Command CommandName | Format-List
```

To search for all commands with a name that contains *text*, surround the text with asterisk characters:

```
Get-Command *text*
```

To search for all commands that use the Get verb, supply Get to the -Verb parameter:

```
Get-Command -Verb Get
```

To search for all commands that act on a service, use Service as the value of the -Noun parameter:

```
Get-Command -Noun Service
```

Discussion

One of the benefits that PowerShell provides administrators is the consistency of its command names. All PowerShell commands (called *cmdlets*) follow a regular *Verb-Noun* pattern, for example: Get-Process, Get-EventLog, and Set-Location. The verbs come from a relatively small set of standard verbs (as listed in Appendix J) and describe what action the cmdlet takes. The nouns are specific to the cmdlet and describe what the cmdlet acts on.

Knowing this philosophy, you can easily learn to work with groups of cmdlets. If you want to start a service on the local machine, the standard verb for that is Start. A good guess would be to first try Start-Service (which in this case would be correct), but typing Get-Command -Verb Start would also be an effective way to see what things you can start. Going the other way, you can see what actions are supported on services by typing Get-Command -Noun Service.

See Recipe 1.8 for a way to list all commands along with a brief description of what they do.

The Get-Command cmdlet is one of the three commands you will use most commonly as you explore Windows PowerShell. The other two commands are Get-Help and Get-Member.

There is one important point when it comes to looking for a PowerShell command to accomplish a particular task. Many times, that PowerShell command does not exist, because the task is best accomplished the same way it always was: ipconfig.exe to get IP configuration information, netstat.exe to list protocol statistics and current TCP/IP network connections, and many more.

For more information about the Get-Command cmdlet, type **Get-Help Get-Command**.

See Also

Recipe 1.8, "Get Help on a Command"

1.8 Get Help on a Command

Problem

You want to learn how a specific command works and how to use it.

Solution

The command that provides help and usage information about a command is called Get-Help. It supports several different views of the help information, depending on your needs.

To get the summary of help information for a specific command, provide the command's name as an argument to the Get-Help cmdlet. This primarily includes its synopsis, syntax, and detailed description:

```
Get-Help CommandName
```

or

```
CommandName -?
```

To get the detailed help information for a specific command, supply the -Detailed flag to the Get-Help cmdlet. In addition to the summary view, this also includes its parameter descriptions and examples:

```
Get-Help CommandName -Detailed
```

To get the full help information for a specific command, supply the -Full flag to the Get-Help cmdlet. In addition to the detailed view, this also includes its full parameter descriptions and additional notes:

```
Get-Help CommandName -Full
```

To get only the examples for a specific command, supply the -Examples flag to the Get-Help cmdlet:

```
Get-Help CommandName -Examples
```

To retrieve the most up-to-date online version of a command's help topic, supply the -Online flag to the Get-Help cmdlet:

```
Get-Help CommandName -Online
```

To find all help topics that contain a given keyword, provide that keyword as an argument to the Get-Help cmdlet. If the keyword isn't also the name of a specific help topic, this returns all help topics that contain the keyword, including its name, category, and synopsis:

```
Get-Help Keyword
```

Discussion

The Get-Help cmdlet is the primary way to interact with the help system in PowerShell. Like the Get-Command cmdlet, the Get-Help cmdlet supports wildcards. If you want to list all commands that match a certain pattern (for example, *process*), you can simply type **Get-Help *process***.

To generate a list of all cmdlets and aliases (along with their brief synopsis), run the following command:

```
Get-Help * -Category Cmdlet | Select-Object Name,Synopsis | Format-Table -Auto
```

If the pattern matches only a single command, PowerShell displays the help for that command. Although command wildcarding and keyword searching is a helpful way to search PowerShell help, see Recipe 1.9 for a script that lets you search the help content for a specified pattern.

In addition to console-based help, PowerShell also offers online and Compiled Help (CHM) versions of its help content. The Solution demonstrates how to quickly access online help content, but accessing the CHM version of help is slightly more difficult.

- If you are working within PowerShell's Integrated Scripting Environment (ISE), accessing the CHM help is as easy as pressing F1.
- If you are working on Windows 7, you can access the CHM help through the Windows PowerShell Help option in PowerShell's *jump list* (Figure 1-1). To open PowerShell's jump list, either right-click on the taskbar icon or click the arrow beside PowerShell's icon in the start menu.

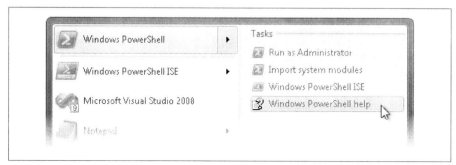

Figure 1-1. Launching PowerShell's Help Viewer

- If you are working within the PowerShell console, you can access the CHM help by launching the *.CHM* file directly. Recipe 1.10 demonstrates how to do this.

The Get-Help cmdlet is one of the three commands you will use most commonly as you explore Windows PowerShell. The other two commands are Get-Command and Get-Member.

For more information about the Get-Help cmdlet, type **Get-Help Get-Help**.

See Also

Recipe 1.9, "Program: Search Help for Text"

Recipe 1.10, "Program: View PowerShell's HTML Help"

1.9 Program: Search Help for Text

Both the Get-Command and Get-Help cmdlets let you search for command names that match a given pattern. However, when you don't know exactly what portions of a command name you are looking for, you will more often have success searching through the help *content* for an answer. On Unix systems, this command is called Apropos.

The Get-Help cmdlet automatically searches the help database for keyword references when it can't find a help topic for the argument you supply. In addition to that, you might want to extend this even further to search for text *patterns* or even help topics that talk *about* existing help topics. PowerShell's help facilities don't support this type of search.

That doesn't need to stop us, though, as we can write the functionality ourselves.

To run this program, supply a search string to the Search-Help script (given in Example 1-4). The search string can be either simple text or a regular expression. The script then displays the name and synopsis of all help topics that match. To see the help content for that topic, use the Get-Help cmdlet.

Example 1-4. Search-Help.ps1

```
##############################################################################
##
## Search-Help
##
## From Windows PowerShell Cookbook (O'Reilly)
## by Lee Holmes (http://www.leeholmes.com/guide)
##
##############################################################################

<#

.SYNOPSIS

Search the PowerShell help documentation for a given keyword or regular
expression.

.EXAMPLE

Search-Help hashtable
Searches help for the term 'hashtable'

.EXAMPLE

Search-Help "(datetime|ticks)"
Searches help for the term datetime or ticks, using the regular expression
syntax.

#>

param(
    ## The pattern to search for
    [Parameter(Mandatory = $true)]
    $Pattern
)

Set-StrictMode -Version Latest

$helpNames = $(Get-Help * | Where-Object { $_.Category -ne "Alias" })

## Go through all of the help topics
foreach($helpTopic in $helpNames)
{
    ## Get their text content, search for the specified pattern
    $content = Get-Help -Full $helpTopic.Name | Out-String
    if($content -match "(.{0,30}$pattern.{0,30})")
    {
```

```
        $helpTopic | Add-Member NoteProperty Match $matches[0].Trim()
        $helpTopic | Select-Object Name,Match
    }
}
```

For more information about running scripts, see Recipe 1.1.

See Also

Recipe 1.1, "Run Programs, Scripts, and Existing Tools"

1.10 Program: View PowerShell's HTML Help

PowerShell's compiled help (CHM) offers many useful features: a table of contents, an index, full-text search, and more. While easy to launch from the Integrated Scripting Environment (ISE) and the Windows 7 jump list, discoverability is still a problem from console windows.

To easily launch PowerShell's CHM help, use the Show-HtmlHelp script shown in Example 1-5.

Example 1-5. Show-HtmlHelp.ps1

```
##############################################################################
##
## Show-HtmlHelp
##
## From Windows PowerShell Cookbook (O'Reilly)
## by Lee Holmes (http://www.leeholmes.com/guide)
##
##############################################################################

<#

.SYNOPSIS

Launches the CHM version of PowerShell help.

.EXAMPLE

Show-HtmlHelp

#>

Set-StrictMode -Version Latest

$path = (Resolve-Path c:\windows\help\mui\*\WindowsPowerShellHelp.chm).Path
hh "$path::/html/defed09e-2acd-4042-bd22-ce4bf92c2f24.htm"
```

For more information about running scripts, see Recipe 1.1.

See Also

Recipe 1.1, "Run Programs, Scripts, and Existing Tools"

1.11 Launch PowerShell at a Specific Location

Problem

You want to launch a PowerShell session in a specific location.

Solution

Both Windows and PowerShell offer several ways to launch PowerShell in a specific location:

- Explorer's address bar
- PowerShell's command-line arguments
- Community extensions

Discussion

If you are browsing the filesystem with Windows Explorer, typing `PowerShell` into the address bar launches PowerShell in that location (as shown in Figure 1-2).

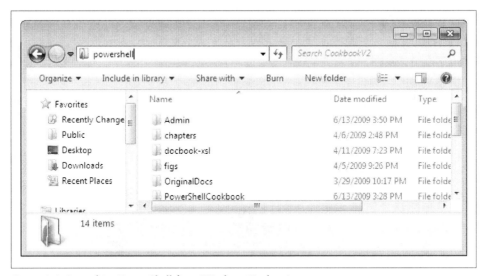

Figure 1-2. Launching PowerShell from Windows Explorer

The resulting session lacks the console window customizations defined by PowerShell's Start menu link (as does launching PowerShell from the Start→Run dialog), but Recipe 1.13 shows how to make even these PowerShell windows display in PowerShell's signature blue.

For another way to launch PowerShell from Windows Explorer, several members of the PowerShell community have written power toys and Windows Explorer extensions that provide a "Launch PowerShell Here" option when you right-click on a folder from Windows Explorer. An Internet search for "PowerShell Here" turns up several.

If you aren't browsing the desired folder with Windows Explorer, use PowerShell's -NoExit parameter, along with the implied -Command parameter. In the -Command parameter, call the Set-Location cmdlet to initially move to your desired location. From Start→Run (or any other means of launching an application), type:

```
PowerShell -NoExit Set-Location 'C:\Program Files'
```

1.12 Invoke a PowerShell Command or Script from Outside PowerShell

Problem

You want to invoke a PowerShell command or script from a batch file, a logon script, a scheduled task, or any other non-PowerShell application.

Solution

To invoke a PowerShell command, use the -Command parameter:

```
PowerShell -Command Get-Process; Read-Host
```

To launch a PowerShell script, use the -File parameter:

```
PowerShell -File 'full path to script' arguments
```

For example:

```
PowerShell -File 'c:\shared scripts\Get-Report.ps1' Hello World
```

Discussion

By default, any arguments to *PowerShell.exe* get interpreted as commands to run. PowerShell runs the command as though you had typed it in the interactive shell, and then exits. You can customize this behavior by supplying other parameters to *PowerShell.exe*, such as -NoExit, -NoProfile, and more.

Since launching a script is so common, PowerShell provides the -File parameter to eliminate the complexities that arise from having to invoke a script from the -Command parameter. This technique lets you invoke a PowerShell script as the target of a logon script, advanced file association, scheduled task, and more.

When PowerShell detects that its input or output streams have been redirected, it suppresses any prompts that it might normally display. If you want to host an interactive PowerShell prompt inside another application (such as Emacs), use - as the argument for the -File parameter. In PowerShell (as with traditional Unix shells), this implies "taken from standard input."

```
powershell -File -
```

If the script is for background automation or a scheduled task, these scripts can sometimes interfere with (or become influenced by) the user's environment. For these situations, three parameters come in handy:

-NoProfile
  Runs the command or script without loading user profile scripts. This makes the script launch faster, but it primarily prevents user preferences (e.g., aliases and preference variables) from interfering with the script's working environment.

-WindowStyle
  Runs the command or script with the specified window style—most commonly Hidden. When run with a window style of Hidden, PowerShell hides its main window immediately. For more ways to control the window style from *within* PowerShell, see Recipe 24.3.

-ExecutionPolicy
  Runs the command or script with a specified execution policy applied only to this instance of PowerShell. This lets you write PowerShell scripts to manage a system without having to change the system-wide execution policy. For more information about scoped execution policies, see Recipe 18.1.

If you are the author of the program that needs to run PowerShell scripts or commands, PowerShell lets you call these scripts and commands much more easily than calling its command-line interface. For more information about this approach, see Recipe 17.10.

If the arguments to the -Command parameter become complex, special character handling in the application calling PowerShell (such as *cmd.exe*) might interfere with the command you want to send to PowerShell. For this situation, PowerShell supports an EncodedCommand parameter: a Base64-encoded representation of the Unicode string you want to run. Example 1-6 demonstrates how to convert a string containing PowerShell commands to a Base64-encoded form.

Example 1-6. Converting PowerShell commands into a Base64-encoded form

```
$commands = '1..10 | % { "PowerShell Rocks" }'
$bytes = [System.Text.Encoding]::Unicode.GetBytes($commands)
$encodedString = [Convert]::ToBase64String($bytes)
```

Once you have the encoded string, you can use it as the value of the EncodedCommand parameter, as shown in Example 1-7.

Example 1-7. Launching PowerShell with an encoded command from cmd.exe

```
Microsoft Windows [Version 6.0.6000]
Copyright (c) 2006 Microsoft Corporation. All rights reserved.

C:\Users\Lee>PowerShell -EncodedCommand MQAuAC4AMQAwACAAfAAgACUAIAB7ACAAIgBQAG8AdwBlAHIAUwBoA
    GUAbABsACAAUgBvAGMAawBzACIAIAB9AA==
PowerShell Rocks
PowerShell Rocks
PowerShell Rocks
PowerShell Rocks
PowerShell Rocks
PowerShell Rocks
PowerShell Rocks
PowerShell Rocks
PowerShell Rocks
PowerShell Rocks
```

For more information about running scripts, see Recipe 1.1.

See Also

Recipe 1.1, "Run Programs, Scripts, and Existing Tools"

Recipe 17.10, "Add PowerShell Scripting to Your Own Program"

1.13 Customize the Shell to Improve Your Productivity

Problem

You want to use the PowerShell console more efficiently for copying, pasting, history management, and scrolling.

Solution

Run the commands shown in Example 1-8 to permanently customize your PowerShell console windows and make many tasks easier.

Example 1-8. Set-ConsoleProperties.ps1

```
Push-Location
Set-Location HKCU:\Console
New-Item '.\%SystemRoot%_system32_WindowsPowerShell_v1.0_powershell.exe'
```

```
Set-Location '.\%SystemRoot%_system32_WindowsPowerShell_v1.0_powershell.exe'

New-ItemProperty . ColorTable00 -type DWORD -value 0x00562401
New-ItemProperty . ColorTable07 -type DWORD -value 0x00f0edee
New-ItemProperty . FaceName -type STRING -value "Lucida Console"
New-ItemProperty . FontFamily -type DWORD -value 0x00000036
New-ItemProperty . FontSize -type DWORD -value 0x000c0000
New-ItemProperty . FontWeight -type DWORD -value 0x00000190
New-ItemProperty . HistoryNoDup -type DWORD -value 0x00000000
New-ItemProperty . QuickEdit -type DWORD -value 0x00000001
New-ItemProperty . ScreenBufferSize -type DWORD -value 0x0bb80078
New-ItemProperty . WindowSize -type DWORD -value 0x00320078
Pop-Location
```

These commands customize the console color, font, history storage properties, Quick-Edit mode, buffer size, and window size.

With these changes in place, you can also improve your productivity by learning some of the hotkeys for common tasks, listed in Table 1-2. PowerShell uses the same input facilities as *cmd.exe*, and so it brings with it all the input features that you are already familiar with—and some that you aren't!

Table 1-2. Partial list of Windows PowerShell hotkeys

Hotkey	Meaning
Up arrow	Scan backward through your command history.
Down arrow	Scan forward through your command history.
PgUp	Display the first command in your command history.
PgDown	Display the last command in your command history.
Left arrow	Move cursor one character to the left on your command line.
Right arrow	Move cursor one character to the right on your command line.
Home	Move the cursor to the beginning of the command line.
End	Move the cursor to the end of the command line.
Ctrl + Left arrow	Move the cursor one word to the left on your command line.
Ctrl + Right arrow	Move the cursor one word to the right on your command line.

Discussion

When you launch PowerShell from the link on your Windows Start menu, it customizes several aspects of the console window:

- Foreground and background color, to make the console more visually appealing
- QuickEdit mode, to make copying and pasting with the mouse easier
- Buffer size, to make PowerShell retain the output of more commands in your console history

By default, these customizations do not apply when you run PowerShell from the Start→Run dialog. The commands given in the solution section improve the experience by applying these changes to all PowerShell windows that you open.

The hotkeys do, however, apply to all PowerShell windows (and any other application that uses Windows' *cooked* input mode). The most common are given in the solution section, but "Common Customization Points" on page 761 provides the full list.

See Also

"Common Customization Points" on page 761

1.14 Program: Learn Aliases for Common Commands

In interactive use, full cmdlet names (such as Get-ChildItem) are cumbersome and slow to type. Although aliases are much more efficient, it takes a while to discover them. To learn aliases more easily, you can modify your prompt to remind you of the shorter version of any aliased commands that you use.

This involves two steps:

1. Add the program Get-AliasSuggestion.ps1, shown in Example 1-9, to your tools directory or another directory.

   Example 1-9. Get-AliasSuggestion.ps1

   ```
   ##############################################################################
   ##
   ## Get-AliasSuggestion
   ##
   ## From Windows PowerShell Cookbook (O'Reilly)
   ## by Lee Holmes (http://www.leeholmes.com/guide)
   ##
   ##############################################################################

   <#

   .SYNOPSIS

   Get an alias suggestion from the full text of the last command. Intended to
   be added to your prompt function to help learn aliases for commands.

   .EXAMPLE

   Get-AliasSuggestion Remove-ItemProperty
   Suggestion: An alias for Remove-ItemProperty is rp

   #>

   param(
       ## The full text of the last command
       $LastCommand
   ```

```
    )

    Set-StrictMode -Version Latest

    $helpMatches = @()

    ## Find all of the commands in their last input
    $tokens = [Management.Automation.PSParser]::Tokenize(
        $lastCommand, [ref] $null)
    $commands = $tokens | Where-Object { $_.Type -eq "Command" }

    ## Go through each command
    foreach($command in $commands)
    {
        ## Get the alias suggestions
        foreach($alias in Get-Alias -Definition $command.Content)
        {
            $helpMatches += "Suggestion: An alias for " +
                "$($alias.Definition) is $($alias.Name)"
        }
    }

    $helpMatches
```

2. Add the text from Example 1-10 to the Prompt function in your profile. If you do not yet have a Prompt function, see Recipe 1.6 to learn how to add one.

Example 1-10. A useful prompt to teach you aliases for common commands

```
function Prompt
{
    ## Get the last item from the history
    $historyItem = Get-History -Count 1

    ## If there were any history items
    if($historyItem)
    {
        ## Get the training suggestion for that item
        $suggestions = @(Get-AliasSuggestion $historyItem.CommandLine)
        ## If there were any suggestions
        if($suggestions)
        {
            ## For each suggestion, write it to the screen
            foreach($aliasSuggestion in $suggestions)
            {
                Write-Host "$aliasSuggestion"
            }
            Write-Host ""

        }
    }

    ## Rest of prompt goes here
    "PS [$env:COMPUTERNAME] >"
}
```

For more information about running scripts, see Recipe 1.1.

See Also

Recipe 1.1, "Run Programs, Scripts, and Existing Tools"

Recipe 1.6, "Customize Your Shell, Profile, and Prompt"

1.15 Program: Learn Aliases for Common Parameters

Problem

You want to learn aliases defined for command parameters.

Solution

Use the `Get-ParameterAlias` script to return all aliases for parameters used by the previous command in your session history.

Example 1-11. Get-ParameterAlias.ps1

```
##############################################################################
##
## Get-ParameterAlias
##
## From Windows PowerShell Cookbook (O'Reilly)
## by Lee Holmes (http://www.leeholmes.com/guide)
##
##############################################################################

<#

.SYNOPSIS

Looks in the session history, and returns any aliases that apply to
parameters of commands that were used.

.EXAMPLE

PS >dir -ErrorAction SilentlyContinue
PS >Get-ParameterAlias
An alias for the 'ErrorAction' parameter of 'dir' is ea

#>

Set-StrictMode -Version Latest

## Get the last item from their session history
$history = Get-History -Count 1
if(-not $history)
{
    return
```

```
}

## And extract the actual command line they typed
$lastCommand = $history.CommandLine

## Use the Tokenizer API to determine which portions represent
## commands and parameters to those commands
$tokens = [System.Management.Automation.PsParser]::Tokenize(
    $lastCommand, [ref] $null)
$currentCommand = $null

## Now go through each resulting token
foreach($token in $tokens)
{
    ## If we've found a new command, store that.
    if($token.Type -eq "Command")
    {
        $currentCommand = $token.Content
    }

    ## If we've found a command parameter, start looking for aliases
    if(($token.Type -eq "CommandParameter") -and ($currentCommand))
    {
        ## Remove the leading "-" from the parameter
        $currentParameter = $token.Content.TrimStart("-")

        ## Determine all of the parameters for the current command.
        (Get-Command $currentCommand).Parameters.GetEnumerator() |

            ## For parameters that start with the current parameter name,
            Where-Object { $_.Key -like "$currentParameter*" } |

            ## return all of the aliases that apply. We use "starts with"
            ## because the user might have typed a shortened form of
            ## the parameter name.
            Foreach-Object {
                $_.Value.Aliases | Foreach-Object {
                    "Suggestion: An alias for the '$currentParameter' " +
                    "parameter of '$currentCommand' is '$_'"
                }
            }
    }
}
}
```

Discussion

To make it easy to type command parameters, PowerShell lets you type only as much of the command parameter as is required to disambiguate it from other parameters of that command. In addition to shortening implicitly supported by the shell, cmdlet authors can also define explicit aliases for their parameters—for example, CN as a short form for ComputerName.

While helpful, these aliases are difficult to discover.

If you want to see the aliases for a specific command, you can access its `Parameters` collection:

```
PS > (Get-Command New-TimeSpan).Parameters.Values | Select Name,Aliases

Name                              Aliases
----                              -------
Start                             {LastWriteTime}
End                               {}
Days                              {}
Hours                             {}
Minutes                           {}
Seconds                           {}
Verbose                           {vb}
Debug                             {db}
ErrorAction                       {ea}
WarningAction                     {wa}
ErrorVariable                     {ev}
WarningVariable                   {wv}
OutVariable                       {ov}
OutBuffer                         {ob}
```

If you want to learn any aliases for parameters in your previous command, simply run `Get-ParameterAlias.ps1`. To make PowerShell do this automatically, add a call to `Get-ParameterAlias.ps1` in your prompt.

This script builds on two main features: PowerShell's *Tokenizer API*, and the rich information returned by the `Get-Command` cmdlet. PowerShell's Tokenizer API examines its input and returns PowerShell's interpretation of the input: commands, parameters, parameter values, operators, and more. Like the rich output produced by most of PowerShell's commands, `Get-Command` returns information about a command's parameters, parameter sets, output type (if specified), and more.

For more information about the Tokenizer API, see Recipe 10.9.

See Also

Recipe 1.1, "Run Programs, Scripts, and Existing Tools"

"Structured Commands (Cmdlets)" on page 7

1.16 Access and Manage Your Console History

Problem

After working in the shell for a while, you want to invoke commands from your history, view your command history, and save your command history.

Solution

The shortcuts given in Recipe 1.13 let you manage your history, but PowerShell offers several features to help you work with your console in even more detail.

To get the most recent commands from your session, use the Get-History cmdlet:

    Get-History

To rerun a specific command from your session history, provide its *Id* to the Invoke-History cmdlet:

    Invoke-History *Id*

To increase (or limit) the number of commands stored in your session history, assign a new value to the $MaximumHistoryCount variable:

    $MaximumHistoryCount = *Count*

To save your command history to a file, pipe the output of Get-History to the Export-CliXml cmdlet:

    Get-History | Export-CliXml *Filename*

To add a previously saved command history to your current session history, call the Import-CliXml cmdlet and then pipe that output to the Add-History cmdlet:

    Import-CliXml *Filename* | Add-History

To clear all commands from your session history, use the Clear-History cmdlet:

    Clear-History

Discussion

Unlike the console history hotkeys discussed in Recipe 1.13, the Get-History cmdlet produces rich objects that represent information about items in your history. Each object contains that item's ID, command line, start of execution time, and end of execution time.

Once you know the ID of a history item (as shown in the output of Get-History), you can pass it to Invoke-History to execute that command again. The example prompt function shown in Recipe 1.6 makes working with prior history items easy—as the prompt for each command includes the history ID that will represent it.

The IDs provided by the Get-History cmdlet differ from the IDs given by the Windows console common history hotkeys (such as F7), because their history management techniques differ.

By default, PowerShell stores only the last 64 entries of your command history. If you want to raise or lower this amount, set the $MaximumHistoryCount variable to the size you desire. To make this change permanent, set the variable in your PowerShell profile script.

See Also

Recipe 1.6, "Customize Your Shell, Profile, and Prompt"

Recipe 1.13, "Customize the Shell to Improve Your Productivity"

Recipe 1.18, "Invoke a Command from Your Session History"

1.17 Program: Create Scripts from Session History

After interactively experimenting at the command line for a while to solve a multistep task, you'll often want to keep or share the exact steps you used to eventually solve the problem. The script smiles at you from your history buffer, but it is unfortunately surrounded by many more commands that you *don't* want to keep.

To solve this problem, use the Get-History cmdlet to view the recent commands that you've typed. Then, call Copy-History with the IDs of the commands you want to keep, as shown in Example 1-12.

Example 1-12. Copy-History.ps1

```
#############################################################################
##
## Copy-History
##
## From Windows PowerShell Cookbook (O'Reilly)
## by Lee Holmes (http://www.leeholmes.com/guide)
##
#############################################################################

<#

.SYNOPSIS

Copy selected commands from the history buffer into the clipboard as a script.

.EXAMPLE

Copy-History
Copies the entire contents of the history buffer into the clipboard.

.EXAMPLE

Copy-History -5
Copies the last five commands into the clipboard.

.EXAMPLE

Copy-History 2,5,8,4
Copies commands 2,5,8, and 4.

.EXAMPLE

Copy-History (1..10+5+6)
```

Copies commands 1 through 10, then 5, then 6, using PowerShell's array
slicing syntax.

```
#>

param(
    ## The range of history IDs to copy
    [int[]] $Range
)

Set-StrictMode -Version Latest

$history = @()

## If they haven't specified a range, assume it's everything
if((-not $range) -or ($range.Count -eq 0))
{
    $history = @(Get-History -Count ([Int16]::MaxValue))
}
## If it's a negative number, copy only that many
elseif(($range.Count -eq 1) -and ($range[0] -lt 0))
{
    $count = [Math]::Abs($range[0])
    $history = (Get-History -Count $count)
}
## Otherwise, go through each history ID in the given range
## and add it to our history list.
else
{
    foreach($commandId in $range)
    {
        if($commandId -eq -1) { $history += Get-History -Count 1 }
        else { $history += Get-History -Id $commandId }
    }
}

## Finally, export the history to the clipboard.
$history | Foreach-Object { $_.CommandLine } | clip.exe
```

For more information about running scripts, see Recipe 1.1.

See Also

Recipe 1.1, "Run Programs, Scripts, and Existing Tools"

1.18 Invoke a Command from Your Session History

Problem

You want to run a command from the history of your current session.

Solution

To invoke a specific command by its *ID*:

```
Invoke-History ID
```

To search through your history for a command containing *text*:

```
PS > #text<TAB>
```

To repopulate your command with the text of a previous command by its *ID*:

```
PS > #ID<TAB>
```

Discussion

Once you've had your shell open for a while, your history buffer quickly fills with useful commands. The history management hotkeys described in Recipe 1.13 show one way to navigate your history, but this type of history navigation works only for command lines you've typed in that specific session. If you keep a persistent command history (as shown in Recipe 1.26), these shortcuts do not apply.

The Invoke-History cmdlet illustrates the simplest example of working with your command history. Given a specific history ID (perhaps shown in your prompt function), calling Invoke-History with that ID will run that command again. For more information about this technique, see Recipe 1.6.

As part of its tab-completion support, PowerShell gives you easy access to previous commands as well. If you prefix your command with the # character, tab completion takes one of two approaches:

ID completion

> If you type a number, tab completion finds the entry in your command history with that ID, and then replaces your command line with the text of that history entry. This is especially useful when you want to slightly modify a previous history entry, since Invoke-History by itself doesn't support that.

Pattern completion

> If you type anything else, tab completion searches for entries in your command history that contain that text. Under the hood, PowerShell uses the -like operator to match your command entries, so you can use all of the wildcard characters supported by that operator. For more information on searching text for patterns, see Recipe 5.7.

PowerShell's tab completion is largely driven by the fully customizable TabExpansion function. You can easily change this function to include more advanced functionality, or even just customize specific behaviors to suit your personal preferences. For more information, see "Tab Completion" on page 764.

See Also

Recipe 1.6

Recipe 5.7

"Tab Completion" on page 764

1.19 Program: Search Formatted Output for a Pattern

While PowerShell's built-in filtering facilities are incredibly flexible (for example, the `Where-Object` cmdlet), they generally operate against specific properties of the incoming object. If you are searching for text in the object's formatted output, or don't know which property contains the text you are looking for, simple text-based filtering is sometimes helpful.

To solve this problem, you can pipe the output into the `Out-String` cmdlet before passing it to the `Select-String` cmdlet. `Select-TextOutput` (shown in Example 1-13) does exactly this, and it lets you search for a pattern in the visual representation of command output.

Example 1-13. Select-TextOutput.ps1

```
##############################################################################
##
## Select-TextOutput
##
## From Windows PowerShell Cookbook (O'Reilly)
## by Lee Holmes (http://www.leeholmes.com/guide)
##
##############################################################################

<#

.SYNOPSIS

Searches the textual output of a command for a pattern.

.EXAMPLE

Get-Service | Select-TextOutput audio
Finds all references to "Audio" in the output of Get-Service

#>

param(
    ## The pattern to search for
    $Pattern
)

Set-StrictMode -Version Latest
$input | Out-String -Stream | Select-String $pattern
```

For more information about running scripts, see Recipe 1.1.

See Also

Recipe 1.1, "Run Programs, Scripts, and Existing Tools"

1.20 Interactively View and Process Command Output

Problem

You want to graphically explore and analyze the output of a command.

Solution

Use the `Out-GridView` cmdlet to interactively explore the output of a command.

Discussion

The `Out-GridView` cmdlet is one of the rare PowerShell cmdlets that displays a graphical user interface. While the `Where-Object` and `Sort-Object` cmdlets are the most common way to sort and filter lists of items, the `Out-GridView` cmdlet is very effective at the style of repeated refinement that sometimes helps you develop complex queries. Figure 1-3 shows the `Out-GridView` cmdlet in action.

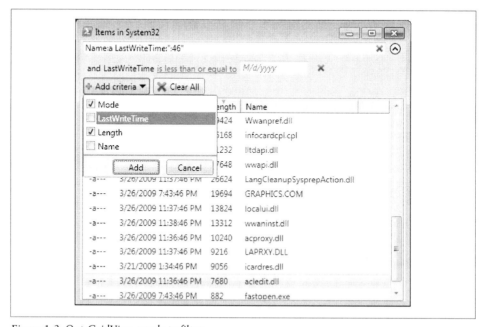

Figure 1-3. Out-GridView, ready to filter

Out-GridView lets you primarily filter your command output in two ways: a *quick filter* expression and a *criteria filter*.

Quick filters are fairly simple. As you type text in the topmost "Filter" window, Out-GridView filters the list to contain only items that match that text. If you want to restrict this text filtering to specific columns, simply provide a column name before your search string and separate the two with a colon. You can provide multiple search strings, in which case Out-GridView returns only rows that match all of the required strings.

 Unlike most filtering cmdlets in PowerShell, the quick filters in the Out-GridView cmdlet do not support wildcards or regular expressions. For this type of advanced query, criteria-based filtering can help.

Criteria filters give fine-grained control over the filtering used by the Out-GridView cmdlet. To apply a criteria filter, click the "Add criteria" button and select a property to filter on. Out-GridView adds a row below the quick filter field and lets you pick one of several operations to apply to this property:

- Less than or equal to
- Greater than or equal to
- Between
- Equals
- Does not equal
- Contains
- Does not contain

In addition to these filtering options, Out-GridView also lets you click and rearrange the header columns to sort by them.

Processing output

Once you've sliced and diced your command output, you can select any rows you want to keep and press Ctrl-C to copy them to the clipboard. Out-GridView copies the items to the clipboard as tab-separated data, so you can easily paste the information into a spreadsheet or other file for further processing.

Despite its clipboard output, exporting items to the Out-GridView cmdlet is primarily a one-way operation. While you can process items somewhat further by exporting them to a spreadsheet or text file, there is no way to access the results of sorting and filtering as full-fidelity objects. For an approach that supports this type of full-fidelity filtering, see Recipe 2.4. Additionally, a graphical version is shown in Recipe 13.10.

See Also

Recipe 2.4, "Program: Interactively Filter Lists of Objects"

Recipe 13.10, "Program: Add a Graphical User Interface to Your Script"

1.21 Store the Output of a Command into a File

Problem

You want to redirect the output of a pipeline into a file.

Solution

To redirect the output of a command into a file, use either the Out-File cmdlet or one of the redirection operators.

Out-File:

```
Get-ChildItem | Out-File unicodeFile.txt
Get-Content filename.cs | Out-File -Encoding ASCII file.txt
Get-ChildItem | Out-File -Width 120 unicodeFile.cs
```

Redirection operators:

```
Get-ChildItem > files.txt
Get-ChildItem 2> errors.txt
```

Discussion

The Out-File cmdlet and redirection operators share a lot in common. For the most part, you can use either. The redirection operators are unique because they give the greatest amount of control over redirecting individual streams. The Out-File cmdlet is unique primarily because it lets you easily configure the formatting width and encoding.

The default formatting width and the default output encoding are two aspects of output redirection that can sometimes cause difficulty.

The default formatting width sometimes causes problems because redirecting PowerShell-formatted output into a file is designed to mimic what you see on the screen. If your screen is 80 characters wide, the file will be 80 characters wide as well. Examples of PowerShell-formatted output include directory listings (that are implicitly formatted as a table) as well as any commands that you explicitly format using one of the *Format-** set of cmdlets. If this causes problems, you can customize the width of the file with the -Width parameter on the Out-File cmdlet.

The default output encoding sometimes causes unexpected results because PowerShell creates all files using the UTF-16 Unicode encoding by default. This allows PowerShell to fully support the entire range of international characters, cmdlets, and output. Although this is a great improvement on traditional shells, it may cause an unwanted surprise when running large search and replace operations on ASCII source code files, for example. To force PowerShell to send its output to a file in the ASCII encoding, use the `-Encoding` parameter on the `Out-File` cmdlet.

For more information about the `Out-File` cmdlet, type **Get-Help Out-File**. For a full list of supported redirection operators, see "Capturing Output" on page 760.

See Also

"Capturing Output" on page 760

1.22 Add Information to the End of a File

Problem

You want to redirect the output of a pipeline into a file but add the information to the end of that file.

Solution

To redirect the output of a command into a file, use either the `-Append` parameter of the `Out-File` cmdlet or one of the appending redirection operators described in "Capturing Output" on page 760. Both support options to append text to the end of a file.

`Out-File`:

```
Get-ChildItem | Out-File -Append files.txt
```

Redirection operators:

```
Get-ChildItem >> files.txt
```

Discussion

The `Out-File` cmdlet and redirection operators share a lot in common. For the most part, you can use either. See the discussion in Recipe 1.21 for a more detailed comparison of the two approaches, including reasons that you would pick one over the other.

See Also

Recipe 1.21, "Store the Output of a Command into a File"

"Capturing Output" on page 760

1.23 Record a Transcript of Your Shell Session

Problem

You want to record a log or transcript of your shell session.

Solution

To record a transcript of your shell session, run the command `Start-Transcript`. It has an optional `-Path` parameter that defaults to a filename based on the current system time. By default, PowerShell places this file in the *My Documents* directory. To stop recording the transcript of your shell system, run the command `Stop-Transcript`.

Discussion

Although the `Get-History` cmdlet is helpful, it does not record the output produced during your PowerShell session. To accomplish that, use the `Start-Transcript` cmdlet. In addition to the `Path` parameter described previously, the `Start-Transcript` cmdlet also supports parameters that let you control how PowerShell interacts with the output file.

1.24 Extend Your Shell with Additional Commands

Problem

You want to use PowerShell cmdlets, providers, or script-based extensions written by a third party.

Solution

Use the `Import-Module` command to import third-party commands into your PowerShell session.

To import a registered module by name:

```
Import-Module Name
```

To import a module from a specific directory:

```
Import-Module c:\path\to\module
```

To import a module from a specific file (module, script, or assembly):

```
Import-Module c:\path\to\module\file.ext
```

Discussion

PowerShell supports two sets of commands that enable additional cmdlets and providers: *-Module and *-PsSnapin. Snapins were the packages for extensions in version one of PowerShell. They supported only compiled extensions and had onerous installation requirements.

Version two of PowerShell introduces *modules* that support everything that snapins support (and more) without the associated installation pain.

The most common way to import a module is by name. PowerShell searches through every directory listed in the PSModulePath environment variable, looking for subdirectories that match the name you specify. Inside those directories, it looks for the module (*.psd1, *.psm1, and *.dll) with the same name and loads it.

 When you install a module on your own system, the most common place to put it is in the *WindowsPowerShell\Modules* directory in your *My Documents* directory.

To have PowerShell look in another directory for modules, add it to your personal PSModulePath environment variable, just as you would add a *Tools* directory to your personal Path.

If you want to load a module from a directory not in PSModulePath, you can provide the entire directory name and module name to the Import-Module command. For example, for a module named Test, use Import-Module *c:\path\to\Test*. As with loading modules by name, PowerShell looks in *c:\temp\path\to* for a module (*.psd1, *.psm1, or *.dll) named Test and loads it.

If you know the specific module file you want to load, you can also specify the full path to that module.

One popular source of additional commands is the PowerShell Community Extensions project, located at *http://www.codeplex.com/PowerShellCX*.

If you want to import these commands for every PowerShell session, add a call to Import-Module to your PowerShell Profile.

See Also

Recipe 1.6, "Customize Your Shell, Profile, and Prompt"

Recipe 11.6, "Package Common Commands in a Module"

1.25 Use Commands from Customized Shells

Problem

You want to use the commands from a PowerShell-based product that launches a customized version of the PowerShell console, but in a regular PowerShell session.

Solution

Launch the customized version of the PowerShell console, and then use the Get-Module and Get-PsSnapin commands to see what additional modules and/or snapins it loaded.

Discussion

As described in Recipe 1.24, PowerShell modules and snapins are the two ways that third parties can distribute and add additional PowerShell commands. Products that provide customized versions of the PowerShell console do this by calling `Power Shell.exe` with one of three parameters:

- `-PSConsoleFile`, to load a console file that provides a list of snapins to load.
- `-Command`, to specify an initial startup command (that then loads a snapin or module)
- `-File`, to specify an initial startup script (that then loads a snapin or module)

Regardless of which one it used, you can examine the resulting set of loaded extensions to see which ones you can import into your other PowerShell sessions.

Detecting loaded snapins

The `Get-PsSnapin` command returns all snapins loaded in the current session. It always returns the set of core PowerShell snapins, but it will also return any additional snapins loaded by the customized environment. For example, if the name of a snapin you recognize is *Product.Feature.Commands*, you can load that into future PowerShell sessions by typing `Add-PsSnapin` *Product.Feature.Commands*. To automate this, add the command into your PowerShell profile.

If you are uncertain of which snapin to load, you can also use the `Get-Command` command to discover which snapin defines a specific command:

```
PS > Get-Command Get-Counter | Select PsSnapin

PSSnapIn
--------
Microsoft.PowerShell.Diagnostics
```

Detecting loaded modules

Like the `Get-PsSnapin` command, the `Get-Module` command returns all modules loaded in the current session. It returns any modules you've added so far into that session, but it will also return any additional modules loaded by the customized environment. For example, if the name of a module you recognize is *ProductModule*, you can load that into future PowerShell sessions by typing `Import-Module` *ProductModule*. To automate this, add the command into your PowerShell profile.

If you are uncertain of which module to load, you can also use the `Get-Command` command to discover which module defines a specific command:

```
PS > Get-Command Start-BitsTransfer | Select Module

Module
------
BitsTransfer
```

See Also

Recipe 1.24, "Extend Your Shell with Additional Commands"

1.26 Save State Between Sessions

Problem

You want to save state or history between PowerShell sessions.

Solution

Subscribe to the `PowerShell.Exiting` engine event to have PowerShell invoke a script or script block that saves any state you need.

To have PowerShell save your command history, place a call to `Enable-HistoryPersistence` in your profile, as in Example 1-14.

Example 1-14. Enable-HistoryPersistence.ps1

```
##############################################################################
##
## Enable-HistoryPersistence
##
## From Windows PowerShell Cookbook (O'Reilly)
## by Lee Holmes (http://www.leeholmes.com/guide)
##
##############################################################################

<#

.SYNOPSIS

Reloads any previously saved command history and registers for the
PowerShell.Exiting engine event to save new history when the shell
exits.

#>

Set-StrictMode -Version Latest

## Load our previous history
$GLOBAL:maximumHistoryCount = 32767
$historyFile = (Join-Path (Split-Path $profile) "commandHistory.clixml")
if(Test-Path $historyFile)
{
    Import-CliXml $historyFile | Add-History
}

## Register for the engine shutdown event
$null = Register-EngineEvent -SourceIdentifier `
    ([System.Management.Automation.PsEngineEvent]::Exiting) -Action {
```

```
## Save our history
$historyFile = (Join-Path (Split-Path $profile) "commandHistory.clixml")
$maximumHistoryCount = 1kb

## Get the previous history items
$oldEntries = @()
if(Test-Path $historyFile)
{
    $oldEntries = Import-CliXml $historyFile -ErrorAction SilentlyContinue
}

## And merge them with our changes
$currentEntries = Get-History -Count $maximumHistoryCount
$additions = Compare-Object $oldEntries $currentEntries `
    -Property CommandLine | Where-Object { $_.SideIndicator -eq "=>" } |
    Foreach-Object { $_.CommandLine }

$newEntries = $currentEntries | ? { $additions -contains $_.CommandLine }

## Keep only unique command lines. First sort by CommandLine in
## descending order (so that we keep the newest entries,) and then
## re-sort by StartExecutionTime.
$history = @($oldEntries + $newEntries) |
    Sort -Unique -Descending CommandLine | Sort StartExecutionTime

## Finally, keep the last 100
Remove-Item $historyFile
$history | Select -Last 100 | Export-CliXml $historyFile
}
```

Discussion

PowerShell provides easy script-based access to a broad variety of system, engine, and other events. You can register for notification of these events and even automatically process any of those events. In this example, we subscribe to the only one currently available, which is called PowerShell.Exiting. PowerShell generates this event when you close a session.

For PowerShell to handle this event, you must use the exit keyword to close your session, rather than the X button at the top right of the console window. In the Integrated Scripting Environment, the close button generates this event as well.

This script could do anything, but in this example we have it save our command history and restore it when we launch PowerShell. Why would we want to do this? Well, with a rich history buffer, we can more easily find and reuse commands we've previously run. For two examples of doing this, see Recipes 1.16 and 1.18.

Example 1-14 takes two main actions. First, we load our stored command history (if any exists). Then, we register an automatic action to be processed whenever the engine generates its PowerShell.Exiting event. The action itself is relatively straightforward, although exporting our new history does take a little finesse. If you have several sessions open at the same time, each will update the saved history file when it exits. Since we don't want to overwrite the history saved by the other shells, we first reload the history from disk and combine it with the history from the current shell.

Once we have the combined list of command lines, we sort them and pick out the unique ones before storing them back in the file.

For more information about working with PowerShell engine events, see Recipe 31.2.

See Also

Recipe 1.1, "Run Programs, Scripts, and Existing Tools"

Recipe 1.16, "Access and Manage Your Console History"

Recipe 31.2, "Create and Respond to Custom Events"

Pipelines

2.0 Introduction

One of the fundamental concepts in a shell is called the *pipeline*. It also forms the basis of one of PowerShell's most significant advances. A pipeline is a big name for a simple concept—a series of commands where the output of one becomes the input of the next. A pipeline in a shell is much like an assembly line in a factory: it successively refines something as it passes between the stages, as shown in Example 2-1.

Example 2-1. A PowerShell pipeline

```
Get-Process | Where-Object { $_.WorkingSet -gt 500kb } | Sort-Object -Descending Name
```

In PowerShell, you separate each stage in the pipeline with the pipe (|) character.

In Example 2-1, the Get-Process cmdlet generates objects that represent actual processes on the system. These process objects contain information about the process's name, memory usage, process ID, and more. As the Get-Process cmdlet generates output, it passes it along. Simultaneously, the Where-Object cmdlet gets to work directly with those processes, testing easily for those that use more than 500 kb of memory. It passes those along immediately as it processes them, allowing the Sort-Object cmdlet to also work directly with those processes and sort them by name in descending order.

This brief example illustrates a significant advancement in the power of pipelines: PowerShell passes full-fidelity objects along the pipeline, not their text representations.

In contrast, all other shells pass data as plain text between the stages. Extracting meaningful information from plain-text output turns the authoring of pipelines into a black art. Expressing the previous example in a traditional Unix-based shell is exceedingly difficult and it is nearly impossible in *cmd.exe*.

Traditional text-based shells make writing pipelines so difficult because they require you to deeply understand the peculiarities of output formatting for each command in the pipeline, as shown in Example 2-2.

Example 2-2. A traditional text-based pipeline

```
lee@trinity:~$ ps -F | awk '{ if($5 > 500) print }' | sort -r -k 64,70
UID         PID PPID C    SZ   RSS PSR STIME TTY          TIME CMD
lee        8175 7967 0   965  1036   0 21:51 pts/0     00:00:00 ps -F
lee        7967 7966 0  1173  2104   0 21:38 pts/0     00:00:00 -bash
```

In this example, you have to know that, for every line, group number five represents the memory usage. You have to know another language (that of the awk tool) to filter by that column. Finally, you have to know the column range that contains the process name (columns 64 to 70 on this system) and then provide that to the sort command. And that's just a simple example.

An object-based pipeline opens up enormous possibilities, making system administration both immensely more simple and more powerful.

2.1 Filter Items in a List or Command Output

Problem

You want to filter the items in a list or command output.

Solution

Use the Where-Object cmdlet to select items in a list (or command output) that match a condition you provide. The Where-Object cmdlet has the standard aliases where and ?.

To list all running processes that have "search" in their name, use the -like operator to compare against the process's Name property:

```
Get-Process | Where-Object { $_.Name -like "*Search*" }
```

To list all directories in the current location, test the PsIsContainer property:

```
Get-ChildItem | Where-Object { $_.PsIsContainer }
```

To list all stopped services, use the -eq operator to compare against the service's Status property:

```
Get-Service | Where-Object { $_.Status -eq "Stopped" }
```

Discussion

For each item in its input (which is the output of the previous command), the Where-Object cmdlet evaluates that input against the script block that you specify. If the script block returns True, then the Where-Object cmdlet passes the object along. Otherwise, it does not. A script block is a series of PowerShell commands enclosed by the { and } characters. You can write any PowerShell commands inside the script block. In the script block, the $_ variable represents the current input object. For each item in the incoming set of objects, PowerShell assigns that item to the $_ variable and then runs your script block. In the preceding examples, this incoming object represents the process, file, or service that the previous cmdlet generated.

This script block can contain a great deal of functionality, if desired. It can combine multiple tests, comparisons, and much more. For more information about script blocks, see Recipe 11.4. For more information about the type of comparisons available to you, see "Comparison Operators" on page 731.

For simple filtering, the syntax of the Where-Object cmdlet may sometimes seem overbearing. Recipe 2.3 shows a script that can make simple filtering (such as the previous examples) easier to work with.

For complex filtering (for example, the type you would normally rely on a mouse to do with files in an Explorer window), writing the script block to express your intent may be difficult or even infeasible. If this is the case, Recipe 2.4 shows a script that can make manual filtering easier to accomplish.

For more information about the Where-Object cmdlet, type **Get-Help Where-Object**.

See Also

Recipe 2.3, "Program: Simplify Most Where-Object Filters"

Recipe 2.4, "Program: Interactively Filter Lists of Objects"

Recipe 11.4, "Write a Script Block"

"Comparison Operators" on page 731

2.2 Group and Pivot Data by Name

Problem

You want to easily access items in a list by a property name.

Solution

Use the Group-Object cmdlet (which has the standard alias group) with the -AsHash and -AsString parameters. This creates a hashtable with the selected property (or expression) used as keys in that hashtable.

```
PS > $h = dir | group -AsHash -AsString Length
PS > $h

Name                    Value
----                    -----
746                     {ReplaceTest.ps1}
499                     {Format-String.ps1}
20494                   {test.dll}
```

```
PS > $h["499"]


    Directory: C:\temp


Mode                LastWriteTime     Length Name
----                -------------     ------ ----
-a---        10/18/2009    9:57 PM       499 Format-String.ps1


PS > $h["746"]


    Directory: C:\temp


Mode                LastWriteTime     Length Name
----                -------------     ------ ----
-a---        10/18/2009    9:51 PM       746 ReplaceTest.ps1
```

Discussion

In some situations, you might find yourself repeatedly calling the Where-Object cmdlet to interact with the same list or output:

```
PS > $processes = Get-Process
PS > $processes | Where-Object { $_.Id -eq 1216 }

Handles  NPM(K)    PM(K)      WS(K) VM(M)   CPU(s)     Id ProcessName
-------  ------    -----      ----- -----   ------     -- -----------
     62       3     1012       3132    50     0.20   1216 dwm


PS > $processes | Where-Object { $_.Id -eq 212 }

Handles  NPM(K)    PM(K)      WS(K) VM(M)   CPU(s)     Id ProcessName
-------  ------    -----      ----- -----   ------     -- -----------
    614      10    28444       5484   117     1.27    212 SearchIndexer
```

In these situations, you can instead use the -AsHash parameter of the Group-Object cmdlet. When you use this parameter, PowerShell creates a hashtable to hold your results, which creates a map between the property you are interested in and the object it represents:

```
PS > $processes = Get-Process | Group-Object -AsHash Id
PS > $processes[1216]

Handles  NPM(K)    PM(K)      WS(K) VM(M)   CPU(s)     Id ProcessName
-------  ------    -----      ----- -----   ------     -- -----------
     62       3     1012       3132    50     0.20   1216 dwm


PS > $processes[212]
```

```
Handles  NPM(K)    PM(K)      WS(K) VM(M)   CPU(s)     Id ProcessName
-------  ------    -----      ----- -----   ------     -- -----------
    610      10    28444       5488   117     1.27    212 SearchIndexer
```

For simple types of data, this approach works well. Depending on your data, though, the -AsHash parameter alone can run into difficulties.

The first issue you might run into comes from when the value of a property is $null. Hashtables in PowerShell (and the .NET Framework that provides the underlying support) do not support $null as a value, so you get a misleading error message:

```
PS > "Hello",(Get-Process -id $pid) | Group-Object -AsHash Id
Group-Object : The objects grouped by this property cannot be expanded
since there is a duplication of the key. Please give a valid property and try
again.
```

A second issue comes when more complex data gets stored within the hashtable. This can unfortunately be true even of data that *appears* to be simple.

```
PS > $result = dir | Group-Object -AsHash Length
PS > $result

Name                       Value
----                       -----
746                        {ReplaceTest.ps1}
499                        {Format-String.ps1}
20494                      {test.dll}

PS > $result[746]
(Nothing appears)
```

This missing result is caused by an incompatibility between the information in the hashtable and the information you typed. This is normally not an issue in hashtables that you create yourself, because you provided all of the information to populate them. In this case, though, the Length values stored in the hashtable come from the directory listing and are of the type Int64. An explicit cast resolves the issue but takes a great deal of trial and error to discover:

```
PS > $result[ [int64] 746 ]


    Directory: C:\temp


Mode                LastWriteTime     Length Name
----                -------------     ------ ----
-a---         10/18/2009   9:51 PM       746 ReplaceTest.ps1
```

It is difficult to avoid both of these issues, so the `Group-Object` cmdlet also offers an `-AsString` parameter to convert all of the values to their string equivalents. With that parameter, you can always assume that the values will be treated as (and accessible by) strings:

```
PS > $result = dir | Group-Object -AsHash -AsString Length
PS > $result["746"]


    Directory: C:\temp


Mode                LastWriteTime     Length Name
----                -------------     ------ ----
-a---        10/18/2009    9:51 PM       746 ReplaceTest.ps1
```

For more information about the `Group-Object` cmdlet, type **Get-Help Group-Object**. For more information about PowerShell hashtables, see Recipe 7.13.

See Also

Recipe 7.13, "Create a Hashtable or Associative Array"

"Hashtables (Associative Arrays)" on page 723

2.3 Program: Simplify Most Where-Object Filters

The `Where-Object` cmdlet is incredibly powerful, in that it allows you to filter your output based on arbitrary criteria. For extremely simple filters (such as filtering based only on a comparison to a single property), though, the syntax can get a little ungainly:

```
Get-Process | Where-Object { $_.Handles -gt 1000 }
```

For this type of situation, it is easy to write a script (as shown in Example 2-3) to offload all the syntax to the script itself:

```
Get-Process | Compare-Property Handles gt 1000
Get-ChildItem | Compare-Property PsIsContainer
```

With a shorter alias, this becomes even easier to type:

```
PS > Set-Alias wheres Compare-Property
PS > Get-ChildItem | wheres Length gt 100
```

Example 2-3 implements this "simple where" functionality. Note that supplying a non-existing operator as the `$operator` parameter will generate an error message.

Example 2-3. Compare-Property.ps1

```
###############################################################################
##
## Compare-Property
##
## From Windows PowerShell Cookbook (O'Reilly)
## by Lee Holmes (http://www.leeholmes.com/guide)
##
###############################################################################

<#

.SYNOPSIS

Compare the property you provide against the input supplied to the script.
This provides the functionality of simple Where-Object comparisons without
the syntax required for that cmdlet.

.EXAMPLE

Get-Process | Compare-Property Handles gt 1000

.EXAMPLE

PS >Set-Alias ?? Compare-Property
PS >dir | ?? PsIsContainer

#>

param(
    ## The property to compare
    $Property,

    ## The operator to use in the comparison
    $Operator = "eq",

    ## The value to compare with
    $MatchText = "$true"
)

Begin { $expression = "`$_.$property -$operator `"$matchText`"" }
Process { if(Invoke-Expression $expression) { $_ } }
```

For more information about running scripts, see Recipe 1.1.

See Also

Recipe 1.1, "Run Programs, Scripts, and Existing Tools"

2.4 Program: Interactively Filter Lists of Objects

There are times when the Where-Object cmdlet is too powerful. In those situations, the Compare-Property script shown in Recipe 2.3 provides a much simpler alternative. There are also times when the Where-Object cmdlet is too simple—when expressing your selection logic as code is more cumbersome than selecting it manually. In those situations, an interactive filter can be much more effective.

Example 2-4 implements this interactive filter. It uses several concepts not covered yet in this book, so feel free to just consider it a neat script for now. To learn more about a part that you don't yet understand, look it up in the Table of Contents or the Index.

Example 2-4. Select-FilteredObject.ps1

```
##############################################################################
##
## Select-FilteredObject
##
## From Windows PowerShell Cookbook (O'Reilly)
## by Lee Holmes (http://www.leeholmes.com/guide)
##
##############################################################################

<#

.SYNOPSIS

Provides an interactive window to help you select complex sets of objects.
To do this, it takes all the input from the pipeline, and presents it in a
notepad window.  Keep any lines that represent objects you want to retain,
delete the rest, then save the file and exit notepad.

The script then passes the original objects that you kept along the
pipeline.

.EXAMPLE

Get-Process | Select-FilteredObject | Stop-Process -WhatIf
Gets all of the processes running on the system, and displays them to you.
After you've selected the ones you want to stop, it pipes those into the
Stop-Process cmdlet.

#>

## PowerShell runs your "begin" script block before it passes you any of the
## items in the pipeline.
begin
{
    Set-StrictMode -Version Latest

    ## Create a temporary file
    $filename = [System.IO.Path]::GetTempFileName()

    ## Define a header in a "here string" that explains how to interact with
```

```
        ## the file
        $header = @"
#############################################################
## Keep any lines that represent obects you want to retain,
## and delete the rest.
##
## Once you finish selecting objects, save this file and
## exit.
#############################################################

"@

        ## Place the instructions into the file
        $header > $filename

        ## Initialize the variables that will hold our list of objects, and
        ## a counter to help us keep track of the objects coming down the
        ## pipeline
        $objectList = @()
        $counter = 0
}

## PowerShell runs your "process" script block for each item it passes down
## the pipeline. In this block, the "$_" variable represents the current
## pipeline object
process
{
        ## Add a line to the file, using PowerShell's format (-f) operator.
        ## When provided the ouput of Get-Process, for example, these lines look
        ## like:
        ## 30: System.Diagnostics.Process (powershell)
        "{0}: {1}" -f $counter,$_.ToString() >> $filename

        ## Add the object to the list of objects, and increment our counter.
        $objectList += $_
        $counter++
}

## PowerShell runs your "end" script block once it completes passing all
## objects down the pipeline.
end
{
        ## Start notepad, then call the process's WaitForExit() method to
        ## pause the script until the user exits notepad.
        $process = Start-Process Notepad -Args $filename -PassThru
        $process.WaitForExit()

        ## Go over each line of the file
        foreach($line in (Get-Content $filename))
        {
                ## Check if the line is of the special format: numbers, followed by
                ## a colon, followed by extra text.
                if($line -match "^(\d+?):.*")
                {
                        ## If it did match the format, then $matches[1] represents the
```

```
            ## number -- a counter into the list of objects we saved during
            ## the "process" section.
            ## So, we output that object from our list of saved objects.
            $objectList[$matches[1]]
        }
    }

    ## Finally, clean up the temporary file.
    Remove-Item $filename
}
```

For more information about running scripts, see Recipe 1.1.

See Also

Recipe 1.1, "Run Programs, Scripts, and Existing Tools"

Recipe 2.3, "Program: Simplify Most Where-Object Filters"

2.5 Work with Each Item in a List or Command Output

Problem

You have a list of items and want to work with each item in that list.

Solution

Use the Foreach-Object cmdlet (which has the standard aliases foreach and %) to work with each item in a list.

To apply a calculation to each item in a list, use the $_ variable as part of a calculation in the script block parameter:

```
PS > 1..10 | Foreach-Object { $_ * 2 }
2
4
6
8
10
12
14
16
18
20
```

To run a program on each file in a directory, use the $_ variable as a parameter to the program in the script block parameter:

```
Get-ChildItem *.txt | Foreach-Object { attrib -r $_ }
```

To access a method or property for each object in a list, access that method or property on the `$_` variable in the script block parameter. In this example, you get the list of running processes called notepad, and then wait for each of them to exit:

```
$notepadProcesses = Get-Process notepad
$notepadProcesses | Foreach-Object { $_.WaitForExit() }
```

Discussion

Like the `Where-Object` cmdlet, the `Foreach-Object` cmdlet runs the script block that you specify for each item in the input. A script block is a series of PowerShell commands enclosed by the { and } characters. For each item in the set of incoming objects, PowerShell assigns that item to the `$_` variable, one element at a time. In the examples given by the solution, the `$_` variable represents each file or process that the previous cmdlet generated.

This script block can contain a great deal of functionality, if desired. You can combine multiple tests, comparisons, and much more. For more information about script blocks, see Recipe 11.4. For more information about the type of comparisons available to you, see "Comparison Operators" on page 731.

 The first example in the solution demonstrates a neat way to generate ranges of numbers: `1..10`

This is PowerShell's array range syntax, which you can learn more about in Recipe 7.3.

The `Foreach-Object` cmdlet isn't the only way to perform actions on items in a list. The PowerShell scripting language supports several other keywords, such as `for`, (a different) `foreach`, `do`, and `while`. For information on how to use those keywords, see Recipe 4.4.

For more information about the `Foreach-Object` cmdlet, type **Get-Help Foreach-Object**.

For more information about dealing with pipeline input in your own scripts, functions, and script blocks, see Recipe 11.18.

See Also

Recipe 4.4, "Repeat Operations with Loops"

Recipe 7.3, "Access Elements of an Array"

Recipe 11.4, "Write a Script Block"

Recipe 11.18, "Access Pipeline Input"

"Comparison Operators" on page 731

2.6 Automate Data-Intensive Tasks

Problem

You want to invoke a simple task on large amounts of data.

Solution

If only one piece of data changes (such as a server name or username), store the data in a text file. Use the Get-Content cmdlet to retrieve the items, and then use the Foreach-Object cmdlet (which has the standard aliases foreach and %) to work with each item in that list. Example 2-5 illustrates this technique.

Example 2-5. Using information from a text file to automate data-intensive tasks

```
PS > Get-Content servers.txt
SERVER1
SERVER2
PS > $computers = Get-Content servers.txt
PS > $computers | Foreach-Object { Get-WmiObject Win32_OperatingSystem -Computer $_ }

SystemDirectory : C:\WINDOWS\system32
Organization    :
BuildNumber     : 2600
Version         : 5.1.2600

SystemDirectory : C:\WINDOWS\system32
Organization    :
BuildNumber     : 2600
Version         : 5.1.2600
```

If it becomes cumbersome (or unclear) to include the actions in the Foreach-Object cmdlet, you can also use the foreach scripting keyword, as illustrated in Example 2-6.

Example 2-6. Using the foreach scripting keyword to make a looping statement easier to read

```
$computers = Get-Content servers.txt

foreach($computer in $computers)
{
    ## Get the information about the operating system from WMI
    $system = Get-WmiObject Win32_OperatingSystem -Computer $computer

    ## Determine if it is running Windows XP
    if($system.Version -eq "5.1.2600")
    {
        "$computer is running Windows XP"
    }
}
```

If several aspects of the data change per task (for example, both the WMI class and the computer name for computers in a large report), create a CSV file with a row for each task. Use the `Import-Csv` cmdlet to import that data into PowerShell, and then use properties of the resulting objects as multiple sources of related data. Example 2-7 illustrates this technique.

Example 2-7. Using information from a CSV to automate data-intensive tasks

```
PS > Get-Content WmiReport.csv
ComputerName,Class
LEE-DESK,Win32_OperatingSystem
LEE-DESK,Win32_Bios
PS > $data = Import-Csv WmiReport.csv
PS > $data

ComputerName                    Class
------------                    -----
LEE-DESK                        Win32_OperatingSystem
LEE-DESK                        Win32_Bios


PS > $data |
    Foreach-Object { Get-WmiObject $_.Class -Computer $_.ComputerName }



SystemDirectory : C:\WINDOWS\system32
Organization    :
BuildNumber     : 2600
Version         : 5.1.2600

SMBIOSBIOSVersion : ASUS A7N8X Deluxe ACPI BIOS Rev 1009
Manufacturer      : Phoenix Technologies, LTD
Name              : Phoenix - AwardBIOS v6.00PG
SerialNumber      : xxxxxxxxxxx
Version           : Nvidia - 42302e31
```

Discussion

One of the major benefits of PowerShell is its capability to automate repetitive tasks. Sometimes these repetitive tasks are action-intensive (such as system maintenance through registry and file cleanup) and consist of complex sequences of commands that will always be invoked together. In those situations, you can write a script to combine these operations to save time and reduce errors.

Other times, you need only to accomplish a single task (for example, retrieving the results of a WMI query) but need to invoke that task repeatedly for a large amount of data. In those situations, PowerShell's scripting statements, pipeline support, and data management cmdlets help automate those tasks.

One of the options given by the solution is the `Import-Csv` cmdlet. The `Import-Csv` cmdlet reads a CSV file and, for each row, automatically creates an object with properties that correspond to the names of the columns. Example 2-8 shows the results of a CSV that contains a `ComputerName` and `Class` header.

Example 2-8. The Import-Csv cmdlet creating objects with Computer Name and Class properties

```
PS > $data = Import-Csv WmiReport.csv
PS > $data

ComputerName                    Class
------------                    -----
LEE-DESK                        Win32_OperatingSystem
LEE-DESK                        Win32_Bios


PS > $data[0].ComputerName
LEE-DESK
```

As the solution illustrates, you can use the `Foreach-Object` cmdlet to provide data from these objects to repetitive cmdlet calls. It does this by specifying each parameter name, followed by the data (taken from a property of the current CSV object) that applies to it.

While this is the most general solution, many cmdlet parameters can automatically retrieve their value from incoming objects if any property of that object has the same name. This can let you omit the `Foreach-Object` and property mapping steps altogether. Parameters that support this feature are said to support *value from pipeline by property name*. The `Move-Item` cmdlet is one example of a cmdlet with parameters that support this, as shown by the `Accept pipeline input` rows in Example 2-9.

Example 2-9. Help content of the Move-Item showing a parameter that accepts value from pipeline by property name

```
PS > Get-Help Move-Item -Full
(...)
PARAMETERS

    -path <string[]>
        Specifies the path to the current location of the items. The default
        is the current directory. Wildcards are permitted.

        Required?                  true
        Position?                  1
        Default value              <current location>
        Accept pipeline input?     true (ByValue, ByPropertyName)
        Accept wildcard characters? true

    -destination <string>
        Specifies the path to the location where the items are being moved.
        The default is the current directory. Wildcards are permitted, but
        the result must specify a single location.

        To rename the item being moved, specify a new name in the value of
        Destination.

        Required?                  false
        Position?                  2
        Default value              <current location>
```

```
Accept pipeline input?      true (ByPropertyName)
Accept wildcard characters?  True
(...)
```

If you purposefully name the columns in the CSV to correspond to parameters that take their value from pipeline by property name, PowerShell can do some (or all) of the parameter mapping for you. Example 2-10 demonstrates a CSV file that moves items in bulk.

Example 2-10. Using the Import-Csv cmdlet to automate a cmdlet that accepts value from pipeline by property name

```
PS > Get-Content ItemMoves.csv
Path,Destination
test.txt,Test1Directory
test2.txt,Test2Directory
PS > dir test.txt,test2.txt | Select Name

Name
----
test.txt
test2.txt


PS > Import-Csv ItemMoves.csv | Move-Item
PS > dir Test1Directory | Select Name

Name
----
test.txt


PS > dir Test2Directory | Select Name
Name
----
test2.txt
```

For more information about the Foreach-Object cmdlet and foreach scripting keyword, see Recipe 2.5. For more information about working with CSV files, see Recipe 10.7. For more information about working with Windows Management Instrumentation (WMI), see Chapter 28.

See Also

Recipe 2.5, "Work with Each Item in a List or Command Output"

Recipe 10.7, "Import CSV and Delimited Data from a File"

Chapter 28, *Windows Management Instrumentation*

2.7 Program: Simplify Most Foreach-Object Pipelines

Problem

You want to access methods and retrieve properties of each pipeline object without the overhead required by the Foreach-Object cmdlet.

Solution

Use the Invoke-Member script (Example 2-11) to avoid the need for script blocks and pipeline variables ($_) for simple property and method access.

Example 2-11. Invoke-Member.ps1

```
##############################################################################
##
## Invoke-Member
##
## From Windows PowerShell Cookbook (O'Reilly)
## by Lee Holmes (http://www.leeholmes.com/guide)
##
##############################################################################

<#

.SYNOPSIS

Enables easy access to methods and properties of pipeline objects.

.EXAMPLE

PS >"Hello","World" | .\Invoke-Member Length
5
5

.EXAMPLE

PS >"Hello","World" | .\Invoke-Member -m ToUpper
HELLO
WORLD

.EXAMPLE

PS >"Hello","World" | .\Invoke-Member Replace l w
Hewwo
Worwd

#>

[CmdletBinding(DefaultParameterSetName= "Member")]
param(

    ## A switch parameter to identify the requested member as a method.
```

```
    ## Only required for methods that take no arguments.
    [Parameter(ParameterSetName = "Method")]
    [Alias("M","Me")]
    [switch] $Method,

    ## The name of the member to retrieve
    [Parameter(ParameterSetName = "Method", Position = 0)]
    [Parameter(ParameterSetName = "Member", Position = 0)]
    [string] $Member,

    ## Arguments for the method, if any
    [Parameter(
        ParameterSetName = "Method", Position = 1,
        Mandatory = $false, ValueFromRemainingArguments = $true)]
    [object[]] $ArgumentList = @(),

    ## The object from which to retrieve the member
    [Parameter(ValueFromPipeline = $true)]
    $InputObject
    )

begin
{
    Set-StrictMode -Version Latest
}

process
{
    ## If the user specified a method, invoke it
    ## with any required arguments.
    if($psCmdlet.ParameterSetName -eq "Method")
    {
        $inputObject.$member.Invoke(@($argumentList))
    }
    ## Otherwise, retrieve the property
    else
    {
        $inputObject.$member
    }
}
```

Discussion

As shown in Recipe 2.6, the Foreach-Object cmdlet literally supports the entire
PowerShell scripting language when working with objects in a pipeline. However, the
syntax and nonalphabetic characters required for simple expressions can sometimes
feel overbearing.

In addition to the `Foreach-Object` cmdlet, you can use the `-ExpandProperty` parameter of the `Select-Object` cmdlet to retrieve the value of properties:

```
PS > "Hello","World" | Select-Object -Expand Length
5
5
```

While its main intent is to include the properties of nested objects as through they were properties of the parent object, it is a useful shortcut for this situation as well.

To remove this syntax overhead, the `Invoke-Member` script supports simple method and property access as its main (and only) function. To make this even easier to type, give it a short alias, such as:

```
PS > Set-Alias :: Invoke-Member
PS > dir | :: Length
907
1425
1641
2057
2286
1854
11220
1562
248
985
560
524
```

For an example of applying this type of simplification to the `Where-Object` cmdlet, see Recipe 2.3.

See Also

Recipe 1.1, "Run Programs, Scripts, and Existing Tools"

Recipe 2.3, "Program: Simplify Most Where-Object Filters"

2.8 Intercept Stages of the Pipeline

Problem

You want to intercept or take some action at different stages of the PowerShell pipeline.

Solution

Use the `New-CommandWrapper` script given in Recipe 11.23 to wrap the `Out-Default` command, and place your custom functionality in that.

Discussion

For any pipeline, PowerShell adds an implicit call to the `Out-Default` cmdlet at the end. By adding a command wrapper over this function we can heavily customize the pipeline processing behavior.

When PowerShell creates a pipeline, it first calls the `BeginProcessing()` method of each command in the pipeline. For advanced functions (the type created by the `New-Command Wrapper` script), PowerShell invokes the `Begin` block. If you want to do anything at the beginning of the pipeline, then put your customizations in that block.

For each object emitted by the pipeline, PowerShell sends that object to the `ProcessRecord()` method of the next command in the pipeline. For advanced functions (the type created by the `New-CommandWrapper` script), PowerShell invokes the `Process` block. If you want to do anything for each element in the pipeline, put your customizations in that block.

Finally, when PowerShell has processed all items in the pipeline, it calls the `EndProcessing()` method of each command in the pipeline. For advanced functions (the type created by the `New-CommandWrapper` script), PowerShell invokes the `End` block. If you want to do anything at the end of the pipeline, then put your customizations in that block.

For two examples of this approach, see Recipe 2.9 and Recipe 11.22.

For more information about running scripts, see Recipe 1.1.

See Also

Recipe 1.1, "Run Programs, Scripts, and Existing Tools"

Recipe 2.9, "Automatically Capture Pipeline Output"

Recipe 11.22, "Invoke Dynamically Named Commands"

Recipe 11.23, "Program: Enhance or Extend an Existing Cmdlet"

2.9 Automatically Capture Pipeline Output

Problem

You want to automatically capture the output of the last command without explicitly storing its output in a variable.

Solution

Invoke the `Add-ObjectCollector` script, which in turn builds upon the `New-CommandWrapper` script.

Example 2-12. Add-ObjectCollector.ps1

```
##############################################################################
##
## Add-ObjectCollector
##
## From Windows PowerShell Cookbook (O'Reilly)
## by Lee Holmes (http://www.leeholmes.com/guide)
##
##############################################################################

<#

.SYNOPSIS

Adds a new Out-Default command wrapper to store up to 500 elements from
the previous command. This wrapper stores output in the $ll variable.

.EXAMPLE

PS >Get-Command $pshome\powershell.exe

CommandType     Name                        Definition
-----------     ----                        ----------
Application     powershell.exe              C:\Windows\System32\Windo...

PS >$ll.Definition
C:\Windows\System32\WindowsPowerShell\v1.0\powershell.exe

.NOTES

This command builds on New-CommandWrapper, also included in the Windows
PowerShell Cookbook.

#>

Set-StrictMode -Version Latest

New-CommandWrapper Out-Default `
    -Begin {
        $cachedOutput = New-Object System.Collections.ArrayList
    } `
    -Process {
        ## If we get an input object, add it to our list of objects
        if($_ -ne $null) { $null = $cachedOutput.Add($_) }
        while($cachedOutput.Count -gt 500) { $cachedOutput.RemoveAt(0) }
    } `
    -End {
        ## Be sure we got objects that were not just errors (
        ## so that we don't wipe out the saved output when we get errors
        ## trying to work with it.)
        ## Also don't capture formatting information, as those objects
        ## can't be worked with.
        $uniqueOutput = $cachedOutput | Foreach-Object {
            $_.GetType().FullName } | Select -Unique
        $containsInterestingTypes = ($uniqueOutput -notcontains `
```

```
        "System.Management.Automation.ErrorRecord") -and
        ($uniqueOutput -notlike `
            "Microsoft.PowerShell.Commands.Internal.Format.*")

    ## If we actually had output, and it was interesting information,
    ## save the output into the $ll variable
    if(($cachedOutput.Count -gt 0) -and $containsInterestingTypes)
    {
        $GLOBAL:ll = $cachedOutput | % { $_ }
    }
}
```

Discussion

The example in the Solution builds a command wrapper over the `Out-Default` command by first creating an `ArrayList` during the `Begin` stage of the pipeline.

As each object passes down the pipeline (and is processed by the `Process` block of `Out-Default`), the wrapper created by `Add-ObjectCollector` adds the object to the `ArrayList`.

Once the pipeline completes, the `Add-ObjectCollector` wrapper stores the saved items in the $ll variable, making them always available at the next prompt.

See Also

Recipe 1.1, "Run Programs, Scripts, and Existing Tools"

Recipe 2.8, "Intercept Stages of the Pipeline"

Recipe 11.23, "Program: Enhance or Extend an Existing Cmdlet"

2.10 Capture and Redirect Binary Process Output

Problem

You want to run programs that transfer complex binary data between themselves.

Solution

Use the `Invoke-BinaryProcess` script to invoke the program. If it is the source of binary data, use the `-RedirectOutput` parameter. If it consumes binary data, use the `-RedirectInput` parameter.

Example 2-13. Invoke-BinaryProcess.ps1

```
###############################################################################
##
## Invoke-BinaryProcess
##
## From Windows PowerShell Cookbook (O'Reilly)
## by Lee Holmes (http://www.leeholmes.com/guide)
##
###############################################################################

<#

.SYNOPSIS

Invokes a process that emits or consumes binary data.

.EXAMPLE

Invoke-BinaryProcess binaryProcess.exe -RedirectOutput |
     Invoke-BinaryProcess binaryProcess.exe -RedirectInput

#>

param(
    ## The name of the process to invoke
    [string] $ProcessName,

    ## Specifies that input to the process should be treated as
    ## binary
    [Alias("Input")]
    [switch] $RedirectInput,

    ## Specifies that the output of the process should be treated
    ## as binary
    [Alias("Output")]
    [switch] $RedirectOutput,

    ## Specifies the arguments for the process
    [string] $ArgumentList
)

Set-StrictMode -Version Latest

## Prepare to invoke the process
$processStartInfo = New-Object System.Diagnostics.ProcessStartInfo
$processStartInfo.FileName = (Get-Command $processname).Definition
$processStartInfo.WorkingDirectory = (Get-Location).Path
if($argumentList) { $processStartInfo.Arguments = $argumentList }
$processStartInfo.UseShellExecute = $false

## Always redirect the input and output of the process.
## Sometimes we will capture it as binary, other times we will
## just treat it as strings.
$processStartInfo.RedirectStandardOutput = $true
$processStartInfo.RedirectStandardInput = $true
```

```
$process = [System.Diagnostics.Process]::Start($processStartInfo)

## If we've been asked to redirect the input, treat it as bytes.
## Otherwise, write any input to the process as strings.
if($redirectInput)
{
    $inputBytes = @($input)
    $process.StandardInput.BaseStream.Write($inputBytes, 0, $inputBytes.Count)
    $process.StandardInput.Close()
}
else
{

    $input | % { $process.StandardInput.WriteLine($_) }
    $process.StandardInput.Close()
}

## If we've been asked to redirect the output, treat it as bytes.
## Otherwise, read any input from the process as strings.
if($redirectOutput)
{
    $byteRead = -1
    do
    {
        $byteRead = $process.StandardOutput.BaseStream.ReadByte()
        if($byteRead -ge 0) { $byteRead }
    } while($byteRead -ge 0)
}
else
{
    $process.StandardOutput.ReadToEnd()
}
```

Discussion

When PowerShell launches a native application, one of the benefits it provides is allowing you to use PowerShell commands to work with the output. For example:

```
PS > (ipconfig)[7]
   Link-local IPv6 Address . . . . . : fe80::20f9:871:8365:f368%8
PS > (ipconfig)[8]
   IPv4 Address. . . . . . . . . . : 10.211.55.3
```

PowerShell enables this by splitting the output of the program on its newline characters, and then passing each line independently down the pipeline. This includes programs that use the Unix newline (\n) as well as the Windows newline (\r\n).

If the program outputs binary data, however, that reinterpretation can corrupt data as it gets redirected to another process or file. For example, some programs communicate between themselves through complicated binary data structures that cannot be modified along the way. This is common in some image editing utilities and other non-PowerShell tools designed for pipelined data manipulation.

We can see this through an example `BinaryProcess.exe` that either emits binary data or consumes it. Here is the C# source code to the `BinaryProcess.exe` application:

```csharp
using System;
using System.IO;

public class BinaryProcess
{
    public static void Main(string[] args)
    {
        if(args[0] == "-consume")
        {
            using(Stream inputStream = Console.OpenStandardInput())
            {
                for(byte counter = 0; counter < 255; counter++)
                {
                    byte received = (byte) inputStream.ReadByte();
                    if(received != counter)
                    {
                        Console.WriteLine(
                            "Got an invalid byte: {0}, expected {1}.",
                            received, counter);
                        return;
                    }
                    else
                    {
                        Console.WriteLine(
                            "Properly received byte: {0}.", received, counter);
                    }
                }
            }
        }

        if(args[0] == "-emit")
        {
            using(Stream outputStream = Console.OpenStandardOutput())
            {
                for(byte counter = 0; counter < 255; counter++)
                {
                    outputStream.WriteByte(counter);
                }
            }
        }
    }
}
```

When we run it with the -emit parameter, PowerShell breaks the output into three objects:

```
PS > $output = .\binaryprocess.exe -emit
PS > $output.Count
3
```

We would expect this output to contain the numbers 0 through 254, but we see that it does not:

```
PS > $output | Foreach-Object { "------------";
    $_.ToCharArray() | Foreach-Object { [int] $_ } }
------------
0
1
2
3
4
5
6
7
8
9
------------
11
12
------------
14
15
16
17
18
19
20
21
22
(...)
255
214
220
162
163
165
8359
402
225
```

At number 10, PowerShell interprets that byte as the end of the line, and uses that to split the output into a new element. It does the same for number 13. Things appear to get even stranger when we get to the higher numbers and PowerShell starts to interpret combinations of bytes as Unicode characters from another language.

The solution resolves this behavior by managing the output of the binary process directly. If you supply the -RedirectInput parameter, the script assumes an incoming stream of binary data and passes it to the program directly. If you supply the -RedirectOutput parameter, the script assumes that the output is binary data, and likewise reads it from the process directly.

See Also

Recipe 1.1, "Run Programs, Scripts, and Existing Tools"

Variables and Objects

3.0 Introduction

As touched on in Chapter 2, PowerShell makes life immensely easier by keeping information in its native form: *objects*. Users expend most of their effort in traditional shells just trying to resuscitate information that the shell converted from its native form to plain text. Tools have evolved that ease the burden of working with plain text, but that job is still significantly more difficult than it needs to be.

Since PowerShell builds on Microsoft's .NET Framework, native information comes in the form of .NET *objects*—packages of information and functionality closely related to that information.

Let's say that you want to get a list of running processes on your system. In other shells, your command (such as `tlist.exe` or `/bin/ps`) generates a plain-text report of the running processes on your system. To work with that output, you send it through a bevy of text processing tools—if you are lucky enough to have them available.

PowerShell's `Get-Process` cmdlet generates a list of the running processes on your system.

In contrast to other shells, though, these are full-fidelity `System.Diagnostics.Process` objects straight out of the .NET Framework. The .NET Framework documentation describes them as objects that "[provide] access to local and remote processes, and [enable] you to start and stop local system processes." With those objects in hand, PowerShell makes it trivial for you to access properties of objects (such as their process name or memory usage) and to access functionality on these objects (such as stopping them, starting them, or waiting for them to exit).

3.1 Display the Properties of an Item as a List

Problem

You have an item (for example, an error record, directory item, or .NET object), and you want to display detailed information about that object in a list format.

Solution

To display detailed information about an item, pass that item to the `Format-List` cmdlet. For example, to display an error in list format, type the following commands:

```
$currentError = $error[0]
$currentError | Format-List -Force
```

Discussion

Many commands by default display a summarized view of their output in a table format, for example, the `Get-Process` cmdlet:

```
PS > Get-Process PowerShell

Handles  NPM(K)    PM(K)    WS(K) VM(M)   CPU(s)     Id ProcessName
-------  ------    -----    ----- -----   ------     -- -----------
    920      10    43808    48424   183     4.69   1928 powershell
    149       6    18228     8660   146     0.48   1940 powershell
    431      11    33308    19072   172            2816 powershell
```

In most cases, the output actually contains a great deal more information. You can use the `Format-List` cmdlet to view it:

```
PS > Get-Process PowerShell | Format-List *


__NounName                 : Process
Name                       : powershell
Handles                    : 443
VM                         : 192176128
WS                         : 52363264
PM                         : 47308800
NPM                        : 9996
Path                       : C:\WINDOWS\system32\WindowsPowerShell\v1.0\power
                             shell.exe
Company                    : Microsoft Corporation
CPU                        : 4.921875
FileVersion                : 6.0.6002.18139 (vistasp2_gdr_win7ip_winman(wmbla
                             ).090902-1426)
ProductVersion             : 6.0.6002.18139
Description                : Windows PowerShell
(...)
```

The `Format-List` cmdlet is one of the four PowerShell formatting cmdlets. These cmdlets are `Format-Table`, `Format-List`, `Format-Wide`, and `Format-Custom`. The `Format-List` cmdlet takes input and displays information about that input as a list.

By default, PowerShell takes the list of properties to display from the *.format.ps1xml* files in PowerShell's installation directory. In many situations, you'll only get a small set of the properties:

```
PS > Get-Process PowerShell | Format-List

Id      : 2816
Handles : 431
CPU     :
Name    : powershell

Id      : 5244
Handles : 665
CPU     : 10.296875
Name    : powershell
```

To display all properties of the item, type **Format-List ***. If you type `Format-List *` but still do not get a list of the item's properties, then the item is defined in the *.format.ps1xml* files, but does not define anything to be displayed for the list command. In that case, type **Format-List -Force**.

One common stumbling block in PowerShell's formatting cmdlets comes from putting them in the middle of a script or pipeline:

```
PS > Get-Process PowerShell | Format-List | Sort Name
out-lineoutput : The object of type "Microsoft.PowerShell.Commands.Internal.
Format.FormatEntryData" is not valid or not in the correct sequence. This is
likely caused by a user-specified "format-*" command which is conflicting with
the default formatting.
```

Internally, PowerShell's formatting commands generate a new type of object: `Microsoft.PowerShell.Commands.Internal.Format.*`. When these objects make it to the end of the pipeline, PowerShell automatically sends them to an output cmdlet: by default, `Out-Default`. These `Out-*` cmdlets assume that the objects arrive in a certain order, so doing anything with the output of the formatting commands causes an error the output system.

To resolve this problem, try to avoid calling the formatting cmdlets in the middle of a script or pipeline. When you do this, the output of your script no longer lends itself to the object-based manipulation so synonymous with PowerShell. If you want to display formatted output anyway, send the output through the `Out-String` cmdlet:

```
Get-Process PowerShell | Format-List | Out-String -Stream
```

Object-manipulation commands still will not work (since the objects have been converted to strings), but at least the script will not generate errors.

For more information about the Format-List cmdlet, type **Get-Help Format-List**.

3.2 Display the Properties of an Item as a Table

Problem

You have a set of items (for example, error records, directory items, or .NET objects), and you want to display summary information about them in a table format.

Solution

To display summary information about a set of items, pass those items to the Format-Table cmdlet. This is the default type of formatting for sets of items in PowerShell and provides several useful features.

To use PowerShell's default formatting, pipe the output of a cmdlet (such as the Get-Process cmdlet) to the Format-Table cmdlet:

```
Get-Process | Format-Table
```

To display specific properties (such as Name and WorkingSet) in the table formatting, supply those property names as parameters to the Format-Table cmdlet:

```
Get-Process | Format-Table Name,WS
```

To instruct PowerShell to format the table in the most readable manner, supply the -Auto flag to the Format-Table cmdlet. PowerShell defines WS as an alias of the Working Set property for processes:

```
Get-Process | Format-Table Name,WS -Auto
```

To define a custom column definition (such as a process's WorkingSet in megabytes), supply a custom formatting expression to the Format-Table cmdlet:

```
$fields = "Name",@{Label = "WS (MB)"; Expression = {$_.WS / 1mb}; Align = "Right"}
Get-Process | Format-Table $fields -Auto
```

Discussion

The Format-Table cmdlet is one of the four PowerShell formatting cmdlets. These cmdlets are Format-Table, Format-List, Format-Wide, and Format-Custom. The Format-Table cmdlet takes input and displays information about that input as a table. By default, PowerShell takes the list of properties to display from the *.format.ps1xml files in PowerShell's installation directory. You can display all properties of the items if you type **Format-Table ***, although this is rarely a useful view.

The -Auto parameter to Format-Table is a helpful way to automatically format the table in the most readable way possible. It does come at a cost, however. To figure out the best table layout, PowerShell needs to examine each item in the incoming set of items. For small sets of items, this doesn't make much difference, but for large sets (such as a recursive directory listing) it does. Without the -Auto parameter, the Format-Table

---

cmdlet can display items as soon as it receives them. With the -Auto flag, the cmdlet displays results only after it receives all the input.

Perhaps the most interesting feature of the Format-Table cmdlet is illustrated by the last example: the ability to define completely custom table columns. You define a custom table column similarly to the way that you define a custom column list. Rather than specify an existing property of the items, you provide a hashtable. That hashtable includes up to three keys: the column's label, a formatting expression, and alignment. The Format-Table cmdlet shows the label as the column header and uses your expression to generate data for that column. The label must be a string, the expression must be a script block, and the alignment must be either "Left", "Center", or "Right". In the expression script block, the $_ variable represents the current item being formatted.

The Select-Object cmdlet supports a similar hashtable to add calculated properties, but uses Name (rather than Label) as the key to identify the property. After realizing how confusing this was, version two of PowerShell updated both cmdlets to accept both Name and Label.

The expression shown in the last example takes the working set of the current item and divides it by 1 megabyte (1 MB).

One common stumbling block in PowerShell's formatting cmdlets comes from putting them in the middle of a script or pipeline:

```
PS > Get-Process PowerShell | Format-Table | Sort Name
out-lineoutput : The object of type "Microsoft.PowerShell.Commands.Internal.
Format.FormatEntryData" is not valid or not in the correct sequence. This is
likely caused by a user-specified "format-*" command which is conflicting with
the default formatting.
```

Internally, PowerShell's formatting commands generate a new type of object: Microsoft.PowerShell.Commands.Internal.Format.*. When these objects make it to the end of the pipeline, PowerShell then automatically sends them to an output cmdlet: by default, Out-Default. These Out-* cmdlets assume that the objects arrive in a certain order, so doing anything with the output of the formatting commands causes an error in the output system.

To resolve this problem, try to avoid calling the formatting cmdlets in the middle of a script or pipeline. When you do this, the output of your script no longer lends itself to the object-based manipulation so synonymous with PowerShell. If you want to display formatted output anyway, send the output through the Out-String cmdlet:

```
Get-Process PowerShell | Format-Table | Out-String -Stream
```

Object-manipulation commands still will not work (since the objects have been converted to strings), but at least the script will not generate errors.

For more information about the Format-Table cmdlet, type **Get-Help Format-Table**. For more information about hashtables, see Recipe 7.13. For more information about script blocks, see Recipe 11.4.

See Also

Recipe 7.13, "Create a Hashtable or Associative Array"

Recipe 11.4, "Write a Script Block"

3.3 Store Information in Variables

Problem

You want to store the output of a pipeline or command for later use or to work with it in more detail.

Solution

To store output for later use, store the output of the command in a variable. You can access this information later, or even pass it down the pipeline as though it were the output of the original command:

```
PS > $result = 2 + 2
PS > $result
4
PS > $processes = Get-Process
PS > $processes.Count
85
PS > $processes | Where-Object { $_.ID -eq 0 }

Handles  NPM(K)    PM(K)     WS(K) VM(M)   CPU(s)    Id ProcessName
-------  ------    -----     ----- -----   -----     -- -----------
      0       0        0        16     0               0 Idle
```

Discussion

Variables in PowerShell (and all other scripting and programming languages) let you store the output of something so that you can use it later. A variable name starts with a dollar sign ($) and can be followed by nearly any character. A small set of characters have special meaning to PowerShell, so PowerShell provides a way to make variable names that include even these.

For more information about the syntax and types of PowerShell variables, see "Variables" on page 716.

You can store the result of any pipeline or command in a variable to use it later. If that command generates simple data (such as a number or string), then the variable contains simple data. If the command generates rich data (such as the objects that represent system processes from the `Get-Process` cmdlet), then the variable contains that list of rich data. If the command (such as a traditional executable) generates plain text (such as the output of traditional executable), then the variable contains plain text.

 If you've stored a large amount of data into a variable but no longer need that data, assign a new value (such as `$null`) to that variable. That will allow PowerShell to release the memory it was using to store that data.

In addition to variables that you create, PowerShell automatically defines several variables that represent things such as the location of your profile file, the process ID of PowerShell, and more. For a full list of these automatic variables, type **`Get-Help about_automatic_variables`**.

See Also

"Variables" on page 716

`Get-Help about_automatic_variables`

3.4 Access Environment Variables

Problem

You want to use an environment variable (such as the system path or the current user's name) in your script or interactive session.

Solution

PowerShell offers several ways to access environment variables.

To list all environment variables, list the children of the env drive:

```
Get-ChildItem env:
```

To get an environment variable using a more concise syntax, precede its name with `$env`:

```
$env:variablename
```

(for example, `$env:username`).

To get an environment variable using its provider path, supply env: or `Environment::` to the `Get-ChildItem` cmdlet:

```
Get-ChildItem env:variablename
Get-ChildItem Environment::variablename
```

Discussion

PowerShell provides access to environment variables through its *environment provider*. Providers let you work with data stores (such as the registry, environment variables, and aliases) much as you would access the filesystem.

By default, PowerShell creates a drive (called env) that works with the *environment provider* to let you access environment variables. The environment provider lets you access items in the env: drive as you would any other drive: dir env:*variablename* or dir env:*variablename*. If you want to access the provider directly (rather than go through its drive), you can also type **dir Environment::*variablename***.

However, the most common (and easiest) way to work with environment variables is by typing **$env:*variablename***. This works with any provider but is most typically used with environment variables.

This is because the environment provider shares something in common with several other providers—namely support for the *-Content set of core cmdlets (see Example 3-1).

Example 3-1. Working with content on different providers

```
PS > "hello world" > test
PS > Get-Content test
hello world
PS > Get-Content c:test
hello world
PS > Get-Content variable:ErrorActionPreference
Continue
PS > Get-Content function:more
param([string[]]$paths)
$OutputEncoding = [System.Console]::OutputEncoding

if($paths)
{
    foreach ($file in $paths)
    {
        Get-Content $file | more.com
    }
}
else
{
    $input | more.com
}
PS > Get-Content env:systemroot
C:\WINDOWS
```

For providers that support the content cmdlets, PowerShell lets you interact with this content through a special variable syntax (see Example 3-2).

Example 3-2. Using PowerShell's special variable syntax to access content

```
PS > $function:more
param([string[]]$paths); if(($paths -ne $null) -and ($paths.length -ne 0)) { ...
    Get-Content $local:file | Out-Host -p } } else { $input | Out-Host ...
PS > $variable:ErrorActionPreference
Continue
PS > $c:test
hello world
PS > $env:systemroot
C:\WINDOWS
```

This variable syntax for content management lets you both get and set content:

```
PS > $function:more = { $input | less.exe }
PS > $function:more
$input | less.exe
```

Now, when it comes to accessing complex provider paths using this method, you'll quickly run into naming issues (even if the underlying file exists):

```
PS > $c:\temp\test.txt
Unexpected token '\temp\test.txt' in expression or statement.
At line:1 char:17
+ $c:\temp\test.txt <<<<
```

The solution to that lies in PowerShell's escaping support for complex variable names. To define a complex variable name, enclose it in braces:

```
PS > ${1234123!@#$!@#$12$!@#$@!} = "Crazy Variable!"
PS > ${1234123!@#$!@#$12$!@#$@!}
Crazy Variable!
PS > dir variable:\1*

Name                            Value
----                            -----
1234123!@#$!@#$12$!@#$@!        Crazy Variable!
```

The following is the content equivalent (assuming that the file exists):

```
PS > ${c:\temp\test.txt}
hello world
```

Since environment variable names do not contain special characters, this Get-Content variable syntax is the best (and easiest) way to access environment variables.

For more information about working with PowerShell variables, see "Variables" on page 716. For more information about working with environment variables, type **Get-Help About_Environment_Variable**.

See Also

"Variables" on page 716

Get-Help About_Environment_Variable

3.5 Program: Retain Changes to Environment Variables Set by a Batch File

When a batch file modifies an environment variable, *cmd.exe* retains this change even after the script exits. This often causes problems, as one batch file can accidentally pollute the environment of another. That said, batch file authors sometimes intentionally change the global environment to customize the path and other aspects of the environment to suit a specific task.

However, environment variables are private details of a process and disappear when that process exits. This makes the environment customization scripts mentioned earlier stop working when you run them from PowerShell—just as they fail to work when you run them from another *cmd.exe* (for example, cmd.exe /c MyScript.cmd).

The script in Example 3-3 lets you run batch files that modify the environment and retain their changes even after *cmd.exe* exits. It accomplishes this by storing the environment variables in a text file once the batch file completes, and then setting all those environment variables again in your PowerShell session.

To run this script, type **Invoke-CmdScript *Scriptname.cmd*** or **Invoke-CmdScript *Scriptname.bat***—whichever extension the batch files uses.

 If this is the first time you've run a script in PowerShell, you will need to configure your Execution Policy. For more information about selecting an execution policy, see Recipe 18.1.

Notice that this script uses the full names for cmdlets: Get-Content, Foreach-Object, Set-Content, and Remove-Item. This makes the script readable and is ideal for scripts that somebody else will read. It is by no means required, though. For quick scripts and interactive use, shorter aliases (such as gc, %, sc, and ri) can make you more productive.

Example 3-3. Invoke-CmdScript.ps1

```
##############################################################################
##
## Invoke-CmdScript
##
## From Windows PowerShell Cookbook (O'Reilly)
## by Lee Holmes (http://www.leeholmes.com/guide)
##
##############################################################################

<#

.SYNOPSIS

Invoke the specified batch file (and parameters), but also propagate any
```

environment variable changes back to the PowerShell environment that called it.

.EXAMPLE

```
PS >type foo-that-sets-the-FOO-env-variable.cmd
@set FOO=%*
echo FOO set to %FOO%.

PS >$env:FOO
PS >Invoke-CmdScript "foo-that-sets-the-FOO-env-variable.cmd" Test

C:\Temp>echo FOO set to Test.
FOO set to Test.

PS > $env:FOO
Test

#>

param(
    ## The path to the script to run
    [Parameter(Mandatory = $true)]
    [string] $Path,

    ## The arguments to the script
    [string] $ArgumentList
)

Set-StrictMode -Version Latest

$tempFile = [IO.Path]::GetTempFileName()

## Store the output of cmd.exe.  We also ask cmd.exe to output
## the environment table after the batch file completes
cmd /c " `"$Path`" $argumentList && set > `"$tempFile`" "

## Go through the environment variables in the temp file.
## For each of them, set the variable in our local environment.
Get-Content $tempFile | Foreach-Object {
    if($_ -match "^(.*?)=(.*)$")
    {
        Set-Content "env:\$($matches[1])" $matches[2]
    }
}

Remove-Item $tempFile
```

For more information about running scripts, see Recipe 1.1.

See Also

Recipe 1.1, "Run Programs, Scripts, and Existing Tools"

Recipe 18.1, "Enable Scripting Through an Execution Policy"

3.6 Control Access and Scope of Variables and Other Items

Problem

You want to control how you define (or interact with) the visibility of variables, aliases, functions, and drives.

Solution

PowerShell offers several ways to access variables.

To create a variable with a specific scope, supply that scope before the variable name:

```
$SCOPE:variable = value
```

To access a variable at a specific scope, supply that scope before the variable name:

```
$SCOPE:variable
```

To create a variable that remains even after the script exits, create it in the GLOBAL scope:

```
$GLOBAL:variable = value
```

To change a scriptwide variable from within a function, supply SCRIPT as its scope name:

```
$SCRIPT:variable = value
```

Discussion

PowerShell controls access to variables, functions, aliases, and drives through a mechanism known as *scoping*. The *scope* of an item is another term for its visibility. You are always in a scope (called the *current* or *local* scope), but some actions change what that means.

When your code enters a nested prompt, script, function, or script block, PowerShell creates a new scope. That scope then becomes the local scope. When it does this, PowerShell remembers the relationship between your old scope and your new scope. From the view of the new scope, the old scope is called the *parent scope*. From the view of the old scope, the new scope is called a *child scope*. Child scopes get access to all the variables in the parent scope, but changing those variables in the child scope doesn't change the version in the parent scope.

 Trying to change a scriptwide variable from a function is often a "gotcha" because a function is a new scope. As mentioned previously, changing something in a child scope (the function) doesn't affect the parent scope (the script). The rest of this discussion describes ways to change the value for the entire script.

When your code exits a nested prompt, script, function, or script block, the opposite happens. PowerShell removes the old scope, then changes the local scope to be the scope that originally created it—the parent of that old scope.

Some scopes are so common that PowerShell gives them special names:

Global
>The outermost scope. Items in the global scope are visible from all other scopes.

Script
>The scope that represents the current script. Items in the script scope are visible from all other scopes in the script.

Local
>The current scope.

When you define the scope of an item, PowerShell supports two additional scope names that act more like options: `Private` and `AllScope`. When you define an item to have a `Private` scope, PowerShell does not make that item directly available to child scopes. PowerShell does not *hide* it from child scopes, though, as child scopes can still use the `-Scope` parameter of the `Get-Variable` cmdlet to get variables from parent scopes. When you specify the `AllScope` option for an item (through one of the `*-Variable`, `*-Alias`, or `*-Drive` cmdlets), child scopes that change the item also affect the value in parent scopes.

With this background, PowerShell provides several ways for you to control access and scope of variables and other items.

Variables

To define a variable at a specific scope (or access a variable at a specific scope), use its scope name in the variable reference. For example:

```
$SCRIPT:myVariable = value
```

As illustrated in "Variables" on page 716, the `*-Variable` set of cmdlets also let you specify scope names through their `-Scope` parameter.

Functions

To define a function at a specific scope (or access a function at a specific scope), use its scope name when creating the function. For example:

```
function GLOBAL:MyFunction { ... }
GLOBAL:MyFunction args
```

Aliases and drives

To define an alias or drive at a specific scope, use the `Option` parameter of the `*-Alias` and `*-Drive` cmdlets. To access an alias or drive at a specific scope, use the `Scope` parameter of the `*-Alias` and `*-Drive` cmdlets.

For more information about scopes, type **Get-Help About-Scope**.

See Also

"Variables" on page 716

3.7 Program: Create a Dynamic Variable

When working with variables and commands, some concepts feel too minor to deserve an entire new command or function, but the readability of your script suffers without them.

A few examples where this becomes evident are date math (*yesterday* becomes (Get-Date).AddDays(-1)) and deeply nested variables (*window title* becomes $host.UI.RawUI.WindowTitle).

Although we could write our own extensions to make these easier to access, Get-Yesterday, Get-WindowTitle, and Set-WindowTitle feel too insignificant to deserve their own commands.

PowerShell lets you define your own types of variables by extending its PSVariable class, but that functionality is largely designed for developer scenarios, and not for scripting scenarios. Example 3-4 resolves this quandary by creating a new variable type (DynamicVariable) that supports dynamic script actions when you get or set the variable's value.

Example 3-4. New-DynamicVariable.ps1

```
##############################################################################
##
## New-DynamicVariable
##
## From Windows PowerShell Cookbook (O'Reilly)
## by Lee Holmes (http://www.leeholmes.com/guide)
##
##############################################################################

<#

.SYNOPSIS

Creates a variable that supports scripted actions for its getter and setter

.EXAMPLE

PS >.\New-DynamicVariable GLOBAL:WindowTitle `
    -Getter { $host.UI.RawUI.WindowTitle } `
    -Setter { $host.UI.RawUI.WindowTitle = $args[0] }

PS >$windowTitle
Administrator: C:\Windows\System32\WindowsPowerShell\v1.0\powershell.exe
```

```
PS >$windowTitle = "Test"
PS >$windowTitle
Test

#>

param(
    ## The name for the dynamic variable
    [Parameter(Mandatory = $true)]
    $Name,

    ## The scriptblock to invoke when getting the value of the variable
    [Parameter(Mandatory = $true)]
    [ScriptBlock] $Getter,

    ## The scriptblock to invoke when setting the value of the variable
    [ScriptBlock] $Setter
)

Set-StrictMode -Version Latest

Add-Type @"
using System;
using System.Collections.ObjectModel;
using System.Management.Automation;

namespace Lee.Holmes
{
    public class DynamicVariable : PSVariable
    {
        public DynamicVariable(
            string name,
            ScriptBlock scriptGetter,
            ScriptBlock scriptSetter)
                : base(name, null, ScopedItemOptions.AllScope)
        {
            getter = scriptGetter;
            setter = scriptSetter;
        }
        private ScriptBlock getter;
        private ScriptBlock setter;

        public override object Value
        {
            get
            {
                if(getter != null)
                {
                    Collection<PSObject> results = getter.Invoke();
                    if(results.Count == 1)
                    {
                        return results[0];
                    }
                    else
                    {
```

```
                        PSObject[] returnResults =
                            new PSObject[results.Count];
                        results.CopyTo(returnResults, 0);
                        return returnResults;
                    }
                }
                else { return null; }
            }
            set
            {
                if(setter != null) { setter.Invoke(value); }
            }
        }
    }
}
"@

## If we've already defined the variable, remove it.
if(Test-Path variable:\$name)
{
    Remove-Item variable:\$name -Force
}

## Set the new variable, along with its getter and setter.
$executioncontext.SessionState.PSVariable.Set(
    (New-Object Lee.Holmes.DynamicVariable $name,$getter,$setter))
```

3.8 Work with .NET Objects

Problem

You want to use and interact with one of the features that makes PowerShell so powerful—its intrinsic support for .NET objects.

Solution

PowerShell offers ways to access methods (both static and instance) and properties.

To call a static method on a class, place the type name in square brackets, and then separate the class name from the method name with two colons:

```
[ClassName]::MethodName(parameter list)
```

To call a method on an object, place a dot between the variable that represents that object and the method name:

```
$objectReference.MethodName(parameter list)
```

To access a static property on a class, place the type name in square brackets, and then separate the class name from the property name with two colons:

```
[ClassName]::PropertyName
```

To access a property on an object, place a dot between the variable that represents that object and the property name:

```
$objectReference.PropertyName
```

Discussion

One feature that gives PowerShell its incredible reach into both system administration and application development is its capability to leverage Microsoft's enormous and broad .NET Framework. The .NET Framework is a large collection of classes. Each class embodies a specific concept and groups closely related functionality and information. Working with the .NET Framework is one aspect of PowerShell that introduces a revolution to the world of management shells.

An example of a class from the .NET Framework is `System.Diagnostics.Process`—the grouping of functionality that "provides access to local and remote processes, and enables you to start and stop local system processes."

 The terms *type* and *class* are often used interchangeably.

Classes contain *methods* (which let you perform operations) and *properties* (which let you access information).

For example, the `Get-Process` cmdlet generates `System.Diagnostics.Process` objects, not a plain-text report like traditional shells. Managing these processes becomes incredibly easy, as they contain a rich mix of information (properties) and operations (methods). You no longer have to parse a stream of text for the ID of a process; you can just ask the object directly!

```
PS > $process = Get-Process Notepad
PS > $process.Id
3872
```

Static methods

```
[ClassName]::MethodName(parameter list)
```

Some methods apply only to the concept the class represents. For example, retrieving all running processes on a system relates to the general concept of processes instead of a specific process. Methods that apply to the class/type as a whole are called *static methods*.

For example:

```
PS > [System.Diagnostics.Process]::GetProcessById(0)
```

This specific task is better handled by the Get-Process cmdlet, but it demonstrates PowerShell's capability to call methods on .NET classes. It calls the static GetProcessById method on the System.Diagnostics.Process class to get the process with the ID of 0. This generates the following output:

```
Handles NPM(K) PM(K) WS(K) VM(M) CPU(s) Id ProcessName
------- ------ ----- ----- ----- ------ -- -----------
      0      0     0    16     0         0 Idle
```

Instance methods

$objectReference.MethodName(parameter list)

Some methods relate only to specific, tangible realizations (called instances) of a class. An example of this would be stopping a process actually running on the system, as opposed to the general concept of processes. If *$objectReference* refers to a specific System.Diagnostics.Process (as output by the Get-Process cmdlet, for example), you may call methods to start it, stop it, or wait for it to exit. Methods that act on instances of a class are called *instance methods*.

The term *object* is often used interchangeably with the term *instance*.

For example:

```
PS > $process = Get-Process Notepad
PS > $process.WaitForExit()
```

stores the Notepad process into the $process variable. It then calls the WaitForExit() instance method on that specific process to pause PowerShell until the process exits.

To learn about the different sets of parameters (overloads) that a given method supports, type that method name without any parameters. For an even cleaner view, access the OverloadDefinitions property of the method:

```
PS > $now = Get-Date
PS > $now.AddDays

MemberType : Method
OverloadDefinitions : {System.DateTime AddDays(Double value)}
TypeNameOfValue : System.Management.Automation.PSMethod
Value : System.DateTime AddDays(Double value)
Name : AddDays
IsInstance : True

PS > $now.AddDays.OverloadDefinitions
System.DateTime AddDays(double value)
```

For both static methods and instance methods, you may sometimes run into situations where PowerShell either generates an error or fails to invoke the method you expected. In this case, review the output of the Trace-Command cmdlet, with MemberResolution as the trace type (see Example 3-5).

Example 3-5. Investigating PowerShell's method resolution

```
PS > Trace-Command MemberResolution -PsHost {
    [System.Diagnostics.Process]::GetProcessById(0) }

DEBUG: MemberResolution Information: 0 : cache hit, Calling Method: static
 System.Diagnostics.Process GetProcessById(int processId)
DEBUG: MemberResolution Information: 0 : Method argument conversion.
DEBUG: MemberResolution Information: 0 :    Converting parameter "0" to
"System.Int32".
DEBUG: MemberResolution Information: 0 : Checking for possible references.

Handles  NPM(K)   PM(K)    WS(K) VM(M)   CPU(s)     Id ProcessName
-------  ------   -----    ----- -----   ------     -- -----------
      0       0       0       12     0                0 Idle
```

Static properties

> [*ClassName*]::*PropertyName*

or:

> [*ClassName*]::*PropertyName* = *value*

Like static methods, some properties relate only to information about the concept that the class represents. For example, the System.DateTime class "represents an instant in time, typically expressed as a date and time of day." It provides a Now static property that returns the current time:

```
PS > [System.DateTime]::Now
Saturday, June 2, 2010 4:57:20 PM
```

This specific task is better handled by the Get-Date cmdlet, but it demonstrates PowerShell's capability to access properties on .NET objects.

Although they are relatively rare, some types let you set the value of some static properties as well: for example, the [System.Environment]::CurrentDirectory property. This property represents the process's current directory—which represents PowerShell's startup directory, as opposed to the path you see in your prompt.

Instance properties

> $*objectReference*.*PropertyName*

or:

> $*objectReference*.*PropertyName* = *value*

Like instance methods, some properties relate only to specific, tangible realizations (called *instances*) of a class. An example of this would be the day of an actual instant in time, as opposed to the general concept of dates and times. If *$objectReference* refers to a specific System.DateTime (as output by the Get-Date cmdlet or [System.Date Time]::Now, for example), you may want to retrieve its day of week, day, or month. Properties that return information about instances of a class are called *instance properties*.

For example:

```
PS > $today = Get-Date
PS > $today.DayOfWeek
Saturday
```

This example stores the current date in the $today variable. It then calls the DayOf Week instance property to retrieve the day of the week for that specific date.

With this knowledge, the next questions are: "How do I learn about the functionality available in the .NET Framework?" and "How do I learn what an object does?"

For an answer to the first question, see Appendix F for a hand-picked list of the classes in the .NET Framework most useful to system administrators. For an answer to the second, see Recipes 3.13 and 3.14.

See Also

Recipe 3.13, "Learn About Types and Objects"

Recipe 3.14, "Get Detailed Documentation About Types and Objects"

Appendix F, *Selected .NET Classes and Their Uses*

3.9 Create an Instance of a .NET Object

Problem

You want to create an instance of a .NET object to interact with its methods and properties.

Solution

Use the New-Object cmdlet to create an instance of an object.

To create an instance of an object using its default constructor, use the New-Object cmdlet with the class name as its only parameter:

```
PS > $generator = New-Object System.Random
PS > $generator.NextDouble()
0.853699042859347
```

To create an instance of an object that takes parameters for its constructor, supply those parameters to the `New-Object` cmdlet. In some instances, the class may exist in a separate library not loaded in PowerShell by default, such as the `System.Windows.Forms` assembly. In that case, you must first load the assembly that contains the class:

```
Add-Type -Assembly System.Windows.Forms
$image = New-Object System.Drawing.Bitmap source.gif
$image.Save("source_converted.jpg","JPEG")
```

To create an object and use it at the same time (without saving it for later), wrap the call to `New-Object` in parentheses:

```
PS > (New-Object Net.WebClient).DownloadString("http://live.com")
```

Discussion

Many cmdlets (such as `Get-Process` and `Get-ChildItem`) generate live .NET objects that represent tangible processes, files, and directories. However, PowerShell supports much more of the .NET Framework than just the objects that its cmdlets produce. These additional areas of the .NET Framework supply a huge amount of functionality that you can use in your scripts and general system administration tasks.

When it comes to using most of these classes, the first step is often to create an instance of the class, store that instance in a variable, and then work with the methods and properties on that instance. To create an instance of a class, you use the `New-Object` cmdlet. The first parameter to the `New-Object` cmdlet is the type name, and the second parameter is the list of arguments to the constructor, if it takes any. The `New-Object` cmdlet supports PowerShell's *type shortcuts*, so you never have to use the fully qualified type name. For more information about type shortcuts, see "Type Shortcuts" on page 743.

 A common pattern when working with .NET objects is to create them, set a few properties, and then use them. The `-Property` parameter of the `New-Object` cmdlet lets you combine steps:

```
$startInfo = New-Object Diagnostics.ProcessStartInfo -Property @{
    'Filename' = "powershell.exe";
    'WorkingDirectory' = $pshome;
    'Verb' = "RunAs"
}
[Diagnostics.Process]::Start($startInfo)
```

Since the second parameter to the `New-Object` cmdlet is an array of parameters to the type's constructor, you might encounter difficulty when trying to specify a parameter that itself is a list. Assuming `$byte` is an array of bytes:

```
PS > $memoryStream = New-Object System.IO.MemoryStream $bytes
New-Object : Cannot find an overload for ".ctor" and the argument count: "11".
At line:1 char:27
+ $memoryStream = New-Object <<<< System.IO.MemoryStream $bytes
```

To solve this, provide an array that contains an array:

```
PS > $parameters = ,$bytes
PS > $memoryStream = New-Object System.IO.MemoryStream $parameters
```

or:

```
PS > $memoryStream = New-Object System.IO.MemoryStream @(,$bytes)
```

Load types from another assembly

PowerShell makes most common types available by default. However, many are available only after you load the library (called the assembly) that defines them. The MSDN documentation for a class includes the assembly that defines it. For more information about loading types from another assembly, see Recipe 17.8.

For a hand-picked list of the classes in the .NET Framework most useful to system administrators, see Appendix F. To learn more about the functionality that a class supports, see Recipe 3.13.

For more information about the New-Object cmdlet, type **Get-Help New-Object**. For more information about the Add-Type cmdlet, type **Get-Help Add-Type**.

See Also

Recipe 3.8, "Work with .NET Objects"

Recipe 3.13, "Learn About Types and Objects"

Recipe 17.8, "Access a .NET SDK Library"

Appendix F, *Selected .NET Classes and Their Uses*

3.10 Program: Create Instances of Generic Objects

When you work with the .NET Framework, you'll often run across classes that have the primary responsibility of managing other objects. For example, the System.Collections.ArrayList class lets you manage a dynamic list of objects. You can add objects to an ArrayList, remove objects from it, sort the objects inside, and more. These objects can be any type of object: String objects, integers, DateTime objects, and many others. However, working with classes that support arbitrary objects can sometimes be a little awkward. One example is *type safety*. If you accidentally add a String to a list of integers, you might not find out until your program fails.

Although the issue becomes largely moot when working only inside PowerShell, a more common complaint in strongly typed languages (such as C#) is that you have to remind the environment (through explicit casts) about the type of your object when you work with it again:

```
// This is C# code
System.Collections.ArrayList list =
```

```
    new System.Collections.ArrayList();
list.Add("Hello World");

string result = (String) list[0];
```

To address these problems, the .NET Framework introduced a feature called *generic types*: classes that support arbitrary types of objects but let you specify *which type* of object. In this case, a collection of strings:

```
// This is C# code
System.Collections.ObjectModel.Collection<String> list =
    new System.Collections.ObjectModel.Collection<String>();
list.Add("Hello World");

string result = list[0];
```

PowerShell version one did not handle this directly, but version two lets you define generic parameters by placing them between square brackets, as demonstrated in Example 3-6.

Example 3-6. Creating a generic object

```
PS > $coll = New-Object System.Collections.ObjectModel.Collection[Int]
PS > $coll.Add(15)
PS > $coll.Add("Test")
Cannot convert argument "0", with value: "Test", for "Add" to type "System
.Int32": "Cannot convert value "Test" to type "System.Int32". Error: "Input
string was not in a correct format.""
At line:1 char:10
+ $coll.Add <<<< ("Test")
    + CategoryInfo          : NotSpecified: (:) [], MethodException
    + FullyQualifiedErrorId : MethodArgumentConversionInvalidCastArgument
```

For a generic type that takes two or more parameters, provide a comma-separated list of types, enclosed in quotes (see Example 3-7).

Example 3-7. Creating a multi-parameter generic object

```
PS > $map = New-Object System.Collections.Generic.Dictionary["String,Int"]
PS > $map.Add("Test", 15)
PS > $map.Add("Test2", "Hello")
Cannot convert argument "1", with value: "Hello", for "Add" to type "System
.Int32": "Cannot convert value "Hello" to type "System.Int32". Error:
"Input string was not in a correct format.""
At line:1 char:9
+ $map.Add <<<< ("Test2", "Hello")
    + CategoryInfo          : NotSpecified: (:) [], MethodException
    + FullyQualifiedErrorId : MethodArgumentConversionInvalidCastArgument
```

PowerShell version one does not support generic types very elegantly. For a simple generic type, you can use the syntax that the .NET Framework uses under the hood:

```
$coll = New-Object 'System.Collections.ObjectModel.Collection`1[System.String]'
```

However, that begins to fall apart if you want to use types defined outside the main `mscorlib` assembly or want to create complex generic types (for example, ones that refer to other generic types).

Example 3-8 lets you easily create instances of generic types.

Example 3-8. New-GenericObject.ps1

```
##############################################################################
##
## New-GenericObject
##
## From Windows PowerShell Cookbook (O'Reilly)
## by Lee Holmes (http://www.leeholmes.com/guide)
##
##############################################################################

<#

.SYNOPSIS

Creates an object of a generic type:

.EXAMPLE

PS >New-GenericObject System.Collections.ObjectModel.Collection System.Int32
Creates a simple generic collection

.EXAMPLE

PS >New-GenericObject System.Collections.Generic.Dictionary `
      System.String,System.Int32
Creates a generic dictionary with two types

.EXAMPLE

PS >$secondType = New-GenericObject System.Collections.Generic.List Int32
PS >New-GenericObject System.Collections.Generic.Dictionary `
      System.String,$secondType.GetType()
Creates a generic list as the second type to a generic dictionary

.EXAMPLE

PS >New-GenericObject System.Collections.Generic.LinkedListNode `
      System.String "Hi"
Creates a generic type with a non-default constructor

#>

param(
    ## The generic type to create
    [Parameter(Mandatory = $true)]
    [string] $TypeName,
```

```
    ## The types that should be applied to the generic object
    [Parameter(Mandatory = $true)]
    [string[]] $TypeParameters,

    ## Arguments to be passed to the constructor
    [object[]] $ConstructorParameters
)

Set-StrictMode -Version Latest

## Create the generic type name
$genericTypeName = $typeName + '`' + $typeParameters.Count
$genericType = [Type] $genericTypeName

if(-not $genericType)
{
    throw "Could not find generic type $genericTypeName"
}

## Bind the type arguments to it
[type[]] $typedParameters = $typeParameters
$closedType = $genericType.MakeGenericType($typedParameters)
if(-not $closedType)
{
    throw "Could not make closed type $genericType"
}

## Create the closed version of the generic type
,[Activator]::CreateInstance($closedType, $constructorParameters)
```

3.11 Reduce Typing for Long Class Names

Problem

You want to reduce the amount of redundant information in your script when you
interact with classes that have long type names.

Solution

To reduce typing for static methods, store the type name in a variable:

```
$math = [System.Math]
$math::Min(1,10)
$math::Max(1,10)
```

To reduce typing for multiple objects in a namespace, use the -f operator:

```
$namespace = "System.Collections.{0}"
$arrayList = New-Object ($namespace -f "ArrayList")
$queue = New-Object ($namespace -f "Queue")
```

To reduce typing for static methods of multiple types in a namespace, use the -f operator along with a cast:

```
$namespace = "System.Diagnostics.{0}"
([Type] ($namespace -f "EventLog"))::GetEventLogs()
([Type] ($namespace -f "Process"))::GetCurrentProcess()
```

Discussion

One thing you will notice when working with some .NET classes (or classes from a third-party SDK) is that it quickly becomes tiresome to specify their fully qualified type names. For example, many useful collection classes in the .NET Framework start with "System.Collections". This is called the *namespace* of that class. Most programming languages solve this problem with a *using* directive that lets you specify a list of namespaces for that language to search when you type a plain class name such as "Array List". PowerShell lacks a using directive, but there are several options to get the benefits of one.

If you are repeatedly working with static methods on a specific type, you can store that type in a variable to reduce typing, as shown in the Solution:

```
$math = [System.Math]
$math::Min(1,10)
$math::Max(1,10)
```

If you are creating instances of different classes from a namespace, you can store the namespace in a variable and then use the PowerShell -f *(format)* operator to specify the unique class name:

```
$namespace = "System.Collections.{0}"
$arrayList = New-Object ($namespace -f "ArrayList")
$queue = New-Object ($namespace -f "Queue")
```

If you are working with static methods from several types in a namespace, you can store the namespace in a variable, use the -f operator to specify the unique class name, and then finally cast that into a type:

```
$namespace = "System.Diagnostics.{0}"
([Type] ($namespace -f "EventLog"))::GetEventLogs()
([Type] ($namespace -f "Process"))::GetCurrentProcess()
```

For more information about PowerShell's format operator, see Recipe 5.6.

See Also

Recipe 5.6, "Place Formatted Information in a String"

3.12 Use a COM Object

Problem

You want to create a COM object to interact with its methods and properties.

Solution

Use the `New-Object` cmdlet (with the `-ComObject` parameter) to create a COM object from its *ProgID*. You can then interact with the methods and properties of the COM object as you would any other object in PowerShell.

```
$object = New-Object -ComObject ProgId
```

For example:

```
PS > $sapi = New-Object -Com Sapi.SpVoice
PS > $sapi.Speak("Hello World")
```

Discussion

Historically, many applications have exposed their scripting and administration interfaces as COM objects. While .NET APIs (and PowerShell cmdlets) are becoming more common, interacting with COM objects is still a routine administrative task.

As with classes in the .NET Framework, it is difficult to know what COM objects you can use to help you accomplish your system administration tasks. For a hand-picked list of the COM objects most useful to system administrators, see Appendix H.

For more information about the `New-Object` cmdlet, type **Get-Help New-Object**.

See Also

Appendix H, *Selected COM Objects and Their Uses*

3.13 Learn About Types and Objects

Problem

You have an instance of an object and want to know what methods and properties it supports.

Solution

The most common way to explore the methods and properties supported by an object is through the `Get-Member` cmdlet.

To get the instance members of an object you've stored in the $*object* variable, pipe it to the Get-Member cmdlet:

```
$object | Get-Member
Get-Member -InputObject $object
```

To get the static members of an object you've stored in the $*object* variable, supply the -Static flag to the Get-Member cmdlet:

```
$object | Get-Member -Static
Get-Member -Static -InputObject $object
```

To get the static members of a specific type, pipe that type to the Get-Member cmdlet, and also specify the -Static flag:

```
[Type] | Get-Member -Static
Get-Member -InputObject [Type]
```

To get members of the specified member type (for example, Method or Property) from an object you have stored in the $*object* variable, supply that member type to the -MemberType parameter:

```
$object | Get-Member -MemberType MemberType
Get-Member -MemberType MemberType -InputObject $object
```

Discussion

The Get-Member cmdlet is one of the three commands you will use most commonly as you explore Windows PowerShell. The other two commands are Get-Command and Get-Help.

If you pass the Get-Member cmdlet a collection of objects (such as an Array or Array List) through the pipeline, PowerShell extracts each item from the collection and then passes them to the Get-Member cmdlet one by one. The Get-Member cmdlet then returns the members of each unique type that it receives. Although helpful the vast majority of the time, this sometimes causes difficulty when you want to learn about the members or properties of the collection class itself.

If you want to see the properties of a collection (as opposed to the elements it contains), provide the collection to the -InputObject parameter instead. Alternatively, you can wrap the collection in an array (using PowerShell's *unary comma operator*) so that the collection class remains when the Get-Member cmdlet unravels the outer array:

```
PS > $files = Get-ChildItem
PS > ,$files | Get-Member


   TypeName: System.Object[]

Name            MemberType    Definition
----            ----------    ----------
Count           AliasProperty Count = Length
Address         Method        System.Object& Address(Int32 )
(...)
```

For another way to learn detailed information about types and objects, see Recipe 3.14.

For more information about the Get-Member cmdlet, type **Get-Help Get-Member**.

See Also

Recipe 3.14, "Get Detailed Documentation About Types and Objects"

3.14 Get Detailed Documentation About Types and Objects

Problem

You have a type of object and want to know detailed information about the methods and properties it supports.

Solution

The documentation for the .NET Framework (available at *http://msdn.microsoft.com*) is the best way to get detailed documentation about the methods and properties supported by an object. That exploration generally comes in two stages:

1. Find the type of the object.

   To determine the type of an object, you can either use the type name shown by the Get-Member cmdlet (as described in Recipe 3.13) or call the GetType() method of an object (if you have an instance of it):

   ```
   PS > $date = Get-Date
   PS > $date.GetType().ToString()
   System.DateTime
   ```

2. Enter that type name into the search box at *http://msdn.microsoft.com*.

Discussion

When the Get-Member cmdlet does not provide the information you need, the MSDN documentation for a type is a great alternative. It provides much more detailed information than the help offered by the Get-Member cmdlet—usually including detailed descriptions, related information, and even code samples. MSDN documentation focuses on developers using these types through a language such as C#, though, so you may find interpreting the information for use in PowerShell to be a little difficult at first.

Typically, the documentation for a class first starts with a general overview, and then provides a hyperlink to the members of the class—the list of methods and properties it supports.

To get to the documentation for the members quickly, search for them more explicitly by adding the term "members" to your MSDN search term:

typename members

Documentation for the members of a class lists the class's methods and properties, as does the output of the Get-Member cmdlet. The S icon represents static methods and properties. Click the member name for more information about that method or property.

Public constructors

This section lists the constructors of the type. You use a constructor when you create the type through the New-Object cmdlet. When you click on a constructor, the documentation provides all the different ways that you can create that object, including the parameter list that you will use with the New-Object cmdlet.

Public fields/public properties

This section lists the names of the fields and properties of an object. The S icon represents a static field or property. When you click on a field or property, the documentation also provides the type returned by this field or property.

For example, you might see the following in the definition for System.DateTime.Now:

```C#
public static DateTime Now { get; }
```

Public means that the Now property is public—that everybody can access it. Static means that the property is static (as described in Recipe 3.8). DateTime means that the property returns a DateTime object when you call it. get; means that you can get information from this property but cannot set the information. Many properties support a set; as well (such as the IsReadOnly property on System.IO.FileInfo), which means that you can change its value.

Public methods

This section lists the names of the methods of an object. The S icon represents a static method. When you click on a method, the documentation provides all the different ways that you can call that method, including the parameter list that you will use to call that method in PowerShell.

For example, you might see the following in the definition for System.DateTime.AddDays():

```C#
public DateTime AddDays (
```

```
            double value
    )
```

`Public` means that the `AddDays` method is public—that everybody can access it. `Date Time` means that the method returns a `DateTime` object when you call it. The text `double value` means that this method requires a parameter (of type `double`). In this case, that parameter determines the number of days to add to the `DateTime` object on which you call the method.

See Also

Recipe 3.8, "Work with .NET Objects"

Recipe 3.13, "Learn About Types and Objects"

3.15 Add Custom Methods and Properties to Objects

Problem

You have an object and want to add your own custom properties or methods (*members*) to that object.

Solution

Use the `Add-Member` cmdlet to add custom members to an object.

Discussion

The `Add-Member` cmdlet is extremely useful in helping you add custom members to individual objects. For example, imagine that you want to create a report from the files in the current directory, and that report should include each file's owner. The `Owner` property is not standard on the objects that `Get-ChildItem` produces, but you could write a small script to add them, as shown in Example 3-9.

Example 3-9. A script that adds custom properties to its output of file objects

```
###############################################################################
##
## Get-OwnerReport
##
## From Windows PowerShell Cookbook (O'Reilly)
## by Lee Holmes (http://www.leeholmes.com/guide)
##
###############################################################################

<#

.SYNOPSIS

Gets a list of files in the current directory, but with their owner added
to the resulting objects.
```

```
.EXAMPLE

Get-OwnerReport | Format-Table Name,LastWriteTime,Owner
Retrieves all files in the current directory, and displays the
Name, LastWriteTime, and Owner

#>

Set-StrictMode -Version Latest

$files = Get-ChildItem
foreach($file in $files)
{
    $owner = (Get-Acl $file).Owner
    $file | Add-Member NoteProperty Owner $owner
    $file
}
```

For more information about running scripts, see Recipe 1.1.

Although it is most common to add static information (such as a NoteProperty), the Add-Member cmdlet supports several other property and method types, including Alias Property, ScriptProperty, CodeProperty, CodeMethod, and ScriptMethod. For a more detailed description of these other property types, see "Working with the .NET Framework" on page 741, as well as the help documentation for the Add-Member cmdlet.

 To create entirely new objects (instead of adding information to existing ones), see Recipe 3.16.

Although the Add-Member cmdlet lets you customize specific objects, it does not let you customize all objects of that type. For information on how to do that, see Recipe 3.17.

Calculated properties

Calculated properties are another useful way to add information to output objects. If your script or command uses a Format-Table or Select-Object command to generate its output, you can create additional properties by providing an expression that generates their value. For example:

```
Get-ChildItem |
    Select-Object Name,
        @{Name="Size (MB)"; Expression={ "{0,8:0.00}" -f ($_.Length / 1MB) } }
```

In this command, we get the list of files in the directory. We use the Select-Object command to retrieve its name and a calculated property called Size (MB). This calculated property returns the size of the file in megabytes, rather than the default (bytes).

The Format-Table cmdlet supports a similar hashtable to add calculated properties, but uses Label (rather than Name) as the key to identify the property. After it was realized how confusing this was, version two of PowerShell updated both cmdlets to accept both Name and Label.

For more information about the Add-Member cmdlet, type **Get-Help Add-Member**.

For more information about adding calculated properties, type **Get-Help Select-Object** or **Get-Help Format-Table**.

See Also

Recipe 1.1, "Run Programs, Scripts, and Existing Tools"

Recipe 3.17, "Add Custom Methods and Properties to Types"

"Working with the .NET Framework" on page 741

3.16 Create and Initialize Custom Objects

Problem

You want to return structured results from a command so that users can easily sort, group, and filter them.

Solution

Use the New-Object cmdlet to create a new PsObject, and then supply a hashtable with the custom information to the -Property parameter, as in Example 3-10.

Example 3-10. Creating a custom object

```
$output = @{
    'User' = 'DOMAIN\User';
    'Quota' = 100MB;
    'ReportDate' = Get-Date;
}

New-Object PsObject -Property $output
```

If you want to create a custom object with associated functionality, place the functionality in a module, and load that module with the -AsCustomObject parameter:

```
$obj = Import-Module PlottingObject -AsCustomObject
$obj.Move(10,10)

$obj.Points = SineWave
while($true) { $obj.Rotate(10); $obj.Draw(); Sleep -m 20 }
```

Discussion

When your script outputs information to the user, always prefer richly structured data over hand-formatted reports. By emitting custom objects, you give the end user as much control over your script's output as PowerShell gives you over the output of its own commands.

Despite the power afforded by the output of custom objects, user-written scripts have frequently continued to generate plain-text output. This can be partly blamed on PowerShell's previously cumbersome support for the creation and initialization of custom objects, as shown in Example 3-11.

Example 3-11. Creating a custom object in PowerShell version one

```
$output = New-Object PsObject
Add-Member -InputObject $output NoteProperty User 'DOMAIN\user'
Add-Member -InputObject $output NoteProperty Quota 100MB
Add-Member -InputObject $output NoteProperty ReportDate (Get-Date)

$output
```

In PowerShell version one, creating a custom object required creating a new object (of the type `PsObject`), and then calling the `Add-Member` cmdlet multiple times to add the desired properties. As shown in Example 3-10, PowerShell version two makes this immensely easier by adding the `-Property` parameter to the `New-Object` cmdlet.

As described in Recipe 7.14, a unique aspect of hashtables is that they don't retain the order of the items you put in them. As a result, custom objects that you define also will have their properties in no specific order:

```
PS > $customObject = New-Object PsObject -Property @{
    FirstProperty = "One";
    SecondProperty = "Two";
    ThirdProperty = "Three"
}
PS > $customObject | Format-Table

SecondProperty          FirstProperty          ThirdProperty
--------------          -------------          -------------
Two                     One                    Three
```

For many objects, this makes no difference. If you do want your custom object to have properties in a specific order, use the `Select-Object` cmdlet:

```
PS > $customObject = $customObject |
    Select-Object FirstProperty,SecondProperty,ThirdProperty
PS > $customObject | Format-Table

FirstProperty           SecondProperty         ThirdProperty
-------------           --------------         -------------
One                     Two                    Three
```

While creating a new `PsObject` makes it easy to create data-centric objects (often called *property bags*), it does not let you add functionality to those objects. When you need functionality as well, the next step is to create a module and import that module with the `-AsCustomObject` parameter (see Example 3-12). Any variables exported by that module become properties on the resulting object, and any functions exported by that module become methods on the resulting object.

 An important point about importing a module as a custom object is that variables defined in that custom object are shared by all versions of that object. If you import the module again as a custom object (but store the result in another variable), the two objects will share their internal state.

Example 3-12. Creating a module designed to be used as a custom object

```
##############################################################################
##
## PlottingObject.psm1
## Demonstrates a module designed to be imported as a custom object
##
## From Windows PowerShell Cookbook (O'Reilly)
## by Lee Holmes (http://www.leeholmes.com/guide)
##
##############################################################################

<#

.EXAMPLE

Remove-Module PlottingObject
function SineWave { -15..15 | % { ,($_,(10 * [Math]::Sin($_ / 3))) } }
function Box { -5..5 | % { ($_,-5),($_,5),(-5,$_),(5,$_) } }

$obj = Import-Module PlottingObject -AsCustomObject
$obj.Move(10,10)

$obj.Points = SineWave
while($true) { $obj.Rotate(10); $obj.Draw(); Sleep -m 20 }

$obj.Points = Box
while($true) { $obj.Rotate(10); $obj.Draw(); Sleep -m 20 }

#>

## Declare some internal variables
$SCRIPT:x = 0
$SCRIPT:y = 0
$SCRIPT:angle = 0
$SCRIPT:xScale = -50,50
$SCRIPT:yScale = -50,50

## And a variable that we will later export
$SCRIPT:Points = @()
```

```
Export-ModuleMember -Variable Points

## A function to rotate the points by a certain amount
function Rotate($angle)
{
    $SCRIPT:angle += $angle
}
Export-ModuleMember -Function Rotate

## A function to move the points by a certain amount
function Move($xDelta, $yDelta)
{
    $SCRIPT:x += $xDelta
    $SCRIPT:y += $yDelta
}
Export-ModuleMember -Function Move

## A function to draw the given points
function Draw
{
    $degToRad = 180 * [Math]::Pi
    Clear-Host

    ## Draw the origin
    PutPixel 0 0 +

    ## Go through each of the supplied points,
    ## move them the amount specified, and then rotate them
    ## by the angle specified
    foreach($point in $points)
    {
        $pointX,$pointY = $point
        $pointX = $pointX + $SCRIPT:x
        $pointY = $pointY + $SCRIPT:y

        $newX = $pointX * [Math]::Cos($SCRIPT:angle / $degToRad ) -
            $pointY * [Math]::Sin($SCRIPT:angle / $degToRad )
        $newY = $pointY * [Math]::Cos($SCRIPT:angle / $degToRad ) +
            $pointX * [Math]::Sin($SCRIPT:angle / $degToRad )

        PutPixel $newX $newY 0
    }

    [Console]::WriteLine()
}
Export-ModuleMember -Function Draw

## A helper function to draw a pixel on the screen
function PutPixel($x, $y, $character)
{
    $scaledX = ($x - $xScale[0]) / ($xScale[1] - $xScale[0])
    $scaledX *= [Console]::WindowWidth

    $scaledY = (($y * 4 / 3) - $yScale[0]) / ($yScale[1] - $yScale[0])
    $scaledY *= [Console]::WindowHeight
```

```
    try
    {
        [Console]::SetCursorPosition($scaledX,
            [Console]::WindowHeight - $scaledY)
        [Console]::Write($character)
    }
    catch
    {
        ## Take no action on error. We probably just rotated a point
        ## out of the screen boundary.
    }
}
```

For more information about creating modules, see Recipe 11.6.

If neither of these options suit your requirements (or if you need to create an object that can be consumed by other .NET libraries), use the `Add-Type` cmdlet. For more information about this approach, see Recipe 17.6.

See Also

Recipe 7.13, "Create a Hashtable or Associative Array"

Recipe 11.6, "Package Common Commands in a Module"

Recipe 17.6, "Define or Extend a .NET Class"

3.17 Add Custom Methods and Properties to Types

Problem

You want to add your own custom properties or methods to all objects of a certain type.

Solution

Use custom type extension files to add custom members to all objects of a type.

Discussion

Although the `Add-Member` cmdlet is extremely useful in helping you add custom members to individual objects, it requires that you add the members to each object that you want to interact with. It does not let you automatically add them to all objects of that type. For that purpose, PowerShell supports another mechanism—*custom type extension* files.

Type extensions are simple XML files that PowerShell interprets. They let you (as the administrator of the system) easily add your own features to any type exposed by the system. If you write code (for example, a script or function) that primarily interacts with a single type of object, then that code might be better suited as an extension to the type instead.

 Since type extension files are XML files, make sure that your customizations properly encode the characters that have special meaning in XML files, such as <, >, and &.

For example, imagine a script that returns the free disk space on a given drive. That might be helpful as a script, but instead you might find it easier to make PowerShell's PSDrive objects themselves tell you how much free space they have left.

Getting started

If you haven't already, the first step in creating a type extension file is to create an empty one. The best location for this is probably in the same directory as your custom profile, with the filename *Types.Custom.ps1xml*, as shown in Example 3-13.

Example 3-13. Sample Types.Custom.ps1xml file

```
<?xml version="1.0" encoding="utf-8" ?>
<Types>
</Types>
```

Next, add a few lines to your PowerShell profile so that PowerShell loads your type extensions during startup:

```
$typeFile = (Join-Path (Split-Path $profile) "Types.Custom.ps1xml")
Update-TypeData -PrependPath $typeFile
```

By default, PowerShell loads several type extensions from the *Types.ps1xml* file in PowerShell's installation directory. The Update-TypeData cmdlet tells PowerShell to also look in your *Types.Custom.ps1xml* file for extensions. The -PrependPath parameter makes PowerShell favor your extensions over the built-in ones in case of conflict.

Once you have a custom types file to work with, adding functionality becomes relatively straightforward. As a theme, these examples do exactly what we alluded to earlier: add functionality to PowerShell's PSDrive type.

 PowerShell version two does this automatically. Type **Get-PSDrive** to see the result.

To support this, you need to extend your custom types file so that it defines additions to the System.Management.Automation.PSDriveInfo type, as shown in Example 3-14. The System.Management.Automation.PSDriveInfo type is the type that the Get-PSDrive cmdlet generates.

Example 3-14. A template for changes to a custom types file

```xml
<?xml version="1.0" encoding="utf-8" ?>
<Types>
  <Type>
    <Name>System.Management.Automation.PSDriveInfo</Name>
    <Members>
        add members such as <ScriptProperty> here
    </Members>
  </Type>
</Types>
```

Add a ScriptProperty

A *ScriptProperty* lets you add properties (that get and set information) to types, using PowerShell script as the extension language. It consists of three child elements: the Name of the property, the *Getter* of the property (via the GetScriptBlock child), and the *Setter* of the property (via the SetScriptBlock child).

In both the GetScriptBlock and SetScriptBlock sections, the $this variable refers to the current object being extended. In the SetScriptBlock section, the $args[0] variable represents the value that the user supplied as the righthand side of the assignment.

Example 3-15 adds an AvailableFreeSpace ScriptProperty to PSDriveInfo, and should be placed within the members section of the template given in Example 3-14. When you access the property, it returns the amount of free space remaining on the drive. When you set the property, it outputs what changes you must make to obtain that amount of free space.

Example 3-15. A ScriptProperty for the PSDriveInfo type

```
<ScriptProperty>
  <Name>AvailableFreeSpace</Name>
  <GetScriptBlock>
    ## Ensure that this is a FileSystem drive
    if($this.Provider.ImplementingType -eq
      [Microsoft.PowerShell.Commands.FileSystemProvider])
    {
       ## Also ensure that it is a local drive
       $driveRoot = $this.Root
       $fileZone = [System.Security.Policy.Zone]::CreateFromUrl(`
                $driveRoot).SecurityZone
       if($fileZone -eq "MyComputer")
       {
          $drive = New-Object System.IO.DriveInfo $driveRoot
          $drive.AvailableFreeSpace
       }
    }
  </GetScriptBlock>
  <SetScriptBlock>
   ## Get the available free space
   $availableFreeSpace = $this.AvailableFreeSpace
```

```
## Find out the difference between what is available, and what they
## asked for.
$spaceDifference = (([long] $args[0]) - $availableFreeSpace) / 1MB

## If they want more free space than they have, give that message
if($spaceDifference -gt 0)
{
    $message = "To obtain $args bytes of free space, " +
        " free $spaceDifference megabytes."
    Write-Host $message
  }
## If they want less free space than they have, give that message
else
{
    $spaceDifference = $spaceDifference * -1
    $message = "To obtain $args bytes of free space, " +
        " use up $spaceDifference more megabytes."
     Write-Host $message
  }
  </SetScriptBlock>
</ScriptProperty>
```

Add an AliasProperty

An *AliasProperty* gives an alternative name (alias) for a property. The referenced property does not need to exist when PowerShell processes your type extension file, since you (or another script) might later add the property through mechanisms such as the Add-Member cmdlet.

Example 3-16 adds a Free AliasProperty to PSDriveInfo, and it should also be placed within the members section of the template given in Example 3-14. When you access the property, it returns the value of the AvailableFreeSpace property. When you set the property, it sets the value of the AvailableFreeSpace property.

Example 3-16. An AliasProperty for the PSDriveInfo type

```
<AliasProperty>
  <Name>Free</Name>
  <ReferencedMemberName>AvailableFreeSpace</ReferencedMemberName>
</AliasProperty>
```

Add a ScriptMethod

A *ScriptMethod* lets you define an action on an object, using PowerShell script as the extension language. It consists of two child elements: the Name of the property and the Script.

In the script element, the $this variable refers to the current object you are extending. Like a standalone script, the $args variable represents the arguments to the method. Unlike standalone scripts, ScriptMethods do not support the param statement for parameters.

Example 3-17 adds a `Remove` ScriptMethod to `PSDriveInfo`. Like the other additions, place these customizations within the members section of the template given in Example 3-14. When you call this method with no arguments, the method simulates removing the drive (through the `-WhatIf` option to `Remove-PSDrive`). If you call this method with `$true` as the first argument, it actually removes the drive from the PowerShell session.

Example 3-17. A ScriptMethod for the PSDriveInfo type

```
<ScriptMethod>
  <Name>Remove</Name>
  <Script>
    $force = [bool] $args[0]
    ## Remove the drive if they use $true as the first parameter
    if($force)
    {
        $this | Remove-PSDrive
    }
    ## Otherwise, simulate the drive removal
    else
    {
        $this | Remove-PSDrive -WhatIf
    }
  </Script>
</ScriptMethod>
```

Add other extension points

PowerShell supports several additional features in the types extension file, including `CodeProperty`, `NoteProperty`, `CodeMethod`, and `MemberSet`. Although not generally useful to end users, developers of PowerShell providers and cmdlets will find these features helpful. For more information about these additional features, see the Windows PowerShell SDK or the MSDN documentation.

Looping and Flow Control

4.0 Introduction

As you begin to write scripts or commands that interact with unknown data, the concepts of looping and flow control become increasingly important.

PowerShell's looping statements and commands let you perform an operation (or set of operations) without having to repeat the commands themselves. This includes, for example, doing something a specified number of times, processing each item in a collection, or working until a certain condition comes to pass.

PowerShell's flow control and comparison statements let you adapt your script or command to unknown data. They let you execute commands based on the value of that data, skip commands based on the value of that data, and more.

Together, looping and flow control statements add significant versatility to your PowerShell toolbox.

4.1 Make Decisions with Comparison and Logical Operators

Problem

You want to compare some data with other data and make a decision based on that comparison.

Solution

Use PowerShell's logical operators to compare pieces of data and make decisions based on them.

Comparison operators

```
-eq, -ne, -ge, -gt, -lt, -le, -like, -notlike, -match, -notmatch, -contains,
-notcontains, -is, -isnot
```

Logical operators
```
-and, -or, -xor, -not
```

For a detailed description (and examples) of these operators, see "Comparison Operators" on page 731.

Discussion

PowerShell's logical and comparison operators let you compare pieces of data or test data for some condition. An operator either compares two pieces of data (a *binary* operator) or tests one piece of data (a *unary* operator). All comparison operators are binary operators (they compare two pieces of data), as are most of the logical operators. The only unary logical operator is the `-not` operator, which returns the `true`/`false` opposite of the data that it tests.

Comparison operators compare two pieces of data and return a result that depends on the specific comparison operator. For example, you might want to check whether a collection has at least a certain number of elements:

```
PS > (dir).Count -ge 4
True
```

or check whether a string matches a given regular expression:

```
PS > "Hello World" -match "H.*World"
True
```

Most comparison operators also adapt to the type of their input. For example, when you apply them to simple data such as a string, the `-like` and `-match` comparison operators determine whether the string matches the specified pattern. When you apply them to a collection of simple data, those same comparison operators return all elements in that collection that match the pattern you provide.

The `-match` operator takes a regular expression as its argument. One of the more common regular expression symbols is the $ character, which represents the end of line. The $ character also represents the start of a PowerShell variable, though! To prevent PowerShell from interpreting characters as language terms or escape sequences, place the string in single quotes rather than double quotes:

```
PS > "Hello World" -match "Hello"
True
PS > "Hello World" -match 'Hello$'
False
```

By default, PowerShell's comparison operators are case-insensitive. To use the case-sensitive versions, prefix them with the character c:

```
-ceq, -cne, -cge, -cgt, -clt, -cle, -clike, -cnotlike,
-cmatch, -cnotmatch, -ccontains, -cnotcontains
```

For a detailed description of the comparison operators, their case-sensitive counterparts, and how they adapt to their input, see "Comparison Operators" on page 731.

Logical operators combine `true` or `false` statements and return a result that depends on the specific logical operator. For example, you might want to check whether a string matches the wildcard pattern you supply *and* that it is longer than a certain number of characters:

```
PS > $data = "Hello World"
PS > ($data -like "*llo W*") -and ($data.Length -gt 10)
True
PS > ($data -like "*llo W*") -and ($data.Length -gt 20)
False
```

Some of the comparison operators actually incorporate aspects of the logical operators. Since using the opposite of a comparison (such as -like) is so common, PowerShell provides comparison operators (such as -notlike) that save you from having to use the -not operator explicitly.

For a detailed description of the individual logical operators, see "Comparison Operators" on page 731.

Comparison operators and logical operators (when combined with flow control statements) form the core of how we write a script or command that adapts to its data and input.

See also "Conditional Statements" on page 733 for detailed information about these statements.

For more information about PowerShell's operators, type **Get-Help About_Operators**.

See Also

"Comparison Operators" on page 731

"Conditional Statements" on page 733

4.2 Adjust Script Flow Using Conditional Statements

Problem

You want to control the conditions under which PowerShell executes commands or portions of your script.

Solution

Use PowerShell's `if`, `elseif`, and `else` conditional statements to control the flow of execution in your script.

For example:

```
$temperature = 90

if($temperature -le 0)
{
    "Balmy Canadian Summer"
}
elseif($temperature -le 32)
{
    "Freezing"
}
elseif($temperature -le 50)
{
    "Cold"
}
elseif($temperature -le 70)
{
    "Warm"
}
else
{
    "Hot"
}
```

Discussion

Conditional statements include the following:

if *statement*
> Executes the script block that follows it if its *condition* evaluates to true

elseif *statement*
> Executes the script block that follows it if its *condition* evaluates to true and none of the conditions in the if or elseif statements before it evaluate to true

else *statement*
> Executes the script block that follows it if none of the conditions in the if or elseif statements before it evaluate to true

In addition to being useful for script control flow, conditional statements are often a useful way to assign data to a variable. PowerShell version two makes this significantly easier by letting you assign the results of a conditional statement directly to a variable:

```
$result = if(Get-Process -Name notepad) { "Running" } else { "Not running" }
```

For more information about these flow control statements, type **Get-Help About_Flow_Control.**

4.3 Manage Large Conditional Statements with Switches

Problem

You want to find an easier or more compact way to represent a large if ... elseif ... else conditional statement.

Solution

Use PowerShell's switch statement to more easily represent a large if ... elseif ... else conditional statement.

For example:

```
$temperature = 20

switch($temperature)
{
    { $_ -lt 32 }   { "Below Freezing"; break }
    32              { "Exactly Freezing"; break }
    { $_ -le 50 }   { "Cold"; break }
    { $_ -le 70 }   { "Warm"; break }
    default         { "Hot" }
}
```

Discussion

PowerShell's switch statement lets you easily test its input against a large number of comparisons. The switch statement supports several options that let you configure how PowerShell compares the input against the conditions—such as with a wildcard, regular expression, or even arbitrary script block. Since scanning through the text in a file is such a common task, PowerShell's switch statement supports that directly. These additions make PowerShell switch statements a great deal more powerful than those in C and C++.

As another example of the switch statement in action, consider how to determine the SKU of the current operating system. For example, is the script running on Windows 7 Ultimate? Windows Server Cluster Edition? The Get-WmiObject cmdlet lets you determine the operating system SKU, but unfortunately returns its result as a simple number. A switch statement lets you map these to their English equivalents:

```
$sku = Get-WmiObject Win32_OperatingSystem
switch ($sku.OperatingSystemSKU)
{
    0   {"Undefined"; break}
    1   {"Ultimate Edition"; break}
    2   {"Home Basic Edition"; break}
    3   {"Home Basic Premium Edition"; break}
    4   {"Enterprise Edition"; break}
    5   {"Home Basic N Edition"; break}
    6   {"Business Edition"; break}
```

```
 7  {"Standard Server Edition"; break}
 8  {"Datacenter Server Edition"; break}
 9  {"Small Business Server Edition"; break}
10  {"Enterprise Server Edition"; break}
11  {"Starter Edition"; break}
12  {"Datacenter Server Core Edition"; break}
13  {"Standard Server Core Edition"; break}
14  {"Enterprise Server Core Edition"; break}
15  {"Enterprise Server Edition for Itanium-Based Systems"; break}
16  {"Business N Edition"; break}
17  {"Web Server Edition"; break}
18  {"Cluster Server Edition"; break}
19  {"Home Server Edition"; break}
20  {"Storage Express Server Edition"; break}
21  {"Storage Standard Server Edition"; break}
22  {"Storage Workgroup Server Edition"; break}
23  {"Storage Enterprise Server Edition"; break}
24  {"Server For Small Business Edition"; break}
25  {"Small Business Server Premium Edition"; break}
default {"UNKNOWN: " + $SKU.OperatingSystemSKU}
}
```

Although used as a way to express large conditional statements more cleanly, a switch statement operates much like a large sequence of if statements, as opposed to a large sequence of if ... elseif ... elseif ... else statements. Given the input that you provide, PowerShell evaluates that input against *each* of the comparisons in the switch statement. If the comparison evaluates to true, PowerShell then executes the script block that follows it. Unless that script block contains a break statement, PowerShell continues to evaluate the following comparisons.

For more information about PowerShell's switch statement, see "Conditional Statements" on page 733 or type Get-Help About_Switch.

See Also

"Conditional Statements" on page 733

4.4 Repeat Operations with Loops

Problem

You want to execute the same block of code more than once.

Solution

Use one of PowerShell's looping statements (for, foreach, while, and do) or Power-Shell's Foreach-Object cmdlet to run a command or script block more than once. For a detailed description of these looping statements, see "Looping State-ments" on page 736. For example:

for *loop*

```
for($counter = 1; $counter -le 10; $counter++)
{
  "Loop number $counter"
}
```

foreach *loop*

```
foreach($file in dir)
{
  "File length: " + $file.Length
}
```

Foreach-Object *cmdlet*

```
Get-ChildItem | Foreach-Object { "File length: " + $_.Length }
```

while *loop*

```
$response = ""
while($response -ne "QUIT")
{
  $response = Read-Host "Type something"
}
```

do..while *loop*

```
$response = ""
do
{
  $response = Read-Host "Type something"
} while($response -ne "QUIT")
```

do..until *loop*

```
$response = ""
do
{
  $response = Read-Host "Type something"
} until($response -eq "QUIT")
```

Discussion

Although any of the looping statements can be written to be functionally equivalent to any of the others, each lends itself to certain problems.

You usually use a for loop when you need to perform an operation an exact number of times. Because using it this way is so common, it is often called a *counted for loop*.

You usually use a foreach loop when you have a collection of objects and want to visit each item in that collection. If you do not yet have that entire collection in memory (as in the dir collection from the foreach example shown earlier), the Foreach-Object cmdlet is usually a more efficient alternative.

Unlike the foreach loop, the Foreach-Object cmdlet lets you process each element in the collection *as PowerShell generates it*. This is an important distinction; asking PowerShell to collect the entire output of a large command (such as Get-Content *hugefile.txt*) in a foreach loop can easily drag down your system.

 A handy shortcut to repeat an operation on the command line is:

```
PS > 1..10 | foreach { "Working" }
Working
Working
Working
Working
Working
Working
Working
Working
Working
Working
```

Like pipeline-oriented functions, the Foreach-Object cmdlet lets you define commands to execute before the looping begins, during the looping, and after the looping completes:

```
PS > "a","b","c" | Foreach-Object `
    -Begin { "Starting"; $counter = 0 } `
    -Process { "Processing $_"; $counter++ } `
    -End { "Finishing: $counter" }

Starting
Processing a
Processing b
Processing c
Finishing: 3
```

The while and do..while loops are similar, in that they continue to execute the loop as long as its condition evaluates to true. A while loop checks for this before running your script block, whereas a do..while loop checks the condition after running your script block. A do..until loop is exactly like a do..while loop, except that it exits when its condition returns $true, rather than when its condition returns $false.

For a detailed description of these looping statements, see "Looping State-ments" on page 736 or type **Get-Help About_For**, **Get-Help About_Foreach**, **Get-Help about_While**, or **Get-Help about_Do**.

See Also

"Looping Statements" on page 736

4.5 Add a Pause or Delay

Problem

You want to pause or delay your script or command.

Solution

To pause until the user presses the Enter key, use the Read-Host cmdlet:

```
PS > Read-Host "Press ENTER"
Press ENTER:
```

To pause until the user presses a key, use the ReadKey() method on the $host object:

```
PS > $host.UI.RawUI.ReadKey()
```

To pause a script for a given amount of time, use the Start-Sleep cmdlet:

```
PS > Start-Sleep 5
PS > Start-Sleep -Milliseconds 300
```

Discussion

When you want to pause your script until the user presses a key or for a set amount of time, Read-Host and Start-Sleep are the two cmdlets you are most likely to use. For more information about using the Read-Host cmdlet to read input from the user, see Recipe 13.1.

In other situations, you may sometimes want to write a loop in your script that runs at a constant speed—such as once per minute or 30 times per second. That is typically a difficult task, as the commands in the loop might take up a significant amount of time, or even an inconsistent amount of time.

In the past, many computer games suffered from solving this problem incorrectly. To control their game speed, game developers added commands to slow down their game. For example, after much tweaking and fiddling, the developers might realize that the game plays correctly on a typical machine if they make the computer count to 1 million every time it updates the screen. Unfortunately, the speed of these commands (such as counting) depend heavily on the speed of the computer. Since a fast computer can count to 1 million much more quickly than a slow computer, the game ends up running much quicker (often to the point of incomprehensibility) on faster computers!

To make your loop run at a regular speed, you can measure how long the commands in a loop take to complete, and then delay for whatever time is left, as shown in Example 4-1.

Example 4-1. Running a loop at a constant speed

```
$loopDelayMilliseconds = 650
while($true)
{
    $startTime = Get-Date

    ## Do commands here
    "Executing"

    $endTime = Get-Date
    $loopLength = ($endTime - $startTime).TotalMilliseconds
    $timeRemaining = $loopDelayMilliseconds - $loopLength

    if($timeRemaining -gt 0)
    {
        Start-Sleep -Milliseconds $timeRemaining
    }
}
```

For more information about the Start-Sleep cmdlet, type **Get-Help Start-Sleep**.

See Also

Recipe 13.1, "Read a Line of User Input"

Strings and Unstructured Text

5.0 Introduction

Creating and manipulating text has long been one of the primary tasks of scripting languages and traditional shells. In fact, Perl (the language) started as a simple (but useful) tool designed for text processing. It has grown well beyond those humble roots, but its popularity provides strong evidence of the need it fills.

In text-based shells, this strong focus continues. When most of your interaction with the system happens by manipulating the text-based output of programs, powerful text processing utilities become crucial. These text parsing tools, such as `awk`, `sed`, and `grep`, form the keystones of text-based systems management.

In PowerShell's object-based environment, this traditional tool chain plays a less critical role. You can accomplish most of the tasks that previously required these tools much more effectively through other PowerShell commands. However, being an object-oriented shell does not mean that PowerShell drops all support for text processing. Dealing with strings and unstructured text continues to play an important part in a system administrator's life. Since PowerShell lets you manage the majority of your system in its full fidelity (using cmdlets and objects), the text processing tools can once again focus primarily on actual text processing tasks.

5.1 Create a String

Problem

You want to create a variable that holds text.

Solution

Use PowerShell string variables as a way to store and work with text.

To define a string that supports variable expansion and escape characters in its definition, surround it with double quotes:

```
$myString = "Hello World"
```

To define a literal string (one that does not interpret variable expansion or escape characters), surround it with single quotes:

```
$myString = 'Hello World'
```

Discussion

String literals come in two varieties: *literal (nonexpanding)* and *expanding* strings. To create a literal string, place single quotes (`$myString = 'Hello World'`) around the text. To create an expanding string, place double quotes (`$myString = "Hello World"`) around the text.

In a literal string, all the text between the single quotes becomes part of your string. In an expanding string, PowerShell expands variable names (such as `$replacement String`) and escape sequences (such as `` `n ``) with their values (such as the content of `$replacementString` and the newline character, respectively).

For a detailed explanation of the escape sequences and replacement rules inside PowerShell strings, see "Strings" on page 718.

One exception to the "all text in a literal string is literal" rule comes from the quote characters themselves. In either type of string, PowerShell lets you place two of that string's quote characters together to add the quote character itself:

```
$myString = "This string includes ""double quotes"" because it combined quote
characters."
$myString = 'This string includes ''single quotes'' because it combined quote
characters.'
```

This helps prevent escaping atrocities that would arise when you try to include a single quote in a single-quoted string. For example:

```
$myString = 'This string includes ' + "'" + 'single quotes' + "'"
```

 This example shows how easy PowerShell makes it to create new strings by adding other strings together. This is an attractive way to build a formatted report in a script but should be used with caution. Because of the way that the .NET Framework (and therefore PowerShell) manages strings, adding information to the end of a large string this way causes noticeable performance problems. If you intend to create large reports, see Recipe 5.15.

See Also

Recipe 5.15, "Generate Large Reports and Text Streams"

"Strings" on page 718

5.2 Create a Multiline or Formatted String

Problem

You want to create a variable that holds text with newlines or other explicit formatting.

Solution

Use a PowerShell *here string* to store and work with text that includes newlines and other formatting information.

```
$myString = @"
This is the first line
of a very long string. A "here string"
lets you create blocks of text
that span several lines.
"@
```

Discussion

PowerShell begins a *here string* when it sees the characters @" followed by a newline. It ends the string when it sees the characters "@ on their own line. These seemingly odd restrictions let you create strings that include quote characters, newlines, and other symbols that you commonly use when you create large blocks of preformatted text.

 These restrictions, while useful, can sometimes cause problems when you copy and paste PowerShell examples from the Internet. Web pages often add spaces at the end of lines, which can interfere with the strict requirements of the beginning of a here string. If PowerShell produces an error when your script defines a here string, check that the here string does not include an errant space after its first quote character.

Like string literals, here strings may be literal (and use single quotes) or expanding (and use double quotes).

In PowerShell version one, here strings were frequently used as the equivalent of block comments to disable lines in a script. PowerShell version two now supports this fully through multiline comments. For more information, see "Comments" on page 716.

See Also

"Comments" on page 716

5.3 Place Special Characters in a String

Problem

You want to place special characters (such as tab and newline) in a string variable.

Solution

In an expanding string, use PowerShell's escape sequences to include special characters such as tab and newline.

```
PS > $myString = "Report for Today`n---------------"
PS > $myString
Report for Today
---------------
```

Discussion

As discussed in Recipe 5.1, PowerShell strings come in two varieties: *literal* (or *nonexpanding*) and *expanding* strings. A literal string uses single quotes around its text, whereas an expanding string uses double quotes around its text.

In a literal string, all the text between the single quotes becomes part of your string. In an expanding string, PowerShell expands variable names (such as `$ENV:SystemRoot`) and escape sequences (such as `` `n ``) with their values (such as the `SystemRoot` environment variable and the newline character).

 Unlike many languages that use a backslash character (\) for escape sequences, PowerShell uses a backtick (`` ` ``) character. This stems from its focus on system administration, where backslashes are ubiquitous in pathnames.

For a detailed explanation of the escape sequences and replacement rules inside PowerShell strings, see "Strings" on page 718.

See Also

Recipe 5.1, "Create a String"

"Strings" on page 718

5.4 Insert Dynamic Information in a String

Problem

You want to place dynamic information (such as the value of another variable) in a string.

Solution

In an expanding string, include the name of a variable in the string to insert the value of that variable:

```
PS > $header = "Report for Today"
PS > $myString = "$header`n----------------"
PS > $myString
Report for Today
----------------
```

To include information more complex than just the value of a variable, enclose it in a subexpression:

```
PS > $header = "Report for Today"
PS > $myString = "$header`n$('-' * $header.Length)"
PS > $myString
Report for Today
----------------
```

Discussion

Variable substitution in an expanding string is a simple enough concept, but subexpressions deserve a little clarification.

A *subexpression* is the dollar sign character, followed by a PowerShell command (or set of commands) contained in parentheses:

```
$(subexpression)
```

When PowerShell sees a subexpression in an expanding string, it evaluates the subexpression and places the result in the expanding string. In the solution, the expression `'-' * $header.Length` tells PowerShell to make a line of dashes `$header.Length` long.

Another way to place dynamic information inside a string is to use PowerShell's string formatting operator, which is based on the rules of the .NET string formatting:

```
PS > $header = "Report for Today"
PS > $myString = "{0}`n{1}" -f $header,('-' * $header.Length)
PS > $myString
Report for Today
----------------
```

For an explanation of PowerShell's formatting operator, see Recipe 5.6. For more information about PowerShell's escape characters, type **Get-Help About_Escape_Characters** or type **Get-Help About_Special_Characters**.

See Also

Recipe 5.6, "Place Formatted Information in a String"

5.5 Prevent a String from Including Dynamic Information

Problem

You want to prevent PowerShell from interpreting special characters or variable names inside a string.

Solution

Use a nonexpanding string to have PowerShell interpret your string exactly as entered. A nonexpanding string uses the single quote character around its text.

```
PS > $myString = 'Useful PowerShell characters include: $, `, " and { }'
PS > $myString
Useful PowerShell characters include: $, `, " and { }
```

If you want to include newline characters as well, use a nonexpanding *here string*, as in Example 5-1.

Example 5-1. A nonexpanding here string that includes newline characters

```
PS > $myString = @'
Tip of the Day
--------------
Useful PowerShell characters include: $, `, ', " and { }
'@

PS > $myString
Tip of the Day
Useful PowerShell characters include: $, `, ', " and { }
```

Discussion

In a literal string, all the text between the single quotes becomes part of your string. This is in contrast to an expanding string, where PowerShell expands variable names (such as $myString) and escape sequences (such as `n) with their values (such as the content of $myString and the newline character).

 Nonexpanding strings are a useful way to manage files and folders containing special characters that might otherwise be interpreted as escape sequences. For more information about managing files with special characters in their name, see Recipe 20.7.

As discussed in Recipe 5.1, one exception to the "all text in a literal string is literal" rule comes from the quote characters themselves. In either type of string, PowerShell lets you place two of that string's quote characters together to include the quote character itself:

```
$myString = "This string includes ""double quotes"" because it combined quote
characters."
$myString = 'This string includes ''single quotes'' because it combined quote
characters.'
```

See Also

Recipe 5.1, "Create a String"

Recipe 20.7, "Manage Files That Include Special Characters"

5.6 Place Formatted Information in a String

Problem

You want to place formatted information (such as right-aligned text or numbers rounded to a specific number of decimal places) in a string.

Solution

Use PowerShell's formatting operator to place formatted information inside a string:

```
PS > $formatString = "{0,8:D4} {1:C}`n"
PS > $report = "Quantity Price`n"
PS > $report += "--------------`n"
PS > $report += $formatString -f 50,2.5677
PS > $report += $formatString -f 3,9
PS > $report
Quantity Price
--------------
    0050 $2.57
    0003 $9.00
```

Discussion

PowerShell's string formatting operator (-f) uses the same string formatting rules as the String.Format() method in the .NET Framework. It takes a format string on its left side and the items you want to format on its right side.

In the solution, you format two numbers: a quantity and a price. The first number ({0}) represents the quantity and is right-aligned in a box of eight characters (,8). It is formatted as a decimal number with four digits (:D4). The second number ({1}) represents the price, which you format as currency (:C).

> If you find yourself hand-crafting text-based reports, STOP! Let PowerShell's built-in commands do all the work for you. Instead, emit custom objects so that your users can work with your script as easily as they work with regular PowerShell commands. For more information, see Recipe 3.16.

For a detailed explanation of PowerShell's formatting operator, see "Simple Operators" on page 725. For a detailed list of the formatting rules, see Appendix D.

Although primarily used to control the layout of information, the string-formatting operator is also a readable replacement for what is normally accomplished with string concatenation:

```
PS > $number1 = 10
PS > $number2 = 32
PS > "$number2 divided by $number1 is " + $number2 / $number1
32 divided by 10 is 3.2
```

The string formatting operator makes this much easier to read:

```
PS > "{0} divided by {1} is {2}" -f $number2, $number1, ($number2 / $number1)
32 divided by 10 is 3.2
```

In addition to the string formatting operator, PowerShell provides three formatting commands (`Format-Table`, `Format-Wide`, and `Format-List`) that let you easily generate formatted reports. For detailed information about those cmdlets, see "Custom Formatting Files" on page 760.

See Also

Recipe 3.16, "Create and Initialize Custom Objects"

"Simple Operators" on page 725

"Custom Formatting Files" on page 760

Appendix D, *.NET String Formatting*

5.7 Search a String for Text or a Pattern

Problem

You want to determine whether a string contains another string, or you want to find the position of a string within another string.

Solution

PowerShell provides several options to help you search a string for text.

Use the `-like` operator to determine whether a string matches a given DOS-like wildcard:

```
PS > "Hello World" -like "*llo W*"
True
```

Use the `-match` operator to determine whether a string matches a given regular expression:

```
PS > "Hello World" -match '.*l[l-z]o W.*$'
True
```

Use the `Contains()` method to determine whether a string contains a specific string:

```
PS > "Hello World".Contains("World")
True
```

Use the `IndexOf()` method to determine the location of one string within another:

```
PS > "Hello World".IndexOf("World")
6
```

Discussion

Since PowerShell strings are fully featured .NET objects, they support many string-oriented operations directly. The `Contains()` and `IndexOf()` methods are two examples of the many features that the `String` class supports. To learn what other functionality the `String` class supports, see Recipe 3.13.

 To search entire files for text or a pattern, see Recipe 9.2.

Although they use similar characters, simple wildcards and regular expressions serve significantly different purposes. Wildcards are much more simple than regular expressions, and because of that, more constrained. While you can summarize the rules for wildcards in just four bullet points, entire books have been written to help teach and illuminate the use of regular expressions.

 A common use of regular expressions is to search for a string that spans multiple lines. By default, regular expressions do not search across lines, but you can use the *singleline* (?s) option to instruct them to do so:

```
PS > "Hello `n World" -match "Hello.*World"
False
PS > "Hello `n World" -match "(?s)Hello.*World"
True
```

Wildcards lend themselves to simple matches, whereas regular expressions lend themselves to more complex matches.

For a detailed description of the `-like` operator, see "Comparison Operators" on page 731. For a detailed description of the `-match` operator, see "Simple Operators" on page 725. For a detailed list of the regular expression rules and syntax, see Appendix B.

One difficulty sometimes arises when you try to store the result of a PowerShell command in a string, as shown in Example 5-2.

Example 5-2. Attempting to store output of a PowerShell command in a string

```
PS > Get-Help Get-ChildItem

NAME
    Get-ChildItem

SYNOPSIS
    Gets the items and child items in one or more specified locations.

(...)

PS > $helpContent = Get-Help Get-ChildItem
PS > $helpContent -match "location"
False
```

The -match operator searches a string for the pattern you specify but seems to fail in this case. This is because all PowerShell commands generate objects. If you don't store that output in another variable or pass it to another command, PowerShell converts the output to a text representation before it displays it to you. In Example 5-2, $help Content is a fully featured object, not just its string representation:

```
PS > $helpContent.Name
Get-ChildItem
```

To work with the text-based representation of a PowerShell command, you can explicitly send it through the Out-String cmdlet. The Out-String cmdlet converts its input into the text-based form you are used to seeing on the screen:

```
PS > $helpContent = Get-Help Get-ChildItem | Out-String
PS > $helpContent -match "location"
True
```

For a script that makes searching textual command output easier, see Recipe 1.19.

See Also

Recipe 1.19, "Program: Search Formatted Output for a Pattern"

Recipe 3.13, "Learn About Types and Objects"

"Simple Operators" on page 725

"Comparison Operators" on page 731

Appendix B, *Regular Expression Reference*

5.8 Replace Text in a String

Problem

You want to replace a portion of a string with another string.

Solution

PowerShell provides several options to help you replace text in a string with other text.

Use the `Replace()` method on the string itself to perform simple replacements:

```
PS > "Hello World".Replace("World", "PowerShell")
Hello PowerShell
```

Use PowerShell's regular expression `-replace` operator to perform more advanced regular expression replacements:

```
PS > "Hello World" -replace '(.*) (.*)','$2 $1'
World Hello
```

Discussion

The `Replace()` method and the `-replace` operator both provide useful ways to replace text in a string. The `Replace()` method is the quickest but also the most constrained. It replaces every occurrence of the exact string you specify with the exact replacement string that you provide. The `-replace` operator provides much more flexibility, since its arguments are regular expressions that can match and replace complex patterns.

Given the power of the regular expressions it uses, the `-replace` operator carries with it some pitfalls of regular expressions as well.

First, the regular expressions that you use with the `-replace` operator often contain characters (such as the dollar sign, which represents a group number) that PowerShell normally interprets as variable names or escape characters. To prevent PowerShell from interpreting these characters, use a nonexpanding string (single quotes) as shown in the solution.

Another, less common pitfall is wanting to use characters that have special meaning to regular expressions as part of your replacement text. For example:

```
PS > "Power[Shell]" -replace "[Shell]","ful"
Powfulr[fulfulfulfulful]
```

That's clearly not what we intended. In regular expressions, square brackets around a set of characters means "match any of the characters inside of the square brackets." In our example, this translates to "Replace the characters S, h, e, and l with 'ful'."

To avoid this, we can use the regular expression escape character to escape the square brackets:

```
PS > "Power[Shell]" -replace "\[Shell\]","ful"
Powerful
```

However, this means knowing all of the regular expression special characters and modifying the input string. Sometimes we don't control that, so the [Regex]::Escape() method comes in handy:

```
PS > "Power[Shell]" -replace ([Regex]::Escape("[Shell]")),"ful"
Powerful
```

For more information about the -replace operator, see "Simple Operators" on page 725 and Appendix B.

See Also

"Simple Operators" on page 725

Appendix B, *Regular Expression Reference*

5.9 Split a String on Text or a Pattern

Problem

You want to split a string based on some literal text or a regular expression pattern.

Solution

Use PowerShell's -split operator to split on a sequence of characters or specific string:

```
PS > "a-b-c-d-e-f" -split "-c-"
a-b
d-e-f
```

To split on a pattern, supply a regular expression as the first argument:

```
PS > "a-b-c-d-e-f" -split "b|[d-e]"
a-
-c-
-
-f
```

Discussion

In PowerShell version one, the String.Split() and [Regex]::Split() methods were the two options available for splitting strings. While still available in PowerShell version two, PowerShell's -split operator provides a more natural way to split a string into smaller strings. When used with no arguments (the *unary* split operator), it splits a string on whitespace characters, as in Example 5-3.

Example 5-3. PowerShell's unary split operator

```
PS > -split "Hello World `t How `n are you?"
Hello
World
How
are
you?
```

When used with an argument, it treats the argument as a regular expression and then splits based on that pattern.

```
PS > "a-b-c-d-e-f" -split 'b|[d-e]'
a-
-c-
-
-f
```

If the replacement pattern avoids characters that have special meaning in a regular expression, you can use it to split a string based on another string.

```
PS > "a-b-c-d-e-f" -split '-c-'
a-b
d-e-f
```

If the replacement pattern has characters that have special meaning in a regular expression (such as the . character, which represents "any character"), use the -split operator's SimpleMatch option, as in Example 5-4.

Example 5-4. PowerShell's SimpleMatch split option

```
PS > "a.b.c" -split '.'
(A bunch of newlines. Something went wrong!)



PS > "a.b.c" -split '.',0,"SimpleMatch"
a
b
c
```

For more information about the -split operator's options, see **Get-Help about_split**.

While regular expressions offer an enormous amount of flexibility, the -split operator gives you ultimate flexibility by letting you supply a script block for split operation. For each character, it invokes the script block and splits the string based on the result. In the script block, $_ represents the current character. For example, Example 5-5 splits a string on even numbers.

Example 5-5. Using a script block to split a string

```
PS > "1234567890" -split { ($_ % 2) -eq 0 }
1
3
5
7
9
```

To split an entire file by a pattern, use the -Delimiter parameter of the Get-Content cmdlet:

```
PS > Get-Content test.txt
Hello
World
PS > (Get-Content test.txt)[0]
Hello
PS > Get-Content test.txt -Delimiter l
Hel
l
o
Worl
d
PS > (Get-Content test.txt -Delimiter l)[0]
Hel
PS > (Get-Content test.txt -Delimiter l)[1]
l
PS > (Get-Content test.txt -Delimiter l)[2]
o
Worl
PS > (Get-Content test.txt -Delimiter l)[3]
d
```

For more information about the -split operator, see "Simple Operators" on page 725 and Get-Help about_split.

See Also

"Simple Operators" on page 725

Appendix B, *Regular Expression Reference*

5.10 Combine Strings into a Larger String

Problem

You want to combine several separate strings into a single string.

Solution

Use PowerShell's *unary* -join operator to combine separate strings into a larger string using the default empty separator:

```
PS > -join ("A","B","C")
ABC
```

If you want to define the string that PowerShell uses to combine the strings, use PowerShell's *binary* `-join` operator.

```
PS > ("A","B","C") -join "`n"
A
B
C
```

Discussion

In PowerShell version one, the `[String]::Join()` method was the primary option available for joining strings. While still available in PowerShell version two, PowerShell's `-join` operator provides a more natural way to combine strings. When used with no arguments (the *unary* join operator), it joins the list using the default empty separator. When used between a list and a separator (the *binary* join operator), it joins the strings using the provided separator.

Aside from its performance benefit, the `-join` operator solves an extremely common difficulty that arises from trying to combine strings by hand.

When first writing the code to join a list with a separator (for example, a comma and a space), you usually end up leaving a lonely separator at the beginning or ending of the output:

```
PS > $list = "Hello","World"
PS > $output = ""
PS >
PS > foreach($item in $list)
{
    $output += $item + ", "
}

PS > $output
Hello, World,
```

You can resolve this by adding some extra logic to the `foreach` loop:

```
PS > $list = "Hello","World"
PS > $output = ""
PS >
PS > foreach($item in $list)
{
    if($output -ne "") { $output += ", " }
    $output += $item
}

PS > $output
Hello, World
```

Or, save yourself the trouble and use the -join operator directly:

```
PS > $list = "Hello","World"
PS > $list -join ", "
Hello, World
```

For more a more structured way to join strings into larger strings or reports, see Recipe 5.6.

See Also

Recipe 5.6, "Place Formatted Information in a String"

5.11 Convert a String to Upper/Lowercase

Problem

You want to convert a string to uppercase or lowercase.

Solution

Use the ToUpper() or ToLower() methods of the string to convert it to uppercase or lowercase, respectively.

To convert a string to uppercase, use the ToUpper() method:

```
PS > "Hello World".ToUpper()
HELLO WORLD
```

To convert a string to lowercase, use the ToLower() method:

```
PS > "Hello World".ToLower()
hello world
```

Discussion

Since PowerShell strings are fully featured .NET objects, they support many string-oriented operations directly. The ToUpper() and ToLower() methods are two examples of the many features that the String class supports. To learn what other functionality the String class supports, see Recipe 3.13.

Neither PowerShell nor the methods of the .NET String class directly support capitalizing only the first letter of a word. If you want to capitalize only the first character of a word or sentence, try the following commands:

```
PS > $text = "hello"
PS > $newText = $text.Substring(0,1).ToUpper() +
    $text.Substring(1)
$newText

Hello
```

One thing to keep in mind as you convert a string to uppercase or lowercase is your motivation for doing it. One of the most common reasons is for comparing strings, as shown in Example 5-6.

Example 5-6. Using the ToUpper() method to normalize strings

```
## $text comes from the user, and contains the value "quit"
if($text.ToUpper() -eq "QUIT") { ... }
```

Unfortunately, explicitly changing the capitalization of strings fails in subtle ways when your script runs in different cultures. Many cultures follow different capitalization and comparison rules than you may be used to. For example, the Turkish language includes two types of the letter "I": one with a dot and one without. The uppercase version of the lowercase letter "i" corresponds to the version of the capital I with a dot, not the capital I used in QUIT. Those capitalization rules cause the string comparison code in Example 5-6 to fail in the Turkish culture.

To compare some input against a hardcoded string in a case-insensitive manner, the better solution is to use PowerShell's -eq operator without changing any of the casing yourself. The -eq operator is case-insensitive and culture-neutral by default:

```
PS > $text1 = "Hello"
PS > $text2 = "HELLO"
PS > $text1 -eq $text2
True
```

For more information about writing culture-aware scripts, see Recipe 13.6.

See Also

Recipe 3.13, "Learn About Types and Objects"

Recipe 13.6, "Write Culture-Aware Scripts"

5.12 Trim a String

Problem

You want to remove leading or trailing spaces from a string or user input.

Solution

Use the Trim() method of the string to remove all leading and trailing whitespace characters from that string.

```
PS > $text = " `t Test String`t `t"
PS > "|" + $text.Trim() + "|"
|Test String|
```

Discussion

The `Trim()` method cleans all whitespace from the beginning *and* end of a string. If you want just one or the other, you can call the `TrimStart()` or `TrimEnd()` method to remove whitespace from the beginning or the end of the string, respectively. If you want to remove specific characters from the beginning or end of a string, the `Trim()`, `Trim Start()`, and `TrimEnd()` methods provide options to support that. To trim a list of specific characters from the end of a string, provide that list to the method, as shown in Example 5-7.

Example 5-7. Trimming a list of characters from the end of a string

```
PS > "Hello World".TrimEnd('d','l','r','o','W',' ')
He
```

 At first blush, the following command that attempts to trim the text "World" from the end of a string appears to work incorrectly:

```
PS > "Hello World".TrimEnd(" World")
He
```

This happens because the `TrimEnd()` method takes a list of characters to remove from the end of a string. PowerShell automatically converts a string to a list of characters if required, and in this case converts your string to the characters `W`, `o`, `r`, `l`, `d`, and a space. These are in fact the same characters as were used in Example 5-7, so it has the same effect.

If you want to replace text anywhere in a string (and not just from the beginning or end), see Recipe 5.8.

See Also

Recipe 5.8, "Replace Text in a String"

5.13 Format a Date for Output

Problem

You want to control the way that PowerShell displays or formats a date.

Solution

To control the format of a date, use one of the following options:

• The `Get-Date` cmdlet's `-Format` parameter:

```
PS > Get-Date -Date "05/09/1998 1:23 PM" -Format "dd-MM-yyyy @ hh:mm:ss"
09-05-1998 @ 01:23:00
```

- PowerShell's string formatting (-f) operator:

```
PS > $date = [DateTime] "05/09/1998 1:23 PM"
PS > "{0:dd-MM-yyyy @ hh:mm:ss}" -f $date
09-05-1998 @ 01:23:00
```

- The object's ToString() method:

```
PS > $date = [DateTime] "05/09/1998 1:23 PM"
PS > $date.ToString("dd-MM-yyyy @ hh:mm:ss")
09-05-1998 @ 01:23:00
```

- The Get-Date cmdlet's -UFormat parameter, which supports Unix date format strings:

```
PS > Get-Date -Date "05/09/1998 1:23 PM" -UFormat "%d-%m-%Y @ %I:%M:%S"
09-05-1998 @ 01:23:00
```

Discussion

Except for the -UFormat parameter of the Get-Date cmdlet, all date formatting in PowerShell uses the standard .NET DateTime format strings. These format strings let you display dates in one of many standard formats (such as your system's short or long date patterns), or in a completely custom manner. For more information on how to specify standard .NET DateTime format strings, see Appendix E.

If you are already used to the Unix-style date formatting strings (or are converting an existing script that uses a complex one), the -UFormat parameter of the Get-Date cmdlet may be helpful. It accepts the format strings accepted by the Unix date command, but does not provide any functionality that standard .NET date formatting strings cannot.

When working with the string version of dates and times, be aware that they are the most common source of internationalization issues—problems that arise from running a script on a machine with a different culture than the one it was written on. In North America, "05/09/1998" means "May 9, 1998." In many other cultures, though, it means "September 5, 1998." Whenever possible, use and compare DateTime objects (rather than strings) to other DateTime objects, as that avoids these cultural differences. Example 5-8 demonstrates this approach.

Example 5-8. Comparing DateTime objects with the -gt operator

```
PS > $dueDate = [DateTime] "01/01/2006"
PS > if([DateTime]::Now -gt $dueDate)
{
    "Account is now due"
}

Account is now due
```

PowerShell *always* assumes the North American date format when it interprets a DateTime constant such as [DateTime] "05/09/1998". This is for the same reason that all languages interpret numeric constants (such as 12.34) in the North American format. If it did otherwise, nearly every script that dealt with dates and times would fail on international systems.

For more information about the Get-Date cmdlet, type **Get-Help Get-Date**. For more information about dealing with dates and times in a culturally aware manner, see Recipe 13.6.

See Also

Recipe 13.6, "Write Culture-Aware Scripts"

Appendix E, *.NET DateTime Formatting*

5.14 Program: Convert Text Streams to Objects

One of the strongest features of PowerShell is its object-based pipeline. You don't waste your energy creating, destroying, and recreating the object representation of your data. In other shells, you lose the full-fidelity representation of data when the pipeline converts it to pure text. You can regain some of it through excessive text parsing, but not all of it.

However, you still often have to interact with low-fidelity input that originates from outside PowerShell. Text-based data files and legacy programs are two examples.

PowerShell offers great support for two of the three text-parsing staples:

Sed
    Replaces text. For that functionality, PowerShell offers the -replace operator.
Grep
    Searches text. For that functionality, PowerShell offers the Select-String cmdlet, among others.

The third traditional text-parsing tool, *Awk*, lets you chop a line of text into more intuitive groupings. PowerShell offers the -split operator for strings, but that lacks some of the power you usually need to break a string into groups.

The Convert-TextObject script presented in Example 5-9 lets you convert text streams into a set of objects that represent those text elements according to the rules you specify. From there, you can use all of PowerShell's object-based tools, which gives you even more power than you would get with the text-based equivalents.

Example 5-9. Convert-TextObject.ps1

```
##############################################################################
##
## Convert-TextObject
##
## From Windows PowerShell Cookbook (O'Reilly)
## by Lee Holmes (http://www.leeholmes.com/guide)
##
##############################################################################

<#

.SYNOPSIS

Convert a simple string into a custom PowerShell object.

.EXAMPLE

"Hello World" | Convert-TextObject
Generates an Object with "P1=Hello" and "P2=World"

.EXAMPLE

"Hello World" | Convert-TextObject -Delimiter "ll"
Generates an Object with "P1=He" and "P2=o World"

.EXAMPLE

"Hello World" | Convert-TextObject -Pattern "He(ll.*o)r(ld)"
Generates an Object with "P1=llo Wo" and "P2=ld"

.EXAMPLE

"Hello World" | Convert-TextObject -PropertyName FirstWord,SecondWord
Generates an Object with "FirstWord=Hello" and "SecondWord=World

.EXAMPLE

"123 456" | Convert-TextObject -PropertyType $([string],[int])
Generates an Object with "Property1=123" and "Property2=456"
The second property is an integer, as opposed to a string

.EXAMPLE

PS >$ipAddress = (ipconfig | Convert-TextObject -Delim ": ")[2].P2
PS >$ipAddress
192.168.1.104

#>

[CmdletBinding(DefaultParameterSetName = "ByDelimiter")]
param(
    ## If specified, gives the .NET Regular Expression with which to
    ## split the string. The script generates properties for the
    ## resulting object out of the elements resulting from this split.
```

```
    ## If not specified, defaults to splitting on the maximum amount
    ## of whitespace: "\s+", as long as Pattern is not
    ## specified either.
    [Parameter(ParameterSetName = "ByDelimiter", Position = 0)]
    [string] $Delimiter = "\s+",

    ## If specified, gives the .NET Regular Expression with which to
    ## parse the string. The script generates properties for the
    ## resulting object out of the groups captured by this regular
    ## expression.
    [Parameter(Mandatory = $true,
        ParameterSetName = "ByPattern",
        Position = 0)]
    [string] $Pattern,

    ## If specified, the script will pair the names from this object
    ## definition with the elements from the parsed string.  If not
    ## specified (or the generated object contains more properties
    ## than you specify), the script uses property names in the
    ## pattern of P1,P2,...,PN
    [Parameter(Position = 1)]
    [Alias("PN")]
    [string[]] $PropertyName = @(),

    ## If specified, the script will pair the types from this list with
    ## the properties from the parsed string.  If not specified (or the
    ## generated object contains more properties than you specify), the
    ## script sets the properties to be of type [string]
    [Parameter(Position = 2)]
    [Alias("PT")]
    [type[]] $PropertyType = @(),

    ## The input object to process
    [Parameter(ValueFromPipeline = $true)]
    [string] $InputObject
)

begin {
    Set-StrictMode -Version Latest
}

process {
    $returnObject = New-Object PSObject

    $matches = $null
    $matchCount = 0

    if($PSBoundParameters["Pattern"])
    {
        ## Verify that the input contains the pattern
        ## Populates the matches variable by default
        if(-not ($InputObject -match $pattern))
        {
            return
        }
```

```
        $matchCount = $matches.Count
        $startIndex = 1
    }
    else
    {
        ## Verify that the input contains the delimiter
        if(-not ($InputObject -match $delimiter))
        {
            return
        }

        ## If so, split the input on that delimiter
        $matches = $InputObject -split $delimiter
        $matchCount = $matches.Length
        $startIndex = 0
    }

    ## Go through all of the matches, and add them as notes to the output
    ## object.
    for($counter = $startIndex; $counter -lt $matchCount; $counter++)
    {
        $currentPropertyName = "P$($counter - $startIndex + 1)"
        $currentPropertyType = [string]

        ## Get the property name
        if($counter -lt $propertyName.Length)
        {
            if($propertyName[$counter])
            {
            $currentPropertyName = $propertyName[$counter]
            }
        }

        ## Get the property value
        if($counter -lt $propertyType.Length)
        {
            if($propertyType[$counter])
            {
            $currentPropertyType = $propertyType[$counter]
            }
        }

        Add-Member -InputObject $returnObject NoteProperty `
            -Name $currentPropertyName `
            -Value ($matches[$counter].Trim() -as $currentPropertyType)
    }

    $returnObject
}
```

See Also

Recipe 1.1, "Run Programs, Scripts, and Existing Tools"

5.15 Generate Large Reports and Text Streams

Problem

You want to write a script that generates a large report or large amount of data.

Solution

The best approach to generating a large amount of data is to take advantage of PowerShell's streaming behavior whenever possible. Opt for solutions that pipeline data between commands:

```
Get-ChildItem C:\ *.txt -Recurse | Out-File c:\temp\AllTextFiles.txt
```

rather than collect the output at each stage:

```
$files = Get-ChildItem C:\ *.txt -Recurse
$files | Out-File c:\temp\AllTextFiles.txt
```

If your script generates a large text report (and streaming is not an option), use the StringBuilder class:

```
$output = New-Object System.Text.StringBuilder
Get-ChildItem C:\ *.txt -Recurse |
    Foreach-Object { [void] $output.AppendLine($_.FullName) }
$output.ToString()
```

rather than simple text concatenation:

```
$output = ""
Get-ChildItem C:\ *.txt -Recurse | Foreach-Object { $output += $_.FullName }
$output
```

Discussion

In PowerShell, combining commands in a pipeline is a fundamental concept. As scripts and cmdlets generate output, PowerShell passes that output to the next command in the pipeline as soon as it can. In the solution, the Get-ChildItem commands that retrieve all text files on the C: drive take a very long time to complete. However, since they *begin* to generate data almost immediately, PowerShell can pass that data on to the next command as soon as the Get-ChildItem cmdlet produces it. This is true of any commands that generate or consume data and is called *streaming*. The pipeline completes almost as soon as the Get-ChildItem cmdlet finishes producing its data and uses memory very efficiently as it does so.

The second Get-ChildItem example (which collects its data) prevents PowerShell from taking advantage of this streaming opportunity. It first stores all the files in an array, which, because of the amount of data, takes a long time and an enormous amount of memory. Then, it sends all those objects into the output file, which takes a long time as well.

However, most commands can consume data produced by the pipeline directly, as illustrated by the `Out-File` cmdlet. For those commands, PowerShell provides streaming behavior as long as you combine the commands into a pipeline. For commands that do not support data coming from the pipeline directly, the `Foreach-Object` cmdlet (with the aliases of `foreach` and `%`) lets you work with each piece of data as the previous command produces it, as shown in the `StringBuilder` example.

Creating large text reports

When you generate large reports, it is common to store the entire report into a string, and then write that string out to a file once the script completes. You can usually accomplish this most effectively by streaming the text directly to its destination (a file or the screen), but sometimes this is not possible.

Since PowerShell makes it so easy to add more text to the end of a string (as in `$output += $_.FullName`), many initially opt for that approach. This works great for small-to-medium strings, but it causes significant performance problems for large strings.

 As an example of this performance difference, compare the following:

```
PS > Measure-Command {
    $output = New-Object Text.StringBuilder
    1..10000 |
        Foreach-Object { $output.Append("Hello World") }
}

(...)
TotalSeconds : 2.3471592

PS > Measure-Command {
    $output = ""
    1..10000 | Foreach-Object { $output += "Hello World" }
}

(...)
TotalSeconds     : 4.9884882
```

In the .NET Framework (and therefore PowerShell), strings never change after you create them. When you add more text to the end of a string, PowerShell has to build a *new* string by combining the two smaller strings. This operation takes a long time for large strings, which is why the .NET Framework includes the `System.Text.String Builder` class. Unlike normal strings, the `StringBuilder` class assumes that you will modify its data—an assumption that allows it to adapt to change much more efficiently.

5.16 Generate Source Code and Other Repetitive Text

Problem

You want to simplify the creation of large amounts of repetitive source code or other text.

Solution

Use PowerShell's string formatting operator (-f) to place dynamic information inside of a preformatted string, and then repeat that replacement for each piece of dynamic information.

Discussion

Code generation is a useful technique in nearly any technology that produces output from some text-based input. For example, imagine having to create an HTML report to show all of the processes running on your system at that time. In this case, "code" is the HTML code understood by a web browser.

HTML pages start with some standard text (`<html>`, `<head>`, `<body>`), and then you would likely include the processes in an HTML `<table>`. Each row would include columns for each of the properties in the process you're working with.

Generating this by hand would be mind-numbing and error-prone. Instead, you can write a function to generate the code for the row:

```
function Get-HtmlRow($process)
{
    $template = "<TR> <TD>{0}</TD> <TD>{1}</TD> </TR>"
    $template -f $process.Name,$process.ID
}
```

and then generate the report in milliseconds, rather than hours:

```
"<HTML><BODY><TABLE>" > report.html
Get-Process | Foreach-Object { Get-HtmlRow $_ } >> report.html
"</TABLE></BODY></HTML>" >> report.html
Invoke-Item .\report.html
```

In addition to the formatting operator, you can sometimes use the `String.Replace` method:

```
$string = @'
Name is __NAME__
Id is __ID__
'@

$string = $string.Replace("__NAME__", $process.Name)
$string = $string.Replace("__ID__", $process.Id)
```

This works well (and is very readable) if you have tight control over the data you'll be using as replacement text. If it is at all possible for the replacement text to contain one of the special tags ("__NAME__" or "__ID__", for example), then they will *also* get replaced by further replacements and corrupt your final output.

To avoid this issue, you can use the `Format-String` script shown in Example 5-10.

Example 5-10. Format-String.ps1

```
#############################################################################
##
## Format-String
##
## From Windows PowerShell Cookbook (O'Reilly)
## by Lee Holmes (http://www.leeholmes.com/guide)
##
#############################################################################

<#

.SYNOPSIS

Replaces text in a string based on named replacement tags

.EXAMPLE

Format-String "Hello {NAME}" @{ NAME = 'PowerShell' }
Hello PowerShell

.EXAMPLE

Format-String "Your score is {SCORE:P}" @{ SCORE = 0.85 }
Your score is 85.00 %

#>

param(
    ## The string to format. Any portions in the form of {NAME}
    ## will be automatically replaced by the corresponding value
    ## from the supplied hashtable.
    $String,

    ## The named replacements to use in the string
    [hashtable] $Replacements
)

Set-StrictMode -Version Latest

$currentIndex = 0
$replacementList = @()

## Go through each key in the hashtable
foreach($key in $replacements.Keys)
{
    ## Convert the key into a number, so that it can be used by
```

```
## String.Format
$inputPattern = '{(.*)' + $key + '(.*)}'
$replacementPattern = '{${1}' + $currentIndex + '${2}}'
$string = $string -replace $inputPattern,$replacementPattern
$replacementList += $replacements[$key]

    $currentIndex++
}

## Now use String.Format to replace the numbers in the
## format string.
$string -f $replacementList
```

PowerShell includes several commands for code generation that you've probably used without recognizing their "code generation" aspect. The ConvertTo-Html cmdlet applies code generation of incoming objects to HTML reports. The ConvertTo-Csv cmdlet applies code generation to CSV files. The ConvertTo-Xml cmdlet applies code generation to XML files.

Code generation techniques seem to come up naturally when you realize you are writing a report, but they are often missed when writing source code of another programming or scripting language. For example, imagine you need to write a C# function that outputs all of the details of a process. The System.Diagnostics.Process class has a lot of properties, so that's going to be a long function. Writing it by hand is going to be difficult, so you can have PowerShell do most of it for you.

For any object (for example, a process that you've retrieved from the Get-Process command), you can access its PsObject.Properties property to get a list of all of its properties. Each of those has a Name property, so you can use that to generate the C# code:

```
$process.PsObject.Properties |
    Foreach-Object {
        'Console.WriteLine("{0}: " + process.{0});' -f $_.Name }
```

This generates more than 60 lines of C# source code, rather than having you do it by hand:

```
Console.WriteLine("Name: " + process.Name);
Console.WriteLine("Handles: " + process.Handles);
Console.WriteLine("VM: " + process.VM);
Console.WriteLine("WS: " + process.WS);
Console.WriteLine("PM: " + process.PM);
Console.WriteLine("NPM: " + process.NPM);
Console.WriteLine("Path: " + process.Path);
Console.WriteLine("Company: " + process.Company);
Console.WriteLine("CPU: " + process.CPU);
Console.WriteLine("FileVersion: " + process.FileVersion);
Console.WriteLine("ProductVersion: " + process.ProductVersion);
(...)
```

Similar benefits come from generating bulk SQL statements, repetitive data structures, and more.

PowerShell code generation can still help you with large-scale administration tasks, even when PowerShell is not available. Given a large list of input (for example, a complex list of files to copy), you can easily generate a *cmd.exe* batch file or Unix shell script to automate the task. Generate the script in PowerShell, and then invoke it on the system of your choice!

Calculations and Math

6.0 Introduction

Math is an important feature in any scripting language. Math support in a language includes addition, subtraction, multiplication, and division, of course, but extends into more advanced mathematical operations. So it should not surprise you that PowerShell provides a strong suite of mathematical and calculation-oriented features.

Since PowerShell provides full access to its scripting language from the command line, this keeps a powerful and useful command-line calculator always at your fingertips! In addition to its support for traditional mathematical operations, PowerShell also caters to system administrators by working natively with concepts such as megabytes and gigabytes, simple statistics (such as sum and average), and conversions between bases.

6.1 Perform Simple Arithmetic

Problem

You want to use PowerShell to calculate simple mathematical results.

Solution

Use PowerShell's arithmetic operators:

+	Addition
-	Subtraction
*	Multiplication
/	Division
%	Modulus
+=, -=, *=, /=, and %=	Assignment variations of the previously listed operators
()	Precedence/order of operations

For a detailed description of these mathematical operators, see "Simple Operators" on page 725.

Discussion

One difficulty in many programming languages comes from the way that they handle data in variables. For example, this C# snippet stores the value of "1" in the result variable, when the user probably wanted the result to hold the floating-point value of 1.5:

```
double result = 0;
result = 3/2;
```

This is because C# (along with many other languages) determines the result of the division from the type of data being used in the division. In the previous example, it decides that you want the answer to be an integer because you used two integers in the division.

PowerShell, on the other hand, avoids this problem. Even if you use two integers in a division, PowerShell returns the result as a floating-point number if required. This is called *widening*.

```
PS > $result = 0
PS > $result = 3/2
PS > $result
1.5
```

One exception to this automatic widening is when you explicitly tell PowerShell the type of result you want. For example, you might use an integer cast ([int]) to say that you want the result to be an integer after all:

```
PS > $result = [int] (3/2)
PS > $result
2
```

Many programming languages drop the portion after the decimal point when they convert them from floating-point numbers to integers. This is called *truncation*. PowerShell, on the other hand, uses *banker's rounding* for this conversion. It converts floating-point numbers to their nearest integer, rounding to the nearest even number in case of a tie.

Several programming techniques use truncation, though, so it is still important that a scripting language somehow support it. PowerShell does not have a built-in operator that performs truncation-style division, but it does support it through the [Math]::Truncate() method in the .NET Framework:

```
PS > $result = 3/2
PS > [Math]::Truncate($result)
1
```

If that syntax seems burdensome, the following example defines a trunc function that truncates its input:

```
PS > function trunc($number) { [Math]::Truncate($number) }
PS > $result = 3/2
PS > trunc $result
1
```

See Also

"Simple Operators" on page 725

6.2 Perform Complex Arithmetic

Problem

You want to use PowerShell to calculate more complex or advanced mathematical results.

Solution

PowerShell supports more advanced mathematical tasks primarily through its support for the `System.Math` class in the .NET Framework.

To find the absolute value of a number, use the `[Math]::Abs()` method:

```
PS > [Math]::Abs(-10.6)
10.6
```

To find the power (such as the square or the cube) of a number, use the `[Math]::Pow()` method. In this case, the method is finding 123 squared:

```
PS > [Math]::Pow(123, 2)
15129
```

To find the square root of a number, use the `[Math]::Sqrt()` method:

```
PS > [Math]::Sqrt(100)
10
```

To find the sine, cosine, or tangent of an angle (given in radians), use the `[Math]::Sin()`, `[Math]::Cos()`, or `[Math]::Tan()` method:

```
PS > [Math]::Sin( [Math]::PI / 2 )
1
```

To find the angle (given in radians) of a sine, cosine, or tangent value, use the `[Math]::ASin()`, `[Math]::ACos()`, or `[Math]::ATan()` method:

```
PS > [Math]::ASin(1)
1.5707963267949
```

See Recipe 3.13 to learn how to find out what other features the `System.Math` class provides.

Discussion

Once you start working with the System.Math class, it may seem as though its designers left out significant pieces of functionality. The class supports the square root of a number, but doesn't support other roots (such as the cube root). It supports sine, cosine, and tangent (and their inverses) in radians, but not in the more commonly used measure of degrees.

Working with any root

To determine any root (such as the cube root) of a number, you can use the function given in Example 6-1.

Example 6-1. A root function and some example calculations

```
PS > function root($number, $root) { [Math]::Pow($number, 1 / $root) }
PS > root 64 3
4
PS > root 25 5
1.90365393871588
PS > [Math]::Pow(1.90365393871588, 5)
25.0000000000001
PS > [Math]::Pow( $(root 25 5), 5)
25
```

This function applies the mathematical fact that the square root of a number is the same as raising that number to the power of 1/2, the cube of a number is the same as raising it to the power of 1/3, etc.

The example also illustrates a very important point about math on computers. When you use this function (or anything else that manipulates floating-point numbers), always be aware that the results of floating-point answers are only ever approximations of the actual result. If you combine multiple calculations in the same statement (or store intermediate results into variables), programming and scripting languages can sometimes keep an accurate answer (such as in the second [Math]::Pow() attempt), but that exception is rare.

Some mathematical systems avoid this problem by working with equations and calculations as symbols (and not numbers). Like humans, these systems know that taking the square of a number that you just took the square root of gives you the original number right back—so they don't actually have to do either of those operations. These systems, however, are extremely specialized and usually very expensive.

Working with degrees instead of radians

Converting radians (the way that mathematicians commonly measure angles) to degrees (the way that most people commonly measure angles) is much more straightforward than the root function. A circle has 2 * Pi radians if you measure in radians, and 360 degrees if you measure in degrees. That gives the following two functions:

```
PS > function Convert-RadiansToDegrees($angle) { $angle / (2 * [Math]::Pi) * 360 }
PS > function Convert-DegreesToRadians($angle) { $angle / 360 * (2 * [Math]::Pi) }
```

and their usage:

```
PS > Convert-RadiansToDegrees ([Math]::Pi)
180
PS > Convert-RadiansToDegrees ([Math]::Pi / 2)
90
PS > Convert-DegreesToRadians 360
6.28318530717959
PS > Convert-DegreesToRadians 45
0.785398163397448
PS > [Math]::Tan( (Convert-DegreesToRadians 45) )
1
```

See Also

Recipe 3.13, "Learn About Types and Objects"

6.3 Measure Statistical Properties of a List

Problem

You want to measure the numeric (minimum, maximum, sum, average) or textual (characters, words, lines) features of a list of objects.

Solution

Use the `Measure-Object` cmdlet to measure these statistical properties of a list.

To measure the numeric features of a stream of objects, pipe those objects to the `Measure-Object` cmdlet:

```
PS > 1..10 | Measure-Object -Average -Sum


Count    : 10
Average  : 5.5
Sum      : 55
Maximum  :
Minimum  :
Property :
```

To measure the numeric features of a specific property in a stream of objects, supply that property name to the `-Property` parameter of the `Measure-Object` cmdlet. For example, in a directory with files:

```
PS > Get-ChildItem | Measure-Object -Property Length -Max -Min -Average -Sum


Count    : 427
Average  : 10617025.4918033
```

```
Sum      : 4533469885
Maximum  : 647129088
Minimum  : 0
Property : Length
```

To measure the textual features of a stream of objects, use the -Character, -Word, and -Line parameters of the Measure-Object cmdlet:

```
PS > Get-ChildItem > output.txt
PS > Get-Content output.txt | Measure-Object -Character -Word -Line

          Lines          Words      Characters Property
          -----          -----      ---------- --------
            964           6083           33484
```

Discussion

By default, the Measure-Object cmdlet counts only the number of objects it receives. If you want to measure additional properties (such as the maximum, minimum, average, sum, characters, words, or lines) of those objects, then you need to specify them as options to the cmdlet.

For the numeric properties, though, you usually don't want to measure the objects themselves. Instead, you probably want to measure a specific property from the list—such as the Length property of a file. For that purpose, the Measure-Object cmdlet supports the -Property parameter to which you provide the property you want to measure.

Sometimes you might want to measure a property that isn't a simple number—such as the LastWriteTime property of a file. Since the LastWriteTime property is a DateTime, you can't determine its average immediately. However, if any property allows you to convert it to a number and back in a meaningful way (such as the Ticks property of a DateTime), then you can still compute its statistical properties. Example 6-2 shows how to get the average LastWriteTime from a list of files.

Example 6-2. Using the Ticks property of the DateTime class to determine the average LastWriteTime of a list of files

```
PS > ## Get the LastWriteTime from each file
PS > $times = dir | Foreach-Object { $_.LastWriteTime }

PS > ## Measure the average Ticks property of those LastWriteTime
PS > $results = $times | Measure-Object Ticks -Average

PS > ## Create a new DateTime out of the average Ticks
PS > New-Object DateTime $results.Average

Sunday, June 11, 2006 6:45:01 AM
```

For more information about the Measure-Object cmdlet, type **Get-Help Measure-Object**.

6.4 Work with Numbers as Binary

Problem

You want to work with the individual bits of a number or work with a number built by combining a series of flags.

Solution

To directly enter a hexadecimal number, use the 0x prefix:

```
PS > $hexNumber = 0x1234
PS > $hexNumber
4660
```

To convert a number to its binary representation, supply a base of 2 to the [Convert]::ToString() method:

```
PS > [Convert]::ToString(1234, 2)
10011010010
```

To convert a binary number into its decimal representation, supply a base of 2 to the [Convert]::ToInt32() method:

```
PS > [Convert]::ToInt32("10011010010", 2)
1234
```

To manage the individual bits of a number, use PowerShell's binary operators. In this case, the Archive flag is just one of the many possible attributes that may be true of a given file:

```
PS > $archive = [System.IO.FileAttributes] "Archive"
PS > attrib +a test.txt
PS > Get-ChildItem | Where { $_.Attributes -band $archive } | Select Name

Name
----
test.txt
PS > attrib -a test.txt
PS > Get-ChildItem | Where { $_.Attributes -band $archive } | Select Name
PS >
```

Discussion

In some system administration tasks, it is common to come across numbers that seem to mean nothing by themselves. The attributes of a file are a perfect example:

```
PS > (Get-Item test.txt).Encrypt()
PS > (Get-Item test.txt).IsReadOnly = $true
PS > [int] (Get-Item test.txt -force).Attributes
16417
PS > (Get-Item test.txt -force).IsReadOnly = $false
PS > (Get-Item test.txt).Decrypt()
```

```
PS > [int] (Get-Item test.txt).Attributes
32
```

What can the numbers 16417 and 32 possibly tell us about the file?

The answer to this comes from looking at the attributes in another light—as a set of features that can be either true or false. Take, for example, the possible attributes for an item in a directory shown by Example 6-3.

Example 6-3. Possible attributes of a file

```
PS > [Enum]::GetNames([System.IO.FileAttributes])
ReadOnly
Hidden
System
Directory
Archive
Device
Normal
Temporary
SparseFile
ReparsePoint
Compressed
Offline
NotContentIndexedEncrypted
```

If a file is `ReadOnly`, `Archive`, and `Encrypted`, then you might consider the following as a succinct description of the attributes on that file:

```
ReadOnly = True
Archive = True
Encrypted = True
```

It just so happens that computers have an extremely concise way of representing sets of true and false values—a representation known as *binary*. To represent the attributes of a directory item as binary, you simply put them in a table. We give the item a "1" if the attribute applies to the item and a "0" otherwise (see Table 6-1).

Table 6-1. Attributes of a directory item

Attribute	True (1) or false (0)
Encrypted	1
NotContentIndexed	0
Offline	0
Compressed	0
ReparsePoint	0
SparseFile	0
Temporary	0
Normal	0
Device	0

Attribute	True (1) or false (0)
Archive	1
Directory	0
<Unused>	0
System	0
Hidden	0
ReadOnly	1

If we treat those features as the individual binary digits in a number, that gives us the number 100000000100001. If we convert that number to its decimal form, it becomes clear where the number 16417 came from:

```
PS > [Convert]::ToInt32("100000000100001", 2)
16417
```

This technique sits at the core of many properties that you can express as a combination of features or flags. Rather than list the features in a table, though, documentation usually describes the number that would result from that feature being the only one active—such as FILE_ATTRIBUTE_REPARSEPOINT = 0x400. Example 6-4 shows the various representations of these file attributes.

Example 6-4. Integer, hexadecimal, and binary representations of possible file attributes

```
PS > $attributes = [Enum]::GetValues([System.IO.FileAttributes])
PS > $attributes | Select-Object `
  @{"Name"="Property";
     "Expression"= { $_ } },
  @{"Name"="Integer";
     "Expression"= { [int] $_ } },
  @{"Name"="Hexadecimal";
     "Expression"= { [Convert]::ToString([int] $_, 16) } },
  @{"Name"="Binary";
     "Expression"= { [Convert]::ToString([int] $_, 2) } } |
  Format-Table -auto


    Property Integer Hexadecimal Binary
    -------- ------- ----------- ------
    ReadOnly       1 1           1
      Hidden       2 2           10
      System       4 4           100
   Directory      16 10          10000
     Archive      32 20          100000
      Device      64 40          1000000
      Normal     128 80          10000000
   Temporary     256 100         100000000
  SparseFile     512 200         1000000000
 ReparsePoint   1024 400         10000000000
  Compressed    2048 800         100000000000
     Offline    4096 1000        1000000000000
```

```
NotContentIndexed    8192 2000         10000000000000
       Encrypted    16384 4000         100000000000000
```

Knowing how that 16417 number was formed, you can now use the properties in meaningful ways. For example, PowerShell's -band operator allows you to check whether a certain bit has been set:

```
PS > $encrypted = 16384
PS > $attributes = (Get-Item test.txt -force).Attributes
PS > ($attributes -band $encrypted) -eq $encrypted
True
PS > $compressed = 2048
PS > ($attributes -band $compressed) -eq $compressed
False
PS >
```

Although that example uses the numeric values explicitly, it would be more common to enter the number by its name:

```
PS > $archive = [System.IO.FileAttributes] "Archive"
PS > ($attributes -band $archive) -eq $archive
True
```

For more information about PowerShell's binary operators, see "Simple Operators" on page 725.

See Also

"Simple Operators" on page 725

6.5 Simplify Math with Administrative Constants

Problem

You want to work with common administrative numbers (that is, kilobytes, megabytes, gigabytes, terabytes, and petabytes) without having to remember or calculate those numbers.

Solution

Use PowerShell's administrative constants (KB, MB, GB, TB, and PB) to help work with these common numbers.

For example, we can calculate the download time (in seconds) of a 10.18 megabyte file over a connection that gets 215 kilobytes per second:

```
PS > 10.18mb / 215kb
48.4852093023256
```

Discussion

PowerShell's administrative constants are based on powers of two, since they are the type most commonly used when working with computers. Each is 1,024 times bigger than the one before it:

```
1kb = 1024
1mb = 1024 * 1 kb
1gb = 1024 * 1 mb
1tb = 1024 * 1 gb
1pb = 1024 * 1 tb
```

Some people (such as hard drive manufacturers) prefer to call numbers based on powers of two "kibibytes," "mebibytes," and "gibibytes." They use the terms "kilobytes," "megabytes," and "gigabytes" to mean numbers that are 1,000 times bigger than the ones before them—numbers based on powers of 10.

Although not represented by administrative constants, PowerShell still makes it easy to work with these numbers in powers of 10—for example, to figure out how big a "300 GB" hard drive is when reported by Windows. To do this, use scientific (exponential) notation:

```
PS > $kilobyte = 1e3
PS > $kilobyte
1000
PS > $megabyte = 1e6
PS > $megabyte
1000000
PS > $gigabyte = 1e9
PS > $gigabyte
1000000000
PS > (300 * $gigabyte) / 1GB
279.396772384644
```

See Also

"Simple Assignment" on page 720

6.6 Convert Numbers Between Bases

Problem

You want to convert a number to a different base.

Solution

The PowerShell scripting language allows you to enter both decimal and hexadecimal numbers directly. It does not natively support other number bases, but its support for interaction with the .NET Framework enables conversion both to and from binary, octal, decimal, and hexadecimal.

To convert a hexadecimal number into its decimal representation, prefix the number with 0x to enter the number as hexadecimal:

```
PS > $myErrorCode = 0xFE4A
PS > $myErrorCode
65098
```

To convert a binary number into its decimal representation, supply a base of 2 to the [Convert]::ToInt32() method:

```
PS > [Convert]::ToInt32("10011010010", 2)
1234
```

To convert an octal number into its decimal representation, supply a base of 8 to the [Convert]::ToInt32() method:

```
PS > [Convert]::ToInt32("1234", 8)
668
```

To convert a number into its hexadecimal representation, use either the [Convert] class or PowerShell's format operator:

```
PS > ## Use the [Convert] class
PS > [Convert]::ToString(1234, 16)
4d2

PS > ## Use the formatting operator
PS > "{0:X4}" -f 1234
04D2
```

To convert a number into its binary representation, supply a base of 2 to the [Convert]::ToString() method:

```
PS > [Convert]::ToString(1234, 2)
10011010010
```

To convert a number into its octal representation, supply a base of 8 to the [Convert]::ToString() method:

```
PS > [Convert]::ToString(1234, 8)
2322
```

Discussion

It is most common to want to convert numbers between bases when you are dealing with numbers that represent binary combinations of data, such as the attributes of a file. For more information on how to work with binary data like this, see Recipe 6.4.

See Also

Recipe 6.4, "Work with Numbers as Binary"

Lists, Arrays, and Hashtables

7.0 Introduction

Most scripts deal with more than one thing—lists of servers, lists of files, lookup codes, and more. To enable this, PowerShell supports many features to help you through both its language features and utility cmdlets.

PowerShell makes working with arrays and lists much like working with other data types: you can easily create an array or list and then add or remove elements from it. You can just as easily sort it, search it, or combine it with another array. When you want to store a mapping between one piece of data and another, a hashtable fulfills that need perfectly.

7.1 Create an Array or List of Items

Problem

You want to create an array or list of items.

Solution

To create an array that holds a given set of items, separate those items with commas:

```
PS > $myArray = 1,2,"Hello World"
PS > $myArray
1
2
Hello World
```

To create an array of a specific size, use the New-Object cmdlet:

```
PS > $myArray = New-Object string[] 10
PS > $myArray[5] = "Hello"
PS > $myArray[5]
Hello
```

To create an array of a specific type, use a strongly typed collection:

```
PS > $list = New-Object Collections.Generic.List[Int]
PS > $list.Add(10)
PS > $list.Add("Hello")
Cannot convert argument "0", with value: "Hello", for "Add" to type "System
.Int32": "Cannot convert value "Hello" to type "System.Int32". Error:
"Input string was not in a correct format.""
```

To store the output of a command that generates a list, use variable assignment:

```
PS > $myArray = Get-Process
PS > $myArray

Handles  NPM(K)    PM(K)    WS(K) VM(M)  CPU(s)     Id ProcessName
-------  ------    -----    ----- -----  ------     -- -----------
    274       6     1316     3908    33            3164 alg
    983       7     3636     7472    30             688 csrss
     69       4      924     3332    30    0.69    2232 ctfmon
    180       5     2220     6116    37            2816 dllhost
(...)
```

To create an array that you plan to modify frequently, use an ArrayList, as shown by Example 7-1.

Example 7-1. Using an ArrayList to manage a dynamic collection of items

```
PS > $myArray = New-Object System.Collections.ArrayList
PS > [void] $myArray.Add("Hello")
PS > [void] $myArray.AddRange( ("World","How","Are","You") )
PS > $myArray
Hello
World
How
Are
You
PS > $myArray.RemoveAt(1)
PS > $myArray
Hello
How
Are
You
```

Discussion

Aside from the primitive data types (such as strings, integers, and decimals), lists of items are a common concept in the scripts and commands that you write. Most commands generate lists of data: the Get-Content cmdlet generates a list of strings in a file, the Get-Process cmdlet generates a list of processes running on the system, and the Get-Command cmdlet generates a list of commands, just to name a few.

The solution shows how to store the output of a command that generates a list. If a command outputs only one item (such as a single line from a file, a single process, or a single command), then that output is no longer a list. If you want to treat that output as a list even when it is not, use the list evaluation syntax (@()) to force PowerShell to interpret it as an array:

```
$myArray = @(Get-Process Explorer)
```

When you want to create a list of a specific type, the solution demonstrates how to use the System.Collections.Generic.List collection to do that. After the type name, you define the type of the list in square brackets, such as [Int], [String], or whichever type you want to restrict your collection to. These types of specialized objects are called *generic objects*. For more information about creating generic objects, see "Creating Instances of Types" on page 744.

For more information on lists and arrays in PowerShell, see "Arrays and Lists" on page 721.

See Also

"Arrays and Lists" on page 721

"Creating Instances of Types" on page 744

7.2 Create a Jagged or Multidimensional Array

Problem

You want to create an array of arrays or an array of multiple dimensions.

Solution

To create an array of arrays (a *jagged* array), use the @() array syntax:

```
PS > $jagged = @(
    (1,2,3,4),
    (5,6,7,8)
)

PS > $jagged[0][1]
2
PS > $jagged[1][3]
8
```

To create a (nonjagged) multidimensional array, use the New-Object cmdlet:

```
PS > $multidimensional = New-Object "int32[,]" 2,4
PS > $multidimensional[0,1] = 2
PS > $multidimensional[1,3] = 8
```

```
PS >
PS > $multidimensional[0,1]
2
PS > $multidimensional[1,3]
8
```

Discussion

Jagged and multidimensional arrays are useful for holding lists of lists and arrays of arrays. Jagged arrays are arrays of arrays, where each array has only as many elements as it needs. A nonjagged array is more like a grid or matrix, where every array needs to be the same size. Jagged arrays are much easier to work with (and use less memory), but nonjagged multidimensional arrays are sometimes useful for dealing with large grids of data.

Since a jagged array is an array of arrays, creating an item in a jagged array follows the same rules as creating an item in a regular array. If any of the arrays are single-element arrays, use the unary comma operator. For example, to create a jagged array with one nested array of one element:

```
PS > $oneByOneJagged = @(
  ,(,1)
)

PS > $oneByOneJagged[0][0]
```

For more information on lists and arrays in PowerShell, see "Arrays and Lists" on page 721.

See Also

"Arrays and Lists" on page 721

7.3 Access Elements of an Array

Problem

You want to access the elements of an array.

Solution

To access a specific element of an array, use PowerShell's array access mechanism:

```
PS > $myArray = 1,2,"Hello World"
PS > $myArray[1]
2
```

To access a range of array elements, use array ranges and array slicing:

```
PS > $myArray = 1,2,"Hello World"
PS > $myArray[1..2 + 0]
2
```

```
Hello World
1
```

Discussion

PowerShell's array access mechanisms provide a convenient way to access either specific elements of an array or more complex combinations of elements in that array. In PowerShell (as with most other scripting and programming languages), the item at index 0 represents the first item in the array.

For long lists of items, knowing the index of an element can sometimes pose a problem. For a solution to this, see the Add-FormatTableIndexParameter script included with this book's code examples. This script adds a new -IncludeIndex parameter to the Format-Table cmdlet:

```
PS > $items = Get-Process outlook,powershell,emacs,notepad
PS > $items

Handles  NPM(K)    PM(K)      WS(K) VM(M)    CPU(s)     Id ProcessName
-------  ------    -----      ----- -----    ------     -- -----------
    163       6    17660      24136   576      7.63   7136 emacs
     74       4     1252       6184    56      0.19  11820 notepad
   3262      48    46664      88280   376     20.98   8572 OUTLOOK
    285      11    31328      21952   171    613.71   4716 powershell
    767      14    56568      66032   227    104.10  11368 powershell


PS > $items | Format-Table -IncludeIndex

PSIndex Handles  NPM(K)    PM(K)      WS(K) VM(M)    CPU(s)     Id ProcessName
------- -------  ------    -----      ----- -----    ------     -- -----------
0           163       6    17660      24136   576      7.63   7136 emacs
1            74       4     1252       6184    56      0.19  11820 notepad
2          3262      48    46664      88280   376     20.98   8572 OUTLOOK
3           285      11    31328      21952   171    613.71   4716 powershell
4           767      14    56568      66032   227    104.15  11368 powershell


PS > $items[2]

Handles  NPM(K)    PM(K)      WS(K) VM(M)    CPU(s)     Id ProcessName
-------  ------    -----      ----- -----    ------     -- -----------
   3262      48    46664      88280   376     20.98   8572 OUTLOOK
```

Although working with the elements of an array by their numerical index is helpful, you may find it useful to refer to them by something else—such as their name, or even a custom label. This type of array is known as an *associative array* (or *hashtable*). For more information about working with hashtables and associative arrays, see Recipe 7.13.

For more information on lists and arrays in PowerShell (including the array ranges and slicing syntax), see "Arrays and Lists" on page 721. For more information about obtaining the code examples for this book, see "Code Examples" on page xxviii.

See Also

Recipe 7.13, "Create a Hashtable or Associative Array"

"Arrays and Lists" on page 721

7.4 Visit Each Element of an Array

Problem

You want to work with each element of an array.

Solution

To access each item in an array one by one, use the `Foreach-Object` cmdlet:

```
PS > $myArray = 1,2,3
PS > $sum = 0
PS > $myArray | Foreach-Object { $sum += $_ }
PS > $sum
6
```

To access each item in an array in a more script-like fashion, use the `foreach` scripting keyword:

```
PS > $myArray = 1,2,3
PS > $sum = 0
PS > foreach($element in $myArray) { $sum += $element }
PS > $sum
6
```

To access items in an array by position, use a `for` loop:

```
PS > $myArray = 1,2,3
PS > $sum = 0
PS > for($counter = 0; $counter -lt $myArray.Count; $counter++) {
    $sum += $myArray[$counter]
}

PS > $sum
6
```

Discussion

PowerShell provides three main alternatives to working with elements in an array. The `Foreach-Object` cmdlet and `foreach` scripting keyword techniques visit the items in an array one element at a time, whereas the `for` loop (and related looping constructs) lets you work with the items in an array in a less structured way.

For more information about the `Foreach-Object` cmdlet, see Recipe 2.5.

For more information about the `foreach` scripting keyword, the `for` keyword, and other looping constructs, see Recipe 4.4.

See Also

Recipe 2.5, "Work with Each Item in a List or Command Output"

Recipe 4.4, "Repeat Operations with Loops"

7.5 Sort an Array or List of Items

Problem

You want to sort the elements of an array or list.

Solution

To sort a list of items, use the `Sort-Object` cmdlet:

```
PS > Get-ChildItem | Sort-Object -Descending Length | Select Name,Length

Name                                                          Length
----                                                          ------
Convert-TextObject.ps1                                          6868
Connect-WebService.ps1                                         4178
Select-FilteredObject.ps1                                      3252
Get-PageUrls.ps1                                              2878
Get-Characteristics.ps1                                       2515
Get-Answer.ps1                                               1890
New-GenericObject.ps1                                         1490
Invoke-CmdScript.ps1                                          1313
```

Discussion

The `Sort-Object` cmdlet provides a convenient way for you to sort items by a property that you specify. If you don't specify a property, the `Sort-Object` cmdlet follows the sorting rules of those items if they define any.

The `Sort-Object` cmdlet also supports custom sort expressions, rather than just sorting on existing properties. To sort by your own logic, use a script block as the sort expression. This example sorts by the second character:

```
PS > "Hello","World","And","PowerShell" | Sort-Object { $_.Substring(1,1) }
Hello
And
PowerShell
World
```

If you want to sort a list that you've saved in a variable, you can either store the results back in that variable or use the `[Array]::Sort()` method from the .NET Framework:

```
PS > $list = "Hello","World","And","PowerShell"
PS > $list = $list | Sort-Object
PS > $list
And
```

```
Hello
PowerShell
World
PS > $list = "Hello","World","And","PowerShell"
PS > [Array]::Sort($list)
PS > $list
And
Hello
PowerShell
World
```

In addition to sorting by a property or expression in ascending or descending order, the Sort-Object cmdlet's -Unique switch also allows you to remove duplicates from the sorted collection.

For more information about the Sort-Object cmdlet, type **Get-Help Sort-Object**.

7.6 Determine Whether an Array Contains an Item

Problem

You want to determine whether an array or list contains a specific item.

Solution

To determine whether a list contains a specific item, use the -contains operator:

```
PS > "Hello","World" -contains "Hello"
True
PS > "Hello","World" -contains "There"
False
```

Discussion

The -contains operator is a useful way to quickly determine whether a list contains a specific element. To search a list for items that instead match a pattern, use the -match or -like operators.

For more information about the -contains, -match, and -like operators, see "Comparison Operators" on page 731.

See Also

"Comparison Operators" on page 731

7.7 Combine Two Arrays

Problem

You have two arrays and want to combine them into one.

Solution

To combine PowerShell arrays, use the addition operator (+):

```
PS > $firstArray = "Element 1","Element 2","Element 3","Element 4"
PS > $secondArray = 1,2,3,4
PS >
PS > $result = $firstArray + $secondArray
PS > $result
Element 1
Element 2
Element 3
Element 4
1
2
3
4
```

Discussion

One common reason to combine two arrays is when you want to add data to the end of one of the arrays. For example:

```
PS > $array = 1,2
PS > $array = $array + 3,4
PS > $array
1
2
3
4
```

You can write this more clearly as:

```
PS > $array = 1,2
PS > $array += 3,4
PS > $array
1
2
3
4
```

When this is written in the second form, however, you might think that PowerShell simply adds the items to the end of the array while keeping the array itself intact. This is not true, since arrays in PowerShell (like most other languages) stay the same length once you create them. To combine two arrays, PowerShell creates a new array large enough to hold the contents of both arrays and then copies both arrays into the destination array.

If you plan to add and remove data from an array frequently, the System.Collections.ArrayList class provides a more dynamic alternative. For more information about using the ArrayList class, see Recipe 7.12.

See Also

Recipe 7.12, "Use the ArrayList Class for Advanced Array Tasks"

7.8 Find Items in an Array That Match a Value

Problem

You have an array and want to find all elements that match a given item or term—either exactly, by pattern, or by regular expression.

Solution

To find all elements that match an item, use the -eq, -like, and -match comparison operators:

```
PS > $array = "Item 1","Item 2","Item 3","Item 1","Item 12"
PS > $array -eq "Item 1"
Item 1
Item 1
PS > $array -like "*1*"
Item 1
Item 1
Item 12
PS > $array -match "Item .."
Item 12
```

Discussion

The -eq, -like, and -match operators are useful ways to find elements in a collection that match your given term. The -eq operator returns all elements that are equal to your term, the -like operator returns all elements that match the wildcard given in your pattern, and the -match operator returns all elements that match the regular expression given in your pattern.

For more complex comparison conditions, the Where-Object cmdlet lets you find elements in a list that satisfy much more complex conditions:

```
PS > $array = "Item 1","Item 2","Item 3","Item 1","Item 12"
PS > $array | Where-Object { $_.Length -gt 6 }
Item 12
```

For more information, see Recipe 2.1.

For more information about the -eq, -like, and -match operators, see "Comparison Operators" on page 731.

See Also

Recipe 2.1, "Filter Items in a List or Command Output"

"Comparison Operators" on page 731

7.9 Compare Two Lists

Problem

You have two lists and want to find items that exist in only one or the other list.

Solution

To compare two lists, use the `Compare-Object` cmdlet:

```
PS > $array1 = "Item 1","Item 2","Item 3","Item 1","Item 12"
PS > $array2 = "Item 1","Item 8","Item 3","Item 9","Item 12"
PS > Compare-Object $array1 $array2

InputObject                          SideIndicator
-----------                          -------------
Item 8                               =>
Item 9                               =>
Item 2                               <=
Item 1                               <=
```

Discussion

The `Compare-Object` cmdlet lets you compare two lists. By default, it shows only the items that exist exclusively in one of the lists, although its `-IncludeEqual` parameter lets you include items that exist in both. If it returns no results, the two lists are equal.

For more information, see Chapter 22.

See Also

Chapter 22, *Comparing Data*

7.10 Remove Elements from an Array

Problem

You want to remove all elements from an array that match a given item or term—either exactly, by pattern, or by regular expression.

Solution

To remove all elements from an array that match a pattern, use the -ne, -notlike, and -notmatch comparison operators, as shown in Example 7-2.

Example 7-2. Removing elements from an array using the -ne, -notlike, and -notmatch operators

```
PS > $array = "Item 1","Item 2","Item 3","Item 1","Item 12"
PS > $array -ne "Item 1"
Item 2
Item 3
Item 12
PS > $array -notlike "*1*"
Item 2
Item 3
PS > $array -notmatch "Item .."
Item 1
Item 2
Item 3
Item 1
```

To actually remove the items from the array, store the results back in the array:

```
PS > $array = "Item 1","Item 2","Item 3","Item 1","Item 12"
PS > $array = $array -ne "Item 1"
PS > $array
Item 2
Item 3
Item 12
```

Discussion

The -eq, -like, and -match operators are useful ways to find elements in a collection that match your given term. Their opposites, the -ne, -notlike, and -notmatch operators, return all elements that do not match that given term.

To remove all elements from an array that match a given pattern, you can then save all elements that *do not* match that pattern.

For more information about the -ne, -notlike, and -notmatch operators, see "Comparison Operators" on page 731.

See Also

"Comparison Operators" on page 731

7.11 Find Items in an Array Greater or Less Than a Value

Problem

You have an array and want to find all elements greater or less than a given item or value.

Solution

To find all elements greater or less than a given value, use the -gt, -ge, -lt, and -le comparison operators:

```
PS > $array = "Item 1","Item 2","Item 3","Item 1","Item 12"
PS > $array -ge "Item 3"
Item 3
PS > $array -lt "Item 3"
Item 1
Item 2
Item 1
Item 12
```

Discussion

The -gt, -ge, -lt, and -le operators are useful ways to find elements in a collection that are greater or less than a given value. Like all other PowerShell comparison operators, these use the comparison rules of the items in the collection. Since the array in the solution is an array of strings, this result can easily surprise you:

```
PS > $array -lt "Item 2"
Item 1
Item 1
Item 12
```

The reason for this becomes clear when you look at the sorted array—"Item 12" comes before "Item 2" *alphabetically*, which is the way that PowerShell compares arrays of strings.

```
PS > $array | Sort-Object
Item 1
Item 1
Item 12
Item 2
Item 3
```

For more information about the -gt, -ge, -lt, and -le operators, see "Comparison Operators" on page 731.

See Also

"Comparison Operators" on page 731

7.12 Use the ArrayList Class for Advanced Array Tasks

Problem

You have an array that you want to frequently add elements to, remove elements from, search, and modify.

Solution

To work with an array frequently after you define it, use the System.Collections.Array List class:

```
PS > $myArray = New-Object System.Collections.ArrayList
PS > [void] $myArray.Add("Hello")
PS > [void] $myArray.AddRange( ("World","How","Are","You") )
PS > $myArray
Hello
World
How
Are
You
PS > $myArray.RemoveAt(1)
PS > $myArray
Hello
How
Are
You
```

Discussion

Like in most other languages, arrays in PowerShell stay the same length once you create them. PowerShell allows you to add items, remove items, and search for items in an array, but these operations may be time-consuming when you are dealing with large amounts of data. For example, to combine two arrays, PowerShell creates a new array large enough to hold the contents of both arrays and then copies both arrays into the destination array.

In comparison, the ArrayList class is designed to let you easily add, remove, and search for items in a collection.

 PowerShell passes along any data that your script generates, unless you capture it or cast it to [void]. Since it is designed primarily to be used from programming languages, the System.Collections.ArrayList class produces output, even though you may not expect it to. To prevent it from sending data to the output pipeline, either capture the data or cast it to [void]:

```
PS > $collection = New-Object System.Collections.ArrayList
PS > $collection.Add("Hello")
0
PS > [void] $collection.Add("World")
```

If you plan to add and remove data to and from an array frequently, the System.Collections.ArrayList class provides a more dynamic alternative.

For more information about working with classes from the .NET Framework, see Recipe 3.8.

See Also

Recipe 3.8, "Work with .NET Objects"

7.13 Create a Hashtable or Associative Array

Problem

You have a collection of items that you want to access through a label that you provide.

Solution

To define a mapping between labels and items, use a hashtable (associative array):

```
PS > $myHashtable = @{ Key1 = "Value1"; "Key 2" = 1,2,3 }
PS > $myHashtable["New Item"] = 5
PS >
PS > $myHashTable

Name                    Value
----                    -----
Key 2                   {1, 2, 3}
New Item                5
Key1                    Value1
```

Discussion

Hashtables are much like arrays that let you access items by whatever label you want—not just through their index in the array. Because of that freedom, they form the keystone of a huge number of scripting techniques. Since they let you map names to values, they form the natural basis for lookup tables such as those for zip codes and area codes. Since they let you map names to fully featured objects and script blocks, they can often take the place of custom objects. And since you can map rich objects to other rich objects, they can even form the basis of more advanced data structures such as caches and object graphs.

The solution demonstrates how to create and initialize a hashtable at the same time, but you can also create one and work with it incrementally:

```
PS > $myHashtable = @{}
PS > $myHashtable["Hello"] = "World"
PS > $myHashtable.AnotherHello = "AnotherWorld"
PS > $myHashtable

Name                    Value
----                    -----
AnotherHello            AnotherWorld
Hello                   World
```

This ability to map labels to structured values also proves helpful in interacting with cmdlets that support advanced configuration parameters, such as the calculated property parameters available on the `Format-Table` and `Select-Object` cmdlets. For an example of this use, see Recipe 3.2.

For more information about working with hashtables, see "Hashtables (Associative Arrays)" on page 723.

See Also

Recipe 3.2, "Display the Properties of an Item as a Table"

"Hashtables (Associative Arrays)" on page 723

7.14 Sort a Hashtable by Key or Value

Problem

You have a hashtable of keys and values, and you want to get the list of values that result from sorting the keys in order.

Solution

To sort a hashtable, use the `GetEnumerator()` method on the hashtable to gain access to its individual elements. Then, use the `Sort-Object` cmdlet to sort by `Name` or `Value`.

```
foreach($item in $myHashtable.GetEnumerator() | Sort Name)
{
    $item.Value
}
```

Discussion

Since the primary focus of a hashtable is to simply map keys to values, you should not depend on it to retain any ordering whatsoever—such as the order you added the items, the sorted order of the keys, or the sorted order of the values.

This becomes clear in Example 7-3.

Example 7-3. A demonstration of hashtable items not retaining their order

```
PS > $myHashtable = @{}
PS > $myHashtable["Hello"] = 3
PS > $myHashtable["Ali"] = 2
PS > $myHashtable["Alien"] = 4
PS > $myHashtable["Duck"] = 1
PS > $myHashtable["Hectic"] = 11
PS > $myHashtable

Name                      Value
----                      -----
Hectic                    11
Duck                      1
```

```
Alien               4
Hello               3
Ali                 2
```

However, the hashtable object supports a GetEnumerator() method that lets you deal with the individual hashtable entries—all of which have a Name and Value property. Once you have those, we can sort by them as easily as we can sort any other PowerShell data. Example 7-4 demonstrates this technique.

Example 7-4. Sorting a hashtable by name and value

```
PS > $myHashtable.GetEnumerator() | Sort Name

Name                        Value
----                        -----
Ali                         2
Alien                       4
Duck                        1
Hectic                      11
Hello                       3

PS > $myHashtable.GetEnumerator() | Sort Value

Name                        Value
----                        -----
Duck                        1
Ali                         2
Hello                       3
Alien                       4
Hectic                      11
```

For more information about working with hashtables, see "Hashtables (Associative Arrays)" on page 723.

See Also

"Hashtables (Associative Arrays)" on page 723

Utility Tasks

8.0 Introduction

When scripting or just using the interactive shell, a handful of needs arise that are simple but useful: measuring commands, getting random numbers, and more.

8.1 Get the System Date and Time

Problem

You want to get the system date.

Solution

To get the system date, run the command Get-Date.

Discussion

The Get-Date command generates rich object-based output, so you can use its result for many date-related tasks. For example, to determine the current day of the week:

```
PS > $date = Get-Date
PS > $date.DayOfWeek
Sunday
```

For more information about the Get-Date cmdlet, type **Get-Help Get-Date**.

For more information about working with classes from the .NET Framework, see Recipe 3.8.

See Also

Recipe 3.8, "Work with .NET Objects"

8.2 Measure the Duration of a Command

Problem

You want to know how long a command takes to execute.

Solution

To measure the duration of a command, use the `Measure-Command` cmdlet:

```
PS > Measure-Command { Start-Sleep -Milliseconds 337 }
```

```
Days              : 0
Hours             : 0
Minutes           : 0
Seconds           : 0
Milliseconds      : 339
Ticks             : 3392297
TotalDays         : 3.92626967592593E-06
TotalHours        : 9.42304722222222E-05
TotalMinutes      : 0.00565382833333333
TotalSeconds      : 0.3392297
TotalMilliseconds : 339.2297
```

Discussion

In interactive use, it is common to want to measure the duration of a command. An example of this might be running a performance benchmark on an application you've developed. The `Measure-Command` cmdlet makes this easy to do. Because the command generates rich object-based output, you can use its output for many date-related tasks. See Recipe 3.8 for more information.

If the accuracy of a command measurement is important, general system activity can easily influence the timing of the result. To improve accuracy, a common technique is to repeat the measurement many times, ignore the outliers (the top and bottom 10 percent), and then average the remaining results. Example 8-1 implements this technique.

Example 8-1. Measure-CommandPerformance.ps1

```
##############################################################################
##
## Measure-CommandPerformance
##
## From Windows PowerShell Cookbook (O'Reilly)
## by Lee Holmes (http://www.leeholmes.com/guide)
##
##############################################################################

<#

.SYNOPSIS
```

Measures the average time of a command, accounting for natural variability by automatically ignoring the top and bottom ten percent.

.EXAMPLE

PS >Measure-CommandPerformance.ps1 { Start-Sleep -m 300 }

```
Count    : 30
Average  : 312.10155
(...)
```

#>

```
param(
    ## The command to measure
    [Scriptblock] $Scriptblock,

    ## The number of times to measure the command's performance
    [int] $Iterations = 30
)

Set-StrictMode -Version Latest

## Figure out how many extra iterations we need to account for the outliers
$buffer = [int] ($iterations * 0.1)
$totalIterations = $iterations + (2 * $buffer)

## Get the results
$results = 1..$totalIterations |
    Foreach-Object { Measure-Command $scriptblock }

## Sort the results, and skip the outliers
$middleResults = $results | Sort TotalMilliseconds |
    Select -Skip $buffer -First $iterations

## Show the average
$middleResults | Measure-Object -Average TotalMilliseconds
```

For more information about the Measure-Command cmdlet, type **Get-Help Measure-Command**.

See Also

Recipe 3.8, "Work with .NET Objects"

8.3 Read and Write from the Windows Clipboard

Problem

You want to interact with the Windows clipboard.

Solution

Use the Get-Clipboard and Set-Clipboard scripts, as shown in Examples 8-2 and 8-3.

Example 8-2. Get-Clipboard.ps1

```
##############################################################################
##
## Get-Clipboard
##
## From Windows PowerShell Cookbook (O'Reilly)
## by Lee Holmes (http://www.leeholmes.com/guide)
##
##############################################################################

<#

.SYNOPSIS

Retrieve the text contents of the Windows Clipboard.

.EXAMPLE

PS >Get-Clipboard
Hello World

#>

Set-StrictMode -Version Latest

PowerShell -NoProfile -STA -Command {
    Add-Type -Assembly PresentationCore
    [Windows.Clipboard]::GetText()
}
```

Example 8-3. Set-Clipboard.ps1

```
##############################################################################
##
## Set-Clipboard
##
## From Windows PowerShell Cookbook (O'Reilly)
## by Lee Holmes (http://www.leeholmes.com/guide)
##
##############################################################################

<#

.SYNOPSIS

Sends the given input to the Windows clipboard.

.EXAMPLE

dir | Set-Clipboard
This example sends the view of a directory listing to the clipboard
```

```
.EXAMPLE

Set-Clipboard "Hello World"
This example sets the clipboard to the string, "Hello World".

#>

param(
    ## The input to send to the clipboard
    [Parameter(ValueFromPipeline = $true)]
    [object[]] $InputObject
)

begin
{
    Set-StrictMode -Version Latest
    $objectsToProcess = @()
}

process
{
    ## Collect everything sent to the script either through
    ## pipeline input, or direct input.
    $objectsToProcess += $inputObject
}

end
{
    ## Launch a new instance of PowerShell in STA mode.
    ## This lets us interact with the Windows clipboard.
    $objectsToProcess | PowerShell -NoProfile -STA -Command {
        Add-Type -Assembly PresentationCore

        ## Convert the input objects to a string representation
        $clipText = ($input | Out-String -Stream) -join "`r`n"

        ## And finally set the clipboard text
        [Windows.Clipboard]::SetText($clipText)
    }
}
```

Discussion

While Windows includes a command-line utility (clip.exe) to place text in the Windows clipboard, it doesn't support direct input (e.g., clip.exe "Hello World"), and it doesn't have a corresponding utility to retrieve the contents from the Windows clipboard.

The Set-Clipboard and Get-Clipboard scripts given in the solution resolve both of these issues.

Both rely on the System.Windows.Clipboard class, which has a special requirement that it must be run from an application in single-threaded apartment (STA) mode. To support that, the scripts launch a new instance of PowerShell in this mode. For more information about interacting with this type of class, see Recipe 13.11.

For more information about working with classes from the .NET Framework, see Recipe 3.8.

See Also

Recipe 3.8, "Work with .NET Objects"

Recipe 13.11, "Interact with UI Frameworks and STA Objects"

8.4 Generate a Random Number or Object

Problem

You want to generate a random number or pick a random element from a set of objects.

Solution

Call the Get-Random cmdlet to generate a random positive integer:

```
Get-Random
```

Use the -Minimum and -Maximum parameters to generate a number between Minimum and up to (but not including) Maximum:

```
Get-Random -Minimum 1 -Maximum 21
```

Use simple pipeline input to pick a random element from a list:

```
PS > $suits = "Hearts","Clubs","Spades","Diamonds"
PS > $faces = (2..10)+"A","J","Q","K"
PS > $cards = foreach($suit in $suits) { foreach($face in $faces) { "$face of $suit" } }
PS > $cards | Get-Random
A of Spades
PS > $cards | Get-Random
2 of Clubs
```

Discussion

The Get-Random cmdlet solves the problems usually associated with picking random numbers or random elements from a collection: *scaling* and *seeding*.

Most random number generators only generate numbers between 0 and 1. If you need a number from a different range, you have to go through a separate scaling step to map those numbers to the appropriate range. Although not terribly difficult, it's a usability hurdle that requires more than trivial knowledge to do properly.

Ensuring that the random number generator picks *good* random numbers is a different problem entirely. All general-purpose random number generators use mathematical

---

equations to generate their values. They make new values by incorporating the number they generated just before that—a feedback process that guarantees evenly distributed sequences of numbers. Maintaining this internal state is critical, as restarting from a specific point will always generate the same number, which is not very random at all! You lose this internal state every time you create a new random number generator.

To create their first value, generators need a random number *seed*. You can supply a seed directly (for example, through the -SetSeed parameter of the Get-Random cmdlet) for testing purposes, but it is usually derived from the system time.

Unless you reuse the same random number generator, this last point usually leads to the downfall of realistically random numbers. When you generate them quickly, you create new random number generators that are likely to have the same seed:

```
PS > 1..10 | Foreach-Object { (New-Object System.Random).Next(1, 21) }
20
7
7
15
15
11
11
18
18
18
```

The Get-Random cmdlet saves you from this issue by internally maintaining a random number generator and its state:

```
PS > 1..10 | Foreach-Object { Get-Random -Min 1 -Max 21 }
20
18
7
12
16
10
9
13
16
14
```

For more information about working with classes from the .NET Framework, see Recipe 3.8.

See Also

Recipe 3.8, "Work with .NET Objects"

8.5 Program: Search the Windows Start Menu

When working at the command line, you might want to launch a program that is normally found only on your Start menu. While you could certainly click through the Start menu to find it, you could also search the Start menu with a script, as shown in Example 8-4.

Example 8-4. Search-StartMenu.ps1

```
##############################################################################
##
## Search-StartMenu
##
## From Windows PowerShell Cookbook (O'Reilly)
## by Lee Holmes (http://www.leeholmes.com/blog)
##
##############################################################################

<#

.SYNOPSIS

Search the Start Menu for items that match the provided text. This script
searches both the name (as displayed on the Start Menu itself), and the
destination of the link.

.Example

Search-StartMenu "Character Map" | Invoke-Item
Searches for the "Character Map" application, and then runs it

Search-StartMenu PowerShell | Select-FilteredObject | Invoke-Item
Searches for anything with "PowerShell" in the application name, lets you
pick which one to launch, and then launches it.

#>

param(
    ## The pattern to match
    [Parameter(Mandatory = $true)]
    $Pattern
)

Set-StrictMode -Version Latest

## Get the locations of the start menu paths
$myStartMenu = [Environment]::GetFolderPath("StartMenu")
$shell = New-Object -Com WScript.Shell
$allStartMenu = $shell.SpecialFolders.Item("AllUsersStartMenu")

## Escape their search term, so that any regular expression
## characters don't affect the search
$escapedMatch = [Regex]::Escape($pattern)
```

```
## Search for text in the link name
dir $myStartMenu *.lnk -rec | ? { $_.Name -match "$escapedMatch" }
dir $allStartMenu *.lnk -rec | ? { $_.Name -match "$escapedMatch" }

## Search for text in the link destination
dir $myStartMenu *.lnk -rec |
    Where-Object { $_ | Select-String "\\[^\\]*$escapedMatch\." -Quiet }
dir $allStartMenu *.lnk -rec |
    Where-Object { $_ | Select-String "\\[^\\]*$escapedMatch\." -Quiet }
```

For more information about running scripts, see Recipe 1.1.

See Also

Recipe 1.1, "Run Programs, Scripts, and Existing Tools"

8.6 Program: Show Colorized Script Content

Discussion

When viewing or demonstrating scripts, syntax highlighting makes the information immensely easier to read. Viewing the scripts in the PowerShell Integrated Scripting Environment (ISE) is the most natural (and powerful) option, but you might want to view them in the console as well.

In addition to basic syntax highlighting, other useful features during script review are line numbers and highlighting ranges of lines. Range highlighting is especially useful when discussing portions of a script in a larger context.

Example 8-5 enables all of these scenarios by providing syntax highlighting of scripts in a console session. Figure 8-1 shows a sample of the colorized content.

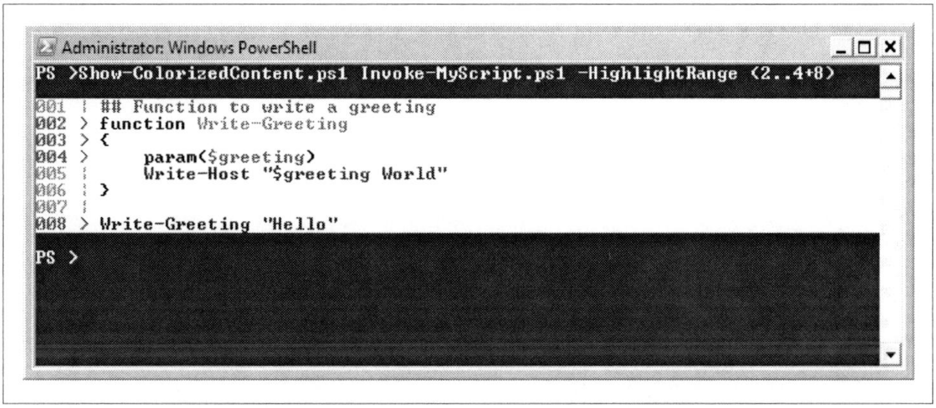

Figure 8-1. Sample colorized content

In addition to having utility all on its own, Show-ColorizedContent.ps1 demonstrates how to use PowerShell's Tokenizer API, introduced in Recipe 10.9. While many of the techniques in this example are specific to syntax highlighting in a PowerShell console, many more apply to all forms of script manipulation.

Example 8-5. Show-ColorizedContent.ps1

```
##############################################################################
##
## Show-ColorizedContent
##
## From Windows PowerShell Cookbook (O'Reilly)
## by Lee Holmes (http://www.leeholmes.com/guide)
##
##############################################################################

<#

.SYNOPSIS

Displays syntax highlighting, line numbering, and range highlighting for
PowerShell scripts.

.EXAMPLE

PS >Show-ColorizedContent Invoke-MyScript.ps1

001 | function Write-Greeting
002 | {
003 |     param($greeting)
004 |     Write-Host "$greeting World"
005 | }
006 |
007 | Write-Greeting "Hello"

.EXAMPLE

PS >Show-ColorizedContent Invoke-MyScript.ps1 -highlightRange (1..3+7)

001 > function Write-Greeting
002 > {
003 >     param($greeting)
004 |     Write-Host "$greeting World"
005 | }
006 |
007 > Write-Greeting "Hello"

#>

param(
    ## The path to colorize
    [Parameter(Mandatory = $true)]
    $Path,

    ## The range of lines to highlight
```

```
    $HighlightRange = @(),

    ## Switch to exclude line numbers
    [Switch] $ExcludeLineNumbers
)

Set-StrictMode -Version Latest

## Colors to use for the different script tokens.
## To pick your own colors:
## [Enum]::GetValues($host.UI.RawUI.ForegroundColor.GetType()) |
##      Foreach-Object { Write-Host -Fore $_ "$_" }
$replacementColors = @{
    'Attribute' = 'DarkCyan'
    'Command' = 'Blue'
    'CommandArgument' = 'Magenta'
    'CommandParameter' = 'DarkBlue'
    'Comment' = 'DarkGreen'
    'GroupEnd' = 'Black'
    'GroupStart' = 'Black'
    'Keyword' = 'DarkBlue'
    'LineContinuation' = 'Black'
    'LoopLabel' = 'DarkBlue'
    'Member' = 'Black'
    'NewLine' = 'Black'
    'Number' = 'Magenta'
    'Operator' = 'DarkGray'
    'Position' = 'Black'
    'StatementSeparator' = 'Black'
    'String' = 'DarkRed'
    'Type' = 'DarkCyan'
    'Unknown' = 'Black'
    'Variable' = 'Red'
}

$highlightColor = "Red"
$highlightCharacter = ">"
$highlightWidth = 6
if($excludeLineNumbers) { $highlightWidth = 0 }

## Read the text of the file, and tokenize it
$file = (Resolve-Path $Path).Path
$content = [IO.File]::ReadAllText($file)
$parsed = [System.Management.Automation.PsParser]::Tokenize(
    $content, [ref] $null) | Sort StartLine,StartColumn

## Write a formatted line -- in the format of:
## <Line Number> <Separator Character> <Text>
function WriteFormattedLine($formatString, [int] $line)
{
    if($excludeLineNumbers) { return }

    ## By default, write the line number in gray, and use
    ## a simple pipe as the separator
    $hColor = "DarkGray"
```

```
    $separator = "|"

    ## If we need to highlight the line, use the highlight
    ## color and highlight separator as the separator
    if($highlightRange -contains $line)
    {
        $hColor = $highlightColor
        $separator = $highlightCharacter
    }

    ## Write the formatted line
    $text = $formatString -f $line,$separator
    Write-Host -NoNewLine -Fore $hColor -Back White $text
}

## Complete the current line with filler cells
function CompleteLine($column)
{
    ## Figure how much space is remaining
    $lineRemaining = $host.UI.RawUI.WindowSize.Width -
        $column - $highlightWidth + 1

    ## If we have less than 0 remaining, we've wrapped onto the
    ## next line. Add another buffer width worth of filler
    if($lineRemaining -lt 0)
    {
        $lineRemaining += $host.UI.RawUI.WindowSize.Width
    }

    Write-Host -NoNewLine -Back White (" " * $lineRemaining)
}


## Write the first line of context information (line number,
## highlight character.)
Write-Host
WriteFormattedLine "{0:D3} {1} " 1

## Now, go through each of the tokens in the input
## script
$column = 1
foreach($token in $parsed)
{
    $color = "Gray"

    ## Determine the highlighting color for that token by looking
    ## in the hashtable that maps token types to their color
    $color = $replacementColors[[string]$token.Type]
    if(-not $color) { $color = "Gray" }

    ## If it's a newline token, write the next line of context
    ## information
    if(($token.Type -eq "NewLine") -or ($token.Type -eq "LineContinuation"))
    {
        CompleteLine $column
```

```
    WriteFormattedLine "{0:D3} {1} " ($token.StartLine + 1)
    $column = 1
}
else
{
    ## Do any indenting
    if($column -lt $token.StartColumn)
    {
        $text = " " * ($token.StartColumn - $column)
        Write-Host -Back White -NoNewLine $text
        $column = $token.StartColumn
    }

    ## See where the token ends
    $tokenEnd = $token.Start + $token.Length - 1

    ## Handle the line numbering for multi-line strings and comments
    if(
        (($token.Type -eq "String") -or
        ($token.Type -eq "Comment")) -and
        ($token.EndLine -gt $token.StartLine))
    {
        ## Store which line we've started at
        $lineCounter = $token.StartLine

        ## Split the content of this token into its lines
        ## We use the start and end of the tokens to determine
        ## the position of the content, but use the content
        ## itself (rather than the token values) for manipulation.
        $stringLines = $(
            -join $content[$token.Start..$tokenEnd] -split "`n")

        ## Go through each of the lines in the content
        foreach($stringLine in $stringLines)
        {
            $stringLine = $stringLine.Trim()

            ## If we're on a new line, fill the righthand
            ## side of the line with spaces, and write the header
            ## for the new line.
            if($lineCounter -gt $token.StartLine)
            {
                CompleteLine $column
                WriteFormattedLine "{0:D3} {1} " $lineCounter
                $column = 1
            }

            ## Now write the text of the current line
            Write-Host -NoNewLine -Fore $color -Back White $stringLine
            $column += $stringLine.Length
            $lineCounter++
        }
    }
    ## Write out a regular token
    else
```

```
    {
        ## We use the start and end of the tokens to determine
        ## the position of the content, but use the content
        ## itself (rather than the token values) for manipulation.
        $text = (-join $content[$token.Start..$tokenEnd])
        Write-Host -NoNewLine -Fore $color -Back White $text
    }

    ## Update our position in the column
    $column = $token.EndColumn
    }
}

CompleteLine $column
Write-Host
```

For more information about running scripts, see Recipe 1.1.

See Also

Recipe 1.1, "Run Programs, Scripts, and Existing Tools"

Recipe 10.9, "Parse and Interpret PowerShell Scripts"

Common Tasks

Simple Files

9.0 Introduction

When administering a system, you naturally spend a significant amount of time working with the files on that system. Many of the things you want to do with these files are simple: get their content, search them for a pattern, or replace text inside them.

For even these simple operations, PowerShell's object-oriented flavor adds several unique and powerful twists.

9.1 Get the Content of a File

Problem

You want to get the content of a file.

Solution

Provide the filename as an argument to the Get-Content cmdlet:

```
PS > $content = Get-Content c:\temp\file.txt
```

Place the filename in a ${} section to use the cmdlet Get-Content variable syntax:

```
PS > $content = ${c:\temp\file.txt}
```

Provide the filename as an argument to the ReadAllText() method to use the System.IO.File class from the .NET Framework:

```
PS > $content = [System.IO.File]::ReadAllText("c:\temp\file.txt")
```

Discussion

PowerShell offers three primary ways to get the content of a file. The first is the Get-Content cmdlet—the cmdlet designed for this purpose. In fact, the Get-Content cmdlet works on any PowerShell drive that supports the concept of items with content. This includes `Alias:`, `Function:`, and more. The second and third ways are the `Get-Content` variable syntax and the `ReadAllText()` method.

When working against files, the `Get-Content` cmdlet returns the content of the file line by line. When it does this, PowerShell supplies additional information about that output line. This information, which PowerShell attaches as properties to each output line, includes the drive and path from where that line originated, among other things.

 If you want PowerShell to split the file content based on a string that you choose (rather than the default of newlines), the `Get-Content` cmdlet's `-Delimiter` parameter lets you provide one.

While useful, having PowerShell attach this extra information when you are not using it can sometimes slow down scripts that operate on large files. If you need to process a large file more quickly, the `Get-Content` cmdlet's `ReadCount` parameter lets you control how many lines PowerShell reads from the file at once. With a `ReadCount` of 1 (which is the default), PowerShell returns each line one by one. With a `ReadCount` of 2, PowerShell returns two lines at a time. With a `ReadCount` of less than 1, PowerShell returns all lines from the file at once.

 Beware of using a `ReadCount` of less than 1 for extremely large files. One of the benefits of the `Get-Content` cmdlet is its streaming behavior. No matter how large the file, you will still be able to process each line of the file without using up all your system's memory. Since a `ReadCount` of less than 1 reads the entire file before returning any results, large files have the potential to use up your system's memory. For more information about how to effectively take advantage of PowerShell's streaming capabilities, see Recipe 5.15.

If performance is a primary concern, the `[File]::ReadAllText()` method from the .NET Framework reads a file most quickly from the disk. Unlike the `Get-Content` cmdlet, it does not split the file into newlines, attach any additional information, or work against any other PowerShell drives. Like the `Get-Content` cmdlet with a `ReadCount` of less than 1, it reads all the content from the file before it returns it to you—so be cautious when using it on extremely large files.

For more information about the `Get-Content` cmdlet, type **Get-Help Get-Content**. For information on how to work with more structured files (such as XML and CSV), see Chapter 10. For more information on how to work with binary files, see Recipe 9.4.

See Also

Recipe 5.15, "Generate Large Reports and Text Streams"

Recipe 9.4, "Parse and Manage Binary Files"

9.2 Search a File for Text or a Pattern

Problem

You want to find a string or regular expression in a file.

Solution

To search a file for an exact (but case-insensitive) match, use the -Simple parameter of the Select-String cmdlet:

```
PS > Select-String -Simple SearchText file.txt
```

To search a file for a regular expression, provide that pattern to the Select-String cmdlet:

```
PS > Select-String "\(...\) ...-...." phone.txt
```

To recursively search all *.txt* files for a regular expression, pipe the results of Get-ChildItem to the Select-String cmdlet:

```
PS > Get-ChildItem -Filter *.txt -Recurse | Select-String pattern
```

Discussion

The Select-String cmdlet is the easiest way to search files for a pattern or specific string. In contrast to the traditional text-matching utilities (such as grep) that support the same type of functionality, the matches returned by the Select-String cmdlet include detailed information about the match itself.

```
PS > $matches = Select-String "output file" transcript.txt
PS > $matches | Select LineNumber,Line

                    LineNumber Line
                    ---------- ----
                             7 Transcript started, output file...
```

With a regular expression match, you'll often want to find out exactly what text was matched by the regular expression. PowerShell captures this in the Matches property of the result. For each match, the Value property represents the text matched by your pattern.

```
PS > Select-String "\(...\) ...-...." phone.txt | Select -Expand Matches

...
Value     : (425) 555-1212

...
Value     : (416) 556-1213
```

If your regular expression defines groups (portions of the pattern enclosed in parentheses), you can access the text matched by those groups through the Groups property. The first group (Group[0]) represents all of the text matched by your pattern. Additional groups (1 and on) represent the groups you defined. In this case, we add additional parentheses around the area code to capture it.

```
PS > Select-String "\((...)\) ...-...." phone.txt |
    Select -Expand Matches | Foreach { $_.Groups[1] }


Success   : True
Captures  : {425}
Index     : 1
Length    : 3
Value     : 425

Success   : True
Captures  : {416}
Index     : 1
Length    : 3
Value     : 416
```

If your regular expression defines a *named capture* (with the text ?<Name> at the beginning of a group), the Groups collection lets you access those by name. In this example, we capture the area code using AreaCode as the capture name.

```
PS > Select-String "\((?<AreaCode>...)\) ...-...." phone.txt |
    Select -Expand Matches | Foreach { $_.Groups["AreaCode"] }


Success   : True
Captures  : {425}
Index     : 1
Length    : 3
Value     : 425

Success   : True
Captures  : {416}
Index     : 1
Length    : 3
Value     : 416
```

By default, the Select-String cmdlet captures only the first match per line of input. If the input can have multiple matches per line, use the -AllMatches parameter.

```
PS > Get-Content phone.txt
(425) 555-1212
(416) 556-1213 (416) 557-1214

PS > Select-String "\((...)\) ...-...." phone.txt |
    Select -Expand Matches | Select -Expand Value
```

```
(425) 555-1212
(416) 556-1213

PS > Select-String "\((...)\) ...-...." phone.txt -AllMatches |
    Select -Expand Matches | Select -Expand Value

(425) 555-1212
(416) 556-1213
(416) 557-1214
```

For more information about captures, named captures, and other aspects of regular expressions, see Appendix B.

 If the information you need is on a different line than the line that has the match, use the -Context parameter to have that line included in Select-String's output. PowerShell places the result in the Context.PreContext and Context.PostContext properties of Select-String's output.

If you want to search multiple files of a specific extension, the Select-String cmdlet lets you use wildcards (such as *.txt) on the filename. For more complicated lists of files (which includes searching all files in the directory), it is usually better to use the Get-ChildItem cmdlet to generate the list of files as shown previously in the solution.

Since the Select-String cmdlet outputs the filename, line number, and matching line for every match it finds, this output may sometimes include too much detail. A perfect example is when you are searching for a binary file that contains a specific string. A binary file (such as a DLL or EXE) rarely makes sense when displayed as text, so your screen quickly fills with apparent garbage.

The solution to this problem comes from Select-String's -Quiet switch. It simply returns true or false, depending on whether the file contains the string. So, to find the DLL or EXE in the current directory that contains the text "Debug":

```
Get-ChildItem | Where { $_ | Select-String "Debug" -Quiet }
```

Two other common tools used to search files for text are the -match operator and the switch statement with the -file option. For more information about those, see Recipes 5.7 and 4.3. For more information about the Select-String cmdlet, type **Get-Help Select-String**.

See Also

Recipe 4.3, "Manage Large Conditional Statements with Switches"

Recipe 5.7, "Search a String for Text or a Pattern"

Appendix B, *Regular Expression Reference*

9.3 Parse and Manage Text-Based Logfiles

Problem

You want to parse and analyze a text-based logfile using PowerShell's standard object management commands.

Solution

Use the Convert-TextObject script given in Recipe 5.14 to work with text-based logfiles. With your assistance, it converts streams of text into streams of objects, which you can then easily work with using PowerShell's standard commands.

The Convert-TextObject script primarily takes two arguments:

- A regular expression that describes how to break the incoming text into groups
- A list of property names that the script then assigns to those text groups

As an example, you can use patch logs from the Windows directory. These logs track the patch installation details from updates applied to the machine (except for Windows Vista). One detail included in these logfiles is the names and versions of the files modified by that specific patch, as shown in Example 9-1.

Example 9-1. Getting a list of files modified by hotfixes

```
PS > cd $env:WINDIR
PS > $parseExpression = "(.*): Destination:(.*) \((.*)\)"
PS > $files = dir kb*.log -Exclude *uninst.log
PS > $logContent = $files | Get-Content | Select-String $parseExpression
PS > $logContent

(...)
0.734: Destination:C:\WINNT\system32\shell32.dll (6.0.3790.205)
0.734: Destination:C:\WINNT\system32\wininet.dll (6.0.3790.218)
0.734: Destination:C:\WINNT\system32\urlmon.dll (6.0.3790.218)
0.734: Destination:C:\WINNT\system32\shlwapi.dll (6.0.3790.212)
0.734: Destination:C:\WINNT\system32\shdocvw.dll (6.0.3790.214)
0.734: Destination:C:\WINNT\system32\digest.dll (6.0.3790.0)
0.734: Destination:C:\WINNT\system32\browseui.dll (6.0.3790.218)
(...)
```

Like most logfiles, the format of the text is very regular but hard to manage. In this example, you have:

- A number (the number of seconds since the patch started)
- The text ": Destination:"
- The file being patched

- An open parenthesis
- The version of the file being patched
- A close parenthesis

You don't care about any of the text, but the time, file, and file version are useful properties to track:

```
$properties = "Time","File","FileVersion"
```

So now, you use the `Convert-TextObject` script to convert the text output into a stream of objects:

```
PS > $logObjects = $logContent |
    Convert-TextObject -ParseExpression $parseExpression -PropertyName $properties
```

We can now easily query those objects using PowerShell's built-in commands. For example, you can find the files most commonly affected by patches and service packs, as shown by Example 9-2.

Example 9-2. Finding files most commonly affected by hotfixes

```
PS > $logObjects | Group-Object file | Sort-Object -Descending Count |
    Select-Object Count,Name | Format-Table -Auto


Count Name
----- ----
  152 C:\WINNT\system32\shdocvw.dll
  147 C:\WINNT\system32\shlwapi.dll

  128 C:\WINNT\system32\wininet.dll
  116 C:\WINNT\system32\shell32.dll
   92 C:\WINNT\system32\rpcss.dll
   92 C:\WINNT\system32\olecli32.dll
   92 C:\WINNT\system32\ole32.dll
   84 C:\WINNT\system32\urlmon.dll
(...)
```

Using this technique, you can work with most text-based logfiles.

Discussion

In Example 9-2, you got all the information you needed by splitting the input text into groups of simple strings. The time offset, file, and version information served their purposes as is. In addition to the features used by Example 9-2, however, the `Convert-TextObject` script also supports a parameter that lets you control the data types of those properties. If one of the properties should be treated as a number or a `DateTime`, you may get incorrect results if you work with that property as a string. For more information about this functionality, see the description of the -`PropertyType` parameter in the `Convert-TextObject` script.

Although most logfiles have entries designed to fit within a single line, some span multiple lines. When a logfile contains entries that span multiple lines, it includes some sort of special marker to separate log entries from each other. Look at this example:

```
PS > Get-Content AddressBook.txt
Name: Chrissy
Phone: 555-1212
----
Name: John
Phone: 555-1213
```

The key to working with this type of logfile comes from two places. The first is the -Delimiter parameter of the Get-Content cmdlet, which makes it split the file based on that delimiter instead of newlines. The second is to write a ParseExpression regular expression that ignores the newline characters that remain in each record:

```
PS > $records = gc AddressBook.txt -Delimiter "----"
PS > $parseExpression = "(?s)Name: (\S*).*Phone: (\S*).*"
PS > $records | Convert-TextObject -ParseExpression $parseExpression

Property1                                          Property2
---------                                          ---------
Chrissy                                            555-1212
John                                               555-1213
```

The parse expression in this example uses the *single line* option (?s) so that the (.*) portion of the regular expression accepts newline characters as well. For more information about these (and other) regular expression options, see Appendix B.

For extremely large logfiles, handwritten parsing tools may not meet your needs. In those situations, specialized log management tools can prove helpful. One example is Microsoft's free Log Parser (*http://www.logparser.com*). Another common alternative is to import the log entries to a SQL database, and then perform ad hoc queries on database tables instead.

See Also

Recipe 5.14, "Program: Convert Text Streams to Objects"

Appendix B, *Regular Expression Reference*

9.4 Parse and Manage Binary Files

Problem

You want to work with binary data in a file.

Solution

There are two main techniques when working with binary data in a file. The first is to read the file using the `Byte` encoding, so that PowerShell does not treat the content as text. The second is to use the `BitConverter` class to translate these bytes back and forth into numbers that you more commonly care about.

Example 9-3 displays the "characteristics" of a Windows executable. The beginning section of any executable (a .DLL, .EXE, or any of several others) starts with a binary section known as the *portable executable (PE) header*. Part of this header includes characteristics about that file, such as whether the file is a DLL.

For more information about the PE header format, see *http://www.microsoft.com/whdc/ system/platform/firmware/PECOFF.mspx*.

Example 9-3. Get-Characteristics.ps1

```
##############################################################################
##
## Get-Characteristics
##
## From Windows PowerShell Cookbook (O'Reilly)
## by Lee Holmes (http://www.leeholmes.com/guide)
##
##############################################################################

<#

.SYNOPSIS

Get the file characteristics of a file in the PE Executable File Format.

.EXAMPLE

Get-Characteristics $env:WINDIR\notepad.exe
IMAGE_FILE_LOCAL_SYMS_STRIPPED
IMAGE_FILE_RELOCS_STRIPPED
IMAGE_FILE_EXECUTABLE_IMAGE
IMAGE_FILE_32BIT_MACHINE
IMAGE_FILE_LINE_NUMS_STRIPPED

#>

param(
    ## The path to the file to check
    [Parameter(Mandatory = $true)]
    [string] $Path
)

Set-StrictMode -Version Latest

## Define the characteristics used in the PE file file header.
## Taken from:
## http://www.microsoft.com/whdc/system/platform/firmware/PECOFF.mspx
```

```
$characteristics = @{}
$characteristics["IMAGE_FILE_RELOCS_STRIPPED"] = 0x0001
$characteristics["IMAGE_FILE_EXECUTABLE_IMAGE"] = 0x0002
$characteristics["IMAGE_FILE_LINE_NUMS_STRIPPED"] = 0x0004
$characteristics["IMAGE_FILE_LOCAL_SYMS_STRIPPED"] = 0x0008
$characteristics["IMAGE_FILE_AGGRESSIVE_WS_TRIM"] = 0x0010
$characteristics["IMAGE_FILE_LARGE_ADDRESS_AWARE"] = 0x0020
$characteristics["RESERVED"] = 0x0040
$characteristics["IMAGE_FILE_BYTES_REVERSED_LO"] = 0x0080
$characteristics["IMAGE_FILE_32BIT_MACHINE"] = 0x0100
$characteristics["IMAGE_FILE_DEBUG_STRIPPED"] = 0x0200
$characteristics["IMAGE_FILE_REMOVABLE_RUN_FROM_SWAP"] = 0x0400
$characteristics["IMAGE_FILE_NET_RUN_FROM_SWAP"] = 0x0800
$characteristics["IMAGE_FILE_SYSTEM"] = 0x1000
$characteristics["IMAGE_FILE_DLL"] = 0x2000
$characteristics["IMAGE_FILE_UP_SYSTEM_ONLY"] = 0x4000
$characteristics["IMAGE_FILE_BYTES_REVERSED_HI"] = 0x8000

## Get the content of the file, as an array of bytes
$fileBytes = Get-Content $path -ReadCount 0 -Encoding byte

## The offset of the signature in the file is stored at location 0x3c.
$signatureOffset = $fileBytes[0x3c]

## Ensure it is a PE file
$signature = [char[]] $fileBytes[$signatureOffset..($signatureOffset + 3)]
if([String]::Join('', $signature) -ne "PE`0`0")
{
    throw "This file does not conform to the PE specification."
}

## The location of the COFF header is 4 bytes into the signature
$coffHeader = $signatureOffset + 4

## The characteristics data are 18 bytes into the COFF header. The
## BitConverter class manages the conversion of the 4 bytes into an integer.
$characteristicsData = [BitConverter]::ToInt32($fileBytes, $coffHeader + 18)

## Go through each of the characteristics. If the data from the file has that
## flag set, then output that characteristic.
foreach($key in $characteristics.Keys)
{
    $flag = $characteristics[$key]
    if(($characteristicsData -band $flag) -eq $flag)
    {
        $key
    }
}
```

Discussion

For most files, this technique is the easiest way to work with binary data. If you actually modify the binary data, then you will also want to use the Byte encoding when you send it back to disk:

```
$fileBytes | Set-Content modified.exe -Encoding Byte
```

For extremely large files, though, it may be unacceptably slow to load the entire file into memory when you work with it. If you begin to run against this limit, the solution is to use file management classes from the .NET Framework. These classes include `BinaryReader`, `StreamReader`, and others. For more information about working with classes from the .NET Framework, see Recipe 3.8. For more information about running scripts, see Recipe 1.1.

See Also

Recipe 1.1, "Run Programs, Scripts, and Existing Tools"

Recipe 3.8, "Work with .NET Objects"

9.5 Create a Temporary File

Problem

You want to create a file for temporary purposes and want to be sure that the file does not already exist.

Solution

Use the `[System.IO.Path]::GetTempFilename()` method from the .NET Framework to create a temporary file:

```
$filename = [System.IO.Path]::GetTempFileName()
 (... use the file ...)
Remove-Item -Force $filename
```

Discussion

It is common to want to create a file for temporary purposes. For example, you might want to search and replace text inside a file. Doing this to a large file requires a temporary file (see Recipe 9.6). Another example is the temporary file used by Recipe 2.4.

Often, people create this temporary file wherever they can think of: in *C:*, the script's current location, or any number of other places. Although this may work on the author's system, it rarely works well elsewhere. For example, if the user does not use their Administrator account for day-to-day tasks, your script will not have access to *C:* and will fail.

Another difficulty comes from trying to create a unique name for the temporary file. If your script just hardcodes a name (no matter how many random characters it has), it will fail if you run two copies at the same time. You might even craft a script smart enough to search for a filename that does not exist, create it, and then use it.

Unfortunately, this could still break if another copy of your script creates that file after you see that it is missing but before you actually create the file.

Finally, there are several security vulnerabilities that your script might introduce should it write its temporary files to a location that other users can read or write.

Luckily, the authors of the .NET Framework provided the [System.IO.Path]::GetTemp Filename() method to resolve these problems for you. It creates a unique filename in a reliable location and in a secure manner. The method returns a filename, which you can then use as you want.

 Remember to delete this file when your script no longer needs it; otherwise, your script will waste disk space and cause needless clutter on your users' systems. Remember: your scripts should solve the administrator's problems, not cause them!

By default, the GetTempFilename() method returns a file with a *.tmp* extension. For most purposes, the file extension does not matter, and this works well. In the rare instances when you need to create a file with a specific extension, the [System.IO.Path]::Change Extension() method lets you change the extension of that temporary file. The following example creates a new temporary file that uses the *.cs* file extension:

```
$filename = [System.IO.Path]::GetTempFileName()
$newname = [System.IO.Path]::ChangeExtension($filename, ".cs")
Move-Item $filename $newname
(... use the file ...)
Remove-Item $newname
```

See Also

Recipe 2.4, "Program: Interactively Filter Lists of Objects"

Recipe 9.6, "Search and Replace Text in a File"

9.6 Search and Replace Text in a File

Problem

You want to search for text in a file and replace that text with something new.

Solution

To search and replace text in a file, first store the content of the file in a variable, and then store the replaced text back in that file, as shown in Example 9-4.

Example 9-4. Replacing text in a file

```
PS > $filename = "file.txt"
PS > $match = "source text"
PS > $replacement = "replacement text"
PS >
PS > $content = Get-Content $filename
PS > $content
This is some source text that we want
to replace. One of the things you may need
to be careful about with Source
Text is when it spans multiple lines,
and may have different Source Text
capitalization.
PS >
PS > $content = $content -creplace $match,$replacement
PS > $content
This is some replacement text that we want
to replace. One of the things you may need
to be careful about with Source
Text is when it spans multiple lines,
and may have different Source Text
capitalization.
PS > $content | Set-Content $filename
```

Discussion

Using PowerShell to search and replace text in a file (or many files!) is one of the best examples of using a tool to automate a repetitive task. What could literally take months by hand can be shortened to a few minutes (or hours, at most).

 Notice that the solution uses the -creplace operator to replace text in a case-sensitive manner. This is almost always what you will want to do, as the replacement text uses the exact capitalization that you provide. If the text you want to replace is capitalized in several different ways (as in the term "Source Text" from the solution), then search and replace several times with the different possible capitalizations.

Example 9-4 illustrates what is perhaps the simplest (but actually most common) scenario:

- You work with an ASCII text file.
- You replace some literal text with a literal text replacement.
- You don't worry that the text match might span multiple lines.
- Your text file is relatively small.

If some of those assumptions don't hold true, then this discussion shows you how to tailor the way you search and replace within this file.

Work with files encoded in Unicode or another (OEM) code page

By default, the Set-Content cmdlet assumes that you want the output file to contain plain ASCII text. If you work with a file in another encoding (for example, Unicode or an OEM code page such as Cyrillic), use the -Encoding parameter of the Out-File cmdlet to specify that:

```
$content | Out-File -Encoding Unicode $filename
$content | Out-File -Encoding OEM $filename
```

Replace text using a pattern instead of plain text

Although it is most common to replace one literal string with another literal string, you might want to replace text according to a pattern in some advanced scenarios. One example might be swapping first name and last name. PowerShell supports this type of replacement through its support of regular expressions in its replacement operator:

```
PS > $content = Get-Content names.txt
PS > $content
John Doe
Mary Smith
PS > $content -replace '(.*) (.*)','$2, $1'
Doe, John
Smith, Mary
```

Replace text that spans multiple lines

The Get-Content cmdlet used in the solution retrieves a list of lines from the file. When you use the -replace operator against this array, it replaces your text in each of those lines individually. If your match spans multiple lines, as shown between lines 3 and 4 in Example 9-4, the -replace operator will be unaware of the match and will not perform the replacement.

If you want to replace text that spans multiple lines, then it becomes necessary to stop treating the input text as a collection of lines. Once you stop treating the input as a collection of lines, it is also important to use a replacement expression that can ignore line breaks, as shown in Example 9-5.

Example 9-5. Replacing text across multiple lines in a file

```
$filename = Get-Item file.txt
$singleLine = [System.IO.File]::ReadAllText($filename.FullName)
$content = $singleLine -creplace "(?s)Source(\s*)Text",'Replacement$1Text'
```

The first and second lines of Example 9-5 read the entire content of the file as a single string. They do this by calling the [System.IO.File]::ReadAllText() method from the .NET Framework, since the Get-Content cmdlet splits the content of the file into individual lines.

The third line of this solution replaces the text by using a regular expression pattern. The section Source(\s*)Text scans for the word Source, followed optionally by some whitespace, followed by the word Text. Since the whitespace portion of the regular expression has parentheses around it, we want to remember exactly what that whitespace was. By default, regular expressions do not let newline characters count as whitespace, so the first portion of the regular expression uses the *single-line option* (?s) to allow newline characters to count as whitespace. The replacement portion of the -replace operator replaces that match with Replacement, followed by the exact whitespace from the match that we captured ($1), followed by Text. For more information, see "Simple Operators" on page 725.

Replace text in large files

The approaches used so far store the entire contents of the file in memory as they replace the text in them. Once we've made the replacements in memory, we write the updated content back to disk. This works well when replacing text in small, medium, and even moderately large files. For extremely large files (for example, more than several hundred megabytes), using this much memory may burden your system and slow down your script. To solve that problem, you can work on the files line by line, rather than with the entire file at once.

Since you're working with the file line by line, it will still be in use when you try to write replacement text back into it. You can avoid this problem if you write the replacement text into a temporary file until you've finished working with the main file. Once you've finished scanning through your file, you can delete it and replace it with the temporary file.

```
$filename = "file.txt"
$temporaryFile = [System.IO.Path]::GetTempFileName()

$match = "source text"
$replacement = "replacement text"

Get-Content $filename |
    Foreach-Object { $_ -creplace $match,$replacement | Add-Content $temporaryFile }

Remove-Item $filename
Move-Item $temporaryFile $filename
```

See Also

"Simple Operators" on page 725

9.7 Program: Get the Encoding of a File

Both PowerShell and the .NET Framework do a lot of work to hide from you the complexities of file encodings. The Get-Content cmdlet automatically detects the encoding of a file, and then handles all encoding issues before returning the content to you. When you do need to know the encoding of a file, though, the solution requires a bit of work.

Example 9-6 resolves this by doing the hard work for you. Files with unusual encodings are supposed to (and almost always do) have a *byte order mark* to identify the encoding. After the byte order mark, they have the actual content. If a file lacks the byte order mark (no matter how the content is encoded), Get-FileEncoding assumes the .NET Framework's default encoding of UTF-7. If the content is not actually encoded as defined by the byte order mark, Get-FileEncoding still outputs the declared encoding.

Example 9-6. Get-FileEncoding.ps1

```
##############################################################################
##
## Get-FileEncoding
##
## From Windows PowerShell Cookbook (O'Reilly)
## by Lee Holmes (http://www.leeholmes.com/guide)
##
##############################################################################

<#

.SYNOPSIS

Gets the encoding of a file

.EXAMPLE

Get-FileEncoding.ps1 .\UnicodeScript.ps1

BodyName          : unicodeFFFE
EncodingName      : Unicode (Big-Endian)
HeaderName        : unicodeFFFE
WebName           : unicodeFFFE
WindowsCodePage   : 1200
IsBrowserDisplay  : False
IsBrowserSave     : False
IsMailNewsDisplay : False
IsMailNewsSave    : False
IsSingleByte      : False
EncoderFallback   : System.Text.EncoderReplacementFallback
DecoderFallback   : System.Text.DecoderReplacementFallback
IsReadOnly        : True
CodePage          : 1201

#>

param(
    ## The path of the file to get the encoding of.
    $Path
)

Set-StrictMode -Version Latest

## The hashtable used to store our mapping of encoding bytes to their
## name. For example, "255-254 = Unicode"
```

```
$encodings = @{}

## Find all of the encodings understood by the .NET Framework. For each,
## determine the bytes at the start of the file (the preamble) that the .NET
## Framework uses to identify that encoding.
$encodingMembers = [System.Text.Encoding] |
    Get-Member -Static -MemberType Property

$encodingMembers | Foreach-Object {
    $encodingBytes = [System.Text.Encoding]::($_.Name).GetPreamble() -join '-'
    $encodings[$encodingBytes] = $_.Name
}

## Find out the lengths of all of the preambles.
$encodingLengths = $encodings.Keys | Where-Object { $_ } |
    Foreach-Object { ($_ -split "-").Count }

## Assume the encoding is UTF7 by default
$result = "UTF7"

## Go through each of the possible preamble lengths, read that many
## bytes from the file, and then see if it matches one of the encodings
## we know about.
foreach($encodingLength in $encodingLengths | Sort -Descending)
{
    $bytes = (Get-Content -encoding byte -readcount $encodingLength $path)[0]
    $encoding = $encodings[$bytes -join '-']

    ## If we found an encoding that had the same preamble bytes,
    ## save that output and break.
    if($encoding)
    {
        $result = $encoding
        break
    }
}

## Finally, output the encoding.
[System.Text.Encoding]::$result
```

For more information about running scripts, see Recipe 1.1.

See Also

Recipe 1.1, "Run Programs, Scripts, and Existing Tools"

9.8 Program: View the Hexadecimal Representation of Content

When dealing with binary data, it is often useful to see the value of the actual bytes being used in that binary data. In addition to the value of the data, finding its offset in the file or content is usually important as well.

Example 9-7 enables both scenarios by displaying content in a report that shows all of this information. The leftmost column displays the offset into the content, increasing by 16 bytes at a time. The middle 16 columns display the hexadecimal representation of the byte at that position in the content. The header of each column shows how far into the 16-byte chunk that character is. The far-right column displays the ASCII representation of the characters in that row.

To determine the position of a byte within the input, add the number at the far-left of the row to the number at the top of the column for that character. For example, 0000230 (shown at the far left) + C (shown at the top of the column) = 000023C. Therefore, the byte in this example is at offset 23C in the content.

Example 9-7. Format-Hex.ps1

```
##############################################################################
##
## Format-Hex
##
## From Windows PowerShell Cookbook (O'Reilly)
## by Lee Holmes (http://www.leeholmes.com/guide)
##
##############################################################################

<#

.SYNOPSIS

Outputs a file or pipelined input as a hexadecimal display. To determine the
offset of a character in the input, add the number at the far-left of the row
with the the number at the top of the column for that character.

.EXAMPLE

"Hello World" | Format-Hex

              0  1  2  3  4  5  6  7  8  9  A  B  C  D  E  F

00000000      48 00 65 00 6C 00 6C 00 6F 00 20 00 57 00 6F 00   H.e.l.l.o. .W.o.
00000010      72 00 6C 00 64 00                                 r.l.d.

.EXAMPLE

Format-Hex c:\temp\example.bmp

#>

[CmdletBinding(DefaultParameterSetName = "ByPath")]
param(
    ## The file to read the content from
    [Parameter(ParameterSetName = "ByPath", Position = 0)]
    [string] $Path,

    ## The input (bytes or strings) to format as hexadecimal
```

```
    [Parameter(
        ParameterSetName = "ByInput", Position = 0,
        ValueFromPipeline = $true)]
    [Object] $InputObject
)

begin
{
    Set-StrictMode -Version Latest

    ## Create the array to hold the content. If the user specified the
    ## -Path parameter, read the bytes from the path.
    [byte[]] $inputBytes = $null
    if($Path) { $inputBytes = [IO.File]::ReadAllBytes((Resolve-Path $Path)) }

    ## Store our header, and formatting information
    $counter = 0
    $header = "            0 1 2 3 4 5 6 7 8 9 A B C D E F"
    $nextLine = "{0}    " -f [Convert]::ToString(
        $counter, 16).ToUpper().PadLeft(8, '0')
    $asciiEnd = ""

    ## Output the header
    "`r`n$header`r`n"
}

process
{
    ## If they specified the -InputObject parameter, retrieve the bytes
    ## from that input
    if(Test-Path variable:\InputObject)
    {
        ## If it's an actual byte, add it to the inputBytes array.
        if($InputObject -is [Byte])
        {
            $inputBytes = $InputObject
        }
        else
        {
            ## Otherwise, convert it to a string and extract the bytes
            ## from that.
            $inputString = [string] $InputObject
            $inputBytes = [Text.Encoding]::Unicode.GetBytes($inputString)
        }
    }

    ## Now go through the input bytes
    foreach($byte in $inputBytes)
    {
        ## Display each byte, in 2-digit hexidecimal, and add that to the
        ## left-hand side.
        $nextLine += "{0:X2} " -f $byte

        ## If the character is printable, add its ascii representation to
        ## the righthand side.  Otherwise, add a dot to the righthand side.
```

```
if(($byte -ge 0x20) -and ($byte -le 0xFE))
{
    $asciiEnd += [char] $byte
}
else
{
    $asciiEnd += "."
}

$counter++;

## If we've hit the end of a line, combine the right half with the
## left half, and start a new line.
if(($counter % 16) -eq 0)
{

    "$nextLine $asciiEnd"
    $nextLine = "{0}    " -f [Convert]::ToString(
        $counter, 16).ToUpper().PadLeft(8, '0')
    $asciiEnd = "";
}
    }
}

end
{
    ## At the end of the file, we might not have had the chance to output
    ## the end of the line yet. Only do this if we didn't exit on the 16-byte
    ## boundary, though.
    if(($counter % 16) -ne 0)
    {
        while(($counter % 16) -ne 0)
        {
            $nextLine += "    "
            $asciiEnd += " "
            $counter++;
        }
        "$nextLine $asciiEnd"
    }

    ""
}
```

For more information about running scripts, see Recipe 1.1.

See Also

Recipe 1.1, "Run Programs, Scripts, and Existing Tools"

Structured Files

10.0 Introduction

In the world of text-only system administration, managing structured files is often a pain. For example, working with (or editing) an XML file means either loading it into an editor to modify by hand or writing a custom tool that can do that for you. Even worse, it may mean modifying the file as though it were plain text while hoping to not break the structure of the XML itself.

In that same world, working with a file in comma-separated values (CSV) format means going through the file yourself, splitting each line by the commas in it. It's a seemingly great approach, until you find yourself faced with anything but the simplest of data.

Structure and structured files don't come only from other programs, either. When writing scripts, one common goal is to save structured data so that you can use it later. In most scripting (and programming) languages, this requires that you design a data structure to hold that data, design a way to store and retrieve it from disk, and bring it back to a usable form when you want to work with it again.

Fortunately, working with XML, CSV, and even your own structured files becomes much easier with PowerShell at your side.

10.1 Access Information in an XML File

Problem

You want to work with and access information in an XML file.

Solution

Use PowerShell's XML cast to convert the plain-text XML into a form that you can more easily work with. In this case, we use the RSS feed downloaded from the Windows PowerShell blog:

```
PS > $xml = [xml] (Get-Content powershell_blog.xml)
```

 See Recipe 12.1 for an example of how to use PowerShell to download this file!

Like other rich objects, PowerShell displays the properties of the XML as you explore. These properties are child nodes and attributes in the XML, as shown by Example 10-1.

Example 10-1. Accessing properties of an XML document

```
PS > $xml
xml                    xml-stylesheet        rss
---                    --------------        ---
                                             rss

PS > $xml.rss

version : 2.0
dc      : http://purl.org/dc/elements/1.1/
slash   : http://purl.org/rss/1.0/modules/slash/
wfw     : http://wellformedweb.org/CommentAPI/
channel : channel
```

If more than one node shares the same name (as in the item nodes of an RSS feed), then the property name represents a collection of nodes:

```
PS > ($xml.rss.channel.item).Count
15
```

You can access those items individually, like you would normally work with an array, as shown in Example 10-2.

Example 10-2. Accessing individual items in an XML document

```
PS > ($xml.rss.channel.item)[0]

title       : Windows Management Framework is here!
link        : http://blogs.msdn.com/powershell/archive/2009/10/27/windows-
              management-framework-is-here.aspx
pubDate     : Tue, 27 Oct 2009 18:25:13 GMT
guid        : guid
creator     : PowerShellTeam
comments    : {15, http://blogs.msdn.com/powershell/comments/9913618.aspx}
commentRss  : http://blogs.msdn.com/powershell/commentrss.aspx?PostID=9913
              618
```

```
comment     : http://blogs.msdn.com/powershell/rsscomments.aspx?PostID=991
              3618
description : <p>Windows Management Framework, which includes Windows Power
              Shell 2.0, WinRM 2.0, and BITS 4.0, was officially released
              to the world this morning.
(...)
```

You can access properties of those elements the same way you would normally work with an object:

```
PS > ($xml.rss.channel.item)[0].title
Windows Management Framework is here!
```

Since these are rich PowerShell objects, Example 10-3 demonstrates how you can use PowerShell's advanced object-based cmdlets for further work, such as sorting and filtering.

Example 10-3. Sorting and filtering items in an XML document

```
PS > $xml.rss.channel.item | Sort-Object title | Select-Object title

title
-----
Analyzing Weblog Data Using the Admin Development Model
Announcing: Open Source PowerShell Cmdlet and Help Designer
Help Us Improve Microsoft Windows Management Framework
Introducing the Windows 7 Resource Kit PowerShell Pack
New and Improved PowerShell Connect Site
PowerShell V2 Virtual Launch Party
Remoting for non-Admins
Select -ExpandProperty <PropertyName>
The Glory of Quick and Dirty Scripting
Tonight is the Virtual Launch Party @ PowerScripting Podcast
Understanding the Feedback Process
What's New in PowerShell V2 -  By Joel "Jaykul" Bennett
What's Up With Command Prefixes?
Windows Management Framework is here!
XP and W2K3 Release Candidate Versions of PowerShell Are Now Available ...
```

Discussion

PowerShell's native XML support provides an excellent way to easily navigate and access XML files. By exposing the XML hierarchy as properties, you can perform most tasks without having to resort to text-only processing or custom tools.

In fact, PowerShell's support for interaction with XML goes beyond just presenting your data in an object-friendly way. The objects created by the [xml] cast in fact represent fully featured System.Xml.XmlDocument objects from the .NET Framework. Each property of the resulting objects represents a System.Xml.XmlElement object from the .NET Framework as well. The underlying objects provide a great deal of additional functionality that you can use to perform both common and complex tasks on XML files.

The underlying `System.Xml.XmlDocument` and `System.Xml.XmlElement` objects that support your XML also provide useful properties in their own right: `Attributes`, `Name`, `OuterXml`, and more.

```
PS > $xml.rss.Attributes

#text
-----
2.0
http://purl.org/dc/elements/1.1/
http://purl.org/rss/1.0/modules/slash/
http://wellformedweb.org/CommentAPI/
```

 In PowerShell version one, PowerShell hid these underlying properties by default. To access them in PowerShell version one, use the `PsBase` property on any node. The `PsBase` property works on any object in PowerShell and represents the object underneath the PowerShell abstraction.

For more information about using the underlying .NET objects for more advanced tasks, see Recipe 10.2 and Recipe 10.4.

For more information about working with XML in PowerShell, see Table F-11 in Appendix F.

See Also

Recipe 10.2, "Perform an XPath Query Against XML"

Recipe 10.4, "Modify Data in an XML File"

Recipe 12.1, "Download a File from the Internet"

Table F-11

10.2 Perform an XPath Query Against XML

Problem

You want to perform an advanced query against an XML file, using XML's standard *XPath syntax*.

Solution

Use PowerShell's `Select-Xml` cmdlet to perform an XPath query against a file.

For example, to find all post titles shorter than 30 characters in an RSS feed:

```
PS > $query = "/rss/channel/item[string-length(title) < 30]/title"
PS > Select-Xml -XPath $query -Path .\powershell_blog.xml | Select -Expand Node
```

```
#text
-----
Remoting for non-Admins
```

Discussion

Although a language all its own, the XPath query syntax provides a powerful, XML-centric way to write advanced queries for XML files. The Select-Xml cmdlet lets you apply these concepts to files, XML nodes, or simply plain text.

 The XPath queries supported by the Select-Xml cmdlet are a popular industry standard. Beware, though. Unlike those in the rest of Power-Shell, these queries are case-sensitive!

The Select-Xml cmdlet generates a SelectXmlInfo object. This lets you chain separate XPath queries together. To retrieve the actual result of the selection, access the Node property.

```
PS > Get-Content page.html
<HTML>
    <HEAD>
        <TITLE>Welcome to my Website</TITLE>
    </HEAD>
    <BODY>
        <P>...</P>
    </BODY>
</HTML>
PS > $content = [xml] (Get-Content page.html)
PS > $result = $content | Select-Xml "/HTML/HEAD" | Select-Xml "TITLE"
PS > $result

Node                    Path                    Pattern
----                    ----                    -------
TITLE                   InputStream             TITLE


PS > $result.Node

#text
-----
Welcome to my Website
```

This works even for content accessed through PowerShell's XML support, as in this case, which uses the RSS feed downloaded from the Windows PowerShell blog:

```
PS > $xml = [xml] (Get-Content powershell_blog.xml)
PS > $xml | Select-Xml $query | Select -Expand Node

#text
-----
Remoting for non-Admins
```

If you are limited to PowerShell version one, you can use the `SelectNodes()` method on an XML result to perform the query. For example, to find all post titles shorter than 30 characters:

```
PS > $xml.SelectNodes($query)

#text
-----
Remoting for non-Admins
```

For simpler queries, you may find PowerShell's object-based XML navigation concepts easier to work with. For more information about working with XML through Power-Shell's XML type, see Table F-11 in Appendix F. For more information about XPath syntax, see Appendix C.

See Also

Appendix C, *XPath Quick Reference*

Table F-11

10.3 Convert Objects to XML

Problem

You want to convert command output to XML for further processing or viewing.

Solution

Use PowerShell's `ConvertTo-Xml` cmdlet to save the output of a command as XML:

```
$xml = Get-Process | ConvertTo-Xml
```

You can then use PowerShell's XML support (XML navigation, `Select-Xml`, and more) to work with the content.

Discussion

Although it is usually easiest to work with objects in their full fidelity, you may some-times want to convert them to XML for further processing by other programs. The solution is the `ConvertTo-Xml` cmdlet.

PowerShell includes another similar-sounding cmdlet called `Export-CliXml`. Unlike the `ConvertTo-Xml` cmdlet, which is intended to produce useful output for humans and programs alike, the `Export-CliXml` cmdlet is designed for PowerShell-centric data interchange. For more informa-tion, see Recipe 10.5.

The ConvertTo-Xml cmdlet gives you two main targets for this conversion. The default is an XML document, which is the same type of object created by the [xml] cast in PowerShell. This is also the format supported by the Select-Xml cmdlet, so you can pipe the output of ConvertTo-Xml directly into it.

```
PS > $xml = Get-Process | ConvertTo-Xml
PS > $xml | Select-Xml '//Property[@Name = "Name"]' | Select -Expand Node

Name                    Type                    #text
----                    ----                    -----
Name                    System.String           audiodg
Name                    System.String           csrss
Name                    System.String           dwm
(...)
```

The second format is a simple string, and it is suitable for redirection into a file. To save the XML into a file, use the -As parameter with String as the argument, and then use the file redirection operator:

```
Get-Process | ConvertTo-Xml -As String > c:\temp\processes.xml
```

If you already have an XML document that you obtained from ConvertTo-Xml or PowerShell's [xml] cast, you can still save it into a file by calling its Save() method:

```
$xml = Get-Process | ConvertTo-Xml
$xml.Save("c:\temp\output.xml")
```

For more information on how to work with XML data in PowerShell, see Recipe 10.1.

See Also

Recipe 10.1, "Access Information in an XML File"

Recipe 10.5, "Easily Import and Export Your Structured Data"

10.4 Modify Data in an XML File

Problem

You want to use PowerShell to modify the data in an XML file.

Solution

To modify data in an XML file, load the file into PowerShell's XML data type, change the content you want, and then save the file back to disk. Example 10-4 demonstrates this approach.

Example 10-4. Modifying an XML file from PowerShell

```
PS > ## Store the filename
PS > $filename = (Get-Item phone.xml).FullName
PS >
```

```
PS > ## Get the content of the file, and load it
PS > ## as XML
PS > Get-Content $filename
<AddressBook>
  <Person contactType="Personal">
    <Name>Lee</Name>
    <Phone type="home">555-1212</Phone>
    <Phone type="work">555-1213</Phone>
  </Person>
  <Person contactType="Business">
    <Name>Ariel</Name>
    <Phone>555-1234</Phone>
  </Person>
</AddressBook>
PS > $phoneBook = [xml] (Get-Content $filename)
PS >
PS > ## Get the part with data we want to change
PS > $person = $phoneBook.AddressBook.Person[0]
PS >
PS > ## Change the text part of the information,
PS > ## and the type (which was an attribute)
PS > $person.Phone[0]."#text" = "555-1214"
PS > $person.Phone[0].type = "mobile"
PS >
PS > ## Add a new phone entry
PS > $newNumber = [xml] '<Phone type="home">555-1215</Phone>'
PS > $newNode = $phoneBook.ImportNode($newNumber.Phone, $true)
PS > [void] $person.AppendChild($newNode)
PS >
PS > ## Save the file to disk
PS > $phoneBook.Save($filename)
PS > Get-Content $filename
<AddressBook>
  <Person contactType="Personal">
    <Name>Lee</Name>
    <Phone type="mobile">555-1214</Phone>
    <Phone type="work">555-1213</Phone>
    <Phone type="home">555-1215</Phone>
  </Person>
  <Person contactType="Business">
    <Name>Ariel</Name>
    <Phone>555-1234</Phone>
  </Person>
</AddressBook>
```

Discussion

In the preceding solution, you change Lee's phone number (which was the "text" portion of the XML's original first Phone node) from 555-1212 to 555-1214. You also change the type of the phone number (which was an attribute of the Phone node) from "home" to "mobile".

Adding new information to the XML is nearly as easy. To add information to an XML file, you need to add it as a *child node* to another node in the file. The easiest way to get that child node is to write the string that represents the XML and then create a temporary PowerShell XML document from that. From that temporary document, you use the main XML document's ImportNode() function to import the node you care about—specifically, the Phone node in this example.

Once we have the child node, you need to decide where to put it. Since we want this Phone node to be a child of the Person node for Lee, we will place it there. To add a child node ($newNode in Example 10-4) to a destination node ($person in the example), use the AppendChild() method from the destination node.

 The Save() method on the XML document allows you to save to more than just files. For a quick way to convert XML into a "beautified" form, save it to the console:

```
$phoneBook.Save([Console]::Out)
```

Finally, we save the XML back to the file from which it came.

10.5 Easily Import and Export Your Structured Data

Problem

You have a set of data (such as a hashtable or array) and want to save it to disk so that you can use it later. Conversely, you have saved structured data to a file and want to import it so that you can use it.

Solution

Use PowerShell's Export-CliXml cmdlet to save structured data to disk, and the Import-CliXml cmdlet to import it again from disk.

For example, imagine storing a list of your favorite directories in a hashtable, so that you can easily navigate your system with a "Favorite CD" function. Example 10-5 shows this function.

Example 10-5. A function that requires persistent structured data

```
PS > $favorites = @{}
PS > $favorites["temp"] = "c:\temp"
PS > $favorites["music"] = "h:\lee\my music"
PS > function fcd {
   param([string] $location) Set-Location $favorites[$location]
}

PS > Get-Location
```

```
Path
----
HKLM:\software

PS > fcd temp
PS > Get-Location

Path
----
C:\temp
```

Unfortunately, the `$favorites` variable vanishes whenever you close PowerShell.

To get around this, you could recreate the `$favorites` variable in your profile, but another approach is to export it directly to a file. This command assumes that you have already created a profile, and it places the file in the same location as that profile:

```
PS > $filename = Join-Path (Split-Path $profile) favorites.clixml
PS > $favorites | Export-CliXml $filename
PS > $favorites = $null
PS > $favorites
PS >
```

Once the file is on disk, you can reload it using the `Import-CliXml` cmdlet, as shown in Example 10-6.

Example 10-6. Restoring structured data from disk

```
PS > $favorites = Import-CliXml $filename
PS > $favorites


Name                      Value
----                      -----
music                     h:\lee\my music
temp                      c:\temp

PS > fcd music
PS > Get-Location

Path
----
H:\lee\My Music
```

Discussion

PowerShell provides the `Export-CliXml` and `Import-CliXml` cmdlets to let you easily move structured data into and out of files. These cmdlets accomplish this in a very data-centric and future-proof way—by storing only the names, values, and basic data types for the properties of that data.

By default, PowerShell stores one level of data: all directly accessible simple properties (such as the WorkingSet of a process) but a plain-text representation for anything deeper (such as a process's Threads collection). For information on how to control the depth of this export, type Get-Help Export-CliXml and see the explanation of the -Depth parameter.

After you import data saved by Export-CliXml, you again have access to the properties and values from the original data. PowerShell converts some objects back to their fully featured objects (such as System.DateTime objects), but for the most part does not retain functionality (for example, methods) from the original objects.

10.6 Store the Output of a Command in a CSV or Delimited File

Problem

You want to store the output of a command in a CSV file for later processing. This is helpful when you want to export the data for later processing outside PowerShell.

Solution

Use PowerShell's Export-Csv cmdlet to save the output of a command into a CSV file. For example, to create an inventory of the processes running on a system:

```
Get-Process | Export-Csv c:\temp\processes.csv
```

You can then review this output in a tool such as Excel, mail it to others, or do whatever else you might want to do with a CSV file.

Discussion

The CSV file format is one of the most common formats for exchanging semistructured data between programs and systems.

PowerShell's Export-Csv cmdlet provides an easy way to export data from the Power-Shell environment while still allowing you to keep a fair amount of your data's structure. When PowerShell exports your data to the CSV, it creates a row for each object that you provide. For each row, PowerShell creates columns in the CSV that represent the values of your object's properties.

If you want to use the CSV-structured data as input to another tool that supports direct CSV pipeline input, you can use the ConvertTo-Csv cmdlet to bypass the step of storing it in a file.

If you want to separate the data with a character *other than* a comma, use the `-Delimiter` parameter.

One thing to keep in mind is that the CSV file format supports only plain strings for property values. If a property on your object isn't actually a string, PowerShell converts it to a string for you. Having PowerShell convert rich property values (such as integers) to strings, however, does mean that a certain amount of information is not preserved. If your ultimate goal is to load this unmodified data again in PowerShell, the `Export-CliXml` cmdlet provides a much better alternative. For more information about the `Export-CliXml` cmdlet, see Recipe 10.5.

For more information on how to import data from a CSV file into PowerShell, see Recipe 10.7.

See Also

Recipe 10.5, "Easily Import and Export Your Structured Data"

Recipe 10.7, "Import CSV and Delimited Data from a File"

10.7 Import CSV and Delimited Data from a File

Problem

You want to import structured data that has been stored in a CSV file or a file that uses some other character as its delimiter.

Solution

Use PowerShell's `Import-Csv` cmdlet to import structured data from a CSV file. Use the `-Delimiter` parameter if fields are separated by a character other than a comma.

For example, to load the (tab-separated) Windows Update log:

```
$header = "Date","Time","PID","TID","Component","Text"
$log = Import-Csv $env:WINDIR\WindowsUpdate.log -Delimiter "`t" -Header $header
```

Then, manage the log as you manage other rich PowerShell output:

```
$log | Group-Object Component
```

Discussion

As mentioned in Recipe 10.6, the CSV file format is one of the most common formats for exchanging semistructured data between programs and systems.

PowerShell's `Import-Csv` cmdlet provides an easy way to import this data into the PowerShell environment from other programs. When PowerShell imports your data from the CSV, it creates a new object for each row in the CSV. For each object, PowerShell creates properties on the object from the values of the columns in the CSV.

If the names of the CSV columns match parameter names, many commands let you pipe this output to automatically set the values of parameters.

For more information about this feature, see Recipe 2.6.

If you are dealing with data in a CSV format that is the output of another tool or command, the Import-Csv cmdlet's file-based behavior won't be of much help. In this case, use the ConvertFrom-Csv cmdlet.

One thing to keep in mind is that the CSV file format supports only plain strings for property values. When you import data from a CSV, properties that look like dates will still only be strings. Properties that look like numbers will only be strings. Properties that look like any sort of rich data type will only be strings. This means that sorting on any property will always be an *alphabetical* sort, which is usually not the same as the sorting rules for the rich data types that the property might look like.

If your ultimate goal is to load rich unmodified data from something that you've previously exported from PowerShell, the Import-CliXml cmdlet provides a much better alternative. For more information about the Import-CliXml cmdlet, see Recipe 10.5.

For more information on how to export data from PowerShell to a CSV file, see Recipe 10.6.

See Also

Recipe 2.6, "Automate Data-Intensive Tasks"

Recipe 10.5, "Easily Import and Export Your Structured Data"

Recipe 10.6, "Store the Output of a Command in a CSV or Delimited File"

10.8 Use Excel to Manage Command Output

Problem

You want to use Excel to manipulate or visualize the output of a command.

Solution

Use PowerShell's Export-Csv cmdlet to save the output of a command in a CSV file, and then load that CSV in Excel. If you have Excel associated with *.CSV* files, the Invoke-Item cmdlet launches Excel when you provide it with a *.CSV* file as an argument.

Example 10-7 demonstrates how to generate a CSV containing the disk usage for subdirectories of the current directory.

Example 10-7. Using Excel to visualize disk usage on the system

```
PS > $filename = "c:\temp\diskusage.csv"
PS >
PS > $output = Get-ChildItem | Where-Object { $_.PsIsContainer } |
    Select-Object Name,
        @{ Name="Size";
            Expression={ ($_ | Get-ChildItem -Recurse |
                Measure-Object -Sum Length).Sum + 0 } }

PS > $output | Export-Csv $filename
PS >
PS > Invoke-Item $filename
```

In Excel, you can manipulate or format the data as you wish. As Figure 10-1 shows, we can manually create a pie chart.

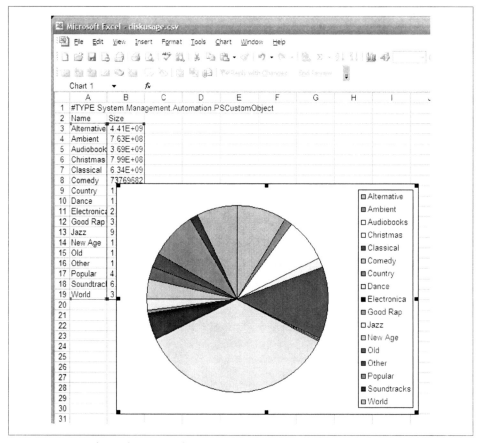

Figure 10-1. Visualizing data in Excel

Discussion

Although used only as a demonstration, Example 10-7 packs quite a bit into just a few lines.

The first `Get-ChildItem` line gets a list of all the files in the current directory and uses the `Where-Object` cmdlet to restrict those to directories. For each of those directories, you use the `Select-Object` cmdlet to pick out the `Name` and `Size` of that directory.

Directories don't have a `Size` property, though. To get that, we use `Select-Object`'s hashtable syntax to generate a *calculated property*. This calculated property (as defined by the `Expression` script block) uses the `Get-ChildItem` and `Measure-Object` cmdlets to add up the `Length` of all files in the given directory.

For more information about creating and working with calculated properties, see Recipe 3.15.

See Also

Recipe 3.15, "Add Custom Methods and Properties to Objects"

10.9 Parse and Interpret PowerShell Scripts

Problem

You want to access detailed structural and language-specific information about the content of a PowerShell script.

Solution

Use PowerShell's Tokenizer API to convert the script into the same internal representation that PowerShell uses to understand the script's structure.

```
PS > $script = '$myVariable = 10'
PS > $errors = [System.Management.Automation.PSParseError[]] @()
PS > [Management.Automation.PsParser]::Tokenize($script, [ref] $errors)


Content     : myVariable
Type        : Variable
Start       : 0
Length      : 11
StartLine   : 1
StartColumn : 1
EndLine     : 1
EndColumn   : 12

Content     : =
Type        : Operator
Start       : 12
```

```
Length       : 1
StartLine    : 1
StartColumn  : 13
EndLine      : 1
EndColumn    : 14

Content      : 10
Type         : Number
Start        : 14
Length       : 2
StartLine    : 1
StartColumn  : 15
EndLine      : 1
EndColumn    : 17
```

Discussion

When PowerShell loads a script, one of its first steps is to *tokenize* that script. Tokenization determines which portions of the script represent variables, numbers, operators, commands, parameters, aliases, and more.

While this is a fairly advanced concept, the Tokenizer API exposes the results of this step. This lets you work with the rich structure of PowerShell scripts the same way that the PowerShell engine does.

Without the support of a Tokenizer API, tool authors are usually required to build complicated regular expressions that attempt to emulate the PowerShell engine. This was true of PowerShell version one. Although these regular expressions are helpful for many situations, they tend to fall apart on more complex scripts.

In the first line of Figure 10-2, "Write-Host" is an argument to the **Write-Host** cmdlet, but gets parsed as a string. The second line, while still providing an argument to the **Write-Host** cmdlet, does not treat the argument the same way. In fact, since it matches a cmdlet name, the argument gets interpreted as another call to the **Write-Host** cmdlet. In the here string that follows, the **Write-Host** cmdlet name gets highlighted again, even though it is really just part of a string.

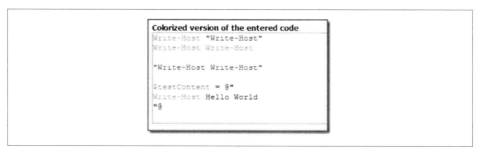

Figure 10-2. Tokenization errors in a complex script

Since the Tokenizer API follows the same rules as the PowerShell engine, it avoids the pitfalls of the regular-expression-based approach while producing output that is much easier to consume. When run on the same input, it produces the output shown in Example 10-8.

Example 10-8. Successfully tokenizing a complex script

```
PS > [Management.Automation.PsParser]::Tokenize($content, [ref] $errors) | ft -auto
```

Content	Type	Start	Length	StartLine	StartColumn	EndLine	EndColumn
Write-Host	Command	0	10	1	1	1	11
Write-Host	String	11	12	1	12	1	24
...	NewLine	23	2	1	24	2	1
Write-Host	Command	25	10	2	1	2	11
Write-Host	CommandArgument	36	10	2	12	2	22
...	NewLine	46	2	2	22	3	1
...	NewLine	48	2	3	1	4	1
Write-Host Write-Host	String	50	23	4	1	4	24
...	NewLine	73	2	4	24	5	1
...	NewLine	75	2	5	1	6	1
testContent	Variable	77	12	6	1	6	13
=	Operator	90	1	6	14	6	15
Write-Host Hello World	String	92	30	6	16	8	3
...	NewLine	122	2	8	3	9	1

This adds a whole new dimension to the way you can interact with PowerShell scripts. Some natural outcomes are:

- Syntax highlighting
- Automated script editing (for example, replacing aliased commands with their expanded equivalents)
- Script style and form verification

If the script contains any errors, PowerShell captures those in the $errors collection you are required to supply. If you don't want to keep track of errors, you can supply [ref] $null as the value for that parameter.

For an example of the Tokenizer API in action, see Recipe 8.6.

See Also

Recipe 8.6, "Program: Show Colorized Script Content"

Code Reuse

11.0 Introduction

One thing that surprises many people is how much you can accomplish in PowerShell from the interactive prompt alone. Since PowerShell makes it so easy to join its powerful commands together into even more powerful combinations, enthusiasts grow to relish this brevity. In fact, there is a special place in the heart of most scripting enthusiasts set aside entirely for the most compact expressions of power: the *one-liner*.

Despite its interactive efficiency, you obviously don't want to retype all your brilliant ideas anew each time you need them. When you want to save or reuse the commands that you've written, PowerShell provides many avenues to support you: scripts, modules, functions, script blocks, and more.

11.1 Write a Script

Problem

You want to store your commands in a script so that you can share them or reuse them later.

Solution

To write a PowerShell script, create a plain-text file with your editor of choice. Add your PowerShell commands to that script (the same PowerShell commands you use from the interactive shell), and then save it with a *.ps1* extension.

Discussion

One of the most important things to remember about PowerShell is that running scripts and working at the command line are essentially equivalent operations. If you see it in a script, you can type it or paste it at the command line. If you typed it on the command line, you can paste it into a text file and call it a script.

Once you write your script, PowerShell lets you call it in the same way that you call other programs and existing tools. Running a script does the same thing as running all the commands in that script.

 PowerShell introduces a few features related to running scripts and tools that may at first confuse you if you aren't aware of them. For more information about how to call scripts and existing tools, see Recipe 1.1.

The first time you try to run a script in PowerShell, you'll likely see the following error message:

```
File c:\tools\myFirstScript.ps1 cannot be loaded because the execution of
scripts is disabled on this system. Please see "get-help about_signing" for
more details.
At line:1 char:12
+ myFirstScript <<<<
```

Since relatively few computer users write scripts, PowerShell's default security policies prevent scripts from running. Once you begin writing scripts, though, you should configure this policy to something less restrictive. For information on how to configure your execution policy, see Recipe 18.1.

When it comes to the filename of your script, picking a descriptive name is the best way to guarantee that you will always remember what that script does—or at least have a good idea. This is an issue that PowerShell tackles elegantly, by naming every cmdlet in the *Verb-Noun* pattern: a command that performs an action (*verb*) on an item (*noun*). As an example of the usefulness of this philosophy, consider the names of typical Windows commands given in Example 11-1.

Example 11-1. The names of some standard Windows commands

```
PS > dir $env:WINDIR\System32\*.exe | Select-Object Name

Name
----
accwiz.exe
actmovie.exe
ahui.exe
alg.exe
append.exe
arp.exe
asr_fmt.exe
asr_ldm.exe
asr_pfu.exe
at.exe
atmadm.exe
attrib.exe
(...)
```

Compare this to the names of some standard Windows PowerShell cmdlets, given in Example 11-2.

Example 11-2. The names of some standard Windows PowerShell cmdlets

```
PS > Get-Command | Select-Object Name

Name
----
Add-Content
Add-History
Add-Member
Add-PSSnapin
Clear-Content
Clear-Item
Clear-ItemProperty
Clear-Variable
Compare-Object
ConvertFrom-SecureString
Convert-Path
ConvertTo-Html
(...)
```

As an additional way to improve discovery, PowerShell takes this even further with the philosophy (and explicit goal) that "you can manage 80 percent of your system with less than 50 verbs." As you learn the standard verbs for a concept, such as Get (which represents the standard concepts of Read, Open, and so on), you can often guess the verb of a command as the first step in discovering it.

When you name your script (*especially* if you intend to share it), make every effort to pick a name that follows these conventions. Recipe 11.3 shows a useful cmdlet to help you find a verb to name your scripts properly. As evidence of its utility for scripts, consider some of the scripts included in this book:

```
PS > dir | select Name

Name
----
Compare-Property.ps1
Connect-WebService.ps1
Convert-TextObject.ps1
Get-AliasSuggestion.ps1
Get-Answer.ps1
Get-Characteristics.ps1
Get-OwnerReport.ps1
Get-PageUrls.ps1
Invoke-CmdScript.ps1
New-GenericObject.ps1
Select-FilteredObject.ps1
(...)
```

Like the PowerShell cmdlets, the names of these scripts are clear, are easy to understand, and use verbs from PowerShell's standard verb list.

See Also

Recipe 1.1, "Run Programs, Scripts, and Existing Tools"

Recipe 11.3, "Find a Verb Appropriate for a Command Name"

Appendix J, *Standard PowerShell Verbs*

11.2 Write a Function

Problem

You have commands in your script that you want to call multiple times or a section of your script that you consider to be a "helper" for the main purpose of your script.

Solution

Place this common code in a function, and then call that function instead. For example, this Celsius conversion code in a script:

```
param([double] $fahrenheit)

## Convert it to Celsius
$celsius= $fahrenheit - 32
$celsius = $celsius / 1.8

## Output the answer
"$fahrenheit degrees Fahrenheit is $celsius degrees Celsius."
```

could be placed in a function (itself placed in a script):

```
param([double] $fahrenheit)

## Convert Fahrenheit to Celsius
function ConvertFahrenheitToCelsius([double] $fahrenheit)
{
    $celsius = $fahrenheit - 32
    $celsius = $celsius / 1.8
    $celsius
}

$celsius = ConvertFahrenheitToCelsius $fahrenheit

## Output the answer
"$fahrenheit degrees Fahrenheit is $celsius degrees Celsius."
```

Although using a function arguably makes this specific script longer and more difficult to understand, the technique is extremely valuable (and used) in almost all nontrivial scripts.

Discussion

Once you define a function, any command after that definition can use it. This means that you must define your function *before* any part of your script that uses it. You might find this unwieldy if your script defines many functions, as the function definitions obscure the main logic portion of your script. If this is the case, you can put your main logic in a "Main" function, as described in Recipe 11.21.

 A common question that comes from those accustomed to batch scripting in cmd.exe is, "What is the PowerShell equivalent of a GOTO?" In situations where the GOTO is used to call subroutines or other isolated helper parts of the batch file, use a PowerShell function to accomplish that task. If the GOTO is used as a way to loop over something, PowerShell's looping mechanisms are more appropriate.

In PowerShell, calling a function is designed to feel just like calling a cmdlet or a script. As a user, you should not have to know whether a little helper routine was written as a cmdlet, script, or function. When you call a function, simply add the parameters after the function name, with spaces separating each one (as shown in the solution). This is in contrast to the way that you call functions in many programming languages (such as C#), where you use parentheses after the function name and commas between each parameter.

```
## Correct
ConvertFahrenheitToCelsius $fahrenheit

## Incorrect
ConvertFahrenheitToCelsius($fahrenheit)
```

Also, notice that the return value from a function is anything that the function writes to the output pipeline (such as `$celsius` in the solution). You can write `return $celsius` if you want, but it is unnecessary.

For more information about writing functions, see "Writing Scripts, Reusing Functionality" on page 746. For more information about PowerShell's looping statements, see Recipe 4.4.

See Also

Recipe 4.4, "Repeat Operations with Loops"

"Writing Scripts, Reusing Functionality" on page 746

11.3 Find a Verb Appropriate for a Command Name

Problem

You are writing a new script or function and want to select an appropriate verb for that command.

Solution

Review the output of the Get-Verb command to find a verb appropriate for your command:

```
PS > Get-Verb In* | Format-Table -Auto

Verb       Group
----       -----
Initialize Data
Install    Lifecycle
Invoke     Lifecycle
```

Discussion

Consistency of command names is one of PowerShell's most beneficial features, largely due to its standard set of verbs. While descriptive command names (such as Stop-Process) make it clear what a command does, standard verbs make commands easier to discover.

For example, many technologies have their own words for creating something: *New*, *Create*, *Instantiate*, *Build*, and more. When a user looks for a command (without the benefit of standard verbs), the user has to know the domain-specific terminology for that action. If the user doesn't know the domain-specific verb, the user is forced to page through long lists of commands in the hope that something rings a bell.

When commands use PowerShell's standard verbs, however, discovery becomes much easier. Once users learn the *standard verb* for an action, they don't need to search for its domain-specific alternatives. Most importantly, the time they invest (actively or otherwise) learning the standard PowerShell verbs improves their efficiency with *all* commands, not just commands from a specific domain.

 This discoverability issue is so important that PowerShell generates a warning message when a module defines a command with a nonstandard verb. To support domain-specific names for your commands *in addition* to the standard names, simply define an alias. For more information, see Recipe 11.8.

To make it easier to select a standard verb while writing a script or function, PowerShell provides a Get-Verb function. You can review the output of that function to find a verb suitable for your command. For an even more detailed description of the standard verbs, see Appendix J.

See Also

Recipe 11.8, "Selectively Export Commands from a Module"

Appendix J, *Standard PowerShell Verbs*

11.4 Write a Script Block

Problem

You have a section of your script that works nearly the same for all input, aside from a minor change in logic.

Solution

As shown in Example 11-3, place the minor logic differences in a script block, and then pass that script block as a parameter to the code that requires it. Use the invoke operator (&) to execute the script block.

Example 11-3. A script that applies a script block to each element in the pipeline

```
##############################################################################
##
## Invoke-ScriptBlock
##
## From Windows PowerShell Cookbook (O'Reilly)
## by Lee Holmes (http://www.leeholmes.com/guide)
##
##############################################################################

<#

.SYNOPSIS

Apply the given mapping command to each element of the input. (Note that
PowerShell includes this command natively, and calls it Foreach-Object)

.EXAMPLE

1,2,3 | Invoke-ScriptBlock { $_ * 2 }

#>

param(
    ## The scriptblock to apply to each incoming element
    [ScriptBlock] $MapCommand
)

begin
```

```
{
    Set-StrictMode -Version Latest
}
process
{
    & $mapCommand
}
```

Discussion

Imagine a script that needs to multiply all the elements in a list by two:

```
function MultiplyInputByTwo
{
    process
    {
        $_ * 2
    }
}
```

but it also needs to perform a more complex calculation:

```
function MultiplyInputComplex
{
    process
    {
        ($_ + 2) * 3
    }
}
```

These two functions are strikingly similar, except for the single line that actually performs the calculation. As we add more calculations, this quickly becomes more evident. Adding each new seven-line function gives us only one unique line of value!

```
PS > 1,2,3 | MultiplyInputByTwo
2
4
6
PS > 1,2,3 | MultiplyInputComplex
9
12
15
```

If we instead use a script block to hold this "unknown" calculation, we don't need to keep on adding new functions:

```
PS > 1,2,3 | Invoke-ScriptBlock { $_ * 2 }
2
4
6
PS > 1,2,3 | Invoke-ScriptBlock { ($_ + 2) * 3 }
9
12
15
```

```
PS > 1,2,3 | Invoke-ScriptBlock { ($_ + 3) * $_ }
4
10
18
```

In fact, the functionality provided by `Invoke-ScriptBlock` is so helpful that it is a stand-ard PowerShell cmdlet—called `Foreach-Object`. For more information about script blocks, see "Writing Scripts, Reusing Functionality" on page 746. For more informa-tion about running scripts, see Recipe 1.1.

See Also

Recipe 1.1, "Run Programs, Scripts, and Existing Tools"

"Writing Scripts, Reusing Functionality" on page 746

11.5 Return Data from a Script, Function, or Script Block

Problem

You want your script or function to return data to whatever called it.

Solution

To return data from a script or function, write that data to the output pipeline:

```
##############################################################################
##
## Get-Tomorrow
##
## Get the date that represents tomorrow
##
## From Windows PowerShell Cookbook (O'Reilly)
## by Lee Holmes (http://www.leeholmes.com/guide)
##
##############################################################################

Set-StrictMode -Version Latest

function GetDate
{
    Get-Date
}

$tomorrow = (GetDate).AddDays(1)
$tomorrow
```

Discussion

In PowerShell, any data that your function or script generates gets sent to the output pipeline, unless something captures that output. The `GetDate` function generates data (a date) and does not capture it, so that becomes the output of the function. The portion of the script that calls the `GetDate` function captures that output and then manipulates it.

Finally, the script writes the `$tomorrow` variable to the pipeline without capturing it, so that becomes the return value of the script itself.

Some .NET methods—such as the `System.Collections.ArrayList` class —produce output, even though you may not expect them to. To prevent these methods from sending data to the output pipeline, either capture the data or cast it to [**void**]:

```
PS > $collection = New-Object System.Collections.ArrayList
PS > $collection.Add("Hello")
0
PS > [void] $collection.Add("Hello")
```

Even with this "pipeline output becomes the return value" philosophy, PowerShell continues to support the traditional **return** keyword as a way to return from a function or script. If you specify anything after the keyword (such as **return** "Hello"), PowerShell treats that as a "Hello" statement followed by a **return** statement.

If you want to make your intention clear to other readers of your script, you can use the `Write-Output` cmdlet to explicitly send data down the pipeline. Both produce the same result, so this is only a matter of preference.

If you write a collection (such as an array or `ArrayList`) to the output pipeline, Power-Shell in fact writes each element of that collection to the pipeline. To keep the collection intact as it travels down the pipeline, prefix it with a comma when you return it. This returns a collection (that will be unraveled) with one element: the collection you wanted to keep intact.

```
function WritesObjects
{
    $arrayList = New-Object System.Collections.ArrayList
    [void] $arrayList.Add("Hello")
    [void] $arrayList.Add("World")

    $arrayList
}

function WritesArrayList
{
    $arrayList = New-Object System.Collections.ArrayList
    [void] $arrayList.Add("Hello")
    [void] $arrayList.Add("World")

    ,$arrayList
```

```
    }

    $objectOutput = WritesObjects

    # The following command would generate an error
    # $objectOutput.Add("Extra")

    $arrayListOutput = WritesArrayList
    $arrayListOutput.Add("Extra")
```

Although relatively uncommon in PowerShell's world of fully structured data, you may sometimes want to use an exit code to indicate the success or failure of your script. For this, PowerShell offers the **exit** keyword.

For more information about the **return** and **exit** statements, see "Writing Scripts, Reusing Functionality" on page 746 and Recipe 15.1.

See Also

Recipe 15.1, "Determine the Status of the Last Command"

"Writing Scripts, Reusing Functionality" on page 746

11.6 Package Common Commands in a Module

Problem

You've developed a useful set of commands or functions. You want to offer them to the user or share them between multiple scripts.

Solution

First, place these common function definitions by themselves in a file with the extension *.psm1*, as shown in Example 11-4.

Example 11-4. A module of temperature commands

```
##############################################################################
##
## Temperature.psm1
## Commands that manipulate and convert temperatures
##
## From Windows PowerShell Cookbook (O'Reilly)
## by Lee Holmes (http://www.leeholmes.com/guide)
##
##############################################################################

## Convert Fahrenheit to Celsius
function Convert-FahrenheitToCelsius([double] $fahrenheit)
{
    $celsius = $fahrenheit - 32
    $celsius = $celsius / 1.8
```

```
        $celsius
}

## Convert Celsius to Fahrenheit
function Convert-CelsiusToFahrenheit([double] $celsius) `
{
    $fahrenheit = $celsius * 1.8
    $fahrenheit = $fahrenheit + 32
    $fahrenheit
}
```

Next, place that file in your *Modules* directory (as defined in the `PSModulePath` environment variable), in a subdirectory with the same name. For example, place *Temperature.psm1* in *<My Documents>\WindowsPowerShell\Modules\Temperature*. Call the `Import-Module` command to import the module (and its commands) into your session, as shown by Example 11-5.

Example 11-5. Importing a module

```
PS > Import-Module Temperature
PS > Convert-FahrenheitToCelsius 81
27.2222222222222
```

Discussion

PowerShell modules give you an easy way to package related commands and functionality. As the solution demonstrates, writing a module is as simple as adding functions to a file.

As with the naming of core commands, the naming of commands packaged in a module plays a critical role in giving users a consistent and discoverable PowerShell experience. When you name the commands in your module, ensure that they follow a `Verb-Noun` syntax and that you select verbs from PowerShell's standard set of verbs. If your module does not follow these standards, your users will receive a warning message when they load your module. For information about how make your module commands discoverable (and as domain-specific as required), see Recipe 11.8.

In addition to creating the *.psm1* file that contains your module's commands, you should also create a *module manifest* to describe its contents and system requirements. Module manifests let you define the module's author, company, copyright information, and more. For more information, see the `New-ModuleManifest` cmdlet.

After writing a module, the last step is making it available to the system. When you call `Import-Module <module name>` to load a module, PowerShell looks through each directory listed in the `PSModulePath` environment variable.

The PSModulePath variable is an environment variable, just like the system's PATH environment variable. For more information on how to view and modify environment variables, see Recipe 16.1.

If PowerShell finds a directory named *<module name>*, it looks in that directory for a *psm1* file with that name as well. Once it finds the *psm1* file, it loads that module into your session. In addition to *psm1* files, PowerShell also supports *module manifest* (*psd1*) files that let you define a great deal of information *about* the module: its author, description, nested modules, version requirements, and much more. For more information, type **Get-Help New-ModuleManifest**.

If you want to make your module available to just yourself (or the "current user" if installing your module as part of a setup process), place it in the per-user modules folder: *<My Documents>\WindowsPowerShell\Modules\<module name>*. If you want to make the module available to all users of the system, place your module in its own directory under the *Program Files* directory, and then add that directory to the system-wide PSModulePath environment variable.

If you don't want to permanently install your module, you can instead specify the complete path to the *psm1* file when you load the module. For example:

```
Import-Module c:\tools\Temperature.psm1
```

If you want to load a module from the same directory that your script is in, see Recipe 16.5.

When you load a module from a script, PowerShell makes the commands from that module available to the entire session. If your script loads the Temperature module, for example, the functions in that module will still be available after your script exits. To ensure that your script doesn't accidentally influence the user's session after it exits, you should remove any modules that you load:

```
$moduleToRemove = $null
if(-not (Get-Module <Module Name>))
{
    $moduleToRemove = Import-Module <Module Name> -Passthru
}


######################
##
## script goes here
##
######################

if($moduleToRemove)
{
    $moduleToRemove | Remove-Module
}
```

If you have a *module* that loads a helper module (as opposed to a *script* that loads a helper module), this step is not required. Modules loaded by a module impact only the module that loads them.

If you want to let users configure your module when they load it, you can define a parameter block at the beginning of your module. These parameters then get filled through the -ArgumentList parameter of the Import-Module command. For example, a module that takes a "retry count" and website as parameters:

```
param(
    [int] $RetryCount,
    [URI] $Website
)

function Get-Page
{
    ....
```

The user would load the module with the following command line:

```
Import-Module <module name> -ArgumentList 10,"http://www.example.com"
Get-Page "/index.html"
```

One important point when it comes to the -ArgumentList parameter is that its support for user input is much more limited than support offered for most scripts, functions, and script blocks. PowerShell lets you access the parameters in most param() statements by name, by alias, and in or out of order. Arguments supplied to the Import-Module command, on the other hand, must be supplied as values only, and in the exact order the module defines them.

For more information about accessing arguments of a command, see Recipe 11.11. For more information about importing a module (and the different types of modules available), see Recipe 1.24. For more information about modules, type **Get-Help about_Modules**.

See Also

Recipe 1.24, "Extend Your Shell with Additional Commands"

Recipe 11.11, "Access Arguments of a Script, Function, or Script Block"

Get-Help about_Modules

11.7 Write Commands That Maintain State

Problem

You have a function or script that needs to maintain state between invocations.

Solution

Place those commands in a *module*. Store any information you want to retain in a variable, and give that variable a SCRIPT scope. See Example 11-6.

Example 11-6. A module that maintains state

```
#############################################################################
##
## PersistentState.psm1
## Demonstrates persistent state through module-scoped variables
##
## From Windows PowerShell Cookbook (O'Reilly)
## by Lee Holmes (http://www.leeholmes.com/guide)
##
#############################################################################

$SCRIPT:memory = $null

function Set-Memory
{
    param(
        [Parameter(ValueFromPipeline = $true)]
        $item
    )

    begin { $SCRIPT:memory = New-Object System.Collections.ArrayList }
    process { $null = $memory.Add($item) }
}

function Get-Memory
{
    $memory.ToArray()
}

Set-Alias remember Set-Memory
Set-Alias recall Get-Memory

Export-ModuleMember -Function Set-Memory,Get-Memory
Export-ModuleMember -Alias remember,recall
```

Discussion

When writing scripts or commands, you'll frequently need to maintain state between the invocation of those commands. For example, your commands might remember user preferences, cache configuration data, or store other types of module state. See Example 11-7.

Example 11-7. Working with commands that maintain state

```
PS > Import-Module PersistentState
PS > Get-Process -Name PowerShell | remember
PS > recall
```

```
Handles  NPM(K)    PM(K)    WS(K) VM(M)   CPU(s)    Id ProcessName
-------  ------    -----    ----- -----   ------    -- -----------
    527       6    32704    44140   172     2.13  2644 powershell
    517       7    23080    33328   154     1.81  2812 powershell
    357       6    31848    33760   165     1.42  3576 powershell
```

In PowerShell version one, the only way to accomplish these goals was to store the information in a global variable. This introduces two problems, though.

The first problem is that global variables impact much more than just the script that defines them. Once your script stores information in a global variable, it pollutes the user's session. If the user has a variable with the same name, your script overwrites its contents. The second problem is the natural counterpart to this pollution. When your script stores information in a global variable, both the user and other scripts have access to it. Due to accident or curiosity, it is quite easy for these "internal" global variables to be damaged or corrupted.

PowerShell version two resolves this issue through the introduction of modules. By placing your commands in a module, PowerShell makes variables with a *script* scope available to all commands in that module. In addition to making script-scoped variables available to all of your commands, PowerShell maintains their value between invocations of those commands.

 Like variables, PowerShell drives obey the concept of scope. When you use the New-PSDrive cmdlet from within a module, that drive stays private to that module. To create a new drive that is visible from outside your module as well, create it with a *global* scope:

```
New-PSDrive -Name Temp FileSystem -Root C:\Temp -Scope Global
```

For more information about variables and their scopes, see Recipe 3.6. For more information about defining a module, see Recipe 11.6.

See Also

Recipe 3.6, "Control Access and Scope of Variables and Other Items"

Recipe 11.6, "Package Common Commands in a Module"

11.8 Selectively Export Commands from a Module

Problem

You have a module and want to export only certain commands from that module.

Solution

Use the `Export-ModuleMember` cmdlet to declare the specific commands you want exported. All other commands then remain internal to your module. See Example 11-8.

Example 11-8. Exporting specific commands from a module

```
##############################################################################
##
## SelectiveCommands.psm1
## Demonstrates the selective export of module commands
##
## From Windows PowerShell Cookbook (O'Reilly)
## by Lee Holmes (http://www.leeholmes.com/guide)
##
##############################################################################

## An internal helper function
function MyInternalHelperFunction
{
    "Result from my internal helper function"
}

## A command exported from the module
function Get-SelectiveCommandInfo
{
    "Getting information from the SelectiveCommands module"
    MyInternalHelperFunction
}

## Alternate names for our standard command
Set-Alias gsci Get-SelectiveCommandInfo
Set-Alias DomainSpecificVerb-Info Get-SelectiveCommandInfo

## Export specific commands
Export-ModuleMember -Function Get-SelectiveCommandInfo
Export-ModuleMember -Alias gsci,DomainSpecificVerb-Info
```

Discussion

When PowerShell imports a module, it imports all functions defined in that module by default. This makes it incredibly simple (as module authors) to create a library of related commands.

Once your module commands get more complex, you'll often write helper functions and support routines. Since these commands aren't intended to be exposed directly to users, you'll instead need to selectively export commands from your module. The `Export-ModuleMember` command allows exactly that.

Once your module includes a call to `Export-ModuleMember`, PowerShell no longer exports all functions in your module. Instead, it exports only the commands that you define. The first call to `Export-ModuleMember` in Example 11-8 demonstrates how to selectively export a function from a module.

Since consistency of command names is one of PowerShell's most beneficial features, PowerShell generates a warning message if your module exports functions (either explicitly or by default) that use nonstandard verbs. For example, imagine that you have a technology that uses *regenerate configuration* as a highly specific phrase for a task. In addition, it already has a `regen` command to accomplish this task.

You might naturally consider `Regenerate-Configuration` and `regen` as function names to export from your module, but doing that would alienate users who don't have a strong background in your technology. Without your same technical expertise, they wouldn't know the name of the command, and instead would instinctively look for `Reset-Configuration`, `Restore-Configuration`, or `Initialize-Configuration` based on their existing PowerShell knowledge. In this situation, the solution is to name your functions with a standard verb and *also* use command aliases to support your domain-specific experts.

The `Export-ModuleMember` cmdlet supports this situation as well. In addition to letting you selectively export commands from your module, it also lets you export alternative names (*aliases*) for your module commands. The second call to `Export-ModuleMember` in Example 11-8 (along with the alias definitions that precede it) demonstrates how to export aliases from a module.

For more information about command naming, see Recipe 11.3. For more information about writing a module, see Recipe 11.6.

See Also

Recipe 3.6, "Control Access and Scope of Variables and Other Items"

Recipe 11.3, "Find a Verb Appropriate for a Command Name"

Recipe 11.6, "Package Common Commands in a Module"

11.9 Diagnose and Interact with Internal Module State

Problem

You have a module and want to examine its internal variables and functions.

Solution

Use the `Enter-Module` script (Example 11-9) to temporarily enter the module and invoke commands within its scope.

Example 11-9. Invoking commands from within the scope of a module

```
#############################################################################
##
## Enter-Module
##
## From Windows PowerShell Cookbook (O'Reilly)
## by Lee Holmes (http://www.leeholmes.com/guide)
##
#############################################################################

<#

.SYNOPSIS

Lets you examine internal module state and functions by executing user
input in the scope of the supplied module.

.EXAMPLE

PS >Import-Module PersistentState
PS >Get-Module PersistentState

ModuleType Name                      ExportedCommands
---------- ----                      ----------------
Script     PersistentState           {Set-Memory, Get-Memory}


PS >"Hello World" | Set-Memory
PS >$m = Get-Module PersistentState
PS >Enter-Module $m
PersistentState: dir variable:\mem*

Name                      Value
----                      -----
memory                    {Hello World}

PersistentState: exit
PS >

#>

param(
    ## The module to examine
    [System.Management.Automation.PSModuleInfo] $Module
)

Set-StrictMode -Version Latest

$userInput = Read-Host $($module.Name)
while($userInput -ne "exit")
{
    $scriptblock = [ScriptBlock]::Create($userInput)
    & $module $scriptblock
```

```
    $userInput = Read-Host $($module.Name)
}
```

Discussion

PowerShell modules are an effective way to create sets of related commands that share private state. While commands in a module can share private state between themselves, PowerShell prevents that state from accidentally impacting the rest of your PowerShell session.

When you are developing a module, though, you might sometimes need to interact with this internal state for diagnostic purposes. To support this, PowerShell lets you target a specific module with the invocation (&) operator:

```
PS > $m = Get-Module PersistentState
PS > & $m { dir variable:\mem* }

Name                            Value
----                            -----
memory                          {Hello World}
```

This syntax gets cumbersome for more detailed investigation tasks, so Enter-Module automates the prompting and invocation for you.

For more information about writing a module, see Recipe 11.6.

See Also

Recipe 11.6, "Package Common Commands in a Module"

11.10 Handle Cleanup Tasks When a Module Is Removed

Problem

You have a module and want to perform some action (such as cleanup tasks) when that module is removed.

Solution

Assign a script block to the $MyInvocation.MyCommand.ScriptBlock.Module.OnRemove event. Place any cleanup commands in that script block. See Example 11-10.

Example 11-10. Handling cleanup tasks from within a module

```
##############################################################################
##
## TidyModule.psm1
## Demonstrates how to handle cleanup tasks when a module is removed
##
## From Windows PowerShell Cookbook (O'Reilly)
## by Lee Holmes (http://www.leeholmes.com/guide)
##
##############################################################################

<#

.EXAMPLE

PS >Import-Module TidyModule
PS >$TidyModuleStatus
Initialized
PS >Remove-Module TidyModule
PS >$TidyModuleStatus
Cleaned Up

#>

## Perform some initialization tasks
$GLOBAL:TidyModuleStatus = "Initialized"

## Register for cleanup
$MyInvocation.MyCommand.ScriptBlock.Module.OnRemove = {
    $GLOBAL:TidyModuleStatus = "Cleaned Up"
}
```

Discussion

PowerShell modules have a natural way to define initialization requirements (any script written in the body of the module), but cleanup requirements are not as simple.

During module creation, you can access your module through the $My Invocation.MyCommand.ScriptBlock.Module property. Each module has an OnRemove event, which you can then subscribe to by assigning it a script block. When PowerShell unloads your module, it invokes that script block.

Beware of using this technique for extremely sensitive cleanup requirements. If the user simply exits the PowerShell window, the OnRemove event is not processed. If this is a concern, register for the PowerShell.Exiting engine event and remove your module from there:

```
Register-EngineEvent PowerShell.Exiting { Remove-Module TidyModule }
```

For PowerShell to handle this event, the user must use the exit keyword to close the session, rather than the X button at the top right of the console window. In the

Integrated Scripting Environment, the close button generates this event as well. This saves the user from having to remember to call `Remove-Module`.

For more information about writing a module, see Recipe 11.6. For more information about PowerShell events, see Recipe 31.2.

See Also

Recipe 11.6, "Package Common Commands in a Module"

Recipe 31.2, "Create and Respond to Custom Events"

11.11 Access Arguments of a Script, Function, or Script Block

Problem

You want to access the arguments provided to a script, function, or script block.

Solution

To access arguments by name, use a `param` statement:

```
param($firstNamedArgument, [int] $secondNamedArgument = 0)

"First named argument is: $firstNamedArgument"
"Second named argument is: $secondNamedArgument"
```

To access unnamed arguments by position, use the `$args` array:

```
"First positional argument is: " + $args[0]
"Second positional argument is: " + $args[1]
```

You can use these techniques in exactly the same way with scripts, functions, and script blocks, as illustrated by Example 11-11.

Example 11-11. Working with arguments in scripts, functions, and script blocks

```
##############################################################################
##
## Get-Arguments
##
## From Windows PowerShell Cookbook (O'Reilly)
## by Lee Holmes (http://www.leeholmes.com/guide)
##
##############################################################################

<#

.SYNOPSIS

Uses command-line arguments

#>
```

```
param(
    ## The first named argument
    $FirstNamedArgument,

    ## The second named argument
    [int] $SecondNamedArgument = 0
)

Set-StrictMode -Version Latest

## Display the arguments by name
"First named argument is: $firstNamedArgument"
"Second named argument is: $secondNamedArgument"

function GetArgumentsFunction
{
    ## We could use a param statement here, as well
    ## param($firstNamedArgument, [int] $secondNamedArgument = 0)

    ## Display the arguments by position
    "First positional function argument is: " + $args[0]
    "Second positional function argument is: " + $args[1]
}

GetArgumentsFunction One Two

$scriptBlock =
{
    param($firstNamedArgument, [int] $secondNamedArgument = 0)

    ## We could use $args here, as well
    "First named scriptblock argument is: $firstNamedArgument"
    "Second named scriptblock argument is: $secondNamedArgument"
}

& $scriptBlock -First One -Second 4.5
```

Example 11-11 produces the following output:

```
PS > Get-Arguments First 2
First named argument is: First
Second named argument is: 2
First positional function argument is: One
Second positional function argument is: Two
First named scriptblock argument is: One
Second named scriptblock argument is: 4
```

Discussion

Although PowerShell supports both the param keyword and the $args array, you will most commonly want to use the param keyword to define and access script, function, and script block parameters.

In most languages, the most common reason to access parameters through an $args array is to determine the name of the currently running script. For information about how to do this in PowerShell, see Recipe 16.2.

When you use the param keyword to define your parameters, PowerShell provides your script or function with many useful features that allow users to work with your script much as they work with cmdlets:

- Users need to specify only enough of the parameter name to disambiguate it from other parameters.
- Users can understand the meaning of your parameters much more clearly.
- You can specify the type of your parameters, which PowerShell uses to convert input if required.
- You can specify default values for your parameters.

Supporting PowerShell's common parameters

In addition to the parameters you define, you might also want to support PowerShell's standard parameters: -Verbose, -Debug, -ErrorAction, -WarningAction, -ErrorVariable, -WarningVariable, -OutVariable, and -OutBuffer.

To get these additional parameters, add the [CmdletBinding()] attribute inside your function, or declare it at the top of your script. The param() statement is required, even if your function or script declares no parameters. These (and other associated) additional features now make your function an *advanced function*. See Example 11-12.

Example 11-12. Declaring an advanced function

```
function Invoke-MyAdvancedFunction
{
    [CmdletBinding()]
    param()

    Write-Verbose "Verbose Message"
}
```

If your function defines a parameter with advanced *validation*, you don't need to explicitly add the [CmdletBinding()] attribute. In that case, PowerShell already knows to treat your command as an advanced function.

 During PowerShell's beta phases, *advanced functions* were known as *script cmdlets*. We decided to change the name because the term *script cmdlets* caused a sense of fear of the great unknown. Users would be comfortable writing functions, but "didn't have the time to learn those new script cmdlet things." Because script cmdlets were just regular functions with additional power, the new name made a lot more sense.

Although PowerShell adds all of its common parameters to your function, you don't actually need to implement the code to support them. For example, calls to Write-Verbose usually generate no output. When the user specifies the -Verbose parameter to your function, PowerShell then automatically displays the output of the Write-Verbose cmdlet.

```
PS > Invoke-MyAdvancedFunction
PS > Invoke-MyAdvancedFunction -Verbose
VERBOSE: Verbose Message
```

If your cmdlet modifies system state, it is extremely helpful to support the standard -WhatIf and -Confirm parameters. For information on how to accomplish this, see Recipe 11.15.

Using the $args array

Despite all of the power exposed by named parameters, common parameters, and advanced functions, the $args array is still sometimes helpful. For example, it provides a clean way to deal with all arguments at once:

```
function Reverse
{
    $argsEnd = $args.Length - 1
    $args[$argsEnd..0]
}
```

This produces:

```
PS > Reverse 1 2 3 4
4
3
2
1
```

For more information about the param statement, see "Writing Scripts, Reusing Functionality" on page 746. For more information about running scripts, see Recipe 1.1. For more information about functionality (such as -Whatif and -Confirm) exposed by the PowerShell engine, see Recipe 11.15.

For information about how to declare parameters with rich validation and behavior, see Recipe 11.12.

See Also

Recipe 1.1, "Run Programs, Scripts, and Existing Tools"

Recipe 11.12, "Add Validation to Parameters"

Recipe 11.15, "Provide -WhatIf, -Confirm, and Other Cmdlet Features"

Recipe 16.2, "Access Information About Your Command's Invocation"

"Writing Scripts, Reusing Functionality" on page 746

11.12 Add Validation to Parameters

Problem

You want to ensure that user input to a parameter satisfies certain restrictions or constraints.

Solution

Use the [Parameter()] attribute to declare the parameter as mandatory, positional, part of a mutually exclusive set of parameters, or able to receive its input from the pipeline.

```
param(
    [Parameter(
        Mandatory = $true,
        Position = 0,
        ValueFromPipeline = $true,
        ValueFromPipelineByPropertyName = $true)]
    [string[]] $Name
)
```

Use additional validation attributes to define aliases, support for null or empty values, count restrictions (for collections), length restrictions (for strings), regular expression requirements, range requirements (for numbers), permissible value requirements, or even arbitrary script requirements.

```
param(
    [ValidateLength(5,10)]
    [string] $Name
)

"Hello $Name"
```

Discussion

Traditional shells require extensions (scripts and commands) to write their parameter support by hand, resulting in a wide range of behavior. Some implement a bare, confusing minimum of support. Others implement more complex features, but differently than any other command. The bare, confusing minimum is by far the most common, as writing fully featured parameter support is a complex endeavor.

Luckily, the PowerShell engine already wrote all of the complex parameter handling support and manages all of this detail for you. Rather than write the code to enforce it, you can simply mark parameters as mandatory or positional or state their validation requirements. This built-in support for parameter behavior and validation forms a centerpiece of PowerShell's unique consistency.

Parameter validation is one of the main distinctions between scripts that are well behaved and those that are not. When running a new script (or one you wrote distantly in the past), reviewing the parameter definitions and validation requirements is one of the quickest ways to familiarize yourself with how that script behaves.

From the script author's perspective, validation requirements save you from writing verification code that you'll need to write anyway.

Defining parameter behavior

The elements of the [`Parameter()`] attribute mainly define how your parameter behaves in relation to other parameters. All elements are optional.

`Mandatory` = *$true*
> Defines the parameter as mandatory. If the user doesn't supply a value to this parameter, PowerShell automatically prompts the user for it. When not specified, the parameter is optional.

`Position` = *position*
> Defines the position of this parameter. This applies when the user provides parameter values without specifying the parameter they apply to (for example, *Argument2* in `Invoke-MyFunction` *-Param1 Argument1 Argument2*). PowerShell supplies these values to parameters that have defined a *Position*, from lowest to highest. When not specified, the name of this parameter must be supplied by the user.

`ParameterSetName` = *name*
> Defines this parameter as a member of a set of other related parameters. Parameter behavior for this parameter is then specific to this related set of parameters, and the parameter exists only in parameter sets in which it is defined. This feature is used, for example, when the user may supply only a Name *or* ID. To include a parameter in two or more specific parameter sets, use two or more [`Parameter()`] attributes. When not specified, this parameter is a member of all parameter sets. To define the default parameter set name of your cmdlet, supply it in the `CmdletBinding` attribute: [`CmdletBinding(DefaultParameterSetName` = *"Name"*)].

`ValueFromPipeline` = *$true*
> Declares this parameter as one that directly accepts pipeline input. If the user pipes data into your script or function, PowerShell assigns this input to your parameter in your command's `process {}` block. For more information about accepting pipeline input, see Recipe 11.18. Beware of applying this parameter to `String` parameters, as almost all input can be converted to strings—often producing a result that doesn't make much sense. When not specified, this parameter does not accept pipeline input directly.

`ValueFromPipelineByPropertyName` = *$true*
> Declares this parameter as one that accepts pipeline input if a property of an incoming object matches its name. If this is true, PowerShell assigns the value of that property to your parameter in your command's `process {}` block. For more

information about accepting pipeline input, see Recipe 11.18. When not specified, this parameter does not accept pipeline input by property name.

ValueFromRemainingArguments = *$true*

Declares this parameter as one that accepts all remaining input that has not otherwise been assigned to positional or named parameters. Only one parameter can have this element. If no parameter declares support for this capability, PowerShell generates an error for arguments that cannot be assigned.

Defining parameter validation

In addition to the [Parameter()] attribute, PowerShell lets you apply other attributes that add additional behavior or validation constraints to your parameters. All validation attributes are optional.

[Alias("*name*")]

Defines an alternate name for this parameter. This is especially helpful for long parameter names that are descriptive but have a more common colloquial term. When not specified, the parameter can be referred to only by the name you originally declared. You can supply many aliases to a parameter. To learn about aliases for command parameters, see Recipe 1.15.

[AllowNull()]

Allows this parameter to receive $null as its value. This is required only for mandatory parameters. When not specified, mandatory parameters cannot receive $null as their value, although optional parameters can.

[AllowEmptyString()]

Allows this string parameter to receive an empty string as its value. This is required only for mandatory parameters. When not specified, mandatory string parameters cannot receive an empty string as their value, although optional string parameters can. You can apply this to parameters that are not strings, but it has no impact.

[AllowEmptyCollection()]

Allows this collection parameter to receive an empty collection as its value. This is required only for mandatory parameters. When not specified, mandatory collection parameters cannot receive an empty collection as their value, although optional collection parameters can. You can apply this to parameters that are not collections, but it has no impact.

[ValidateCount(*lower limit, upper limit*)]

Restricts the number of elements that can be in a collection supplied to this parameter. When not specified, mandatory parameters have a lower limit of one element. Optional parameters have no restrictions. You can apply this to parameters that are not collections, but it has no impact.

[ValidateLength(*lower limit, upper limit*)]

Restricts the length of strings that this parameter can accept. When not specified, mandatory parameters have a lower limit of one character. Optional parameters have no restrictions. You can apply this to parameters that are not strings, but it has no impact.

[ValidatePattern("*regular expression*")]

Enforces a pattern that input to this string parameter must match. When not specified, string inputs have no pattern requirements. You can apply this to parameters that are not strings, but it has no impact.

If your parameter has a pattern requirement, though, it may be more effective to validate the parameter in the body of your script or function instead. The error message that PowerShell generates when a parameter fails [ValidatePattern()] validation is not very user-friendly ("The argument ... does not match the *<pattern>* pattern"). Instead, it might be more helpful to generate a message explaining the *intent* of the pattern:

```
if($EmailAddress -notmatch Pattern)
{
    throw "Please specify a valid email address."
}
```

[ValidateRange(*lower limit, upper limit*)]

Restricts the upper and lower limit of numerical arguments that this parameter can accept. When not specified, parameters have no range limit. You can apply this to parameters that are not numbers, but it has no impact.

[ValidateScript({ *script block* })]

Ensures that input supplied to this parameter satisfies the condition that you supply in the script block. PowerShell assigns the proposed input to the $_ variable, and then invokes your script block. If the script block returns $true (or anything that can be converted to $true, such as nonempty strings), PowerShell considers the validation to have been successful.

[ValidateSet("*First Option*", "*Second Option*", ..., "*Last Option*")]

Ensures that input supplied to this parameter is equal to one of the options in the set. PowerShell uses its standard meaning of equality during this comparison (the same rules used by the -eq operator). If your validation requires nonstandard rules (such as case-sensitive comparison of strings), you can instead write the validation in the body of the script or function.

[ValidateNotNull()]

Ensures that input supplied to this parameter is not null. This is the default behavior of mandatory parameters, and this attribute is useful only for optional parameters. When applied to string parameters, a $null parameter value instead gets converted to an empty string.

[ValidateNotNullOrEmpty()]

Ensures that input supplied to this parameter is neither null nor empty. This is the default behavior of mandatory parameters, and this attribute is useful only for optional parameters. When applied to string parameters, the input must be a string with a length greater than one. When applied to collection parameters, the

collection must have at least one element. When applied to other types of parameters, this attribute is equivalent to the `[ValidateNotNull()]` attribute.

See Also

Recipe 1.15, "Program: Learn Aliases for Common Parameters"

Recipe 11.18, "Access Pipeline Input"

"Providing Input to Commands" on page 750

`Get-Help about_functions_advanced_parameters`

11.13 Accept Script Block Parameters with Local Variables

Problem

Your command takes a script block as a parameter. When you invoke that script block,
you want variables to refer to variables from the user's session, not your script.

Solution

Call the `GetNewClosure()` method on the supplied script block before either defining
any of your own variables or invoking the script block. See Example 11-13.

Example 11-13. A command that supports variables from the user's session

```
###############################################################################
##
## Invoke-ScriptBlockClosure
##
## From Windows PowerShell Cookbook (O'Reilly)
## by Lee Holmes (http://www.leeholmes.com/guide)
##
###############################################################################

<#

.SYNOPSIS

Demonstrates the GetNewClosure() method on a script block that pulls variables
in from the user's session (if they are defined).

.EXAMPLE

PS >$name = "Hello There"
PS >Invoke-ScriptBlockClosure { $name }
Hello There
Hello World
Hello There

#>
```

```
param(
    ## The script block to invoke
    [ScriptBlock] $ScriptBlock
)

Set-StrictMode -Version Latest

## Create a new script block that pulls variables
## from the user's scope (if defined).
$closedScriptBlock = $scriptBlock.GetNewClosure()

## Invoke the script block normally. The contents of
## the $name variable will be from the user's session.
& $scriptBlock

## Define a new variable
$name = "Hello World"

## Invoke the script block normally. The contents of
## the $name variable will be "Hello World", now from
## our scope.
& $scriptBlock

## Invoke the "closed" script block. The contents of
## the $name variable will still be whatever was in the user's session
## (if it was defined).
& $closedScriptBlock
```

Discussion

Whenever you invoke a script block (for example, one passed by the user as a parameter value), PowerShell treats variables in that script block as though you had typed them yourself. For example, if a variable referenced by the script block is defined in your script or module, PowerShell will use that value when it evaluates the variable.

This is often desirable behavior, although its use ultimately depends on your script. For example, Recipe 11.4 accepts a script block parameter that is intended to refer to variables defined *within* the script: $_, specifically.

Alternatively, this might not always be what you want. Sometimes, you might prefer that variable names refer to variables from the *user's session*, rather than potentially from your script.

The solution, in this case, is to call the GetNewClosure() method. This method makes the script block self-contained, or *closed*. Variables maintain the value they had when the GetNewClosure() method was called, even if a new variable with that name is created.

See Also

Recipe 3.6, "Control Access and Scope of Variables and Other Items"

Recipe 11.4, "Write a Script Block"

11.14 Dynamically Compose Command Parameters

Problem

You want to specify the parameters of a command you are about to invoke but don't know beforehand what those parameters will be.

Solution

Define the parameters and their values as elements of a hashtable, and then use the @ character to pass that hashtable to a command:

```
PS > $parameters = @{
    Name = "PowerShell";
    WhatIf = $true
}

PS > Stop-Process @parameters
What if: Performing operation "Stop-Process" on Target "powershell (2380)".
What if: Performing operation "Stop-Process" on Target "powershell (2792)".
```

Discussion

When writing commands that call other commands, a common problem is not knowing the exact parameter values that you'll pass to a target command. The solution to this is simple, and comes by storing the parameter values in variables:

```
PS > function Stop-ProcessWhatIf($name)
{
    Stop-Process -Name $name -Whatif
}

PS > Stop-ProcessWhatIf PowerShell
What if: Performing operation "Stop-Process" on Target "powershell (2380)".
What if: Performing operation "Stop-Process" on Target "powershell (2792)".
```

In version one of PowerShell, things were unreasonably more difficult if you didn't know beforehand which parameter *names* you wanted to pass along. Version two of PowerShell significantly improves the situation through a technique called *splatting* that lets you pass along parameter values *and* names.

The first step is to define a variable, for example, `parameters`. In that variable, store a hashtable of parameter names and their values. When you call a command, you can pass the hashtable of parameter names and values with the @ character and the variable name that stores them. Note that you use the @ character to represent the variable, instead of the usual $ character:

```
Stop-Process @parameters
```

This is a common need when writing commands that are designed to enhance or extend existing commands. In that situation, you simply want to pass all of the user's input (parameter values *and* names) on to the existing command, even though you don't know exactly what they supplied.

To simplify this situation even further, *advanced functions* have access to an automatic variable called PSBoundParameters. This automatic variable is a hashtable that stores all parameters passed to the current command, and it is suitable for both tweaking and splatting. For an example of this approach, see Recipe 11.23. For more information about advanced functions, see Recipe 11.11.

See Also

Recipe 11.11, "Access Arguments of a Script, Function, or Script Block"

Recipe 11.23, "Program: Enhance or Extend an Existing Cmdlet"

11.15 Provide -WhatIf, -Confirm, and Other Cmdlet Features

Problem

You want to support the standard -WhatIf and -Confirm parameters, and access cmdlet-centric support in the PowerShell engine.

Solution

Ensure your script or function declares the [CmdletBinding()] attribute, and then access engine features through the $psCmdlet automatic variable.

```
function Invoke-MyAdvancedFunction
{
    [CmdletBinding(SupportsShouldProcess = $true)]
    param()

    if($psCmdlet.ShouldProcess("test.txt", "Remove Item"))
    {
        "Removing test.txt"
    }

    Write-Verbose "Verbose Message"
}
```

Discussion

When a script or function progresses to an *advanced function*, PowerShell defines an additional $psCmdlet automatic variable. This automatic variable exposes support for the -ShouldProcess and -Confirm automatic parameters. If your command defined parameter sets, it also exposes the parameter set name that PowerShell selected based on the user's choice of parameters. For more information about advanced functions, see Recipe 11.11.

To support the -WhatIf and -Confirm parameters, add the [CmdletBinding(Supports ShouldProcess = $true)] attribute inside of your script or function. You should support this on any scripts or functions that modify system state, as they let your users investigate what your script will do before actually doing it. Then, you simply surround the portion of your script that changes the system with an if($psCmdlet.ShouldProcess(...)) { } block. Example 11-14 demonstrates this approach.

Example 11-14. Adding support for -WhatIf and -Confirm

```
function Invoke-MyAdvancedFunction
{
    [CmdletBinding(SupportsShouldProcess = $true)]
    param()

    if($psCmdlet.ShouldProcess("test.txt", "Remove Item"))
    {
        "Removing test.txt"
    }

    Write-Verbose "Verbose Message"
}
```

Now your advanced function is as well-behaved as built-in PowerShell cmdlets!

```
PS > Invoke-MyAdvancedFunction -WhatIf
What if: Performing operation "Remove Item" on Target "test.txt".
```

If your command causes a high-impact result that should be evaluated with caution, call the $psCmdlet.ShouldContinue() method. This generates a warning for users—but be sure to support a -Force parameter that lets them bypass this message.

```
function Invoke-MyDangerousFunction
{
    [CmdletBinding()]
    param(
        [Switch] $Force
    )

    if($Force -or $psCmdlet.ShouldContinue(
        "Do you wish to invoke this dangerous operation? Changes can not be undone.",
        "Invoke dangerous action?"))
    {
        "Invoking dangerous action"
    }
}
```

This generates a standard PowerShell confirmation message:

```
PS > Invoke-MyDangerousFunction

Invoke dangerous action?
Do you wish to invoke this dangerous operation? Changes can not be undone.
[Y] Yes  [N] No  [S] Suspend  [?] Help (default is "Y"):
```

```
Invoking dangerous action

PS > Invoke-MyDangerousFunction -Force
Invoking dangerous action
```

To explore the $psCmdlet automatic variable further, you can use Example 11-15. This command creates the bare minimum of advanced function, and then invokes whatever script block you supply within it.

Example 11-15. Invoke-AdvancedFunction.ps1

```
param(
    [Parameter(Mandatory = $true)]
    [ScriptBlock] $Scriptblock
    )

## Invoke the script block supplied by the user.
& $scriptblock
```

For open-ended exploration, use `$host.EnterNestedPrompt()` as the script block:

```
PS > Invoke-AdvancedFunction { $host.EnterNestedPrompt() }
PS > $psCmdlet | Get-Member


    TypeName: System.Management.Automation.PSScriptCmdlet

Name                         MemberType Definition
----                         ---------- ----------
(...)
WriteDebug                   Method     System.Void WriteDebug(s...
WriteError                   Method     System.Void WriteError(S...
WriteObject                  Method     System.Void WriteObject(...
WriteProgress                Method     System.Void WriteProgres...
WriteVerbose                 Method     System.Void WriteVerbose...
WriteWarning                 Method     System.Void WriteWarning...
(...)
ParameterSetName             Property   System.String ParameterS...

PS > >exit
PS >
```

For more about cmdlet support in the PowerShell engine, see the developer's reference at *http://msdn.microsoft.com/en-us/library/dd878294%28VS.85%29.aspx*.

See Also

Recipe 11.11, "Access Arguments of a Script, Function, or Script Block"

11.16 Add Help to Scripts or Functions

Problem

You want to make your command and usage information available to the Get-Help command.

Solution

Add descriptive help comments at the beginning of your script for its synopsis, description, examples, notes, and more. Add descriptive help comments before parameters to describe their meaning and behavior.

```
##############################################################################
##
##    Measure-CommandPerformance
##
##    From Windows PowerShell Cookbook (O'Reilly)
##    by Lee Holmes (http://www.leeholmes.com/guide)
##
##############################################################################

<#

.SYNOPSIS
Measures the average time of a command, accounting for natural variability by
automatically ignoring the top and bottom ten percent.

.EXAMPLE
PS > .\Measure-CommandPerformance.ps1 { Start-Sleep -m 300 }

Count    : 30
Average  : 312.10155
(...)

#>

param(
    ## The command to measure
    [Scriptblock] $command,

    ## The number of times to measure the command's performance
    [int] $iterations = 30)

(...)
```

Discussion

Like parameter validation, discussed in Recipe 11.12, rich help is something traditionally supported in only the most high-end commands. For most commands, you're lucky if you can figure out how to get some form of usage message.

As with PowerShell's easy-to-define support for advanced parameter validation, adding help to commands and functions is extremely simple. Despite its simplicity, comment-based help provides all the power you've come to expect of fully featured PowerShell commands: overview, description, examples, parameter-specific details, and more.

PowerShell creates help for your script or function by looking at its comments. If the comments include any supported help tags, PowerShell adds those to the help for your command.

 To speed up processing of these help comments, PowerShell places restrictions on where they may appear. In addition, if it encounters a comment that is *not* a help-based comment, it stops searching that block of comments for help tags. This may come as a surprise if you are used to placing headers or copyright information at the beginning of your script. The solution demonstrates how to avoid this problem by putting the header and comment-based help in separate comment blocks. For more information about these guidelines, type **Get-Help about_Comment_Based_Help**.

You can place your help tags in either single-line comments or multiline (block) comments. You may find multiline comments easier to work with, as you can write them in editors that support spelling and grammar checks and then simply paste them into your script. Also, adjusting the word-wrapping of your comment is easier when you don't have to repair comment markers at the beginning of the line. From the user's perspective, multiline comments offer a significant benefit for the .EXAMPLES section because they require much less modification before being tried.

Comment-based help supports the following tags, which are all case-insensitive.

.SYNOPSIS
    A short summary of the command, ideally a single sentence.

.DESCRIPTION
    A more detailed description of the command.

.PARAMETER *name*
    A description of parameter *name*, with one for each parameter you want to describe. While you can write a .PARAMETER comment for each parameter, PowerShell also supports comments written directly above the parameter (as shown in the solution). Putting parameter help alongside the actual parameter makes it easier to read and maintain.

.EXAMPLE
    An example of this command in use, with one for each example you want to provide. PowerShell treats the line immediately beneath the .EXAMPLE tag as the example command. If this line doesn't contain any text that looks like a prompt,

PowerShell adds a prompt before it. It treats lines that follow the initial line as additional output and example commentary.

.INPUTS

A short summary of pipeline input(s) supported by this command. For each input type, PowerShell's built-in help follows this convention:

```
System.String
    You can pipe a string that contains a path to Get-ChildItem.
```

.OUTPUTS

A short summary of items generated by this command. For each output type, PowerShell's built-in help follows this convention:

```
System.ServiceProcess.ServiceController
    Get-Service returns objects that represent the services on the computer.
```

.NOTES

Any additional notes or remarks about this command.

.LINK

A link to a related help topic or command, with one .LINK tag per link. If the related help topic is a URL, PowerShell launches that URL when the user supplies the -Online parameter to Get-Help for your command.

Although these are all of the supported help tags you are likely to use, comment-based help also supports tags for some of Get-Help's more obscure features: .COMPONENT, .ROLE, .FUNCTIONALITY, .FORWARDHELPTARGETNAME, .FORWARDHELPCATE GORY, .REMOTEHELPRUNSPACE, and .EXTERNALHELP. For more information about these, type **Get-Help about_Comment_Based_Help**.

See Also

Recipe 11.12, "Add Validation to Parameters"

Get-Help about_Comment_Based_Help

11.17 Add Custom Tags to a Function or Script Block

Problem

You want to tag or add your own custom information to a function or script block.

Solution

If you want the custom information to always be associated with the function or script block, declare a System.ComponentModel.Description attribute inside that function:

```
function TestFunction
{
    [System.ComponentModel.Description("Information I care about")]
```

```
    param()

    "Some function with metadata"
}
```

If you don't control the source code of the function, create a new System.ComponentModel.Description attribute, and add it to the script block's Attributes collection manually:

```
$testFunction = Get-Command TestFunction
$newAttribute =
    New-Object ComponentModel.DescriptionAttribute "More information I care about"
$testFunction.ScriptBlock.Attributes.Add($newAttribute)
```

To retrieve any attributes associated with a function or script block, access the Script Block.Attributes property:

```
PS > $testFunction = Get-Command TestFunction
PS > $testFunction.ScriptBlock.Attributes

Description                      TypeId
-----------                      ------
Information I care about         System.ComponentModel.Description...
```

Discussion

Although a specialized need for sure, it is sometimes helpful to add your own custom information to functions or script blocks. For example, once you've built up a large set of functions, many are really useful only in a specific context. Some functions might apply to only one of your clients, whereas others are written for a custom website you're developing. If you forget the name of a function, you might have difficulty going through all of your functions to find the ones that apply to your current context.

You might find it helpful to write a new function, Get-CommandForContext, that takes a context (for example, *website*) and returns only commands that apply to that context.

```
function Get-CommandForContext($context)
{
    Get-Command -CommandType Function |
        Where-Object { $_.ScriptBlock.Attributes |
            Where-Object { $_.Description -eq "Context=$context" } }
}
```

Then write some functions that apply to specific contexts:

```
function WebsiteFunction
{
    [System.ComponentModel.Description("Context=Website")]
    param()

    "Some function I use with my website"
}

function ExchangeFunction
{
```

```
        [System.ComponentModel.Description("Context=Exchange")]
        param()

        "Some function I use with Exchange"
    }
```

Then, by building on these two, we have a context-sensitive equivalent to Get-Command:

```
PS > Get-CommandForContext Website

CommandType    Name                        Definition
-----------    ----                        ----------
Function       WebsiteFunction             ...


PS > Get-CommandForContext Exchange

CommandType    Name                        Definition
-----------    ----                        ----------
Function       ExchangeFunction            ...
```

While the System.ComponentModel.Description attribute is the most generically useful, PowerShell lets you place any attribute in a function. You can define your own (by deriving from the System.Attribute class in the .NET Framework) or use any of the other attributes included in the .NET Framework. Example 11-16 shows the Power-Shell commands to find all attributes that have a constructor that takes a single string as its argument. These attributes are likely to be generally useful.

Example 11-16. Finding all useful attributes

```
$types = [Appdomain]::CurrentDomain.GetAssemblies() |
    Foreach-Object { $_.GetTypes() }

foreach($type in $types)
{
    if($type.BaseType -eq [System.Attribute])
    {
        foreach($constructor in $type.GetConstructors())
        {
            if($constructor.ToString() -match "\(System.String\)")
            {
                $type
            }
        }
    }
}
```

For more information about working with .NET objects, see Recipe 3.8.

See Also

Recipe 3.8, "Work with .NET Objects"

11.18 Access Pipeline Input

Problem

You want to interact with input that a user sends to your function, script, or script block via the pipeline.

Solution

To access pipeline input, use the $input variable, as shown in Example 11-17.

Example 11-17. Accessing pipeline input

```
function InputCounter
{
    $count = 0

    ## Go through each element in the pipeline, and add up
    ## how many elements there were.
    foreach($element in $input)
    {
        $count++
    }

    $count
}
```

This function produces the following (or similar) output when run against your Windows system directory:

```
PS > dir $env:WINDIR | InputCounter
295
```

Discussion

In your scripts, functions, and script blocks, the $input variable represents an *enumerator* (as opposed to a simple array) for the pipeline input the user provides. An enumerator lets you use a foreach statement to efficiently scan over the elements of the input (as shown in Example 11-17) but does not let you directly access specific items (such as the fifth element in the input, for example).

> An enumerator only lets you scan forward through its contents. Once you access an element, PowerShell automatically moves on to the next one. If you need to access an item that you've already accessed, you must either call $input.Reset() to scan through the list again from the beginning or store the input in an array.

If you need to access specific elements in the input (or access items multiple times), the best approach is to store the input in an array. This prevents your script from taking advantage of the $input enumerator's streaming behavior, but is sometimes the only alternative. To store the input in an array, use PowerShell's list evaluation syntax (@()) to force PowerShell to interpret it as an array.

```
function ReverseInput
{
    $inputArray = @($input)
    $inputEnd = $inputArray.Count - 1

    $inputArray[$inputEnd..0]
}
```

This produces:

```
PS > 1,2,3,4 | ReverseInput
4
3
2
1
```

If dealing with pipeline input plays a major role in your script, function, or script block, PowerShell provides an alternative means of dealing with pipeline input that may make your script easier to write and understand. For more information, see Recipe 11.19.

See Also

Recipe 11.19, "Write Pipeline-Oriented Scripts with Cmdlet Keywords"

11.19 Write Pipeline-Oriented Scripts with Cmdlet Keywords

Problem

Your script, function, or script block primarily takes input from the pipeline, and you want to write it in a way that makes this intention both easy to implement and easy to read.

Solution

To cleanly separate your script into regions that deal with the initialization, per-record processing, and cleanup portions, use the begin, process, and end keywords, respectively. For example, a pipeline-oriented conversion of the solution in Recipe 11.18 looks like Example 11-18.

Example 11-18. A pipeline-oriented script that uses cmdlet keywords

```
function InputCounter
{
    begin
    {
        $count = 0
        {
```

```
## Go through each element in the pipeline, and add up
## how many elements there were.
process
{
    Write-Debug "Processing element $_"
    $count++
}

end
{
    $count
}
}
```

This produces the following output:

```
PS > $debugPreference = "Continue"
PS > dir | InputCounter
DEBUG: Processing element Compare-Property.ps1
DEBUG: Processing element Connect-WebService.ps1
DEBUG: Processing element Convert-TextObject.ps1
DEBUG: Processing element ConvertFrom-FahrenheitWithFunction.ps1
DEBUG: Processing element ConvertFrom-FahrenheitWithoutFunction.ps1
DEBUG: Processing element Get-AliasSuggestion.ps1
(...)
DEBUG: Processing element Select-FilteredObject.ps1
DEBUG: Processing element Set-ConsoleProperties.ps1
20
```

Discussion

If your script, function, or script block deals primarily with input from the pipeline, the begin, process, and end keywords let you express your solution most clearly. Readers of your script (including you!) can easily see which portions of your script deal with initialization, per-record processing, and cleanup. In addition, separating your code into these blocks lets your script consume elements from the pipeline as soon as the previous script produces them.

Take, for example, the Get-InputWithForeach and Get-InputWithKeyword functions shown in Example 11-19. The first function visits each element in the pipeline with a foreach statement over its input, whereas the second uses the begin, process, and end keywords.

Example 11-19. Two functions that take different approaches to processing pipeline input

```
## From Windows PowerShell Cookbook (O'Reilly)
## by Lee Holmes (http://www.leeholmes.com/guide)

Set-StrictMode -Version Latest

## Process each element in the pipeline, using a
## foreach statement to visit each element in $input
function Get-InputWithForeach($identifier)
```

```
{
    Write-Host "Beginning InputWithForeach (ID: $identifier)"

    foreach($element in $input)
    {
        Write-Host "Processing element $element (ID: $identifier)"
        $element
    }

    Write-Host "Ending InputWithForeach (ID: $identifier)"
}

## Process each element in the pipeline, using the
## cmdlet-style keywords to visit each element in $input
function Get-InputWithKeyword($identifier)
{
    begin
    {
        Write-Host "Beginning InputWithKeyword (ID: $identifier)"
    }

    process
    {
        Write-Host "Processing element $_ (ID: $identifier)"
        $_
    }

    end
    {
        Write-Host "Ending InputWithKeyword (ID: $identifier)"
    }
}
```

Both of these functions act the same when run individually, but the difference becomes clear when we combine them with other scripts or functions that take pipeline input. When a script uses the $input variable, it must wait until the previous script finishes producing output before it can start. If the previous script takes a long time to produce all its records (for example, a large directory listing), then your user must wait until the entire directory listing completes to see any results, rather than seeing results for each item as the script generates it.

 If a script, function, or script block uses the cmdlet-style keywords, it must place all its code (aside from comments or its param statement if it uses one) inside one of the three blocks. If your code needs to define and initialize variables or define functions, place them in the begin block. Unlike most blocks of code contained within curly braces, the code in the begin, process, and end blocks has access to variables and functions defined within the blocks before it.

When we chain together two scripts that process their input with the begin, process, and end keywords, the second script gets to process input as soon as the first script produces it.

```
PS > 1,2,3 | Get-InputWithKeyword 1 | Get-InputWithKeyword 2
Starting InputWithKeyword (ID: 1)
Starting InputWithKeyword (ID: 2)
Processing element 1 (ID: 1)
Processing element 1 (ID: 2)
1
Processing element 2 (ID: 1)
Processing element 2 (ID: 2)
2
Processing element 3 (ID: 1)
Processing element 3 (ID: 2)
3
Stopping InputWithKeyword (ID: 1)
Stopping InputWithKeyword (ID: 2)
```

When we chain together two scripts that process their input with the $input variable, the second script can't start until the first completes.

```
PS > 1,2,3 | Get-InputWithForeach 1 | Get-InputWithForeach 2
Starting InputWithForeach (ID: 1)
Processing element 1 (ID: 1)
Processing element 2 (ID: 1)
Processing element 3 (ID: 1)
Stopping InputWithForeach (ID: 1)
Starting InputWithForeach (ID: 2)
Processing element 1 (ID: 2)
1
Processing element 2 (ID: 2)
2
Processing element 3 (ID: 2)
3
Stopping InputWithForeach (ID: 2)
```

When the first script uses the cmdlet-style keywords, and the second script uses the $input variable, the second script can't start until the first completes.

```
PS > 1,2,3 | Get-InputWithKeyword 1 | Get-InputWithForeach 2
Starting InputWithKeyword (ID: 1)
Processing element 1 (ID: 1)
Processing element 2 (ID: 1)
Processing element 3 (ID: 1)
Stopping InputWithKeyword (ID: 1)
Starting InputWithForeach (ID: 2)
Processing element 1 (ID: 2)
1
Processing element 2 (ID: 2)
2
Processing element 3 (ID: 2)
3
Stopping InputWithForeach (ID: 2)
```

When the first script uses the $input variable and the second script uses the cmdlet-style keywords, the second script gets to process input as soon as the first script produces it. Notice, however, that InputWithKeyword starts before InputWithForeach. This is because functions with no explicit begin, process, or end blocks have all of their code placed in an end block by default.

```
PS > 1,2,3 | Get-InputWithForeach 1 | Get-InputWithKeyword 2
Starting InputWithKeyword (ID: 2)
Starting InputWithForeach (ID: 1)
Processing element 1 (ID: 1)
Processing element 1 (ID: 2)
1
Processing element 2 (ID: 1)
Processing element 2 (ID: 2)
2
Processing element 3 (ID: 1)
Processing element 3 (ID: 2)
3
Stopping InputWithForeach (ID: 1)
Stopping InputWithKeyword (ID: 2)
```

For more information about dealing with pipeline input, see "Writing Scripts, Reusing Functionality" on page 746.

See Also

Recipe 11.18, "Access Pipeline Input"

"Writing Scripts, Reusing Functionality" on page 746

11.20 Write a Pipeline-Oriented Function

Problem

Your function primarily takes its input from the pipeline, and you want it to perform the same steps for each element of that input.

Solution

To write a pipeline-oriented function, define your function using the filter keyword, rather than the function keyword. PowerShell makes the current pipeline object available as the $_ variable.

```
filter Get-PropertyValue($property)
{
    $_.$property
}
```

Discussion

A filter is the equivalent of a function that uses the cmdlet-style keywords and has all its code inside the process section.

The solution demonstrates an extremely useful filter: one that returns the value of a property for each item in a pipeline.

```
PS > Get-Process | Get-PropertyValue Name
audiodg
avgamsvr
avgemc
avgrssvc
avgrssvc
avgupsvc
(...)
```

For a more complete example of this approach, see Recipe 2.7. For more information about the cmdlet-style keywords, see Recipe 11.19.

See Also

Recipe 2.7, "Program: Simplify Most Foreach-Object Pipelines"

Recipe 11.19, "Write Pipeline-Oriented Scripts with Cmdlet Keywords"

11.21 Organize Scripts for Improved Readability

Problem

You have a long script that includes helper functions, but those helper functions obscure the main intent of the script.

Solution

Place the main logic of your script in a function called Main, and place that function at the top of your script. At the bottom of your script (after all the helper functions have also been defined), dot source the Main function.

```
## LongScript.ps1

function Main
{
    "Invoking the main logic of the script"
    CallHelperFunction1
    CallHelperFunction2
}

function CallHelperFunction1
{
    "Calling the first helper function"
}
```

```
function CallHelperFunction2
{
    "Calling the second helper function"
}

. Main
```

Discussion

When PowerShell invokes a script, it executes it in order from the beginning to the end. Just as when you type commands in the console, PowerShell generates an error if you try to call a function that you haven't yet defined.

When writing a long script with lots of helper functions, this usually results in those helper functions migrating to the top of the script so that they are all defined by the time your main logic finally executes them. When reading the script, then, you are forced to wade through pages of seemingly unrelated helper functions just to reach the main logic of the script.

You might wonder why PowerShell requires this strict ordering of function definitions and when they are called. After all, a script is self-contained, and it would be possible for PowerShell to process all of the function definitions before invoking the script.

The reason is parity with the interactive environment. Pasting a script into the console window is a common diagnostic or experimental technique, as is highlighting portions of a script in the Integrated Scripting Environment and selecting "Run Selection." If PowerShell did something special in an imaginary *script mode*, these techniques would not be possible.

To resolve this problem, you can place the main script logic in a function of its own. The name doesn't matter, but Main is a traditional name. If you place this function at the top of the script, your main logic is visible immediately.

Functions aren't automatically executed, so the final step is to invoke the Main function. Place this call at the end of your script, and you can be sure that all the required helper functions have been defined. Dot sourcing this function ensures that it is processed in the *script scope*, rather than the isolated function scope that would normally be created for it.

For more information about dot sourcing and script scopes, see Recipe 3.6.

See Also

Recipe 3.6, "Control Access and Scope of Variables and Other Items"

11.22 Invoke Dynamically Named Commands

Problem

You want to take an action based on the *pattern* of a command name, as opposed to the name of the command itself.

Solution

Add a command wrapper for the `Out-Default` cmdlet that intercepts `CommandNotFound` errors and takes action based on the `TargetObject` of that error.

Example 11-20 illustrates this technique by supporting relative path navigation without an explicit call to `Set-Location`.

Example 11-20. Add-RelativePathCapture.ps1

```
##############################################################################
##
## Add-RelativePathCapture
##
## From Windows PowerShell Cookbook (O'Reilly)
## by Lee Holmes (http://www.leeholmes.com/guide)
##
##############################################################################

<#

.SYNOPSIS

Adds a new Out-Default command wrapper that captures relative path
navigation without having to explicitly call 'Set-Location'

.EXAMPLE

PS C:\Users\Lee\Documents>..
PS C:\Users\Lee>...
PS C:\>

.NOTES

This commands builds on New-CommandWrapper, also included in the Windows
PowerShell Cookbook.

#>

Set-StrictMode -Version Latest

New-CommandWrapper Out-Default `
    -Process {
        if(($_ -is [System.Management.Automation.ErrorRecord]) -and
            ($_.FullyQualifiedErrorId -eq "CommandNotFoundException"))
        {
```

```
## Intercept all CommandNotFound exceptions, where the actual
## command consisted solely of dots.
$command = $_.TargetObject
if($command -match '^(\.)+$')
{
    ## Count the number of dots, and go that many levels (minus
    ## one) up the directory hierarchy.
    $newLocation = "..\" * ($command.Length - 1)
    if($newLocation) { Set-Location $newLocation }

    ## Handle the error
    $error.RemoveAt(0)
    $_ = $null
}
        }
    }
}
```

Discussion

PowerShell supports several useful forms of named commands (cmdlets, functions, and aliases), but you may find yourself wanting to write extensions that alter their behavior based on the *form* of the name, rather than the arguments passed to it. For example, you might want to automatically launch URLs just by typing them or navigate around providers just by typing relative path locations.

While this is not a built-in feature of PowerShell, it is possible to get a very reasonable alternative by intercepting the errors that PowerShell generates when it can't find a command. The example in the Solution does just this, by building a command wrapper over the Out-Default command to intercept and act on commands that consist solely of dots.

See Also

Recipe 2.8, "Intercept Stages of the Pipeline"

Recipe 11.23, "Program: Enhance or Extend an Existing Cmdlet"

11.23 Program: Enhance or Extend an Existing Cmdlet

While PowerShell's built-in commands are useful, you may sometimes wish they had included an additional parameter or supported a minor change to their functionality. This was difficult in version one of PowerShell, since "wrapping" another command was technical and error-prone. In addition to the complexity of parsing parameters and passing only the correct ones along, previous solutions also prevented wrapped commands from benefiting from the streaming nature of PowerShell's pipeline.

Version two of PowerShell significantly improves the situation by combining three new features:

Steppable pipelines

> Given a script block that contains a single pipeline, the GetSteppablePipeline()
> method returns a **SteppablePipeline** object that gives you control over the Begin,
> Process, and End stages of the pipeline.

Argument splatting

> Given a hashtable of names and values, PowerShell lets you pass the entire
> hashtable to a command. If you use the @ symbol to identify the hashtable variable
> name (rather than the $ symbol), PowerShell then treats each element of the
> hashtable as though it were a parameter to the command.

Proxy command APIs

> With enough knowledge of steppable pipelines, splatting, and parameter valida-
> tion, you can write your own function that can effectively wrap another command.
> The proxy command APIs make this significantly easier by auto-generating large
> chunks of the required boilerplate script.

These three features finally enable the possibility of powerful command extensions,
but putting them together still requires a fair bit of technical expertise. To make things
easier, use the **New-CommandWrapper** script (Example 11-21) to easily create commands
that wrap (and extend) existing commands.

Example 11-21. New-CommandWrapper.ps1

```
##############################################################################
##
## New-CommandWrapper
##
## From Windows PowerShell Cookbook (O'Reilly)
## by Lee Holmes (http://www.leeholmes.com/guide)
##
##############################################################################

<#

.SYNOPSIS

Adds parameters and functionality to existing cmdlets and functions.

.EXAMPLE

New-CommandWrapper Get-Process `
    -AddParameter @{
       SortBy = {
           $newPipeline = {
               __ORIGINAL_COMMAND__ | Sort-Object -Property $SortBy
           }
       }
    }

This example adds a 'SortBy' parameter to Get-Process. It accomplishes
this by adding a Sort-Object command to the pipeline.
```

```
.EXAMPLE

$parameterAttributes = @'
        [Parameter(Mandatory = $true)]
        [ValidateRange(50,75)]
        [Int]
'@

New-CommandWrapper Clear-Host `
    -AddParameter @{
        @{
            Name = 'MyMandatoryInt';
            Attributes = $parameterAttributes
        } = {
            Write-Host $MyMandatoryInt
            Read-Host "Press ENTER"
        }
    }

This example adds a new mandatory 'MyMandatoryInt' parameter to
Clear-Host. This parameter is also validated to fall within the range
of 50 to 75. It doesn't alter the pipeline, but does display some
information on the screen before processing the original pipeline.

#>

param(
    ## The name of the command to extend
    [Parameter(Mandatory = $true)]
    $Name,

    ## Script to invoke before the command begins
    [ScriptBlock] $Begin,

    ## Script to invoke for each input element
    [ScriptBlock] $Process,

    ## Script to invoke at the end of the command
    [ScriptBlock] $End,

    ## Parameters to add, and their functionality.
    ##
    ## The Key of the hashtable can be either a simple parameter name,
    ## or a more advanced parameter description.
    ##
    ## If you want to add additional parameter validation (such as a
    ## parameter type,) then the key can itself be a hashtable with the keys
    ## 'Name' and 'Attributes'. 'Attributes' is the text you would use when
    ## defining this parameter as part of a function.
    ##
    ## The Value of each hashtable entry is a script block to invoke
    ## when this parameter is selected. To customize the pipeline,
    ## assign a new script block to the $newPipeline variable. Use the
    ## special text, __ORIGINAL_COMMAND__, to represent the original
```

```
    ## command. The $targetParameters variable represents a hashtable
    ## containing the parameters that will be passed to the original
    ## command.
    [HashTable] $AddParameter
)

Set-StrictMode -Version Latest

## Store the target command we are wrapping and its command type
$target = $Name
$commandType = "Cmdlet"

## If a function already exists with this name (perhaps it's already been
## wrapped), rename the other function and chain to its new name.
if(Test-Path function:\$Name)
{
    $target = "$Name" + "-" + [Guid]::NewGuid().ToString().Replace("-","")
    Rename-Item function:\GLOBAL:$Name GLOBAL:$target
    $commandType = "Function"
}

## The template we use for generating a command proxy
$proxy = @'

__CMDLET_BINDING_ATTRIBUTE__
param(
__PARAMETERS__
)
begin
{
    try {
        __CUSTOM_BEGIN__

        ## Access the REAL Foreach-Object command, so that command
        ## wrappers do not interfere with this script
        $foreachObject = $executionContext.InvokeCommand.GetCmdlet(
            "Microsoft.PowerShell.Core\Foreach-Object")

        $wrappedCmd = $ExecutionContext.InvokeCommand.GetCommand(
            '__COMMAND_NAME__',
            [System.Management.Automation.CommandTypes]::__COMMAND_TYPE__)

        ## TargetParameters represents the hashtable of parameters that
        ## we will pass along to the wrapped command
        $targetParameters = @{}
        $PSBoundParameters.GetEnumerator() |
            & $foreachObject {
                if($command.Parameters.ContainsKey($_.Key))
                {
                    $targetParameters.Add($_.Key, $_.Value)
                }
            }

        ## finalPipeline represents the pipeline we wil ultimately run
        $newPipeline = { & $wrappedCmd @targetParameters }
```

```
        $finalPipeline = $newPipeline.ToString()

        __CUSTOM_PARAMETER_PROCESSING__

        $steppablePipeline = [ScriptBlock]::Create(
            $finalPipeline).GetSteppablePipeline()
        $steppablePipeline.Begin($PSCmdlet)
    } catch {
        throw
    }
}

process
{
    try {
        __CUSTOM_PROCESS__
        $steppablePipeline.Process($_)
    } catch {
        throw
    }
}

end
{
    try {
        __CUSTOM_END__
        $steppablePipeline.End()
    } catch {
        throw
    }
}

dynamicparam
{
    ## Access the REAL Get-Command, Foreach-Object, and Where-Object
    ## commands, so that command wrappers do not interfere with this script
    $getCommand = $executionContext.InvokeCommand.GetCmdlet(
        "Microsoft.PowerShell.Core\Get-Command")
    $foreachObject = $executionContext.InvokeCommand.GetCmdlet(
        "Microsoft.PowerShell.Core\Foreach-Object")
    $whereObject = $executionContext.InvokeCommand.GetCmdlet(
        "Microsoft.PowerShell.Core\Where-Object")

    ## Find the parameters of the original command, and remove everything
    ## else from the bound parameter list so we hide parameters the wrapped
    ## command does not recognize.
    $command = & $getCommand __COMMAND_NAME__ -Type __COMMAND_TYPE__
    $targetParameters = @{}
    $PSBoundParameters.GetEnumerator() |
        & $foreachObject {
            if($command.Parameters.ContainsKey($_.Key))
            {
                $targetParameters.Add($_.Key, $_.Value)
            }
        }
```

```
    ## Get the argument list as it would be passed to the target command
    $argList = @($targetParameters.GetEnumerator() |
        Foreach-Object { "-$($_.Key)"; $_.Value })

    ## Get the dynamic parameters of the wrapped command, based on the
    ## arguments to this command
    $command = $null
    try
    {
        $command = & $getCommand __COMMAND_NAME__ -Type __COMMAND_TYPE__ `
            -ArgumentList $argList
    }
    catch
    {

    }

    $dynamicParams = @($command.Parameters.GetEnumerator() |
        & $whereObject { $_.Value.IsDynamic })

    ## For each of the dynamic parameters, add them to the dynamic
    ## parameters that we return.
    if ($dynamicParams.Length -gt 0)
    {
        $paramDictionary = `
            New-Object Management.Automation.RuntimeDefinedParameterDictionary
        foreach ($param in $dynamicParams)
        {
            $param = $param.Value
            $arguments = $param.Name, $param.ParameterType, $param.Attributes
            $newParameter = `
                New-Object Management.Automation.RuntimeDefinedParameter `
                $arguments
            $paramDictionary.Add($param.Name, $newParameter)
        }
        return $paramDictionary
    }
}

<#

.ForwardHelpTargetName __COMMAND_NAME__
.ForwardHelpCategory __COMMAND_TYPE__

#>

'@

## Get the information about the original command
$originalCommand = Get-Command $target
$metaData = New-Object System.Management.Automation.CommandMetaData `
    $originalCommand
$proxyCommandType = [System.Management.Automation.ProxyCommand]
```

```
## Generate the cmdlet binding attribute, and replace information
## about the target
$proxy = $proxy.Replace("__CMDLET_BINDING_ATTRIBUTE__",
    $proxyCommandType::GetCmdletBindingAttribute($metaData))
$proxy = $proxy.Replace("__COMMAND_NAME__", $target)
$proxy = $proxy.Replace("__COMMAND_TYPE__", $commandType)

## Stores new text we'll be putting in the param() block
$newParamBlockCode = ""

## Stores new text we'll be putting in the begin block
## (mostly due to parameter processing)
$beginAdditions = ""

## If the user wants to add a parameter
$currentParameter = $originalCommand.Parameters.Count
if($AddParameter)
{
    foreach($parameter in $AddParameter.Keys)
    {
        ## Get the code associated with this parameter
        $parameterCode = $AddParameter[$parameter]

        ## If it's an advanced parameter declaration, the hashtable
        ## holds the validation and / or type restrictions
        if($parameter -is [Hashtable])
        {
            ## Add their attributes and other information to
            ## the variable holding the parameter block additions
            if($currentParameter -gt 0)
            {
                $newParamBlockCode += ","
            }

            $newParamBlockCode += "`n`n        " +
                $parameter.Attributes + "`n" +
                '        $' + $parameter.Name

            $parameter = $parameter.Name
        }
        else
        {
            ## If this is a simple parameter name, add it to the list of
            ## parameters. The proxy generation APIs will take care of
            ## adding it to the param() block.
            $newParameter =
                New-Object System.Management.Automation.ParameterMetadata `
                    $parameter
            $metaData.Parameters.Add($parameter, $newParameter)
        }

        $parameterCode = $parameterCode.ToString()

        ## Create the template code that invokes their parameter code if
        ## the parameter is selected.
```

```
        $templateCode = @"

        if(`$PSBoundParameters['$parameter'])
        {
            $parameterCode

            ## Replace the __ORIGINAL_COMMAND__ tag with the code
            ## that represents the original command
            `$alteredPipeline = `$newPipeline.ToString()
            `$finalPipeline = `$alteredPipeline.Replace(
                '__ORIGINAL_COMMAND__', `$finalPipeline)
        }
"@

        ## Add the template code to the list of changes we're making
        ## to the begin() section.
        $beginAdditions += $templateCode
        $currentParameter++
    }
}

## Generate the param() block
$parameters = $proxyCommandType::GetParamBlock($metaData)
if($newParamBlockCode) { $parameters += $newParamBlockCode }
$proxy = $proxy.Replace('__PARAMETERS__', $parameters)

## Update the begin, process, and end sections
$proxy = $proxy.Replace('__CUSTOM_BEGIN__', $Begin)
$proxy = $proxy.Replace('__CUSTOM_PARAMETER_PROCESSING__', $beginAdditions)
$proxy = $proxy.Replace('__CUSTOM_PROCESS__', $Process)
$proxy = $proxy.Replace('__CUSTOM_END__', $End)

## Save the function wrapper
Write-Verbose $proxy
Set-Content function:\GLOBAL:$NAME $proxy

## If we were wrapping a cmdlet, hide it so that it doesn't conflict with
## Get-Help and Get-Command
if($commandType -eq "Cmdlet")
{
    $originalCommand.Visibility = "Private"
}
```

See Also

Recipe 1.1, "Run Programs, Scripts, and Existing Tools"

Internet-Enabled Scripts

12.0 Introduction

Although PowerShell provides an enormous benefit even when your scripts interact only with the local system, working with data sources from the Internet opens exciting and unique opportunities. For example, you might download files or information from the Internet, interact with a web service, store your output as HTML, or even send an email that reports the results of a long-running script.

Through its cmdlets and access to the networking support in the .NET Framework, PowerShell provides ample opportunities for Internet-enabled administration.

12.1 Download a File from the Internet

Problem

You want to download a file from a website on the Internet.

Solution

Use the `DownloadFile()` method from the .NET Framework's `System.Net.WebClient` class to download a file:

```
PS > $source = "http://www.leeholmes.com/favicon.ico"
PS > $destination = "c:\temp\favicon.ico"
PS >
PS > $wc = New-Object System.Net.WebClient
PS > $wc.DownloadFile($source, $destination)
```

Discussion

The `System.Net.WebClient` class from the .NET Framework lets you easily upload and download data from remote web servers.

The WebClient class acts much like a web browser, in that you can specify a user agent, a proxy (if your outgoing connection requires one), and even credentials.

All web browsers send a user agent identifier along with their web request. This identifier tells the website what application is making the request—such as Internet Explorer, Firefox, or an automated crawler from a search engine. Many websites check this user agent identifier to determine how to display the page. Unfortunately, many fail entirely if they can't determine the user agent for the incoming request. To make the System.Net.WebClient identify itself as Internet Explorer, use the following commands instead:

```
$userAgent = "Mozilla/4.0 (compatible; MSIE 6.0; Windows NT 5.2;)"
$wc = New-Object System.Net.WebClient
$wc.Headers.Add("user-agent", $userAgent)
```

Notice that the solution uses a fully qualified path for the destination file. This is an important step, as otherwise the DownloadFile() method saves its files to the directory in which *PowerShell.exe* started (the root of your user profile directory by default).

You can use the DownloadFile() method to download web pages just as easily as you download files. Just supply a URL as a source (such as *http://blogs.msdn.com/power shell/rss.xml*) instead of a filename. If you ultimately intend to parse or read through the downloaded page, the DownloadString() method may be more appropriate.

For more information on how to download and parse web pages, see Recipe 12.2.

See Also

Recipe 12.2, "Download a Web Page from the Internet"

12.2 Download a Web Page from the Internet

Problem

You want to download a web page from the Internet and work with the content as a plain string.

Solution

Use the DownloadString() method from the .NET Framework's System.Net.WebClient class to download a web page or plain text file into a string.

```
PS > $source = "http://blogs.msdn.com/powershell/rss.xml"
PS >
PS > $wc = New-Object System.Net.WebClient
PS > $content = $wc.DownloadString($source)
```

Discussion

The most common reason to download a web page from the Internet is to extract unstructured information from it. Although web services are becoming increasingly popular, they are still far less common than web pages that display useful data. Because of this, retrieving data from services on the Internet often comes by means of *screen scraping:* downloading the HTML of the web page and then carefully separating out the content you want from the vast majority of the content that you do not.

The technique of screen scraping has been around much longer than the Internet! As long as computer systems have generated output designed primarily for humans, screen scraping tools have risen to make this output available to other computer programs.

Unfortunately, screen scraping is an error-prone way to extract content.

 That's not an exaggeration! As proof, Example 12-2 (shown later in this recipe) broke four or five times while the first edition of this book was being written, and then again after it was published. Such are the perils of screen scraping.

If the web page authors change the underlying HTML, your code will usually stop working correctly. If the site's HTML is written as valid XHTML, you may be able to use PowerShell's built-in XML support to more easily parse the content.

For more information about PowerShell's built-in XML support, see Recipe 10.1.

Despite its fragility, pure screen scraping is often the only alternative. Since screen scraping is just text manipulation, you have the same options you do with other text reports. For some fairly structured web pages, you can get away with a single regular expression replacement (plus cleanup), as shown in Example 12-1.

Example 12-1. Search-Twitter.ps1

```
##############################################################################
##
## Search-Twitter
##
## From Windows PowerShell Cookbook (O'Reilly)
## by Lee Holmes (http://www.leeholmes.com/guide)
##
##############################################################################

<#

.SYNOPSIS

Search Twitter for recent mentions of a search term
```

```
.EXAMPLE

Search-Twitter PowerShell
Searches Twitter for the term "PowerShell"

#>

param(
    ## The term to search for
    $Pattern = "PowerShell"
)

Set-StrictMode -Version Latest

## Create the URL that contains the Twitter search results
Add-Type -Assembly System.Web
$queryUrl = 'http://integratedsearch.twitter.com/search.html?q={0}'
$queryUrl = $queryUrl -f ([System.Web.HttpUtility]::UrlEncode($pattern))

## Download the web page
$wc = New-Object System.Net.WebClient
$wc.Encoding = [System.Text.Encoding]::UTF8
$results = $wc.DownloadString($queryUrl)

## Extract the text of the messages, which are contained in
## segments that look like "<div class='msg'>...</div>"
$matches = $results |
    Select-String -Pattern '(?s)<div[^>]*msg[^>]*>.*?</div>' -AllMatches

foreach($match in $matches.Matches)
{
    ## Replace anything in angle brackets with an empty string,
    ## leaving just plain text remaining.
    $tweet = $match.Value -replace '<[^>]*>', ''

    ## Output the text
    [System.Web.HttpUtility]::HtmlDecode($tweet.Trim()) + "`n"
}
```

Text parsing on less structured web pages, while possible to accomplish with complicated regular expressions, can often be made much simpler through more straightforward text manipulation. Example 12-2 uses this second approach to fetch "Instant Answers" from Bing.

Example 12-2. Get-Answer.ps1

```
##############################################################################
##
## Get-Answer
##
## From Windows PowerShell Cookbook (O'Reilly)
## by Lee Holmes (http://www.leeholmes.com/guide)
##
##############################################################################
```

```
<#

.SYNOPSIS

Uses Bing Answers to answer your question

.EXAMPLE

Get-Answer "(5 + e) * sqrt(x) = Pi"
Calculation
(5+e )*sqrt ( x)=pi  : x=0.165676

.EXAMPLE

Get-Answer msft stock
Microsoft Corp (US:MSFT) NASDAQ
29.66  -0.35 (-1.17%)
After Hours: 30.02 +0.36 (1.21%)
Open: 30.09    Day's Range: 29.59 - 30.20
Volume: 55.60 M    52 Week Range: 17.27 - 31.50
P/E Ratio: 16.30    Market Cap: 260.13 B

#>

Set-StrictMode -Version Latest

$question = $args -join " "

function Main
{
    ## Load the System.Web.HttpUtility DLL, to let us URLEncode
    Add-Type -Assembly System.Web

    ## Get the web page into a single string with newlines between
    ## the lines.
    $encoded = [System.Web.HttpUtility]::UrlEncode($question)
    $url = "http://www.bing.com/search?q=$encoded"
    $text = (new-object System.Net.WebClient).DownloadString($url)

    ## Find the start of the answers section
    $startIndex = $text.IndexOf('<div class="ans">')

    ## The end is either defined by an "attribution" div
    ## or the start of a "results" div
    $endIndex = $text.IndexOf('<div class="sn_att2">')
    if($endIndex -lt 0) { $endIndex = $text.IndexOf('<div id="results">') }

    ## If we found a result, then filter the result
    if(($startIndex -ge 0) -and ($endIndex -ge 0))
    {
        ## Pull out the text between the start and end portions
        $partialText = $text.Substring($startIndex, $endIndex - $startIndex)

        ## Very fragile screen scraping here. Replace a bunch of
        ## tags that get placed on new lines with the newline
```

```
## character, and a few others with spaces.
$partialText = $partialText -replace '<div[^>]*>',"`n"
$partialText = $partialText -replace '<tr[^>]*>',"`n"
$partialText = $partialText -replace '<li[^>]*>',"`n"
$partialText = $partialText -replace '<br[^>]*>',"`n"
$partialText = $partialText -replace '<span[^>]*>'," "
$partialText = $partialText -replace '<td[^>]*>',"    "

$partialText = CleanHtml $partialText

## Now split the results on newlines, trim each line, and then
## join them back.
$partialText = $partialText -split "`n" |
    Foreach-Object { $_.Trim() } | Where-Object { $_ }
$partialText = $partialText -join "`n"

[System.Web.HttpUtility]::HtmlDecode($partialText.Trim())
    }
    else
    {
        "`nNo answer found."
    }
}

## Clean HTML from a text chunk
function CleanHtml ($htmlInput)
{
    $tempString = [Regex]::Replace($htmlInput, "(?s)<[^>]*>", "")
    $tempString.Replace("  ", "")
}

. Main
```

For more information about running scripts, see Recipe 1.1.

See Also

Recipe 1.1, "Run Programs, Scripts, and Existing Tools"

Recipe 10.1, "Access Information in an XML File"

12.3 Program: Get-PageUrls

When working with HTML, it is common to require advanced regular expressions that separate the content you care about from the content you don't. A perfect example of this is extracting all the HTML links from a web page.

Links come in many forms, depending on how lenient you want to be. They may be well-formed according to the various HTML standards. They may use relative paths or they may use absolute paths. They may place double quotes around the URL or they may place single quotes around the URL. If you're really unlucky, they may accidentally include quotes on only one side of the URL.

Example 12-3 demonstrates some approaches for dealing with this type of advanced parsing task. Given a web page that you've downloaded from the Internet, it extracts all links from the page and returns a list of the URLs on that page. It also fixes URLs that were originally written as relative URLs (for example, /file.zip) to include the server from which they originated.

Example 12-3. Get-PageUrls.ps1

```
##############################################################################
##
## Get-PageUrls
##
## From Windows PowerShell Cookbook (O'Reilly)
## by Lee Holmes (http://www.leeholmes.com/guide)
##############################################################################

<#

.SYNOPSIS

Parse all of the URLs out of a given file.

.EXAMPLE

Get-PageUrls microsoft.html http://www.microsoft.com
Gets all of the URLs from HTML stored in microsoft.html, and converts relative
URLs to the domain of http://www.microsoft.com

.EXAMPLE

Get-PageUrls microsoft.html http://www.microsoft.com 'aspx$'
Gets all of the URLs from HTML stored in microsoft.html, converts relative
URLs to the domain of http://www.microsoft.com, and returns only URLs that end
in 'aspx'.

#>

param(
    ## The filename to parse
    [Parameter(Mandatory = $true)]
    [string] $Path,

    ## The URL from which you downloaded the page.
    ## For example, http://www.microsoft.com
    [Parameter(Mandatory = $true)]
    [string] $BaseUrl,

    ## The Regular Expression pattern with which to filter
    ## the returned URLs
    [string] $Pattern = ".*"
)

Set-StrictMode -Version Latest
```

```
## Load the System.Web DLL so that we can decode URLs
Add-Type -Assembly System.Web

## Defines the regular expression that will parse an URL
## out of an anchor tag.
$regex = "<\s*a\s*[^>]*?href\s*=\s*[`""']*([^`""'>]+)[^>]*?>"

## Parse the file for links
function Main
{
    ## Do some minimal source URL fixups, by switching backslashes to
    ## forward slashes
    $baseUrl = $baseUrl.Replace("\", "/")

    if($baseUrl.IndexOf("://") -lt 0)
    {
        throw "Please specify a base URL in the form of " +
            "http://server/path_to_file/file.html"
    }

    ## Determine the server from which the file originated. This will
    ## help us resolve links such as "/somefile.zip"
    $baseUrl = $baseUrl.Substring(0, $baseUrl.LastIndexOf("/") + 1)
    $baseSlash = $baseUrl.IndexOf("/", $baseUrl.IndexOf("://") + 3)

    if($baseSlash -ge 0)
    {
        $domain = $baseUrl.Substring(0, $baseSlash)
    }
    else
    {
        $domain = $baseUrl
    }


    ## Put all of the file content into a big string, and
    ## get the regular expression matches
    $content = [String]::Join(' ', (Get-Content $path))
    $contentMatches = @(GetMatches $content $regex)

    foreach($contentMatch in $contentMatches)
    {
        if(-not ($contentMatch -match $pattern)) { continue }
        if($contentMatch -match "javascript:") { continue }

        $contentMatch = $contentMatch.Replace("\", "/")

        ## Hrefs may look like:
        ## ./file
        ## file
        ## ../../../file
        ## /file
        ## url
        ## We'll keep all of the relative paths, as they will resolve.
        ## We only need to resolve the ones pointing to the root.
```

```
            if($contentMatch.IndexOf("://") -gt 0)
            {
                $url = $contentMatch
            }
            elseif($contentMatch[0] -eq "/")
            {
                $url = "$domain$contentMatch"
            }
            else
            {
                $url = "$baseUrl$contentMatch"
                $url = $url.Replace("/./", "/")
            }

            ## Return the URL, after first removing any HTML entities
            [System.Web.HttpUtility]::HtmlDecode($url)
        }
    }

    function GetMatches([string] $content, [string] $regex)
    {
        $returnMatches = new-object System.Collections.ArrayList

        ## Match the regular expression against the content, and
        ## add all trimmed matches to our return list
        $resultingMatches = [Regex]::Matches($content, $regex, "IgnoreCase")
        foreach($match in $resultingMatches)
        {
            $cleanedMatch = $match.Groups[1].Value.Trim()
            [void] $returnMatches.Add($cleanedMatch)
        }

        $returnMatches
    }

    . Main
```

For more information about running scripts, see Recipe 1.1.

See Also

Recipe 1.1, "Run Programs, Scripts, and Existing Tools"

12.4 Connect to a Web Service

Problem

You want to connect to and interact with an Internet web service.

Solution

Use the New-WebserviceProxy cmdlet to work with a web service.

```
PS > $url = "http://terraservice.net/TerraService.asmx"
PS > $terraServer = New-WebserviceProxy $url -Namespace Cookbook
PS > $place = New-Object Cookbook.Place
PS > $place.City = "Redmond"
PS > $place.State = "WA"
PS > $place.Country = "USA"
PS > $facts = $terraserver.GetPlaceFacts($place)
PS > $facts.Center
```

Lon	Lat
-122.110000610352	47.6699981689453

Discussion

Although screen scraping (parsing the HTML of a web page) is the most common way to obtain data from the Internet, web services are becoming increasingly common. Web services provide a significant advantage over HTML parsing, as they are much less likely to break when the web designer changes minor features in a design.

The benefit to web services isn't just their more stable interface, however. When working with web services, the .NET Framework lets you generate *proxies* that let you interact with the web service as easily as you would work with a regular .NET object. That is because to you, the web service user, these proxies act almost exactly the same as any other .NET object. To call a method on the web service, simply call a method on the proxy.

The New-WebserviceProxy cmdlet simplifies all of the work required to connect to a web service, making it just as easy as a call to the New-Object cmdlet.

The primary differences you will notice when working with a web service proxy (as opposed to a regular .NET object) are the speed and Internet connectivity requirements. Depending on conditions, a method call on a web service proxy could easily take several seconds to complete. If your computer (or the remote computer) experiences network difficulties, the call might even return a network error message (such as a timeout) instead of the information you had hoped for.

If the web service requires authentication in a domain, specify the -UseDefaultCredential parameter. If it requires explicit credentials, use the -Credential parameter.

When you create a new web service proxy, PowerShell creates a new .NET object on your behalf that connects to that web service. All .NET types live within a *namespace* to prevent them from conflicting with other types that have the same name, so PowerShell automatically generates the namespace name for you. You normally won't need to pay attention to this namespace. However, some web services require input objects that the web service also defines, such as the Place object in the solution. For these web services, use the -Namespace parameter to place the web service (and its support objects) in a namespace of your choice.

Support objects from one web service proxy cannot be consumed by a different web service proxy, even if they are two proxies to a web service at the same URL. If you need to work with two connections to a web service at the same URL, and your task requires creating support objects for that service, be sure to use two different namespaces for those proxies.

The New-WebserviceProxy cmdlet was introduced in version two of PowerShell. If you need to connect to a web service from version one of PowerShell, see Recipe 12.5.

For more information about running scripts, see Recipe 1.1.

See Also

Recipe 1.1, "Run Programs, Scripts, and Existing Tools"

Recipe 12.5, "Program: Connect-WebService"

12.5 Program: Connect-WebService

Recipe 12.4 discusses how to connect to a web service on the Internet. However, the New-WebserviceProxy cmdlet in that recipe was introduced in version two of PowerShell. If you need to connect to a web service from version one of PowerShell, Example 12-4 is your solution. It lets you connect to a remote web service if you know the location of its service description file (WSDL). It generates the web service proxy for you, letting you interact with it as you would any other .NET object.

Example 12-4. Connect-WebService.ps1

```
##############################################################################
## Connect-WebService
##
## From Windows PowerShell Cookbook (O'Reilly)
## by Lee Holmes (http://www.leeholmes.com/guide)
##
## Connect to a given web service, and create a type that allows you to
## interact with that web service. In PowerShell version two, use the
## New-WebserviceProxy cmdlet.
##
## Example:
##
## $wsdl = "http://terraservice.net/TerraService.asmx?WSDL"
## $terraServer = Connect-WebService $wsdl
## $place = New-Object Place
## $place.City = "Redmond"
## $place.State = "WA"
## $place.Country = "USA"
## $facts = $terraserver.GetPlaceFacts($place)
## $facts.Center
##############################################################################
```

```
param(
    ## The URL that contains the WSDL
    [string] $WsdlLocation = $(throw "Please specify a WSDL location"),

    ## The namespace to use to contain the web service proxy
    [string] $Namespace,

    ## Switch to identify web services that require authentication
    [Switch] $RequiresAuthentication
)

## Create the web service cache, if it doesn't already exist
if(-not (Test-Path Variable:\Lee.Holmes.WebServiceCache))
{
    ${GLOBAL:Lee.Holmes.WebServiceCache} = @{}
}

## Check if there was an instance from a previous connection to
## this web service. If so, return that instead.
$oldInstance = ${GLOBAL:Lee.Holmes.WebServiceCache}[$wsdlLocation]
if($oldInstance)
{
    $oldInstance
    return
}

## Load the required Web Services DLL
Add-Type -Assembly System.Web.Services

## Download the WSDL for the service, and create a service description from
## it.
$wc = New-Object System.Net.WebClient

if($requiresAuthentication)
{
    $wc.UseDefaultCredentials = $true
}

$wsdlStream = $wc.OpenRead($wsdlLocation)

## Ensure that we were able to fetch the WSDL
if(-not (Test-Path Variable:\wsdlStream))
{
    return
}

$serviceDescription =
    [Web.Services.Description.ServiceDescription]::Read($wsdlStream)
$wsdlStream.Close()

## Ensure that we were able to read the WSDL into a service description
if(-not (Test-Path Variable:\serviceDescription))
{
    return
```

```powershell
}

## Import the web service into a CodeDom
$serviceNamespace = New-Object System.CodeDom.CodeNamespace
if($namespace)
{
    $serviceNamespace.Name = $namespace
}

$codeCompileUnit = New-Object System.CodeDom.CodeCompileUnit
$serviceDescriptionImporter =
    New-Object Web.Services.Description.ServiceDescriptionImporter
$serviceDescriptionImporter.AddServiceDescription(
    $serviceDescription, $null, $null)
[void] $codeCompileUnit.Namespaces.Add($serviceNamespace)
[void] $serviceDescriptionImporter.Import(
    $serviceNamespace, $codeCompileUnit)

## Generate the code from that CodeDom into a string
$generatedCode = New-Object Text.StringBuilder
$stringWriter = New-Object IO.StringWriter $generatedCode
$provider = New-Object Microsoft.CSharp.CSharpCodeProvider
$provider.GenerateCodeFromCompileUnit($codeCompileUnit, $stringWriter, $null)

## Compile the source code.
$references = @("System.dll", "System.Web.Services.dll", "System.Xml.dll")
$compilerParameters = New-Object System.CodeDom.Compiler.CompilerParameters
$compilerParameters.ReferencedAssemblies.AddRange($references)
$compilerParameters.GenerateInMemory = $true

$compilerResults =
    $provider.CompileAssemblyFromSource($compilerParameters, $generatedCode)

## Write any errors if generated.
if($compilerResults.Errors.Count -gt 0)
{
    $errorLines = ""
    foreach($error in $compilerResults.Errors)
    {
        $errorLines += "`n`t" + $error.Line + ":`t" + $error.ErrorText
    }

    Write-Error $errorLines
    return
}
## There were no errors. Create the webservice object and return it.
else
{
    ## Get the assembly that we just compiled
    $assembly = $compilerResults.CompiledAssembly

    ## Find the type that had the WebServiceBindingAttribute.
    ## There may be other "helper types" in this file, but they will
    ## not have this attribute
    $type = $assembly.GetTypes() |
```

```
            Where-Object { $_.GetCustomAttributes(
                [System.Web.Services.WebServiceBindingAttribute], $false) }

    if(-not $type)
    {
        Write-Error "Could not generate web service proxy."
        return
    }

    ## Create an instance of the type, store it in the cache,
    ## and return it to the user.
    $instance = $assembly.CreateInstance($type)

    ## Many services that support authentication also require it on the
    ## resulting objects
    if($requiresAuthentication)
    {
        if(@($instance.PsObject.Properties |
            where { $_.Name -eq "UseDefaultCredentials" }).Count -eq 1)
        {
            $instance.UseDefaultCredentials = $true
        }
    }

    ${GLOBAL:Lee.Holmes.WebServiceCache}[$wsdlLocation] = $instance

    $instance
}
```

For more information about running scripts, see Recipe 1.1.

See Also

Recipe 1.1, "Run Programs, Scripts, and Existing Tools"

12.6 Export Command Output as a Web Page

Problem

You want to export the results of a command as a web page so that you can post it to a web server.

Solution

Use PowerShell's ConvertTo-Html cmdlet to convert command output into a web page. For example, to create a quick HTML summary of PowerShell's commands:

```
PS > $filename = "c:\temp\help.html"
PS >
PS > $commands = Get-Command | Where { $_.CommandType -ne "Alias" }
PS > $summary = $commands | Get-Help | Select Name,Synopsis
PS > $summary | ConvertTo-Html | Set-Content $filename
```

Discussion

When you use the `ConvertTo-Html` cmdlet to export command output to a file, Power-Shell generates an HTML table that represents the command output. In the table, it creates a row for each object that you provide. For each row, PowerShell creates columns to represent the values of your object's properties.

If the table format makes the output difficult to read, `ConvertTo-Html` offers the `-As` parameter that lets you set the output style to either `Table` or `List`.

While the default output is useful, you can customize the structure and style of the resulting HTML as much as you see fit. For example, the `-PreContent` and `-PostContent` parameters let you include additional text before and after the resulting table or list. The `-Head` parameter lets you define the content of the HEAD section of the HTML. Even if you want to generate most of the HTML from scratch, you can still use the `-Fragment` parameter to generate just the inner table or list.

For more information about the `ConvertTo-Html` cmdlet, type **Get-Help ConvertTo-Html**.

12.7 Send an Email

Problem

You want to send an email.

Solution

Use the `Send-MailMessage` cmdlet to send an email.

```
PS > Send-MailMessage -To guide@leeholmes.com `
    -From user@example.com `
    -Subject "Hello!" `
    -Body "Hello, from another satisfied Cookbook reader!" `
    -SmtpServer mail.example.com
```

Discussion

The `Send-MailMessage` cmdlet supports everything you would expect an email-centric cmdlet to support: attachments, plain text messages, HTML messages, priority, receipt requests, and more. The most difficult aspect usually is remembering the correct SMTP server to use.

The `Send-MailMessage` cmdlet helps solve this problem as well. If you don't specify the `-SmtpServer` parameter, it uses the server specified in the `$PSEmailServer` variable, if any.

The `Send-MailMessage` cmdlet was introduced in version two of PowerShell. If you need to send an email from version one of PowerShell, see Recipe 12.8.

See Also

Recipe 12.8, "Program: Send-MailMessage"

12.8 Program: Send-MailMessage

The Send-MailMessage cmdlet is the easiest way to send an email from PowerShell, but was introduced in version two of PowerShell. If you need to send an email from version one of PowerShell, you can use Example 12-5.

In addition to the fields shown in the script, the System.Net.Mail.MailMessage class supports properties that let you add attachments, set message priority, and much more. For more information about working with classes from the .NET Framework, see Recipe 3.8.

Example 12-5. Send-MailMessage.ps1

```
##############################################################################
##
## Send-MailMessage
##
## From Windows PowerShell Cookbook (O'Reilly)
## by Lee Holmes (http://www.leeholmes.com/guide)
##
## Illustrate the techniques used to send an email in PowerShell.
## In version two, use the Send-MailMessage cmdlet.
##
## Example:
##
## PS >$body = @"
## >> Hi from another satisfied customer of The PowerShell Cookbook!
## >> "@
## >>
## PS >$to = "guide_feedback@leeholmes.com"
## PS >$subject = "Thanks for all of the scripts."
## PS >$mailHost = "mail.leeholmes.com"
## PS >Send-MailMessage $to $subject $body $mailHost
##
##############################################################################

param(
    ## The recipient of the mail message
    [string[]] $To = $(throw "Please specify the destination mail address"),

    ## The subject of the message
    [string] $Subject = "<No Subject>",

    ## The body of the message
    [string] $Body = $(throw "Please specify the message content"),

    ## The SMTP host that will transmit the message
    [string] $SmtpHost = $(throw "Please specify a mail server."),
```

```
    ## The sender of the message
    [string] $From = "$($env:UserName)@example.com"
)

## Create the mail message
$email = New-Object System.Net.Mail.MailMessage

## Populate its fields
foreach($mailTo in $to)
{
    $email.To.Add($mailTo)
}

$email.From = $from
$email.Subject = $subject
$email.Body = $body

## Send the mail
$client = New-Object System.Net.Mail.SmtpClient $smtpHost
$client.UseDefaultCredentials = $true
$client.Send($email)
```

For more information about running scripts, see Recipe 1.1.

See Also

Recipe 1.1, "Run Programs, Scripts, and Existing Tools"

Recipe 3.8, "Work with .NET Objects"

12.9 Program: Interact with Internet Protocols

Although it is common to work at an abstract level with websites and web services, an entirely separate style of Internet-enabled scripting comes from interacting with the remote computer at a much lower level. This lower level (called the TCP level, for *Transmission Control Protocol*) forms the communication foundation of most Internet protocols—such as Telnet, SMTP (sending mail), POP3 (receiving mail), and HTTP (retrieving web content).

The .NET Framework provides classes that let you interact with many of the Internet protocols directly: the `System.Web.Mail.SmtpMail` class for SMTP, the `System.Net.Web Client` class for HTTP, and a few others. When the .NET Framework does not support an Internet protocol that you need, though, you can often script the application protocol directly if you know the details of how it works.

Example 12-6 shows how to receive information about mail waiting in a remote POP3 mailbox, using the `Send-TcpRequest` script given in Example 12-7.

Example 12-6. Interacting with a remote POP3 mailbox

```
## Get the user credential
if(-not (Test-Path Variable:\mailCredential))
{
    $mailCredential = Get-Credential
}
$address = $mailCredential.UserName
$password = $mailCredential.GetNetworkCredential().Password

## Connect to the remote computer, send the commands, and receive the
## output
$pop3Commands = "USER $address","PASS $password","STAT","QUIT"
$output = $pop3Commands | Send-TcpRequest mail.myserver.com 110
$inbox = $output.Split("`n")[3]

## Parse the output for the number of messages waiting and total bytes
$status = $inbox |
    Convert-TextObject -PropertyName "Response","Waiting","BytesTotal","Extra"
"{0} messages waiting, totaling {1} bytes." -f $status.Waiting, $status.BytesTotal
```

In Example 12-6, you connect to port 110 of the remote mail server. You then issue commands to request the status of the mailbox in a form that the mail server understands. The format of this network conversation is specified and required by the standard POP3 protocol. Example 12-6 uses the `Convert-TextObject` command, which is provided in Recipe 5.14.

Example 12-7 supports the core functionality of Example 12-6. It lets you easily work with plain-text TCP protocols.

Example 12-7. Send-TcpRequest.ps1

```
##############################################################################
##
## Send-TcpRequest
##
## From Windows PowerShell Cookbook (O'Reilly)
## by Lee Holmes (http://www.leeholmes.com/guide)
##
##############################################################################

<#

.SYNOPSIS

Send a TCP request to a remote computer, and return the response.
If you do not supply input to this script (via either the pipeline or the
-InputObject parameter), the script operates in interactive mode.

.EXAMPLE

PS >$http = @"
  GET / HTTP/1.1
  Host:bing.com
  `n`n
```

```
"@

$http | Send-TcpRequest bing.com 80

#>

param(
    ## The computer to connect to
    [string] $ComputerName = "localhost",

    ## A switch to determine if you just want to test the connection
    [switch] $Test,

    ## The port to use
    [int] $Port = 80,

    ## A switch to determine if the connection should be made using SSL
    [switch] $UseSSL,

    ## The input string to send to the remote host
    [string] $InputObject,

    ## The delay, in milliseconds, to wait between commands
    [int] $Delay = 100
)

Set-StrictMode -Version Latest

[string] $SCRIPT:output = ""

## Store the input into an array that we can scan over. If there was no input,
## then we will be in interactive mode.
$currentInput = $inputObject
if(-not $currentInput)
{
    $currentInput = @($input)
}
$scriptedMode = ([bool] $currentInput) -or $test

function Main
{
    ## Open the socket, and connect to the computer on the specified port
    if(-not $scriptedMode)
    {
        write-host "Connecting to $computerName on port $port"
    }

    try
    {
        $socket = New-Object Net.Sockets.TcpClient($computerName, $port)
    }
    catch
    {
        if($test) { $false }
        else { Write-Error "Could not connect to remote computer: $_" }
```

```
    return
}

## If we're just testing the connection, we've made the connection
## successfully, so just return $true
if($test) { $true; return }

## If this is interactive mode, supply the prompt
if(-not $scriptedMode)
{
    write-host "Connected.  Press ^D followed by [ENTER] to exit.`n"
}

$stream = $socket.GetStream()

## If we wanted to use SSL, set up that portion of the connection
if($UseSSL)
{
    $sslStream = New-Object System.Net.Security.SslStream $stream,$false
    $sslStream.AuthenticateAsClient($computerName)
    $stream = $sslStream
}

$writer = new-object System.IO.StreamWriter $stream

while($true)
{
    ## Receive the output that has buffered so far
    $SCRIPT:output += GetOutput

    ## If we're in scripted mode, send the commands,
    ## receive the output, and exit.
    if($scriptedMode)
    {
        foreach($line in $currentInput)
        {
            $writer.WriteLine($line)
            $writer.Flush()
            Start-Sleep -m $Delay
            $SCRIPT:output += GetOutput
        }

        break
    }
    ## If we're in interactive mode, write the buffered
    ## output, and respond to input.
    else
    {
        if($output)
        {
            foreach($line in $output.Split("`n"))
            {
                write-host $line
            }
```

```
                $SCRIPT:output = ""
            }

            ## Read the user's command, quitting if they hit ^D
            $command = read-host
            if($command -eq ([char] 4)) { break; }

            ## Otherwise, write their command to the remote host
            $writer.WriteLine($command)
            $writer.Flush()
        }
    }

    ## Close the streams
    $writer.Close()
    $stream.Close()

    ## If we're in scripted mode, return the output
    if($scriptedMode)
    {
        $output
    }
}

## Read output from a remote host
function GetOutput
{
    ## Create a buffer to receive the response
    $buffer = new-object System.Byte[] 1024
    $encoding = new-object System.Text.AsciiEncoding

    $outputBuffer = ""
    $foundMore = $false

    ## Read all the data available from the stream, writing it to the
    ## output buffer when done.
    do
    {
        ## Allow data to buffer for a bit
        start-sleep -m 1000

        ## Read what data is available
        $foundmore = $false
        $stream.ReadTimeout = 1000

        do
        {
            try
            {
                $read = $stream.Read($buffer, 0, 1024)

                if($read -gt 0)
                {
                    $foundmore = $true
                    $outputBuffer += ($encoding.GetString($buffer, 0, $read))
```

```
        }
      } catch { $foundMore = $false; $read = 0 }
    } while($read -gt 0)
  } while($foundmore)

  $outputBuffer
}

. Main
```

For more information about running scripts, see Recipe 1.1.

See Also

Recipe 1.1, "Run Programs, Scripts, and Existing Tools"

Recipe 5.14, "Program: Convert Text Streams to Objects"

User Interaction

13.0 Introduction

Although most scripts are designed to run automatically, you will frequently find it useful to have your scripts interact with the user.

 The best way to get input from your user is through the arguments and parameters to your script or function. This lets your users run your script without having to be there as it runs!

If your script greatly benefits from (or requires) an interactive experience, PowerShell offers a range of possibilities. This might be simply waiting for a keypress, prompting for input, or displaying a richer choice-based prompt.

User input isn't the only aspect of interaction, though. In addition to its input facilities, PowerShell supports output as well—from displaying simple text strings to much more detailed progress reporting and interaction with UI frameworks.

13.1 Read a Line of User Input

Problem

You want to use input from the user in your script.

Solution

To obtain user input, use the Read-Host cmdlet:

```
PS > $directory = Read-Host "Enter a directory name"
Enter a directory name: C:\MyDirectory
PS > $directory
C:\MyDirectory
```

Discussion

The Read-Host cmdlet reads a single line of input from the user. If the input contains sensitive data, the cmdlet supports an -AsSecureString parameter to read this input as a SecureString.

If the user input represents a date, time, or number, be aware that most cultures represent these data types differently. For more information about writing culturally aware scripts, see Recipe 13.6.

For more information about the Read-Host cmdlet, type **Get-Help Read-Host**. For an example of reading user input through a graphical prompt, see the Read-InputBox script included in this book's code examples. For more information about obtaining these examples, see "Code Examples" on page xxviii.

See Also

Recipe 13.6, "Write Culture-Aware Scripts"

13.2 Read a Key of User Input

Problem

You want your script to get a single keypress from the user.

Solution

For most purposes, use the [Console]::ReadKey() method to read a key:

```
PS > $key = [Console]::ReadKey($true)
PS > $key
```

KeyChar	Key	Modifiers
h	H	Alt

For highly interactive use (for example, when you care about key down and key up), use:

```
PS > $key = $host.UI.RawUI.ReadKey("NoEcho,IncludeKeyDown")
PS > $key
```

VirtualKeyCode	Character	ControlKeyState	KeyDown
16		...ssed, NumLockOn	True

```
PS > $key.ControlKeyState
ShiftPressed, NumLockOn
```

Discussion

For most purposes, the `[Console]::ReadKey()` is the best way to get a keystroke from a user, as it accepts simple keypresses and more complex keypresses that might include the Ctrl, Alt, and Shift keys. We pass the `$true` parameter to tell the method to not display the character on the screen, and only to return it to us.

The following function emulates the DOS pause command:

```
function Pause
{
    Write-Host -NoNewLine "Press any key to continue . . . "
    [Console]::ReadKey($true) | Out-Null
    Write-Host
}
```

If you need to capture individual key down and key up events (including those of the Ctrl, Alt, and Shift keys), use the `$host.UI.RawUI.ReadKey()` method.

13.3 Program: Display a Menu to the User

It is often useful to read input from the user but restrict input to a list of choices that you specify. The following script lets you access PowerShell's prompting functionality in a manner that is friendlier than what PowerShell exposes by default. It returns a number that represents the position of the user's choice from the list of options you provide.

PowerShell's prompting requires that you include an accelerator key (the & before a letter in the option description) to define the keypress that represents that option. Since you don't always control the list of options (for example, a list of possible directories), Example 13-1 automatically generates sensible accelerator characters for any descriptions that lack them.

Example 13-1. Read-HostWithPrompt.ps1

```
#############################################################################
##
## Read-HostWithPrompt
##
## From Windows PowerShell Cookbook (O'Reilly)
## by Lee Holmes (http://www.leeholmes.com/guide)
##
#############################################################################

<#

.SYNOPSIS

Read user input, with choices restricted to the list of options you
provide.
```

```
.EXAMPLE

PS >$caption = "Please specify a task"
PS >$message = "Specify a task to run"
PS >$option = "&Clean Temporary Files","&Defragment Hard Drive"
PS >$helptext = "Clean the temporary files from the computer",
>>              "Run the defragment task"
>>
PS >$default = 1
PS >Read-HostWithPrompt $caption $message $option $helptext $default

Please specify a task
Specify a task to run
[C] Clean Temporary Files  [D] Defragment Hard Drive  [?] Help
(default is "D"):?
C - Clean the temporary files from the computer
D - Run the defragment task
[C] Clean Temporary Files  [D] Defragment Hard Drive  [?] Help
(default is "D"):C
0

#>

param(
    ## The caption for the prompt
    $Caption = $null,

    ## The message to display in the prompt
    $Message = $null,

    ## Options to provide in the prompt
    [Parameter(Mandatory = $true)]
    $Pption,

    ## Any help text to provide
    $HelpText = $null,

    ## The default choice
    $Default = 0
)

Set-StrictMode -Version Latest

## Create the list of choices
$choices = New-GenericObject `
    Collections.ObjectModel.Collection `
    Management.Automation.Host.ChoiceDescription

## Go through each of the options, and add them to the choice collection
for($counter = 0; $counter -lt $option.Length; $counter++)
{
    $choice = New-Object Management.Automation.Host.ChoiceDescription `
        $option[$counter]

    if($helpText -and $helpText[$counter])
```

```
    {
        $choice.HelpMessage = $helpText[$counter]
    }

    $choices.Add($choice)
}

## Prompt for the choice, returning the item the user selected
$host.UI.PromptForChoice($caption, $message, $choices, $default)
```

For more information about running scripts, see Recipe 1.1.

See Also

Recipe 1.1, "Run Programs, Scripts, and Existing Tools"

13.4 Display Messages and Output to the User

Problem

You want to display messages and other information to the user.

Solution

Simply have your script output the string information. If you like to be more explicit in your scripting, call the Write-Output cmdlet:

```
PS > function Get-Information
{
    "Hello World"
    Write-Output (1 + 1)
}

PS > Get-Information
Hello World
2
PS > $result = Get-Information
PS > $result[1]
2
```

Discussion

Most scripts that you write should output richly structured data, such as the actual count of bytes in a directory (if you are writing a directory information script). That way, other scripts can use the output of that script as a building block for their functionality.

When you do want to provide output specifically to the user, use the `Write-Host`, `Write-Debug`, and `Write-Verbose` cmdlets:

```
PS > function Get-DirectorySize
{
    $size = (Get-ChildItem | Measure-Object -Sum Length).Sum
    Write-Host ("Directory size: {0:N0} bytes" -f $size)
}

PS > Get-DirectorySize
Directory size: 46,581 bytes
PS > $size = Get-DirectorySize
Directory size: 46,581 bytes
```

If you want a message to help you (or the user) diagnose and debug your script, use the `Write-Debug` cmdlet. If you want a message to provide detailed trace-type output, use the `Write-Verbose` cmdlet, as shown in Example 13-2.

Example 13-2. A function that provides debug and verbose output

```
PS > function Get-DirectorySize
{
    Write-Debug "Current Directory: $(Get-Location)"

    Write-Verbose "Getting size"
    $size = (Get-ChildItem | Measure-Object -Sum Length).Sum
    Write-Verbose "Got size: $size"

    Write-Host ("Directory size: {0:N0} bytes" -f $size)
}

PS > $DebugPreference = "Continue"
PS > Get-DirectorySize
DEBUG: Current Directory: D:\lee\OReilly\Scripts\Programs
Directory size: 46,581 bytes
PS > $DebugPreference = "SilentlyContinue"
PS > $VerbosePreference = "Continue"
PS > Get-DirectorySize
VERBOSE: Getting size
VERBOSE: Got size: 46581
Directory size: 46,581 bytes
PS > $VerbosePreference = "SilentlyContinue"
```

However, be aware that this type of output bypasses normal file redirection and is therefore difficult for the user to capture. In the case of the `Write-Host` cmdlet, use it only when your script already generates other structured data that the user would want to capture in a file or variable.

Most script authors eventually run into the problem illustrated by Example 13-3 when their script tries to output formatted data to the user.

Example 13-3. An error message caused by formatting statements

```
PS > ## Get the list of items in a directory, sorted by length
PS > function Get-ChildItemSortedByLength($path = (Get-Location))
{
    Get-ChildItem $path | Format-Table | Sort Length
}

PS > Get-ChildItemSortedByLength
out-lineoutput : Object of type "Microsoft.PowerShell.Commands.Internal.
Format.FormatEntryData" is not legal or not in the correct sequence. This is
likely caused by a user-specified "format-*" command which is conflicting
with the default formatting.
```

This happens because the Format-* cmdlets actually generate formatting information for the Out-Host cmdlet to consume. The Out-Host cmdlet (which PowerShell adds automatically to the end of your pipelines) then uses this information to generate formatted output. To resolve this problem, always ensure that formatting commands are the last commands in your pipeline, as shown in Example 13-4.

Example 13-4. A function that does not generate formatting errors

```
PS > ## Get the list of items in a directory, sorted by length
PS > function Get-ChildItemSortedByLength($path = (Get-Location))
{
    ## Problematic version
    ## Get-ChildItem $path | Format-Table | Sort Length

    ## Fixed version
    Get-ChildItem $path | Sort Length | Format-Table
}

PS > Get-ChildItemSortedByLength

(...)

Mode                LastWriteTime     Length Name
----                -------------     ------ ----
-a---        3/11/2007   3:21 PM         59 LibraryProperties.ps1
-a---         3/6/2007  10:27 AM        150 Get-Tomorrow.ps1
-a---         3/4/2007   3:10 PM        194 ConvertFrom-FahrenheitWithout
                                            Function.ps1
-a---         3/4/2007   4:40 PM        257 LibraryTemperature.ps1
-a---         3/4/2007   4:57 PM        281 ConvertFrom-FahrenheitWithLib
                                            rary.ps1
-a---         3/4/2007   3:14 PM        337 ConvertFrom-FahrenheitWithFunc
                                            tion.ps1
(...)
```

These examples are included as *LibraryDirectory.ps1* in this book's code examples. For more information about obtaining these examples, see "Code Examples" on page xxviii.

When it comes to producing output for the user, a common reason is to provide progress messages. PowerShell actually supports this in a much richer way, through its `Write-Progress` cmdlet. For more information about the `Write-Progress` cmdlet, see Recipe 13.5.

See Also

Recipe 13.5, "Provide Progress Updates on Long-Running Tasks"

13.5 Provide Progress Updates on Long-Running Tasks

Problem

You want to display status information to the user for long-running tasks.

Solution

To provide status updates, use the `Write-Progress` cmdlet shown in Example 13-5.

Example 13-5. Using the Write-Progress cmdlet to display status updates

```
##############################################################################
##
## Invoke-LongRunningOperation
##
## From Windows PowerShell Cookbook (O'Reilly)
## by Lee Holmes (http://www.leeholmes.com/guide)
##
##############################################################################

<#

.SYNOPSIS

Demonstrates the functionality of the Write-Progress cmdlet

#>

Set-StrictMode -Version Latest

$activity = "A long running operation"
$status = "Initializing"

## Initialize the long-running operation
for($counter = 0; $counter -lt 100; $counter++)
{
    $currentOperation = "Initializing item $counter"
    Write-Progress $activity $status -PercentComplete $counter `
        -CurrentOperation $currentOperation
    Start-Sleep -m 20
}
```

```
$status = "Running"

## Initialize the long-running operation
for($counter = 0; $counter -lt 100; $counter++)
{
    $currentOperation = "Running task $counter"
    Write-Progress $activity $status -PercentComplete $counter `
        -CurrentOperation $currentOperation
    Start-Sleep -m 20
}
```

Discussion

The Write-Progress cmdlet provides a way for you to provide structured status information to the users of your script for long-running operations (see Figure 13-1).

Like the other detailed information channels (Write-Debug, Write-Verbose, and the other *Write-** cmdlets), PowerShell lets users control how much of this information they see.

For more information about the Write-Progress cmdlet, type **Get-Help Write-Progress**.

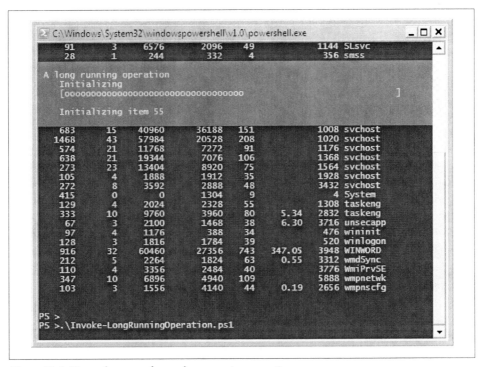

Figure 13-1. Example output from a long-running operation

13.6 Write Culture-Aware Scripts

Problem

You want to ensure that your script works well on computers around the world.

Solution

To write culture-aware scripts, keep the following guidelines in mind as you develop your scripts:

- Create dates, times, and numbers using PowerShell's language primitives.
- Compare strings using PowerShell's built-in operators.
- Avoid treating user input as a collection of characters.
- Use Parse() methods to convert user input to dates, times, and numbers.

Discussion

Writing culture-aware programs has long been isolated to the world of professional software developers. It's not that users of simple programs and scripts can't benefit from culture awareness, though. It has just frequently been too difficult for nonprofessional programmers to follow the best practices. However, PowerShell makes this much easier than traditional programming languages.

As your script travels between different cultures, several things change.

Date, time, and number formats

Most cultures have unique date, time, and number formats. To ensure that your script works in all cultures, PowerShell first ensures that its language primitives remain consistent no matter where your script runs. Even if your script runs on a machine in France (which uses a comma for its decimal separator), you can always rely on the statement $myDouble = 3.5 to create a number halfway between three and four. Likewise, you can always count on the statement $christmas = [DateTime]"12/25/2007" to create a date that represents Christmas in 2007—even in cultures that write dates in the order of day, month, year.

Culturally aware programs always display dates, times, and numbers using the preferences of that culture. This doesn't break scripts as they travel between cultures and is an important aspect of writing culture-aware scripts. PowerShell handles this for you, as it uses the current culture's preferences whenever it displays data.

If your script asks the user for a date, time, or number, make sure that you respect the format of the user's culture's when you do so. To convert user input to a specific type of data, use the [DateTime]::Parse() method:

```
$userInput = Read-Host "Please enter a date"
$enteredDate = [DateTime]::Parse($userInput)
```

So, to ensure that your script remains culture-aware with respect to dates, times, and number formats, simply use PowerShell's language primitives when you define them in your script. When you read them from the user, use `Parse()` methods when you convert them from strings.

Complexity of user input and file content

English is a rare language in that its alphabet is so simple. This leads to all kinds of programming tricks that treat user input and file content as arrays of bytes or simple plain-text (ASCII) characters. In most international languages, these tricks fail. In fact, many international symbols take up two characters' worth of data in the string that contains them.

PowerShell uses the standard Unicode character set for all string-based operations: reading input from the user, displaying output to the user, sending data through the pipeline, and working with files.

 Although PowerShell fully supports Unicode, the `powershell.exe` command-line host does not output some characters correctly, because of limitations in the Windows console system. Graphical PowerShell hosts (such as the Integrated Scripting Environment and the many third-party PowerShell IDEs) are not affected by these limitations, however.

If you use PowerShell's standard features when working with user input, you do not have to worry about its complexity. If you want to work with individual characters or words in the input, though, you will need to take special precautions. The `System.Globalization.StringInfo` class lets you do this in a culturally aware way. For more information about working with the `StringInfo` class, see *http://msdn.microsoft .com/en-us/library/7h9tk6x8.aspx*.

So, to ensure that your script remains culturally aware with respect to user input, simply use PowerShell's support for string operations whenever possible.

Capitalization rules

A common requirement in scripts is to compare user input against some predefined text (such as a menu selection). You normally want this comparison to be case insensitive, so that "QUIT" and "qUiT" mean the same thing.

A traditional way to accomplish this is to convert the user input to uppercase or lowercase:

```
## $text comes from the user, and contains the value "quit"
if($text.ToUpper() -eq "QUIT") { ... }
```

Unfortunately, explicitly changing the capitalization of strings fails in subtle ways when run in different cultures, as many cultures have different capitalization and comparison rules. For example, the Turkish language includes two types of the letter "I": one with a dot and one without. The uppercase version of the lowercase letter "i" corresponds to the version of the capital "I" with a dot, not the capital "I" used in QUIT. That example causes the preceding string comparison to fail on a Turkish system.

To compare some input against a hard-coded string in a case-insensitive manner, the better solution is to use PowerShell's -eq operator without changing any of the casing yourself. The -eq operator is case-insensitive and culture-neutral by default:

```
PS > $text1 = "Hello"
PS > $text2 = "HELLO"
PS > $text1 -eq $text2
True
```

So, to ensure that your script remains culturally aware with respect to capitalization rules, simply use PowerShell's case-insensitive comparison operators whenever possible.

Sorting rules

Sorting rules frequently change between cultures. For example, compare English and Danish with the script given in Recipe 13.8.

```
PS > Use-Culture en-US { "Apple","Æble" | Sort-Object }
Æble
Apple
PS > Use-Culture da-DK { "Apple","Æble" | Sort-Object }
Apple
Æble
```

To ensure that your script remains culturally aware with respect to sorting rules, assume that output is sorted correctly after you sort it—but don't depend on the actual order of sorted output.

Other guidelines

For other resources on writing culturally aware programs, see *http://msdn.microsoft .com/en-us/library/h6270d0z.aspx* and *http://msdn.microsoft.com/en-us/goglobal/ bb688110.aspx.*

See Also

Recipe 13.8, "Program: Invoke a Script Block with Alternate Culture Settings"

13.7 Support Other Languages in Script Output

Problem

You are displaying text messages to the user and want to support international languages.

Solution

Use the `Import-LocalizedData` cmdlet, shown in Example 13-6.

Example 13-6. Importing culture-specific strings for a script or module

```
Set-StrictMode -Version Latest

## Create some default messages for English cultures, and
## when culture-specific messages are not available.
$messages = DATA {
    @{
        Greeting = "Hello, {0}"
        Goodbye = "So long."
    }
}

## Import localized messages for the current culture.
Import-LocalizedData messages -ErrorAction SilentlyContinue

## Output the localized messages
$messages.Greeting -f "World"
$messages.Goodbye
```

Discussion

The `Import-LocalizedData` cmdlet lets you easily write scripts that display different messages for different languages.

The core of this localization support comes from the concept of a *message table*: a simple mapping of message IDs (such as a `"Greeting"` or `"Goodbye"` message) to the actual message it represents. Instead of directly outputting a string to the user, you instead retrieve the string from the message table and output that. Localization of your script comes from replacing the message table with one that contains messages appropriate for the current language.

PowerShell uses standard hashtables to define message tables. Keys and values in the hashtable represent message IDs and their corresponding strings, respectively.

 The solution defines the default message table within a DATA section. As with loading messages from *.psd1* files, this places PowerShell in a data-centric subset of the full PowerShell language. While not required, it is a useful practice for both error detection and consistency.

After defining a default message table in your script, the next step is to create localized versions and place them in language-specific directories alongside your script. The real magic of the Import-LocalizedData cmdlet comes from the intelligence it applies when loading the appropriate message file.

As a background, the standard way to refer to a culture (for localization purposes) is an identifier that combines the *culture* and *region*. For example, German as spoken in Germany is defined by the identifier de-DE. English as spoken in the United States is defined by the identifier en-US, whereas English as spoken in Canada is defined by the identifier en-CA. Most languages are spoken in many regions.

When you call the Import-LocalizedData cmdlet, PowerShell goes to the same directory as your script, and first tries to load your messages from a directory with a name that matches the full name of the current culture (for example, en-CA or en-GB). If that fails, it falls back to the region-neutral directory (such as en or de) and on to the other fallback languages defined by the operating system.

To make your efforts available to the broadest set of languages, place your localized messages in the most general directory that applies. For example, place French messages (first) in the "fr" directory so that all French-speaking regions can benefit. If you want to customize your messages to a specific region after that, place them in a region-specific directory.

Rather than define these message tables in script files (like your main script), place them in *.psd1* files that have the same name as your script. For example, Example 13-6 places its localized messages in *Import-LocalizedData.psd1*. PowerShell's *psd1* files represent a data-centric subset of the full PowerShell language and are ideally suited for localization. In the *.psd1* file, define a hashtable (Example 13-7)—but do not store it in a variable like you do for the default message table.

Example 13-7. A localized .psd1 file that defines a message table

```
@{
    Greeting = "Guten Tag, {0}"
    Goodbye = "Auf Wiedersehen."
}
```

If you already use a set of tools to help you manage the software localization process, they may not understand the PowerShell *.psd1* file format. Another standard message format is simple name-value mapping, so PowerShell supports that through the ConvertFrom-StringData cmdlet:

```
ConvertFrom-StringData @'
Greeting = Guten Tag, {0}
Goodbye = Auf Wiedersehen
'@
```

Notice that the Greeting message in Example 13-6 uses {0}-style placeholders (and PowerShell's string formatting operator) to output strings with replaceable text. Using this technique is vastly preferable to using string concatenation (e.g.,

$messages.GreetingBeforeName + " World " + $messages.GreetingAftername) because it gives additional flexibility during localization of languages with different sentence structures.

To test your script under different languages, you can use Recipe 13.8, as in this example:

```
PS > Use-Culture de-DE { Invoke-LocalizedScript }
Guten Tag, World
Auf Wiedersehen.
```

For more information about script internationalization, type **Get-Help about_Script_Internationalization**.

See Also

Recipe 13.8, "Program: Invoke a Script Block with Alternate Culture Settings"

Get-Help about_Script_Internationalization

13.8 Program: Invoke a Script Block with Alternate Culture Settings

Given PowerShell's diverse user community, scripts that you share will often be run on a system set to a language other than English. To ensure that your script runs properly in other languages, it is helpful to give it a test run in that culture. Example 13-8 lets you run the script block you provide in a culture of your choosing.

Example 13-8. Use-Culture.ps1

```
#############################################################################
##
## Use-Culture
##
## From Windows PowerShell Cookbook (O'Reilly)
## by Lee Holmes (http://www.leeholmes.com/guide)
##
#############################################################################

<#

.SYNOPSIS

Invoke a script block under the given culture

.EXAMPLE

Use-Culture fr-FR { [DateTime]::Parse("25/12/2007") }
mardi 25 decembre 2007 00:00:00

#>
```

```
param(
    ## The culture in which to evaluate the given script block
    [Parameter(Mandatory = $true)]
    [System.Globalization.CultureInfo] $Culture,

    ## The code to invoke in the context of the given culture
    [Parameter(Mandatory = $true)]
    [ScriptBlock] $ScriptBlock
)

Set-StrictMode -Version Latest

## A helper function to set the current culture
function Set-Culture([System.Globalization.CultureInfo] $culture)
{
    [System.Threading.Thread]::CurrentThread.CurrentUICulture = $culture
    [System.Threading.Thread]::CurrentThread.CurrentCulture = $culture
}

## Remember the original culture information
$oldCulture = [System.Threading.Thread]::CurrentThread.CurrentUICulture

## Restore the original culture information if
## the user's script encounters errors.
trap { Set-Culture $oldCulture }

## Set the current culture to the user's provided
## culture.
Set-Culture $culture

## Invoke the user's script block
& $ScriptBlock

## Restore the original culture information.
Set-Culture $oldCulture
```

For more information about running scripts, see Recipe 1.1.

See Also

Recipe 1.1, "Run Programs, Scripts, and Existing Tools"

13.9 Access Features of the Host's User Interface

Problem

You want to interact with features in the user interface of the hosting application, but
PowerShell doesn't directly provide cmdlets for them.

Solution

To access features of the host's user interface, use the `$host.UI.RawUI` variable:

```
$host.UI.RawUI.WindowTitle = (Get-Location)
```

Discussion

PowerShell itself consists of two main components. The first is an engine that interprets commands, executes pipelines, and performs other similar actions. The second is the hosting application—the way that users interact with the PowerShell engine.

The default shell, *PowerShell.exe*, is a user interface based on the traditional Windows console. The graphical Integrated Scripting Environment hosts PowerShell in a graphical user interface. In fact, PowerShell makes it relatively simple for developers to build their own hosting applications, or even to embed the PowerShell engine features into their own applications.

You (and your scripts) can always depend on the functionality available through the `$host.UI` variable, as that functionality remains the same for all hosts. Example 13-9 shows the features available to you in all hosts.

Example 13-9. Functionality available through the $host.UI property

```
PS > $host.UI | Get-Member | Select Name,MemberType | Format-Table -Auto

Name                    MemberType
----                    ----------
(...)
Prompt                  Method
PromptForChoice         Method
PromptForCredential     Method
ReadLine                Method
ReadLineAsSecureString  Method
Write                   Method
WriteDebugLine          Method
WriteErrorLine          Method
WriteLine               Method
WriteProgress           Method
WriteVerboseLine        Method
WriteWarningLine        Method
RawUI                   Property
```

If you (or your scripts) want to interact with portions of the user interface specific to the current host, PowerShell provides that access through the `$host.UI.RawUI` variable. Example 13-10 shows the features available to you in the PowerShell console host.

Example 13-10. Functionality available through the default console host

```
PS > $host.UI.RawUI | Get-Member |
    Select Name,MemberType | Format-Table -Auto
```

```
Name                         MemberType
----                         ----------
(...)
FlushInputBuffer                Method
GetBufferContents               Method
GetHashCode                     Method
GetType                         Method
LengthInBufferCells             Method
NewBufferCellArray              Method
ReadKey                         Method
ScrollBufferContents            Method
SetBufferContents               Method
BackgroundColor               Property
BufferSize                    Property
CursorPosition                Property
CursorSize                    Property
ForegroundColor               Property
KeyAvailable                  Property
MaxPhysicalWindowSize         Property
MaxWindowSize                 Property
WindowPosition                Property
WindowSize                    Property
WindowTitle                   Property
```

If you rely on the host-specific features from $host.UI.RawUI, be aware that your script will require modifications (perhaps major modifications) before it will run properly on other hosts.

13.10 Program: Add a Graphical User Interface to Your Script

Although the techniques provided in the rest of this chapter usually are all you need, it is sometimes helpful to provide a graphical user interface to interact with the user.

Since PowerShell fully supports traditional executables, simple programs usually can fill this need. If creating a simple program in an environment such as Visual Studio is inconvenient, you can often use PowerShell to create these applications directly.

In addition to creating Windows Forms applications through PowerShell scripts, two community projects (PowerBoots and WPK) let you easily create rich WPF (Windows Presentation Foundation) interfaces for your PowerShell scripts. For more information, search the Internet for "PowerShell PowerBoots" and "PowerShell WPK."

Example 13-11 demonstrates the techniques you can use to develop a Windows Forms application using PowerShell scripting alone.

Example 13-11. Select-GraphicalFilteredObject.ps1

```
##############################################################################
##
## Select-GraphicalFilteredObject
##
## From Windows PowerShell Cookbook (O'Reilly)
## by Lee Holmes (http://www.leeholmes.com/guide)
##
##############################################################################

<#

.SYNOPSIS

Display a Windows Form to help the user select a list of items piped in.
Any selected items get passed along the pipeline.

.EXAMPLE

dir | Select-GraphicalFilteredObject

    Directory: C:\

Mode                LastWriteTime     Length Name
----                -------------     ------ ----
d----         10/7/2006    4:30 PM           Documents and Settings
d----         3/18/2007    7:56 PM           Windows

#>

Set-StrictMode -Version Latest

$objectArray = @($input)

## Ensure that they've piped information into the script
if($objectArray.Count -eq 0)
{
    Write-Error "This script requires pipeline input."
    return
}

## Load the Windows Forms assembly
Add-Type -Assembly System.Windows.Forms

## Create the main form
$form = New-Object Windows.Forms.Form
$form.Size = New-Object Drawing.Size @(600,600)

## Create the listbox to hold the items from the pipeline
$listbox = New-Object Windows.Forms.CheckedListBox
$listbox.CheckOnClick = $true
$listbox.Dock = "Fill"
$form.Text = "Select the list of objects you wish to pass down the pipeline"
$listBox.Items.AddRange($objectArray)
```

```
## Create the button panel to hold the OK and Cancel buttons
$buttonPanel = New-Object Windows.Forms.Panel
$buttonPanel.Size = New-Object Drawing.Size @(600,30)
$buttonPanel.Dock = "Bottom"

## Create the Cancel button, which will anchor to the bottom right
$cancelButton = New-Object Windows.Forms.Button
$cancelButton.Text = "Cancel"
$cancelButton.DialogResult = "Cancel"
$cancelButton.Top = $buttonPanel.Height - $cancelButton.Height - 5
$cancelButton.Left = $buttonPanel.Width - $cancelButton.Width - 10
$cancelButton.Anchor = "Right"

## Create the OK button, which will anchor to the left of Cancel
$okButton = New-Object Windows.Forms.Button
$okButton.Text = "Ok"
$okButton.DialogResult = "Ok"
$okButton.Top = $cancelButton.Top
$okButton.Left = $cancelButton.Left - $okButton.Width - 5
$okButton.Anchor = "Right"

## Add the buttons to the button panel
$buttonPanel.Controls.Add($okButton)
$buttonPanel.Controls.Add($cancelButton)

## Add the button panel and list box to the form, and also set
## the actions for the buttons
$form.Controls.Add($listBox)
$form.Controls.Add($buttonPanel)
$form.AcceptButton = $okButton
$form.CancelButton = $cancelButton
$form.Add_Shown( { $form.Activate() } )

## Show the form, and wait for the response
$result = $form.ShowDialog()

## If they pressed OK (or Enter), go through all the
## checked items and send the corresponding object down the pipeline
if($result -eq "OK")
{
    foreach($index in $listBox.CheckedIndices)
    {
        $objectArray[$index]
    }
}
```

For more information about running scripts, see Recipe 1.1.

See Also

Recipe 1.1, "Run Programs, Scripts, and Existing Tools"

13.11 Interact with UI Frameworks and STA Objects

Problem

You want to interact with a user interface framework or other object that requires that the current thread be in single-threaded apartment (STA) mode.

```
PS > Add-Type -Assembly PresentationCore
PS > [Windows.Clipboard]::SetText("Hello World")
Exception calling "SetText" with "1" argument(s): "Current thread must be
set to single thread apartment (STA) mode before OLE calls can be made."
At line:1 char:29
+ [Windows.Clipboard]::SetText <<<< ("Hello World")
    + CategoryInfo          : NotSpecified: (:) [], MethodInvocationExcep
   tion
    + FullyQualifiedErrorId : DotNetMethodException
```

Solution

Launch PowerShell with the -STA switch. If you do this as part of a script or helper command, also use the -NoProfile switch to avoid the performance impact and side effects of loading the user's profile:

```
PS > PowerShell -NoProfile -STA -Command {
    Add-Type -Assembly PresentationCore
    [Windows.Clipboard]::SetText("Hello World")
}

PS > PowerShell -NoProfile -STA -Command {
    Add-Type -Assembly PresentationCore
    [Windows.Clipboard]::GetText()
}

Hello World
```

Discussion

Threading modes define an agreement between an application and how it interacts with some of its objects. Most objects in the .NET Framework (and thus, PowerShell and nearly everything it interacts with) ignore the threading mode and are not impacted by it.

Many user interface frameworks (such as WPF and WinForms) do require a specific threading mode, though, called *single-threaded apartment*. PowerShell uses a threading mode called *multi-threaded apartment* (MTA) by default, so you'll sometimes run into an error similar to the code example shown in the problem.

If you frequently find that you need to use STA mode, you can simply modify the PowerShell link on your start menu to always load PowerShell with the -STA parameter. It is incredibly rare for a component to require MTA mode rather than STA mode, and always loading PowerShell with the -STA parameter has no performance impact.

You might wonder why we didn't just change PowerShell's default if it is so safe. Although it is very rare for a component to run into additional issues in STA mode, some advanced threading situations cease to work. Since components with these advanced requirements worked in version one of PowerShell, changing the default would have introduced compatibility issues.

If your entire script requires STA mode, you have two primary options: detect the current threading mode or relaunch yourself under STA mode.

To detect the current threading mode, you can access the `$host.Runspace.Apartment State` variable. If its value is `"STA"`, the current threading mode is STA.

If your script has simple parameter requirements, you may be able to relaunch yourself automatically, as in Example 13-12.

Example 13-12. A script that relaunches itself in STA mode

```
##############################################################################
##
## Invoke-ScriptThatRequiresSta
##
## From Windows PowerShell Cookbook (O'Reilly)
## by Lee Holmes (http://www.leeholmes.com/guide)
##
##############################################################################

<#

.SYNOPSIS

Demonstrates a technique to relaunch a script that requires STA mode.
This is useful only for simple parameter definitions that can be
specified positionally.

#>

param(
    $Parameter1,
    $Parameter2
)

Set-StrictMode -Version Latest

"Current threading mode: " + $host.Runspace.ApartmentState
"Parameter1 is: $parameter1"
"Parameter2 is: $parameter2"

if($host.Runspace.ApartmentState -ne "STA")
{
    "Relaunching"
    $file = $myInvocation.MyCommand.Path
    powershell -NoProfile -Sta -File $file $parameter1 $parameter2
```

```
    return
}

"After relaunch - current threading mode: " + $host.Runspace.ApartmentState
```

When you run this script, you get the following output:

```
PS > .\Invoke-ScriptThatRequiresSta.ps1 Test1 Test2
Current threading mode: Unknown
Parameter1 is: Test1
Parameter2 is: Test2
Relaunching
Current threading mode: STA
Parameter1 is: Test1
Parameter2 is: Test2
After relaunch - current threading mode: STA
```

For more information about PowerShell's command-line parameters, see
Recipe 1.12. For more information about running scripts, see Recipe 1.1.

See Also

Recipe 1.1, "Run Programs, Scripts, and Existing Tools"

Recipe 1.12, "Invoke a PowerShell Command or Script from Outside PowerShell"

Debugging

14.0 Introduction

While developing scripts and functions, you'll often find yourself running into behavior that you didn't intend. This is a natural part of software development, and the path to diagnosing these issues is the fine art known as debugging.

For the simplest of problems, a well-placed call to `Write-Host` can answer many of your questions. Did your script get to the places you thought it should? Were the variables set to the values you thought they should be?

Once problems get more complex, print-style debugging quickly becomes cumbersome and unwieldy. Rather than continually modifying your script to diagnose its behavior, you can leverage PowerShell's much more extensive debugging facilities to help you get to the root of the problem.

```
PS > Set-PsBreakPoint .\Invoke-ComplexDebuggerScript.ps1 -Line 14

  ID Script            Line Command        Variable        Action
  -- ------            ---- -------        --------        ------
   0 Invoke-Comple...   14


PS > .\Invoke-ComplexDebuggerScript.ps1
Calculating lots of complex information
1225
89
Entering debug mode. Use h or ? for help.

Hit Line breakpoint on
'Z:\Documents\CookbookV2\chapters\current\PowerShellCookbook\Invoke-Complex
DebuggerScript.ps1:14'

Invoke-ComplexDebuggerScript.ps1:14       $dirCount = 0
```

```
PS > ?

s, stepInto          Single step (step into functions, scripts, etc.)
v, stepOver          Step to next statement (step over functions, scripts,
                     etc.)
o, stepOut           Step out of the current function, script, etc.

c, continue          Continue execution
q, quit              Stop execution and exit the debugger

k, Get-PSCallStack   Display call stack

l, list              List source code for the current script.
                     Use "list" to start from the current line, "list <m>"
                     to start from line <m>, and "list <m> <n>" to list <n>
                     lines starting from line <m>

<enter>              Repeat last command if it was stepInto, stepOver or
                     list

?, h                 Displays this help message


For instructions about how to customize your debugger prompt, type "help
about_prompt".

PS > k

Command                  Arguments          Location
-------                  ---------          --------
HelperFunction           {}                 Invoke-ComplexDebugge...
Invoke-ComplexDebugge... {}                 Invoke-ComplexDebugge...
prompt                   {}                 prompt
```

By leveraging strict mode, you can often save yourself from writing bugs in the first place. Once you discover an issue, script tracing can help you get a quick overview of the execution flow taken by your script. For interactive diagnosis, PowerShell's Integrated Scripting Environment (ISE) offers full-featured graphical debugging support. From the command line, the *-PsBreakPoint cmdlets let you investigate your script when it hits a specific line, condition, or error.

14.1 Prevent Common Scripting Errors

Problem

You want to have PowerShell warn you when your script contains an error likely to result in a bug.

Solution

Use the `Set-StrictMode` cmdlet to place PowerShell in a mode that prevents many of the scripting errors that tend to introduce bugs.

```
PS > function BuggyFunction
{
    $testVariable = "Hello"
    if($testVariab1e -eq "Hello")
    {
        "Should get here"
    }
    else
    {
        "Should not get here"
    }
}

PS > BuggyFunction
Should not get here

PS > Set-StrictMode -Version Latest
PS > BuggyFunction
The variable '$testVariab1e' cannot be retrieved because it has not been set.
At line:4 char:21
+     if($testVariab1e <<<<  -eq "Hello")
    + CategoryInfo          : InvalidOperation: (testVariab1e:Token) [], RuntimeException
    + FullyQualifiedErrorId : VariableIsUndefined
```

Discussion

By default, PowerShell allows you to assign data to variables you haven't yet created (thereby creating those variables). It also allows you to retrieve data from variables that don't exist—which usually happens by accident and almost always causes bugs. The solution demonstrates this trap, where the L in "variable" was accidentally replaced by the number 1.

To help save you from getting stung by this problem and others like it, PowerShell provides a *strict* mode that generates an error if you attempt to access a nonexisting variable. Example 14-1 demonstrates this mode.

Example 14-1. PowerShell operating in strict mode

```
PS > $testVariable = "Hello"
PS > $tsetVariable += " World"
PS > $testVariable
Hello
PS > Remove-Item Variable:\tsetvariable
PS > Set-StrictMode -Version Latest
PS > $testVariable = "Hello"
PS > $tsetVariable += " World"
The variable '$tsetVariable' cannot be retrieved because it has not been set.
At line:1 char:14
+ $tsetVariable <<<<  += "World"
```

```
  + CategoryInfo          : InvalidOperation: (tsetVariable:Token) [], RuntimeException
  + FullyQualifiedErrorId : VariableIsUndefined
```

In addition to saving you from accessing nonexistent variables, strict mode also detects the following:

- Accessing nonexistent properties on an object
- Calling functions as though they were methods

One unique feature of the `Set-StrictMode` cmdlet is the `-Version` parameter. As PowerShell releases new versions of the `Set-StrictMode` cmdlet, the cmdlet will become more powerful and detect additional scripting errors. Because of this, a script that works with one version of strict mode might not work under a later version. If you won't have the flexibility to modify your script to account for new strict mode rules, use `"-Version 2"` as the value of the `-Version` parameter.

 The `Set-StrictMode` cmdlet is *scoped*, meaning that the strict mode set in one script or function doesn't impact the scripts or functions that call it. To temporarily disable strict mode for a region of a script, do so in a new script block:

```
& { Set-StrictMode -Off; $tsetVariable }
```

For the sake of your script debugging health and sanity, strict mode should be one of the first additions you make to your PowerShell profile.

See Also

Recipe 1.6, "Customize Your Shell, Profile, and Prompt"

`Get-Help Set-StrictMode`

14.2 Trace Script Execution

Problem

You want to review the flow of execution taken by your script as PowerShell runs it.

Solution

Use the `-Trace` parameter of the `Set-PsDebug` cmdlet to have PowerShell trace your script as it executes it:

```
PS > function BuggyFunction
{
    $testVariable = "Hello"
    if($testVariab1e -eq "Hello")
    {
```

```
            "Should get here"
        }
        else
        {
            "Should not get here"
        }
    }

PS > Set-PsDebug -Trace 1
PS > BuggyFunction
DEBUG:    1+  <<<< BuggyFunction
DEBUG:    3+      $testVariable = <<<<  "Hello"
DEBUG:    4+      if <<<< ($testVariable -eq "Hello")
DEBUG:   10+          "Should not get here" <<<<
Should not get here
```

Discussion

When it comes to simple interactive debugging (as opposed to bug prevention), PowerShell supports several of the most useful debugging features that you might be accustomed to. For the full experience, the Integrated Scripting Environment (ISE) offers a full-fledged graphical debugger. For more information about debugging in the ISE, see Recipe 19.1.

From the command line, though, you still have access to tracing (through the Set-PsDebug -Trace statement), stepping (through the Set-PsDebug -Step statement), and environment inspection (through the $host.EnterNestedPrompt() call). The *-PsBreak point cmdlets support much more functionality in addition to these primitives, but the Set-PsDebug cmdlet is useful for some simple problems.

As a demonstration of these techniques, consider Example 14-2.

Example 14-2. A complex script that interacts with PowerShell's debugging features

```
##############################################################################
##
## Invoke-ComplexScript
##
## From Windows PowerShell Cookbook (O'Reilly)
## by Lee Holmes (http://www.leeholmes.com/guide)
##
##############################################################################

<#

.SYNOPSIS

Demonstrates the functionality of PowerShell's debugging support.

#>

Set-StrictMode -Version Latest
```

```
Write-Host "Calculating lots of complex information"

$runningTotal = 0
$runningTotal += [Math]::Pow(5 * 5 + 10, 2)

Write-Debug "Current value: $runningTotal"

Set-PsDebug -Trace 1
$dirCount = @(Get-ChildItem $env:WINDIR).Count

Set-PsDebug -Trace 2
$runningTotal -= 10
$runningTotal /= 2

Set-PsDebug -Step
$runningTotal *= 3
$runningTotal /= 2

$host.EnterNestedPrompt()

Set-PsDebug -off
```

As you try to determine why this script isn't working as you expect, a debugging session might look like Example 14-3.

Example 14-3. Debugging a complex script

```
PS > $debugPreference = "Continue"
PS > Invoke-ComplexScript.ps1
Calculating lots of complex information
DEBUG: Current value: 1225
DEBUG:    17+ $dirCount = @(Get-ChildItem $env:WINDIR).Count
DEBUG:    17+ $dirCount = @(Get-ChildItem $env:WINDIR).Count
DEBUG:    19+ Set-PsDebug -Trace 2
DEBUG:    20+ $runningTotal -= 10
DEBUG:     ! SET $runningTotal = '1215'.
DEBUG:    21+ $runningTotal /= 2
DEBUG:     ! SET $runningTotal = '607.5'.
DEBUG:    23+ Set-PsDebug -Step

Continue with this operation?
  24+ $runningTotal *= 3
[Y] Yes  [A] Yes to All  [N] No  [L] No to All  [S] Suspend  [?] Help
(default is "Y"):y
DEBUG:    24+ $runningTotal *= 3
DEBUG:     !  SET $runningTotal = '1822.5'.

Continue with this operation?
  25+ $runningTotal /= 2
[Y] Yes  [A] Yes to All  [N] No  [L] No to All  [S] Suspend  [?] Help
(default is "Y"):y
DEBUG:    25+ $runningTotal /= 2
DEBUG:     !  SET $runningTotal = '911.25'.

Continue with this operation?
```

```
  27+ $host.EnterNestedPrompt()
[Y] Yes  [A] Yes to All  [N] No  [L] No to All  [S] Suspend [?] Help
(default is "Y"):y
DEBUG:    27+ $host.EnterNestedPrompt()
DEBUG:      ! CALL method 'System.Void EnterNestedPrompt()'
PS > $dirCount
296
PS > $dirCount + $runningTotal
1207.25
PS > exit

Continue with this operation?
  29+ Set-PsDebug -off
[Y] Yes  [A] Yes to All  [N] No  [L] No to All  [S] Suspend [?] Help
(default is "Y"):y
DEBUG:    29+ Set-PsDebug -off
```

Together, these interactive debugging features are bound to help you diagnose and resolve simple problems quickly. For more complex problems, PowerShell's graphical debugger (in the ISE) and the *-PsBreakpoint cmdlets are here to help.

For more information about the Set-PsDebug cmdlet, type **Get-Help Set-PsDebug**. For more information about setting script breakpoints, see Recipe 14.3.

See Also

Recipe 1.1, "Run Programs, Scripts, and Existing Tools"

Recipe 14.3, "Set a Script Breakpoint"

Recipe 19.1, "Debug a Script"

14.3 Set a Script Breakpoint

Problem

You want PowerShell to enter debugging mode when it executes a specific command, executes a particular line in your script, or updates a variable.

Solution

Use the Set-PsBreakpoint cmdlet to set a new breakpoint:

```
Set-PsBreakPoint .\Invoke-ComplexDebuggerScript.ps1 -Line 21
Set-PSBreakpoint -Command Get-ChildItem
Set-PsBreakPoint -Variable dirCount
```

Discussion

When running a script, a breakpoint is a location (or condition) that causes PowerShell to temporarily pause execution of that script. When it does so, it enters debugging mode. Debugging mode lets you investigate the state of the script and also gives you fine-grained control over the script's execution.

For more information about interacting with PowerShell's debugging mode, see Recipe 14.6.

The `Set-PsBreakpoint` cmdlet supports three primary types of breakpoints:

Positional

Positional breakpoints (lines and optionally columns) cause PowerShell to pause execution once it reaches the specified location in the script you identify.

```
PS > Set-PSBreakpoint -Script .\Invoke-ComplexDebuggerScript.ps1 -Line 21

ID Script                          Line Command Variable Action
-- ------                          ---- ------- -------- ------
 0 Invoke-ComplexDebuggerScript.ps1   21


PS > .\Invoke-ComplexDebuggerScript.ps1
Calculating lots of complex information
Entering debug mode. Use h or ? for help.

Hit Line breakpoint on
'(...)\Invoke-ComplexDebuggerScript.ps1:21'

Invoke-ComplexDebuggerScript.ps1:21   $runningTotal
```

When running the debugger from the command line, you can use Recipe 8.6 to determine script line numbers.

Command

Command breakpoints cause PowerShell to pause execution before calling the specified command. This is especially helpful for diagnosing in-memory functions or for pausing before your script invokes a cmdlet. If you specify the `-Script` parameter, PowerShell pauses only when the command is either defined by that script (as in the case of dot-sourced functions) or called by that script. Although command breakpoints do not support the `-Line` parameter, you can get the same effect by setting a positional breakpoint on the script that defines them.

```
PS > Show-ColorizedContent $profile.CurrentUserAllHosts

(...)
084 | function grep(
085 |     [string] $text = $(throw "Specify a search string"),
086 |     [string] $filter = "*",
087 |     [switch] $rec,
088 |     [switch] $edit
089 |     )
090 | {
091 |     $results = & {
092 |         if($rec) { gci . $filter -rec | select-string $text }
093 |         else {gci $filter | select-string $text }
094 |     }
```

```
095 |     $results
096 | }
(...)

PS > Set-PsBreakpoint $profile.CurrentUserAllHosts -Line 92 -Column 18

  ID Script                    Line Command Variable
  -- ------                    ---- ------- --------
   0 profile.ps1                 92


PS > grep "function grep" *.ps1 -rec
Entering debug mode. Use h or ? for help.

Hit Line breakpoint on 'E:\Lee\WindowsPowerShell\profile.ps1:92, 18'

profile.ps1:92        if($rec) { gci . $filter -rec | select-string $text }

(...)
```

Variable

By default, variable breakpoints cause PowerShell to pause execution before changing the value of a variable.

```
PS > Set-PsBreakPoint -Variable dirCount

ID Script Line Command Variable Action
-- ------ ---- ------- -------- ------
 0                      dirCount

PS > .\Invoke-ComplexDebuggerScript.ps1
Calculating lots of complex information
1225
Entering debug mode. Use h or ? for help.

Hit Variable breakpoint on '$dirCount' (Write access)

Invoke-ComplexDebuggerScript.ps1:23
$dirCount = @(Get-ChildItem $env:WINDIR).Count
PS >
```

In addition to letting you break before it changes the value of a variable, PowerShell also lets you break before it accesses the value of a variable.

Once you have a breakpoint defined, you can use the Disable-PsBreakpoint and Enable-PsBreakpoint cmdlets to control how PowerShell reacts to those breakpoints. If a breakpoint is disabled, PowerShell does not pause execution when it reaches that breakpoint. To remove a breakpoint completely, use the Remove-PsBreakpoint cmdlet.

In addition to interactive debugging, PowerShell also lets you define actions to perform automatically when it reaches a breakpoint. For more information, see Recipe 14.5.

For more information about PowerShell's debugging support, type **Get-Help about_Debuggers**.

See Also

Recipe 14.5, "Create a Conditional Breakpoint"

Recipe 14.6, "Investigate System State While Debugging"

Get-Help about_Debuggers

14.4 Debug a Script When It Encounters an Error

Problem

You want PowerShell to enter debugging mode as soon as it encounters an error.

Solution

Run the `Enable-BreakOnError` script (as shown in Example 14-4) to have PowerShell automatically pause script execution when it encounters an error.

Example 14-4. Enable-BreakOnError.ps1

```
##############################################################################
##
## Enable-BreakOnError
##
## From Windows PowerShell Cookbook (O'Reilly)
## by Lee Holmes (http://www.leeholmes.com/guide)
##
##############################################################################

<#

.SYNOPSIS

Creates a breakpoint that only fires when PowerShell encounters an error

.EXAMPLE

PS >Enable-BreakOnError

ID Script          Line Command      Variable        Action
-- ------          ---- -------      --------        ------
 0                      Out-Default                  ...

PS >1/0
Entering debug mode. Use h or ? for help.

Hit Command breakpoint on 'Out-Default'
```

```
PS >$error
Attempted to divide by zero.

#>

Set-StrictMode -Version Latest

## Store the current number of errors seen in the session so far
$GLOBAL:EnableBreakOnErrorLastErrorCount = $error.Count

Set-PSBreakpoint -Command Out-Default -Action {

    ## If we're generating output, and the error count has increased,
    ## break into the debugger.
    if($error.Count -ne $EnableBreakOnErrorLastErrorCount)
    {
        $GLOBAL:EnableBreakOnErrorLastErrorCount = $error.Count
        break
    }
}
```

Discussion

When PowerShell generates an error, its final action is displaying that error to you. This goes through the Out-Default cmdlet, as does all other PowerShell output. Knowing this, Example 14-4 defines a conditional breakpoint. That breakpoint fires only when the number of errors in the global $error collection changes from the last time it checked.

If you don't want PowerShell to break on all errors, you might just want to set a breakpoint on the last error you encountered. For that, run Set-PsBreakpointLastError (Example 14-5) and then run your script again.

Example 14-5. Set-PsBreakpointLastError.ps1

```
Set-StrictMode -Version Latest

$lastError = $error[0]
Set-PsBreakpoint $lastError.InvocationInfo.ScriptName `
    $lastError.InvocationInfo.ScriptLineNumber
```

For more information about intercepting stages of the PowerShell pipeline via the Out-Default cmdlet, see Recipe 2.8. For more information about conditional breakpoints, see Recipe 14.5.

For more information about PowerShell's debugging support, type **Get-Help about_Debuggers**.

See Also

Recipe 2.8, "Intercept Stages of the Pipeline"

Recipe 14.5, "Create a Conditional Breakpoint"

Get-Help about_Debuggers

14.5 Create a Conditional Breakpoint

Problem

You want PowerShell to enter debugging mode when it encounters a breakpoint, but only when certain other conditions hold true as well.

Solution

Use the -Action parameter to define an action that PowerShell should take when it encounters the breakpoint. If the action includes a break statement, PowerShell pauses execution and enters debugging mode.

```
PS > Get-Content .\looper.ps1
for($count = 0; $count -lt 10; $count++)
{
    "Count is: $count"
}
PS > Set-PsBreakpoint .\looper.ps1 -Line 3 -Action {
    if($count -eq 4) { break }
}


  ID Script        Line Command        Variable      Action
  -- ------        ---- -------        --------      ------
   0 looper.ps1       3                              ...


PS > .\looper.ps1
Count is: 0
Count is: 1
Count is: 2
Count is: 3
Entering debug mode. Use h or ? for help.

Hit Line breakpoint on 'C:\temp\looper.ps1:3'

looper.ps1:3      "Count is: $count"
PS > $count
4
PS > c
Count is: 4
Count is: 5
Count is: 6
```

```
Count is: 7
Count is: 8
Count is: 9
```

Discussion

Conditional breakpoints are a great way to automate repetitive interactive debugging. When you are debugging an often-executed portion of your script, the problematic behavior often doesn't occur until that portion of your script has been executed hundreds or thousands of times. By narrowing down the conditions under which the breakpoint should apply (such as the value of an interesting variable), you can drastically simplify your debugging experience.

The solution demonstrates a conditional breakpoint that triggers only when the value of the $count variable is 4. When the -Action script block executes a break statement, PowerShell enters debug mode.

Inside the -Action script block, you have access to all variables that exist at that time. You can review them, or even change them if desired.

In addition to being useful for conditional breakpoints, the -Action script block also proves helpful for generalized logging or automatic debugging. For example, consider the following action that logs the text of a line whenever the script reaches that line:

```
PS > cd c:\temp
PS > Set-PsBreakpoint .\looper.ps1 -line 3 -Action {
    $debugPreference = "Continue"
    Write-Debug (Get-Content .\looper.ps1)[2]
}


  ID Script           Line Command      Variable      Action
  -- ------           ---- -------      --------      ------
   0 looper.ps1          3                            ...


PS > .\looper.ps1
DEBUG:    "Count is: $count"
Count is: 0
DEBUG:    "Count is: $count"
Count is: 1
DEBUG:    "Count is: $count"
Count is: 2
DEBUG:    "Count is: $count"
(...)
```

When we create the breakpoint, we know which line we've set it on. When we hit the breakpoint, we can simply get the content of the script and return the appropriate line.

For an even more complete example of conditional breakpoints being used to perform code coverage analysis, see Recipe 14.8.

For more information about PowerShell's debugging support, type **Get-Help about_Debuggers**.

See Also

Recipe 14.8, "Program: Get Script Code Coverage"

`Get-Help about_Debuggers`

14.6 Investigate System State While Debugging

Problem

PowerShell has paused execution after hitting a breakpoint, and you want to investigate the state of your script.

Solution

Examine the `$PSDebugContext` variable to investigate information about the current breakpoint and script location. Examine other variables to investigate the internal state of your script. Use the debug mode commands (`Get-PsCallstack`, `List`, and others) for more information about how you got to the current breakpoint and what source code corresponds to the current location:

```
PS > Get-Content .\looper.ps1
param($userInput)

for($count = 0; $count -lt 10; $count++)
{
    "Count is: $count"
}

if($userInput -eq "One")
{
    "Got 'One'"
}

if($userInput -eq "Two")
{
    "Got 'Two'"
}

PS > Set-PsBreakpoint c:\temp\looper.ps1 -Line 5

  ID Script            Line Command          Variable         Action
  -- ------            ---- -------          --------         ------
   0 looper.ps1           5


PS > c:\temp\looper.ps1 -UserInput "Hello World"
Entering debug mode. Use h or ? for help.
```

```
Hit Line breakpoint on 'C:\temp\looper.ps1:5'

looper.ps1:5        "Count is: $count"
PS > $PSDebugContext.InvocationInfo.Line
    "Count is: $count"
PS > $PSDebugContext.InvocationInfo.ScriptLineNumber
5
PS > $count
0
PS > s
Count is: 0
looper.ps1:3    for($count = 0; $count -lt 10; $count++)
PS > s
looper.ps1:3    for($count = 0; $count -lt 10; $count++)
PS > s
Hit Line breakpoint on 'C:\temp\looper.ps1:5'

looper.ps1:5        "Count is: $count"
PS > s
Count is: 1
looper.ps1:3    for($count = 0; $count -lt 10; $count++)
PS > $count
1
PS > $userInput
Hello World
PS > Get-PsCallStack

Command                 Arguments               Location
-------                 ---------               --------
looper.ps1              {userInput=Hello World} looper.ps1: Line 3
prompt                  {}                      prompt


PS > l 3 3

    3:* for($count = 0; $count -lt 10; $count++)
    4:  {
    5:      "Count is: $count"

PS >
```

Discussion

When PowerShell pauses your script as it hits a breakpoint, it enters a debugging mode very much like the regular console session you are used to. You can execute commands, get and set variables, and otherwise explore the state of the system.

What makes debugging mode unique, however, is its context. When you enter commands in the PowerShell debugger, you are investigating the live state of the script. If you pause in the middle of a loop, you can view and modify the counter variable that controls that loop. Commands that you enter, in essence, become temporary parts of the script itself.

In addition to the regular variables available to you, PowerShell creates a new $PSDebugContext automatic variable whenever it reaches a breakpoint. The $PSDebugContext.BreakPoints property holds the current breakpoint, whereas the $PSDebugContext.InvocationInfo property holds information about the current location in the script:

```
PS > $PSDebugContext.InvocationInfo


MyCommand          :
BoundParameters    : {}
UnboundArguments   : {}
ScriptLineNumber   : 3
OffsetInLine       : 40
HistoryId          : -1
ScriptName         : C:\temp\looper.ps1
Line               : for($count = 0; $count -lt 10; $count++)
PositionMessage    :
                     At C:\temp\looper.ps1:3 char:40
                     + for($count = 0; $count -lt 10; $count++ <<<< )
InvocationName     : ++
PipelineLength     : 0
PipelinePosition   : 0
ExpectingInput     : False
CommandOrigin      : Internal
```

For information about the nesting of functions and commands that called each other to reach this point (the "call stack"), type Get-PsCallStack.

If you find yourself continually monitoring a specific variable (or set of variables) for changes, Recipe 14.7 shows a script that lets you automatically watch an expression of your choice.

After investigating the state of the script, you can analyze its flow of execution through the three stepping commands: *step into*, *step over*, and *step out*. These functions single-step through your script with three different behaviors: entering functions and scripts as you go, skipping over functions and scripts as you go, or popping out of the current function or script (while still executing its remainder.)

For more information about PowerShell's debugging support, type **Get-Help about_Debuggers**.

See Also

Recipe 14.7, "Program: Watch an Expression for Changes"

Get-Help about_Debuggers

14.7 Program: Watch an Expression for Changes

When debugging a script (or even just generally using the shell), you might find yourself monitoring the same expression very frequently. This gets tedious to type by hand, so Example 14-6 simplifies the task by automatically displaying the value of expressions that interest you as part of your prompt.

Example 14-6. Watch-Expression.ps1

```
###############################################################################
##
## Watch-Expression
##
## From Windows PowerShell Cookbook (O'Reilly)
## by Lee Holmes (http://www.leeholmes.com/guide)
##
###############################################################################

<#

.SYNOPSIS

Updates your prompt to display the values of information you want to track.


.EXAMPLE

PS >Watch-Expression { (Get-History).Count }

Expression          Value
----------          -----
(Get-History).Count     3

PS >Watch-Expression { $count }

Expression          Value
----------          -----
(Get-History).Count     4
$count

PS >$count = 100

Expression          Value
----------          -----
(Get-History).Count     5
$count                100

PS >Watch-Expression -Reset
PS >

#>

param(
    ## The expression to track
```

```
    [ScriptBlock] $ScriptBlock,

    ## Switch to no longer watch an expression
    [Switch] $Reset
)

Set-StrictMode -Version Latest

if($Reset)
{
    Set-Item function:\prompt ([ScriptBlock]::Create($oldPrompt))

    Remove-Item variable:\expressionWatch
    Remove-Item variable:\oldPrompt

    return
}

## Create the variableWatch variable if it doesn't yet exist
if(-not (Test-Path variable:\expressionWatch))
{
    $GLOBAL:expressionWatch = @()
}

## Add the current variable name to the watch list
$GLOBAL:expressionWatch += $scriptBlock

## Update the prompt to display the expression values,
## if needed.
$GLOBAL:oldPrompt = Get-Content function:\prompt
if($oldPrompt -notlike '*$expressionWatch*')
{
    $newPrompt = @'
        $results = foreach($expression in $expressionWatch)
        {
            New-Object PSObject -Property @{
                Expression = $expression.ToString().Trim();
                Value = & $expression
            } | Select Expression,Value
        }
        Write-Host "`n"
        Write-Host ($results | Format-Table -Auto | Out-String).Trim()
        Write-Host "`n"
'@

    $newPrompt += $oldPrompt

    Set-Item function:\prompt ([ScriptBlock]::Create($newPrompt))
}
```

For more information about running scripts, see Recipe 1.1.

See Also

Recipe 1.1, "Run Programs, Scripts, and Existing Tools"

14.8 Program: Get Script Code Coverage

When developing a script, testing it (either automatically or by hand) is a critical step in knowing how well it does the job you think it does. While you can spend enormous amounts of time testing new and interesting variations in your script, how do you know when you are done?

Code coverage is the standard technique to answer this question. You instrument your script so that the system knows what portions it executed, and then review the report at the end to see which portions were *not* executed. If a portion was not executed during your testing, you have untested code and can improve your confidence in its behavior by adding more tests.

In PowerShell, we can combine two powerful techniques to create a code coverage analysis tool: the Tokenizer API and conditional breakpoints.

First, we use the Tokenizer API to discover all of the unique elements of our script: its statements, variables, loops, and more. Each token tells us the line and column that holds it, so we then create breakpoints for all of those line and column combinations.

When we hit a breakpoint, we record that we hit it and then continue.

Once the script in Example 14-7 completes, we can compare the entire set of tokens against the ones we actually hit. Any tokens that were not hit by a breakpoint represent gaps in our tests.

Example 14-7. Get-ScriptCoverage.ps1

```
##############################################################################
##
## Get-ScriptCoverage
##
## From Windows PowerShell Cookbook (O'Reilly)
## by Lee Holmes (http://www.leeholmes.com/guide)
##
##############################################################################

<#

.SYNOPSIS

Uses conditional breakpoints to obtain information about what regions of
a script are executed when run.

.EXAMPLE

PS >Get-Content c:\temp\looper.ps1
```

```
param($userInput)

for($count = 0; $count -lt 10; $count++)
{
    "Count is: $count"
}

if($userInput -eq "One")
{
    "Got 'One'"
}

if($userInput -eq "Two")
{
    "Got 'Two'"
}

PS >$action = { c:\temp\looper.ps1 -UserInput 'One' }
PS >$coverage = Get-ScriptCoverage c:\temp\looper.ps1 -Action $action
PS >$coverage | Select Content,StartLine,StartColumn | Format-Table -Auto

Content   StartLine StartColumn
-------   --------- -----------
param             1           1
(                 1           6
userInput         1           7
)                 1          17
Got 'Two'        15           5
}                16           1
```

This example exercises a 'looper.ps1' script, and supplies it with some
user input. The output demonstrates that we didn't exercise the
"Got 'Two'" statement.

```
#>

param(
    ## The path of the script to monitor
    $Path,

    ## The command to exercise the script
    [ScriptBlock] $Action = { & $path }
)

Set-StrictMode -Version Latest

## Determine all of the tokens in the script
$scriptContent = Get-Content $path
$ignoreTokens = "Comment","NewLine"
$tokens = [System.Management.Automation.PsParser]::Tokenize(
    $scriptContent, [ref] $null) |
    Where-Object { $ignoreTokens -notcontains $_.Type }
$tokens = $tokens | Sort-Object StartLine,StartColumn
```

```
## Create a variable to hold the tokens that PowerShell actually hits
$visited = New-Object System.Collections.ArrayList

## Go through all of the tokens
$breakpoints = foreach($token in $tokens)
{
    ## Create a new action. This action logs the token that we
    ## hit. We call GetNewClosure() so that the $token variable
    ## gets the _current_ value of the $token variable, as opposed
    ## to the value it has when the breakpoints gets hit.
    $breakAction = { $null = $visited.Add($token) }.GetNewClosure()

    ## Set a breakpoint on the line and column of the current token.
    ## We use the action from above, which simply logs that we've hit
    ## that token.
    Set-PsBreakpoint $path -Line `
        $token.StartLine -Column $token.StartColumn -Action $breakAction
}

## Invoke the action that exercises the script
$null = . $action

## Remove the temporary breakpoints we set
$breakpoints | Remove-PsBreakpoint

## Sort the tokens that we hit, and compare them with all of the tokens
## in the script. Output the result of that comparison.
$visited = $visited | Sort-Object -Unique StartLine,StartColumn
Compare-Object $tokens $visited -Property StartLine,StartColumn -PassThru

## Clean up our temporary variable
Remove-Item variable:\visited
```

For more information about running scripts, see Recipe 1.1.

See Also

Recipe 1.1, "Run Programs, Scripts, and Existing Tools"

Recipe 10.9, "Parse and Interpret PowerShell Scripts"

Recipe 14.5, "Create a Conditional Breakpoint"

Tracing and Error Management

15.0 Introduction

What if it doesn't all go according to plan? This is the core question behind error management in any system and it plays a large part in writing PowerShell scripts as well.

Although this is a core concern in many systems, PowerShell's support for error management provides several unique features designed to make your job easier. The primary benefit is a distinction between terminating and nonterminating errors.

When running a complex script or scenario, the last thing you want is for your world to come crashing down because a script can't open one of the 1,000 files it is operating on. Although the system should make you aware of the failure, the script should still continue to the next file. That is an example of a nonterminating error. But what if the script runs out of disk space while running a backup? That should absolutely be an error that causes the script to exit—also known as a terminating error.

Given this helpful distinction, PowerShell provides several features that let you manage errors generated by scripts and programs, and also allows you to generate errors yourself.

15.1 Determine the Status of the Last Command

Problem

You want to get status information about the last command you executed, such as whether it succeeded.

Solution

Use one of the two variables PowerShell provides to determine the status of the last command you executed: the `$lastExitCode` variable and the `$?` variable.

```
$lastExitCode
```
A number that represents the exit code/error level of the last script or application that exited

$? (pronounced "dollar hook")
A Boolean value that represents the success or failure of the last command

Discussion

The `$lastExitCode` PowerShell variable is similar to the `%errorlevel%` variable in DOS. It holds the exit code of the last application to exit. This lets you continue to interact with traditional executables (such as `ping`, `findstr`, and `choice`) that use exit codes as a primary communication mechanism. PowerShell also extends the meaning of this variable to include the exit codes of scripts, which can set their status using the exit statement. Example 15-1 demonstrates this interaction.

Example 15-1. Interacting with the $lastExitCode and $? variables

```
PS > ping localhost

Pinging MyComputer [127.0.0.1] with 32 bytes of data:

Reply from 127.0.0.1: bytes=32 time<1ms TTL=128
Reply from 127.0.0.1: bytes=32 time<1ms TTL=128
Reply from 127.0.0.1: bytes=32 time<1ms TTL=128
Reply from 127.0.0.1: bytes=32 time<1ms TTL=128

Ping statistics for 127.0.0.1:
    Packets: Sent = 4, Received = 4, Lost = 0 (0% loss),
Approximate round trip times in milliseconds:
    Minimum = 0ms, Maximum = 0ms, Average = 0ms
PS > $?
True
PS > $lastExitCode

0
PS > ping missing-host
Ping request could not find host missing-host. Please check the name and try again.
PS > $?
False
PS > $lastExitCode
1
```

The `$?` variable describes the exit status of the last application in a more general manner. PowerShell sets this variable to `False` on error conditions such as the following:

- An application exits with a nonzero exit code.
- A cmdlet or script writes anything to its error stream.
- A cmdlet or script encounters a terminating error or exception.

For commands that do not indicate an error condition, PowerShell sets the $? variable to True.

15.2 View the Errors Generated by a Command

Problem

You want to view the errors generated in the current session.

Solution

To access the list of errors generated so far, use the $error variable, as shown by Example 15-2.

Example 15-2. Viewing errors contained in the $error variable

```
PS > 1/0
Attempted to divide by zero.
At line:1 char:3
+ 1/ <<<< 0
    + CategoryInfo          : NotSpecified: (:) [], ParentContainsError
    RecordException
    + FullyQualifiedErrorId : RuntimeException

PS > $error[0] | Format-List -Force


ErrorRecord             : Attempted to divide by zero.
StackTrace              :    at System.Management.Automation.Expressio
                             (...)
WasThrownFromThrowStatement : False
Message                 : Attempted to divide by zero.
Data                    : {}
InnerException          : System.DivideByZeroException: Attempted to
                          divide by zero.
                             at System.Management.Automation.ParserOps
                          .PolyDiv(ExecutionContext context, Token op
                          Token, Object lval, Object rval)
TargetSite              : System.Collections.ObjectModel.Collection`1[
                          System.Management.Automation.PSObject] Invoke
                          (System.Collections.IEnumerable)
HelpLink                :
Source                  : System.Management.Automation
```

Discussion

The PowerShell $error variable always holds the list of errors generated so far in the current shell session. This list includes both terminating and nonterminating errors.

PowerShell displays fairly detailed information when it encounters an error:

```
PS > Stop-Process -name IDoNotExist
Stop-Process : Cannot find a process with the name "IDoNotExist". Verify
the process name and call the cmdlet again.
At line:1 char:13
+ Stop-Process <<<<  -name IDoNotExist
    + CategoryInfo          : ObjectNotFound: (IDoNotExist:String) [Stop-
Process], ProcessCommandException
    + FullyQualifiedErrorId : NoProcessFoundForGivenName,Microsoft.Power
Shell.Commands.StopProcessCommand
```

One unique feature about these errors is that they benefit from a diverse and international community of PowerShell users. Notice the FullyQualifiedErrorId line: an error identifier that remains the same no matter which language the error occurs in. When a user pastes this error message on an Internet forum, newsgroup, or blog, this fully qualified error ID never changes. English-speaking users can then benefit from errors posted by non-English-speaking PowerShell users, and vice versa.

If you want to view an error in a table or list (through the Format-Table or Format-List cmdlets), you must also specify the -Force option to override this customized view.

If you want to display errors in a more compact manner, PowerShell supports an additional view called CategoryView that you set through the $errorView preference variable:

```
PS > Get-ChildItem IDoNotExist
Get-ChildItem : Cannot find path 'C:\IDoNotExist' because it does not exist.
At line:1 char:14
+ Get-ChildItem <<<<  IDoNotExist
    + CategoryInfo          : ObjectNotFound: (C:\IDoNotExist:String)
  [Get-ChildItem], ItemNotFoundException
    + FullyQualifiedErrorId : PathNotFound,Microsoft.PowerShell.Commands.
  GetChildItemCommand

PS > $errorView = "CategoryView"
PS > Get-ChildItem IDoNotExist
ObjectNotFound: (C:\IDoNotExist:String) [Get-ChildItem], ItemNotFound
Exception
```

To clear the list of errors, call the Clear() method on the $error list:

```
PS > $error.Count
2
PS > $error.Clear()
PS > $error.Count
0
```

For more information about PowerShell's preference variables, type **Get-Help about_automatic_variables**. If you want to determine only the success or failure of the last command, see Recipe 15.1.

See Also

Recipe 15.1, "Determine the Status of the Last Command"

```
Get-Help about_automatic_variables
```

15.3 Manage the Error Output of Commands

Problem

You want to display detailed information about errors that come from commands.

Solution

To list all errors (up to `$MaximumErrorCount`) that have occurred in this session, access the `$error` array:

```
$error
```

To list the last error that occurred in this session, access the first element in the `$error` array:

```
$error[0]
```

To list detailed information about an error, pipe the error into the `Format-List` cmdlet with the -Force parameter:

```
$currentError = $error[0]
$currentError | Format-List -Force
```

To list detailed information about the command that caused an error, access its `InvocationInfo` property:

```
$currentError = $error[0]
$currentError.InvocationInfo
```

To display errors in a more succinct category-based view, change the `$errorView` variable to `"CategoryView"`:

```
$errorView = "CategoryView"
```

To clear the list of errors collected by PowerShell so far, call the `Clear()` method on the `$error` variable:

```
$error.Clear()
```

Discussion

Errors are a simple fact of life in the administrative world. Not all errors mean disaster, though. Because of this, PowerShell separates errors into two categories: *nonterminating* and *terminating*.

Nonterminating errors are the most common type of error. They indicate that the cmdlet, script, function, or pipeline encountered an error that it was able to recover from or was able to continue past. An example of a nonterminating error comes from the Copy-Item cmdlet. If it fails to copy a file from one location to another, it can still proceed with the rest of the files specified.

A terminating error, on the other hand, indicates a deeper, more fundamental error in the operation. An example of this can again come from the Copy-Item cmdlet when you specify invalid command-line parameters.

Digging into an error (and its nested errors) can be cumbersome, so for a script that automates this task, see Recipe 15.4.

See Also

Recipe 15.4, "Program: Resolve an Error"

15.4 Program: Resolve an Error

Analyzing an error frequently requires several different investigative steps: displaying the error, exploring its context, and analyzing its inner exceptions.

Example 15-3 automates these mundane tasks for you.

Example 15-3. Resolve-Error.ps1

```
##############################################################################
##
## Resolve-Error
##
## From Windows PowerShell Cookbook (O'Reilly)
## by Lee Holmes (http://www.leeholmes.com/guide)
##
##############################################################################

<#

.SYNOPSIS

Displays detailed information about an error and its context

#>

param(
    ## The error to resolve
    $ErrorRecord = ($error[0])
)

Set-StrictMode -Off

""
"If this is an error in a script you wrote, use the Set-PsBreakpoint cmdlet"
```

```
"to diagnose it."
""

'Error details ($error[0] | Format-List * -Force)'
"-"*80
$errorRecord | Format-List * -Force

'Information about the command that caused this error ' +
    '($error[0].InvocationInfo | Format-List *)'
"-"*80
$errorRecord.InvocationInfo | Format-List *

'Information about the error''s target ' +
    '($error[0].TargetObject | Format-List *)'
"-"*80
$errorRecord.TargetObject | Format-List *

'Exception details ($error[0].Exception | Format-List * -Force)'
"-"*80

$exception = $errorRecord.Exception

for ($i = 0; $exception; $i++, ($exception = $exception.InnerException))
{
    "$i" * 80
    $exception | Format-List * -Force
}
```

For more information about running scripts, see Recipe 1.1.

See Also

Recipe 1.1, "Run Programs, Scripts, and Existing Tools"

15.5 Configure Debug, Verbose, and Progress Output

Problem

You want to manage the detailed debug, verbose, and progress output generated by cmdlets and scripts.

Solution

To enable debug output for scripts and cmdlets that generate it:

```
$debugPreference = "Continue"
Start-DebugCommand
```

To enable verbose mode for a cmdlet that checks for the -Verbose parameter:

```
Copy-Item c:\temp\*.txt c:\temp\backup\ -Verbose
```

To disable progress output from a script or cmdlet that generates it:

```
$progressPreference = "SilentlyContinue"
Get-Progress.ps1
```

Discussion

In addition to error output (as described in Recipe 15.3), many scripts and cmdlets generate several other types of output. These include the following types:

Debug output

Helps you diagnose problems that may arise and can provide a view into the inner workings of a command. You can use the Write-Debug cmdlet to produce this type of output in a script or the WriteDebug() method to produce this type of output in a cmdlet. PowerShell displays this output in yellow by default, but you can customize it through the $host.PrivateData.Debug* color configuration variables.

Verbose output

Helps you monitor the actions of commands at a finer level than the default. You can use the Write-Verbose cmdlet to produce this type of output in a script or the WriteVerbose() method to produce this type of output in a cmdlet. PowerShell displays this output in yellow by default, but you can customize it through the $host.PrivateData.Verbose* color configuration variables.

Progress output

Helps you monitor the status of long-running commands. You can use the Write-Progress cmdlet to produce this type of output in a script or the WriteProgress() method to produce this type of output in a cmdlet. PowerShell displays this output in yellow by default, but you can customize the color through the $host.PrivateData.Progress* color configuration variables.

Some cmdlets generate verbose and debug output only if you specify the -Verbose and -Debug parameters, respectively.

To configure the debug, verbose, and progress output of a script or cmdlet, modify the $debugPreference, $verbosePreference, and $progressPreference shell variables. These variables can accept the following values:

SilentlyContinue

Do not display this output.

Stop

Treat this output as an error.

Continue

Display this output.

Inquire

Display a continuation prompt for this output.

See Also

Recipe 15.3, "Manage the Error Output of Commands"

15.6 Handle Warnings, Errors, and Terminating Errors

Problem

You want to handle warnings, errors, and terminating errors generated by scripts or other tools that you call.

Solution

To control how your script responds to warning messages, set the $warningPrefer ence variable. In this example, to ignore them:

```
$warningPreference = "SilentlyContinue"
```

To control how your script responds to nonterminating errors, set the $errorAction Preference variable. In this example, to ignore them:

```
$errorActionPreference = "SilentlyContinue"
```

To control how your script responds to terminating errors, you can use either the try / catch / finally statements or the trap statement. In this example, to output a message and continue with the script:

```
try
{
    1 / $null
}
catch [DivideByZeroException]
{
    "Don't divide by zero!"
}
finally
{
    "Script that will be executed even if errors occur in the try statement"
}
```

Use the trap statement if you want its error handling to apply to the entire scope:

```
trap [DivideByZeroException] { "Don't divide by zero!"; continue }
1 / $null
```

Discussion

PowerShell defines several preference variables that help you control how your script reacts to warnings, errors, and terminating errors. As an example of these error management techniques, consider the following script.

```
##############################################################################
##
## Get-WarningsAndErrors
##
## From Windows PowerShell Cookbook (O'Reilly)
## by Lee Holmes (http://www.leeholmes.com/guide)
##
##############################################################################

<#

.SYNOPSIS

Demonstrates the functionality of the Write-Warning, Write-Error, and throw
statements

#>

Set-StrictMode -Version Latest

Write-Warning "Warning: About to generate an error"
Write-Error "Error: You are running this script"
throw "Could not complete operation."
```

For more information about running scripts, see Recipe 1.1.

You can now see how a script might manage those separate types of errors:

```
PS > $warningPreference = "Continue"
PS > Get-WarningsAndErrors
WARNING: Warning: About to generate an error
Get-WarningsAndErrors : Error: You are running this script
At line:1 char:22
+ Get-WarningsAndErrors <<<<
    + CategoryInfo          : NotSpecified: (:) [Write-Error], WriteError
    Exception
    + FullyQualifiedErrorId : Microsoft.PowerShell.Commands.WriteError
    Exception,Get-WarningsAndErrors

Could not complete operation.
At line:15 char:6
+ throw <<<<  "Could not complete operation."
    + CategoryInfo          : OperationStopped: (Could not complete
    operation.:String) [], RuntimeException
    + FullyQualifiedErrorId : Could not complete operation.
```

Once you modify the warning preference, the original warning message gets suppressed. A value of SilentlyContinue is useful when you are expecting an error of some sort.

```
PS > $warningPreference = "SilentlyContinue"
PS > Get-WarningsAndErrors
Get-WarningsAndErrors : Error: You are running this script
At line:1 char:22
+ Get-WarningsAndErrors <<<<
```

```
   + CategoryInfo          : NotSpecified: (:) [Write-Error], WriteError
Exception
   + FullyQualifiedErrorId : Microsoft.PowerShell.Commands.WriteError
Exception,Get-WarningsAndErrors

Could not complete operation.
At line:15 char:6
+ throw <<<<  "Could not complete operation."
   + CategoryInfo          : OperationStopped: (Could not complete
operation.:String) [], RuntimeException
   + FullyQualifiedErrorId : Could not complete operation.
```

When you modify the error preference, you suppress errors and exceptions as well:

```
PS > $errorActionPreference = "SilentlyContinue"
PS > Get-WarningsAndErrors
PS >
```

An addition to the $errorActionPreference variable, all cmdlets let you specify your preference during an individual call:

```
PS > $errorActionPreference = "Continue"
PS > Get-ChildItem IDoNotExist
Get-ChildItem : Cannot find path '...\IDoNotExist' because it does not exist.
At line:1 char:14
+ Get-ChildItem  <<<< IDoNotExist
PS > Get-ChildItem IDoNotExist -ErrorAction SilentlyContinue
PS >
```

If you reset the error preference back to Continue, you can see the impact of a try / catch / finally statement. The message from the Write-Error call makes it through, but the exception does not:

```
PS > $errorActionPreference = "Continue"
PS > try { Get-WarningsAndErrors } catch { "Caught an error" }
Get-WarningsAndErrors : Error: You are running this script
At line:1 char:28
+ try { Get-WarningsAndErrors <<<< } catch { "Caught an error" }
   + CategoryInfo          : NotSpecified: (:) [Write-Error], WriteError
Exception
   + FullyQualifiedErrorId : Microsoft.PowerShell.Commands.WriteError
Exception,Get-WarningsAndErrors

Caught an error
```

The try / catch / finally statement acts like the similar statement in other programming languages. First, it executes the code inside of its script block. If it encounters a terminating error, it executes the code inside of the catch script block. It executes the code in the finally statement no matter what—an especially useful feature for cleanup or error-recovery code.

A similar technique is the **trap** statement:

```
PS > $errorActionPreference = "Continue"
PS > trap { "Caught an error"; continue }; Get-WarningsAndErrors
Get-WarningsAndErrors : Error: You are running this script
At line:1 char:60
+ trap { "Caught an error"; continue }; Get-WarningsAndErrors <<<<
    + CategoryInfo          : NotSpecified: (:) [Write-Error], WriteError
   Exception
    + FullyQualifiedErrorId : Microsoft.PowerShell.Commands.WriteError
   Exception,Get-WarningsAndErrors

Caught an error
```

Unlike the **try** statement, the **trap** statement handles terminating errors for anything in the scope that defines it. For more information about scopes, see Recipe 3.6.

 After handling an error, you can also remove it from the system's error collection by typing `$error.RemoveAt(0)`.

For more information about error management in PowerShell, see "Managing Errors" on page 757. For more detailed information about the valid settings of these preference variables, see Appendix A.

See Also

Recipe 1.1, "Run Programs, Scripts, and Existing Tools"

Recipe 3.6, "Control Access and Scope of Variables and Other Items"

"Managing Errors" on page 757

Get-Help about_automatic_variables

15.7 Output Warnings, Errors, and Terminating Errors

Problem

You want your script to notify its caller of a warning, error, or terminating error.

```
##############################################################################
##
## Get-WarningsAndErrors
##
## From Windows PowerShell Cookbook (O'Reilly)
## by Lee Holmes (http://www.leeholmes.com/guide)
##
##############################################################################
```

```
<#

.SYNOPSIS

Demonstrates the functionality of the Write-Warning, Write-Error, and throw
statements

#>

Set-StrictMode -Version Latest

Write-Warning "Warning: About to generate an error"
Write-Error "Error: You are running this script"
throw "Could not complete operation."
```

Solution

To write warnings and errors, use the `Write-Warning` and `Write-Error` cmdlets, respectively. Use the `throw` statement to generate a terminating error.

Discussion

When you need to notify the caller of your script about an unusual condition, the `Write-Warning`, `Write-Error`, and `throw` statements are the way to do it. If your user should consider the message as more of a warning, use the `Write-Warning` cmdlet. If your script encounters an error (but can reasonably continue past that error), use the `Write-Error` cmdlet. If the error is fatal and your script simply cannot continue, use a `throw` statement.

For information on how to handle these errors when thrown by other scripts, see Recipe 15.6. For more information about error management in PowerShell, see "Managing Errors" on page 757. For more information about running scripts, see Recipe 1.1.

See Also

Recipe 1.1, "Run Programs, Scripts, and Existing Tools"

Recipe 15.6, "Handle Warnings, Errors, and Terminating Errors"

"Managing Errors" on page 757

15.8 Program: Analyze a Script's Performance Profile

When you write scripts that heavily interact with the user, you may sometimes feel that your script could benefit from better performance.

When tackling performance problems, the first rule is to measure the problem. Unless you can guide your optimization efforts with hard performance data, you are almost certainly directing your efforts to the wrong spots. Random cute performance improvements will quickly turn your code into an unreadable mess, often with no appreciable performance gain! Low-level optimization has its place, but it should always be guided by hard data that supports it.

The way to obtain hard performance data is from a profiler. PowerShell doesn't ship with a script profiler, but Example 15-4 uses PowerShell features to implement one.

Example 15-4. Get-ScriptPerformanceProfile.ps1

```
##############################################################################
##
## Get-ScriptPerformanceProfile
##
## From Windows PowerShell Cookbook (O'Reilly)
## by Lee Holmes (http://www.leeholmes.com/guide)
##
##############################################################################

<#

.SYNOPSIS

Computes the performance characteristics of a script, based on the transcript
of it running at trace level 1.

.DESCRIPTION

To profile a script:

    1) Turn on script tracing in the window that will run the script:
       Set-PsDebug -trace 1
    2) Turn on the transcript for the window that will run the script:
       Start-Transcript
       (Note the filename that PowerShell provides as the logging destination.)
    3) Type in the script name, but don't actually start it.
    4) Open another PowerShell window, and navigate to the directory holding
       this script.  Type in '.\Get-ScriptPerformanceProfile <transcript>',
       replacing <transcript> with the path given in step 2.  Don't
       press <Enter> yet.
    5) Switch to the profiled script window, and start the script.
       Switch to the window containing this script, and press <Enter>.
    6) Wait until your profiled script exits, or has run long enough to be
       representative of its work. To be statistically accurate, your script
       should run for at least ten seconds.
    7) Switch to the window running this script, and press a key.
    8) Switch to the window holding your profiled script, and type:
       Stop-Transcript
    9) Delete the transcript.

.NOTES

You can profile regions of code (ie: functions) rather than just lines
by placing the following call at the start of the region:
     Write-Debug "ENTER <region_name>"
and the following call and the end of the region:
     Write-Debug "EXIT"
```

This is implemented to account exclusively for the time spent in that
region, and does not include time spent in regions contained within the
region. For example, if FunctionA calls FunctionB, and you've surrounded
each by region markers, the statistics for FunctionA will not include the
statistics for FunctionB.

```
#>

param(
    ## The path of the transcript log file
    [Parameter(Mandatory = $true)]
    $Path
)

Set-StrictMode -Version Latest

function Main
{
    ## Run the actual profiling of the script. $uniqueLines gets
    ## the mapping of line number to actual script content.
    ## $samples gets a hashtable mapping line number to the number of times
    ## we observed the script running that line.
    $uniqueLines = @{}
    $samples = GetSamples $uniqueLines

    "Breakdown by line:"
    "----------------------------"

    ## Create a new hashtable that flips the $samples hashtable --
    ## one that maps the number of times sampled to the line sampled.
    ## Also, figure out how many samples we got altogether.
    $counts = @{}
    $totalSamples = 0;
    foreach($item in $samples.Keys)
    {
        $counts[$samples[$item]] = $item
        $totalSamples += $samples[$item]
    }

    ## Go through the flipped hashtable, in descending order of number of
    ## samples. As we do so, output the number of samples as a percentage of
    ## the total samples. This gives us the percentage of the time our
    ## script spent executing that line.
    foreach($count in ($counts.Keys | Sort-Object -Descending))
    {
        $line = $counts[$count]
        $percentage = "{0:#0}" -f ($count * 100 / $totalSamples)
        "{0,3}%: Line {1,4} -{2}" -f $percentage,$line,
            $uniqueLines[$line]
    }

    ## Go through the transcript log to figure out which lines are part of
    ## any marked regions. This returns a hashtable that maps region names
    ## to the lines they contain.
    ""
```

```
        "Breakdown by marked regions:"
        "--------------------------"
        $functionMembers = GenerateFunctionMembers

        ## For each region name, cycle through the lines in the region. As we
        ## cycle through the lines, sum up the time spent on those lines and
        ## output the total.
        foreach($key in $functionMembers.Keys)
        {
            $totalTime = 0
            foreach($line in $functionMembers[$key])
            {
                $totalTime += ($samples[$line] * 100 / $totalSamples)
            }

            $percentage = "{0:#0}" -f $totalTime
            "{0,3}%: {1}" -f $percentage,$key
        }
    }

    ## Run the actual profiling of the script. $uniqueLines gets
    ## the mapping of line number to actual script content.
    ## Return a hashtable mapping line number to the number of times
    ## we observed the script running that line.
    function GetSamples($uniqueLines)
    {
        ## Open the log file. We use the .Net file I/O, so that we keep
        ## monitoring just the end of the file. Otherwise, we would make our
        ## timing inaccurate as we scan the entire length of the file every time.
        $logStream = [System.IO.File]::Open($Path, "Open", "Read", "ReadWrite")
        $logReader = New-Object System.IO.StreamReader $logStream

        $random = New-Object Random
        $samples = @{}

        $lastCounted = $null

        ## Gather statistics until the user presses a key.
        while(-not $host.UI.RawUI.KeyAvailable)
        {
            ## We sleep a slightly random amount of time. If we sleep a constant
            ## amount of time, we run the very real risk of improperly sampling
            ## scripts that exhibit periodic behaviour.
            $sleepTime = [int] ($random.NextDouble() * 100.0)
            Start-Sleep -Milliseconds $sleepTime

            ## Get any content produced by the transcript since our last poll.
            ## From that poll, extract the last DEBUG statement (which is the last
            ## line executed).
            $rest = $logReader.ReadToEnd()
            $lastEntryIndex = $rest.LastIndexOf("DEBUG: ")

            ## If we didn't get a new line, then the script is still working on
            ## the last line that we captured.
            if($lastEntryIndex -lt 0)
```

```
    {
        if($lastCounted) { $samples[$lastCounted] ++ }
        continue;
    }

    ## Extract the debug line.
    $lastEntryFinish = $rest.IndexOf("\n", $lastEntryIndex)
    if($lastEntryFinish -eq -1) { $lastEntryFinish = $rest.length }

    $scriptLine = $rest.Substring(
        $lastEntryIndex, ($lastEntryFinish - $lastEntryIndex)).Trim()
    if($scriptLine -match 'DEBUG:[ \t]*([0-9]*)\+(.*)')
    {
        ## Pull out the line number from the line
        $last = $matches[1]

        $lastCounted = $last
        $samples[$last] ++

        ## Pull out the actual script line that matches the line number
        $uniqueLines[$last] = $matches[2]
    }

    ## Discard anything that's buffered during this poll, and start
    ## waiting again
    $logReader.DiscardBufferedData()
}

## Clean up
$logStream.Close()
$logReader.Close()

$samples
}

## Go through the transcript log to figure out which lines are part of any
## marked regions. This returns a hashtable that maps region names to
## the lines they contain.
function GenerateFunctionMembers
{
    ## Create a stack that represents the callstack. That way, if a marked
    ## region contains another marked region, we attribute the statistics
    ## appropriately.
    $callstack = New-Object System.Collections.Stack
    $currentFunction = "Unmarked"
    $callstack.Push($currentFunction)

    $functionMembers = @{}

    ## Go through each line in the transcript file, from the beginning
    foreach($line in (Get-Content $Path))
    {
        ## Check if we're entering a monitor block
        ## If so, store that we're in that function, and push it onto
        ## the callstack.
```

```
if($line -match 'write-debug "ENTER (.*)"')
{
    $currentFunction = $matches[1]
    $callstack.Push($currentFunction)
}
## Check if we're exiting a monitor block
## If so, clear the "current function" from the callstack,
## and store the new "current function" onto the callstack.
elseif($line -match 'write-debug "EXIT"')
{
    [void] $callstack.Pop()
    $currentFunction = $callstack.Peek()
}
## Otherwise, this is just a line with some code.
## Add the line number as a member of the "current function"
else
{
    if($line -match 'DEBUG:[ \t]*([0-9]*)\+')
    {
        ## Create the arraylist if it's not initialized
        if(-not $functionMembers[$currentFunction])
        {
            $functionMembers[$currentFunction] =
                New-Object System.Collections.ArrayList
        }

        ## Add the current line to the ArrayList
        $hitLines = $functionMembers[$currentFunction]
        if(-not $hitLines.Contains($matches[1]))
        {
            [void] $hitLines.Add($matches[1])
        }
    }
}
}
}

    $functionMembers
}

. Main
```

For more information about running scripts, see Recipe 1.1.

See Also

Recipe 1.1, "Run Programs, Scripts, and Existing Tools"

Environmental Awareness

16.0 Introduction

While many of your scripts will be designed to work in isolation, you will often find it helpful to give your script information about its execution environment: its name, current working directory, environment variables, common system paths, and more.

PowerShell offers several ways to get at this information—from its cmdlets and built-in variables to features that it offers from the .NET Framework.

16.1 View and Modify Environment Variables

Problem

You want to interact with your system's environment variables.

Solution

To interact with environment variables, access them in almost the same way that you access regular PowerShell variables. The only difference is that you place env: between the dollar sign ($) and the variable name:

```
PS > $env:Username
Lee
```

You can modify environment variables this way, too. For example, to temporarily add the current directory to the path:

```
PS > Invoke-DemonstrationScript
The term 'Invoke-DemonstrationScript' is not recognized as the name of a
cmdlet, function, script file, or operable program. Check the spelling of
the name, or if a path was included, verify that the path is correct and
try again.
At line:1 char:27
+ Invoke-DemonstrationScript <<<<
    + CategoryInfo          : ObjectNotFound: (Invoke-DemonstrationScript
```

```
 :String) [], CommandNotFoundException
  + FullyQualifiedErrorId : CommandNotFoundException


Suggestion [3,General]: The command Invoke-DemonstrationScript was not
found, but does exist in the current location. Windows PowerShell doesn't load
commands from the current location by default. If you trust this command,
instead type ".\Invoke-DemonstrationScript". See "get-help about_Command_
Precedence" for more details.

PS > $env:PATH = $env:PATH + ".;"
PS > Invoke-DemonstrationScript
The script ran!
```

Discussion

In batch files, environment variables are the primary way to store temporary information or to transfer information between batch files. PowerShell variables and script parameters are more effective ways to solve those problems, but environment variables continue to provide a useful way to access common system settings, such as the system's path, temporary directory, domain name, username, and more.

PowerShell surfaces environment variables through its *environment provider*: a container that lets you work with environment variables much as you would work with items in the filesystem or registry providers. By default, PowerShell defines an env: drive (much like c: or d:) that provides access to this information:

```
PS > dir env:

Name                         Value
----                         -----
Path                         c:\progra~1\ruby\bin;C:\WINDOWS\system32;C:\
TEMP                         C:\DOCUME~1\Lee\LOCALS~1\Temp
SESSIONNAME                  Console
PATHEXT                      .COM;.EXE;.BAT;.CMD;.VBS;.VBE;.JS;.JSE;.WSF;
(...)
```

Since it is a regular PowerShell drive, the full way to get the value of an environment variable looks like this:

```
PS > Get-Content Env:\Username
Lee
```

When it comes to environment variables, though, that is a syntax you will almost never need to use, because of PowerShell's support for the Get-Content and Set-Content variable syntax, which shortens that to:

```
PS > $env:Username
Lee
```

This syntax works for all drives but is used most commonly to access environment variables. For more information about this syntax, see Recipe 16.2.

Some environment variables actually get their values from a combination of two places: the machine-wide settings and the current-user settings. If you want to access environment variable values specifically configured at the machine or user level, use the `[Environment]::GetEnvironmentVariable()` method. For example, if you've defined a *tools* directory in your path, you might see:

```
PS > [Environment]::GetEnvironmentVariable("Path", "User")
d:\lee\tools
```

To set these machine- or user-specific environment variables permanently, use the `[Environment]::SetEnvironmentVariable()` method:

```
[Environment]::SetEnvironmentVariable(<name>, <value>, <target>)
```

The *target* parameter defines where this variable should be stored: User for the current user and Machine for all users on the machine. For example, to permanently add your *tools* directory to your path:

```
PS > $oldPersonalPath = [Environment]::GetEnvironmentVariable("Path", "User")
PS > $oldPersonalPath += "d:\tools"
PS > [Environment]::SetEnvironmentVariable("Path", $oldPersonalPath, "User")
```

For more information about the Get-Content and Set-Content variable syntax, see "Variables" on page 716. For more information about the environment provider, type **Get-Help About_Environment**.

See Also

Recipe 16.2, "Access Information About Your Command's Invocation"

"Variables" on page 716

16.2 Access Information About Your Command's Invocation

Problem

You want to learn about how the user invoked your script, function, or script block.

Solution

To access information about how the user invoked your command, use the `$myInvocation` variable:

```
"You invoked this script by typing: " + $myInvocation.Line
```

Discussion

The $myInvocation variable provides a great deal of information about the current script, function, or script block—and the context in which it was invoked:

MyCommand
> Information about the command (script, function, or script block) itself.

ScriptLineNumber
> The line number in the script that called this command.

ScriptName
> When in a function or script block, the name of the script that called this command.

Line
> The verbatim text used in the line of script (or command line) that called this command.

InvocationName
> The name that the user supplied to invoke this command. This will be different from the information given by MyCommand if the user has defined an alias for the command.

PipelineLength
> The number of commands in the pipeline that invoked this command.

PipelinePosition
> The position of this command in the pipeline that invoked this command.

One important point about working with the $myInvocation variable is that it changes depending on the type of command from which you call it. If you access this information from a function, it provides information specific to that function—not the script from which it was called. Since scripts, functions, and script blocks are fairly unique, information in the $myInvocation.MyCommand variable changes slightly between the different command types.

Scripts

Definition *and* Path
> The full path to the currently running script

Name
> The name of the currently running script

CommandType
> Always ExternalScript

Functions

Definition *and* ScriptBlock
> The source code of the currently running function

Options

> The options (None, ReadOnly, Constant, Private, AllScope) that apply to the currently running function

Name

> The name of the currently running function

CommandType

> Always Function

Script blocks

Definition *and* ScriptBlock

> The source code of the currently running script block

Name

> Empty

CommandType

> Always Script

16.3 Program: Investigate the InvocationInfo Variable

When experimenting with the information available through the $myInvocation variable, it is helpful to see how this information changes between scripts, functions, and script blocks. For a useful deep dive into the resources provided by the $myInvocation variable, review the output of Example 16-1.

Example 16-1. Get-InvocationInfo.ps1

```
##############################################################################
##
## Get-InvocationInfo
##
## From Windows PowerShell Cookbook (O'Reilly)
## by Lee Holmes (http://www.leeholmes.com/guide)
##
##############################################################################

<#

.SYNOPSIS

Display the information provided by the $myInvocation variable

#>

param(
    ## Switch to no longer recursively call ourselves
    [switch] $PreventExpansion
)
```

```
Set-StrictMode -Version Latest

## Define a helper function, so that we can see how $myInvocation changes
## when it is called, and when it is dot-sourced
function HelperFunction
{
    "    MyInvocation from function:"
    "-"*50
    $myInvocation

    "    Command from function:"
    "-"*50
    $myInvocation.MyCommand
}

## Define a script block, so that we can see how $myInvocation changes
## when it is called, and when it is dot-sourced
$myScriptBlock = {
    "    MyInvocation from script block:"
    "-"*50
    $myInvocation

    "    Command from script block:"
    "-"*50
    $myInvocation.MyCommand
}

## Define a helper alias
Set-Alias gii .\Get-InvocationInfo

## Illustrate how $myInvocation.Line returns the entire line that the
## user typed.
"You invoked this script by typing: " + $myInvocation.Line

## Show the information that $myInvocation returns from a script
"MyInvocation from script:"
"-"*50
$myInvocation

"Command from script:"
"-"*50
$myInvocation.MyCommand

## If we were called with the -PreventExpansion switch, don't go
## any further
if($preventExpansion)
{
    return
}

## Show the information that $myInvocation returns from a function
"Calling HelperFunction"
"-"*50
HelperFunction
```

```
## Show the information that $myInvocation returns from a dot-sourced
## function
"Dot-Sourcing HelperFunction"
"-"*50
. HelperFunction

## Show the information that $myInvocation returns from an aliased script
"Calling aliased script"
"-"*50
gii -PreventExpansion

## Show the information that $myInvocation returns from a script block
"Calling script block"
"-"*50
& $myScriptBlock

## Show the information that $myInvocation returns from a dot-sourced
## script block
"Dot-Sourcing script block"
"-"*50
. $myScriptBlock

## Show the information that $myInvocation returns from an aliased script
"Calling aliased script"
"-"*50
gii -PreventExpansion
```

For more information about running scripts, see Recipe 1.1.

See Also

Recipe 1.1, "Run Programs, Scripts, and Existing Tools"

16.4 Find Your Script's Name

Problem

You want to know the name of the currently running script.

Solution

To determine the full path and filename of the currently executing script, use this function:

```
function Get-ScriptName
{
    $myInvocation.ScriptName
}
```

To determine the name that the user actually typed to invoke your script (for example, in a "Usage" message), use the $myInvocation.InvocationName variable.

Discussion

By placing the $myInvocation.ScriptName statement in a function, we drastically simplify the logic it takes to determine the name of the currently running script. If you don't want to use a function, you can invoke a script block directly, which also simplifies the logic required to determine the current script's name:

```
$scriptName = & { $myInvocation.ScriptName }
```

Although this is a fairly complex way to get access to the current script's name, the alternative is a bit more error-prone. If you are in the body of a script, you can directly get the name of the current script by typing:

```
$myInvocation.Path
```

If you are in a function or script block, though, you must use:

```
$myInvocation.ScriptName
```

Working with the $myInvocation.InvocationName variable is sometimes tricky, as it returns the script name when called directly in the script, but not when called from a function in that script. If you need this information from a function, pass it to the function as a parameter.

For more information about working with the $myInvocation variable, see Recipe 16.2.

See Also

Recipe 16.2, "Access Information About Your Command's Invocation"

16.5 Find Your Script's Location

Problem

You want to know the location of the currently running script.

Solution

To determine the location of the currently executing script, use this function:

```
function Get-ScriptPath
{
    Split-Path $myInvocation.ScriptName
}
```

Discussion

Once we know the full path to a script, the Split-Path cmdlet makes it easy to determine its location. Its sibling, the Join-Path cmdlet, makes it easy to form new paths from their components as well.

By accessing the $myInvocation.ScriptName variable in a function, we drastically simplify the logic it takes to determine the location of the currently running script. For a discussion about alternatives to using a function for this purpose, see Recipe 16.4.

For more information about working with the $myInvocation variable, see Recipe 16.2.

For more information about the Join-Path cmdlet, see Recipe 16.8.

See Also

Recipe 16.2, "Access Information About Your Command's Invocation"

Recipe 16.4, "Find Your Script's Name"

Recipe 16.8, "Safely Build File Paths Out of Their Components"

16.6 Find the Location of Common System Paths

Problem

You want to know the location of common system paths and special folders, such as *My Documents* and *Program Files*.

Solution

To determine the location of common system paths and special folders, use the [Environment]::GetFolderPath() method:

```
PS > [Environment]::GetFolderPath("System")
C:\WINDOWS\system32
```

For paths not supported by this method (such as *All Users Start Menu*), use the WScript.Shell COM object:

```
$shell = New-Object -Com WScript.Shell
$allStartMenu = $shell.SpecialFolders.Item("AllUsersStartMenu")
```

Discussion

The [Environment]::GetFolderPath() method lets you access the many common locations used in Windows. To use it, provide the short name for the location (such as System or Personal). Since you probably don't have all these short names memorized, one way to see all these values is to use the [Enum]::GetValues() method, as shown in Example 16-2.

Example 16-2. Folders supported by the [Environment]::GetFolderPath() method

```
PS > [Enum]::GetValues([Environment+SpecialFolder])
Desktop
Programs
Personal
```

```
Favorites
Startup
Recent
SendTo
StartMenu
MyMusic
DesktopDirectory
MyComputer
Templates
ApplicationData
LocalApplicationData
InternetCache
Cookies
History
CommonApplicationData
System
ProgramFiles
MyPictures
CommonProgramFiles
```

Since this is such a common task for all enumerated constants, though, PowerShell actually provides the possible values in the error message if it is unable to convert your input:

```
PS > [Environment]::GetFolderPath("aouaoue")
Cannot convert argument "0", with value: "aouaoue", for "GetFolderPath" to
type "System.Environment+SpecialFolder": "Cannot convert value "aouaoue"
to type "System.Environment+SpecialFolder" due to invalid enumeration values.
Specify one of the following enumeration values and try again. The possible
enumeration values are "Desktop, Programs, Personal, MyDocuments, Favorites, Startup,
Recent, SendTo, StartMenu, MyMusic, DesktopDirectory, MyComputer, Templates, ApplicationData,
LocalApplicationData, InternetCache, Cookies, History, CommonApplicationData, System,
ProgramFiles, MyPictures, CommonProgramFiles"."
At line:1 char:29
+ [Environment]::GetFolderPath( <<<< "aouaoue")
```

Although this method provides access to the most-used common system paths, it does not provide access to all of them. For the paths that the [Environment]:: GetFolder Path() method does not support, use the WScript.Shell COM object. The WScript.Shell COM object supports the following paths: AllUsersDesktop, AllUsers StartMenu, AllUsersPrograms, AllUsersStartup, Desktop, Favorites, Fonts, MyDocuments, NetHood, PrintHood, Programs, Recent, SendTo, StartMenu, Startup, and Templates.

It would be nice if you could use either the [Environment]::GetFolderPath() method *or* the WScript.Shell COM object, but each of them supports a significant number of paths that the other does not, as Example 16-3 illustrates.

Example 16-3. Differences between folders supported by [Environment]::GetFolderPath() and the Wscript.Shell COM object

```
PS > $shell = New-Object -Com WScript.Shell
PS > $shellPaths = $shell.SpecialFolders | Sort-Object
PS >
PS > $netFolders = [Enum]::GetValues([Environment+SpecialFolder])
```

```
PS > $netPaths = $netFolders |
    Foreach-Object { [Environment]::GetFolderPath($_) } | Sort-Object

PS > ## See the shell-only paths
PS > Compare-Object $shellPaths $netPaths |
    Where-Object { $_.SideIndicator -eq "<=" }


InputObject                                              SideIndicator
-----------                                              -------------
C:\Documents and Settings\All Users\Desktop              <=
C:\Documents and Settings\All Users\Start Menu           <=
C:\Documents and Settings\All Users\Start Menu\Programs  <=
C:\Documents and Settings\All Users\Start Menu\Programs\... <=
C:\Documents and Settings\Lee\NetHood                    <=
C:\Documents and Settings\Lee\PrintHood                  <=
C:\Windows\Fonts                                         <=


PS > ## See the .NET-only paths
PS > Compare-Object $shellPaths $netPaths |
    Where-Object { $_.SideIndicator -eq "=>" }


InputObject                                              SideIndicator
-----------                                              -------------
                                                         =>
C:\Documents and Settings\All Users\Application Data     =>
C:\Documents and Settings\Lee\Cookies                    =>
C:\Documents and Settings\Lee\Local Settings\Application... =>
C:\Documents and Settings\Lee\Local Settings\History     =>
C:\Documents and Settings\Lee\Local Settings\Temporary I... =>
C:\Program Files                                         =>
C:\Program Files\Common Files                            =>
C:\WINDOWS\system32                                      =>
d:\lee                                                   =>
D:\Lee\My Music                                          =>
D:\Lee\My Pictures                                       =>
```

For more information about working with classes from the .NET Framework, see Recipe 3.8.

See Also

Recipe 3.8, "Work with .NET Objects"

16.7 Get the Current Location

Problem

You want to determine the current location.

Solution

To determine the current location, use the `Get-Location` cmdlet:

```
PS > Get-Location

Path
----
C:\temp
PS > $currentLocation = (Get-Location).Path
PS > $currentLocation
C:\temp
```

Discussion

One problem that sometimes impacts scripts that work with the .NET Framework is that PowerShell's concept of "current location" isn't always the same as the *Power-Shell.exe* process's "current directory." Take, for example:

```
PS > Get-Location

Path
----
C:\temp

PS > Get-Process | Export-CliXml processes.xml
PS > $reader = New-Object Xml.XmlTextReader processes.xml
PS > $reader.BaseURI
file:///C:/Documents and Settings/Lee/processes.xml
```

PowerShell keeps these concepts separate because it supports multiple pipelines of execution. The process-wide current directory affects the entire process, so you would risk corrupting the environment of all background tasks as you navigate around the shell if that changed the process's current directory.

When you use filenames in most .NET methods, the best practice is to use fully qualified pathnames. The `Resolve-Path` cmdlet makes this easy:

```
PS > Get-Location

Path
----
C:\temp

PS > Get-Process | Export-CliXml processes.xml
PS > $reader = New-Object Xml.XmlTextReader (Resolve-Path processes.xml)
PS > $reader.BaseURI
file:///C:/temp/processes.xml
```

If you want to access a path that doesn't already exist, use the `Join-Path` cmdlet in combination with the `Get-Location` cmdlet:

```
PS > Join-Path (Get-Location) newfile.txt
C:\temp\newfile.txt
```

For more information about the Join-Path cmdlet, see Recipe 16.8.

See Also

Recipe 16.8, "Safely Build File Paths Out of Their Components"

16.8 Safely Build File Paths Out of Their Components

Problem

You want to build a new path out of a combination of subpaths.

Solution

To join elements of a path together, use the Join-Path cmdlet:

```
PS > Join-Path (Get-Location) newfile.txt
C:\temp\newfile.txt
```

Discussion

The usual way to create new paths is by combining strings for each component, placing a path separator between them:

```
PS > "$(Get-Location)\newfile.txt"
C:\temp\newfile.txt
```

Unfortunately, this approach suffers from a handful of problems:

- What if the directory returned by Get-Location already has a slash at the end?
- What if the path contains forward slashes instead of backslashes?
- What if we are talking about registry paths instead of filesystem paths?

Fortunately, the Join-Path cmdlet resolves these issues and more.

For more information about the Join-Path cmdlet, type **Get-Help Join-Path**.

16.9 Interact with PowerShell's Global Environment

Problem

You want to store information in the PowerShell environment so that other scripts have access to it.

Solution

To make a variable available to the entire PowerShell session, use a $GLOBAL: prefix when you store information in that variable:

```
## Create the web service cache, if it doesn't already exist
if(-not (Test-Path Variable:\Lee.Holmes.WebServiceCache))
{
    ${GLOBAL:Lee.Holmes.WebServiceCache} = @{}
}
```

Discussion

The primary guidance when it comes to storing information in the session's global environment is to avoid it when possible. Scripts that store information in the global scope are prone to breaking other scripts and prone to being broken by other scripts.

This is a common practice in batch file programming, but script parameters and return values usually provide a much cleaner alternative.

Most scripts that use global variables do that to maintain state between invocations. PowerShell handles this in a much cleaner way through the use of *Modules*. For information about this technique, see Recipe 11.7.

If you do need to write variables to the global scope, make sure that you create them with a name unique enough to prevent collisions with other scripts, as illustrated in the solution. Good options for naming prefixes are the script name, author's name, or company name.

For more information about setting variables at the global scope (and others), see Recipe 3.6.

See Also

Recipe 3.6, "Control Access and Scope of Variables and Other Items"

Recipe 11.7, "Write Commands That Maintain State"

16.10 Determine PowerShell Version Information

Problem

You want information about the current PowerShell version, CLR version, compatible PowerShell versions, and more.

Solution

Access the $PSVersionTable automatic variable:

```
PS > $psVersionTable

Name                        Value
----                        -----
CLRVersion                  2.0.50727.4200
BuildVersion                6.0.6002.18139
PSVersion                   2.0
WSManStackVersion           2.0
PSCompatibleVersions        {1.0, 2.0}
SerializationVersion        1.1.0.1
PSRemotingProtocolVersion   2.1
```

Discussion

The $PSVersionTable automatic variable holds version information for all of Power-Shell's components: the PowerShell version, its build information, Common Language Runtime (CLR) version, and more.

This automatic variable was introduced in version two of PowerShell, so if your script might be launched in PowerShell version one, you should use the Test-Path cmdlet to test for existence of the $PSVersionTable automatic variable if your script needs to change its behavior:

```
if(Test-Path variable:\PSVersionTable)
{
    ...
}
```

This technique isn't completely sufficient for writing scripts that work in both versions of PowerShell, however. If your script uses language features introduced by PowerShell version two (such as new keywords), the script will fail to load in version one.

If the ability to run your script in both versions of PowerShell is a strong requirement, the best approach is to simply write a script that works in PowerShell version one. It will automatically work in PowerShell version two.

Extend the Reach of Windows PowerShell

17.0 Introduction

The PowerShell environment is phenomenally comprehensive. It provides a great surface of cmdlets to help you manage your system, a great scripting language to let you automate those tasks, and direct access to all the utilities and tools you already know.

The cmdlets, scripting language, and preexisting tools are just part of what makes PowerShell so comprehensive, however. In addition to these features, PowerShell provides access to a handful of technologies that drastically increase its capabilities: the .NET Framework, Windows Management Instrumentation (WMI), COM automation objects, native Windows API calls, and more.

Not only does PowerShell give you access to these technologies, but it also gives you access to them in a consistent way. The techniques you use to interact with properties and methods of PowerShell objects are the same techniques that you use to interact with properties and methods of .NET objects. In turn, those are the same techniques that you use to work with WMI and COM objects.

Working with these techniques and technologies provides another huge benefit—knowledge that easily transfers to working in .NET programming languages such as C#.

17.1 Automate Programs Using COM Scripting Interfaces

Problem

You want to automate a program or system task through its COM automation interface.

Solution

To instantiate and work with COM objects, use the New-Object cmdlet's -ComObject parameter.

```
$shell = New-Object -ComObject "Shell.Application"
$shell.Windows() | Format-Table LocationName,LocationUrl
```

Discussion

Like WMI, COM automation interfaces have long been a standard tool for scripting and system administration. When an application exposes management or automation tasks, COM objects are the second most common interface (right after custom command-line tools).

PowerShell exposes COM objects like it exposes most other management objects in the system. Once you have access to a COM object, you work with its properties and methods in the same way that you work with methods and properties of other objects in PowerShell.

 Some COM objects require a special interaction mode called *single-threaded apartment* (STA) to work correctly. For information about how to interact with components that require STA interaction, see Recipe 13.11.

In addition to automation tasks, many COM objects exist entirely to improve the scripting experience in languages such as VBScript. Two examples are working with files and sorting an array.

Most of these COM objects become obsolete in PowerShell, as PowerShell often provides better alternatives to them! In many cases, PowerShell's cmdlets, scripting language, or access to the .NET Framework provide the same or similar functionality to a COM object that you might be used to.

For more information about working with COM objects, see Recipe 3.12. For a list of the most useful COM objects, see Appendix H.

See Also

Recipe 3.12, "Use a COM Object"

Appendix H, *Selected COM Objects and Their Uses*

17.2 Program: Query a SQL Data Source

It is often helpful to perform ad hoc queries and commands against a data source such as a SQL server, Access database, or even an Excel spreadsheet. This is especially true when you want to take data from one system and put it in another, or when you want to bring the data into your PowerShell environment for detailed interactive manipulation or processing.

Although you can directly access each of these data sources in PowerShell (through its support of the .NET Framework), each data source requires a unique and hard to remember syntax. Example 17-1 makes working with these SQL-based data sources both consistent and powerful.

Example 17-1. Invoke-SqlCommand.ps1

```
##############################################################################
##
## Invoke-SqlCommand
##
## From Windows PowerShell Cookbook (O'Reilly)
## by Lee Holmes (http://www.leeholmes.com/guide)
##
##
##############################################################################

<#

.SYNOPSIS

Return the results of a SQL query or operation

.EXAMPLE

Invoke-SqlCommand.ps1 -Sql "SELECT TOP 10 * FROM Orders"
Invokes a command using Windows authentication

.EXAMPLE

PS >$cred = Get-Credential
PS >Invoke-SqlCommand.ps1 -Sql "SELECT TOP 10 * FROM Orders" -Cred $cred
Invokes a command using SQL Authentication

.EXAMPLE

PS >$server = "MYSERVER"
PS >$database = "Master"
PS >$sql = "UPDATE Orders SET EmployeeID = 6 WHERE OrderID = 10248"
PS >Invoke-SqlCommand $server $database $sql
Invokes a command that performs an update

.EXAMPLE

PS >$sql = "EXEC SalesByCategory 'Beverages'"
PS >Invoke-SqlCommand -Sql $sql
Invokes a stored procedure
```

```
.EXAMPLE

Invoke-SqlCommand (Resolve-Path access_test.mdb) -Sql "SELECT * FROM Users"
Access an Access database

.EXAMPLE

Invoke-SqlCommand (Resolve-Path xls_test.xls) -Sql 'SELECT * FROM [Sheet1$]'
Access an Excel file

#>

param(
    ## The data source to use in the connection
    [string] $DataSource = ".\SQLEXPRESS",

    ## The database within the data source
    [string] $Database = "Northwind",

    ## The SQL statement(s) to invoke against the database
    [Parameter(Mandatory = $true)]
    [string[]] $SqlCommand,

    ## The timeout, in seconds, to wait for the query to complete
    [int] $Timeout = 60,

    ## The credential to use in the connection, if any
    $Credential
)


Set-StrictMode -Version Latest

## Prepare the authentication information. By default, we pick
## Windows authentication
$authentication = "Integrated Security=SSPI;"

## If the user supplies a credential, then they want SQL
## authentication
if($credential)
{
    $credential = Get-Credential $credential
    $plainCred = $credential.GetNetworkCredential()
    $authentication =
        ("uid={0};pwd={1};" -f $plainCred.Username,$plainCred.Password)
}

## Prepare the connection string out of the information they
## provide
$connectionString = "Provider=sqloledb; " +
                    "Data Source=$dataSource; " +
                    "Initial Catalog=$database; " +
                    "$authentication; "

## If they specify an Access database or Excel file as the connection
```

```
## source, modify the connection string to connect to that data source
if($dataSource -match '\.xls$|\.mdb$')
{
    $connectionString = "Provider=Microsoft.Jet.OLEDB.4.0; " +
        "Data Source=$dataSource; "

    if($dataSource -match '\.xls$')
    {
        $connectionString += 'Extended Properties="Excel 8.0;"; '

        ## Generate an error if they didn't specify the sheet name properly
        if($sqlCommand -notmatch '\[.+\$\]')
        {
            $error = 'Sheet names should be surrounded by square brackets, ' +
                'and have a dollar sign at the end: [Sheet1$]'
            Write-Error $error
            return
        }
    }
}

## Connect to the data source and open it
$connection = New-Object System.Data.OleDb.OleDbConnection $connectionString
$connection.Open()

foreach($commandString in $sqlCommand)
{
    $command = New-Object Data.OleDb.OleDbCommand $commandString,$connection
    $command.CommandTimeout = $timeout

    ## Fetch the results, and close the connection
    $adapter = New-Object System.Data.OleDb.OleDbDataAdapter $command
    $dataset = New-Object System.Data.DataSet
    [void] $adapter.Fill($dataSet)

    ## Return all of the rows from their query
    $dataSet.Tables | Select-Object -Expand Rows
}

$connection.Close()
```

For more information about running scripts, see Recipe 1.1.

See Also

Recipe 1.1, "Run Programs, Scripts, and Existing Tools"

17.3 Access Windows Performance Counters

Problem

You want to access system performance counter information from PowerShell.

Solution

To retrieve information about a specific performance counter, use the `Get-Counter` cmdlet, as shown in Example 17-2.

Example 17-2. Accessing performance counter data through the Get-Counter cmdlet

```
PS > $counter = Get-Counter "\System\System Up Time"
PS > $uptime = $counter.CounterSamples[0].CookedValue
PS > New-TimeSpan -Seconds $uptime
```

```
Days               : 8
Hours              : 1
Minutes            : 38
Seconds            : 58
Milliseconds       : 0
Ticks              : 6971380000000
TotalDays          : 8.06872685185185
TotalHours         : 193.649444444444
TotalMinutes       : 11618.9666666667
TotalSeconds       : 697138
TotalMilliseconds  : 697138000
```

Alternatively, WMI's `Win32_Perf*` set of classes support many of the most common performance counters:

```
Get-WmiObject Win32_PerfFormattedData_Tcpip_NetworkInterface
```

Discussion

The `Get-Counter` cmdlet provides handy access to all of Windows' performance counters. With no parameters, it gives a helpful summary of system activity:

```
PS > Get-Counter -Continuous

Timestamp               CounterSamples
---------               --------------
1/9/2010 7:26:49 PM     \\...\network interface(ethernet
                        adapter)\bytes total/sec :
                        102739.3921377

                        \\...\processor(_total)\% processor
                        time :
                        35.6164383561644

                        \\...\memory\% committed bytes in use
                        :
                        29.4531607006855

                        \\...\memory\cache faults/sec :
                        98.1952324093294

                        \\...\physicaldisk(_total)\% disk time
                        :
```

```
                          144.227945205479

                          \\...\physicaldisk(_total)\current disk
                          queue length :
                          0
(...)
```

When you supply a path to a specific counter, the Get-Counter cmdlet retrieves only the samples for that path. The -Computer parameter lets you target a specific remote computer, if desired:

```
PS > $computer = $ENV:Computername
PS > Get-Counter "\\$computer\processor(_total)\% processor time"

Timestamp                   CounterSamples
---------                   --------------
1/9/2010 7:31:58 PM         \\...\processor(_total)\% processor time :
                            15.8710351576814
```

If you don't know the path to the performance counter you want, you can use the -ListSet parameter to search for a counter or set of counters. To see all counter sets, use * as the parameter value:

```
PS > Get-Counter -List * | Format-List CounterSetName,Description


CounterSetName : TBS counters
Description    : Performance counters for the TPM Base Services component.

CounterSetName : WSMan Quota Statistics
Description    : Displays quota usage and violation information for WS-
                 Management processes.

CounterSetName : Netlogon
Description    : Counters for measuring the performance of Netlogon.

(...)
```

If you want to find a specific counter, use the Where-Object cmdlet to compare against the Description or Paths property:

```
Get-Counter -ListSet * | Where-Object { $_.Description -match "garbage" }
Get-Counter -ListSet * | Where-Object { $_.Paths -match "Gen 2 heap" }

CounterSetName      : .NET CLR Memory
MachineName         : .
CounterSetType      : MultiInstance
Description         : Counters for CLR Garbage Collected heap.
Paths               : {\.NET CLR Memory(*)\# Gen 0 Collections, \.NET CLR
                      Memory(*)\# Gen 1 Collections, \.NET CLR Memory(*)\#
                      Gen 2 Collections, \.NET CLR Memory(*)\Promoted Memory
                      from Gen 0...}
PathsWithInstances : {\.NET CLR Memory(_Global_)\# Gen 0 Collections, \.NET
                      CLR Memory(powershell)\# Gen 0 Collections, \.NET CLR
                      Memory(powershell_ise)\# Gen 0 Collections, \.NET
```

```
                     CLR Memory(PresentationFontCache)\# Gen 0 Collections
                     ...}
    Counter        : {\.NET CLR Memory(*)\# Gen 0 Collections, \.NET CLR
                     Memory(*)\# Gen 1 Collections, \.NET CLR Memory(*)\#
                     Gen 2 Collections, \.NET CLR Memory(*)\Promoted Memory
                     from Gen 0...}
```

Once you've retrieved a set of counters, you can use the Export-Counter cmdlet to save them in a format supported by other tools, such as the *.BLG* files supported by the Windows Performance Monitor application.

If you already have a set of performance counters saved in a *.BLG* file or *.TSV* file that were exported from Windows Performance Monitor, you can use the Import-Counter cmdlet to work with those samples in PowerShell.

17.4 Access Windows API Functions

Problem

You want to access functions from the Windows API, as you would access them through a Platform Invoke (P/Invoke) in a .NET language such as C#.

Solution

As shown in Example 17-3, obtain (or create) the signature of the Windows API function, and then pass that to the -MemberDefinition parameter of the Add-Type cmdlet. Store the output object in a variable, and then use the method on that variable to invoke the Windows API function.

Example 17-3. Get-PrivateProfileString.ps1

```
##############################################################################
##
## Get-PrivateProfileString
##
## From Windows PowerShell Cookbook (O'Reilly)
## by Lee Holmes (http://www.leeholmes.com/guide)
##
##############################################################################

<#

.SYNOPSIS

Retrieves an element from a standard .INI file

.EXAMPLE

Get-PrivateProfileString c:\windows\system32\tcpmon.ini `
    "<Generic Network Card>" Name
Generic Network Card
```

```
#>

param(
    ## The INI file to retrieve
    $Path,

    ## The section to retrieve from
    $Category,

    ## The item to retrieve
    $Key
)

Set-StrictMode -Version Latest

## The signature of the Windows API that retrieves INI
## settings
$signature = @'
[DllImport("kernel32.dll")]
public static extern uint GetPrivateProfileString(
    string lpAppName,
    string lpKeyName,
    string lpDefault,
    StringBuilder lpReturnedString,
    uint nSize,
    string lpFileName);
'@

## Create a new type that lets us access the Windows API function
$type = Add-Type -MemberDefinition $signature `
    -Name Win32Utils -Namespace GetPrivateProfileString `
    -Using System.Text -PassThru

## The GetPrivateProfileString function needs a StringBuilder to hold
## its output. Create one, and then invoke the method
$builder = New-Object System.Text.StringBuilder 1024
$null = $type::GetPrivateProfileString($category,
    $key, "", $builder, $builder.Capacity, $path)

## Return the output
$builder.ToString()
```

Discussion

You can access many simple Windows APIs using the script given in Recipe 17.5. This approach is difficult for more complex APIs, however.

In PowerShell version one, it was possible to access these APIs in one of two ways: by generating a dynamic assembly on the fly (you wouldn't really do this for one-off calls, but Recipe 17.5 uses this technique) or by looking up the P/Invoke definition for that API call and compiling the C# to access it.

These are both good approaches, but PowerShell version two introduces the Add-Type cmdlet to make this much easier.

Add-Type offers four basic modes of operation:

```
PS > Get-Command Add-Type | Select -Expand ParameterSets | Select Name

Name
----
FromSource
FromMember
FromPath
FromAssemblyName
```

These modes of operation are:

FromSource

> Compile some C# (or other language) code that completely defines a type. This is useful when you want to define an entire class, its methods, namespace, etc. You supply the actual code as the value to the -TypeDefinition parameter, usually through a variable. For more information about this technique, see Recipe 17.6.

FromPath

> Compile from a file on disk, or load the types from an assembly at that location. For more information about this technique, see Recipe 17.8.

FromAssemblyName

> Load an assembly from the .NET Global Assembly Cache (GAC) by its shorter name. This is not the same as the [Reflection.Assembly]::LoadWithPartialName method, since that method introduces your script to many subtle breaking changes. Instead, PowerShell maintains a large mapping table that converts the shorter name you type into a strongly named assembly reference. For more information about this technique, see Recipe 17.8.

FromMember

> Generates a type out of a member definition (or a set of them). For example, if you specify only a method definition, PowerShell automatically generates the wrapper class for you. This parameter set is explicitly designed to easily support P/Invoke calls.

Now, how do you use the FromMember parameter set to call a Windows API? The solution shows the end result of this process, but let's take it step-by-step. First, imagine that you want to access sections of an INI file.

PowerShell doesn't have a native way to manage INI files, and neither does the .NET Framework. However, the Windows API does, through a call to the function called GetPrivateProfileString. The .NET framework lets you access Windows functions through a technique called *P/Invoke* (Platform Invocation Services). Most calls boil down to a simple *P/Invoke definition*, which usually takes a lot of trial and error. However, a great community has grown around these definitions, resulting in an enormous resource called P/Invoke .NET (*http://www.pinvoke.net/*). The .NET Framework team also supports a tool called the P/Invoke Interop Assistant that generates these definitions as well, but we won't consider that for now.

First, we'll create a script called Get-PrivateProfileString.ps1. It's a template for now:

```
## Get-PrivateProfileString.ps1
param(
    $Path,
    $Category,
    $Key)

$null
```

To start fleshing this out, we visit P/Invoke .NET and search for GetPrivateProfile String, as shown in Figure 17-1.

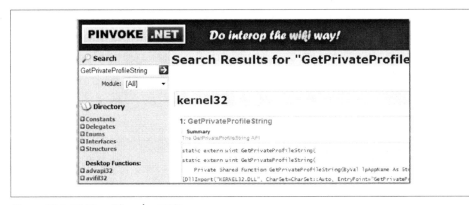

Figure 17-1. Visiting P/Invoke .NET

Click into the definition, and we see the C# signature, as in Figure 17-2.

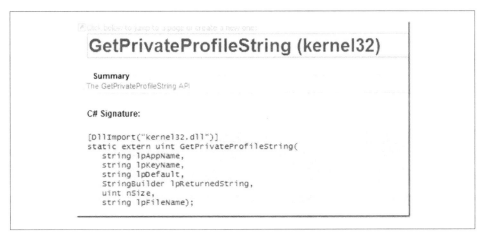

Figure 17-2. The Windows API signature for GetPrivateProfileString

Next, we copy that signature as a here string into our script. Notice in the following code example that we've added `public` to the declaration. The signatures on P/Invoke .NET assume that you'll call the method from within the C# class that defines it. We'll be calling it from scripts (which are outside of the C# class that defines it), so we need to change its visibility.

```
## Get-PrivateProfileString.ps1
param(
    $Path,
    $Category,
    $Key)

$signature = @'
[DllImport("kernel32.dll")]
public static extern uint GetPrivateProfileString(
    string lpAppName,
    string lpKeyName,
    string lpDefault,
    StringBuilder lpReturnedString,
    uint nSize,
    string lpFileName);
'@

$null
```

Now we add the call to `Add-Type`. This signature becomes the building block for a new class, so we only need to give it a name. To prevent its name from colliding with other classes with the same name, we also put it in a namespace. The name of our script is a good choice:

```
## Get-PrivateProfileString.ps1
param(
    $Path,
    $Category,
    $Key)

$signature = @'
[DllImport("kernel32.dll")]
public static extern uint GetPrivateProfileString(
    string lpAppName,
    string lpKeyName,
    string lpDefault,
    StringBuilder lpReturnedString,
    uint nSize,
    string lpFileName);
'@

$type = Add-Type -MemberDefinition $signature `
    -Name Win32Utils -Namespace GetPrivateProfileString `
    -PassThru

$null
```

When we try to run this script, though, we get an error:

```
The type or namespace name 'StringBuilder' could not be found (are you missing a
using directive or an assembly reference?)
c:\Temp\obozeqo1.0.cs(12) :    string lpDefault,
c:\Temp\obozeqo1.0.cs(13) : >>>    StringBuilder lpReturnedString,
c:\Temp\obozeqo1.0.cs(14) :    uint nSize,
```

Indeed we are missing something. The `StringBuilder` class is defined in the `System.Text` namespace, which requires a *using* directive to be placed at the top of the program by the class definition. Since we're letting PowerShell define the type for us, we can either rename `StringBuilder` to `System.Text.StringBuilder` or add a `-UsingNamespace` parameter to have PowerShell add the using statement for us.

 PowerShell adds references to the `System` and `System.Runtime.Interop Services` namespaces by default.

Let's do the latter:

```
## Get-PrivateProfileString.ps1
param(
    $Path,
    $Category,
    $Key)

$signature = @'
[DllImport("kernel32.dll")]
public static extern uint GetPrivateProfileString(
    string lpAppName,
    string lpKeyName,
    string lpDefault,
    StringBuilder lpReturnedString,
    uint nSize,
    string lpFileName);
'@

$type = Add-Type -MemberDefinition $signature `
    -Name Win32Utils -Namespace GetPrivateProfileString `
    -Using System.Text -PassThru

$builder = New-Object System.Text.StringBuilder 1024
$null = $type::GetPrivateProfileString($category,
    $key, "", $builder, $builder.Capacity, $path)

$builder.ToString()
```

Now we can plug in all of the necessary parameters. The `GetPrivateProfileString` function puts its output in a `StringBuilder`, so we'll have to feed it one and return its contents. This gives us the script shown in Example 17-3.

```
PS > Get-PrivateProfileString c:\windows\system32\tcpmon.ini `
    "<Generic Network Card>" Name
Generic Network Card
```

So now we have it. With just a few lines of code, we've defined and invoked a Win32 API call.

For more information about working with classes from the .NET Framework, see Recipe 1.1.

See Also

Recipe 1.1, "Run Programs, Scripts, and Existing Tools"

Recipe 17.5, "Program: Invoke Simple Windows API Calls"

Recipe 17.6, "Define or Extend a .NET Class"

Recipe 17.8, "Access a .NET SDK Library"

17.5 Program: Invoke Simple Windows API Calls

There are times when neither PowerShell's cmdlets nor its scripting language directly support a feature you need. In most of those situations, PowerShell's direct support for the .NET Framework provides another avenue to let you accomplish your task. In some cases, though, even the .NET Framework does not support a feature you need to resolve a problem, and the only solution is to access the core Windows APIs.

For complex API calls (ones that take highly structured data), the solution is to use the `Add-Type` cmdlet (or write a PowerShell cmdlet) that builds on the Platform Invoke (P/Invoke) support in the .NET Framework. The P/Invoke support in the .NET Framework is designed to let you access core Windows APIs directly.

Although it is possible to determine these P/Invoke definitions yourself, it is usually easiest to build on the work of others. If you want to know how to call a specific Windows API from a .NET language, the P/Invoke .NET website (*http://www.pinvoke .net*) is the best place to start.

If the API you need to access is straightforward (one that takes and returns only simple data types), however, Example 17-4 can do most of the work for you.

For an example of this script in action, see Recipe 20.20.

Example 17-4. Invoke-WindowsApi.ps1

```
##############################################################################
##
## Invoke-WindowsApi
##
## From Windows PowerShell Cookbook (O'Reilly)
## by Lee Holmes (http://www.leeholmes.com/guide)
##
##############################################################################
```

```
<#

.SYNOPSIS

Invoke a native Windows API call that takes and returns simple data types.


.EXAMPLE

## Prepare the parameter types and parameters for the CreateHardLink function
PS >$filename = "c:\temp\hardlinked.txt"
PS >$existingFilename = "c:\temp\link_target.txt"
PS >Set-Content $existingFilename "Hard Link target"
PS >$parameterTypes = [string], [string], [IntPtr]
PS >$parameters = [string] $filename, [string] $existingFilename,
    [IntPtr]::Zero

## Call the CreateHardLink method in the Kernel32 DLL
PS >$result = Invoke-WindowsApi "kernel32" ([bool]) "CreateHardLink" `
    $parameterTypes $parameters
PS >Get-Content C:\temp\hardlinked.txt
Hard Link target

#>

param(
    ## The name of the DLL that contains the Windows API, such as "kernel32"
    [string] $DllName,

    ## The return type expected from Windows API
    [Type] $ReturnType,

    ## The name of the Windows API
    [string] $MethodName,

    ## The types of parameters expected by the Windows API
    [Type[]] $ParameterTypes,

    ## Parameter values to pass to the Windows API
    [Object[]] $Parameters
)

Set-StrictMode -Version Latest

## Begin to build the dynamic assembly
$domain = [AppDomain]::CurrentDomain
$name = New-Object Reflection.AssemblyName 'PInvokeAssembly'
$assembly = $domain.DefineDynamicAssembly($name, 'Run')
$module = $assembly.DefineDynamicModule('PInvokeModule')
$type = $module.DefineType('PInvokeType', "Public,BeforeFieldInit")

## Go through all of the parameters passed to us. As we do this,
## we clone the user's inputs into another array that we will use for
## the P/Invoke call.
$inputParameters = @()
```

```
$refParameters = @()

for($counter = 1; $counter -le $parameterTypes.Length; $counter++)
{
    ## If an item is a PSReference, then the user
    ## wants an [out] parameter.
    if($parameterTypes[$counter - 1] -eq [Ref])
    {
        ## Remember which parameters are used for [Out] parameters
        $refParameters += $counter

        ## On the cloned array, we replace the PSReference type with the
        ## .Net reference type that represents the value of the PSReference,
        ## and the value with the value held by the PSReference.
        $parameterTypes[$counter - 1] =
            $parameters[$counter - 1].Value.GetType().MakeByRefType()
        $inputParameters += $parameters[$counter - 1].Value
    }
    else
    {
        ## Otherwise, just add their actual parameter to the
        ## input array.
        $inputParameters += $parameters[$counter - 1]
    }
}

## Define the actual P/Invoke method, adding the [Out]
## attribute for any parameters that were originally [Ref]
## parameters.
$method = $type.DefineMethod(
    $methodName, 'Public,HideBySig,Static,PinvokeImpl',
    $returnType, $parameterTypes)
foreach($refParameter in $refParameters)
{
    [void] $method.DefineParameter($refParameter, "Out", $null)
}

## Apply the P/Invoke constructor
$ctor = [Runtime.InteropServices.DllImportAttribute].GetConstructor([string])
$attr = New-Object Reflection.Emit.CustomAttributeBuilder $ctor, $dllName
$method.SetCustomAttribute($attr)

## Create the temporary type, and invoke the method.
$realType = $type.CreateType()

$realType.InvokeMember(
    $methodName, 'Public,Static,InvokeMethod', $null, $null,$inputParameters)

## Finally, go through all of the reference parameters, and update the
## values of the PSReference objects that the user passed in.
foreach($refParameter in $refParameters)
{
    $parameters[$refParameter - 1].Value = $inputParameters[$refParameter - 1]
}
```

For more information about running scripts, see Recipe 1.1.

See Also

Recipe 1.1, "Run Programs, Scripts, and Existing Tools"

Recipe 20.20, "Program: Create a Filesystem Hard Link"

17.6 Define or Extend a .NET Class

Problem

You want to define a new .NET class or extend an existing one.

Solution

Use the -TypeDefinition parameter of the Add-Type class, as in Example 17-5.

Example 17-5. Invoke-AddTypeTypeDefinition.ps1

```
##############################################################################
##
## Invoke-AddTypeTypeDefinition
##
## From Windows PowerShell Cookbook (O'Reilly)
## by Lee Holmes (http://www.leeholmes.com/guide)
##
##############################################################################

<#

.SYNOPSIS

Demonstrates the use of the -TypeDefinition parameter of the Add-Type
cmdlet.

#>

Set-StrictMode -Version Latest

## Define the new C# class
$newType = @'
using System;

namespace PowerShellCookbook
{
    public class AddTypeTypeDefinitionDemo
    {
        public string SayHello(string name)
        {
            string result = String.Format("Hello {0}", name);
            return result;
        }
```

```
    }
}
'@

## Add it to the Powershell session
Add-Type -TypeDefinition $newType

## Show that we can access it like any other .NET type
$greeter = New-Object PowerShellCookbook.AddTypeTypeDefinitionDemo
$greeter.SayHello("World");
```

Discussion

The Add-Type cmdlet is one of the major new additions to the *glue-like* nature of
PowerShell version two, and it offers several unique ways to interact deeply with
the .NET Framework. One of its major modes of operation comes from the -TypeDefi
nition parameter, which lets you define entirely new .NET classes. In addition to the
example given in the solution, Recipe 3.7 demonstrates an effective use of this
technique.

Once you call the Add-Type cmdlet, PowerShell compiles the source code you provide
into a real .NET class. This action is equivalent to defining the class in a traditional
development environment, such as Visual Studio, and is just as powerful.

 The thought of compiling source code as part of the execution of your
script may concern you because of its performance impact. Fortunately,
PowerShell saves your objects when it compiles them. If you call the
Add-Type cmdlet a second time with the same source code and in the
same session, PowerShell reuses the result of the first call. If you want
to change the behavior of a type you've already loaded, exit your session
and create it again.

PowerShell assumes C# as the default language for source code supplied to the -Type
Definition parameter. In addition to C#, the Add-Type cmdlet also supports C# version
3 (LINQ, the var keyword, etc.), Visual Basic, and JScript. It also supports languages
that implement the .NET-standard CodeProvider requirements (such as F#).

If the code you want to compile already exists in a file, you don't have to specify it inline. Instead, you can provide its path to the -Path parameter. This parameter automatically detects the extension of the file and compiles using the appropriate language
as needed.

In addition to supporting input from a file, you might also want to store the output
into a file—such as a cmdlet DLL or console application. The Add-Type cmdlet makes
this possible through the -OutputAssembly parameter. For example, the following adds
a cmdlet on the fly:

```
PS > $cmdlet = @'
using System.Management.Automation;

namespace PowerShellCookbook
{
    [Cmdlet("Invoke", "NewCmdlet")]
    public class InvokeNewCmdletCommand : Cmdlet
    {
        [Parameter(Mandatory = true)]
        public string Name
        {
            get { return _name; }
            set { _name = value; }
        }
        private string _name;


        protected override void BeginProcessing()
        {
            WriteObject("Hello " + _name);
        }
    }
}

'@

PS > Add-Type -TypeDefinition $cmdlet -OutputAssembly MyNewModule.dll
PS > Import-Module .\MyNewModule.dll
PS > Invoke-NewCmdlet

cmdlet Invoke-NewCmdlet at command pipeline position 1
Supply values for the following parameters:
Name: World
Hello World
```

For advanced scenarios, you might want to customize how PowerShell compiles your source code: embedding resources, changing the warning options, and more. For this, use the -CompilerParameters parameter.

For an example of using the Add-Type cmdlet to generate inline C#, see Recipe 17.7.

See Also

Recipe 1.1, "Run Programs, Scripts, and Existing Tools"

Recipe 17.5, "Program: Invoke Simple Windows API Calls"

Recipe 17.7, "Add Inline C# to Your PowerShell Script"

Recipe 17.9, "Create Your Own PowerShell Cmdlet"

17.7 Add Inline C# to Your PowerShell Script

Problem

You want to write a portion of your script in C# (or another .NET language).

Solution

Use the `-MemberDefinition` parameter of the `Add-Type` class, as in Example 17-6.

Example 17-6. Invoke-Inline.ps1

```
##############################################################################
##
## Invoke-Inline
##
## From Windows PowerShell Cookbook (O'Reilly)
## by Lee Holmes (http://www.leeholmes.com/guide)
##
##############################################################################

<#

.SYNOPSIS

Demonstrates the Add-Type cmdlet to invoke inline C#

#>

Set-StrictMode -Version Latest

$inlineType = Add-Type -Name InvokeInline_Inline -PassThru `
    -MemberDefinition @'
    public static int RightShift(int original, int places)
    {
        return original >> places;
    }
'@

$inlineType::RightShift(1024, 3)
```

Discussion

One of the natural languages to explore after learning PowerShell is C#. It uses many of the same programming techniques as PowerShell, and it also uses the same classes and methods in the .NET Framework. In addition, C# sometimes offers language features or performance benefits that are not available through PowerShell.

Rather than having to move to C# completely for these situations, Example 17-6 demonstrates how you can use the `Add-Type` cmdlet to write and invoke C# directly in your script.

Once you call the `Add-Type` cmdlet, PowerShell compiles the source code you provide into a real .NET class. This action is equivalent to defining the class in a traditional development environment, such as Visual Studio, and gives you equivalent functionality. When you use the `-MemberDefinition` parameter, PowerShell adds the surrounding source code required to create a complete .NET class.

By default, PowerShell will place your resulting type in the `Microsoft.PowerShell.Commands.AddType.AutoGeneratedTypes` namespace. If you use the `-PassThru` parameter (and define your method as `static`), you don't need to pay much attention to the name or namespace of the generated type. However, if you do not define your method as `static`, you will need to use the `New-Object` cmdlet to create a new instance of the object before using it. In this case, you will need to use the full name of the resulting type when creating it. For example:

```
New-Object Microsoft.PowerShell.Commands.AddType.

AutoGeneratedTypes.InvokeInline_Inline
```

 The thought of compiling source code as part of the execution of your script may concern you because of its performance impact. Fortunately, PowerShell saves your objects when it compiles them. If you call the `Add-Type` cmdlet a second time with the same source code and in the same session, PowerShell reuses the result of the first call. If you want to change the behavior of a type you've already loaded, exit your session and create it again.

PowerShell assumes C# as the default language of code supplied to the `-MemberDefinition` parameter. It also supports C# version 3 (LINQ, the `var` keyword, etc.), Visual Basic, and JScript. In addition, it supports languages that implement the .NET-standard CodeProvider requirements (such as F#).

For an example of the `-MemberDefinition` parameter being used as part of a larger script, see Recipe 17.4. For an example of using the `Add-Type` cmdlet to create entire types, see Recipe 17.6.

See Also

Recipe 17.4, "Access Windows API Functions"

Recipe 17.6, "Define or Extend a .NET Class"

17.8 Access a .NET SDK Library

Problem

You want to access the functionality exposed by a .NET DLL, but that DLL is packaged as part of a developer-oriented Software Development Kit (SDK).

Solution

To create objects contained in a DLL, use the -Path parameter of the Add-Type cmdlet to load the DLL and the New-Object cmdlet to create objects contained in it. Example 17-7 illustrates this technique.

Example 17-7. Interacting with classes from the SharpZipLib SDK DLL

```
Add-Type -Path d:\bin\ICSharpCode.SharpZipLib.dll
$namespace = "ICSharpCode.SharpZipLib.Zip.{0}"

$zipName = Join-Path (Get-Location) "PowerShell_TDG_Scripts.zip"
$zipFile = New-Object ($namespace -f "ZipOutputStream") ([IO.File]::Create($zipName))

foreach($file in dir *.ps1)
{
   ## Add the file to the ZIP archive.
   $zipEntry = New-Object ($namespace -f "ZipEntry") $file.Name
   $zipFile.PutNextEntry($zipEntry)
}

$zipFile.Close()
```

Discussion

While C# and VB.Net developers are usually the consumers of SDKs created for the .NET Framework, PowerShell lets you access the SDK features just as easily. To do this, use the -Path parameter of the Add-Type cmdlet to load the SDK assembly, and then work with the classes from that assembly as you would work with other classes in the .NET Framework.

 Although PowerShell lets you access developer-oriented SDKs easily, it can't change the fact that these SDKs are developer-oriented. SDKs and programming interfaces are rarely designed with the administrator in mind, so be prepared to work with programming models that require multiple steps to accomplish your task.

To load any of the typical assemblies included in the .NET Framework, use the -Assembly parameter of the Add-Type cmdlet:

```
PS > Add-Type -Assembly System.Web
```

Like most PowerShell cmdlets, the `Add-Type` cmdlet supports wildcards to make long assembly names easier to type:

```
PS > Add-Type -Assembly system.win*.forms
```

If the wildcard matches more than one assembly, `Add-Type` generates an error.

The .NET Framework offers a similar feature through the `LoadWithPartialName` method of the `System.Reflection.Assembly` class, shown in Example 17-8.

Example 17-8. Loading an assembly by its partial name

```
PS > [Reflection.Assembly]::LoadWithPartialName("System.Web")

GAC     Version      Location
---     -------      --------
True    v2.0.50727   C:\WINDOWS\assembly\GAC_32\(...)\System.Web.dll

PS > [Web.HttpUtility]::UrlEncode("http://www.bing.com")
http%3a%2f%2fwww.bing.com
```

The difference between the two is that the `LoadWithPartialName` method is unsuitable for scripts that you want to share with others or use in a production environment. It loads the most current version of the assembly, which may not be the same as the version you used to develop your script. If that assembly changes between versions, your script will no longer work. The `Add-Type` command, on the other hand, internally maps the short assembly names to the fully qualified assembly names contained in a typical installation of the .NET Framework versions 2.0 and 3.5.

One thing you will notice when working with classes from an SDK is that it quickly becomes tiresome to specify their fully qualified type names. For example, zip-related classes from the SharpZipLib all start with `ICSharpCode.SharpZipLib.Zip`. This is called the *namespace* of that class. Most programming languages solve this problem with a `using` statement that lets you specify a list of namespaces for that language to search when you type a plain class name such as `ZipEntry`. PowerShell lacks a `using` statement, but the solution demonstrates one of several ways to get the benefits of one.

For more information on how to manage these long class names, see Recipe 3.11.

Note that prepackaged SDKs aren't the only DLLs you can load this way. An SDK library is simply a DLL that somebody wrote, compiled, packaged, and released. If you are comfortable with any of the .NET languages, you can also create your own DLL, compile it, and use it exactly the same way. To see an example of this approach, see Recipe 17.6.

For more information about working with classes from the .NET Framework, see Recipe 3.9.

See Also

Recipe 3.9, "Create an Instance of a .NET Object"

Recipe 3.11, "Reduce Typing for Long Class Names"

Recipe 17.6, "Define or Extend a .NET Class"

17.9 Create Your Own PowerShell Cmdlet

Problem

You want to write your own PowerShell cmdlet.

Solution

To create a compiled cmdlet, use the PowerShell SDK (software development kit) as described on MSDN (the Microsoft Developer Network). To create a script-based cmdlet, see Recipe 11.15.

Discussion

As mentioned in "Structured Commands (Cmdlets)" on page 7, PowerShell cmdlets offer several significant advantages over traditional executable programs. From the user's perspective, cmdlets are incredibly consistent. Their support for strongly typed objects as input makes them incredibly powerful, too. From the cmdlet author's perspective, cmdlets are incredibly easy to write when compared to the amount of power they provide. Creating and exposing a new command-line parameter is as easy as creating a new public property on a class. Supporting a rich pipeline model is as easy as placing your implementation logic into one of three standard method overrides.

Although a full discussion on how to implement a cmdlet is outside the scope of this book, the following steps illustrate the process behind implementing a simple cmdlet. While implementation typically happens in a fully featured development environment (such as Visual Studio), Example 17-9 demonstrates how to compile a cmdlet simply through the csc.exe command-line compiler.

For more information on how to write a PowerShell cmdlet, see the MSDN topic "How to Create a Windows PowerShell Cmdlet," available at *http://msdn.microsoft.com/en -us/library/ms714598.aspx*.

Step 1: Download the PowerShell SDK

The PowerShell SDK contains samples, reference assemblies, documentation, and other information used when developing PowerShell cmdlets. Search for "PowerShell 2.0 SDK" on *http://download.microsoft.com* and download the latest PowerShell SDK.

Step 2: Create a file to hold the cmdlet source code

Create a file called *InvokeTemplateCmdletCommand.cs* with the content from Example 17-9 and save it on your hard drive.

Example 17-9. InvokeTemplateCmdletCommand.cs

```
using System;
using System.ComponentModel;
using System.Management.Automation;

/*
To build and install:

1) Set-Alias csc $env:WINDIR\Microsoft.NET\Framework\v2.0.50727\csc.exe
2) $ref = [PsObject].Assembly.Location
3) csc /out:TemplateBinaryModule.dll /t:library InvokeTemplateCmdletCommand.cs /r:$ref
4) Import-Module .\TemplateBinaryModule.dll

To run:

PS >Invoke-TemplateCmdlet
*/

namespace Template.Commands
{
    [Cmdlet("Invoke", "TemplateCmdlet")]
    public class InvokeTemplateCmdletCommand : Cmdlet
    {
        [Parameter(Mandatory=true, Position=0, ValueFromPipeline=true)]
        public string Text
        {
            get
            {
                return text;
            }
            set
            {
                text = value;
            }
        }
        private string text;

        protected override void BeginProcessing()
        {
            WriteObject("Processing Started");
        }

        protected override void ProcessRecord()
        {
            WriteObject("Processing " + text);
        }

        protected override void EndProcessing()
        {
            WriteObject("Processing Complete.");
        }
    }
}
```

Step 3: Compile the DLL

A PowerShell cmdlet is a simple .NET class. The DLL that contains one or more compiled cmdlets is called a *binary module*.

```
Set-Alias csc $env:WINDIR\Microsoft.NET\Framework\v2.0.50727\csc.exe
$ref = [PsObject].Assembly.Location
csc /out:TemplateBinaryModule.dll /t:library InvokeTemplateCmdletCommand.cs /r:$ref
```

For more information about binary modules, see Recipe 1.24.

If you don't want to use csc.exe to compile the DLL, you can also use PowerShell's built-in Add-Type cmdlet. For more information about this approach, see Recipe 17.6.

Step 4: Load the module

Once you have compiled the module, the final step is to load it:

```
Import-Module .\TemplateBinaryModule.dll
```

Step 6: Use the module

Once you've added the module to your session, you can call commands from that module as you would call any other cmdlet.

```
PS > "Hello World" | Invoke-TemplateCmdlet
Processing Started
Processing Hello World
Processing Complete.
```

In addition to binary modules, PowerShell supports almost all of the functionality of cmdlets through advanced functions. If you want to create functions with the power of cmdlets and the ease of scripting, see Recipe 11.15.

See Also

"Structured Commands (Cmdlets)" on page 7

Recipe 1.24, "Extend Your Shell with Additional Commands"

Recipe 11.15, "Provide -WhatIf, -Confirm, and Other Cmdlet Features"

Recipe 17.6, "Define or Extend a .NET Class"

17.10 Add PowerShell Scripting to Your Own Program

Problem

You want to provide your users with an easy way to automate your program, but don't want to write a scripting language on your own.

Solution

To build PowerShell scripting into your own program, use the PowerShell Hosting features as described on MSDN (the Microsoft Developer Network).

Discussion

One of the fascinating aspects of PowerShell is how easily it lets you add many of its capabilities to your own program. This is because PowerShell is, at its core, a powerful engine that any application can use. The PowerShell console application is in fact just a text-based interface to this engine.

Although a full discussion of the PowerShell hosting model is outside the scope of this book, the following example illustrates the techniques behind exposing features of your application for your users to script.

To frame the premise of Example 17-10 (shown later), imagine an email application that lets you run rules when it receives an email. While you will want to design a standard interface that allows users to create simple rules, you also will want to provide a way for users to write incredibly complex rules. Rather than design a scripting language yourself, you can simply use PowerShell's scripting language. In the following example, we provide user-written scripts with a variable called $message that represents the current message and then runs the commands.

```
PS > Get-Content VerifyCategoryRule.ps1
if($message.Body -match "book")
{
    [Console]::WriteLine("This is a message about the book.")
}
else
{
    [Console]::WriteLine("This is an unknown message.")
}
PS > .\RulesWizardExample.exe (Resolve-Path VerifyCategoryRule.ps1)
This is a message about the book.
```

For more information on how to host PowerShell in your own application, see the MSDN topic "How to Create a Windows PowerShell Hosting Application," available at *http://msdn.microsoft.com/en-us/library/ee706563.aspx*.

Step 1: Download the PowerShell SDK

The PowerShell SDK contains samples, reference assemblies, documentation, and other information used when developing PowerShell cmdlets. Search for "PowerShell 2.0 SDK" on *http://download.microsoft.com* and download the latest PowerShell SDK.

Step 2: Create a file to hold the hosting source code

Create a file called *RulesWizardExample.cs* with the content from Example 17-10, and save it on your hard drive.

Example 17-10. RulesWizardExample.cs

```csharp
using System;
using System.Management.Automation;
using System.Management.Automation.Runspaces;

namespace Template
{

    // Define a simple class that represents a mail message
    public class MailMessage
    {
        public MailMessage(string to, string from, string body)
        {
            this.To = to;
            this.From = from;
            this.Body = body;
        }

        public String To;
        public String From;
        public String Body;
    }

    public class RulesWizardExample
    {
        public static void Main(string[] args)
        {
            // Ensure that they've provided some script text
            if(args.Length == 0)
            {
                Console.WriteLine("Usage:");
                Console.WriteLine(" RulesWizardExample <script text>");
                return;
            }

            // Create an example message to pass to our rules wizard
            MailMessage mailMessage =
                        new MailMessage(
                            "guide_feedback@LeeHolmes.com",
                            "guide_reader@example.com",
                            "This is a message about your book.");

            // Create a runspace, which is the environment for
            // running commands
            Runspace runspace = RunspaceFactory.CreateRunspace();
            runspace.Open();

            // Create a variable called "$message" in the Runspace, and populate
            // it with a reference to the current message in our application.
            // Pipeline commands can interact with this object like any other
            // .Net object.
            runspace.SessionStateProxy.SetVariable("message", mailMessage);

            // Create a pipeline, and populate it with the script given in the
            // first command-line argument.
```

```
        Pipeline pipeline = runspace.CreatePipeline(args[0]);

        // Invoke (execute) the pipeline, and close the runspace.
        pipeline.Invoke();
        runspace.Close();
      }
   }
}
```

Step 3: Compile and run the example

Although the example itself provides very little functionality, it demonstrates the core
concepts behind adding PowerShell scripting to your own program.

```
Set-Alias csc $env:WINDIR\Microsoft.NET\Framework\v2.0.50727\csc.exe
$dll = [PsObject].Assembly.Location
Csc RulesWizardExample.cs /reference:$dll
RulesWizardExample.exe <script commands to run>
```

Now we can run Example 17-10. Here we give it a simple rule to just output the sender
of the sample mail message:

```
PS > .\RulesWizardExample.exe '[Console]::WriteLine($message.From)'
guide_reader@example.com
```

See Also

"Structured Commands (Cmdlets)" on page 7

Security and Script Signing

18.0 Introduction

Security plays two important roles in PowerShell. The first role is the security of PowerShell itself. Scripting languages have long been a vehicle of email-based malware on Windows, so PowerShell's security features have been carefully designed to thwart this danger. The second role is the set of security-related tasks you are likely to encounter when working with your computer: script signing, certificates, and credentials, just to name a few.

When it comes to talking about security in the scripting and command-line world, a great deal of folklore and superstition clouds the picture. One of the most common misconceptions is that scripting languages and command-line shells somehow let users bypass the security protections of the Windows graphical user interface.

The Windows security model protects resources—not the way you get to them. That is because, in effect, the programs that you run *are* you. If you can do it, so can a program. If a program can do it, then you can do it without having to use that program. For example, consider the act of changing critical data in the Windows Registry. If you use the Windows Registry Editor graphical user interface, it provides an error message when you attempt to perform an operation that you do not have permission for, as shown in Figure 18-1.

The Registry Editor provides this error message because it is *unable* to delete that key, not because it wanted to prevent you from doing it. Windows itself protects the registry keys, not the programs you use to access them.

Likewise, PowerShell provides an error message when you attempt to perform an operation that you do not have permission for. Not because PowerShell contains extra security checks for that operation, but simply because it is unable to perform the operation:

```
PS > New-Item "HKLM:\Software\Microsoft\Windows\CurrentVersion\Run\New"
New-Item : Requested registry access is not allowed.
```

```
At line:1 char:9
+ New-Item <<<< "HKLM:\Software\Microsoft\Windows\CurrentVersion\Run\New"
```

While perhaps clear after explanation, this misunderstanding often gets used as a reason to prevent users from running command shells or scripting languages altogether.

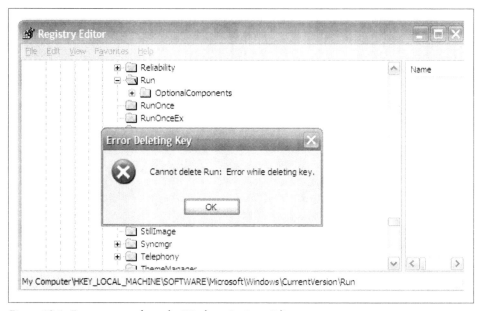

Figure 18-1. Error message from the Windows Registry Editor

18.1 Enable Scripting Through an Execution Policy

Problem

PowerShell provides an error message, such as the following, when you try to run a script:

```
PS > .\Test.ps1
File C:\temp\test.ps1 cannot be loaded because the execution of scripts is
disabled on this system. Please see "get-help about_signing" for more details.
At line:1 char:10
+ .\Test.ps1 <<<<
```

Solution

To prevent this error message, use the Set-ExecutionPolicy cmdlet to change the PowerShell execution policy to one of the policies that allow scripts to run:

```
Set-ExecutionPolicy RemoteSigned
```

Discussion

As normally configured, PowerShell operates strictly as an interactive shell. By disabling the execution of scripts by default, PowerShell prevents malicious PowerShell scripts from affecting users who have PowerShell installed but who may never have used (or even heard of!) PowerShell.

You (as a reader of this book and PowerShell user) are not part of that target audience. You will want to configure PowerShell to run under one of the following five execution policies:

Restricted

> PowerShell operates as an interactive shell only. Attempting to run a script generates an error message. This is PowerShell's default execution policy.

AllSigned

> PowerShell runs only those scripts that contain a digital signature. When you attempt to run a script signed by a publisher that PowerShell hasn't seen before, PowerShell asks whether you trust that publisher to run scripts on your system.

RemoteSigned *(recommended)*

> PowerShell runs most scripts without prompting, but requires that scripts from the Internet contain a digital signature. As in AllSigned mode, PowerShell asks whether you trust that publisher to run scripts on your system when you run a script signed by a publisher it hasn't seen before. PowerShell considers a script to have come from the Internet when it has been downloaded to your computer by a popular communications program such as Internet Explorer, Outlook, or Messenger.

Unrestricted

> PowerShell does not require a digital signature on any script, but (like Windows Explorer) warns you when a script has been downloaded from the Internet.

Bypass

> PowerShell places the responsibility of security validation entirely upon the user.

When it comes to evaluating script signatures, always remember that a signed script does not mean a safe script! The signature on a script gives you a way to verify who the script came from, but not that you can trust its author to run commands on your system. You need to make that decision for yourself, which is why PowerShell asks you.

Run the Set-ExecutionPolicy cmdlet to configure the system's execution policy. It supports three scopes:

Process

> Impacts the current session and any that it launches. This scope modifies the PSExecutionPolicy environment variable and is also supported through the -ExecutionPolicy parameter to *PowerShell.exe*.

`CurrentUser`

Modifies the execution policy for the current user, and stores its value in the `HKEY_CURRENT_USER` hive of the Windows Registry.

`LocalMachine`

Modifies the execution policy for the entire machine, and stores its value in the `HKEY_LOCAL_MACHINE` hive of the Windows Registry. Modifying the execution policy at this scope requires that you launch PowerShell with Administrator privileges. If you want to configure your execution policy on Windows Vista or later, right-click the Windows PowerShell link for the option to launch PowerShell as the Administrator.

If you specify the value `Undefined` for the execution policy at a specific scope, PowerShell removes any execution policy you previously defined for that scope.

Alternatively, you can directly modify the registry key that PowerShell uses to store its execution policy. For the `CurrentUser` and `LocalMachine` scopes, this is the `Execution Policy` property under the registry path *SOFTWARE\Microsoft\PowerShell\1\ShellIds\Microsoft.PowerShell*.

In an enterprise setting, PowerShell also lets you override this local preference through Group Policy. For more information about PowerShell's Group Policy support, see Recipe 18.5.

Execution policies are not user restrictions

It is easy to understand the power of an execution policy to prevent scripts from running, but administrators often forget to consider *from whom*. They might think that enforcing an `AllSigned` policy is a way to prevent the *user* from running unapproved applications, when really it is designed as a way to prevent the *attacker* from running scripts that the user doesn't approve. This misconception is often wrongly reinforced by the location of the `ExecutionPolicy` configuration key in PowerShell version one—in a registry location that only machine administrators have access to.

System-wide PowerShell execution policies cannot prevent the user from doing something the user wants to do. That job is left to the Windows Account Model, which is designed as a security boundary. It controls what users can do: what files can be accessed, what registry keys can be accessed, and more. PowerShell is a user-mode application, and is therefore (as defined by the Windows security model) completely under the user's control.

Instead, execution policies are a user-focused feature, similar to seatbelts or helmets. It's best to keep them on, but you always have the option to take them off. PowerShell's installer sets the execution policy to `Restricted` as a safe default for the vast majority of Windows users who will never run a PowerShell script in their life. A system administrator might set the execution policy to `AllSigned` to define it as a best practice or to let nontechnical users run a subset of safe scripts.

At any time, users can decide otherwise. They can type the commands by hand, paste the script into their PowerShell prompt, or use any of a countless number of other workarounds. These are all direct results of a Windows core security principle: you have complete control over any application you are running. PowerShell version two makes this reality much more transparent through its fine-grained execution policy scopes.

At its core, execution policy scopes let administrators and users tailor their safety harnesses. Jane might be fluent and technical (and opt for a `RemoteSigned` execution policy), whereas Bob (another user of the same machine with different security preferences) can still get the benefits of an `AllSigned` default execution policy. In addition, agents or automation tools can invoke PowerShell commands without having to modify the permanent state of the system.

See Also

Recipe 18.5, "Manage PowerShell Security in an Enterprise"

18.2 Disable Warnings for UNC Paths

Problem

PowerShell warns you when it tries to load a script from an Intranet (UNC) path.

Solution

If it makes sense, copy the file locally and run it from your local location. If you want to keep the script on the UNC path, enable Internet Explorer's `UncAsIntranet` setting, or add the UNC path to the list of trusted sites. Example 18-1 adds *server* to the list of trusted sites.

Example 18-1. Adding a server to the list of trusted hosts

```
$path = "HKLM:\SOFTWARE\Microsoft\Windows\CurrentVersion\Internet Settings\" +
    "ZoneMap\Domains\server"
New-Item -Path $path | New-ItemProperty -Name File -PropertyType DWORD -Value 2
```

Discussion

When using an execution policy that detects Internet-based scripts, you may want to stop PowerShell from treating those scripts as remote.

In an enterprise setting, PowerShell sometimes warns of the dangers of Internet-based scripts even if they are located only on a network share. This is a security precaution, as it is possible for network paths (such as UNC shares) to be spoofed, or for the content of those scripts to be changed without your knowledge. If you have a high trust in your network and the security of the remote system, you might want to avoid these precautions.

To remove this warning, first ensure the scripts have not actually been downloaded from the Internet. Right-click on the file from Windows Explorer, select Properties, and then click Unblock.

If unblocking the file does not resolve the issue (or is not an option), your machine has likely been configured to restrict access to network shares. This is common with Internet Explorer's Enhanced Security Configuration mode. To prevent this message, add the path of the network share to Internet Explorer's Intranet or Trusted Sites zone. For more information on managing Internet Explorer's zone mappings, see Recipe 21.7.

If you are using an Unrestricted execution policy and want to get rid of this warning for remote files without altering the Trusted Sites zone, you can use the Bypass execution policy to bypass PowerShell's security features entirely. For more information about execution policies, see Recipe 18.1.

See Also

Recipe 18.1, "Enable Scripting Through an Execution Policy"

Recipe 21.7, "Add a Site to an Internet Explorer Security Zone"

18.3 Sign a PowerShell Script, Module, or Formatting File

Problem

You want to sign a PowerShell script, module, or formatting file so that it can be run on systems that have their execution policy set to require signed scripts.

Solution

To sign the script with your standard code-signing certificate, use the Set-AuthenticodeSignature cmdlet:

```
$cert = @(Get-ChildItem cert:\CurrentUser\My -CodeSigning)[0]
Set-AuthenticodeSignature file.ps1 $cert
```

Alternatively, you can also use other traditional applications (such as signtool.exe) to sign PowerShell *.ps1*, *.psm1*, *.psd1*, and *.ps1xml* files.

Discussion

Signing a script or formatting file provides you and your customers with two primary benefits: publisher identification and file integrity. When you sign a script, module, or formatting file, PowerShell appends your digital signature to the end of that file. This signature verifies that the file came from you and also ensures that nobody can tamper

---

with the content in the file without detection. If you try to load a file that has been tampered with, PowerShell provides the following error message:

```
File C:\temp\test.ps1 cannot be loaded. The contents of file C:\temp\test.ps1
may have been tampered because the hash of the file does not match the hash
stored in the digital signature. The script will not execute on the system. Please
see "get-help about_signing" for more details.
At line:1 char:10
+ .\test.ps1 <<<<
```

When it comes to the signing of scripts, modules, and formatting files, PowerShell participates in the standard Windows Authenticode infrastructure. Because of that, techniques you may already know for signing files and working with their signatures continue to work with PowerShell scripts and formatting files. Although the Set-AuthenticodeSignature cmdlet is primarily designed to support scripts and formatting files, it also supports DLLs and other standard Windows executable file types.

To sign a file, the Set-AuthenticodeSignature cmdlet requires that you provide it with a valid code-signing certificate. Most certification authorities provide Authenticode code-signing certificates for a fee. By using an Authenticode code-signing certificate from a reputable certification authority (such as VeriSign or Thawte), you can be sure that all users will be able to verify the signature on your script. Some online services offer extremely cheap code-signing certificates, but be aware that many machines may be unable to verify the digital signatures created by those certificates.

 You can still gain many of the benefits of code signing on your own computers by generating your own code-signing certificate. While other computers will not be able to recognize the signature, it still provides tamper protection on your own computer. For more information about this approach, see Recipe 18.4.

The -TimeStampServer parameter lets you sign your script or formatting file in a way that makes the signature on your script or formatting file valid even after your code-signing certificate expires.

For more information about the Set-AuthenticodeSignature cmdlet, type **Get-Help Set-AuthenticodeSignature**.

See Also

Recipe 18.4, "Program: Create a Self-Signed Certificate"

18.4 Program: Create a Self-Signed Certificate

Discussion

It is possible to benefit from the tamper-protection features of signed scripts without having to pay for an official code-signing certificate. You do this by creating a *self-signed* certificate. Scripts signed with a self-signed certificate will not be recognized as valid on other computers, but you can still sign and use them on your own computer.

When Example 18-2 runs, it prompts you for a password. Windows uses this password to prevent malicious programs from automatically signing files on your behalf.

Example 18-2. New-SelfSignedCertificate.ps1

```
##############################################################################
##
## New-SelfSignedCertificate
##
## From Windows PowerShell Cookbook (O'Reilly)
## by Lee Holmes (http://www.leeholmes.com/guide)
##
##############################################################################

<#

.SYNOPSIS

Generate a new self-signed certificate. The certificate generated by these
commands allow you to sign scripts on your own computer for protection
from tampering. Files signed with this signature are not valid on other
computers.

.EXAMPLE

New-SelfSignedCertificate.ps1
Creates a new self-signed certificate

#>

Set-StrictMode -Version Latest

## Ensure we can find makecert.exe
if(-not (Get-Command makecert.exe -ErrorAction SilentlyContinue))
{
    $errorMessage = "Could not find makecert.exe. " +
        "This tool is available as part of Visual Studio, or the Windows SDK."

    Write-Error $errorMessage
    return
}

$keyPath = Join-Path ([IO.Path]::GetTempPath()) "root.pvk"
```

```
## Generate the local certification authority
makecert -n "CN=PowerShell Local Certificate Root" -a sha1 `
    -eku 1.3.6.1.5.5.7.3.3 -r -sv $keyPath root.cer `
    -ss Root -sr localMachine

## Use the local certification authority to generate a self-signed
## certificate
makecert -pe -n "CN=PowerShell User" -ss MY -a sha1 `
    -eku 1.3.6.1.5.5.7.3.3 -iv $keyPath -ic root.cer

## Remove the private key from the filesystem.
Remove-Item $keyPath

## Retrieve the certificate
Get-ChildItem cert:\currentuser\my -codesign |
    Where-Object { $_.Subject -match "PowerShell User" }
```

For more information about running scripts, see Recipe 1.1.

See Also

Recipe 1.1, "Run Programs, Scripts, and Existing Tools"

18.5 Manage PowerShell Security in an Enterprise

Problem

You want to control PowerShell's security features in an enterprise setting.

Solution

You have two ways to manage PowerShell's security features enterprise-wide:

- Apply PowerShell's Group Policy templates to control PowerShell's execution policy through Group Policy.
- Deploy Microsoft Certificate Services to automatically generate Authenticode code-signing certificates for domain accounts.

Discussion

Either separately or together, these features let you customize your PowerShell environment across your entire domain.

Apply PowerShell's Group Policy templates

The administrative templates for Windows PowerShell let you override the machine's local execution policy preference at both the machine and per-user level. To obtain the

PowerShell administrative templates, visit *http://www.microsoft.com/downloads* and search for "Administrative templates for Windows PowerShell".

 Although Group Policy settings override local preferences, PowerShell's execution policy should not be considered a security measure that protects the system from the user. It is a security measure that helps prevent untrusted scripts from running on the system. As mentioned in Recipe 18.1, PowerShell is only a vehicle that allows users to do what they already have the Windows permissions to do.

Once you install the administrative templates for Windows PowerShell, launch the Group Policy Object Editor MMC snap-in. Right-click Administrative Templates, and then select Add/Remove Administrative Templates. You will find the administrative template in the installation location you chose when you installed the administrative templates for Windows PowerShell. Once added, the Group Policy Editor MMC snap-in provides PowerShell as an option under its Administrative Templates node, as shown in Figure 18-2.

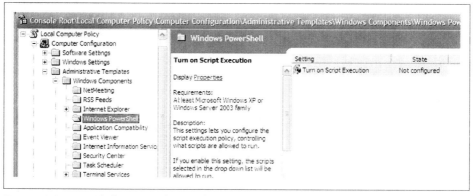

Figure 18-2. PowerShell Group Policy configuration

The default state is Not Configured. In this state, PowerShell takes its execution policy from the machine's local preference (as described in Recipe 18.1). If you change the state to one of the Enabled options (or Disabled), PowerShell uses this configuration instead of the machine's local preference.

 PowerShell respects these Group Policy settings no matter what. This includes settings that the machine's administrator may consider to *reduce* security—such as an Unrestricted group policy overriding an AllSigned local preference.

Per-user Group Policy settings override the machine's local preference, whereas per-machine Group Policy settings override per-user settings.

Deploy Microsoft Certificate Services

Although outside the scope of this book, Microsoft Certificate Services lets you automatically deploy code-signing certificates to any or all domain users. This provides a significant benefit, as it helps protect users from accidental or malicious script tampering.

For an introduction to this topic, visit *http://technet.microsoft.com* and search for "Enterprise Design for Certificate Services". For more information about script signing, see Recipe 18.3.

See Also

Recipe 18.1, "Enable Scripting Through an Execution Policy"

Recipe 18.3, "Sign a PowerShell Script, Module, or Formatting File"

18.6 Block Scripts by Publisher, Path, or Hash

Problem

In addition to PowerShell's execution policy, you want to block scripts by their publisher, location, or similarity to a specific script.

Solution

Create new Software Restriction Policy rules to enforce these requirements.

Discussion

While this is not common, you may sometimes want to prevent PowerShell from running scripts signed by specific publishers, from a certain path, or with specific content. For all execution policies except `Bypass`, PowerShell lets you configure this through the computer's software restriction policies.

To configure these software restriction policies, launch the Local Security Policy MMC snap-in listed in the Administrative Tools group of the Start menu. Expand the Software Restriction Policies node, right-click Additional Rules, and then create the desired rules: certificate rules, path rule, or hash rules.

 In Windows 7, the PowerShell module for the AppLocker feature makes managing software restriction policies immensely easier. For more information, search the Internet for "Applocker PowerShell".

Certificate rules let you configure certain certificates that PowerShell will never trust. Path rules let you define system paths that allow or disallow execution of PowerShell scripts from certain paths. Hash rules let you block specific scripts from execution if they are the same as the script you used to generate the rule.

Figure 18-3 shows how to add a new certificate rule.

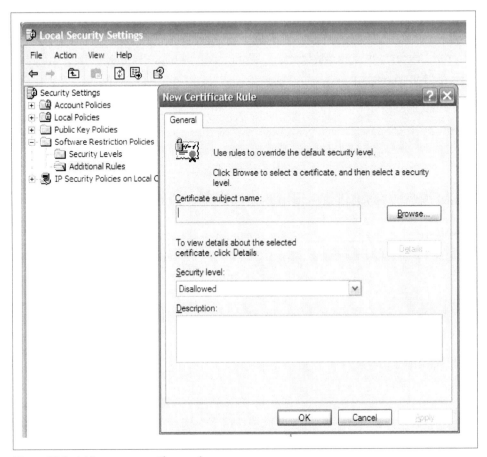

Figure 18-3. Adding a new certificate rule

Browse to the certificate that represents the publisher you want to block, and then click OK to block that publisher.

Rather than block specific certificates, you can also create a certificate policy that allows only certificates from a centrally administered whitelist. To do this, select either *Allow only all administrators to manage Trusted Publishers* or *Allow only enterprise administrators to manage Trusted Publishers* from the Trusted Publishers Management dialog.

See Also

Recipe 18.1, "Enable Scripting Through an Execution Policy"

Recipe 18.3, "Sign a PowerShell Script, Module, or Formatting File"

18.7 Verify the Digital Signature of a PowerShell Script

Problem

You want to verify the digital signature of a PowerShell script or formatting file.

Solution

To validate the signature of a script or formatting file, use the `Get-Authenticode Signature` cmdlet:

```
PS > Get-AuthenticodeSignature .\test.ps1

    Directory: C:\temp

SignerCertificate                          Status    Path
-----------------                          ------    ----
FD48FAA9281A657DBD089B5A008FAFE61D3B32FD   Valid     test.ps1
```

Discussion

The `Get-AuthenticodeSignature` cmdlet gets the Authenticode signature from a file. This can be a PowerShell script or formatting file, but the cmdlet also supports DLLs and other Windows standard executable file types.

By default, PowerShell displays the signature in a format that summarizes the certificate and its status. For more information about the signature, use the `Format-List` cmdlet, as shown in Example 18-3.

Example 18-3. PowerShell displaying detailed information about an Authenticode signature

```
PS > Get-AuthenticodeSignature .\test.ps1 | Format-List

SignerCertificate        : [Subject]
                             CN=PowerShell User

                           [Issuer]
                             CN=PowerShell Local Certificate Root

                           [Serial Number]
                             454D75B8A18FBDB445D8FCEC4942085C

                           [Not Before]
                             4/22/2007 12:32:37 AM

                           [Not After]
                             12/31/2039 3:59:59 PM

                           [Thumbprint]
                             FD48FAA9281A657DBD089B5A008FAFE61D3B32FD
```

```
TimeStamperCertificate :
Status              : Valid
StatusMessage       : Signature verified.
Path                : C:\temp\test.ps1
```

For more information about the Get-AuthenticodeSignature cmdlet, type **Get-Help Get-AuthenticodeSignature**.

18.8 Securely Handle Sensitive Information

Problem

You want to request sensitive information from the user, but want to do this as securely as possible.

Solution

To securely handle sensitive information, store it in a SecureString whenever possible. The Read-Host cmdlet (with the -AsSecureString parameter) lets you prompt the user for (and handle) sensitive information by returning the user's response as a Secure String:

```
PS > $secureInput = Read-Host -AsSecureString "Enter your private key"
Enter your private key:
PS > $secureInput
System.Security.SecureString
```

Discussion

When you use any string in the .NET Framework (and therefore PowerShell), it retains that string so that it can efficiently reuse it later. Unlike most .NET data, unused strings persist even after you finish using them. When this data is in memory, there is always the chance that it could get captured in a crash dump or swapped to disk in a paging operation. Because some data (such as passwords and other confidential information) may be sensitive, the .NET Framework includes the SecureString class: a container for text data that the framework encrypts when it stores it in memory. Code that needs to interact with the plain-text data inside a SecureString does so as securely as possible.

When a cmdlet author asks you for sensitive data (for example, an encryption key), the best practice is to designate that parameter as a SecureString to help keep your information confidential. You can provide the parameter with a SecureString variable as input, or the host prompts you for the SecureString if you do not provide one. PowerShell also supports two cmdlets (ConvertTo-SecureString and ConvertFrom-SecureString) that let you securely persist this data to disk. For more information about securely storing information on disk, see Recipe 18.12.

Credentials are a common source of sensitive information. See Recipe 18.9 for information on how to securely manage credentials in PowerShell.

By default, the SecureString cmdlets use the Windows Data Protection API (DPAPI) when they convert your SecureString to and from its text representation. The key it uses to encrypt your data is based on your Windows logon credentials, so only you can decrypt the data that you've encrypted. If you want the exported data to work on another system or separate user account, you can use the cmdlet options that let you provide an explicit key. PowerShell treats this sensitive data as an opaque blob—and so should you.

However, there are many instances when you may want to automatically provide the SecureString input to a cmdlet rather than have the host prompt you for it. In these situations, the ideal solution is to use the ConvertTo-SecureString cmdlet to import a previously exported SecureString from disk. This retains the confidentiality of your data and still lets you automate the input.

If the data is highly dynamic (for example, coming from a CSV), then the ConvertTo-SecureString cmdlet supports an -AsPlainText parameter:

```
$secureString = ConvertTo-SecureString "Kinda Secret" -AsPlainText-Force
```

Since you've already provided plain-text input in this case, placing this data in a Secure String no longer provides a security benefit. To prevent a false sense of security, the cmdlet requires the -Force parameter to convert plain-text data into a SecureString.

Once you have data in a SecureString, you may want to access its plain-text representation. PowerShell doesn't provide a direct way to do this, as that defeats the purpose of a SecureString. If you still want to convert a SecureString to plain text, you have two options:

- Use the GetNetworkCredential() method of the PsCredential class:

```
$secureString = Read-Host -AsSecureString
$temporaryCredential = New-Object `
    System.Management.Automation.PsCredential "TempUser",$secureString
$unsecureString = $temporaryCredential.GetNetworkCredential().Password
```

- Use the .NET Framework's Marshal class:

```
$secureString = Read-Host -AsSecureString
$unsecureString = [Runtime.InteropServices.Marshal]::PtrToStringAuto(
    [Runtime.InteropServices.Marshal]::SecureStringToBSTR($secureString))
```

See Also

Recipe 18.9, "Securely Request Usernames and Passwords"

Recipe 18.12, "Securely Store Credentials on Disk"

18.9 Securely Request Usernames and Passwords

Problem

Your script requires that users provide it with a username and password, but you want to do this as securely as possible.

Solution

To request a credential from the user, use the Get-Credential cmdlet:

```
$credential = Get-Credential
```

Discussion

The Get-Credential cmdlet reads credentials from the user as securely as possible and ensures that the user's password remains highly protected the entire time. For an example of using the Get-Credential cmdlet effectively in a script, see Recipe 18.10.

Once you have the username and password, you can pass that information around to any other command that accepts a PowerShell credential object without worrying about disclosing sensitive information. If a command doesn't accept a PowerShell credential object (but does support a SecureString for its sensitive information), the resulting PsCredential object provides a Username property that returns the username in the credential and a Password property that returns a SecureString containing the user's password.

Unfortunately, not everything that requires credentials can accept either a PowerShell credential or SecureString. If you need to provide a credential to one of these commands or API calls, the PsCredential object provides a GetNetworkCredential() method to convert the PowerShell credential to a less secure NetworkCredential object. Once you've converted the credential to a NetworkCredential, the UserName and Password properties provide unencrypted access to the username and password from the original credential. Many network-related classes in the .NET Framework support the NetworkCredential class directly.

 The NetworkCredential class is less secure than the PsCredential class because it stores the user's password in plain text. For more information about the security implications of storing sensitive information in plain text, see Recipe 18.8.

If a frequently run script requires credentials, you might consider caching those credentials in memory to improve the usability of that script. For example, in the region of the script that calls the Get-Credential cmdlet, you can instead use the techniques shown by Example 18-4.

Example 18-4. Caching credentials in memory to improve usability

```
$credential = $null
if(Test-Path Variable:\Lee.Holmes.CommonScript.CachedCredential)
{
    $credential = ${GLOBAL:Lee.Holmes.CommonScript.CachedCredential}
}

${GLOBAL:Lee.Holmes.CommonScript.CachedCredential} =
    Get-Credential $credential

$credential = ${GLOBAL:Lee.Holmes.CommonScript.CachedCredential}
```

The script prompts the user for credentials the first time it is called but uses the cached credentials for subsequent calls. If your command is part of a PowerShell module, you can avoid storing the information in a global variable. For more information about this technique, see Recipe 11.7.

To cache these credentials on disk (to support unattended operations), see Recipe 18.12.

For more information about the `Get-Credential` cmdlet, type **Get-Help Get-Credential**.

See Also

Recipe 11.7, "Write Commands That Maintain State"

Recipe 18.8, "Securely Handle Sensitive Information"

Recipe 18.10, "Program: Start a Process as Another User"

Recipe 18.12, "Securely Store Credentials on Disk"

18.10 Program: Start a Process as Another User

If your script requires user credentials, PowerShell offers the `PsCredential` object. This lets you securely store those credentials or pass them to other commands that accept PowerShell credentials. When you write a script that accepts credentials, consider letting the user supply either a username or a preexisting credential. This is the model followed by the `Get-Credential` cmdlet, and it provides an intuitive user experience. Example 18-5 demonstrates a useful approach to support this model. As the framework for this demonstration, the script lets you start a process as another user. While the scenario addressed by this specific script is fully handled by the `Start-Process` cmdlet, it provides a useful framework for discussion.

Example 18-5. Start-ProcessAsUser.ps1

```
###########################################################################
##
## Start-ProcessAsUser
##
## From Windows PowerShell Cookbook (O'Reilly)
## by Lee Holmes (http://www.leeholmes.com/guide)
##
###########################################################################

<#

.SYNOPSIS

Launch a process under alternate credentials, providing functionality
similar to runas.exe.

.EXAMPLE

PS >$file = Join-Path ([Environment]::GetFolderPath("System")) certmgr.msc
PS >Start-ProcessAsUser Administrator mmc $file

#>

param(
    ## The credential to launch the process under
    $Credential = (Get-Credential),

    ## The process to start
    [Parameter(Mandatory = $true)]
    [string] $Process,

    ## Any arguments to pass to the process
    [string] $ArgumentList = ""
)

Set-StrictMode -Version Latest

## Create a real credential if they supplied a username
$credential = Get-Credential $credential

## Exit if they canceled out of the credential dialog
if(-not ($credential -is "System.Management.Automation.PsCredential"))
{
    return
}

## Prepare the startup information (including username and password)
$startInfo = New-Object Diagnostics.ProcessStartInfo
$startInfo.Filename = $process
$startInfo.Arguments = $argumentList

## If we're launching as ourselves, set the "runas" verb
if(($credential.Username -eq "$ENV:Username") -or
    ($credential.Username -eq "\$ENV:Username"))
```

```
{
    $startInfo.Verb = "runas"
}
else
{
    $startInfo.UserName = $credential.Username
    $startInfo.Password = $credential.Password
    $startInfo.UseShellExecute = $false
}

## Start the process
[Diagnostics.Process]::Start($startInfo)
```

For a version of this script that lets you invoke PowerShell commands in an elevated session and easily interact with the results, see Recipe 18.11.

For more information about running scripts, see Recipe 1.1.

See Also

Recipe 1.1, "Run Programs, Scripts, and Existing Tools"

Recipe 18.11, "Program: Run a Temporarily Elevated Command"

18.11 Program: Run a Temporarily Elevated Command

One popular feature of many Unix-like operating systems is the sudo command: a feature that lets you invoke commands as another user without switching context.

This is a common desire in Windows Vista and above, where User Access Control (UAC) means that most interactive sessions do not have their Administrator privileges enabled. Enabling these privileges is often a clumsy task, requiring that you launch a new instance of PowerShell with the "Run as Administrator" option enabled.

Example 18-6 resolves many of these issues by launching an administrative shell for you and letting it participate in a regular (nonelevated) PowerShell pipeline.

To do this, it first streams all of your input into a richly structured CliXml file on disk. It invokes the elevated command and stores its results into another richly structured CliXml file on disk. Finally, it imports the structured data from disk and removes the temporary files.

Example 18-6. Invoke-ElevatedCommand.ps1

```
##############################################################################
##
## Invoke-ElevatedCommand
##
## From Windows PowerShell Cookbook (O'Reilly)
## by Lee Holmes (http://www.leeholmes.com/guide)
##
##############################################################################
```

```
<#

.SYNOPSIS

Runs the provided script block under an elevated instance of PowerShell as
though it were a member of a regular pipeline.

.EXAMPLE

PS >Get-Process | Invoke-ElevatedCommand.ps1 {
    $input | Where-Object { $_.Handles -gt 500 } } | Sort Handles

#>

param(
    ## The script block to invoke elevated
    [Parameter(Mandatory = $true)]
    [ScriptBlock] $Scriptblock,

    ## Any input to give the elevated process
    [Parameter(ValueFromPipeline = $true)]
    $InputObject,

    ## Switch to enable the user profile
    [switch] $EnableProfile
)

begin
{
    Set-StrictMode -Version Latest
    $inputItems = New-Object System.Collections.ArrayList
}

process
{
    $null = $inputItems.Add($inputObject)
}

end
{
    ## Create some temporary files for streaming input and output
    $outputFile = [IO.Path]::GetTempFileName()
    $inputFile = [IO.Path]::GetTempFileName()

    ## Stream the input into the input file
    $inputItems.ToArray() | Export-CliXml -Depth 1 $inputFile

    ## Start creating the command line for the elevated PowerShell session
    $commandLine = ""
    if(-not $EnableProfile) { $commandLine += "-NoProfile " }

    ## Convert the command into an encoded command for PowerShell
    $commandString = "Set-Location '$($pwd.Path)'; " +
        "`$output = Import-CliXml '$inputFile' | " +
```

```
            "& {" + $scriptblock.ToString() + "} 2>&1; " +
            "Export-CliXml -Depth 1 -In `$output '$outputFile'"

        $commandBytes = [System.Text.Encoding]::Unicode.GetBytes($commandString)
        $encodedCommand = [Convert]::ToBase64String($commandBytes)
        $commandLine += "-EncodedCommand $encodedCommand"

        ## Start the new PowerShell process
        $process = Start-Process -FilePath (Get-Command powershell).Definition `
            -ArgumentList $commandLine -Verb RunAs `
            -WindowStyle Hidden `
            -Passthru
        $process.WaitForExit()

        ## Return the output to the user
        if((Get-Item $outputFile).Length -gt 0)
        {
            Import-CliXml $outputFile
        }

        ## Clean up
        Remove-Item $outputFile
        Remove-Item $inputFile
}
```

For more information about the CliXml commands, see Recipe 10.5. For more information about running scripts, see Recipe 1.1.

See Also

Recipe 1.1, "Run Programs, Scripts, and Existing Tools"

Recipe 10.5, "Easily Import and Export Your Structured Data"

18.12 Securely Store Credentials on Disk

Problem

Your script performs an operation that requires credentials, but you don't want it to require user interaction when it runs.

Solution

To securely store the credential's password to disk so that your script can load it automatically, use the ConvertFrom-SecureString and ConvertTo-SecureString cmdlets.

Save the credential's password to disk

The first step for storing a password on disk is usually a manual one. There is nothing mandatory about the file name, but we'll use a convention to name the file *<Current-Script>.ps1.credential*. Given a credential that you've stored in the $credential variable, you can safely export its password to *<CurrentScript>.ps1.credential* using the following command. Replace *CurrentScript* with the name of the script that will be loading it.

```
PS > $credPath = Join-Path (Split-Path $profile) CurrentScript.ps1.credential
PS > $credential.Password | ConvertFrom-SecureString | Set-Content $credPath
```

Recreate the credential from the password stored on disk

In the script that you want to run automatically, add the following commands:

```
$credPath = Join-Path (Split-Path $profile) CurrentScript.ps1.credential
$password = Get-Content $credPath | ConvertTo-SecureString
$credential = New-Object System.Management.Automation.PsCredential `
    "CachedUser",$password
```

These commands create a new credential object (for the *CachedUser* user) and store that object in the $credential variable.

Discussion

When reading the solution, you might at first be wary of storing a password on disk. While it is natural (and prudent) to be cautious of littering your hard drive with sensitive information, the ConvertFrom-SecureString cmdlet encrypts this data using the Windows standard Data Protection API. This ensures that only your user account can properly decrypt its contents.

While keeping a password secure is an important security feature, you may sometimes want to store a password (or other sensitive information) on disk so that other accounts have access to it. This is often the case with scripts run by service accounts or scripts designed to be transferred between computers. The ConvertFrom-SecureString and ConvertTo-SecureString cmdlets support this by letting you specify an encryption key.

 When used with a hardcoded encryption key, this technique no longer acts as a security measure. If a user can access the content of your automated script, that user has access to the encryption key. If the user has access to the encryption key, the user has access to the data you were trying to protect.

Although the solution stores the password in the directory that contains your profile, you could also load it from the same location as your script. To learn how to load it from the same location as your script, see Recipe 16.5.

For more information about the ConvertTo-SecureString and ConvertFrom-Secure
String cmdlets, type **Get-Help ConvertTo-SecureString** or **Get-Help Convert
From-SecureString**.

See Also

Recipe 16.5, "Find Your Script's Location"

18.13 Access User and Machine Certificates

Problem

You want to retrieve information about certificates for the current user or local machine.

Solution

To browse and retrieve certificates on the local machine, use PowerShell's certificate
drive. This drive is created by the certificate provider, as shown in Example 18-7.

Example 18-7. Exploring certificates in the certificate provider

```
PS > Set-Location cert:\CurrentUser\
PS > $cert = Get-ChildItem -Rec -CodeSign
PS > $cert | Format-List

Subject      : CN=PowerShell User
Issuer       : CN=PowerShell Local Certificate Root
Thumbprint   : FD48FAA9281A657DBD089B5A008FAFE61D3B32FD
FriendlyName :
NotBefore    : 4/22/2007 12:32:37 AM
NotAfter     : 12/31/2039 3:59:59 PM
Extensions   : {System.Security.Cryptography.Oid, System.Security.
               Cryptography.Oid}
```

Discussion

The certificate drive provides a useful way to navigate and view certificates for the
current user or local machine. For example, if your execution policy requires the use
of digital signatures, the following command tells you which publishers are trusted to
run scripts on your system:

```
Get-ChildItem cert:\CurrentUser\TrustedPublisher
```

The certificate provider is probably most commonly used to select a code-signing certificate for the Set-AuthenticodeSignature cmdlet. The following command selects the
"best" code-signing certificate (i.e., the one that expires last):

```
$certificates = Get-ChildItem Cert:\CurrentUser\My -CodeSign
$signingCert = @($certificates | Sort -Desc NotAfter)[0]
```

The -CodeSign parameter lets you search for certificates in the certificate store that support code signing. To search for certificates used for other purposes, see Recipe 18.14.

Although the certificate provider is useful for browsing and retrieving information from the computer's certificate stores, it does not let you add or remove items from these locations. If you want to manage certificates in the certificate store, the `System.Security.Cryptography.X509Certificates.X509Store` class (and other related classes from the `System.Security.Cryptography.X509Certificates` namespace) from the .NET Framework supports that functionality. For an example of this approach, see Recipe 18.15.

For more information about the certificate provider, type **Get-Help Certificate**.

See Also

Recipe 18.14, "Program: Search the Certificate Store"

Recipe 18.15, "Add and Remove Certificates"

18.14 Program: Search the Certificate Store

One useful feature of the certificate provider is its support for a -CodeSign parameter that lets you search for certificates in the certificate store that support code signing.

This parameter is called a *dynamic parameter*: one that has been added by a provider to a core PowerShell cmdlet. You can discover the dynamic parameters for a provider by navigating to that provider and then reviewing the output of Get-Command -Syntax. For example:

```
PS > Set-Location cert:\
PS > Get-Command Get-ChildItem -Syntax
Get-ChildItem [[-Path] <String[]>] [[-Filter] <String>] (...) [-CodeSigningCert]
```

In addition to the output of Get-Command, the help topic for the provider often describes the dynamic parameters it supports. For a list of the provider help topics, type **Get-Help -Category Provider**.

Code-signing certificates are not the only kind of certificates, however; other frequently used certificate types are Encrypting File System, Client Authentication, and more.

Example 18-8 lets you search the certificate provider for certificates that support a given Enhanced Key Usage (EKU).

Example 18-8. Search-CertificateStore.ps1

```
##############################################################################
##
## Search-CertificateStore
##
## From Windows PowerShell Cookbook (O'Reilly)
## by Lee Holmes (http://www.leeholmes.com/guide)
##
##############################################################################

<#

.SYNOPSIS

Search the certificate provider for certificates that match the specified
Enhanced Key Usage (EKU).

.EXAMPLE

Search-CertificateStore "Encrypting File System"

#>

param(
    ## The friendly name of an Enhanced Key Usage
    ## (such as 'Code Signing')
    [Parameter(Mandatory = $true)]
    $EkuName
)

Set-StrictMode -Off

## Go through every certificate in the current user's "My" store
foreach($cert in Get-ChildItem cert:\CurrentUser\My)
{
    ## For each of those, go through its extensions
    foreach($extension in $cert.Extensions)
    {
        ## For each extension, go through its Enhanced Key Usages
        foreach($certEku in $extension.EnhancedKeyUsages)
        {
            ## If the friendly name matches, output that certificate
            if($certEku.FriendlyName -eq $ekuName)
            {
                $cert
            }
        }
    }
}
```

For more information about running scripts, see Recipe 1.1.

See Also

Recipe 1.1, "Run Programs, Scripts, and Existing Tools"

18.15 Add and Remove Certificates

Problem

You want to add and remove certificates from the certificate store.

Solution

Use the certificate store APIs from the .NET Framework, as shown in Example 18-9.

Example 18-9. Adding and removing certificates

```
## Removing a certificate
$cert = Get-ChildItem cert:\currentuser\TrustedPublisher\<thumbprint>
$store = New-Object System.Security.Cryptography.X509Certificates.X509Store `
    "TrustedPublisher","CurrentUser"
$store.Open("ReadWrite")
$store.Remove($cert)
$store.Close()

## Adding a certificate from disk
$cert = Get-PfxCertificate <path_to_certificate>
$store = New-Object System.Security.Cryptography.X509Certificates.X509Store `
    "TrustedPublisher","CurrentUser"
$store.Open("ReadWrite")
$store.Add($cert)
$store.Close()
```

Discussion

The certificate drive provides a useful way to navigate and view certificates for the current user or local machine. For example, if your execution policy requires the use of digital signatures, the following command tells you which publishers are trusted to run scripts on your system:

```
Get-ChildItem cert:\CurrentUser\TrustedPublisher
```

The certificate provider is ultimately a read-only view of your certificates, however. After using the certificate provider to retrieve a certificate, you can then use the .NET APIs to remove it from the certificate store permanently.

Likewise, the Get-PfxCertificate cmdlet lets you review a certificate from a file that contains it, but it does not let you install it into the certificate store permanently. The .NET APIs are also the way to import the certificate for good.

For more information about retrieving certificates from the certificate provider, see Recipe 18.13. For more information about working with classes from the .NET Framework, see Recipe 3.8.

See Also

Recipe 3.8, "Work with .NET Objects"

Recipe 18.13, "Access User and Machine Certificates"

18.16 Manage Security Descriptors in SDDL Form

Problem

You want to work with a security identifier in Security Descriptor Definition Language (SDDL) form.

Solution

Use the `System.Security.AccessControl.CommonSecurityDescriptor` class from the .NET Framework, as shown by Example 18-10.

Example 18-10. Automating security configuration of the PowerShell Remoting Users group

```
## Get the SID for the "PowerShell Remoting Users" group
$account = New-Object Security.Principal.NTAccount "PowerShell Remoting Users"
$sid = $account.Translate([Security.Principal.SecurityIdentifier]).Value

## Get the security descriptor for the existing configuration
$config = Get-PsSessionConfiguration Microsoft.PowerShell
$existingSddl = $config.SecurityDescriptorSddl

## Create a CommonSecurityDescriptor object out of the existing SDDL
## so that we don't need to manage the string by hand
$arguments = $false,$false,$existingSddl
$mapper = New-Object Security.AccessControl.CommonSecurityDescriptor $arguments

## Create a new access rule that adds the "PowerShell Remoting Users" group
$mapper.DiscretionaryAcl.AddAccess("Allow",$sid,268435456,"None","None")

## Get the new SDDL for that configuration
$newSddl = $mapper.GetSddlForm("All")

## Update the endpoint configuration
Set-PSSessionConfiguration Microsoft.PowerShell -SecurityDescriptorSddl $newSddl
```

Discussion

Security descriptors are often shown (or requested) in SDDL form. The SDDL form of a security descriptor is cryptic, highly specific, and plain text. All of these aspects make this format difficult to work with reliably, so you can use the `System.Security.Access`

`Control.CommonSecurityDescriptor` class from the .NET Framework to do most of the gritty work for you.

For more information about the SDDL format, see *http://msdn.microsoft.com/en-us/ library/aa379570%28VS.85%29.aspx*. For an example of this in action, see Recipe 29.8.

See Also

Recipe 3.8, "Work with .NET Objects"

Recipe 29.8, "Configure User Permissions for Remoting"

Integrated Scripting Environment

19.0 Introduction

While text-mode PowerShell is great for its efficiency and automation, there's not much to be said for its user interface. Most Windows key combinations don't work. Text selection and editing don't work. Rectangular text selection is strange, as is the lack of support for freely resizing the console window.

All of these are simple side-effects of *PowerShell.exe* being a console application. These problems impact every console application in Windows and likely always will.

Aside from the user interface oddities, the fatal flaw with console applications comes from their lack of support for the Unicode standard: the way that most international languages represent their alphabets. While the Windows console supports a few basic non-English characters (such as accented letters), it provides full support for very little else.

This proves to be quite a problem for worldwide administrators! Since typing international characters directly at the command line was so difficult, administrators in many countries were forced to write scripts in Notepad in order to get full Unicode support, and then use PowerShell to run the scripts, even if the command was ultimately only a single line.

PowerShell version two resolves these issues by introducing the Integrated Scripting Environment (ISE).

The ISE gives PowerShell the user interface you expect from a modern application, supports full Unicode input and multiple tabbed sessions, and provides a great experience for interactive debugging.

Conceptually, the ISE consists of three main components (shown in Figure 19-1).

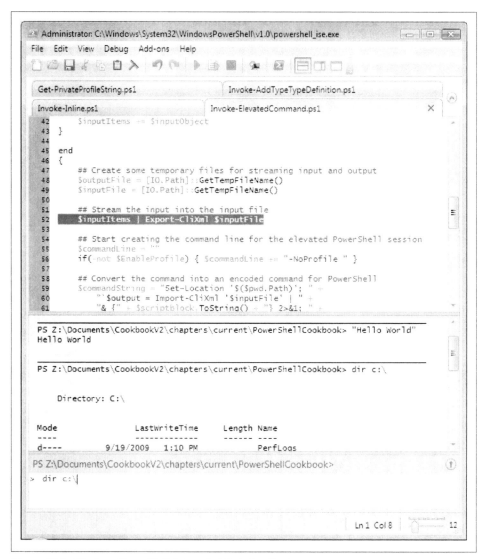

Figure 19-1. Windows PowerShell Integrated Scripting Environment

Scripting pane

The scripting pane is the top pane of the ISE, and it is geared toward multiline script editing and creation. It offers line numbering and syntax highlighting, and it supports a great debugging experience.

One unique aspect of the scripting pane is that it supports *selective execution*: the ability to run just what you've highlighted rather than the entire script you're working on. This makes script authoring a breeze. As you start to write your script, you can interactively experiment with commands until you get them right. Once they work as expected, you can keep them, move on, and then continue to build your script one piece at a time. As you've come to expect from PowerShell's console shell, script editing in the scripting pane supports tab completion of commands, parameters, paths, and more.

Output pane

The output pane sits in the middle of the ISE, and it shows output from commands run in both the scripting pane and the command pane. Unlike PowerShell's console shell, text selection in the output pane acts like text selection in a regular Windows application.

Command pane

The command pane, which sits in the bottom of the application, is where you'll spend most of your interactive sessions in the ISE. Like the command prompt in the PowerShell console, the command pane supports tab completion. Unlike the command pane in the console window, it supports standard Windows hotkeys, text selection, syntax highlighting, and more.

If you find your command growing too long, you can press Shift-Enter to enable multiline editing for the current command.

In addition to these features, the PowerShell ISE offers extensive customization, scripting, and remoting support.

19.1 Debug a Script

Problem

You want to use PowerShell's debugging commands through an interface more friendly than its *-PsBreakpoint cmdlets.

Solution

Use the Debug menu in the ISE to add and remove breakpoints and manage debugging behavior when PowerShell reaches a breakpoint.

Discussion

The PowerShell ISE gives you a rich set of interactive graphical debugging commands to help you diagnose errors in your scripts. It exposes these through the *Debug* menu, and it behaves like many other graphical debugging environments you may have experience with. Figure 19-2 shows the debugging option available in the ISE.

To set a breakpoint, first save your script. Then, select the Toggle Breakpoint menu item, select the Toggle Breakpoint option that shows when you right-click in the left-hand margin of the ISE, or press F9. Once PowerShell hits the breakpoint in your script, it pauses to let you examine variables, script state, and whatever else interests you. To

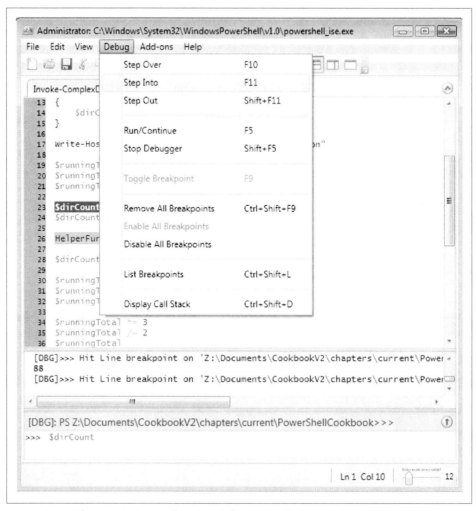

Figure 19-2. Debugging options in the Integrated Scripting Environment

control the flow of execution, you can use the stepping commands: Step Over, Step Into, and Step Out.

Step Over continues to the next line of the script, executing (but not debugging into) any function calls that you come across. Step Into continues to the next line of the script, debugging into any function calls that you come across. If you are in a function, the Step Out command lets PowerShell complete execution of the function and resumes debugging once the function completes.

One unique aspect of debugging in the ISE is that it builds its support entirely on the core debugging cmdlets discussed in Chapter 14. Changes that you make from the debugging menu (such as adding a breakpoint) are immediately reflected in the cmdlets (such as listing breakpoints). Likewise, breakpoints that you add or modify from the integrated command line show up in the user interface as though you had created them from the debug menu itself.

 In fact, the features exposed by PowerShell's breakpoint cmdlets in many cases surpass the functionality exposed by the ISE's debug menu. For example, the Set-PsDebug cmdlet supports command breakpoints, conditional breakpoints, variable breakpoints, and much more. For more information about the Set-PsDebug cmdlet, see Recipe 14.3.

Unlike most graphical debugging environments, the PowerShell ISE makes it incredibly easy to investigate the dynamic state of your script while you are debugging it. For more information about how to investigate the state of your script while debugging, see Recipe 14.6.

See Also

Chapter 14, *Debugging*

Recipe 14.6, "Investigate System State While Debugging"

19.2 Customize Text and User Interface Colors

Problem

You want to change the color scheme of the ISE or change the colors used for syntax highlighting.

Solution

Review the properties of the $psISE.Options automatic variable, and customize the ones you want. For example, to give the output pane the same appearance as the PowerShell console:

```
$psISE.Options.OutputPaneBackgroundColor = "#012456"
$psISE.Options.OutputPaneForegroundColor = "#EEEDF0"
$psISE.Options.OutputPaneTextBackgroundColor = "#012456"
```

Discussion

While working in the ISE, you might sometimes wonder, "Where is the Options dialog?"

The answer is that there isn't one. Instead, the ISE offers a wealth of configuration option through its $psISE automatic variable:

```
PS > $psISE.Options | Format-List
```

```
SelectedScriptPaneState      : Top
ShowToolBar                  : True
TokenColors                  : {[Attribute, #FFADD8E6], [Command, #FF0000FF],
                                 [CommandArgument, #FF8A2BE2], [CommandParameter
                                 , #FF000080]...}
DefaultOptions               : Microsoft.PowerShell.Host.ISE.ISEOptions
FontSize                     : 12
FontName                     : Consolas
ErrorForegroundColor         : #FFFF0000
ErrorBackgroundColor         : #00FFFFFF
WarningForegroundColor       : #FFFF8C00
WarningBackgroundColor       : #00FFFFFF
VerboseForegroundColor       : #FF0000FF
VerboseBackgroundColor       : #00FFFFFF
DebugForegroundColor         : #FF0000FF
DebugBackgroundColor         : #00FFFFFF
OutputPaneBackgroundColor    : #FF012456
OutputPaneTextBackgroundColor : #FF012456
OutputPaneForegroundColor    : #FFEEEDF0
CommandPaneBackgroundColor   : #FFFFFFFF
ScriptPaneBackgroundColor    : #FFFFFFFF
ScriptPaneForegroundColor    : #FF000000
ShowWarningForDuplicateFiles : True
ShowWarningBeforeSavingOnRun : True
UseLocalHelp                 : True
CommandPaneUp                : False
```

You can change these options as easily as you change any other automatic variable—by assigning new values to its properties (as shown in the solution). To make these changes affect all of your ISE sessions, simply store them in the host-specific profile file for the ISE. To edit this file, simply type: **ise $profile.CurrentUserCurrentHost**.

In addition to user interface customization, the ISE also lets you customize the colors it uses for syntax highlighting. It exposes these settings through the $psISE.Options.TokenColors automatic variable. For example, to change the coloring of attributes (such as the [Parameter()] statement) to be more like regular types, type:

```
$psIse.Options.TokenColors["Attribute"] = $psIse.Options.TokenColors["Type"]
```

For more information about modifying your PowerShell profile, see Recipe 1.6.

See Also

Recipe 1.6, "Customize Your Shell, Profile, and Prompt"

19.3 Connect to a Remote Computer

Problem

You want to create a new tab in the ISE that represents a connection to a remote computer.

Solution

Click the New Remote PowerShell Tab icon in the toolbar or File menu.

Discussion

One of the features most requested for the PowerShell console application is support for multiple tabs and multiple sessions. As such, multitab support in the ISE is prominent—and gets a unique treatment.

To create a new tab that represents a local PowerShell session, simply click the New PowerShell Tab icon in the toolbar or File menu. If you want to connect to a remote computer instead, just click the New *Remote* PowerShell Tab menu or toolbar icon.

Once you've connected a remote PowerShell tab, interacting with a remote system is just like interacting with a local one. Prompts from the remote system show up like prompts from the local system, as do progress bars, credential requests, and Power-Shell's other feedback mechanisms.

For more information about PowerShell Remoting, see Chapter 29.

See Also

Chapter 29, *Remoting*

19.4 Extend ISE Functionality Through Its Object Model

Problem

You want to customize the PowerShell ISE to add your own functionality and features.

Solution

Explore and modify properties of the $psISE automatic variable to interact with the ISE's object model. For example, to clean up trailing spaces from the script you are currently editing, use the following:

```
$psISE.CurrentFile.Editor.Text =
    $psise.CurrentFile.Editor.Text -replace '(?m)\s+$',''
```

Discussion

In addition to the features already available, the PowerShell ISE offers many additional customization opportunities through its *object model*. The object model exposes the nuts and bolts you need to create your own functionality—and makes it available through the $psISE automatic variable. Recipe 19.5 demonstrates one aspect of the object model by showing how to add items to the Add-ons menu.

As with other .NET object models, the Get-Member and Format-List cmdlets are the keys to exploring the ISE's object model. At its first level, the object model gives you access to the current file, PowerShell tab, and ISE options:

```
PS > $psISE | Format-List


CurrentPowerShellTab : Microsoft.PowerShell.Host.ISE.PowerShellTab
CurrentFile          : Microsoft.PowerShell.Host.ISE.ISEFile
Options              : Microsoft.PowerShell.Host.ISE.ISEOptions
PowerShellTabs       : {PowerShell 1}
```

For example, the $psISE.CurrentFile.Editor variable provides programmatic access to the text and behavior of the current scripting pane:

```
PS > $psISE.CurrentFile.Editor | Get-Member

   TypeName: Microsoft.Windows.PowerShell.Gui.Internal.ScriptEditor

Name              MemberType Definition
----              ---------- ----------
PropertyChanged   Event      System.ComponentModel.PropertyChangedEventHandler...
Clear             Method     System.Void Clear()
EnsureVisible     Method     System.Void EnsureVisible(int lineNumber)
Equals            Method     bool Equals(System.Object obj)
Focus             Method     System.Void Focus()
GetHashCode       Method     int GetHashCode()
GetLineLength     Method     int GetLineLength(int lineNumber)
GetType           Method     type GetType()
InsertText        Method     System.Void InsertText(string text)
Select            Method     System.Void Select(int startLine, int startColumn,...
SetCaretPosition  Method     System.Void SetCaretPosition(int lineNumber, int c...
ToString          Method     string ToString()
CaretColumn       Property   System.Int32 CaretColumn {get;}
CaretLine         Property   System.Int32 CaretLine {get;}
LineCount         Property   System.Int32 LineCount {get;}
SelectedText      Property   System.String SelectedText {get;}
Text              Property   System.String Text {get;set;}
```

By building on the object model, you can write tools to automatically process your scripts (for example, commenting and uncommenting regions of your script, processing script output, and more).

For more information about working with .NET objects, see Recipe 3.8.

See Also

Recipe 3.8, "Work with .NET Objects"

Recipe 19.5, "Add an Item to the Tools Menu"

19.5 Add an Item to the Tools Menu

Problem

You want to add your own menu items and shortcuts to the ISE.

Solution

Pick a display name, action, and (optional) shortcut, and then add those to the `$psISE.CurrentPowerShellTab.AddOnsMenu.Submenus` collection:

```
$psISE.CurrentPowerShellTab.AddOnsMenu.Submenus.Add(
    "PowerShell Blog",
    { Start-Process http://blogs.msdn.com/PowerShell },
    "Control+Alt+B")
```

Discussion

As part of its extensibility features, the PowerShell ISE gives you complete access to a submenu of your very own: the Add-ons menu.

To work with the Add-ons menu, access the `$psISE.CurrentPowerShellTab.AddOnsMenu` variable.

By default, menu items that get added have no shortcuts, so you must click them to activate them. To add a typical menu shortcut that becomes active once the Add-ons menu is active, put an underscore (_) character before the letter that you want to activate your menu item.

To define a global hotkey (one that is available through the entire application), supply the keys as the third argument for the `Add()` method. If you don't want to assign a global hotkey, use `$null` as the third argument.

For more information about extending the ISE, see Recipe 19.4.

See Also

Recipe 19.4, "Extend ISE Functionality Through Its Object Model"

Administrator Tasks

Files and Directories

20.0 Introduction

One of the most common tasks when administering a system is working with its files and directories. This is true when you administer the computer at the command line, and it is true when you write scripts to administer it automatically.

Fortunately, PowerShell makes scripting files and directories as easy as working at the command line—a point that many seasoned programmers and scripters often miss. A perfect example of this comes when you wrestle with limited disk space and need to find the files taking up the most space.

A typical programmer might approach this task by writing functions to scan a specific directory of a system. For each file, they check whether the file is big enough to care about. If so, they add it to a list. For each directory in the original directory, the programmer repeats this process (until there are no more directories to process).

As the saying goes, though, "You can write C in any programming language." The habits and preconceptions you bring to a language often directly influence how open you are to advances in that language.

Being an administrative shell, PowerShell directly supports tasks such as visiting all the files in a subdirectory or moving a file from one directory to another. That complicated programmer-oriented script turns into a one-liner:

```
Get-ChildItem -Recurse | Sort-Object -Descending Length | Select -First 10
```

Before diving into your favorite programmer's toolkit, check to see what PowerShell supports in that area. In many cases, it can handle the task without requiring your programmer's bag of tricks.

20.1 Determine the Current Location

Problem

You want to determine the current location from a script or command.

Solution

To retrieve the current location, use the Get-Location cmdlet. The Get-Location cmdlet provides the drive and path as two common properties:

```
$currentLocation = (Get-Location).Path
```

As a short form for (Get-Location).Path, use the $pwd automatic variable.

Discussion

The Get-Location cmdlet returns information about the current location. From the information it returns, you can access the current drive, provider, and path.

This current location affects PowerShell commands and programs that you launch from PowerShell. This does not apply when you interact with the .NET Framework, however. If you need to call a .NET method that interacts with the filesystem, always be sure to provide fully qualified paths:

```
[System.IO.File]::ReadAllText("c:\temp\file.txt")
```

If you are sure that the file exists, the Resolve-Path cmdlet lets you translate a relative path to an absolute path:

```
$filePath = (Resolve-Path file.txt).Path
```

If the file does not exist, use the Join-Path cmdlet in combination with the Get-Location cmdlet to specify the file:

```
$filePath = Join-Path (Get-Location) file.txt
```

Another alternative that combines the functionality of both approaches is a bit more advanced but also lets you specify relative locations. It comes from methods in the PowerShell $executionContext variable, which provides functionality normally used by cmdlet and provider authors:

```
$executionContext.SessionState.Path.`
    GetUnresolvedProviderPathFromPSPath("..\file.txt")
```

For more information about the Get-Location cmdlet, type **Get-Help Get-Location**.

20.2 Get the Files in a Directory

Problem

You want to get or list the files in a directory.

Solution

To retrieve the list of files in a directory, use the Get-ChildItem cmdlet. To get a specific item, use the Get-Item cmdlet.

- To list all items in the current directory, use the Get-ChildItem cmdlet:

    ```
    Get-ChildItem
    ```

- To list all items that match a wildcard, supply a wildcard to the Get-ChildItem cmdlet:

    ```
    Get-ChildItem *.txt
    ```

- To list all files that match a wildcard in the current directory (and all its children), use the -Include and -Recurse parameters of the Get-ChildItem cmdlet:

    ```
    Get-ChildItem -Include *.txt -Recurse
    ```

- To list all directories in the current directory, use the Where-Object cmdlet to test the PsIsContainer property:

    ```
    Get-ChildItem | Where { $_.PsIsContainer }
    ```

- To get information about a specific item, use the Get-Item cmdlet:

    ```
    Get-Item test.txt
    ```

Discussion

Although most commonly used on the filesystem, the Get-ChildItem and Get-Item cmdlets in fact work against any items on any of the PowerShell drives. In addition to A: through Z: (the standard filesystem drives), they also work on Alias:, Cert:, Env:, Function:, HKLM:, HKCU:, and Variable:.

 The third example in the Solution lists files that match a wildcard in a directory and all its children. That example works on any PowerShell provider. However, PowerShell can retrieve your results more quickly if you use a provider-specific filter, as described in Recipe 20.6.

The solution demonstrates some simple wildcard scenarios that the Get-ChildItem cmdlet supports, but PowerShell in fact enables several more advanced scenarios. For more information about these scenarios, see Recipe 20.6.

In the filesystem, these cmdlets return objects from the .NET Framework that represent files and directories—instances of System.IO.FileInfo and System.IO.DirectoryInfo classes, respectively. Each provides a great deal of useful information: attributes, modification times, full name, and more. Although the default directory listing exposes a lot of information, PowerShell provides even more. For more information about working with classes from the .NET Framework, see Recipe 3.8.

See Also

Recipe 3.8, "Work with .NET Objects"

Recipe 20.6, "Find Files That Match a Pattern"

20.3 Find All Files Modified Before a Certain Date

Problem

You want to find all files last modified before a certain date.

Solution

To find all files modified before a certain date, use the Get-ChildItem cmdlet to list the files in a directory, and then use the Where-Object cmdlet to compare the LastWrite Time property to the date you are interested in. For example, to find all files created before the year 2007:

```
Get-ChildItem -Recurse | Where-Object { $_.LastWriteTime -lt "01/01/2007" }
```

Discussion

A common reason to compare files against a certain date is to find recently modified (or not recently modified) files. The code for this looks almost the same as the example given by the solution, except your script can't know the exact date to compare against.

In this case, the AddDays() method in the .NET Framework's DateTime class gives you a way to perform some simple calendar arithmetic. If you have a DateTime object, you can add or subtract time from it to represent a different date altogether. For example, to find all files modified in the last 30 days:

```
$compareDate = (Get-Date).AddDays(-30)
Get-ChildItem -Recurse | Where-Object { $_.LastWriteTime -ge $compareDate }
```

Similarly, to find all files more than 30 days old:

```
$compareDate = (Get-Date).AddDays(-30)
Get-ChildItem -Recurse | Where-Object { $_.LastWriteTime -lt $compareDate }
```

In this example, the Get-Date cmdlet returns an object that represents the current date and time. You call the AddDays() method to subtract 30 days from that time, which stores the date representing "30 days ago" in the $compareDate variable. Next, you compare that date against the LastWriteTime property of each file that the Get-ChildItem cmdlet returns.

The DateTime class is the administrator's favorite calendar!

```
PS > [DateTime]::IsLeapYear(2008)
True
PS > $daysTillChristmas = [DateTime] "December 25" - (Get-Date)
PS > $daysTillChristmas.Days
327
```

For more information about the Get-ChildItem cmdlet, type **Get-Help Get-ChildItem**. For more information about the Where-Object cmdlet, see Recipe 2.1.

See Also

Recipe 2.1, "Filter Items in a List or Command Output"

20.4 Clear the Content of a File

Problem

You want to clear the content of a file.

Solution

To clear the content of a file, use the Clear-Content cmdlet, as shown by Example 20-1.

Example 20-1. Clearing content from a file

```
PS > Get-Content test.txt
Hello World
PS > Clear-Content test.txt
PS > Get-Content test.txt
PS > Get-Item test.txt


    Directory: C:\temp


Mode                LastWriteTime     Length Name
----                -------------     ------ ----
-a---         4/23/2007   8:05 PM          0 test.txt
```

Discussion

The (aptly named) Clear-Content cmdlet clears the content from an item. Although the Solution demonstrates this only for files in the filesystem, it in fact applies to any PowerShell providers that support the concept of "content." Examples of other drives that support these content concepts are Function:, Alias:, and Variable:.

For information on how to remove an item entirely, see Recipe 20.13.

For more information about the Remove-Item or Clear-Content cmdlets, type Get-Help Remove-Item or Get-Help Clear-Content.

See Also

Get-Help Remove-Item

Get-Help Clear-Content

20.5 Manage and Change the Attributes of a File

Problem

You want to update the ReadOnly, Hidden, or System attributes of a file.

Solution

Most of the time, you will want to use the familiar *attrib.exe* program to change the attributes of a file:

```
attrib +r test.txt
attrib -s test.txt
```

To set only the ReadOnly attribute, you can optionally set the IsReadOnly property on the file:

```
$file = Get-Item test.txt
$file.IsReadOnly = $true
```

To apply a specific set of attributes, use the Attributes property on the file:

```
$file = Get-Item test.txt
$file.Attributes = "ReadOnly,NotContentIndexed"
```

Directory listings show the attributes on a file, but you can also access the Mode or Attributes property directly:

```
PS > $file.Attributes = "ReadOnly","System","NotContentIndexed"
PS > $file.Mode
--r-s
PS > $file.Attributes
ReadOnly, System, NotContentIndexed
```

Discussion

When the Get-Item or Get-ChildItem cmdlets retrieve a file, the resulting output has an Attributes property. This property doesn't offer much in addition to the regular *attrib.exe* program, although it does make it easier to set the attributes to a specific state.

Be aware that setting the Hidden attribute on a file removes it from most default views. If you want to retrieve it after hiding it, most commands require a -Force parameter. Similarly, setting the ReadOnly attribute on a file causes most write operations on that file to fail unless you call that command with the -Force parameter.

If you want to add an attribute to a file using the Attributes property (rather than *attrib.exe* for some reason), this is how you would do that:

```
$file = Get-Item test.txt
$readOnly = [IO.FileAttributes] "ReadOnly"
$file.Attributes = $file.Attributes -bor $readOnly
```

For more information about working with classes from the .NET Framework, see Recipe 3.8.

See Also

Recipe 3.8, "Work with .NET Objects"

20.6 Find Files That Match a Pattern

Problem

You want to get a list of files that match a specific pattern.

Solution

Use the Get-ChildItem cmdlet for both simple and advanced wildcard support:

- To find all items in the current directory that match a PowerShell wildcard, supply that wildcard to the Get-ChildItem cmdlet:

  ```
  Get-ChildItem *.txt
  ```

- To find all items in the current directory that match a *provider-specific* filter, supply that filter to the -Filter parameter:

  ```
  Get-ChildItem -Filter *~2*
  ```

- To find all items in the current directory that do not match a PowerShell wildcard, supply that wildcard to the -Exclude parameter:

  ```
  Get-ChildItem -Exclude *.txt
  ```

- To find all items in subdirectories that match a PowerShell wildcard, use the -Include and -Recurse parameters:

  ```
  Get-ChildItem -Include *.txt -Recurse
  ```

- To find all items in subdirectories that match a *provider-specific* filter, use the
  -Filter and -Recurse parameters:

      Get-ChildItem -Filter *.txt -Recurse

- To find all items in subdirectories that do not match a PowerShell wildcard, use
  the -Exclude and -Recurse parameters:

      Get-ChildItem -Exclude *.txt -Recurse

Use the Where-Object cmdlet for advanced regular expression support:

- To find all items with a filename that matches a regular expression, use the Where-
  Object cmdlet to compare the Name property to the regular expression:

      Get-ChildItem | Where-Object { $_.Name -match '^KB[0-9]+\.log$' }

- To find all items with a directory name that matches a regular expression, use the
  Where-Object cmdlet to compare the DirectoryName property to the regular expression:

      Get-ChildItem -Recurse | Where-Object { $_.DirectoryName -match 'Release' }

- To find all items with a directory name or filename that matches a regular expression, use the Where-Object cmdlet to compare the FullName property to the regular
  expression:

      Get-ChildItem -Recurse | Where-Object { $_.FullName -match 'temp' }

Discussion

The Get-ChildItem cmdlet supports wildcarding through three parameters:

Path

> The -Path parameter is the first (and default) parameter. While you can enter sim-
> ple paths such as ., C:\, or D:\Documents, you can also supply paths that include
> wildcards—such as *, *.txt, [a-z]???.log, or even C:\win**.N[a-f]?\ F*\v2*
> \csc.exe.

Include/Exclude

> The -Include and -Exclude parameters act as a filter on wildcarding that happens
> on the -Path parameter. If you specify the -Recurse parameter, the -Include and
> -Exclude wildcards apply to all items returned.

 The most common mistake with the -Include parameter comes
when you use it against a path with no wildcards. For example, this
doesn't seem to produce the expected results:

        Get-ChildItem $env:WINDIR -Include *.log

That command produces no results because you have not supplied
an item wildcard to the path. Instead, the correct command is:

        Get-ChildItem $env:WINDIR* -Include *.log

Filter

> The -Filter parameter lets you filter results based on the *provider-specific* filtering language of the provider from which you retrieve items. Since PowerShell's wild-carding support closely mimics filesystem wildcards, and most people use the -Filter parameter only on the filesystem, this seems like a redundant (and equivalent) parameter. A SQL provider, however, would use SQL syntax in its -Filter parameter. Likewise, an Active Directory provider would use LDAP paths in its -Filter parameter.

It may not be obvious, but the filesystem provider's filtering language is not exactly the same as the PowerShell wildcard syntax. For example, the -Filter parameter matches against the short filenames, too:

```
PS > Get-ChildItem | Select-Object Name

Name
----
A Long File Name With Spaces Also.txt
A Long File Name With Spaces.txt

PS > Get-ChildItem *1* | Select-Object Name
PS > Get-ChildItem -Filter *1* | Select-Object Name

Name
----
A Long File Name With Spaces.txt
```

On the other hand, PowerShell's wildcard syntax supports far more than the filesystem's native filtering language. For more information about PowerShell's wildcard syntax, type **Get-Help About_WildCard**.

When you want to perform even more advanced filtering than what PowerShell's wild-carding syntax offers, the Where-Object cmdlet provides infinite possibilities. For example, to exclude certain directories from a search, use the following:

```
Get-ChildItem -Rec | Where-Object { $_.DirectoryName -notmatch "Debug" }
```

To list all directories, use:

```
Get-ChildItem | Where-Object { $_.PsIsContainer }
```

Since the syntax of the Where-Object cmdlet can sometimes be burdensome for simple queries, the Compare-Property script in Recipe 2.3 provides an attractive alternative:

```
Get-ChildItem -Rec | Compare-Property DirectoryName notmatch Debug
```

For a filter that is difficult (or impossible) to specify programmatically, the Select-FilteredObject script provided by Recipe 2.4 lets you interactively filter the output.

Because of PowerShell's pipeline model, an advanced file set generated by Get-ChildItem automatically turns into an advanced file set for other cmdlets to operate on:

```
PS > Get-ChildItem -Rec | Where-Object { $_.Length -gt 20mb } |
Sort-Object -Descending Length | Select-FilteredObject |
Remove-Item -WhatIf

What if: Performing operation "Remove File" on Target "C:\temp\backup092300
.zip".
What if: Performing operation "Remove File" on Target "C:\temp\sp-tricking_
iT2.zip".
What if: Performing operation "Remove File" on Target "C:\temp\slime.mov".
What if: Performing operation "Remove File" on Target "C:\temp\hello-world.
mov".
```

For more information about the Get-ChildItem cmdlet, type **Get-Help Get-ChildItem**.

For more information about the Where-Object cmdlet, type **Get-Help Where-Object**.

See Also

Recipe 2.3, "Program: Simplify Most Where-Object Filters"

Recipe 2.4, "Program: Interactively Filter Lists of Objects"

20.7 Manage Files That Include Special Characters

Problem

You want to use a cmdlet that supports wildcarding but provide a filename that includes wildcard characters.

Solution

To prevent PowerShell from treating those characters as wildcard characters, use the cmdlet's -LiteralPath (or similarly named) parameter if it defines one:

```
Get-ChildItem -LiteralPath '[My File].txt'
```

Discussion

One consequence of PowerShell's advanced wildcard support is that the square brackets used to specify character ranges sometimes conflict with actual filenames. Consider the following example:

```
PS > Get-ChildItem | Select-Object Name

Name
----
[My File].txt
```

```
PS > Get-ChildItem '[My File].txt' | Select-Object Name
PS > Get-ChildItem -LiteralPath '[My File].txt' | Select-Object Name

Name
----
[My File].txt
```

The first command clearly demonstrates that we have a file called *[My File].txt*. When we try to retrieve it (passing its name to the `Get-ChildItem` cmdlet), we see no results. Since square brackets are wildcard characters in PowerShell (as are * and ?), the text we provided turns into a search expression rather than a filename.

The `-LiteralPath` parameter (or a similarly named parameter in other cmdlets) tells PowerShell that the filename is named exactly—not a wildcard search term.

In addition to wildcard matching, filenames may sometimes run afoul of PowerShell escape sequences. For example, the backtick character (`` ` ``) in PowerShell means the start of an escape sequence, such as `` `t `` (tab), `` `n `` (newline), or `` `a `` (alarm). To prevent PowerShell from interpreting a backtick as an escape sequence, surround that string in single quotes instead of double quotes.

For more information about the `Get-ChildItem` cmdlet, type **Get-Help Get-ChildItem**. For more information about PowerShell's special characters, type **Get-Help About_ Special_Characters**.

20.8 Program: Get Disk Usage Information

When disk space starts running low, you'll naturally want to find out where to focus your cleanup efforts. Sometimes you may tackle this by looking for large directories (including the directories in them), but other times, you may solve this by looking for directories that are large simply from the files they contain.

 To review the disk usage statistics for an entire drive, use the `Get-PSDrive` cmdlet.

Example 20-2 collects both types of data. It also demonstrates an effective use of *calculated properties*. Like the **Add-Member** cmdlet, calculated properties let you add properties to output objects by specifying the expression that generates their data.

For more information about calculated properties and the **Add-Member** cmdlet, see Recipe 3.15.

Example 20-2. Get-DiskUsage.ps1

```
##############################################################################
##
## Get-DiskUsage
##
## From Windows PowerShell Cookbook (O'Reilly)
## by Lee Holmes (http://www.leeholmes.com/guide)
##
##############################################################################

<#

.SYNOPSIS

Retrieve information about disk usage in the current directory and all
subdirectories. If you specify the -IncludeSubdirectories flag, this
script accounts for the size of subdirectories in the size of a directory.

.EXAMPLE

Get-DiskUsage
Gets the disk usage for the current directory.

.EXAMPLE

Get-DiskUsage -IncludeSubdirectories
Gets the disk usage for the current directory and those below it,
adding the size of child directories to the directory that contains them.

#>

param(
    ## Switch to include subdirectories in the size of each directory
    [switch] $IncludeSubdirectories
)

Set-StrictMode -Version Latest

## If they specify the -IncludeSubdirectories flag, then we want to account
## for all subdirectories in the size of each directory
if($includeSubdirectories)
{
    Get-ChildItem | Where-Object { $_.PsIsContainer } |
        Select-Object Name,
            @{ Name="Size";
            Expression={ ($_ | Get-ChildItem -Recurse |
                Measure-Object -Sum Length).Sum + 0 } }
}
## Otherwise, we just find all directories below the current directory,
## and determine their size
else
{
    Get-ChildItem -Recurse | Where-Object { $_.PsIsContainer } |
        Select-Object FullName,
            @{ Name="Size";
```

```
            Expression={ ($_ | Get-ChildItem |
               Measure-Object -Sum Length).Sum + 0 } }
}
```

For more information about running scripts, see Recipe 1.1.

See Also

Recipe 1.1, "Run Programs, Scripts, and Existing Tools"

Recipe 3.15, "Add Custom Methods and Properties to Objects"

20.9 Monitor a File for Changes

Problem

You want to monitor the end of a file for new content.

Solution

To monitor the end of a file for new content, use the -Wait parameter of the Get-Content cmdlet:

```
Get-Content log.txt -Wait
```

Discussion

The -Wait parameter of the Get-Content cmdlet acts much like the traditional Unix tail command with the --follow parameter. If you provide the -Wait parameter, the Get-Content cmdlet reads the content of the file but doesn't exit. When a program appends new content to the end of the file, the Get-Content cmdlet returns that content and continues to wait.

 Unlike the Unix tail command, the Get-Content cmdlet does not support a feature to let you start reading from the end of a file. If you need to monitor the end of an extremely large file, a specialized file monitoring utility is a valid option.

For more information about the Get-Content cmdlet, type **Get-Help Get-Content**. For more information about the -Wait parameter, type **Get-Help FileSystem**.

20.10 Get the Version of a DLL or Executable

Problem

You want to examine the version information of a file.

Solution

Use the `Get-Item` cmdlet to retrieve the file, and then access the `VersionInfo` property to retrieve its version information:

```
PS > $file = Get-Item $pshome\powershell.exe
PS > $file.VersionInfo

ProductVersion FileVersion   FileName
-------------- -----------   --------
6.0.6002.18139 6.0.6002.1813 C:\Windows\System32\WindowsPowerShell\v1.0\powershell.exe
```

Discussion

One common task in system administration is identifying file and version information of installed software. PowerShell makes this simple through the `VersionInfo` property that it automatically attaches to files that you retrieve through the `Get-Item` cmdlet. To generate a report for a directory, simply pass the output of `Get-ChildItem` to the `Select-Object` cmdlet, and use the `-ExpandProperty` parameter to expand the `VersionInfo` property.

```
PS > Get-ChildItem $env:WINDIR |
    Select -Expand VersionInfo -ErrorAction SilentlyContinue

ProductVersion   FileVersion      FileName
--------------   -----------      --------
                                  C:\Windows\autologon.log
6.0.6000.16386   6.0.6000.1638... C:\Windows\bfsvc.exe
                                  C:\Windows\bootstat.dat
                                  C:\Windows\DtcInstall.log
6.0.6000.16386   6.0.6000.1638... C:\Windows\explorer.exe
6.0.6000.16386   6.0.6000.1638... C:\Windows\fveupdate.exe
6.0.6000.16386   6.0.6000.1638... C:\Windows\HelpPane.exe
6.0.6000.16386   6.0.6000.1638... C:\Windows\hh.exe
(...)
```

For more information about the `Get-ChildItem` cmdlet, see Recipe 20.2.

See Also

Recipe 20.2, "Get the Files in a Directory"

20.11 Program: Get the MD5 or SHA1 Hash of a File

File hashes provide a useful way to check for damage or modification to a file. A digital hash acts like the fingerprint of a file and detects even minor modifications. If the content of a file changes, then so does its hash. Many online download services provide the hash of a file on that file's download page so you can determine whether the transfer somehow corrupted the file (see Figure 20-1).

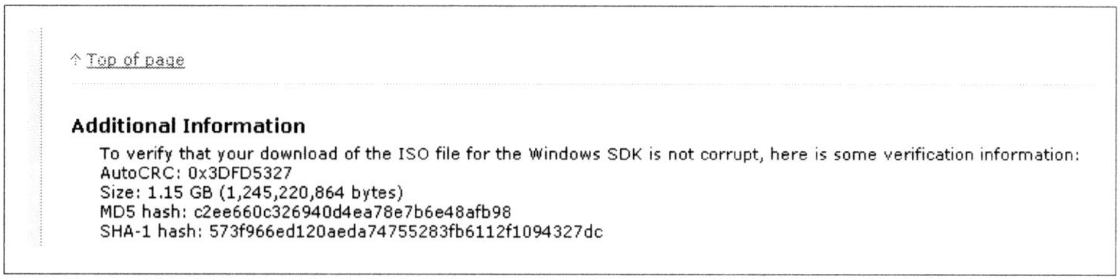

Figure 20-1. File hashes as a verification mechanism

There are three common ways to generate the hash of a file: MD5, SHA1, and SHA256. The most common is MD5, and the next most common is SHA1. While popular, these hash types can be trusted to detect only accidental file modification. They can be fooled if somebody wants to tamper with the file without changing its hash. The SHA256 algorithm can be used to protect against even intentional file tampering.

Example 20-3 lets you determine the hash of a file (or of multiple files if provided by the pipeline).

Example 20-3. Get-FileHash.ps1

```
##############################################################################
##
## Get-FileHash
##
## From Windows PowerShell Cookbook (O'Reilly)
## by Lee Holmes (http://www.leeholmes.com/guide)
##
##############################################################################

<#

.SYNOPSIS

Get the hash of an input file.

.EXAMPLE

Get-FileHash myFile.txt
Gets the hash of a specific file

.EXAMPLE

dir | Get-FileHash
Gets the hash of files from the pipeline

.EXAMPLE

Get-FileHash myFile.txt -Hash SHA1
Gets the hash of myFile.txt, using the SHA1 hashing algorithm

#>
```

```
param(
    ## The path of the file to check
    $Path,

    ## The algorithm to use for hash computation
    [ValidateSet("MD5", "SHA1", "SHA256", "SHA384", "SHA512")]
    $HashAlgorithm = "MD5"
)

Set-StrictMode -Version Latest

## Create the hash object that calculates the hash of our file.
$hashType = [Type] "System.Security.Cryptography.$HashAlgorithm"
$hasher = $hashType::Create()

## Create an array to hold the list of files
$files = @()

## If they specified the file name as a parameter, add that to the list
## of files to process
if($path)
{
    $files += $path
}
## Otherwise, take the files that they piped into the script.
## For each input file, put its full name into the file list
else
{
    $files += @($input | Foreach-Object { $_.FullName })
}

## Go through each of the items in the list of input files
foreach($file in $files)
{
    ## Skip the item if it is not a file
    if(-not (Test-Path $file -Type Leaf)) { continue }

    ## Convert it to a fully qualified path
    $filename = (Resolve-Path $file).Path

    ## Use the ComputeHash method from the hash object to calculate
    ## the hash
    $inputStream = New-Object IO.StreamReader $filename
    $hashBytes = $hasher.ComputeHash($inputStream.BaseStream)
    $inputStream.Close()

    ## Convert the result to hexadecimal
    $builder = New-Object System.Text.StringBuilder
    $hashBytes | Foreach-Object { [void] $builder.Append($_.ToString("X2")) }

    ## Return a custom object with the important details from the
    ## hashing
    $output = New-Object PsObject -Property @{
        Path = ([IO.Path]::GetFileName($file));
        HashAlgorithm = $hashAlgorithm;
```

```
        HashValue = $builder.ToString()
    }

    $output
}
```

For more information about running scripts, see Recipe 1.1.

See Also

Recipe 1.1, "Run Programs, Scripts, and Existing Tools"

20.12 Create a Directory

Problem

You want to create a directory or file folder.

Solution

To create a directory, use the md or mkdir function:

```
PS > md NewDirectory


    Directory: C:\temp


Mode                LastWriteTime     Length Name
----                -------------     ------ ----
d----         4/29/2007   7:31  PM           NewDirectory
```

Discussion

The md and mkdir functions are simple wrappers around the more sophisticated New-Item cmdlet. As you might guess, the New-Item cmdlet creates an item at the location you provide. To create a directory using the New-Item cmdlet directly, supply Directory to the -Type parameter.

```
New-Item -Path C:\Temp\NewDirectory -Type Directory
```

The New-Item cmdlet doesn't work against only the filesystem, however. Any providers that support the concept of items automatically support this cmdlet as well.

For more information about the New-Item cmdlet, type **Get-Help New-Item**.

20.13 Remove a File or Directory

Problem

You want to remove a file or directory.

Solution

To remove a file or directory, use the `Remove-Item` cmdlet:

```
PS > Test-Path NewDirectory
True
PS > Remove-Item NewDirectory
PS > Test-Path NewDirectory
False
```

Discussion

The `Remove-Item` cmdlet removes an item from the location you provide. The `RemoveItem` cmdlet doesn't work against only the filesystem, however. Any providers that support the concept of items automatically support this cmdlet as well.

 The `Remove-Item` cmdlet lets you specify multiple files through its `Path`, `Include`, `Exclude`, and `Filter` parameters. For information on how to use these parameters effectively, see Recipe 20.6.

If the item is a container (for example, a directory), PowerShell warns you that your action will also remove anything inside that container. You can provide the -Recurse flag if you want to prevent this message.

For more information about the `Remove-Item` cmdlet, type **Get-Help Remove-Item**.

See Also

Recipe 20.6, "Find Files That Match a Pattern"

20.14 Rename a File or Directory

Problem

You want to rename a file or directory.

Solution

To rename an item in a provider, use the `Rename-Item` cmdlet:

```
PS > Rename-Item example.txt example2.txt
```

Discussion

The `Rename-Item` cmdlet changes the name of an item.

Some shells let you rename multiple files at the same time. In those shells, the command looks like this:

```
ren *.gif *.jpg
```

PowerShell does not support this syntax, but provides even more power through its `-replace` operator. As a simple example, we can emulate the preceding command:

```
Get-ChildItem *.gif | Rename-Item -NewName { $_.Name -replace '.gif$','.jpg' }
```

This syntax provides an immense amount of power. Consider removing underscores from filenames and replacing them with spaces:

```
Get-ChildItem *_* | Rename-Item -NewName { $_.Name -replace '_',' ' }
```

or restructuring files in a directory with the naming convention of *<Report_Project_Quarter>.txt*:

```
PS > Get-ChildItem | Select Name

Name
----
Report_Project1_Q3.txt
Report_Project1_Q4.txt
Report_Project2_Q1.txt
```

You might want to change that to *<Quarter_Project>.txt* with an advanced replacement pattern:

```
PS > Get-ChildItem |
    Rename-Item -NewName { $_.Name -replace '.*_(.*)_(.*)\.txt','$2_$1.txt' }

PS > Get-ChildItem | Select Name

Name
----
Q1_Project2.txt
Q3_Project1.txt
Q4_Project1.txt
```

For more information about the `-replace` operator, see Recipe 5.8.

Like the other `*-Item` cmdlets, the `Rename-Item` doesn't work against only the filesystem. Any providers that support the concept of items automatically support this cmdlet as well. For more information about the `Rename-Item` cmdlet, type **Get-Help Rename-Item**.

See Also

Recipe 5.8, "Replace Text in a String"

20.15 Move a File or Directory

Problem

You want to move a file or directory.

Solution

To move a file or directory, use the Move-Item cmdlet:

```
PS > Move-Item example.txt c:\temp\example2.txt
```

Discussion

The Move-Item cmdlet moves an item from one location to another. Like the other *-Item cmdlets, Move-Item doesn't work against only the filesystem. Any providers that support the concept of items automatically support this cmdlet as well.

 The Move-Item cmdlet lets you specify multiple files through its Path, Include, Exclude, and Filter parameters. For information on how to use these parameters effectively, see Recipe 20.6.

Although the Move-Item cmdlet works in every provider, you cannot move items between providers. For more information about the Move-Item cmdlet, type **Get-Help Move-Item**.

See Also

Recipe 20.6, "Find Files That Match a Pattern"

20.16 Program: Move or Remove a Locked File

Once in a while, you'll run into a file that's been locked by the operating system, and you'll want to move it or delete it.

This is a common problem encountered by patches, installers, and hotfixes, so Windows has a special mechanism that lets it move files before any process has the chance to lock it. If a file that an installer needs to change is locked, it uses this special mechanism to complete its setup tasks. Windows can do this only during a reboot, which is why you sometimes receive warnings from installers about locked files requiring a restart.

The underlying mechanism that enables this is the MoveFileEx Windows API. Calling this API with the MOVEFILE_DELAY_UNTIL_REBOOT flag tells Windows to move (or delete) your file at the next boot. If you specify a source and destination path, Windows moves the file. If you specify $null as a destination path, Windows deletes the file.

Example 20-4 uses the Add-Type cmdlet to expose this functionality through Power-Shell. While it exposes only the functionality to move locked files, you can easily rename it and modify it to delete locked files.

Example 20-4. Move-LockedFile.ps1

```
###############################################################################
##
## Move-LockedFile
##
## From Windows PowerShell Cookbook (O'Reilly)
## by Lee Holmes (http://www.leeholmes.com/guide)
##
###############################################################################

<#

.SYNOPSIS

Registers a locked file to be moved at the next system restart.

.EXAMPLE

Move-LockedFile c:\temp\locked.txt c:\temp\locked.txt.bak

#>

param(
    ## The current location of the file to move
    $Path,

    ## The target location of the file
    $Destination
)

Set-StrictMode -Version Latest

## Convert the the path and destination to fully qualified paths
$path = (Resolve-Path $path).Path
$destination = $executionContext.SessionState.`
    Path.GetUnresolvedProviderPathFromPSPath($destination)

## Define a new .NET type that calls into the Windows API to
## move a locked file.
$MOVEFILE_DELAY_UNTIL_REBOOT = 0x00000004
$memberDefinition = @'
[DllImport("kernel32.dll", SetLastError=true, CharSet=CharSet.Auto)]
public static extern bool MoveFileEx(
    string lpExistingFileName, string lpNewFileName, int dwFlags);
'@
$type = Add-Type -Name MoveFileUtils `
    -MemberDefinition $memberDefinition -PassThru

## Move the file
$type::MoveFileEx($path, $destination, $MOVEFILE_DELAY_UNTIL_REBOOT)
```

For more information about interacting with the Windows API, see Recipe 17.4. For more information about running scripts, see Recipe 1.1.

See Also

Recipe 1.1, "Run Programs, Scripts, and Existing Tools"

Recipe 17.4, "Access Windows API Functions"

20.17 Get the ACL of a File or Directory

Problem

You want to retrieve the ACL of a file or directory.

Solution

To retrieve the ACL of a file, use the Get-Acl cmdlet:

```
PS > Get-Acl example.txt


    Directory: C:\temp


Path                      Owner                     Access
----                      -----                     ------
example.txt               LEE-DESK\Lee              BUILTIN\Administrator...
```

Discussion

The Get-Acl cmdlet retrieves the security descriptor of an item. This cmdlet doesn't work against only the filesystem, however. Any provider (for example, the Registry provider) that supports the concept of security descriptors also supports the Get-Acl cmdlet.

The Get-Acl cmdlet returns an object that represents the security descriptor of the item and is specific to the provider that contains the item. In the filesystem, this returns a .NET System.Security.AccessControl.FileSecurity object that you can explore for further information. For example, Example 20-5 searches a directory for possible ACL misconfigurations by ensuring that each file contains an Administrator, Full Control ACL.

Example 20-5. Get-AclMisconfiguration.ps1

```
#############################################################################
##
## Get-AclMisconfiguration
##
## From Windows PowerShell Cookbook (O'Reilly)
## by Lee Holmes (http://www.leeholmes.com/guide)
##
#############################################################################

<#

.SYNOPSIS

Demonstration of functionality exposed by the Get-Acl cmdlet. This script
goes through all access rules in all files in the current directory, and
ensures that the Administrator group has full control of that file.

#>

Set-StrictMode -Version Latest

## Get all files in the current directory
foreach($file in Get-ChildItem)
{
    ## Retrieve the ACL from the current file
    $acl = Get-Acl $file
    if(-not $acl)
    {
        continue
    }

    $foundAdministratorAcl = $false

    ## Go through each access rule in that ACL
    foreach($accessRule in $acl.Access)
    {
        ## If we find the Administrator, Full Control access rule,
        ## then set the $foundAdministratorAcl variable
        if(($accessRule.IdentityReference -like "*Administrator*") -and
            ($accessRule.FileSystemRights -eq "FullControl"))
        {
            $foundAdministratorAcl = $true
        }
    }

    ## If we didn't find the administrator ACL, output a message
    if(-not $foundAdministratorAcl)
    {
        "Found possible ACL Misconfiguration: $file"
    }
}
```

For more information about the Get-Acl command, type **Get-Help Get-Acl**. For more information about working with classes from the .NET Framework, see Recipe 3.8. For more information about running scripts, see Recipe 1.1.

See Also

Recipe 1.1, "Run Programs, Scripts, and Existing Tools"

Recipe 3.8, "Work with .NET Objects"

20.18 Set the ACL of a File or Directory

Problem

You want to change the ACL of a file or directory.

Solution

To change the ACL of a file, use the Set-Acl cmdlet. This example prevents the Guest account from accessing a file:

```
$acl = Get-Acl example.txt
$arguments = "LEE-DESK\Guest","FullControl","Deny"
$accessRule =
    New-Object System.Security.AccessControl.FileSystemAccessRule $arguments
$acl.SetAccessRule($accessRule)
$acl | Set-Acl example.txt
```

Discussion

The Set-Acl cmdlet sets the security descriptor of an item. This cmdlet doesn't work against only the filesystem, however. Any provider (for example, the Registry provider) that supports the concept of security descriptors also supports the Set-Acl cmdlet.

The Set-Acl cmdlet requires that you provide it with an ACL to apply to the item. While it is possible to construct the ACL from scratch, it is usually easiest to retrieve it from the item beforehand (as demonstrated in the Solution). To retrieve the ACL, use the Get-Acl cmdlet. Once you've modified the access control rules on the ACL, simply pipe them to the Set-Acl cmdlet to make them permanent.

In the solution, the $arguments list that we provide to the FileSystemAccessRule constructor explicitly sets a Deny rule on the Guest account of the LEE-DESK computer for FullControl permission. For more information about working with classes from the .NET Framework (such as the FileSystemAccessRule class), see Recipe 3.8.

Although the Set-Acl command is powerful, you may already be familiar with command-line tools that offer similar functionality (such as cacls.exe). Although these tools generally do not work on the registry (or other providers that support PowerShell security descriptors), you can of course continue to use these tools from PowerShell.

For more information about the Set-Acl cmdlet, type **Get-Help Set-Acl**. For more information about the Get-Acl cmdlet, see Recipe 20.17.

See Also

Recipe 3.8, "Work with .NET Objects"

Recipe 20.17, "Get the ACL of a File or Directory"

20.19 Program: Add Extended File Properties to Files

The Explorer shell provides useful information about a file when you click on its Properties dialog. It includes the authoring information, image information, music information, and more (see Figure 20-2).

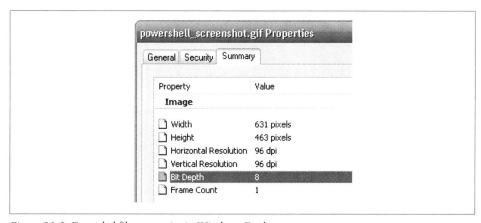

Figure 20-2. Extended file properties in Windows Explorer

PowerShell doesn't expose this information by default, but it is possible to obtain these properties from the Shell.Application COM object. Example 20-6 does just that—and adds this extended information as properties to the files returned by the Get-ChildItem cmdlet.

Example 20-6. Add-ExtendedFileProperties.ps1

```
##############################################################################
##
## Add-ExtendedFileProperties
##
## From Windows PowerShell Cookbook (O'Reilly)
## by Lee Holmes (http://www.leeholmes.com/guide)
##
##############################################################################
```

```
<#

.SYNOPSIS

Add the extended file properties normally shown in Explorer's
"File Properties" tab.

.EXAMPLE

Get-ChildItem | Add-ExtendedFileProperties.ps1 | Format-Table Name,"Bit Rate"

#>

begin
{
    Set-StrictMode -Version Latest

    ## Create the Shell.Application COM object that provides this
    ## functionality
    $shellObject = New-Object -Com Shell.Application

    ## Store the property names and identifiers for all of the shell
    ## properties
    $itemProperties = $null
}

process
{
    ## Get the file from the input pipeline. If it is just a filename
    ## (rather than a real file), piping it to the Get-Item cmdlet will
    ## get the file it represents.
    $fileItem = $_ | Get-Item

    ## Don't process directories
    if($fileItem.PsIsContainer)
    {
        $fileItem
        return
    }

    ## Extract the file name and directory name
    $directoryName = $fileItem.DirectoryName
    $filename = $fileItem.Name

    ## Create the folder object and shell item from the COM object
    $folderObject = $shellObject.NameSpace($directoryName)
    $item = $folderObject.ParseName($filename)

    ## Populate the item properties
    if(-not $itemProperties)
    {
        $itemProperties = @{}

        $counter = 0
        $columnName = ""
```

```
    do
    {
        $columnName = $folderObject.GetDetailsOf(
            $folderObject.Items, $counter)
        if($columnName) { $itemProperties[$counter] = $columnName }

        $counter++
    } while($columnName)
}

## Now, go through each property and add its information as a
## property to the file we are about to return
foreach($itemProperty in $itemProperties.Keys)
{
    $fileItem | Add-Member NoteProperty $itemProperties[$itemProperty] `
        $folderObject.GetDetailsOf($item, $itemProperty) -ErrorAction `
        SilentlyContinue
}

## Finally, return the file with the extra shell information
$fileItem
}
```

For more information about running scripts, see Recipe 1.1.

See Also

Recipe 1.1, "Run Programs, Scripts, and Existing Tools"

20.20 Program: Create a Filesystem Hard Link

It is sometimes useful to refer to the same file by two different names or locations. You can't solve this problem by copying the item, because modifications to one file do not automatically affect the other.

The solution to this is called a *hard link*, an item of a new name that points to the data of another file. The Windows operating system supports hard links, but only Windows Vista includes a utility that lets you create them.

Example 20-7 lets you create hard links without needing to install additional tools. It uses (and requires) the *Invoke-WindowsApi.ps1* script provided in Recipe 17.5.

Example 20-7. New-FilesystemHardLink.ps1

```
##############################################################################
##
## New-FileSystemHardLink
##
## From Windows PowerShell Cookbook (O'Reilly)
## by Lee Holmes (http://www.leeholmes.com/guide)
##
##############################################################################

<#

.SYNOPSIS

Create a new hard link, which allows you to create a new name by which you
can access an existing file. Windows only deletes the actual file once
you delete all hard links that point to it.

.EXAMPLE

PS >"Hello" > test.txt
PS >dir test* | select name

Name
----
test.txt

PS >.\New-FilesystemHardLink.ps1 test.txt test2.txt
PS >type test2.txt
Hello
PS >dir test* | select name

Name
----
test.txt
test2.txt

#>

param(
    ## The existing file that you want the new name to point to
    [string] $Path,

    ## The new filename you want to create
    [string] $Destination
)

Set-StrictMode -Version Latest

## Ensure that the provided names are absolute paths
$filename = $executionContext.SessionState.`
    Path.GetUnresolvedProviderPathFromPSPath($destination)
$existingFilename = Resolve-Path $path

## Prepare the parameter types and parameters for the CreateHardLink function
```

```
$parameterTypes = [string], [string], [IntPtr]
$parameters = [string] $filename, [string] $existingFilename, [IntPtr]::Zero

## Call the CreateHardLink method in the Kernel32 DLL
$currentDirectory = Split-Path $myInvocation.MyCommand.Path
$invokeWindowsApiCommand = Join-Path $currentDirectory Invoke-WindowsApi.ps1
$result = & $invokeWindowsApiCommand "kernel32" `
    ([bool]) "CreateHardLink" $parameterTypes $parameters

## Provide an error message if the call fails
if(-not $result)
{
    $message = "Could not create hard link of $filename to " +
        "existing file $existingFilename"
    Write-Error $message
}
```

For more information about running scripts, see Recipe 1.1.

See Also

Recipe 1.1, "Run Programs, Scripts, and Existing Tools"

Recipe 17.5, "Program: Invoke Simple Windows API Calls"

20.21 Program: Create a ZIP Archive

When transporting or archiving files, it is useful to store those files in an archive. ZIP archives are the most common type of archive, so it would be useful to have a script to help manage them.

For many purposes, traditional command-line ZIP archive utilities may fulfill your needs. If they do not support the level of detail or interaction that you need for administrative tasks, a more programmatic alternative is attractive.

Example 20-8 lets you create ZIP archives simply by piping files into them. It requires that you have the SharpZipLib installed, which you can obtain from *http://www.icsharp code.net/OpenSource/SharpZipLib/*.

Example 20-8. New-ZipFile.ps1

```
###############################################################################
##
## New-ZipFile
##
## From Windows PowerShell Cookbook (O'Reilly)
## by Lee Holmes (http://www.leeholmes.com/guide)
##
###############################################################################
```

```
<#

.SYNOPSIS

Create a ZIP file from any files piped in. Requires that
you have the SharpZipLib installed, which is available from
http://www.icsharpcode.net/OpenSource/SharpZipLib/

.EXAMPLE

dir *.ps1 | New-ZipFile scripts.zip d:\bin\ICSharpCode.SharpZipLib.dll
Copies all PS1 files in the current directory to scripts.zip

.EXAMPLE

"readme.txt" | New-ZipFile docs.zip d:\bin\ICSharpCode.SharpZipLib.dll
Copies readme.txt to docs.zip

#>

param(
    ## The name of the zip archive to create
    $ZipName = $(throw "Specify a zip file name"),

    ## The path to ICSharpCode.SharpZipLib.dll
    $LibPath = $(throw "Specify the path to SharpZipLib.dll")
)

Set-StrictMode -Version Latest

## Load the ZIP library
[void] [Reflection.Assembly]::LoadFile($libPath)
$namespace = "ICSharpCode.SharpZipLib.Zip.{0}"

## Create the ZIP file
$zipName = $executionContext.SessionState.`
    Path.GetUnresolvedProviderPathFromPSPath($zipName)
$zipFile =
    New-Object ($namespace -f "ZipOutputStream") ([IO.File]::Create($zipName))
$zipFullName = (Resolve-Path $zipName).Path

[byte[]] $buffer = New-Object byte[] 4096

## Go through each file in the input, adding it to the ZIP file
## specified
foreach($file in $input)
{
    ## Skip the current file if it is the ZIP file itself
    if($file.FullName -eq $zipFullName)
    {
        continue
    }

    ## Convert the path to a relative path, if it is under the
    ## current location
```

```
    $replacePath = [Regex]::Escape( (Get-Location).Path + "\" )
    $zipName = ([string] $file) -replace $replacePath,""

    ## Create the ZIP entry, and add it to the file
    $zipEntry = New-Object ($namespace -f "ZipEntry") $zipName
    $zipFile.PutNextEntry($zipEntry)

    $fileStream = [IO.File]::OpenRead($file.FullName)
    [ICSharpCode.SharpZipLib.Core.StreamUtils]::Copy(
        $fileStream, $zipFile, $buffer)
    $fileStream.Close()
}

## Close the file
$zipFile.Close()
```

For more information about running scripts, see Recipe 1.1.

See Also

Recipe 1.1, "Run Programs, Scripts, and Existing Tools"

The Windows Registry

21.0 Introduction

As the configuration store for the vast majority of applications, the registry plays a central role in system administration. It is also generally hard to manage.

Although command-line tools (such as `reg.exe`) exist to help you work with the registry, their interfaces are usually inconsistent and confusing. The Registry Editor graphical user interface is easy to use, but it does not support scripted administration.

PowerShell tackles this problem by exposing the Windows Registry as a navigation provider: a data source that you navigate and manage in exactly the same way that you work with the filesystem.

21.1 Navigate the Registry

Problem

You want to navigate and explore the Windows Registry.

Solution

Use the `Set-Location` cmdlet to navigate the registry, just as you would navigate the filesystem:

```
PS > Set-Location HKCU:
PS > Set-Location \Software\Microsoft\Windows\CurrentVersion\Run
PS > Get-Location

Path
----
HKCU:\Software\Microsoft\Windows\CurrentVersion\Run
```

Discussion

PowerShell lets you navigate the Windows Registry in exactly the same way that you navigate the filesystem, certificate drives, and other navigation-based providers. Like these other providers, the registry provider supports the Set-Location cmdlet (with the standard aliases of sl, cd, and chdir), Push-Location (with the standard alias pushd), Pop-Location (with the standard alias popd), and more.

For information about how to change registry keys once you get to a registry location, see Recipe 21.3. For more information about the registry provider, type **Get-Help Registry**.

See Also

Recipe 21.3, "Modify or Remove a Registry Key Value"

21.2 View a Registry Key

Problem

You want to view the value of a specific registry key.

Solution

To retrieve the value(s) of a registry key, use the Get-ItemProperty cmdlet, as shown in Example 21-1.

Example 21-1. Retrieving properties of a registry key

```
PS > Set-Location HKCU:
PS > Set-Location \Software\Microsoft\Windows\CurrentVersion\Run
PS > Get-ItemProperty .

PSPath                : Microsoft.PowerShell.Core\Registry::HKEY_CURRENT_U
                        SER\Software\Microsoft\Windows\CurrentVersion\Run
PSParentPath          : Microsoft.PowerShell.Core\Registry::HKEY_CURRENT_U
                        SER\Software\Microsoft\Windows\CurrentVersion
PSChildName           : Run
PSDrive               : HKCU
PSProvider            : Microsoft.PowerShell.Core\Registry
FolderShare           : "C:\Program Files\FolderShare\FolderShare.exe" /
                        background
TaskSwitchXP          : d:\lee\tools\TaskSwitchXP.exe
ctfmon.exe            : C:\WINDOWS\system32\ctfmon.exe
Ditto                 : C:\Program Files\Ditto\Ditto.exe
QuickTime Task        : "C:\Program Files\QuickTime Alternative\qttask.exe
                        " -atboottime
H/PC Connection Agent : "C:\Program Files\Microsoft ActiveSync\wcescomm.exe"
```

Discussion

In the registry provider, PowerShell treats registry keys as items and key values as properties of those items. To get the properties of an item, use the Get-ItemProperty cmdlet. The Get-ItemProperty cmdlet has the standard alias gp.

Example 21-1 lists all property values associated with that specific key. To retrieve the value of a specific item, access it as you would access a property on a .NET object, or anywhere else in PowerShell:

```
PS > $item = Get-ItemProperty .
PS > $item.TaskSwitchXp
d:\lee\tools\TaskSwitchXP.exe
```

If you want to do this all at once, the command looks like:

```
PS > $runKey = "HKCU:\Software\Microsoft\Windows\CurrentVersion\Run"
PS > (Get-ItemProperty $runKey).TaskSwitchXp
d:\lee\tools\TaskSwitchXP.exe
```

For more information about the Get-ItemProperty cmdlet, type **Get-Help Get-ItemProperty**. For more information about the registry provider, type **Get-Help Registry**.

21.3 Modify or Remove a Registry Key Value

Problem

You want to modify or remove a property of a specific registry key.

Solution

To set the value of a registry key, use the Set-ItemProperty cmdlet:

```
PS > (Get-ItemProperty .).MyProgram
c:\temp\MyProgram.exe
PS > Set-ItemProperty . MyProgram d:\Lee\tools\MyProgram.exe
PS > (Get-ItemProperty .).MyProgram
d:\Lee\tools\MyProgram.exe
```

To remove the value of a registry key, use the Remove-ItemProperty cmdlet:

```
PS > Remove-ItemProperty . MyProgram
PS > (Get-ItemProperty .).MyProgram
```

Discussion

In the registry provider, PowerShell treats registry keys as items and key values as properties of those items. To change the value of a key property, use the Set-ItemProperty cmdlet. The Set-ItemProperty cmdlet has the standard alias sp. To remove a key property altogether, use the Remove-ItemProperty cmdlet.

As always, use caution when changing information in the registry. Deleting or changing the wrong item can easily render your system unbootable.

For more information about the Get-ItemProperty cmdlet, type **Get-Help Get-ItemProperty**. For information about the Set-ItemProperty and Remove-ItemProperty cmdlets, type **Get-Help Set-ItemProperty** or **Get-Help Remove-ItemProperty**, respectively. For more information about the registry provider, type **Get-Help Registry**.

21.4 Create a Registry Key Value

Problem

You want to add a new key value to an existing registry key.

Solution

To add a value to a registry key, use the New-ItemProperty cmdlet. Example 21-2 adds *MyProgram.exe* to the list of programs that start when the current user logs in.

Example 21-2. Creating new properties on a registry key

```
PS > Set-Location HKCU:\Software\Microsoft\Windows\CurrentVersion\Run
PS > New-ItemProperty . -Name MyProgram -Value c:\temp\MyProgram.exe

PSPath        : Microsoft.PowerShell.Core\Registry::HKEY_CURRENT_USER
                \Software\Microsoft\Windows\CurrentVersion\Run
PSParentPath  : Microsoft.PowerShell.Core\Registry::HKEY_CURRENT_USER
                \Software\Microsoft\Windows\CurrentVersion
PSChildName   : Run
PSDrive       : HKCU
PSProvider    : Microsoft.PowerShell.Core\Registry
MyProgram     : c:\temp\MyProgram.exe

PS > Get-ItemProperty .

PSPath             : Microsoft.PowerShell.Core\Registry::HKEY_CURRENT_
                     USER\Software\Microsoft\Windows\CurrentVersion\Run
PSParentPath       : Microsoft.PowerShell.Core\Registry::HKEY_CURRENT_
                     USER\Software\Microsoft\Windows\CurrentVersion
PSChildName        : Run
PSDrive            : HKCU
PSProvider         : Microsoft.PowerShell.Core\Registry
FolderShare        : "C:\Program Files\FolderShare\FolderShare.exe"
                     /background
TaskSwitchXP       : d:\lee\tools\TaskSwitchXP.exe
ctfmon.exe         : C:\WINDOWS\system32\ctfmon.exe
Ditto              : C:\Program Files\Ditto\Ditto.exe
QuickTime Task     : "C:\Program Files\QuickTime Alternative\qttask.exe"
                     -atboottime
```

```
H/PC Connection Agent : "C:\Program Files\Microsoft ActiveSync\wcescomm.exe"
MyProgram             : c:\temp\MyProgram.exe
```

Discussion

In the registry provider, PowerShell treats registry keys as items and key values as properties of those items. To create a key property, use the New-ItemProperty cmdlet.

For more information about the New-ItemProperty cmdlet, type **Get-Help New-ItemProperty**. For more information about the registry provider, type **Get-Help Registry**.

21.5 Remove a Registry Key

Problem

You want to remove a registry key and all its properties.

Solution

To remove a registry key, use the Remove-Item cmdlet:

```
PS > dir

   Hive: HKEY_CURRENT_USER\Software\Microsoft\Windows\CurrentVersion\Run

SKC  VC Name                       Property
---  -- ----                       --------
  0   0 Spyware                     {}

PS > Remove-Item Spyware
```

Discussion

As mentioned in Recipe 21.4, the registry provider lets you remove items and containers with the Remove-Item cmdlet. The Remove-Item cmdlet has the standard aliases rm, rmdir, del, erase, and rd.

 As always, use caution when changing information in the registry. Deleting or changing the wrong item can easily render your system unbootable.

As in the filesystem, the Remove-Item cmdlet lets you specify multiple files through its Path, Include, Exclude, and Filter parameters. For information on how to use these parameters effectively, see Recipe 20.6.

For more information about the Remove-Item cmdlet, type **Get-Help Remove-Item**. For more information about the registry provider, type **Get-Help Registry**.

See Also

Recipe 20.6, "Find Files That Match a Pattern"

Recipe 21.4, "Create a Registry Key Value"

21.6 Safely Combine Related Registry Modifications

Problem

You have several related registry modifications, and you want to group them so that
either they all apply or none apply.

Solution

Use the `Start-Transaction` cmdlet to start a transaction, and make your registry modifications within it. Use the `Complete-Transaction` cmdlet to make the registry modifications permanent:

```
PS > Set-Location HKCU:
PS > Start-Transaction

Suggestion [1,Transactions]: Once a transaction is started, only commands
that get called with the -UseTransaction flag become part of that transaction.
PS > mkdir TempKey -UseTransaction


    Hive: HKEY_CURRENT_USER


SKC  VC Name                        Property
---  -- ----                        --------
  0   0 TempKey                     {}


PS > Set-Location TempKey -UseTransaction
PS > New-Item TempKey2 -UseTransaction


    Hive: HKEY_CURRENT_USER\TempKey


SKC  VC Name                        Property
---  -- ----                        --------
  0   0 TempKey2                    {}


PS > Set-Location \
PS > Get-ChildItem TempKey
Get-ChildItem : Cannot find path 'HKEY_CURRENT_USER\TempKey' because it
does not exist.
At line:1 char:14
```

```
+ Get-ChildItem <<<<  TempKey
    + CategoryInfo          : ObjectNotFound: (HKEY_CURRENT_USER\TempKey:
  String) [Get-ChildItem], ItemNotFoundException
    + FullyQualifiedErrorId : PathNotFound,Microsoft.PowerShell.Commands.
  GetChildItemCommand

PS > Complete-Transaction
PS > Get-ChildItem TempKey


    Hive: HKEY_CURRENT_USER\TempKey


SKC  VC Name                        Property
---  -- ----                        --------
  0   0 TempKey2                     {}
```

Discussion

When working in the registry, you might sometimes want to chain a set of related changes and be sure that they all get applied as a single unit. These are goals known as *atomicity* and *consistency*: the desire to avoid situations where an error during any step of the operation could cause an inconsistent system state if the other operations are not also successful.

To support this type of management task, PowerShell supports a change management strategy known as *transactions*. On Windows Vista and later, PowerShell's registry provider fully supports transactions.

When you start a transaction, any commands in that transaction are virtual and don't actually apply to the system until you complete the transaction. Within the context of the transaction, through, each participating command sees the system as though the state really had changed. Once you complete a transaction, changes are applied as a single unit.

Some systems that support transactions (such as databases) put locks on any resources that are being changed by a transaction. If another user tries to modify the locked resources, the user gets an error message. This is not supported in the Windows Registry. If something alters a resource that your transaction depends on, the changes contained in your transaction will be abandoned and you will receive an error message when you try to complete that transaction.

For more information about transactions, see Chapter 30.

See Also

Chapter 30, *Transactions*

21.7 Add a Site to an Internet Explorer Security Zone

Problem

You want to add a site to a specific Internet Explorer security zone.

Solution

To create the registry keys and properties required to add a site to a specific security zone, use the New-Item and New-ItemProperty cmdlets. Example 21-3 adds *www.example.com* to the list of sites trusted by Internet Explorer.

Example 21-3. Adding www.example.com to the list of trusted sites in Internet Explorer

```
Set-Location "HKCU:\Software\Microsoft\Windows\CurrentVersion\Internet Settings"
Set-Location ZoneMap\Domains
New-Item example.com
Set-Location example.com
New-Item www
Set-Location www
New-ItemProperty . -Name http -Value 2 -Type DWORD
```

Discussion

One task that requires modifying data in the registry is working with Internet Explorer to add and remove sites from its different security zones.

Internet Explorer stores its zone mapping information in the registry at *HKCU:\Software\Microsoft\Windows\CurrentVersion\Internet Settings\ZoneMap\Domains*. Below that key, Explorer stores the domain name (such as leeholmes.com) with the hostname (such as www) as a subkey of that one (see Figure 21-1). In the host key, Explorer stores a property (such as http) with a DWORD value that corresponds to the zone identifier.

The Internet Explorer zone identifiers are:

* My Computer
* Local intranet
* Trusted sites
* Internet
* Restricted sites

When Internet Explorer is configured in its Enhanced Security Configuration mode, you must also update entries under the EscDomains key.

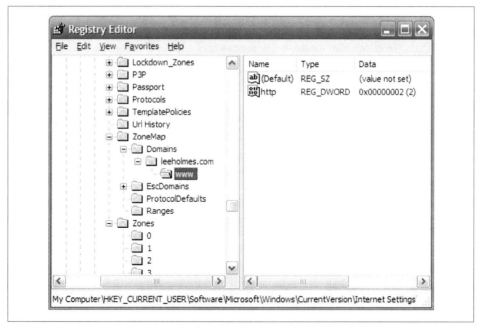

Figure 21-1. Internet Explorer zone configuration

 Once a machine has enabled Internet Explorer's Enhanced Security Configuration, those settings persist even after removing Enhanced Security Configuration. The following commands let your machine trust UNC paths again:

```
Set-Location "HKCU:\Software\Microsoft\Windows\"
Set-Location "CurrentVersion"
Set-Location "Internet Settings"
Set-ItemProperty ZoneMap UNCAsIntranet -Type DWORD 1
Set-ItemProperty ZoneMap IntranetName -Type DWORD 1
```

To remove the zone mapping for a specific domain, use the Remove-Item cmdlet:

```
PS > Get-ChildItem

    Hive: HKEY_CURRENT_USER\Software\...\Internet Settings\ZoneMap\Domains

SKC VC Name                     Property
--- -- ----                     --------
  1  0 example.com              {}

PS > Remove-Item -Recurse example.com
PS > Get-ChildItem
PS >
```

For more information about using the Internet Explorer registry entries to configure security zones, see the Microsoft KB article "Description of Internet Explorer Security

Zones Registry Entries" at *http://support.microsoft.com/kb/182569*. For more information about managing Internet Explorer's Enhanced Security Configuration, search for it on *http://technet.microsoft.com*.

For more information about modifying data in the registry, see Recipe 21.3.

See Also

Recipe 21.3, "Modify or Remove a Registry Key Value"

21.8 Modify Internet Explorer Settings

Problem

You want to modify Internet Explorer's configuration options.

Solution

To modify the Internet Explorer configuration registry keys, use the Set-ItemProperty cmdlet. For example, to update the proxy:

```
Set-Location "HKCU:\Software\Microsoft\Windows\CurrentVersion\Internet Settings"
Set-ItemProperty . -Name ProxyServer -Value http://proxy.example.com
Set-ItemProperty . -Name ProxyEnable -Value 1
```

Discussion

Internet Explorer stores its main configuration information as properties on the registry key *HKCU:\Software\Microsoft\Windows\CurrentVersion\Internet Settings*. To change these properties, use the Set-ItemProperty cmdlet as demonstrated in the solution.

Another common set of properties to tweak are the configuration parameters that define a security zone. An example of this is to prevent scripts from running in the Restricted Sites zone. For each zone, Internet Explorer stores this information as properties of the registry key *HKCU:\Software\Microsoft\Windows\CurrentVersion\Internet Settings\Zones\<Zone>*, where *<Zone>* represents the zone identifier (0, 1, 2, 3, or 4) to manage.

The Internet Explorer zone identifiers are:

- My Computer
- Local intranet
- Trusted sites
- Internet
- Restricted sites

The names of the properties in this key are not designed for human consumption, as they carry illuminating titles such as 1A04 and 1809. While they are not well-named, you can still script them.

For more information about using the Internet Explorer registry settings to configure security zones, see the Microsoft KB article "Description of Internet Explorer Security Zones Registry Entries" at *http://support.microsoft.com/kb/182569*.

For more information about modifying data in the registry, see Recipe 21.3.

See Also

Recipe 21.3, "Modify or Remove a Registry Key Value"

21.9 Program: Search the Windows Registry

Although the Windows Registry Editor is useful for searching the registry, sometimes it might not provide the power you need. For example, the registry editor does not support searches with wildcards or regular expressions.

In the filesystem, we have the Select-String cmdlet to search files for content. Power-Shell does not offer that ability for other stores, but we can write a script to do it. The key here is to think of registry key values like you think of content in a file:

- Directories have items; items have content.
- Registry keys have properties; properties have values.

Example 21-4 goes through all registry keys (and their values) for a search term and returns information about the match.

Example 21-4. Search-Registry.ps1

```
##############################################################################
##
## Search-Registry
##
## From Windows PowerShell Cookbook (O'Reilly)
## by Lee Holmes (http://www.leeholmes.com/guide)
##
##############################################################################

<#

.SYNOPSIS

Search the registry for keys or properties that match a specific value.

.EXAMPLE

PS >Set-Location HKCU:\Software\Microsoft\
PS >Search-Registry Run
```

```
#>

param(
    ## The text to search for
    [Parameter(Mandatory = $true)]
    [string] $Pattern
)

Set-StrictMode -Off

## Helper function to create a new object that represents
## a registry match from this script
function New-RegistryMatch
{
    param( $matchType, $keyName, $propertyName, $line )

    $registryMatch = New-Object PsObject -Property @{
        MatchType = $matchType;
        KeyName = $keyName;
        PropertyName = $propertyName;
        Line = $line
    }

    $registryMatch
}

## Go through each item in the registry
foreach($item in Get-ChildItem -Recurse -ErrorAction SilentlyContinue)
{
    ## Check if the key name matches
    if($item.Name -match $pattern)
    {
        New-RegistryMatch "Key" $item.Name $null $item.Name
    }

    ## Check if a key property matches
    foreach($property in (Get-ItemProperty $item.PsPath).PsObject.Properties)
    {
        ## Skip the property if it was one PowerShell added
        if(($property.Name -eq "PSPath") -or
            ($property.Name -eq "PSChildName"))
        {
            continue
        }

        ## Search the text of the property
        $propertyText = "$($property.Name)=$($property.Value)"
        if($propertyText -match $pattern)
        {
            New-RegistryMatch "Property" $item.Name `
                property.Name $propertyText
        }
    }
}
```

For more information about running scripts, see Recipe 1.1.

See Also

Recipe 1.1, "Run Programs, Scripts, and Existing Tools"

21.10 Get the ACL of a Registry Key

Problem

You want to retrieve the ACL of a registry key.

Solution

To retrieve the ACL of a registry key, use the Get-Acl cmdlet:

```
PS > Get-Acl HKLM:\Software

Path                     Owner                   Access
----                     -----                   ------
Microsoft.PowerShell.... BUILTIN\Administrators   CREATOR OWNER Allow ....
```

Discussion

As mentioned in Recipe 20.17, the Get-Acl cmdlet retrieves the security descriptor of an item. This cmdlet doesn't work against only the registry, however. Any provider (for example, the filesystem provider) that supports the concept of security descriptors also supports the Get-Acl cmdlet.

The Get-Acl cmdlet returns an object that represents the security descriptor of the item and is specific to the provider that contains the item. In the registry provider, this returns a .NET System.Security.AccessControl.RegistrySecurity object that you can explore for further information. For an example of changing the ACL of a registry key with this result, see Recipe 21.11. For an example of a script that works with ACLs, see Recipe 20.17.

For more information about the Get-Acl command, type **Get-Help Get-Acl**. For more information about working with classes from the .NET Framework, see Recipe 3.8.

See Also

Recipe 3.8, "Work with .NET Objects"

Recipe 20.17, "Get the ACL of a File or Directory"

Recipe 21.11, "Set the ACL of a Registry Key"

21.11 Set the ACL of a Registry Key

Problem

You want to change the ACL of a registry key.

Solution

To set the ACL on a registry key, use the `Set-Acl` cmdlet. This example grants an account write access to a registry key under *HKLM:\Software*. This is especially useful for programs that write to administrator-only regions of the registry, which prevents them from running under a nonadministrator account.

```
##############################################################################
##
## Grant-RegistryAccessFullControl
##
## From Windows PowerShell Cookbook (O'Reilly)
## by Lee Holmes (http://www.leeholmes.com/guide)
##
##############################################################################

<#

.SYNOPSIS

Grants full control access to a user for the specified registry key.

.EXAMPLE

PS >$registryPath = "HKLM:\Software\MyProgram"
PS >Grant-RegistryAccessFullControl "LEE-DESK\LEE" $registryPath

#>

param(
    ## The user to grant full control
    [Parameter(Mandatory = $true)]
    $User,

    ## The registry path that should have its permissions modified
    [Parameter(Mandatory = $true)]
    $RegistryPath
)

Set-StrictMode -Version Latest

Push-Location
Set-Location -LiteralPath $registryPath

## Retrieve the ACL from the registry key
$acl = Get-Acl .
```

```
## Prepare the access rule, and set the access rule
$arguments = $user,"FullControl","Allow"
$accessRule = New-Object Security.AccessControl.RegistryAccessRule $arguments
$acl.SetAccessRule($accessRule)

## Apply the modified ACL to the registry key
$acl | Set-Acl  .

Pop-Location
```

Discussion

As mentioned in Recipe 20.18, the Set-Acl cmdlet sets the security descriptor of an item. This cmdlet doesn't work against only the registry, however. Any provider (for example, the filesystem provider) that supports the concept of security descriptors also supports the Set-Acl cmdlet.

The Set-Acl cmdlet requires that you provide it with an ACL to apply to the item. Although it is possible to construct the ACL from scratch, it is usually easiest to retrieve it from the item beforehand (as demonstrated in the Solution). To retrieve the ACL, use the Get-Acl cmdlet. Once you've modified the access control rules on the ACL, simply pipe them to the Set-Acl cmdlet to make them permanent.

In the solution, the $arguments list that we provide to the RegistryAccessRule constructor explicitly sets an Allow rule on the Lee account of the LEE-DESK computer for FullControl permission. For more information about working with classes from the .NET Framework (such as the RegistryAccessRule class), see Recipe 3.8.

Although the Set-Acl command is powerful, you may already be familiar with command-line tools that offer similar functionality (such as SubInAcl.exe). You can of course continue to use these tools from PowerShell.

For more information about the Set-Acl cmdlet, type **Get-Help Set-Acl**. For more information about the Get-Acl cmdlet, see Recipe 21.10.

See Also

Recipe 3.8, "Work with .NET Objects"

Recipe 20.18, "Set the ACL of a File or Directory"

Recipe 21.10, "Get the ACL of a Registry Key"

21.12 Work with the Registry of a Remote Computer

Problem

You want to work with the registry keys and values of a remote computer.

Solution

To work with the registry of a remote computer, use the scripts provided in this chapter: Get-RemoteRegistryChildItem (Recipe 21.13), Get-RemoteRegistryKeyProperty (Recipe 21.14), and Set-RemoteRegistryKeyProperty (Recipe 21.15). These scripts require that the remote computer has the remote registry service enabled and running. Example 21-5 updates the PowerShell execution policy of a remote machine.

Example 21-5. Setting the PowerShell execution policy of a remote machine

```
PS > $registryPath = "HKLM:\Software\Microsoft\PowerShell\1"
PS > Get-RemoteRegistryChildItem LEE-DESK $registryPath

SKC  VC Name                       Property
---  -- ----                       --------
  0   1 1033                       {Install}
  0   5 PowerShellEngine           {ApplicationBase, ConsoleHostAss...
  2   0 PowerShellSnapIns          {}
  1   0 ShellIds                   {}

PS > Get-RemoteRegistryChildItem LEE-DESK $registryPath\ShellIds

SKC  VC Name                       Property
---  -- ----                       --------
  0   2 Microsoft.PowerShell       {Path, ExecutionPolicy}

PS > $registryPath = "HKLM:\Software\Microsoft\PowerShell\1\" +
    "ShellIds\Microsoft.PowerShell"

PS > Get-RemoteRegistryKeyProperty LEE-DESK $registryPath ExecutionPolicy

ExecutionPolicy
---------------
Unrestricted

PS > Set-RemoteRegistryKeyProperty LEE-DESK $registryPath `
    "ExecutionPolicy" "RemoteSigned"

PS > Get-RemoteRegistryKeyProperty LEE-DESK $registryPath ExecutionPolicy


ExecutionPolicy
---------------
RemoteSigned
```

Discussion

Although this specific task is perhaps better solved through PowerShell's Group Policy support, it demonstrates a useful scenario that includes both remote registry exploration and modification.

If the remote computer does not have the Remote Registry service running (but does have WMI enabled), you can use WMI's StdRegProv class to work with the registry as well. The following example demonstrates how to get and set the registry key that controls Remote Desktop:

```
$HKEY_CLASSES_ROOT = [Convert]::ToUInt32(80000000, 16)
$HKEY_CURRENT_USER = [Convert]::ToUInt32(80000001, 16)
$HKEY_LOCAL_MACHINE = [Convert]::ToUInt32(80000002, 16)
$HKEY_USERS = [Convert]::ToUInt32(80000003, 16)
$HKEY_CURRENT_CONFIG = [Convert]::ToUInt32(80000005, 16)

## Connect to the registry via WMI
$reg = Get-WmiObject -ComputerName LEE-DESK `
    -Namespace root\default StdRegProv -List

## Get and set DWORD values on the remote machine
$reg.GetDWORDValue($HKEY_LOCAL_MACHINE,
    "SYSTEM\CurrentControlSet\Control\Terminal Server",
    "fDenyTSConnections")

$reg.SetDWORDValue($HKEY_LOCAL_MACHINE,
    "SYSTEM\CurrentControlSet\Control\Terminal Server",
    "fDenyTSConnections", 0)
```

For more information about the Get-RemoteRegistryChildItem, Get-RemoteRegistryKey Property, and Set-RemoteRegistryKeyProperty scripts, see Recipes 21.13, 21.14, and 21.15.

See Also

Recipe 21.13, "Program: Get Registry Items from Remote Machines"

Recipe 21.14, "Program: Get Properties of Remote Registry Keys"

Recipe 21.15, "Program: Set Properties of Remote Registry Keys"

21.13 Program: Get Registry Items from Remote Machines

Although PowerShell does not directly let you access and manipulate the registry of a remote computer, it still supports this by working with the .NET Framework. The functionality exposed by the .NET Framework is a bit more developer-oriented than we want, so we can instead use a script to make it easier to work with.

Example 21-6 lets you list child items in a remote registry key, much like you do on the local computer. In order for this script to succeed, the target computer must have the remote registry service enabled and running.

Example 21-6. Get-RemoteRegistryChildItem.ps1

```
#############################################################################
##
## Get-RemoteRegistryChildItem
##
## From Windows PowerShell Cookbook (O'Reilly)
## by Lee Holmes (http://www.leeholmes.com/guide)
##
#############################################################################

<#

.SYNOPSIS

Get the list of subkeys below a given key on a remote computer.

.EXAMPLE

Get-RemoteRegistryChildItem LEE-DESK HKLM:\Software

#>

param(
    ## The computer that you wish to connect to
    [Parameter(Mandatory = $true)]
    $ComputerName,

    ## The path to the registry items to retrieve
    [Parameter(Mandatory = $true)]
    $Path
)

Set-StrictMode -Version Latest

## Validate and extract out the registry key
if($path -match "^HKLM:\\(.*)")
{
    $baseKey = [Microsoft.Win32.RegistryKey]::OpenRemoteBaseKey(
        "LocalMachine", $computername)
}
elseif($path -match "^HKCU:\\(.*)")
{
    $baseKey = [Microsoft.Win32.RegistryKey]::OpenRemoteBaseKey(
        "CurrentUser", $computername)
}
else
{
    Write-Error ("Please specify a fully-qualified registry path " +
        "(i.e.: HKLM:\Software) of the registry key to open.")
    return
}

## Open the key
$key = $baseKey.OpenSubKey($matches[1])
```

```
## Retrieve all of its children
foreach($subkeyName in $key.GetSubKeyNames())
{
    ## Open the subkey
    $subkey = $key.OpenSubKey($subkeyName)

    ## Add information so that PowerShell displays this key like regular
    ## registry key
    $returnObject = [PsObject] $subKey
    $returnObject | Add-Member NoteProperty PsChildName $subkeyName
    $returnObject | Add-Member NoteProperty Property $subkey.GetValueNames()

    ## Output the key
    $returnObject

    ## Close the child key
    $subkey.Close()
}

## Close the key and base keys
$key.Close()
$baseKey.Close()
```

For more information about running scripts, see Recipe 1.1.

See Also

Recipe 1.1, "Run Programs, Scripts, and Existing Tools"

21.14 Program: Get Properties of Remote Registry Keys

Although PowerShell does not directly let you access and manipulate the registry of a remote computer, it still supports this by working with the .NET Framework. The functionality exposed by the .NET Framework is a bit more developer-oriented than we want, so we can instead use a script to make it easier to work with.

Example 21-7 lets you get the properties (or a specific property) from a given remote registry key. In order for this script to succeed, the target computer must have the remote registry service enabled and running.

Example 21-7. Get-RemoteRegistryKeyProperty.ps1

```
##############################################################################
##
## Get-RemoteRegistryKeyProperty
##
## From Windows PowerShell Cookbook (O'Reilly)
## by Lee Holmes (http://www.leeholmes.com/guide)
##
##############################################################################
```

```
<#

.SYNOPSIS

Get the value of a remote registry key property

.EXAMPLE

PS >$registryPath =
    "HKLM:\software\Microsoft\PowerShell\1\ShellIds\Microsoft.PowerShell"
PS >Get-RemoteRegistryKeyProperty LEE-DESK $registryPath ExecutionPolicy

#>

param(
    ## The computer that you wish to connect to
    [Parameter(Mandatory = $true)]
    $ComputerName,

    ## The path to the registry item to retrieve
    [Parameter(Mandatory = $true)]
    $Path,

    ## The specific property to retrieve
    $Property = "*"
)

Set-StrictMode -Version Latest

## Validate and extract out the registry key
if($path -match "^HKLM:\\(.*)")
{
    $baseKey = [Microsoft.Win32.RegistryKey]::OpenRemoteBaseKey(
        "LocalMachine", $computername)
}
elseif($path -match "^HKCU:\\(.*)")
{
    $baseKey = [Microsoft.Win32.RegistryKey]::OpenRemoteBaseKey(
        "CurrentUser", $computername)
}
else
{
    Write-Error ("Please specify a fully-qualified registry path " +
        "(i.e.: HKLM:\Software) of the registry key to open.")
    return
}

## Open the key
$key = $baseKey.OpenSubKey($matches[1])
$returnObject = New-Object PsObject

## Go through each of the properties in the key
foreach($keyProperty in $key.GetValueNames())
{
    ## If the property matches the search term, add it as a
```

```
        ## property to the output
        if($keyProperty -like $property)
        {
            $returnObject |
                Add-Member NoteProperty $keyProperty $key.GetValue($keyProperty)
        }
}

## Return the resulting object
$returnObject

## Close the key and base keys
$key.Close()
$baseKey.Close()
```

For more information about running scripts, see Recipe 1.1.

See Also

Recipe 1.1, "Run Programs, Scripts, and Existing Tools"

21.15 Program: Set Properties of Remote Registry Keys

Although PowerShell does not directly let you access and manipulate the registry of a remote computer, it still supports this by working with the .NET Framework. The functionality exposed by the .NET Framework is a bit more developer-oriented than we want, so we can instead use a script to make it easier to work with.

Example 21-8 lets you set the value of a property on a given remote registry key. In order for this script to succeed, the target computer must have the remote registry service enabled and running.

Example 21-8. Set-RemoteRegistryKeyProperty.ps1

```
##############################################################################
##
## Set-RemoteRegistryKeyProperty
##
## From Windows PowerShell Cookbook (O'Reilly)
## by Lee Holmes (http://www.leeholmes.com/guide)
##
##############################################################################

<#

.SYNOPSIS

Set the value of a remote registry key property

.EXAMPLE

PS >$registryPath =
```

```
        "HKLM:\software\Microsoft\PowerShell\1\ShellIds\Microsoft.PowerShell"
PS >Set-RemoteRegistryKeyProperty LEE-DESK $registryPath `
        "ExecutionPolicy" "RemoteSigned"

#>

param(
    ## The computer to connect to
    [Parameter(Mandatory = $true)]
    $ComputerName,

    ## The registry path to modify
    [Parameter(Mandatory = $true)]
    $Path,

    ## The property to modify
    [Parameter(Mandatory = $true)]
    $PropertyName,

    ## The value to set on the property
    [Parameter(Mandatory = $true)]
    $PropertyValue
)

Set-StrictMode -Version Latest

## Validate and extract out the registry key
if($path -match "^HKLM:\\(.*)")
{
    $baseKey = [Microsoft.Win32.RegistryKey]::OpenRemoteBaseKey(
        "LocalMachine", $computername)
}
elseif($path -match "^HKCU:\\(.*)")
{
    $baseKey = [Microsoft.Win32.RegistryKey]::OpenRemoteBaseKey(
        "CurrentUser", $computername)
}
else
{
    Write-Error ("Please specify a fully-qualified registry path " +
        "(i.e.: HKLM:\Software) of the registry key to open.")
    return
}

## Open the key and set its value
$key = $baseKey.OpenSubKey($matches[1], $true)
$key.SetValue($propertyName, $propertyValue)

## Close the key and base keys
$key.Close()
$baseKey.Close()
```

For more information about running scripts, see Recipe 1.1.

See Also

Recipe 1.1, "Run Programs, Scripts, and Existing Tools"

21.16 Discover Registry Settings for Programs

Problem

You want to automate the configuration of a program, but that program does not document its registry configuration settings.

Solution

To discover a registry setting for a program, use the Sysinternals Process Monitor to observe registry access by that program. Process Monitor is available from *http://www .microsoft.com/technet/sysinternals/FileAndDisk/processmonitor.mspx*.

Discussion

In an ideal world, all programs would fully support command-line administration and configuration through PowerShell cmdlets. Many programs do not, however, so the solution is to look through their documentation in the hope that they list the registry keys and properties that control their settings. While many programs document their registry configuration settings, many still do not.

Although these programs may not document their registry settings, you can usually observe their registry access activity to determine the registry paths they use. To illustrate this, we will use the Sysinternals Process Monitor to discover PowerShell's execution policy configuration keys. Although PowerShell documents these keys *and* makes its automated configuration a breeze, this example illustrates the general technique.

Launch and configure Process Monitor

Once you've downloaded Process Monitor, the first step is to filter its output to include only the program you are interested in. By default, Process Monitor logs almost all registry and file activity on the system.

First, launch Process Monitor, and then press Ctrl-E (or click the magnifying glass icon) to temporarily prevent it from capturing any data (see Figure 21-2). Next, press Ctrl-X (or click the white sheet with an eraser icon) to clear the extra information that it captured automatically. Finally, drag the target icon and drop it on top of the application in question. You can press Ctrl-L (or click the funnel icon) to see the filter that Process Monitor now applies to its output.

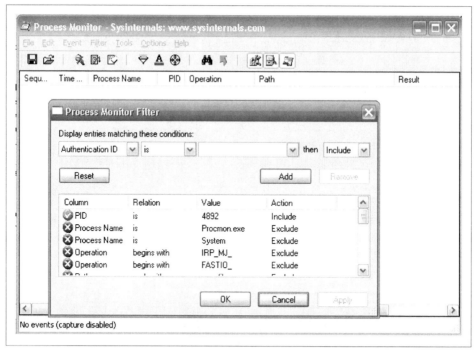

Figure 21-2. Process Monitor ready to capture

Prepare to manually set the configuration option

Next, prepare to manually set the program's configuration option. Usually, this means typing and clicking all the property settings, but just not clicking OK or Apply. For this PowerShell example, type the `Set-ExecutionPolicy` command line, but do not press Enter (see Figure 21-3).

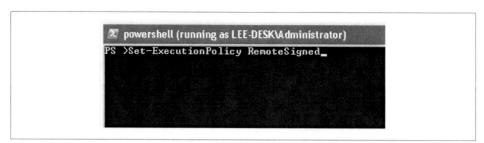

Figure 21-3. Preparing to apply the configuration option

Tell Process Monitor to begin capturing information

Switch to the Process Monitor window, and then press Ctrl-E (or click the magnifying glass icon). Process Monitor now captures all registry access for the program in question.

Manually set the configuration option

Click OK, Apply, or whatever action it takes to actually complete the program's configuration. For the PowerShell example, this means pressing Enter.

Tell Process Monitor to stop capturing information

Switch again to the Process Monitor window, and then press Ctrl-E (or click the magnifying glass icon). Process Monitor now no longer captures the application's activity.

Review the capture logs for registry modification

The Process Monitor window now shows all registry keys that the application interacted with when it applied its configuration setting.

Press Ctrl-F (or click the binoculars icon), and then search for RegSetValue. Process Monitor highlights the first modification to a registry key, as shown in Figure 21-4.

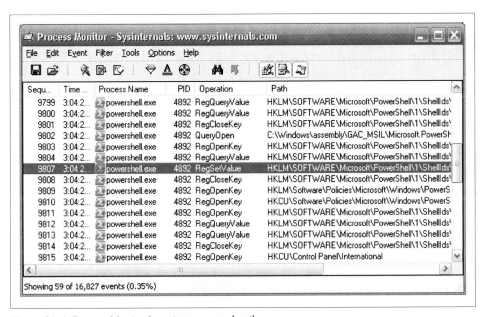

Figure 21-4. Process Monitor's registry access detail

Press Enter (or double-click the highlighted row) to see the details about this specific registry modification. In this example, we can see that PowerShell changed the value of the ExecutionPolicy property (under *HKLM:\Software\Microsoft\PowerShell\1\Shell-Ids\Microsoft.PowerShell*) to RemoteSigned. Press F3 to see the next entry that corresponds to a registry modification.

Automate these registry writes

Now that you know all registry writes that the application performed when it updated its settings, judgment and experimentation will help you determine which modifications actually represent this setting. Since PowerShell performed only one registry write (to a key that very obviously represents the execution policy), the choice is pretty clear in this example.

Once you've discovered the registry keys, properties, and values that the application uses to store its configuration data, you can use the techniques discussed in Recipe 21.3 to automate these configuration settings, as in the following example:

```
PS > $key = "HKLM:\Software\Microsoft\PowerShell\1\" +
    "ShellIds\Microsoft.PowerShell"

PS > Set-ItemProperty $key ExecutionPolicy AllSigned
PS > Get-ExecutionPolicy
AllSigned
PS > Set-ItemProperty $key ExecutionPolicy RemoteSigned
PS > Get-ExecutionPolicy
RemoteSigned
```

See Also

Recipe 21.3, "Modify or Remove a Registry Key Value"

Comparing Data

22.0 Introduction

When working in PowerShell, it is common to work with collections of objects. Most PowerShell commands generate objects, as do many of the methods that you work with in the .NET Framework. To help you work with these object collections, PowerShell introduces the Compare-Object cmdlet. The Compare-Object cmdlet provides functionality similar to the well-known diff commands, but with an object-oriented flavor.

22.1 Compare the Output of Two Commands

Problem

You want to compare the output of two commands.

Solution

To compare the output of two commands, store the output of each command in variables, and then use the Compare-Object cmdlet to compare those variables:

```
PS > notepad
PS > $processes = Get-Process
PS > Stop-Process -ProcessName Notepad
PS > $newProcesses = Get-Process
PS > Compare-Object $processes $newProcesses

InputObject                          SideIndicator
-----------                          -------------
System.Diagnostics.Process (notepad) <=
```

Discussion

The Solution shows how to determine which processes have exited between the two calls to Get-Process. The SideIndicator of <= tells us that the process was present in the left collection ($processes) but not in the right ($newProcesses). To work with the actual object that was different, access the InputObject property:

```
PS > $diff = @(Compare-Object $processes $newProcesses)[0]
PS > $process = $diff.InputObject
PS > $process.Handles
55
```

By default, the Compare-Object cmdlet uses the comparison functionality built into most .NET objects. This works as expected most of the time, but sometimes you might want to override that comparison behavior. For example, you might want two processes to be considered different if their memory usage changes. In that case, use the -Property parameter.

```
PS > Compare-Object $processes $newProcesses -Property Name,WS | Sort Name

Name                          WS SideIndicator
----                          -- -------------
dwm                     31358976 <=
dwm                     29540352 =>
explorer                37969920 <=
explorer                38023168 =>
lsass                    1548288 =>
lsass                    1372160 <=
notepad                  5701632 <=
notepad                  2891776 =>
powershell              44281856 =>
powershell              44290048 <=
SearchIndexer           13606912 =>
SearchIndexer           13619200 <=
svchost                 56061952 <=
svchost                 43982848 <=
svchost                 56037376 =>
svchost                 44048384 =>
svchost                 12193792 <=
svchost                 12201984 =>
taskeng                  9220096 <=
taskeng                  9228288 =>
```

When you use the -Property parameter, the Compare-Object cmdlet outputs custom objects that have only the properties you used in the comparison. If you still want access to the original objects used in the comparison, also use the -PassThru parameter. In that case, PowerShell instead adds the SideIndicator property to the original objects.

 If the objects you are comparing are already in proper order (for example, the lines in a file), you can improve the performance of the comparison process by using the -SyncWindow parameter. A sync window of five, for example, looks for differences only within the surrounding five objects.

For more information about the `Compare-Object` cmdlet, type **Get-Help** **Compare-Object**.

22.2 Determine the Differences Between Two Files

Problem

You want to determine the differences between two files.

Solution

To determine simple differences in the content of each file, store their content in variables, and then use the `Compare-Object` cmdlet to compare those variables:

```
PS > "Hello World" > c:\temp\file1.txt
PS > "Hello World" > c:\temp\file2.txt
PS > "More Information" >> c:\temp\file2.txt
PS > $content1 = Get-Content c:\temp\file1.txt
PS > $content2 = Get-Content c:\temp\file2.txt
PS > Compare-Object $content1 $content2

InputObject                      SideIndicator
-----------                      -------------
More Information                 =>
```

Discussion

The primary focus of the `Compare-Object` cmdlet is to compare two unordered sets of objects. Although those sets of objects can be strings (as in the content of two files), the output of `Compare-Object` when run against files is usually counterintuitive because of the content losing its order.

When comparing large files (or files where the order of comparison matters), you can still use traditional file comparison tools such as `diff.exe` or the `WinDiff` application that comes with both the Windows Support Tools and Visual Studio.

For more information about the `Compare-Object` cmdlet, type **Get-Help** **Compare-Object**.

22.3 Verify Integrity of File Sets

Problem

You want to determine whether any files in a set of files have been modified or damaged.

Solution

To verify the integrity of file sets, use the `Get-FileHash` script provided in Recipe 20.11 to generate the signatures of those files in question. Do the same for the files on a known good system. Finally, use the `Compare-Object` cmdlet to compare those two sets.

Discussion

To generate the information from the files in question, use a command like:

```
dir C:\Windows\System32\WindowsPowerShell\v1.0 | Get-FileHash |
    Export-CliXml c:\temp\PowerShellHashes.clixml
```

This command gets the hash values of the files from *C:\Windows\System32\ WindowsPowerShell\v1.0*, and uses the `Export-CliXml` cmdlet to store that data in a file.

Transport this file to a system with files in a known good state, and then import the data from that file.

```
$otherHashes = Import-CliXml c:\temp\PowerShellHashes.clixml
```

 You can also map a network drive to the files in question and skip the export, transport, and import steps altogether:

```
net use x: \\lee-desk\c$\Windows\System32\WindowsPowerShell\v1.0
$otherHashes = dir x: | Get-FileHash
```

Generate the information from the files you know are in a good state:

```
$knownHashes = dir C:\Windows\System32\WindowsPowerShell\v1.0 |
    Get-FileHash
```

Finally, use the `Compare-Object` cmdlet to detect any differences:

```
Compare-Object $otherHashes $knownHashes -Property Path,HashValue
```

If there are any differences, the `Compare-Object` cmdlet displays them in a list, as shown in Example 22-1.

Example 22-1. The Compare-Object cmdlet showing differences between two files

```
PS > Compare-Object $otherHashes $knownHashes -Property Path,HashValue
Path                     HashValue                SideIndicator
----                     ---------                -------------
system.management.aut... 247F291CCDA8E669FF9FA... =>
system.management.aut... 5A68BC5819E29B8E3648F... <=


PS > Compare-Object $otherHashes $knownHashes -Property Path,HashValue |
Select-Object Path
```

```
Path
----
system.management.automation.dll-help.xml
system.management.automation.dll-help.xml
```

For more information about the Compare-Object cmdlet, type **Get-Help Compare-Object**. For more information about the Export-CliXml and Import-CliXml cmdlets, type **Get-Help Export-CliXml and Get-Help Import-CliXml**, respectively.

See Also

Recipe 20.11, "Program: Get the MD5 or SHA1 Hash of a File"

Event Logs

23.0 Introduction

Event logs form the core of most monitoring and diagnosis on Windows. To support this activity, PowerShell offers both the Get-EventLog and Get-WinEvent cmdlets to let you query and work with event log data on a system. In addition to simple event log retrieval, PowerShell also includes many other cmdlets to create, delete, customize, and interact with event logs.

In addition to the (now "classic") event logs exposed by the *-EventLog cmdlets, Windows Vista and beyond have a significantly expanded and revamped event logging system compared to Windows XP. The features of the new system are different enough that we expose them through an entirely new Get-WinEvent cmdlet. If you need to read events from Vista-style event logs, you'll need the Get-WinEvent cmdlet. If you need to read events from classic event logs, the choice is up to you.

23.1 List All Event Logs

Problem

You want to determine which event logs exist on a system.

Solution

To list all classic event logs on a system, use the -List parameter of the Get-EventLog cmdlet:

```
PS > Get-EventLog -List

Max(K) Retain OverflowAction       Entries Log
------ ------ --------------       ------- ---
20,480      0 OverwriteAsNeeded      1,933 Application
15,168      0 OverwriteAsNeeded          0 DFS Replication
20,480      0 OverwriteAsNeeded          0 HardwareEvents
```

```
   512    7 OverwriteOlder            0 Internet Explorer
20,480    0 OverwriteAsNeeded         0 Key Management Service
 8,192    0 OverwriteAsNeeded         0 Media Center
   128    0 OverwriteAsNeeded         2 OAlerts
 1,024    7 OverwriteOlder          424 ScriptEvents
20,480    0 OverwriteAsNeeded    39,006 Security
20,480    0 OverwriteAsNeeded    55,958 System
15,360    0 OverwriteAsNeeded     2,865 Windows PowerShell
```

On Windows Vista or later, you can also use the Get-WinEvent cmdlet. In addition to classic event logs, the Get-WinEvent cmdlet supports Application and Services event logs:

```
PS > Get-WinEvent -ListLog * | Select LogName,RecordCount

LogName                                       RecordCount
-------                                       -----------
Application                                          1933
DFS Replication                                         0
HardwareEvents                                          0
Internet Explorer                                       0
Key Management Service                                  0
Media Center                                            0
OAlerts                                                 2
ScriptEvents                                          424
Security                                            39005
System                                              55957
Windows PowerShell                                   2865
ForwardedEvents
Microsoft-Windows-Backup                                0
Microsoft-Windows-Bits-Client/Ana ...
Microsoft-Windows-Bits-Client/Oper...                2232
Microsoft-Windows-Bluetooth-MTPEnu...                   0
Microsoft-Windows-CAPI2/Operational
(...)
```

To browse event logs using the Windows Event Viewer graphical user interface, use the Show-EventLog cmdlet.

Discussion

The -List parameter of the Get-EventLog cmdlet generates a list of the event logs registered on the system. In addition to supporting event logs on the current system, all of PowerShell's event log cmdlets let you supply the -ComputerName parameter to interact with event logs on a remote system.

Once you've determined which event log you are interested in, you can use the Get-EventLog and Get-WinEvent cmdlets to search, filter, and retrieve specific entries from those logs. For information on how to retrieve event log entries, see Recipes 23.2, 23.3, and 23.4.

For more information about the Get-EventLog cmdlet, type **Get-Help Get-EventLog**. For more information about the Get-WinEvent cmdlet, type **Get-Help Get-WinEvent**.

See Also

Recipe 23.2, "Get the Newest Entries from an Event Log"

Recipe 23.3, "Find Event Log Entries with Specific Text"

Recipe 23.4, "Retrieve and Filter Event Log Entries"

23.2 Get the Newest Entries from an Event Log

Problem

You want to retrieve the most recent entries from an event log.

Solution

To retrieve the most recent entries from an event log, use the `-Newest` parameter of the `Get-EventLog` cmdlet, as shown in Example 23-1.

Example 23-1. Retrieving the 10 newest entries from the System event log

```
PS > Get-EventLog System -Newest 10 | Format-Table Index,Source,Message -Auto

Index Source                  Message
----- ------                  -------
 2922 Service Control Manager The Background Intelligent Transfer Servi...
 2921 Service Control Manager The Background Intelligent Transfer Servi...
 2920 Service Control Manager The Logical Disk Manager Administrative S...
 2919 Service Control Manager The Logical Disk Manager Administrative S...
 2918 Service Control Manager The Logical Disk Manager Administrative S...
 2917 TermServDevices         Driver Microsoft XPS Document Writer requ...
 2916 Print                   Printer Microsoft Office Document Image W...
 2915 Print                   Printer Microsoft Office Document Image W...
 2914 Print                   Printer Microsoft Office Document Image W...
 2913 TermServDevices         Driver Microsoft Shared Fax Driver requir...
```

Alternatively, use the `-MaxEvents` parameter of the `Get-WinEvent` cmdlet:

```
PS > Get-WinEvent Application -MaxEvents 10 |
    Format-Table ProviderName,Id,Message -Auto


ProviderName               Id Message
------------               -- -------
VSS                      8224 The VSS service is shutting down due to ...
System Restore           8194 Successfully created restore point (Proc...
System Restore           8194 Successfully created restore point (Proc...
VSS                      8224 The VSS service is shutting down due to ...
System Restore           8211 Successfully created scheduled restore p...
System Restore           8194 Successfully created restore point (Proc...
Microsoft-Windows-MSDTC 2 4202 MSDTC started with the following setting...
VSS                      8224 The VSS service is shutting down due to ...
```

```
System Restore              8211 Successfully created scheduled restore p...
System Restore              8194 Successfully created restore point (Proc...
```

Discussion

The -Newest parameter of the Get-EventLog cmdlet retrieves the most recent entries from an event log that you specify. To list the event logs available on the system, see Recipe 23.1. The Get-WinEvent cmdlet returns the most recent entries by default, so no specific parameter is required.

For more information about the Get-EventLog cmdlet, type **Get-Help Get-EventLog**.

See Also

Recipe 23.1, "List All Event Logs"

23.3 Find Event Log Entries with Specific Text

Problem

You want to retrieve all event log entries that contain a given term.

Solution

To find specific event log entries, use the Get-EventLog or Get-WinEvent cmdlet to retrieve the items, and then pipe them to the Where-Object cmdlet to filter them, as shown in Example 23-2.

Example 23-2. Searching the event log for entries that mention the term "disk"

```
PS > Get-EventLog System | Where-Object { $_.Message -match "disk" }

Index Time          Type Source           EventID Message
----- ----          ---- ------           ------- -------
 2920 May 06 09:18  Info Service Control M...  7036 The Logical Disk...
 2919 May 06 09:17  Info Service Control M...  7036 The Logical Disk...
 2918 May 06 09:17  Info Service Control M...  7035 The Logical Disk...
 2884 May 06 00:28  Erro sr                       1 The System Resto...
 2333 Apr 03 00:16  Erro Disk                    11 The driver detec...
 2332 Apr 03 00:16  Erro Disk                    11 The driver detec...
 2131 Mar 27 13:59  Info Service Control M...  7036 The Logical Disk...
 2127 Mar 27 12:48  Info Service Control M...  7036 The Logical Disk...
 2126 Mar 27 12:48  Info Service Control M...  7035 The Logical Disk...
 2123 Mar 27 12:31  Info Service Control M...  7036 The Logical Disk...
 2122 Mar 27 12:29  Info Service Control M...  7036 The Logical Disk...
 2121 Mar 27 12:29  Info Service Control M...  7035 The Logical Disk...
```

Discussion

Since the `Get-EventLog` cmdlet retrieves rich objects that represent event log entries, you can pipe them to the `Where-Object` cmdlet for equally rich filtering.

By default, PowerShell's default table formatting displays a summary of event log entries. If you are searching the event log message, however, you are probably interested in seeing more details about the message itself. In this case, use the `Format-List` cmdlet to format these entries in a more detailed list view. Example 23-3 shows this view.

Example 23-3. A detailed list view of an event log entry

```
PS > Get-EventLog System | Where-Object { $_.Message -match "disk" } |
    Format-List


Index               : 2920
EntryType           : Information
EventID             : 7036
Message             : The Logical Disk Manager Administrative Service
                      service entered the stopped state.
Category            : (0)
CategoryNumber      : 0
ReplacementStrings  : {Logical Disk Manager Administrative Service, stopped
                      }
Source              : Service Control Manager
TimeGenerated       : 5/6/2007 9:18:25 AM
TimeWritten         : 5/6/2007 9:18:25 AM
UserName            :

Index               : 2919
(...)
```

For more information about the `Get-EventLog` cmdlet, type **Get-Help Get-EventLog**. For more information about filtering command output, see Recipe 2.1.

See Also

Recipe 2.1, "Filter Items in a List or Command Output"

23.4 Retrieve and Filter Event Log Entries

Problem

You want to retrieve a specific event log entry or filter a log based on advanced search criteria.

Solution

To retrieve a specific event log entry, use the Get-EventLog cmdlet to retrieve the entries in the event log, and then pipe them to the Where-Object cmdlet to filter them to the one you are looking for.

```
PS > Get-EventLog System | Where-Object { $_.Index -eq 2920 }

Index Time          Type Source              EventID Message
----- ----          ---- ------              ------- -------
 2920 May 06 09:18  Info Service Control M...    7036 The Logical Disk...
```

For more advanced (or performance-sensitive) queries, use the -FilterXml, -FilterHashtable, or -FilterXPath parameters of the Get-WinEvent cmdlet:

```
Get-WinEvent -LogName "System" -FilterXPath "*[System[EventRecordID = 2920]]"
```

Discussion

If you've listed the items in an event log or searched it for entries that have a message with specific text, you often want to get more details about a specific event log entry.

Since the Get-EventLog cmdlet retrieves rich objects that represent event log entries, you can pipe them to the Where-Object cmdlet for equally rich filtering.

By default, PowerShell's default table formatting displays a summary of event log entries. If you are retrieving a specific entry, however, you are probably interested in seeing more details about the entry. In this case, use the Format-List cmdlet to format these entries in a more detailed list view, as shown in Example 23-4.

Example 23-4. A detailed list view of an event log entry

```
PS > Get-EventLog System | Where-Object { $_.Index -eq 2920 } |
    Format-List


Index             : 2920
EntryType         : Information
EventID           : 7036
Message           : The Logical Disk Manager Administrative Service
                    service entered the stopped state.
Category          : (0)
CategoryNumber    : 0
ReplacementStrings : {Logical Disk Manager Administrative Service, stopped
                    }
Source            : Service Control Manager
TimeGenerated     : 5/6/2007 9:18:25 AM
TimeWritten       : 5/6/2007 9:18:25 AM
UserName          :

Index             : 2919
(...)
```

While the `Where-Object` cmdlet works well for simple (or one-off) tasks, the `Get-WinEvent` cmdlet offers three parameters that can make your event log searches both more powerful and more efficient.

Efficiently processing simple queries

If you have a simple event log query, you can use the `-FilterHashtable` parameter of the `Get-WinEvent` cmdlet to filter the event log very efficiently.

 The `-FilterHashtable` parameter works only on Windows 7. On Windows Vista, it generates an error: "The parameter is incorrect."

The hashtable that you supply to this parameter lets you filter on `LogName`, `Provider Name`, `Path`, `Keywords`, `ID`, `Level`, `StartTime`, `EndTime`, and `UserID`. This can replace many `Where-Object` style filtering operations. This example retrieves all critical and error events in the System event log:

```
Get-WinEvent -FilterHashtable @{ LogName = "System"; Level = 1,2 }
```

Automating GUI-generated searches

When you are reviewing an event log, the Windows Event Viewer offers a Filter Current Log action on the righthand side. This interface lets you select data ranges, event severity, keywords, task categories, and more. After customizing a filter, you can click the XML tab to see an XML representation of your query. You can copy and paste that XML directly into a here string in a script, and then pass it to the `-FilterXml` parameter of the `Get-WinEvent` cmdlet:

```
## Gets all Critical and Error events from the last 24 hours
$xml = @'
<QueryList>
  <Query Id="0" Path="System">
    <Select Path="System">
        *[System[(Level=1  or Level=2) and
            TimeCreated[timediff(@SystemTime) &lt;= 86400000]]]
    </Select>
  </Query>
</QueryList>
'@

Get-WinEvent -FilterXml $xml
```

Performing complex event analysis and correlation

Under the covers, event logs store their event information in an XML format. In addition to the `-FilterHashtable` and `-FilterXml` parameters, the `Get-WinEvent` cmdlet lets you filter event logs with a subset of the standard XPath XML querying language. XPath lets your filters describe complex hierarchical queries, value ranges, and more.

 Like regular expressions, the XPath query language is by no means simple or easy to understand. This parameter can help if you already have some degree of knowledge or comfort in XPath, but don't let it intimidate or frustrate you. There is always more than one way to do it.

While the XPath querying language is powerful, the type of rules you can express ultimately depend on what is contained in the XML of the actual events. To see what can be contained in the XML of an event, search MSDN for "windows 'event schema'". The online reference is useful, but actual events tend to contain an extremely small subset of the supported XML nodes. Because of that, you might have more success reviewing the XML of events that interest you and forming XPath queries based on those. Here are some example queries that build on the -FilterXPath parameter:

```
## Search by Event ID
Get-WinEvent -LogName "System" -FilterXPath "*[System[(EventID=1)]]"

## Search for events associated with a given Process ID
Get-WinEvent -LogName "System" -FilterXPath "*[System/Execution[@ProcessID=428]]"

## Search for events that have 'Volume Shadow Copy' as one of the replacement strings
Get-WinEvent -LogName "System" -FilterXPath "*[EventData[Data = 'Volume Shadow Copy']]"

## Search for Windows Installer Events associated with Vista SP1
$query = "*[UserData/CbsPackageInitiateChanges[PackageIdentifier = 'KB936330']]"
Get-WinEvent -LogName "System" -FilterXPath $query
```

See Also

Recipe 2.1, "Filter Items in a List or Command Output"

Appendix C, *XPath Quick Reference*

23.5 Find Event Log Entries by Their Frequency

Problem

You want to find the event log entries that occur most frequently.

Solution

To find event log entries by frequency, use the Get-EventLog cmdlet to retrieve the entries in the event log, and then pipe them to the Group-Object cmdlet to group them by their message.

```
PS > Get-EventLog System | Group-Object Message | Sort-Object -Desc Count

Count Name                     Group
----- ----                     -----
   23 The Background Intelli... {LEE-DESK, LEE-DESK, LEE-DESK, LEE-DESK...
   23 The Background Intelli... {LEE-DESK, LEE-DESK, LEE-DESK, LEE-DESK...
    3 The Logical Disk Manag... {LEE-DESK, LEE-DESK, LEE-DESK}
    3 The Logical Disk Manag... {LEE-DESK, LEE-DESK, LEE-DESK}
    3 The Logical Disk Manag... {LEE-DESK, LEE-DESK, LEE-DESK}
  161 Driver Microsoft XPS D... {LEE-DESK, LEE-DESK, LEE-DESK, LEE-DESK...
(...)
```

Discussion

The Group-Object cmdlet is a useful way to determine which events occur most frequently on your system. It also provides a useful way to summarize the information in the event log.

If you want more information about the items in a specific group, use the Where-Object cmdlet. Since we used the Message property in the Group-Object cmdlet, we need to filter on Message in the Where-Object cmdlet. For example, to learn more about the entries relating to the Microsoft XPS Driver (from the scenario in the solution):

```
PS > Get-EventLog System |
    Where-Object { $_.Message -like "Driver Microsoft XPS*" }


Index Time          Type Source              EventID Message
----- ----          ---- ------              ------- -------
 2917 May 06 09:13  Erro TermServDevices        1111 Driver Microsoft...
 2883 May 05 10:40  Erro TermServDevices        1111 Driver Microsoft...
 2877 May 05 08:10  Erro TermServDevices        1111 Driver Microsoft...
(...)
```

If grouping by message doesn't provide useful information, you can group by any other property—such as source:

```
PS > Get-EventLog Application | Group-Object Source

Count Name                     Group
----- ----                     -----
    4 Application              {LEE-DESK, LEE-DESK, LEE-DESK, LEE-DESK}
  191 Media Center Scheduler   {LEE-DESK, LEE-DESK, LEE-DESK, LEE-DESK...
 1082 MSSQL$SQLEXPRESS         {LEE-DESK, LEE-DESK, LEE-DESK, LEE-DESK...
(...)
```

If you've listed the items in an event log or searched it for entries that have a message with specific text, you often want to get more details about a specific event log entry.

By default, PowerShell's default table formatting displays a summary of event log entries. If you are retrieving a specific entry, however, you are probably interested in seeing more details about the entry. In this case, use the Format-List cmdlet to format these entries in a more detailed list view, as shown in Example 23-5.

Example 23-5. A detailed list view of an event log entry

```
PS > Get-EventLog System | Where-Object { $_.Index -eq 2917 } |
Format-List


Index           : 2917
EntryType       : Error
EventID         : 1111
Message         : Driver Microsoft XPS Document Writer required for printer
                  Microsoft XPS Document Writer is unknown. Contact
                  the administrator to install the driver before you
                  log in again.
Category        : (0)
CategoryNumber  : 0
ReplacementStrings : {Microsoft XPS Document Writer, Microsoft XPS Document
                  Writer}
Source          : TermServDevices
TimeGenerated   : 5/6/2007 9:13:31 AM
TimeWritten     : 5/6/2007 9:13:31 AM
UserName        :
```

For more information about the Get-EventLog cmdlet, type **Get-Help Get-EventLog**. For more information about filtering command output, see Recipe 2.1. For more information about the Group-Object cmdlet, type **Get-Help Group-Object**.

See Also

Recipe 2.1, "Filter Items in a List or Command Output"

23.6 Back Up an Event Log

Problem

You want to store the information in an event log in a file for storage or later review.

Solution

To store event log entries in a file, use the *wevtutil.exe* application:

```
PS > wevtutil epl System c:\temp\system.bak.evtx
```

After exporting the event log, use the Get-WinEvent cmdlet to query the exported log as though it were live:

```
PS > Get-WinEvent -FilterHashtable @{ LogName="System"; Level=1,2 } -MaxEvents 2 |
    Format-Table -Auto

TimeCreated            ProviderName Id Message
-----------            ------------ -- -------
2/15/2010 11:49:31 AM Ntfs         55 The file system structure on the disk is ...
2/15/2010 11:49:31 AM Ntfs         55 The file system structure on the disk is ...
```

```
PS > Get-WinEvent -FilterHashtable @{
    Path="c:\temp\system.bak.evtx"; Level=1,2 } -MaxEvents 2 |
    Format-Table -Auto

TimeCreated            ProviderName Id Message
-----------            ------------ -- -------
2/15/2010 11:49:31 AM Ntfs          55 The file system structure on the disk is ...
2/15/2010 11:49:31 AM Ntfs          55 The file system structure on the disk is ...
```

If you need to process the event logs on a system where the `Get-WinEvent` cmdlet is not available, use the `Get-EventLog` cmdlet to retrieve the entries in the event log, and then pipe them to the `Export-CliXml` cmdlet to store them in a file.

```
Get-EventLog System | Export-CliXml c:\temp\SystemLogBackup.clixml
```

Discussion

While there is no PowerShell cmdlet to export event logs, the *wevtutil.exe* application provides an easy way to save an event log to disk in its full fidelity. After exporting the event log, you can import it again, or even use the `Get-WinEvent` cmdlet to query against it directly.

If you want to analyze the event logs on a machine where the `Get-WinEvent` cmdlet is not available, you can use the `Export-CliXml` cmdlet to save event logs to disk—just as PowerShell lets you save any other structured data to disk. Once you've exported the events from an event log, you can archive them, or use the `Import-CliXml` cmdlet to review them on any machine that has PowerShell installed:

```
PS > $archivedLogs = Import-CliXml c:\temp\SystemLogBackup.clixml
PS > $archivedLogs | Group Source

Count Name                      Group
----- ----                      -----
  856 Service Control Manager   {LEE-DESK, LEE-DESK, LEE-DESK, LEE-DESK...
  640 TermServDevices           {LEE-DESK, LEE-DESK, LEE-DESK, LEE-DESK...
   91 Print                     {LEE-DESK, LEE-DESK, LEE-DESK, LEE-DESK...
  100 WMPNetworkSvc             {LEE-DESK, LEE-DESK, LEE-DESK, LEE-DESK...
  123 Tcpip                     {LEE-DESK, LEE-DESK, LEE-DESK, LEE-DESK...
(...)
```

In addition to the `Export-CliXml` cmdlet, you can also use WMI's `Win32_NTEventLog File` class to back up classic event logs:

```
$log = Get-WmiObject Win32_NTEventLogFile -Filter "LogFileName = 'Application'"
$log.BackupEventlog("c:\temp\application_backup.log")
```

After saving a log, you can use the Open Saved Log feature in the Windows Event Viewer to review it.

For more information about the `Get-EventLog` cmdlet, type **Get-Help Get-EventLog**. For more information about the `Export-CliXml` and `Import-CliXml` cmdlets, type **Get-Help Export-CliXml** and **Get-Help Import-CliXml**, respectively.

23.7 Create or Remove an Event Log

Problem

You want to create or remove an event log.

Solution

Use the `New-EventLog` and `Remove-EventLog` cmdlets to create and remove event logs:

```
PS > New-EventLog -Logname ScriptEvents -Source PowerShellCookbook
PS > Get-EventLog -List

 Max(K) Retain OverflowAction       Entries Log
 ------ ------ --------------       ------- ---
 20,480      0 OverwriteAsNeeded      1,930 Application
(...)
    512      7 OverwriteOlder             0 ScriptEvents
(...)
 15,360      0 OverwriteAsNeeded      2,847 Windows PowerShell


PS > Remove-EventLog ScriptEvents
```

Both cmdlets support remote administration via the `-ComputerName` parameter.

Discussion

Although Windows offers the standard `Application` event log, you might sometimes want to make separate event logs to hold events of special interest. For this, PowerShell includes the `New-EventLog` cmdlet. It takes two parameters: the event log name and the source identifier for events. If the event log does not already exist, PowerShell creates it. If both the event log and event log source already exist, the `New-EventLog` cmdlet generates an error.

After you create the event log, the `Limit-EventLog` cmdlet lets you manage its retention policy. For more information about the `Limit-EventLog` cmdlet, see Recipe 23.10.

The `Remove-EventLog` cmdlet lets you remove both event logs and event log sources.

 Be careful when deleting event logs, as it is difficult to recreate all the event sources if you delete the wrong log by accident. If you delete a standard event log, you have little hope for recovery.

To remove just an event log source, use the `-Source` parameter:

```
Remove-EventLog -Source PowerShellCookbook
```

To remove an event log altogether, specify the log name in the `-Logname` parameter:

```
Remove-EventLog -LogName ScriptEvents
```

Once you have created an event log, you can use the `Write-EventLog` cmdlet to work with it. For more information about writing to event logs, see Recipe 23.8.

See Also

Recipe 23.8, "Write to an Event Log"

23.8 Write to an Event Log

Problem

You want to add an entry to an event log.

Solution

Use the `Write-EventLog` cmdlet to write events to an event log:

```
PS > Write-EventLog -LogName ScriptEvents -Source PowerShellCookbook `
    -EventId 1234 -Message "Hello World"

PS > Get-EventLog ScriptEvents | Select EntryType,Source,InstanceId,Message


    EntryType Source                        InstanceId Message
    --------- ------                        ---------- -------
    Information PowerShellCookbook                 1234 Hello World
```

Discussion

The `Write-EventLog` cmdlet lets you write event log messages to a specified event log. To write an event log message, you must supply a valid log name and a registered event log source. If you need to create a new event log or register a new event source, see Recipe 23.7.

In addition to the log name and source, the `Write-EventLog` cmdlet also requires an event ID and message. Within an event log and event source, each event ID should uniquely identify the situation being logged: for example, *logon failure* or *disk full*. This makes it easy for scripts and other management tasks to automatically respond to system events. The event message should elaborate on the situation being logged (for example, the username or drive letter), but should not be required to identify its reason.

See Also

Recipe 23.7, "Create or Remove an Event Log"

23.9 Run a PowerShell Script for Windows Event Log Entries

Problem

You want to run a PowerShell script when the system generates a specific event log entry.

Solution

Use the *schtasks.exe* tool to define a new task that reacts to event log entries. As its action, call *powershell.exe* with the arguments to disable the profile, customize the execution policy, hide its window, and launch a script:

```
$cred = Get-Credential
$password = $cred.GetNetworkCredential().Password

## Define the command that task scheduler should run when the event
## occurs
$command = "PowerShell -NoProfile -ExecutionPolicy RemoteSigned " +
    "-WindowStyle Hidden -File 'C:\Program Files\TaskScripts\ScriptEvents.ps1'"

## Create a new scheduled task
SCHTASKS /Create /TN "ScriptEvents Monitor" /TR $command /SC ONEVENT `
        /RL Highest /RU $cred.Username /RP $password `
        /EC ScriptEvents /MO *[System/EventID=1010]
```

Discussion

In Vista and beyond, the Windows event log lets you define custom actions that launch when an event is generated. Although you can use the user interface to create these tasks and filters, the *schtasks.exe* tool lets you create them all from the automation-friendly command line.

As an example of this in action, imagine trying to capture the processes running on a system when a problematic event occurs. That script might look like:

```
$logTag = "{0:yyyyMMdd_HHmm}" -f (Get-Date)
$logPath = 'C:\Program Files\TaskScripts\ScriptEvents-{0}.txt' -f $logTag

Start-Transcript -Path $logPath

Get-WmiObject Win32_OperatingSystem | Format-List | Out-String
Get-Process | Format-Table | Out-String

Stop-Transcript
```

After generating an event, we can see the log being created just moments after:

```
PS > dir

    Directory: C:\Program Files\TaskScripts


Mode                LastWriteTime     Length Name
----                -------------     ------ ----
-a---        2/21/2010   8:38 PM        278 ScriptEvents.ps1


PS > Write-EventLog -LogName ScriptEvents -Source PowerShellCookbook `
    -EventId 1010 -Message "Hello World"


PS > dir

    Directory: C:\Program Files\TaskScripts


Mode                LastWriteTime     Length Name
----                -------------     ------ ----
-a---        2/21/2010   9:50 PM      12766 ScriptEvents-20100221_2150.txt
-a---        2/21/2010   8:38 PM        278 ScriptEvents.ps1
```

When we define the task, we use the /TN parameter to define a name for our task. As the command (specified by the /TR parameter), we tell Windows to launch *Power-Shell.exe* with several parameters to customize its environment. We use the /RL parameter to ensure that the task is run with elevated permissions (as it writes to the *Program Files* directory). To define the actual event log filter, we use the /EC parameter to define the event channel—in this case, the ScriptEvents log. In the /MO ("modifier") parameter, we specify the XPath filter required to match events that we care about. In this case, we search for EventId 1010. The System/ prefix doesn't tell Windows to search the System event log; it tells it to look in the standard system properties: EventID, Level, Task, Keywords, Computer, and more.

For more information about the event viewer's XPath syntax, see Recipe 23.4.

See Also

Recipe 1.12, "Invoke a PowerShell Command or Script from Outside PowerShell"

Recipe 23.4, "Retrieve and Filter Event Log Entries"

23.10 Clear or Maintain an Event Log

Problem

You want to clear an event log or manage its retention policy.

Solution

Use the `Limit-EventLog` cmdlet to manage the retention policy (days, size, and overflow behavior) of an event log. Use the `Clear-EventLog` cmdlet to clear it completely:

```
PS > Get-EventLog -List | Where-Object { $_.Log -eq "ScriptEvents" }

  Max(K) Retain OverflowAction        Entries Log
  ------ ------ --------------        ------- ---
   2,048      7 OverwriteOlder            872 ScriptEvents


PS > Clear-EventLog ScriptEvents
PS > Get-EventLog -List | Where-Object { $_.Log -eq "ScriptEvents" }

  Max(K) Retain OverflowAction        Entries Log
  ------ ------ --------------        ------- ---
   2,048      7 OverwriteOlder              0 ScriptEvents


PS > Limit-EventLog -LogName ScriptEvents -MaximumSize 1024kb
PS > 1..10000 | Foreach-Object {
    Write-EventLog -LogName ScriptEvents -Source PowerShellCookbook `
        -EventId 1234 -Message ('A' * 1000)
}

PS > Get-EventLog -List | Where-Object { $_.Log -eq "ScriptEvents" }

  Max(K) Retain OverflowAction        Entries Log
  ------ ------ --------------        ------- ---
   1,024      7 OverwriteOlder            424 ScriptEvents
```

Both cmdlets support remote administration via the `-ComputerName` parameter.

Discussion

While the default policies of most event logs are sensible, PowerShell still provides commands to help you manage how much information each event log retains.

For permanent policy changes, use the `Limit-EventLog` cmdlet. This cmdlet lets you limit the log size, maximum event age, and overwrite behavior for the event log that you apply it to. While the size and age limits are fairly self-describing parameters, configuring the overflow behavior is more subtle.

The `-OverflowAction` parameter supports one of three options. Each describes a different strategy for Windows to take when writing to a full event log:

DoNotOverwrite
: Discards new entries.

OverwriteAsNeeded
: Overwrites the oldest entry.

`OverwriteOlder`

Overwrites entries older than the age limit specified for the event log (via the `RetentionDays` parameter). If there are no old entries to overwrite, Windows discards the new entry.

To clear an event log entirely, use the `Clear-EventLog` cmdlet. If you want to save the contents of the event log before clearing it, see Recipe 23.6. PowerShell does not include a cmdlet to clear the new event logs supported by Vista and later (as exposed by the `Get-WinEvent` cmdlet), but you can use the `[System.Diagnostics.Event ing.Reader.EventLogSession]::GlobalSession.ClearLog()` method from the .NET Framework to clear these event logs. For more information about working with .NET objects, see Recipe 3.8.

If you want to remove an event log entirely, see Recipe 23.7.

See Also

Recipe 3.8, "Work with .NET Objects"

Recipe 23.6, "Back Up an Event Log"

Recipe 23.7, "Create or Remove an Event Log"

23.11 Access Event Logs of a Remote Machine

Problem

You want to access event log entries from a remote machine.

Solution

To access event logs on a remote machine, use the `-ComputerName` parameter of any of the `EventLog` cmdlets:

```
PS > Get-EventLog System -ComputerName LEE-DESK | Group-Object Source

Count Name                      Group
----- ----                      -----
   91 Print                     {LEE-DESK, LEE-DESK, LEE-DESK, LEE-DESK...
  640 TermServDevices           {LEE-DESK, LEE-DESK, LEE-DESK, LEE-DESK...
  148 W32Time                   {LEE-DESK, LEE-DESK, LEE-DESK, LEE-DESK...
  100 WMPNetworkSvc             {LEE-DESK, LEE-DESK, LEE-DESK, LEE-DESK...
  856 Service Control Manager   {LEE-DESK, LEE-DESK, LEE-DESK, LEE-DESK...
  123 Tcpip                     {LEE-DESK, LEE-DESK, LEE-DESK, LEE-DESK...
(...)
```

To use the graphical event log viewer to browse event logs on a remote machine, use the `Show-EventLog` cmdlet:

```
Show-EventLog Computername
```

Discussion

The `-ComputerName` parameter of the `*-EventLog` cmdlets makes it easy to manage event logs of remote computers. Using these cmdlets, you can create event logs, remove event logs, write event log entries, and more.

If you want to use a graphical user interface to work with event logs on a remote machine in a more ad-hoc way, use the `Show-EventLog` cmdlet. If the Remote Eventlog Management firewall rule is enabled on the remote computer (and you have the appropriate permissions), PowerShell launches the Windows Event Viewer targeted to that machine (see Figure 23-1).

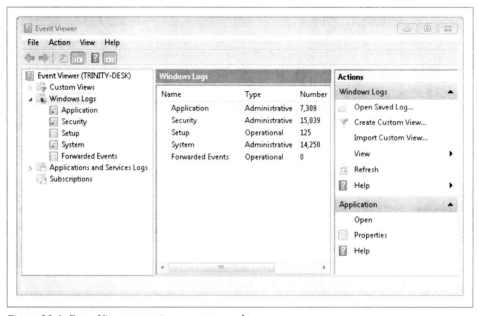

Figure 23-1. Event Viewer targeting a remote machine

By default, the Windows Event Viewer tries to use the credentials of your current account to connect to the remote computer. If you need to connect as another account, click the "Connect to Another Computer" action on the righthand side of the Event Viewer window that opens. In that window, specify both the remote computer name and new user information.

For information about how to get event logs, see Recipe 23.1. For more information about how to create or delete event logs, see Recipe 23.7. For more information about how to write event log entries, see Recipe 23.8.

See Also

Recipe 23.1, "List All Event Logs"

Recipe 23.7, "Create or Remove an Event Log"

Recipe 23.8, "Write to an Event Log"

Processes

24.0 Introduction

Working with system processes is a natural aspect of system administration. It is also the source of most of the regular expression magic and kung fu that make system administrators proud. After all, who wouldn't boast about this Unix one-liner to stop all processes using more than 100 MB of memory:

```
ps -el | awk '{ if ( $6 > (1024*100)) { print $3 } }' | grep -v PID | xargs kill
```

While helpful, it also demonstrates the inherently fragile nature of pure text processing. For this command to succeed, it must:

- Depend on the ps command to display memory usage in column 6
- Depend on column 6 of the ps command's output to represent the memory usage in kilobytes
- Depend on column 3 of the ps command's output to represent the process ID
- Remove the header column from the ps command's output

While the ps command has parameters that simplify some of this work, this form of "prayer-based parsing" is common when manipulating the output of tools that produce only text.

Since PowerShell's Get-Process cmdlet returns information as highly structured .NET objects, fragile text parsing becomes a thing of the past:

```
Get-Process | Where-Object { $_.WorkingSet -gt 100mb } | Stop-Process -WhatIf
```

If brevity is important, PowerShell defines aliases to make most commands easier to type:

```
gps | ? { $_.WS -gt 100mb } | kill -WhatIf
```

In addition to simple process control, PowerShell also offers commands for starting processes, customizing their execution environment, waiting for processes to exit, and more.

24.1 List Currently Running Processes

Problem

You want to see which processes are running on the system.

Solution

To retrieve the list of currently running processes, use the Get-Process cmdlet:

```
PS > Get-Process
```

Handles	NPM(K)	PM(K)	WS(K)	VM(M)	CPU(s)	Id	ProcessName
274	6	1328	3940	33		1084	alg
85	4	3816	6656	57	5.67	3460	AutoHotkey
50	2	2292	1980	14	384.25	1560	BrmfRsmg
71	3	2520	4680	35	0.42	2592	cmd
946	7	3676	6204	32		848	csrss
84	4	732	2248	22		3144	csrss
68	4	936	3364	30	0.38	3904	ctfmon
243	7	3648	9324	48	2.02	2892	Ditto

(...)

Discussion

The Get-Process cmdlet retrieves information about all processes running on the system. Because these are rich .NET objects (of the type System.Diagnostics.Process), advanced filters and operations are easier than ever before.

For example, to find all processes using more than 100 MB of memory:

```
PS > Get-Process | Where-Object { $_.WorkingSet -gt 100mb }
```

Handles	NPM(K)	PM(K)	WS(K)	VM(M)	CPU(s)	Id	ProcessName
1458	29	83468	105824	273	323.80	3992	BigBloatedApp

To group processes by company:

```
PS > Get-Process | Group-Object Company
```

Count	Name	Group
39		{alg, csrss, csrss, dllhost...}
4		{AutoHotkey, Ditto, gnuserv, mafwTray}
1	Brother Industries, Ltd.	{BrmfRsmg}
19	Microsoft Corporation	{cmd, ctfmon, EXCEL, explorer...}
1	Free Software Foundation	{emacs}
1	Microsoft (R) Corporation	{FwcMgmt}

(...)

Or perhaps to sort by start time (with the most recent first):

```
PS > Get-Process | Sort -Descending StartTime | Select-Object -First 10
```

Handles	NPM(K)	PM(K)	WS(K)	VM(M)	CPU(s)	Id	ProcessName
1810	39	53616	33964	193	318.02	1452	iTunes
675	6	41472	50180	146	49.36	296	powershell
1240	35	48220	58860	316	167.58	4012	OUTLOOK
305	8	5736	2460	105	21.22	3384	WindowsSearch...
464	7	29704	30920	153	6.00	3680	powershell
1458	29	83468	105824	273	324.22	3992	iexplore
478	6	24620	23688	143	17.83	3548	powershell
222	8	8532	19084	144	20.69	3924	EXCEL
14	2	396	1600	15	0.06	2900	logon.scr
544	18	21336	50216	294	180.72	2660	WINWORD

These advanced tasks become incredibly simple due to the rich amount of information that PowerShell returns for each process. For more information about the Get-Process cmdlet, type **Get-Help Get-Process**. For more information about filtering, grouping, and sorting in PowerShell commands, see Recipe 2.1.

For more information about working with classes from the .NET Framework, see Recipe 3.8.

See Also

Recipe 2.1, "Filter Items in a List or Command Output"

Recipe 3.8, "Work with .NET Objects"

24.2 Launch the Application Associated with a Document

Problem

You want to launch the application associated with a document or with another shell association.

Solution

Use the Start-Process cmdlet (or its start alias) to launch the document or location:

```
PS > Start-Process http://blogs.msdn.com/powershell
PS > start http://www.bing.com
PS > start c:\temp\output.csv
```

To launch one of the predefined actions for a document (usually exposed through its right-click menu), use the -Verb parameter:

```
start c:\documents\MyDoc.docx -Verb Print
```

Discussion

The Start-Process cmdlet gives you a great deal of flexibility over how you launch an application. In addition to launching applications, it also gives you access to Windows *shell associations*: functionality associated with URLs and documents.

Windows defines many shell associations: for HTTP websites, FTP locations, and even Explorer-specific behavior. For example, to launch the All Tasks view of the Windows control panel:

```
start 'shell:::{ED7BA470-8E54-465E-825C-99712043E01C}'
```

If the document you are launching defines an action (such as Edit or Print), you can use the -Verb parameter to invoke that action.

For more information about the Start-Process cmdlet and launching system processes, see Recipe 24.3.

See Also

Recipe 24.3, "Launch a Process"

24.3 Launch a Process

Problem

You want to launch a new process on the system, but you also want to configure its startup environment.

Solution

To launch a new process, use the Start-Process cmdlet.

```
PS > Start-Process mmc -Verb RunAs -WindowStyle Maximized
```

For advanced tasks not covered by the Start-Process cmdlet, call the [System.Diagnostics.Process]::Start() method. To control the process's startup environment, supply it with a System.Diagnostics.ProcessStartInfo object that you prepare, as shown in Example 24-1.

Example 24-1. Configuring the startup environment of a new process

```
$processname = "powershell.exe"

## Prepare to invoke the process
$processStartInfo = New-Object System.Diagnostics.ProcessStartInfo
$processStartInfo.FileName = (Get-Command $processname).Definition
$processStartInfo.WorkingDirectory = (Get-Location).Path
if($argumentList) { $processStartInfo.Arguments = $argumentList }
$processStartInfo.UseShellExecute = $false
```

```
## Always redirect the input and output of the process.
## Sometimes we will capture it as binary, other times we will
## just treat it as strings.
$processStartInfo.RedirectStandardOutput = $true
$processStartInfo.RedirectStandardInput = $true

$process = [System.Diagnostics.Process]::Start($processStartInfo)
```

Discussion

Normally, launching a process in PowerShell is as simple as typing the program name:

```
PS > notepad c:\temp\test.txt
```

However, you may sometimes need detailed control over the process details, such as its credentials, working directory, window style, and more. In those situations, use the Start-Process cmdlet. It exposes most of these common configuration options through simple parameters.

 For an example of how to start a process as another user (or as an elevated PowerShell command), see Recipe 18.10.

If your needs are more complex than the features offered by the Start-Process cmdlet, you can use the [System.Diagnostics.Process]::Start() method from the .NET Framework to provide that additional functionality. Example 24-1 is taken from Recipe 2.10, and gives an example of this type of advanced requirement.

For more information about launching programs from PowerShell, see Recipe 1.1. For more information about working with classes from the .NET Framework, see Recipe 3.8.

See Also

Recipe 1.1, "Run Programs, Scripts, and Existing Tools"

Recipe 3.8, "Work with .NET Objects"

24.4 Stop a Process

Problem

You want to stop (or kill) a process on the system.

Solution

To stop a process, use the Stop-Process cmdlet, as shown in Example 24-2.

Example 24-2. Stopping a process using the Stop-Process cmdlet

```
PS > notepad
PS > Get-Process Notepad

Handles  NPM(K)  PM(K)  WS(K)  VM(M)  CPU(s)     Id ProcessName
-------  ------  -----  -----  -----  ------     -- -----------
     42       3   1276   3916     32    0.09   3520 notepad


PS > Stop-Process -ProcessName notepad
PS > Get-Process Notepad
Get-Process : Cannot find a process with the name 'Notepad'. Verify the
process name and call the cmdlet again.
At line:1 char:12
+ Get-Process <<<< Notepad
```

Discussion

Although the parameters of the Stop-Process cmdlet are useful in their own right, PowerShell's pipeline model lets you be even more precise. The Stop-Process cmdlet stops any processes that you pipeline into it, so an advanced process set generated by Get-Process automatically turns into an advanced process set for the Stop-Process cmdlet to operate on:

```
PS > Get-Process | Where-Object { $_.WorkingSet -lt 10mb } |
    Sort-Object -Descending Name | Stop-Process -WhatIf

What if: Performing operation "Stop-Process" on Target "svchost (1368)".
What if: Performing operation "Stop-Process" on Target "sqlwriter (1772)".
What if: Performing operation "Stop-Process" on Target "qttask (3672)".
What if: Performing operation "Stop-Process" on Target "Ditto (2892)".
What if: Performing operation "Stop-Process" on Target "ctfmon (3904)".
What if: Performing operation "Stop-Process" on Target "csrss (848)".
What if: Performing operation "Stop-Process" on Target "BrmfRsmg (1560)".
What if: Performing operation "Stop-Process" on Target "AutoHotkey (3460)".
What if: Performing operation "Stop-Process" on Target "alg (1084)".
```

 Notice that this example uses the -WhatIf flag on the Stop-Process cmdlet. This flag lets you see what would happen if you were to run the command, but doesn't actually perform the action.

Another common need when it comes to stopping a process is simply waiting for one to exit. Most scripts handle this by creating a loop that exits only when the Get-Process cmdlet returns no results for the process in question. PowerShell greatly simplifies this need by offering the Wait-Process cmdlet, which lets you pause your script until the specified process has exited. If you still want some degree of control while waiting for the process to stop, the -Timeout parameter lets you control how long PowerShell should wait for the process to exit. When the timeout elapses, PowerShell returns control to your script—giving you the opportunity to continue waiting, forcibly terminate the process, or do whatever else you wish.

For more information about the `Stop-Process` cmdlet, type **`Get-Help Stop-Process`**. For more information about the `Wait-Process` cmdlet, type **`Get-Help Wait-Process`**.

24.5 Debug a Process

Problem

You want to attach a debugger to a running process on the system.

Solution

To debug a process, use the `Debug-Process` cmdlet.

Discussion

If you have a software debugger installed on your computer (such as Visual Studio or the Debugging Tools for Windows), the `Debug-Process` cmdlet lets you start a debugging session from the PowerShell command line. It is not designed to automate the debugging tools after launching them, but it does provide a useful shortcut.

 To debug a PowerShell script, see Chapter 14.

The `Debug-Process` cmdlet launches the system-wide debugger, as configured in the *HKLM:\Software\Microsoft\Windows NT\CurrentVersion\AeDebug* registry key. To change the debugger launched by this cmdlet (and other tools that launch the default debugger), change the `Debugger` property:

```
PS > Get-Location

Path
----
HKLM:\Software\Microsoft\Windows NT\CurrentVersion\AeDebug


PS > Get-ItemProperty .


PSPath          : Microsoft.PowerShell.Core\Registry::HKEY_LOCAL_MACHINE
                  \Software\Microsoft\Windows NT\CurrentVersion\AeDebug
PSParentPath    : Microsoft.PowerShell.Core\Registry::HKEY_LOCAL_MACHINE
                  \Software\Microsoft\Windows NT\CurrentVersion
PSChildName     : AeDebug
PSDrive         : HKLM
```

```
PSProvider          : Microsoft.PowerShell.Core\Registry
UserDebuggerHotKey : 0
Debugger            : "c:\Windows\system32\vsjitdebugger.exe" -p %ld -e %ld
```

For more information about the Debug-Process cmdlet, type **Get-Help Debug-Process**.

See Also

Chapter 14, *Debugging*

System Services

25.0 Introduction

As the support mechanism for many administrative tasks on Windows, managing and working with system services naturally fits into the administrator's toolbox.

PowerShell offers a handful of cmdlets to help make working with system services easier: from listing services to lifecycle management and even to service installation.

25.1 List All Running Services

Problem

You want to see which services are running on the system.

Solution

To list all running services, use the Get-Service cmdlet:

```
PS > Get-Service

Status    Name          DisplayName
------    ----          -----------
Running   ADAM_Test     Test
Stopped   Alerter       Alerter
Running   ALG           Application Layer Gateway Service
Stopped   AppMgmt       Application Management
Stopped   aspnet_state  ASP.NET State Service
Running   AudioSrv      Windows Audio
Running   BITS          Background Intelligent Transfer Ser...
Running   Browser       Computer Browser
(...)
```

Discussion

The `Get-Service` cmdlet retrieves information about all services running on the system. Because these are rich .NET objects (of the type `System.ServiceProcess.ServiceCon troller`), you can apply advanced filters and operations to make managing services straightforward.

For example, to find all running services:

```
PS > Get-Service | Where-Object { $_.Status -eq "Running" }

Status   Name              DisplayName
------   ----              -----------
Running  ADAM_Test         Test
Running  ALG               Application Layer Gateway Service
Running  AudioSrv          Windows Audio
Running  BITS              Background Intelligent Transfer Ser...
Running  Browser           Computer Browser
Running  COMSysApp         COM+ System Application
Running  CryptSvc          Cryptographic Services
```

Or, to sort services by the number of services that depend on them:

```
PS > Get-Service | Sort-Object -Descending { $_.DependentServices.Count }

Status   Name              DisplayName
------   ----              -----------
Running  RpcSs             Remote Procedure Call (RPC)
Running  PlugPlay          Plug and Play
Running  lanmanworkstation Workstation
Running  SSDPSRV           SSDP Discovery Service
Running  TapiSrv           Telephony
(...)
```

Since PowerShell returns full-fidelity .NET objects that represent system services, these tasks and more become incredibly simple due to the rich amount of information that PowerShell returns for each service. For more information about the `Get-Service` cmdlet, type **Get-Help Get-Service**. For more information about filtering, grouping, and sorting in PowerShell commands, see Recipe 2.1.

 The `Get-Service` cmdlet displays most (but not all) information about running services. For additional information (such as the service's start-up mode), use the `Get-WmiObject` cmdlet:

```
$service = Get-WmiObject Win32_Service |
    Where-Object { $_.Name -eq "AudioSrv" }
$service.StartMode
```

In addition to supporting services on the local machine, the `Get-Service` cmdlet lets you retrieve and manage services on a remote machine as well:

```
PS > Get-Service -Computer <Computer> |
    Sort-Object -Descending { $_.DependentServices.Count }
```

```
Status    Name              DisplayName
------    ----              -----------
Running   RpcEptMapper      RPC Endpoint Mapper
Running   DcomLaunch        DCOM Server Process Launcher
Running   RpcSs             Remote Procedure Call (RPC)
Running   PlugPlay          Plug and Play
Running   nsi               Network Store Interface Service
Running   SamSs             Security Accounts Manager
(...)
```

For more information about working with classes from the .NET Framework, see Recipe 3.8. For more information about working with the `Get-WmiObject` cmdlet, see Chapter 28.

See Also

Recipe 2.1, "Filter Items in a List or Command Output"

Recipe 3.8, "Work with .NET Objects"

Chapter 28, *Windows Management Instrumentation*

25.2 Manage a Running Service

Problem

You want to manage a running service.

Solution

To stop a service, use the `Stop-Service` cmdlet:

```
PS > Stop-Service AudioSrv -WhatIf
What if: Performing operation "Stop-Service" on Target "Windows Audio
(AudioSrv)".
```

Likewise, use the `Suspend-Service`, `Restart-Service`, and `Resume-Service` cmdlets to suspend, restart, and resume services, respectively.

Discussion

The `Stop-Service` cmdlet lets you stop a service either by name or display name.

 Notice that the solution uses the -WhatIf flag on the `Stop-Service` cmdlet. This parameter lets you see what would happen if you were to run the command but doesn't actually perform the action.

For more information about the Stop-Service cmdlet, type **Get-Help Stop-Service**. If you want to suspend, restart, or resume a service, see the help for the Suspend-Service, Restart-Service, and Resume-Service cmdlets.

To configure a service (for example, its description or startup type), see Recipe 25.3. In addition to letting you configure a service, the Set-Service cmdlet described in that recipe also lets you stop a service on a remote computer.

See Also

Recipe 25.3, "Configure a Service"

Chapter 28, *Windows Management Instrumentation*

25.3 Configure a Service

Problem

You want to configure properties or startup behavior of a service.

Solution

To configure a service, use the Set-Service cmdlet:

```
PS > Set-Service WinRM -DisplayName 'Windows Remote Management (WS-Management)' `
    -StartupType Manual
```

Discussion

The Set-Service cmdlet lets you manage the configuration of a service: its name, display name, description, and startup type.

If you change the startup type of a service, your natural next step is to verify that the changes were applied correctly. Recipe 25.1 shows how to view the properties of a service, including the WMI-based workaround to examine the startup type.

In addition to letting you configure services on the local computer, the Set-Service cmdlet also offers the -ComputerName parameter to configure services on remote computers.

See Also

Recipe 25.1, "List All Running Services"

Active Directory

26.0 Introduction

By far, the one thing that makes system administration on the Windows platform unique is its interaction with Active Directory. As the centralized authorization, authentication, and information store for Windows networks, Active Directory automation forms the core of many enterprise administration tasks.

In PowerShell version one, the primary way to interact with Active Directory came through its support for Active Directory Service Interface (ADSI) type shortcuts.

While PowerShell version two was under development, the Active Directory team created an immensely feature-filled PowerShell module to manage Active Directory domains. The Active Directory module includes a PowerShell provider (`Set-Location AD:\`) and almost 100 task-specific PowerShell cmdlets.

Working with the Active Directory module has two requirements:

Support from the server
> This module works with any domain that has enabled the Active Directory Web Services feature. Windows Server 2008 R2 enables this feature by default on Active Directory instances, and you can install it on any recent server operating system from Windows Server 2003 on.

Support from the client
> The module itself is included in the Windows 7 Remote Server Administration Tools (RSAT) package. After downloading and installing the package, you can enable it through the "Turn Windows Features On or Off" dialog in the Control Panel.

If working with the Active Directory module is an option at all, import it and use its commands. The `Get-Command` and `Get-Help` commands should be the two key steps you need to get started. In addition to the help built into the commands, MSDN provides a great task-based introduction to the Active Directory Module at *http://go.microsoft.com/fwlink/?linkid=168142*.

If the Active Directory module is not an option, PowerShell provides fluid integration with Active Directory through its [adsi] and [adsisearcher] built-in type shortcuts. This chapter covers their use for most common Active Directory tasks.

26.1 Test Active Directory Scripts on a Local Installation

Problem

You want to test your Active Directory scripts against a local installation.

Solution

To test your scripts against a local system, install Active Directory Lightweight Directory Services (AD LDS) and its sample configuration.

Discussion

For most purposes, Active Directory Lightweight Services works as a lightweight version of Active Directory. Although it doesn't support any of Active Directory's infrastructure features, its programming model is close enough that you can easily use it to experiment with Active Directory scripting. Until recently, Active Directory Lightweight Directory Services was known as Active Directory Application Mode (ADAM). AD LDS is not supported on Windows XP, and so the Microsoft Download Center continues to provide a download of ADAM that supports Windows XP. To test your scripts against a local installation, you'll need to install either AD LDS or ADAM, and then create a test instance.

Verify prerequisites

If you want to test AD LDS on a recent *server* operating system, simply enable it through the Optional Component Manager.

If you want to install it on a client operating system, you have two options. If you have Windows 7 or Windows Vista, download AD LDS. If you have Windows XP (or want to install in Windows XP mode), download ADAM.

Install ADAM

To install AD LDS or ADAM, the first step is to download it. Microsoft provides both free of charge from the Download Center. You can obtain either by searching for "Active Directory Application Mode" or "AD LDS" at *http://download.microsoft.com*.

Once you've downloaded it, run the setup program. Figure 26-1 shows the ADAM setup wizard on Windows XP.

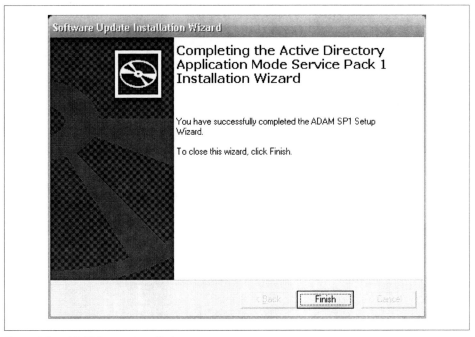

Figure 26-1. ADAM's post-installation screen

Create a test instance

From the ADAM menu in the Windows Start menu, select "Create an ADAM instance." On the Setup Options page that appears next, select "A unique instance." On the Instance Name page, type **Test** as an instance name. On the Ports page, accept the default ports, and then on the Application Directory Partition page, select "Yes, create an application directory partition." As the partition name, type **DC=Fabrikam,DC=COM**, as shown in Figure 26-2.

In the next pages, accept the default file locations, service accounts, and administrators.

When the setup wizard gives you the option to import LDIF files, import all available files except for *MS-AZMan.LDF*. Click Next on this page and the confirmation page to complete the instance setup.

Open a PowerShell window, and test your new instance:

```
PS > [adsi] "LDAP://localhost:389/dc=Fabrikam,dc=COM"

distinguishedName
-----------------
{DC=Fabrikam,DC=COM}
```

The [adsi] tag is a *type shortcut*, like several other type shortcuts in PowerShell. The [adsi] type shortcut provides a quick way to create and work with directory entries through Active Directory Service Interfaces.

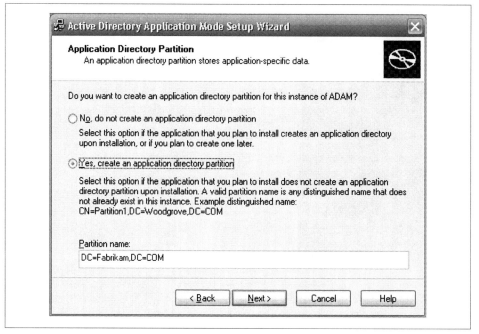

Figure 26-2. Creating a partition of a test ADAM instance

When you first try this shortcut, you may receive this unhelpful error message:

```
format-default : The following exception occurred while retrieving
member "PSComputerName": "Unknown error (0x80005000)"
```

If you receive this error, ensure that you've capitalized the LDAP in LDAP://localhost:389/.

Although scripts that act against an ADAM test environment are almost identical to those that operate directly against Active Directory, there are a few minor differences. ADAM scripts specify the host and port in their binding string (that is, localhost: 389/), whereas Active Directory scripts do not.

For more information about type shortcuts in PowerShell, see "Working with the .NET Framework" on page 741.

See Also

"Working with the .NET Framework" on page 741

26.2 Create an Organizational Unit

Problem

You want to create an organizational unit (OU) in Active Directory.

Solution

To create an organizational unit in a container, use the [adsi] type shortcut to bind to a part of the Active Directory, and then call the Create() method.

```
$domain = [adsi] "LDAP://localhost:389/dc=Fabrikam,dc=COM"
$salesOrg = $domain.Create("OrganizationalUnit", "OU=Sales")
$salesOrg.Put("Description", "Sales Headquarters, SF")
$salesOrg.Put("wwwHomePage", "http://fabrikam.com/sales")
$salesOrg.SetInfo()
```

Discussion

The solution shows an example of creating a Sales organizational unit (OU) at the root of the organization. You can use the same syntax to create OUs under other OUs as well. Example 26-1 demonstrates how to create more sales divisions.

Example 26-1. Creating North, East, and West sales divisions

```
$sales = [adsi] "LDAP://localhost:389/ou=Sales,dc=Fabrikam,dc=COM"

$east = $sales.Create("OrganizationalUnit", "OU=East")
$east.Put("wwwHomePage", "http://fabrikam.com/sales/east")
$east.SetInfo()

$west = $sales.Create("OrganizationalUnit", "OU=West")
$west.Put("wwwHomePage", "http://fabrikam.com/sales/west")
$west.SetInfo()

$north = $sales.Create("OrganizationalUnit", "OU=North")
$north.Put("wwwHomePage", "http://fabrikam.com/sales/north")
$north.SetInfo()
```

When you initially create an item, notice that you need to use the Put() method to set properties on the new item. Once you've created the item, you can instead use simple property access to change those properties. For more information about changing properties of an organizational unit, see Recipe 26.4.

To check that these OUs have been created, see Recipe 26.6.

Using the Active Directory module, the cmdlet to create an organizational unit is New-ADOrganizationalUnit. For more information on how to accomplish these tasks through the Active Directory module, see *http://go.microsoft.com/fwlink/?linkid=168142*.

See Also

Recipe 26.4, "Modify Properties of an Organizational Unit"

Recipe 26.6, "Get the Children of an Active Directory Container"

26.3 Get the Properties of an Organizational Unit

Problem

You want to get and list the properties of a specific OU.

Solution

To list the properties of an OU, use the [adsi] type shortcut to bind to the OU in Active Directory, and then pass the OU to the Format-List cmdlet:

```
$organizationalUnit =
  [adsi] "LDAP://localhost:389/ou=West,ou=Sales,dc=Fabrikam,dc=COM"

$organizationalUnit | Format-List *
```

Discussion

The solution retrieves the Sales West OU. By default, the Format-List cmdlet shows only the distinguished name of the group, so we type **Format-List** * to display all properties.

If you know which property you want the value of, you can specify it by name:

```
PS > $organizationalUnit.wWWHomePage
http://fabrikam.com/sales/west
```

If you are having trouble getting a property that you know exists, you can also retrieve the property using the Get() method on the container. While the name property can be accessed using the usual property syntax, the following example demonstrates the alternative approach:

```
PS > $organizationalUnit.Get("name")
West
```

Using the Active Directory module, the cmdlet to get the properties of an organizational unit is Get-ADOrganizationalUnit. For more information on how to accomplish these tasks through the Active Directory module, see *http://go.microsoft.com/fwlink/?linkid=168142*.

26.4 Modify Properties of an Organizational Unit

Problem

You want to modify properties of a specific OU.

Solution

To modify the properties of an OU, use the [adsi] type shortcut to bind to the OU in Active Directory. If the property has already been set, you can change the value of a property as you would with any other PowerShell object. If you are setting a property for the first time, use the Put() method. Finally, call the SetInfo() method to apply the changes.

```
$organizationalUnit =
   [adsi] "LDAP://localhost:389/ou=West,ou=Sales,dc=Fabrikam,dc=COM"

$organizationalUnit.Put("Description", "Sales West Organization")
$organizationalUnit.wwwHomePage = "http://fabrikam.com/sales/west/fy2012"
$organizationalUnit.SetInfo()
```

Discussion

The solution retrieves the Sales West OU. It then sets the description to Sales West Organization, updates the home page, and then applies those changes to Active Directory.

Using the Active Directory module, the cmdlet to modify the properties of an organizational unit is Set-ADOrganizationalUnit. For more information on how to accomplish these tasks through the Active Directory module, see *http://go.microsoft.com/fwlink/?linkid=168142*.

26.5 Delete an Organizational Unit

Problem

You want to delete a specific OU.

Solution

To delete an OU, use the [adsi] type shortcut to bind to the OU in Active Directory. Finally, call its DeleteTree() method to apply the changes.

```
$organizationalUnit =
   [adsi] "LDAP://localhost:389/ou=North,ou=Sales,dc=Fabrikam,dc=COM"
$organizationalUnit.DeleteTree()
```

Discussion

The solution retrieves the `Sales North` OU. It then calls the `DeleteTree()` method to permanently delete the organizational unit and all of its children.

Using the Active Directory module, the cmdlet to remove an organizational unit is `Remove-ADOrganizationalUnit`. For more information on how to accomplish these tasks through the Active Directory module, see *http://go.microsoft.com/fwlink/?linkid=168142*.

26.6 Get the Children of an Active Directory Container

Problem

You want to list all the children of an Active Directory container.

Solution

To list the items in a container, use the `[adsi]` type shortcut to bind to the OU in Active Directory, and then access the `Children` property of that container:

```
$sales =
  [adsi] "LDAP://localhost:389/ou=Sales,dc=Fabrikam,dc=COM"
$sales.Children
```

Discussion

The solution lists all the children of the `Sales` OU. This is the level of information you typically get from selecting a node in the `ADSIEdit` MMC snap-in. If you want to filter this information to include only users, other organizational units, or more complex queries, see Recipe 26.9.

In PowerShell version one, this solution used to require that you access `$sales.PsBase.Children`. This issue was resolved in PowerShell version two.

Using the Active Directory module, the Active Directory provider lets you get the children of an organizational unit. For example:

```
PS > Set-Location 'AD:\ou=Sales,dc=Fabrikam,dc=COM'
PS > dir
```

For more information on how to accomplish these tasks through the Active Directory module, see *http://go.microsoft.com/fwlink/?linkid=168142*.

See Also

Recipe 26.9, "Search for a User Account"

26.7 Create a User Account

Problem

You want to create a user account in a specific OU.

Solution

To create a user in a container, use the `[adsi]` type shortcut to bind to the OU in Active Directory, and then call the `Create()` method:

```
$salesWest =
  [adsi] "LDAP://localhost:389/ou=West,ou=Sales,dc=Fabrikam,dc=COM"

$user = $salesWest.Create("User", "CN=MyerKen")
$user.Put("userPrincipalName", "Ken.Myer@fabrikam.com")
$user.Put("displayName", "Ken Myer")
$user.SetInfo()
```

Discussion

The solution creates a user under the `Sales West` organizational unit. It sets the `user PrincipalName` (a unique identifier for the user), as well as the user's display name.

 If this step generates an error saying, "The specified directory service attribute or value does not exist," verify that you properly imported the LDIF files at the beginning of the ADAM installation steps. Importing those LDIF files creates the Active Directory schema required for many of these steps.

When you run this script against a real Active Directory deployment (as opposed to an ADAM instance), be sure to update the `sAMAccountName` property, or you'll get an autogenerated default.

To check that these users have been created, see Recipe 26.6. If you need to create users in bulk, see Recipe 26.8.

Using the Active Directory module, the cmdlet to create a user account is `New-ADUser`. For more information on how to accomplish these tasks through the Active Directory module, see *http://go.microsoft.com/fwlink/?linkid=168142*.

See Also

Recipe 26.6, "Get the Children of an Active Directory Container"

Recipe 26.8, "Program: Import Users in Bulk to Active Directory"

26.8 Program: Import Users in Bulk to Active Directory

When importing several users into Active Directory, it quickly becomes tiresome to do it by hand (or even to script the addition of each user one by one). To solve this problem, we can put all our data into a CSV, and then do a bulk import from the information in the CSV.

Example 26-2 supports this in a flexible way. You provide a container to hold the user accounts and a CSV that holds the account information. For each row in the CSV, the script creates a user from the data in that row. The only mandatory column is a CN column to define the common name of the user. Any other columns, if present, represent other Active Directory attributes you want to define for that user.

Example 26-2. Import-ADUser.ps1

```
###########################################################################
##
## Import-AdUser
##
## From Windows PowerShell Cookbook (O'Reilly)
## by Lee Holmes (http://www.leeholmes.com/guide)
##
###########################################################################

<#

.SYNOPSIS

Create users in Active Directory from the content of a CSV.

.DESCRIPTION

In the user CSV, one column must be named "CN" for the user name.
All other columns represent properties in Active Directory for that user.

For example:
CN,userPrincipalName,displayName,manager
MyerKen,Ken.Myer@fabrikam.com,Ken Myer,
DoeJane,Jane.Doe@fabrikam.com,Jane Doe,"CN=MyerKen,OU=West,OU=Sales,DC=..."
SmithRobin,Robin.Smith@fabrikam.com,Robin Smith,"CN=MyerKen,OU=West,OU=..."

.EXAMPLE

PS >$container = "LDAP://localhost:389/ou=West,ou=Sales,dc=Fabrikam,dc=COM"
PS >Import-ADUser.ps1 $container .\users.csv

#>

param(
    ## The container in which to import users
    ## For example:
    ## "LDAP://localhost:389/ou=West,ou=Sales,dc=Fabrikam,dc=COM)")
    [Parameter(Mandatory = $true)]
```

```
        $Container,

        ## The path to the CSV that contains the user records
        [Parameter(Mandatory = $true)]
        $Path
)

Set-StrictMode -Off

## Bind to the container
$userContainer = [adsi] $container

## Ensure that the container was valid
if(-not $userContainer.Name)
{
    Write-Error "Could not connect to $container"
    return
}

## Load the CSV
$users = @(Import-Csv $Path)
if($users.Count -eq 0)
{
    return
}

## Go through each user from the CSV
foreach($user in $users)
{
    ## Pull out the name, and create that user
    $username = $user.CN
    $newUser = $userContainer.Create("User", "CN=$username")

    ## Go through each of the properties from the CSV, and set its value
    ## on the user
    foreach($property in $user.PsObject.Properties)
    {
        ## Skip the property if it was the CN property that sets the
        ## user name
        if($property.Name -eq "CN")
        {
            continue
        }

        ## Ensure they specified a value for the property
        if(-not $property.Value)
        {
            continue
        }

        ## Set the value of the property
        $newUser.Put($property.Name, $property.Value)
    }

    ## Finalize the information in Active Directory
```

```
    $newUser.SetInfo()
}
```

For more information about running scripts, see Recipe 1.1.

See Also

Recipe 1.1, "Run Programs, Scripts, and Existing Tools"

26.9 Search for a User Account

Problem

You want to search for a specific user account, but you don't know the user's distinguished name (DN).

Solution

To search for a user in Active Directory, use the [adsi] type shortcut to bind to a container that holds the user account, and then use the [adsisearcher] type shortcut to search for the user:

```
$domain = [adsi] "LDAP://localhost:389/dc=Fabrikam,dc=COM"
$searcher = [adsisearcher] $domain
$searcher.Filter = '(&(objectClass=User)(displayName=Ken Myer))'
$userResult = $searcher.FindOne()
$user = $userResult.GetDirectoryEntry()
$user
```

Discussion

When you don't know the full distinguished name (DN) of a user account, the [adsi searcher] type shortcut lets you search for it.

You provide an LDAP filter (in this case, searching for users with the display name of Ken Myer), and then call the FindOne() method. The FindOne() method returns the first search result that matches the filter, so we retrieve its actual Active Directory entry. If you expect your query to return multiple results, use the FindAll() method instead. Although the solution searches on the user's display name, you can search on any field in Active Directory—the userPrincipalName and sAMAccountName are two other good choices.

When you do this search, always try to restrict it to the lowest level of the domain possible. If we know that Ken Myer is in the Sales OU, it would be better to bind to that OU instead:

```
$domain = [adsi] "LDAP://localhost:389/ou=Sales,dc=Fabrikam,dc=COM"
```

For more information about the LDAP search filter syntax, search *http://msdn.microsoft .com* for "Search Filter Syntax".

Using the Active Directory module, the cmdlet to search for a user account is Get-ADUser. While you can use a LDAP filter to search for users, the Get-ADUser cmdlet also lets you supply PowerShell expressions:

```
Get-ADUser -Filter { Name -like "*Ken*" }
```

For more information on how to accomplish these tasks through the Active Directory module, see *http://go.microsoft.com/fwlink/?linkid=168142*.

26.10 Get and List the Properties of a User Account

Problem

You want to get and list the properties of a specific user account.

Solution

To list the properties of a user account, use the [adsi] type shortcut to bind to the user in Active Directory, and then pass the user to the Format-List cmdlet:

```
$user =
  [adsi] "LDAP://localhost:389/cn=MyerKen,ou=West,ou=Sales,dc=Fabrikam,dc=COM"

$user | Format-List *
```

Discussion

The solution retrieves the MyerKen user from the Sales West OU. By default, the Format-List cmdlet shows only the distinguished name of the user, so we type **Format-List *** to display all properties.

If you know the property for which you want the value, specify it by name:

```
PS > $user.DirectReports
CN=SmithRobin,OU=West,OU=Sales,DC=Fabrikam,DC=COM
CN=DoeJane,OU=West,OU=Sales,DC=Fabrikam,DC=COM
```

If you are having trouble getting a property that you know exists, you can also retrieve the property using the Get() method on the container. While the userPrincipalName property can be accessed using the usual property syntax, the following example demonstrates the alternate approach:

```
PS > $user.Get("userPrincipalName")
Ken.Myer@fabrikam.com
```

Using the Active Directory module, the cmdlet to retrieve a user account is Get-ADUser. For more information on how to accomplish these tasks through the Active Directory module, see *http://go.microsoft.com/fwlink/?linkid=168142*.

26.11 Modify Properties of a User Account

Problem

You want to modify properties of a specific user account.

Solution

To modify a user account, use the [adsi] type shortcut to bind to the user in Active Directory. If the property has already been set, you can change the value of a property as you would with any other PowerShell object. If you are setting a property for the first time, use the Put() method. Finally, call the SetInfo() method to apply the changes.

```
$user =
  [adsi] "LDAP://localhost:389/cn=MyerKen,ou=West,ou=Sales,dc=Fabrikam,dc=COM"

$user.Put("Title", "Sr. Exec. Overlord")
$user.SetInfo()
```

Discussion

The solution retrieves the MyerKen user from the SalesWest OU. It then sets the user's title to Sr. Exec. Overlord and applies those changes to Active Directory.

Using the Active Directory module, the cmdlet to modify a user account is Set-ADUser. For more information on how to accomplish these tasks through the Active Directory module, see *http://go.microsoft.com/fwlink/?linkid=168142*.

26.12 Change a User Password

Problem

You want to change a user's password.

Solution

To change a user's password, use the [adsi] type shortcut to bind to the user in Active Directory, and then call the SetPassword() method:

```
$user =
  [adsi] "LDAP://localhost:389/cn=MyerKen,ou=West,ou=Sales,dc=Fabrikam,dc=COM"
$user.SetPassword("newpassword")
```

Discussion

Changing a user password in Active Directory is a relatively straightforward operation, requiring simply calling the SetPassword() method.

Unfortunately, configuring your local experimental ADAM instance to support password changes is complicated and beyond the scope of this book.

One thing to notice is that the SetPassword() method takes a plain-text password as its input. Active Directory protects this password as it sends it across the network, but storing passwords securely until needed is a security best practice. Recipe 18.8 discusses how to handle sensitive strings and also shows you how to convert one back to plain text when needed.

Using the Active Directory module, the cmdlet to change a user password is Set-ADAccountPassword. For more information on how to accomplish these tasks through the Active Directory module, see *http://go.microsoft.com/fwlink/?linkid=168142*.

See Also

Recipe 18.8, "Securely Handle Sensitive Information"

26.13 Create a Security or Distribution Group

Problem

You want to create a security or distribution group.

Solution

To create a security or distribution group, use the [adsi] type shortcut to bind to a container in Active Directory, and then call the Create() method:

```
$salesWest =
  [adsi] "LDAP://localhost:389/ou=West,ou=Sales,dc=Fabrikam,dc=COM"
$management = $salesWest.Create("Group", "CN=Management")
$management.SetInfo()
```

Discussion

The solution creates a group named Management in the Sales West OU.

When you run this script against a real Active Directory deployment (as opposed to an ADAM instance), be sure to update the sAMAccountName property, or you'll get an autogenerated default.

When you create a group in Active Directory, it is customary to also set the type of group by defining the groupType attribute on that group. To specify a group type, use the -bor operator to combine group flags, and use the resulting value as the group Type property. Example 26-3 defines the group as a global, security-enabled group.

Example 26-3. Creating an Active Directory security group with a custom groupType

```
$ADS_GROUP_TYPE_GLOBAL_GROUP = 0x00000002
$ADS_GROUP_TYPE_DOMAIN_LOCAL_GROUP = 0x00000004
$ADS_GROUP_TYPE_LOCAL_GROUP = 0x00000004
$ADS_GROUP_TYPE_UNIVERSAL_GROUP = 0x00000008
$ADS_GROUP_TYPE_SECURITY_ENABLED = 0x80000000

$salesWest =
  [adsi] "LDAP://localhost:389/ou=West,ou=Sales,dc=Fabrikam,dc=COM"

$groupType = $ADS_GROUP_TYPE_SECURITY_ENABLED -bor
    $ADS_GROUP_TYPE_GLOBAL_GROUP

$management = $salesWest.Create("Group", "CN=Management")
$management.Put("groupType", $groupType)
$management.SetInfo()
```

If you need to create groups in bulk from the data in a CSV, the Import-ADUser script given in Recipe 26.8 provides an excellent starting point. To make the script create groups instead of users, change this line:

```
$newUser = $userContainer.Create("User", "CN=$username")
```

to this:

```
$newUser = $userContainer.Create("Group", "CN=$username")
```

If you change the script to create groups in bulk, it is helpful to also change the variable names ($user, $users, $username, and $newUser) to correspond to group-related names: $group, $groups, $groupname, and $newgroup.

Using the Active Directory module, the cmdlet to create a group is New-ADGroup. For more information on how to accomplish these tasks through the Active Directory module, see *http://go.microsoft.com/fwlink/?linkid=168142*.

See Also

Recipe 26.8, "Program: Import Users in Bulk to Active Directory"

26.14 Search for a Security or Distribution Group

Problem

You want to search for a specific group, but you don't know its distinguished name (DN).

Solution

To search for a security or distribution group, use the [adsi] type shortcut to bind to a container that holds the group, and then use the [adsisearcher] type shortcut to search for the group:

```
$domain = [adsi] "LDAP://localhost:389/dc=Fabrikam,dc=COM"
$searcher = [adsisearcher] $domain
$searcher.Filter = '(&(objectClass=Group)(name=Management))'
$groupResult = $searcher.FindOne()
$group = $groupResult.GetDirectoryEntry()
$group
```

Discussion

When you don't know the full distinguished name (DN) of a group, the [adsi searcher] type shortcut lets you search for it.

You provide an LDAP filter (in this case, searching for groups with the name of Management), and then call the FindOne() method. The FindOne() method returns the first search result that matches the filter, so we retrieve its actual Active Directory entry. If you expect your query to return multiple results, use the FindAll() method instead. Although the solution searches on the group's name, you can search on any field in Active Directory—the mailNickname and sAMAccountName are two other good choices.

When you do this search, always try to restrict it to the lowest level of the domain possible. If we know that the Management group is in the Sales OU, it would be better to bind to that OU instead:

```
$domain = [adsi] "LDAP://localhost:389/ou=Sales,dc=Fabrikam,dc=COM"
```

For more information about the LDAP search filter syntax, search *http://msdn.microsoft .com* for "Search Filter Syntax".

Using the Active Directory module, the cmdlet to search for a security or distribution group is Get-ADGroup. While you can use a LDAP filter to search for a group, the Get-ADGroup cmdlet also lets you supply PowerShell expressions:

```
Get-ADGroup -Filter { Name -like "*Management*" }
```

For more information on how to accomplish these tasks through the Active Directory module, see *http://go.microsoft.com/fwlink/?linkid=168142*.

26.15 Get the Properties of a Group

Problem

You want to get and list the properties of a specific security or distribution group.

Solution

To list the properties of a group, use the [adsi] type shortcut to bind to the group in Active Directory, and then pass the group to the Format-List cmdlet:

```
$group =
  [adsi] "LDAP://localhost:389/cn=Management,ou=West,ou=Sales,dc=Fabrikam,dc=COM"

$group | Format-List *
```

Discussion

The solution retrieves the Management group from the Sales West OU. By default, the Format-List cmdlet shows only the DN of the group, so we type **Format-List** * to display all properties.

If you know the property for which you want the value, specify it by name:

```
PS > $group.Member
CN=SmithRobin,OU=West,OU=Sales,DC=Fabrikam,DC=COM
CN=MyerKen,OU=West,OU=Sales,DC=Fabrikam,DC=COM
```

If you are having trouble getting a property that you know exists, you can also retrieve the property using the Get() method on the container. While the name property can be accessed using the usual property syntax, the following example demonstrates the alternative approach:

```
PS > $group.Get("name")
Management
```

Using the Active Directory module, the cmdlet to get the properties of a group is Get-ADGroup. For more information on how to accomplish these tasks through the Active Directory module, see *http://go.microsoft.com/fwlink/?linkid=168142*.

26.16 Find the Owner of a Group

Problem

You want to get the owner of a security or distribution group.

Solution

To determine the owner of a group, use the [adsi] type shortcut to bind to the group in Active Directory, and then retrieve the ManagedBy property:

```
$group =
  [adsi] "LDAP://localhost:389/cn=Management,ou=West,ou=Sales,dc=Fabrikam,dc=COM"

$group.ManagedBy
```

Discussion

The solution retrieves the owner of the `Management` group from the `Sales West` OU. To do this, it accesses the `ManagedBy` property of that group. This property exists only when populated by the administrator of the group but is fairly reliable: Active Directory administrators consider it a best practice to create and populate this property.

Using the Active Directory module, the cmdlet to find the owner of a group is `Get-ADGroup`. This cmdlet does not retrieve the `ManagedBy` property by default, so you also need to specify `ManagedBy` as the value of the `-Property` parameter. For more information on how to accomplish these tasks through the Active Directory module, see *http://go .microsoft.com/fwlink/?linkid=168142*.

26.17 Modify Properties of a Security or Distribution Group

Problem

You want to modify properties of a specific security or distribution group.

Solution

To modify a security or distribution group, use the `[adsi]` type shortcut to bind to the group in Active Directory. If the property has already been set, you can change the value of a property as you would with any other PowerShell object. If you are setting a property for the first time, use the `Put()` method. Finally, call the `SetInfo()` method to apply the changes.

```
$group =
  [adsi] "LDAP://localhost:389/cn=Management,ou=West,ou=Sales,dc=Fabrikam,dc=COM"

PS > $group.Put("Description", "Managers in the Sales West Organization")
PS > $group.SetInfo()
PS > $group.Description
```

Discussion

The solution retrieves the `Management` group from the `Sales West` OU. It then sets the description to `Managers in the Sales West Organization`, and then applies those changes to Active Directory.

Using the Active Directory module, the cmdlet to modify the properties of a security or distribution group is `Set-ADGroup`. For more information on how to accomplish these tasks through the Active Directory module, see *http://go.microsoft.com/fwlink/?linkid= 168142*.

26.18 Add a User to a Security or Distribution Group

Problem

You want to add a user to a security or distribution group.

Solution

To add a user to a security or distribution group, use the [adsi] type shortcut to bind to the group in Active Directory, and then call the Add() method:

```
$management =
  [adsi] "LDAP://localhost:389/cn=Management,ou=West,ou=Sales,dc=Fabrikam,dc=COM"

$user = "LDAP://localhost:389/cn=MyerKen,ou=West,ou=Sales,dc=Fabrikam,dc=COM"
$management.Add($user)
```

Discussion

The solution adds the MyerKen user to a group named Management in the SalesWest OU. To check whether you have added the user successfully, see Recipe 26.20.

Using the Active Directory module, the cmdlet to add a user to a security or distribution group is Add-ADGroupMember. For more information on how to accomplish these tasks through the Active Directory module, see *http://go.microsoft.com/fwlink/?linkid= 168142*.

See Also

Recipe 26.20, "List a User's Group Membership"

26.19 Remove a User from a Security or Distribution Group

Problem

You want to remove a user from a security or distribution group.

Solution

To remove a user from a security or distribution group, use the [adsi] type shortcut to bind to the group in Active Directory, and then call the Remove() method:

```
$management =
  [adsi] "LDAP://localhost:389/cn=Management,ou=West,ou=Sales,dc=Fabrikam,dc=COM"

$user = "LDAP://localhost:389/cn=MyerKen,ou=West,ou=Sales,dc=Fabrikam,dc=COM"
$management.Remove($user)
```

Discussion

The solution removes the MyerKen user from a group named Management in the Sales West OU. To check whether you have removed the user successfully, see Recipe 26.20.

Using the Active Directory module, the cmdlet to remove a user from a security or distribution group is Remove-ADGroupMember. For more information on how to accomplish these tasks through the Active Directory module, see *http://go.microsoft.com/ fwlink/?linkid=168142*.

See Also

Recipe 26.20, "List a User's Group Membership"

26.20 List a User's Group Membership

Problem

You want to list the groups to which a user belongs.

Solution

To list a user's group membership, use the [adsi] type shortcut to bind to the user in Active Directory, and then access the MemberOf property:

```
$user =
  [adsi] "LDAP://localhost:389/cn=MyerKen,ou=West,ou=Sales,dc=Fabrikam,dc=COM"
$user.MemberOf
```

Discussion

The solution lists all groups in which the MyerKen user is a member. Since Active Directory stores this information as a user property, this is simply a specific case of retrieving information about the user. For more information about retrieving information about a user, see Recipe 26.10.

Using the Active Directory module, the cmdlet to retrieve a user's group membership is Get-ADUser. This cmdlet does not retrieve the MemberOf property by default, so you also need to specify MemberOf as the value of the -Property parameter. For more information on how to accomplish these tasks through the Active Directory module, see *http://go.microsoft.com/fwlink/?linkid=168142*.

See Also

Recipe 26.10, "Get and List the Properties of a User Account"

26.21 List the Members of a Group

Problem

You want to list all the members in a group.

Solution

To list the members of a group, use the [adsi] type shortcut to bind to the group in Active Directory, and then access the Member property:

```
$group =
  [adsi] "LDAP://localhost:389/cn=Management,ou=West,ou=Sales,dc=Fabrikam,dc=COM"
$group.Member
```

Discussion

The solution lists all members of the Management group in the Sales West OU. Since Active Directory stores this information as a property of the group, this is simply a specific case of retrieving information about the group. For more information about retrieving information about a group, see Recipe 26.15.

Using the Active Directory module, the cmdlet to list the members of a security or distribution group is Get-ADGroupMember. For more information on how to accomplish these tasks through the Active Directory module, see *http://go.microsoft.com/fwlink/ ?linkid=168142*.

See Also

Recipe 26.15, "Get the Properties of a Group"

26.22 List the Users in an Organizational Unit

Problem

You want to list all the users in an OU.

Solution

To list the users in an OU, use the [adsi] type shortcut to bind to the OU in Active Directory. Use the [adsisearcher] type shortcut to create a searcher for that OU, and then set its Filter property to (objectClass=User). Finally, call the searcher's FindAll() method to perform the search.

```
$sales =
  [adsi] "LDAP://localhost:389/ou=Sales,dc=Fabrikam,dc=COM"

$searcher = [adsisearcher] $sales
```

```
$searcher.Filter = '(objectClass=User)'
$searcher.FindAll()
```

Discussion

The solution lists all users in the Sales OU. It does this through the [adsisearcher] type shortcut, which lets you search and query Active Directory. The Filter property specifies an LDAP filter string.

 By default, an [adsisearcher] searches the given container and all containers below it. Set the SearchScope property to change this behavior. A value of Base searches only the current container, whereas a value of OneLevel searches only the immediate children.

For more information about working with classes from the .NET Framework, see Recipe 3.8.

Using the Active Directory module, the cmdlet to list the users in an organizational unit is Get-ADUser. To restrict the results to a specific organizational unit, specify that organizational unit as the -SearchBase parameter. Alternatively, navigate to that path in the Active Directory provider, and then call the Get-ADUser cmdlet. For more information on how to accomplish these tasks through the Active Directory module, see *http://go.microsoft.com/fwlink/?linkid=168142*.

See Also

Recipe 3.8, "Work with .NET Objects"

26.23 Search for a Computer Account

Problem

You want to search for a specific computer account, but you don't know its distinguished name (DN).

Solution

To search for a computer account, use the [adsi] type shortcut to bind to a container that holds the account, and then use the [adsisearcher] type shortcut to search for the account:

```
$domain = [adsi] "LDAP://localhost:389/dc=Fabrikam,dc=COM"
$searcher = [adsisearcher] $domain
$searcher.Filter = '(&(objectClass=Computer)(name=kenmyer_laptop))'
$computerResult = $searcher.FindOne()
$computer = $computerResult.GetDirectoryEntry()
```

Discussion

When you don't know the full distinguished name (DN) of a computer account, the [adsisearcher] type shortcut lets you search for it.

 This recipe requires a full Active Directory instance, as neither ADAM nor AD LDS supports computer objects.

You provide an LDAP filter (in this case, searching for computers with the name of kenmyer_laptop), and then call the FindOne() method. The FindOne() method returns the first search result that matches the filter, so we retrieve its actual Active Directory entry. If you expect your query to return multiple results, use the FindAll() method instead. Although the solution searches on the computer's name, you can search on any field in Active Directory. The sAMAccountName and operating system characteristics (operatingSystem, operatingSystemVersion, operatingSystemServicePack) are other good choices.

When you do this search, always try to restrict it to the lowest level of the domain possible. If you know that the computer is in the Sales OU, it would be better to bind to that OU instead:

```
$domain = [adsi] "LDAP://localhost:389/ou=Sales,dc=Fabrikam,dc=COM"
```

For more information about the LDAP search filter syntax, search *http://msdn.microsoft .com* for "Search Filter Syntax".

Using the Active Directory module, the cmdlet to search for a computer account is Get-ADComputer. While you can use a LDAP filter to search for computer, the Get-ADComputer cmdlet also lets you supply PowerShell expressions:

```
Get-ADComputer -Filter { Name -like "*kenmyer*" }
```

For more information on how to accomplish these tasks through the Active Directory module, see *http://go.microsoft.com/fwlink/?linkid=168142*.

26.24 Get and List the Properties of a Computer Account

Problem

You want to get and list the properties of a specific computer account.

Solution

To list the properties of a computer account, use the [adsi] type shortcut to bind to the computer in Active Directory and then pass the computer to the Format-List cmdlet:

```
$computer =
  [adsi] "LDAP://localhost:389/cn=kenmyer_laptop,ou=West,ou=Sales,dc=Fabrikam,dc=COM"

$computer | Format-List *
```

Discussion

The solution retrieves the kenmyer_laptop computer from the Sales West OU. By default, the Format-List cmdlet shows only the distinguished name of the computer, so we type **Format-List** * to display all properties.

This recipe requires a full Active Directory instance, as neither ADAM nor AD LDS supports computer objects.

If you know the property for which you want the value, specify it by name:

```
PS > $computer.OperatingSystem
Windows Server 2003
```

If you are having trouble getting a property that you know exists, you can also retrieve the property using the Get() method on the container. While the operatingSystem property can be accessed using the usual property syntax, the following example demonstrates the alternative approach:

```
PS > $computer.Get("operatingSystem")
Windows Server 2003
```

Using the Active Directory module, the cmdlet to list the properties of a computer account is Get-ADComputer. For more information on how to accomplish these tasks through the Active Directory module, see *http://go.microsoft.com/fwlink/?linkid=168142*.

Enterprise Computer Management

27.0 Introduction

When working with Windows systems across an enterprise, this question often arises: "How do I do <some task> in PowerShell?" In an administrator's perfect world, anybody who designs a feature with management implications also supports (via PowerShell cmdlets) the tasks that manage that feature. Many management tasks have been around longer than PowerShell, though, so the answer can sometimes be, "The same way you did it before PowerShell."

That's not to say that your life as an administrator doesn't improve with the introduction of PowerShell, however. Pre-PowerShell administration tasks generally fall into one of several models: command-line utilities, Windows Management Instrumentation (WMI) interaction, registry manipulation, file manipulation, interaction with COM objects, or interaction with .NET objects.

PowerShell makes it easier to interact with all these task models, and therefore makes it easier to manage functionality that depends on them.

27.1 Join a Computer to a Domain or Workgroup

Problem

You want to join a computer to a domain or workgroup.

Solution

Use the -DomainName parameter of the Add-Computer cmdlet to add a computer to a domain. Use the -WorkGroupName parameter to add it to a workgroup.

```
PS > Add-Computer -DomainName MyDomain -Credential MyDomain\MyUser
PS > Restart-Computer
```

Discussion

The `Add-Computer` cmdlet's name is fairly self-descriptive: it lets you add a computer to a domain or workgroup. Since a domain join only takes effect once you restart the computer, always call the `Restart-Computer` cmdlet after joining a domain.

Perhaps the most complex parameter of the `Add-Computer` cmdlet is the `-Unsecure` parameter. When you add a computer to a domain, a machine account is normally created with a unique password. An unsecure join (as enabled by the `-Unsecure` parameter) instead uses a default password: the first 14 characters of the computer name, all in lowercase. Once the domain join is complete, the system automatically changes the password. This parameter is primarily intended for unattended installations.

To remove a computer from a domain, see Recipe 27.2.

See Also

Recipe 27.2, "Remove a Computer from a Domain"

27.2 Remove a Computer from a Domain

Problem

You want to remove a computer from a domain.

Solution

Use the `Remove-Computer` cmdlet to depart a domain.

```
PS > Remove-Computer
PS > Restart-Computer
```

Discussion

The `Remove-Computer` lets you remove the current computer from a domain. Once you do so, it reverts back to its default workgroup. Since domain changes only take effect once you restart the computer, always call the `Restart-Computer` cmdlet after departing a domain.

Once you remove a computer from a domain, you can no longer use domain credentials to manage that computer. Before departing a domain, make sure that you know (or create) a local administrator's account for that machine.

To rejoin a domain, see Recipe 27.1.

See Also

Recipe 27.1, "Join a Computer to a Domain or Workgroup"

27.3 Program: List Logon or Logoff Scripts for a User

The Group Policy system in Windows stores logon and logoff scripts under the two registry keys *HKLM:\SOFTWARE\Microsoft\Windows\CurrentVersion\Group Policy \State\<User SID>\Scripts\Logon* and *HKLM:\SOFTWARE\Microsoft\Windows \CurrentVersion\Group Policy\State\<User SID>\Scripts\Logoff*. Each key has a subkey for each group policy object that applies. Each of those child keys has another level of keys that correspond to individual scripts that apply to the user.

This can be difficult to investigate when you don't know the SID of the user in question, so Example 27-1 automates the mapping of username to SID, as well as all the registry manipulation tasks required to access this information.

Example 27-1. Get-UserLogonLogoffScript.ps1

```
##############################################################################
##
## Get-UserLogonLogoffScript
##
## From Windows PowerShell Cookbook (O'Reilly)
## by Lee Holmes (http://www.leeholmes.com/guide)
##
##############################################################################

<#

.SYNOPSIS

Get the logon or logoff scripts assigned to a specific user

.EXAMPLE

Get-UserLogonLogoffScript LEE-DESK\LEE Logon
Gets all logon scripts for the user 'LEE-DESK\Lee'

#>

param(
    ## The username to examine
    [Parameter(Mandatory = $true)]
    $Username,

    [Parameter(Mandatory = $true)]
    [ValidateSet("Logon","Logoff")]
    $ScriptType
)

Set-StrictMode -Version Latest

## Find the SID for the username
$account = New-Object System.Security.Principal.NTAccount $username
$sid =
    $account.Translate([System.Security.Principal.SecurityIdentifier]).Value
```

```
## Map that to their group policy scripts
$registryKey = "HKLM:\SOFTWARE\Microsoft\Windows\CurrentVersion\" +
    "Group Policy\State\$sid\Scripts"

if(-not (Test-Path $registryKey))
{
    return
}

## Go through each of the policies in the specified key
foreach($policy in Get-ChildItem $registryKey\$scriptType)
{
    ## For each of the scripts in that policy, get its script name
    ## and parameters
    foreach($script in Get-ChildItem $policy.PsPath)
    {
        Get-ItemProperty $script.PsPath | Select Script,Parameters
    }
}
```

For more information about working with the Windows Registry in PowerShell, see Chapter 21. For more information about running scripts, see Recipe 1.1.

See Also

Recipe 1.1, "Run Programs, Scripts, and Existing Tools"

Chapter 21, *The Windows Registry*

27.4 Program: List Startup or Shutdown Scripts for a Machine

The Group Policy system in Windows stores startup and shutdown scripts under the registry keys *HKLM:\SOFTWARE\Policies\Microsoft\Windows\System\Scripts\Startup* and *HKLM:\SOFTWARE\Policies\Microsoft\Windows\System\Scripts\Shutdown*. Each key has a subkey for each group policy object that applies. Each of those child keys has another level of keys that correspond to individual scripts that apply to the machine.

Example 27-2 allows you to easily retrieve and access the startup and shutdown scripts for a machine.

Example 27-2. Get-MachineStartupShutdownScript.ps1

```
##############################################################################
##
## Get-MachineStartupShutdownScript
##
## From Windows PowerShell Cookbook (O'Reilly)
## by Lee Holmes (http://www.leeholmes.com/guide)
##
##############################################################################
```

```
<#

.SYNOPSIS

Get the startup or shutdown scripts assigned to a machine

.EXAMPLE

Get-MachineStartupShutdownScript -ScriptType Startup
Gets startup scripts for the machine

#>

param(
    ## The type of script to search for: Startup or Shutdown.
    [Parameter(Mandatory = $true)]
    [ValidateSet("Startup","Shutdown")]
    $ScriptType
)

Set-StrictMode -Version Latest

## Store the location of the group policy scripts for the machine
$registryKey = "HKLM:\SOFTWARE\Policies\Microsoft\Windows\System\Scripts"

## There may be no scripts defined
if(-not (Test-Path $registryKey))
{
    return
}

## Go through each of the policies in the specified key
foreach($policy in Get-ChildItem $registryKey\$scriptType)
{
    ## For each of the scripts in that policy, get its script name
    ## and parameters
    foreach($script in Get-ChildItem $policy.PsPath)
    {
        Get-ItemProperty $script.PsPath | Select Script,Parameters
    }
}
```

For more information about working with the Windows Registry in PowerShell, see Chapter 21. For more information about running scripts, see Recipe 1.1.

See Also

Recipe 1.1, "Run Programs, Scripts, and Existing Tools"

Chapter 21, *The Windows Registry*

27.5 Deploy PowerShell-Based Logon Scripts

Problem

You want to use a PowerShell script in a logon, logoff, startup, or shutdown script.

Solution

In Windows 7 (and Windows Server 2008 R2), simply add a new script in the Power-Shell Scripts tab.

For other operating systems, open the Scripts tab, and click "Add a Script." Use `power shell.exe` as the script name, and the following as its parameters:

```
-NoProfile -NonInteractive -ExecutionPolicy ByPass -File "script" arguments
```

Discussion

Before PowerShell version two, launching a PowerShell script as a Group Policy script was a difficult task. Although you could use the `-Command` parameter of *powershell.exe* to invoke a command, the quoting rules made it difficult to specify the script correctly. After getting the quoting rules correct, you still had to contend with the Execution Policy of the client computer.

While PowerShell version two was under development, the situation improved significantly. First of all, Group Policy now supports PowerShell scripts as first-class citizens for the four different user and computer scripts.

When Group Policy's native support is not an option, *PowerShell.exe* includes two new parameters that make it easier to control the execution environment: `-ExecutionPolicy` and `-File`. For more information about these (and PowerShell's other) parameters, see Recipe 1.12.

See Also

Recipe 1.12, "Invoke a PowerShell Command or Script from Outside PowerShell"

27.6 Enable or Disable the Windows Firewall

Problem

You want to enable or disable the Windows Firewall.

Solution

To manage the Windows Firewall, use the `LocalPolicy.CurrentProfile.FirewallEna bled` property of the `HNetCfg.FwMgr` COM object:

```
PS > $firewall = New-Object -com HNetCfg.FwMgr
PS > $firewall.LocalPolicy.CurrentProfile.FirewallEnabled = $true
PS > $firewall.LocalPolicy.CurrentProfile.FirewallEnabled
True
```

Discussion

The `HNetCfg.FwMgr` COM object provides programmatic access to the Windows Firewall in Windows XP SP2 and later. The `LocalPolicy.CurrentProfile` property provides the majority of its functionality.

For more information about managing the Windows Firewall through its COM API, visit *http://msdn.microsoft.com* and search for "Using Windows Firewall API." The documentation provides examples in VBScript but gives a useful overview of the functionality available.

If you are unfamiliar with the VBScript-specific portions of the documentation, the Microsoft Script Center provides a useful guide to help you convert from VBScript to PowerShell. You can find that document at *http://www.microsoft.com/technet/scriptcenter/topics/winpsh/convert/default.mspx*.

For more information about working with COM objects in PowerShell, see Recipe 17.1.

See Also

Recipe 17.1, "Automate Programs Using COM Scripting Interfaces"

27.7 Open or Close Ports in the Windows Firewall

Problem

You want to open or close ports in the Windows Firewall.

Solution

To open or close ports in the Windows Firewall, use the `LocalPolicy.CurrentProfile.GloballyOpenPorts` collection of the `HNetCfg.FwMgr` COM object.

To open a port, create a `HNetCfg.FWOpenPort` COM object to represent the port, and then add it to the `GloballyOpenPorts` collection:

```
$PROTOCOL_TCP = 6
$firewall = New-Object -com HNetCfg.FwMgr
$port = New-Object -com HNetCfg.FWOpenPort
```

```
$port.Name = "Webserver at 8080"
$port.Port = 8080
$port.Protocol = $PROTOCOL_TCP

$firewall.LocalPolicy.CurrentProfile.GloballyOpenPorts.Add($port)
```

To close a port, remove it from the `GloballyOpenPorts` collection:

```
$PROTOCOL_TCP = 6
$firewall.LocalPolicy.CurrentProfile.GloballyOpenPorts.Remove(8080, $PROTOCOL_TCP)
```

Discussion

The `HNetCfg.FwMgr` COM object provides programmatic access to the Windows Firewall in Windows XP SP2 and later. The `LocalPolicy.CurrentProfile` property provides the majority of its functionality.

For more information about managing the Windows Firewall through its COM API, visit *http://msdn.microsoft.com* and search for "Using Windows Firewall API." The documentation provides examples in VBScript but gives a useful overview of the functionality available.

If you are unfamiliar with the VBScript-specific portions of the documentation, the Microsoft Script Center provides a useful guide to help you convert from VBScript to PowerShell. You can find that document at *http://www.microsoft.com/technet/scriptcenter/topics/winpsh/convert/default.mspx*.

For more information about working with COM objects in PowerShell, see Recipe 17.1.

See Also

Recipe 17.1, "Automate Programs Using COM Scripting Interfaces"

27.8 Program: List All Installed Software

The best place to find information about currently installed software is actually from the place that stores information about how to uninstall it: the *HKLM:\SOFTWARE\Microsoft\Windows\CurrentVersion\Uninstall* registry key.

Each child of that registry key represents a piece of software you can uninstall—traditionally through the Add/Remove Programs entry in the Control Panel. In addition to the `DisplayName` of the application, other useful properties usually exist (depending on the application). Examples include `Publisher`, `UninstallString`, and `HelpLink`.

To see all the properties available from software installed on your system, type the following:

```
$properties = Get-InstalledSoftware |
    Foreach-Object { $_.PsObject.Properties }

$properties | Select-Object Name | Sort-Object -Unique Name
```

This lists all properties mentioned by at least one installed application (although very few are shared by all installed applications).

To work with this data, though, you first need to retrieve it. Example 27-3 provides a script to list all installed software on the current system, returning all information as properties of PowerShell objects.

Example 27-3. Get-InstalledSoftware.ps1

```
##############################################################################
##
## Get-InstalledSoftware
##
## From Windows PowerShell Cookbook (O'Reilly)
## by Lee Holmes (http://www.leeholmes.com/guide)
##
##############################################################################

<#

.SYNOPSIS

Lists installed software on the current computer.

.EXAMPLE

Get-InstalledSoftware *Frame* | Select DisplayName

DisplayName
-----------
Microsoft .NET Framework 3.5 SP1
Microsoft .NET Framework 3.5 SP1
Hotfix for Microsoft .NET Framework 3.5 SP1 (KB953595)
Hotfix for Microsoft .NET Framework 3.5 SP1 (KB958484)
Update for Microsoft .NET Framework 3.5 SP1 (KB963707)

#>

param(
    ## The name of the software to search for
    $DisplayName = "*"
)

Set-StrictMode -Off

## Get all the listed software in the Uninstall key
$keys =
    Get-ChildItem HKLM:\SOFTWARE\Microsoft\Windows\CurrentVersion\Uninstall

## Get all of the properties from those items
$items = $keys | Foreach-Object { Get-ItemProperty $_.PsPath }

## For each of those items, display the DisplayName and Publisher
foreach($item in $items)
{
```

```
        if(($item.DisplayName) -and ($item.DisplayName -like $displayName))
        {
            $item
        }
    }
}
```

For more information about working with the Windows Registry in PowerShell, see Chapter 21. For more information about running scripts, see Recipe 1.1.

See Also

Recipe 1.1, "Run Programs, Scripts, and Existing Tools"

Chapter 21, *The Windows Registry*

27.9 Uninstall an Application

Problem

You want to uninstall a specific software application.

Solution

To uninstall an application, use the `Get-InstalledSoftware` script provided in Recipe 27.8 to retrieve the command that uninstalls the software. Since the `Uninstall String` uses batch file syntax, use *cmd.exe* to launch the uninstaller:

```
PS > $software = Get-InstalledSoftware UnwantedProgram
PS > cmd /c $software.UninstallString
```

Alternatively, use the `Win32_Product` WMI class for an unattended installation:

```
$application = Get-WmiObject Win32_Product -filter "Name='UnwantedProgram'"
$application.Uninstall()
```

Discussion

The `UninstallString` provided by applications starts the interactive experience you would see if you were to uninstall the application through the Add/Remove Programs entry in the Control Panel. If you need to remove the software in an unattended manner, you have two options: use the "quiet mode" of the application's uninstaller (for example, the /quiet switch to *msiexec.exe*) or use the software removal functionality of the `Win32_Product` WMI class as demonstrated in the solution.

For more information about working with WMI in PowerShell, see Recipe 28.1.

See Also

Recipe 27.8, "Program: List All Installed Software"

Recipe 28.1, "Access Windows Management Instrumentation Data"

27.10 Manage Computer Restore Points

Problem

You want to create a computer restore point, restore a computer to a previous restore point, or manage the schedule for automatic restore points.

Solution

Use the `Enable-ComputerRestore` and `Disable-ComputerRestore` cmdlets to enable and disable automatic computer checkpoints. Use the `Get-ComputerRestorePoint` and `Restore-Computer` cmdlets to list all restore points and to restore a computer to one of them, respectively. Use the `Checkpoint-Computer` cmdlet to create a new system restore point.

```
PS > Get-ComputerRestorePoint |
    Select Description,SequenceNumber,RestorePointType |
    Format-Table -Auto


Description          SequenceNumber RestorePointType
-----------          -------------- ----------------
Windows Update                  122                0
Windows Update                  123                0
Scheduled Checkpoint            124                7
Scheduled Checkpoint            125                7
Windows Update                  126                0
Scheduled Checkpoint            127                7
Scheduled Checkpoint            128                7
Windows Update                  129                0
Scheduled Checkpoint            130                7
Windows Update                  131                0
Scheduled Checkpoint            132                7
Windows Update                  133                0
Manual Checkpoint               134                0
Before driver updates           135                0


PS > Checkpoint-Computer "Before driver updates"
```

Discussion

The computer restore point cmdlets give you an easy way to manage Windows' system restore points. You can use the `Checkpoint-Computer` to create a new restore point before a potentially disruptive installation or system change. Figure 27-1 shows the `Checkpoint-Computer` cmdlet in progress. If you need to restore the computer to a previous state, you can use the `Get-ComputerRestorePoint` cmdlet to list existing restore points, and then use the `Restore-Computer` cmdlet to restore the computer to its previously saved state.

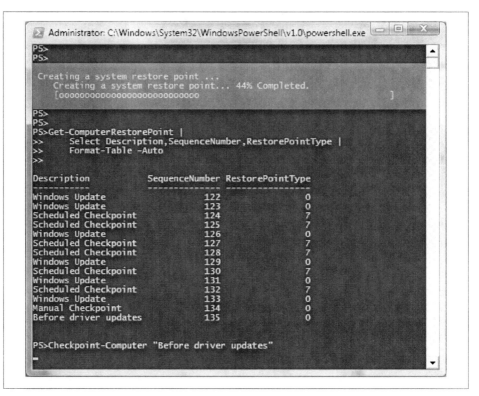

Figure 27-1. Managing computer restore points

System restore points are finely tuned toward managing the state of the operating system, and are not designed to protect user data. System restore points primarily protect the Windows Registry, core operating system files, local user profiles, and COM and WMI registration databases.

To conserve disk space, Windows limits the amount of space consumed by restore points, and removes the oldest restore points as needed. If you plan to create manual checkpoints more frequently than the ones automatically scheduled by Windows, consider increasing the amount of space dedicated to system restore points. If you don't, you run the risk of being unable to recover from system errors that took you a long time to detect.

By default, Windows schedules automatic restore points for your main system volume. To enable or disable these automatic checkpoints for this (or any) volume, use the Enable-ComputerRestore and Disable-ComputerRestore cmdlets.

On Windows 7, the Control Panel lets you configure how much space Windows reserves for restore points. To do this, open the System group in the Control Panel, and then open System Protection. On Windows Vista, use the *vssadmin.exe* tool to manage this policy.

27.11 Reboot or Shut Down a Computer

Problem

You want to restart or shut down a local or remote computer.

Solution

Use the `Restart-Computer` cmdlet to restart a computer:

```
PS > Restart-Computer -ComputerName Computer
```

Use the Stop-Computer cmdlet to shut it down entirely:

```
PS > Stop-Computer -ComputerName Computer
```

If you want to perform the same action on many computers, use the cmdlet's throttling support:

```
PS > $computers = Get-Content computers.txt
PS > Restart-Computer -ComputerName $computers -ThrottleLimit
```

Discussion

Both the `Restart-Computer` and `Stop-Computer` cmdlets let you manage the reboot and shutdown process of a local or remote computer. Since they build on PowerShell's WMI support, they also offer the `-ThrottleLimit` parameter to let you control how many machines should be controlled at a time.

By default, these cmdlets reject a restart or a shutdown if a user is logged on to the computer. To restart the computer anyway, use the `-Force` parameter to override this behavior.

> While restarting a computer, you might sometimes want to have the computer take some action after it comes back online. To do this, create a new scheduled task (using the *schtasks.exe* application) with `ONSTART` as the value of its schedule (`/SC`) parameter. For more information, see Recipe 27.13.

Rather than shut down or restart a computer, you might instead want to suspend or hibernate it. While neither the `Restart-Computer` nor `Stop-Computer` cmdlets support this, you can use the `System.Windows.Forms.Application` class from the .NET Framework to do so:

```
Add-Type -Assembly System.Windows.Forms
[System.Windows.Forms.Application]::SetSuspendState("Suspend", $false, $false)

Add-Type -Assembly System.Windows.Forms
[System.Windows.Forms.Application]::SetSuspendState("Hibernate", $false, $false)
```

This technique does not let you suspend or hibernate remote computers, but you can use PowerShell Remoting to invoke those commands on remote systems.

For more information about PowerShell Remoting, see Chapter 29.

See Also

Recipe 27.13, "Manage Scheduled Tasks on a Computer"

Chapter 29, *Remoting*

27.12 Determine Whether a Hotfix Is Installed

Problem

You want to determine whether a specific hotfix is installed on a system.

Solution

To retrieve a list of hotfixes applied to the system, use the Get-Hotfix cmdlet:

```
PS > Get-HotFix KB968930 | Format-List


Description          : Windows Management Framework Core
FixComments          : Update
HotFixID             : KB968930
InstallDate          :
InstalledBy          : XPMUser
InstalledOn          :
Name                 :
ServicePackInEffect  : SP10
Status               :
```

To search by description, use the -Description parameter:

```
PS > Get-HotFix -Description *Framework* | Format-List


Description          : Windows Management Framework Core
FixComments          : Update
HotFixID             : KB968930
InstallDate          :
InstalledBy          : XPMUser
InstalledOn          :
Name                 :
ServicePackInEffect  : SP10
Status               :
```

Discussion

The Get-Hotfix cmdlet lets you determine whether a hotfix is installed on a specific system. By default, it retrieves hotfixes from the local system, but you can use the -ComputerName parameter to retrieve hotfix information from a remote system.

27.13 Manage Scheduled Tasks on a Computer

Problem

You want to schedule a task on a computer.

Solution

To manage scheduled tasks, use the *schtasks.exe* application.

To view the list of scheduled tasks:

```
PS > schtasks

TaskName                             Next Run Time            Status
==================================== ======================== =============
Defrag C                             03:00:00, 5/21/2007
User_Feed_Synchronization-{CA4D6D9C- 18:34:00, 5/20/2007
User_Feed_Synchronization-{CA4D6D9C- 18:34:00, 5/20/2007
```

To schedule a task to defragment *C:* every day at 3:00 a.m.:

```
schtasks /create /tn "Defrag C" /sc DAILY `
    /st 03:00:00 /tr "defrag c:" /ru Administrator
```

To remove a scheduled task by name:

```
schtasks /delete /tn "Defrag C"
```

Discussion

The example in the solution tells the system to defragment *C:* every day at 3:00 a.m. It runs this command under the Administrator account, since the *defrag.exe* command requires administrative privileges. In addition to scheduling tasks on the local computer, the *schtasks.exe* application also allows you to schedule tasks on remote computers.

On Windows Vista, the *schtasks.exe* application has been enhanced to support event triggers, conditions, and additional settings.

Although the *schtasks.exe* application doesn't support PowerShell scripts directly, you can always use PowerShell's command-line parameters to launch a script of your choice. For example:

```
powershell -noprofile -noexit -windowstyle hidden
    -file e:\lee\tools\Start-Scheduler.ps1
```

For more information about automating PowerShell from other applications, see Recipe 1.12.

For more information about the *schtasks.exe* application, type **schtasks /?**.

See Also

Recipe 1.12, "Invoke a PowerShell Command or Script from Outside PowerShell"

27.14 Retrieve Printer Information

Problem

You want to get information about printers on the current system.

Solution

To retrieve information about printers attached to the system, use the Win32_Printer WMI class:

```
PS > Get-WmiObject Win32_Printer | Select-Object Name,PrinterStatus

Name                                              PrinterStatus
----                                              -------------
Microsoft Office Document Image Wr...                         3
Microsoft Office Document Image Wr...                         3
CutePDF Writer                                               3
Brother DCP-1000                                             3
```

To retrieve information about a specific printer, apply a filter based on its name:

```
PS > $device = Get-WmiObject Win32_Printer -Filter "Name='Brother DCP-1000'"
PS > $device | Format-List *
Status                 : Unknown
Name                   : Brother DCP-1000
Attributes             : 588
Availability           :
AvailableJobSheets     :
AveragePagesPerMinute  : 0
Capabilities           : {4, 2, 5}
CapabilityDescriptions : {Copies, Color, Collate}
Caption                : Brother DCP-1000
(...)
```

To retrieve specific properties, access them as you would access properties on other PowerShell objects:

```
PS > $device.VerticalResolution
600
PS > $device.HorizontalResolution
600
```

Discussion

The example in the solution uses the `Win32_Printer` WMI class to retrieve information about installed printers on the computer. While the `Win32_Printer` class gives access to the most commonly used information, WMI supports several additional printer-related classes: `Win32_TCPIPPrinterPort`, `Win32_PrinterDriver`, `CIM_Printer`, `Win32_PrinterConfiguration`, `Win32_PrinterSetting`, `Win32_PrinterController`, `Win32_PrinterShare`, and `Win32_PrinterDriverDll`. For more information about working with WMI in PowerShell, see Recipe 28.1.

See Also

Recipe 28.1, "Access Windows Management Instrumentation Data"

27.15 Retrieve Printer Queue Statistics

Problem

You want to get information about print queues for printers on the current system.

Solution

To retrieve information about printers attached to the system, use the `Win32_PerfFormattedData_Spooler_PrintQueue` WMI class:

```
PS > Get-WmiObject Win32_PerfFormattedData_Spooler_PrintQueue |
Select Name,TotalJobsPrinted


Name                                         TotalJobsPrinted
----                                         ----------------
Microsoft Office Document Image Wr...                       0
Microsoft Office Document Image Wr...                       0
CutePDF Writer                                             0
Brother DCP-1000                                           2
_Total                                                     2
```

To retrieve information about a specific printer, apply a filter based on its name, as shown in Example 27-4.

Example 27-4. Retrieving information about a specific printer

```
PS > $queueClass = "Win32_PerfFormattedData_Spooler_PrintQueue"
PS > $filter = "Name='Brother DCP-1000'"
PS > $stats = Get-WmiObject $queueClass -Filter $filter
PS > $stats | Format-List *

AddNetworkPrinterCalls    : 129
BytesPrintedPersec        : 0
Caption                   :
Description               :
```

```
EnumerateNetworkPrinterCalls : 0
Frequency_Object             :
Frequency_PerfTime           :
Frequency_Sys100NS           :
JobErrors                    : 0
Jobs                         : 0
JobsSpooling                 : 0
MaxJobsSpooling              : 1
MaxReferences                : 3
Name                         : Brother DCP-1000
NotReadyErrors               : 0
OutofPaperErrors             : 0
References                   : 2
Timestamp_Object             :
Timestamp_PerfTime           :
Timestamp_Sys100NS           :
TotalJobsPrinted             : 2
TotalPagesPrinted            : 0
```

To retrieve specific properties, access them as you would access properties on other PowerShell objects:

```
PS > $stats.TotalJobsPrinted
2
```

Discussion

The `Win32_PerfFormattedData_Spooler_PrintQueue` WMI class provides access to the various Windows performance counters associated with print queues. Because of this, you can also access them through the .NET Framework, as mentioned in Recipe 17.3:

```
PS > Get-Counter "\Print Queue($printer)\Jobs" | Select -Expand CounterSamples |
    Select InstanceName,CookedValue | Format-Table -Auto


InstanceName         CookedValue
------------         -----------
brother dcp-1000 usb           1
```

For more information about working with WMI in PowerShell, see Recipe 28.1.

See Also

Recipe 17.3, "Access Windows Performance Counters"

Recipe 28.1, "Access Windows Management Instrumentation Data"

27.16 Manage Printers and Print Queues

Problem

You want to clear pending print jobs from a printer.

Solution

To manage printers attached to the system, use the `Win32_Printer` WMI class. By default, the WMI class lists all printers:

```
PS > Get-WmiObject Win32_Printer | Select-Object Name,PrinterStatus

Name                                              PrinterStatus
----                                              -------------
Microsoft Office Document Image Wr...                         3
Microsoft Office Document Image Wr...                         3
CutePDF Writer                                               3
Brother DCP-1000                                             3
```

To clear the print queue of a specific printer, apply a filter based on its name and call the `CancelAllJobs()` method:

```
PS > $device = Get-WmiObject Win32_Printer -Filter "Name='Brother DCP-1000'"
PS > $device.CancelAllJobs()


__GENUS          : 2
__CLASS          : __PARAMETERS
__SUPERCLASS     :
__DYNASTY        : __PARAMETERS
__RELPATH        :
__PROPERTY_COUNT : 1
__DERIVATION     : {}
__SERVER         :
__NAMESPACE      :
__PATH           :
ReturnValue      : 5
```

Discussion

The example in the solution uses the `Win32_Printer` WMI class to cancel all jobs for a printer. In addition to cancelling all print jobs, the `Win32_Printer` class supports other tasks:

```
PS > $device | Get-Member -MemberType Method


   TypeName: System.Management.ManagementObject#root\cimv2\Win32_Printer

Name              MemberType Definition
----              ---------- ----------
CancelAllJobs     Method     System.Management.ManagementBaseObject Can...
Pause             Method     System.Management.ManagementBaseObject Pau...
PrintTestPage     Method     System.Management.ManagementBaseObject Pri...
RenamePrinter     Method     System.Management.ManagementBaseObject Ren...
Reset             Method     System.Management.ManagementBaseObject Res...
Resume            Method     System.Management.ManagementBaseObject Res...
SetDefaultPrinter Method     System.Management.ManagementBaseObject Set...
SetPowerState     Method     System.Management.ManagementBaseObject Set...
```

For more information about working with WMI in PowerShell, see Recipe 28.1.

See Also

Recipe 28.1, "Access Windows Management Instrumentation Data"

27.17 Program: Summarize System Information

WMI provides an immense amount of information about the current system or remote systems. In fact, the *msinfo32.exe* application traditionally used to gather system information is based largely on WMI.

The script shown in Example 27-5 summarizes the most common information, but WMI provides a great deal more than that. For a list of other commonly used WMI classes, see Appendix G. For more information about working with WMI in Power-Shell, see Recipe 28.1.

Example 27-5. Get-DetailedSystemInformation.ps1

```
##############################################################################
##
## Get-DetailedSystemInformation
##
## From Windows PowerShell Cookbook (O'Reilly)
## by Lee Holmes (http://www.leeholmes.com/guide)
##
##############################################################################

<#

.SYNOPSIS

Get detailed information about a system.

.EXAMPLE

Get-DetailedSystemInformation LEE-DESK > output.txt
Gets detailed information about LEE-DESK and stores the output into output.txt

#>

param(
    ## The computer to analyze
    $Computer = "."
)

Set-StrictMode -Version Latest

"#"*80
"System Information Summary"
"Generated $(Get-Date)"
"#"*80
""
""
```

```
"#"*80
"Computer System Information"
"#"*80
Get-WmiObject Win32_ComputerSystem -Computer $computer | Format-List *

"#"*80
"Operating System Information"
"#"*80
Get-WmiObject Win32_OperatingSystem -Computer $computer | Format-List *

"#"*80
"BIOS Information"
"#"*80
Get-WmiObject Win32_Bios -Computer $computer | Format-List *

"#"*80
"Memory Information"
"#"*80
Get-WmiObject Win32_PhysicalMemory -Computer $computer | Format-List *

"#"*80
"Physical Disk Information"
"#"*80
Get-WmiObject Win32_DiskDrive -Computer $computer | Format-List *

"#"*80
"Logical Disk Information"
"#"*80
Get-WmiObject Win32_LogicalDisk -Computer $computer | Format-List *
```

For more information about running scripts, see Recipe 1.1.

See Also

Recipe 1.1, "Run Programs, Scripts, and Existing Tools"

Recipe 28.1, "Access Windows Management Instrumentation Data"

Appendix G, *WMI Reference*

27.18 Renew a DHCP Lease

Problem

You want to renew the DHCP lease for a connection on a computer.

Solution

To renew DHCP leases, use the `ipconfig` application. To renew the lease on all connections:

```
PS > ipconfig /renew
```

To renew the lease on a specific connection:

```
PS > ipconfig /renew "Wireless Network Connection 4"
```

Discussion

The standard `ipconfig` application works well to manage network configuration options on a local machine. To renew the lease on a remote computer, you have two options.

Use the Win32_NetworkAdapterConfiguration WMI class

In order to renew the lease on a remote computer, use the `Win32_NetworkAdapterConfiguration` WMI class. The WMI class requires that you know the description of the network adapter, so first obtain that by reviewing the output of `Get-WmiObject Win32_NetworkAdapterConfiguration -Computer ComputerName`:

```
PS > Get-WmiObject Win32_NetworkAdapterConfiguration -Computer LEE-DESK

(...)
DHCPEnabled     : True
IPAddress       : {192.168.1.100}
DefaultIPGateway : {192.168.1.1}
DNSDomain       : hsd1.wa.comcast.net.
ServiceName     : USB_RNDIS
Description     : Linksys Wireless-G USB Network Adapter with (...)
Index           : 13
(...)
```

Knowing which adapter you want to renew, call its `RenewDHCPLease()` method:

```
$description = "Linksys Wireless-G USB"
$adapter = Get-WmiObject Win32_NetworkAdapterConfiguration -Computer LEE-DESK |
    Where-Object { $_.Description -match $description}
$adapter.RenewDHCPLease()
```

Run ipconfig on the remote computer

Another way to renew the DHCP lease on a remote computer is to use either PowerShell Remoting or the solution offered by Recipe 29.2:

```
PS > Invoke-Command LEE-DESK { ipconfig /renew }
PS > Invoke-RemoteExpression \\LEE-DESK { ipconfig /renew }
```

For more information about working with WMI in PowerShell, see Recipe 28.1.

See Also

Recipe 28.1, "Access Windows Management Instrumentation Data"

Recipe 29.2, "Program: Invoke a PowerShell Expression on a Remote Machine"

27.19 Assign a Static IP Address

Problem

You want to assign a static IP address to a computer.

Solution

Use the Win32_NetworkAdapterConfiguration WMI class to manage network settings for a computer:

```
$description = "Linksys Wireless-G USB"
$staticIp = "192.168.1.100"
$subnetMask = "255.255.255.0"
$gateway = "192.168.1.1"

$adapter = Get-WmiObject Win32_NetworkAdapterConfiguration -Computer LEE-DESK |
    Where-Object { $_.Description -match $description}
$adapter.EnableStatic($staticIp, $subnetMask)
$adapter.SetGateways($gateway, [UInt16] 1)
```

Discussion

When you are managing network settings for a computer, the Win32_NetworkAdapterConfiguration WMI class requires that you know the description of the network adapter. Obtain that by reviewing the output of Get-WmiObject Win32_NetworkAdapterConfiguration -Computer *ComputerName*:

```
PS > Get-WmiObject Win32_NetworkAdapterConfiguration -Computer LEE-DESK

(...)
DHCPEnabled      : True
IPAddress        : {192.168.1.100}
DefaultIPGateway : {192.168.1.1}
DNSDomain        : hsd1.wa.comcast.net.
ServiceName      : USB_RNDIS
Description      : Linksys Wireless-G USB Network Adapter with (...)
Index            : 13
(...)
```

Knowing which adapter you want to renew, you can now call methods on that object as illustrated in the solution. To enable DHCP on an adapter again, use the EnableDHCP() method:

```
PS > $adapter.EnableDHCP()
```

For more information about working with WMI in PowerShell, see Recipe 28.1.

See Also

Recipe 28.1, "Access Windows Management Instrumentation Data"

27.20 List All IP Addresses for a Computer

Problem

You want to list all IP addresses for a computer.

Solution

To list IP addresses assigned to a computer, use the `ipconfig` application:

```
PS > ipconfig
```

Discussion

The standard `ipconfig` application works well to manage network configuration options on a local machine. To view IP addresses on a remote computer, you have two options.

Use the Win32_NetworkAdapterConfiguration WMI class

To view IP addresses of a remote computer, use the `Win32_NetworkAdapterConfiguration` WMI class. Since that lists all network adapters, use the `Where-Object` cmdlet to restrict the results to those with an IP address assigned to them:

```
PS > Get-WmiObject Win32_NetworkAdapterConfiguration -Computer LEE-DESK |
    Where-Object { $_.IpEnabled }


DHCPEnabled       : True
IPAddress         : {192.168.1.100}
DefaultIPGateway  : {192.168.1.1}
DNSDomain         : hsd1.wa.comcast.net.
ServiceName       : USB_RNDIS
Description       : Linksys Wireless-G USB Network Adapter with SpeedBooste
                    r v2 - Packet Scheduler Miniport
Index             : 13
```

Run ipconfig on the remote computer

Another way to view the IP addresses of a remote computer is to use either PowerShell Remoting or the solution offered by Recipe 29.2:

```
PS > Invoke-Command LEE-DESK { ipconfig }
PS > Invoke-RemoteExpression \\LEE-DESK { ipconfig }
```

For more information about working with WMI in PowerShell, see Recipe 28.1.

See Also

Recipe 28.1, "Access Windows Management Instrumentation Data"

Recipe 29.2, "Program: Invoke a PowerShell Expression on a Remote Machine"

27.21 List Network Adapter Properties

Problem

You want to retrieve information about network adapters on a computer.

Solution

To retrieve information about network adapters on a computer, use the Win32_NetworkAdapterConfiguration WMI class:

```
Get-WmiObject Win32_NetworkAdapterConfiguration -Computer <ComputerName>
```

To list only those with IP addresses assigned to them, use the Where-Object cmdlet to filter on the IpEnabled property:

```
PS > Get-WmiObject Win32_NetworkAdapterConfiguration -Computer LEE-DESK |
    Where-Object { $_.IpEnabled }


DHCPEnabled     : True
IPAddress       : {192.168.1.100}
DefaultIPGateway : {192.168.1.1}
DNSDomain       : hsd1.wa.comcast.net.
ServiceName     : USB_RNDIS
Description     : Linksys Wireless-G USB Network Adapter with SpeedBooster
                  v2 - Packet Scheduler Miniport
Index           : 13
```

Discussion

The solution uses the Win32_NetworkAdapterConfiguration WMI class to retrieve information about network adapters on a given system. By default, PowerShell displays only the most important information about the network adapter, but it provides access to much more.

To see all information available, use the Format-List cmdlet, as shown in Example 27-6.

Example 27-6. Using the Format-List cmdlet to see detailed information about a network adapter

```
PS > $adapter = Get-WmiObject Win32_NetworkAdapterConfiguration |
    Where-Object { $_.IpEnabled }

PS > $adapter
DHCPEnabled     : True
IPAddress       : {192.168.1.100}
DefaultIPGateway : {192.168.1.1}
DNSDomain       : hsd1.wa.comcast.net.
ServiceName     : USB_RNDIS
Description     : Linksys Wireless-G USB Network Adapter with SpeedBooster
                  v2 - Packet Scheduler Miniport
Index           : 13
```

```
PS > $adapter | Format-List *

DHCPLeaseExpires             : 20070521221927.000000-420
Index                        : 13
Description                  : Linksys Wireless-G USB Network Adapter with
                                 SpeedBooster v2 - Packet Scheduler Miniport
DHCPEnabled                  : True
DHCPLeaseObtained            : 20070520221927.000000-420
DHCPServer                   : 192.168.1.1
DNSDomain                    : hsd1.wa.comcast.net.
DNSDomainSuffixSearchOrder   :
DNSEnabledForWINSResolution  : False
DNSHostName                  : Lee-Desk
DNSServerSearchOrder         : {68.87.69.146, 68.87.85.98}
DomainDNSRegistrationEnabled : False
FullDNSRegistrationEnabled   : True
IPAddress                    : {192.168.1.100}
IPConnectionMetric           : 25
IPEnabled                    : True
IPFilterSecurityEnabled      : False
WINSEnableLMHostsLookup      : True
(...)
```

To retrieve specific properties, access them as you would access properties on other PowerShell objects:

```
PS > $adapter.MacAddress
00:12:17:77:B4:EB
```

For more information about working with WMI in PowerShell, see Recipe 28.1.

See Also

Recipe 28.1, "Access Windows Management Instrumentation Data"

Windows Management Instrumentation

28.0 Introduction

Windows Management Instrumentation (WMI) has long been a core management feature in Windows. It offers amazing breadth, wide reach, and ubiquitous remoting.

What WMI lacked in the past, though, was a good way to get to it. Graphically, the *wbemtest.exe* utility lets you experiment with WMI, its namespaces, and classes. It truly is a testing tool, though, as its complex user interface makes it impractical to use for most scenarios (see Figure 28-1).

A more user-friendly alternative is the *wmic.exe* command-line tool. The WMIC tool lets you interactively query WMI—but more importantly, automate its behavior. As with PowerShell, results within WMIC retain a great deal of their structured information and let you write fairly detailed queries:

```
PS > WMIC logicaldisk WHERE drivetype=3 `
    GET "name,freespace,SystemName,FileSystem,Size"

FileSystem  FreeSpace    Name  Size        SystemName
NTFS        10587656192  C:    34357637120 LEEHOLMES1C23
```

The language is limited, however, and all of the data's structure is lost once WMIC converts its output to text.

By far, the most popular user interface for WMI has been VBScript, the administrator's traditional scripting language. VBScript offers much richer language facilities than WMIC and retains WMI's structured data for the entire duration of your script.

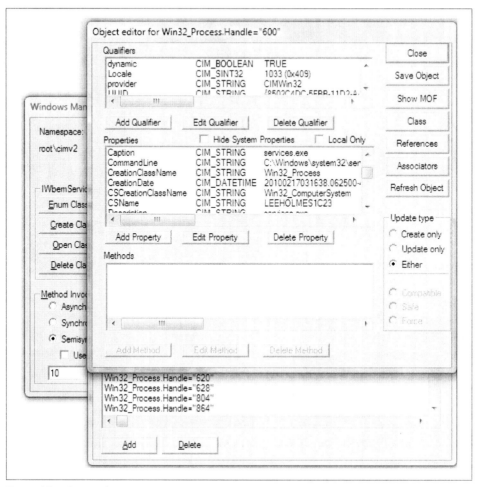

Figure 28-1. Using wbemtest.exe to retrieve a Win32_Process

VBScript has its own class of usability difficulties, however. For example, generating a report of the processes running on a computer often ends up looking like this:

```
strComputer = "atl-dc-01"
Set objWMIService = GetObject("winmgmts:" _
    & "{impersonationLevel=impersonate}!\\" _
    & strComputer & "\root\cimv2")
Set colProcessList = objWMIService.ExecQuery _
    ("Select * from Win32_Process")
For Each objProcess in colProcessList
    Wscript.Echo "Process: " & objProcess.Name
    Wscript.Echo "Process ID: " & objProcess.ProcessID
    Wscript.Echo "Thread Count: " & objProcess.ThreadCount
    Wscript.Echo "Page File Size: " _
        & objProcess.PageFileUsage
    Wscript.Echo "Page Faults: " _
```

```
        & objProcess.PageFaults
    Wscript.Echo "Working Set Size: " _
        & objProcess.WorkingSetSize
Next
```

It also requires that you write an entire *script*, and it offers no lightweight interactive experience. The Microsoft Scripting Guys' Scriptomatic tool helps make it easier to create many of these mundane scripts, but it still doesn't address one-off queries.

Enter PowerShell.

PowerShell elevates WMI to a first-class citizen for both ad-hoc and structured queries. Since most of the template VBScript for dealing with WMI instances ends up being used to display the results, PowerShell eliminates this step completely. The PowerShell equivalent of the preceding VBScript is simply:

```
Get-WmiObject Win32_Process -Computer atl-dc-01
```

Or, if you want a subset of properties:

```
Get-WmiObject Win32_Process | Select Name,ProcessId,ThreadCount
```

By providing a deep and user-friendly integration with WMI, PowerShell puts a great deal of functionality at the fingertips of every administrator.

28.1 Access Windows Management Instrumentation Data

Problem

You want to work with data and functionality provided by the WMI facilities in Windows.

Solution

To retrieve all instances of a WMI class, use the Get-WmiObject cmdlet:

```
Get-WmiObject -ComputerName Computer -Class Win32_Bios
```

To retrieve specific instances of a WMI class using a WMI filter, supply an argument to the -Filter parameter of the Get-WmiObject cmdlet. This is the WHERE clause of a WQL statement, but without the WHERE keyword:

```
Get-WmiObject Win32_Service -Filter "StartMode = 'Auto'"
```

To retrieve instances of a WMI class using WMI's WQL language, use the [Wmi Searcher] type shortcut:

```
$query = [WmiSearcher] "SELECT * FROM Win32_Service WHERE StartMode = 'Auto'"
$query.Get()
```

To retrieve a specific instance of a WMI class using a WMI filter, use the [Wmi] type shortcut:

```
[Wmi] 'Win32_Service.Name="winmgmt"'
```

To retrieve a property of a WMI instance, access that property as you would access a .NET property:

```
$service = [Wmi] 'Win32_Service.Name="winmgmt"'
$service.StartMode
```

To invoke a method on a WMI instance, invoke that method as you would invoke a .NET method:

```
$service = [Wmi] 'Win32_Service.Name="winmgmt"'
$service.ChangeStartMode("Manual")
$service.ChangeStartMode("Automatic")
```

To invoke a method on a WMI class, use the Invoke-WmiMethod cmdlet. Alternatively, use the [WmiClass] type shortcut to access that WMI class. Then, invoke that method as you would invoke a .NET method:

```
Invoke-WmiMethod Win32_Process Create notepad

$class = [WmiClass] "Win32_Process"
$class.Create("Notepad")
```

To retrieve a WMI class from a specific namespace, use its fully qualified name along with the [WmiClass] type shortcut:

```
[WmiClass] "\\COMPUTER\Root\Cimv2:Win32_Process"
```

Discussion

Working with WMI has long been a staple of managing Windows systems—especially systems that are part of corporate domains or enterprises. WMI supports a huge number of Windows management tasks, albeit not in a very user-friendly way.

Traditionally, administrators required either VBScript or the WMIC command-line tool to access and manage these systems through WMI. While powerful and useful, these techniques still provided plenty of opportunities for improvement. VBScript lacks support for an ad-hoc investigative approach, and WMIC fails to provide (or take advantage of) knowledge that applies to anything outside WMIC.

In comparison, PowerShell lets you work with WMI just like you work with the rest of the shell. WMI instances provide methods and properties, and you work with them the same way you work with methods and properties of other objects in PowerShell.

Not only does PowerShell make working with WMI instances and classes easy once you have them, but it also provides a clean way to access them in the first place. For most tasks, you need only to use the simple [Wmi], [WmiClass], or [WmiSearcher] syntax as shown in the solution.

Along with WMI's huge scope, though, comes a related problem: finding the WMI class that accomplishes your task. To assist you in learning what WMI classes are available, Appendix G provides a helpful listing of the most common ones. For a script that helps you search for WMI classes by name, description, property name, or property description, see Recipe 28.5.

Some advanced WMI tasks require that you enable your security privileges or adjust the packet privacy settings used in your request. All of PowerShell's WMI cmdlets support these options through built-in parameters.

When you want to access a specific WMI instance with the [Wmi] accelerator, you might at first struggle to determine what properties WMI lets you search on. These properties are called key properties on the class. For a script that lists these key properties, see Recipe 28.4.

For more information about the Get-WmiObject cmdlet, type **Get-Help Get-WmiObject**.

See Also

Recipe 28.4, "Program: Determine Properties Available to WMI Filters"

Recipe 28.5, "Program: Search for WMI Classes"

Appendix G, *WMI Reference*

28.2 Modify the Properties of a WMI Instance

Problem

You want to modify the properties of a WMI instance.

Solution

Use the Set-WmiInstance cmdlet:

```
PS > $bootVolume = Get-WmiObject Win32_LogicalDisk |
    Where-Object { $_.DeviceID -eq 'C:' }

PS > $bootVolume

DeviceID     : C:
DriveType    : 3
ProviderName :
FreeSpace    : 10587656192
Size         : 34357637120
VolumeName   : Boot Volume

PS > $bootVolume | Set-WmiInstance -Arguments @{ VolumeName = 'Vista' }

DeviceID     : C:
DriveType    : 3
```

```
ProviderName :
FreeSpace    : 10587656192
Size         : 34357637120
VolumeName   : Vista
```

Discussion

Although you can assign new property values to the objects output by Get-WmiObject, changes you make ultimately are not reflected in the permanent system state, as this example shows:

```
PS > $bootVolume = Get-WmiObject Win32_LogicalDisk |
    Where-Object { $_.DeviceID -eq 'C:' }

PS > $bootVolume

DeviceID     : C:
DriveType    : 3
ProviderName :
FreeSpace    : 10587656192
Size         : 34357637120
VolumeName   : Vista

PS > $bootVolume.VolumeName = "Boot Volume"

PS > Get-WmiObject Win32_LogicalDisk |
    Where-Object { $_.DeviceID -eq 'C:' }


DeviceID     : C:
DriveType    : 3
ProviderName :
FreeSpace    : 10587652096
Size         : 34357637120
VolumeName   : Vista
```

Instead, the Set-WmiInstance cmdlet lets you permanently modify values of WMI instances. While the Set-WmiInstance cmdlet supports WMI instances as pipeline input, you can also pass the fully qualified path to the -Path parameter:

```
Set-WmiInstance -Path "Win32_LogicalDisk.DeviceID='C:'" `
    -Argument @{ VolumeName="Vista" }
```

To determine which properties can be modified on an instance, you need to investigate the WMI class that defines it. Each WMI class has a Properties collection, and each property has a Qualifiers collection. If Write is one of the qualifiers, then that property is writeable:

```
PS > [WmiClass] "Win32_LogicalDisk" | Select -Expand Properties

(...)
Name    : VolumeName
Value   :
Type    : String
```

```
IsLocal    : True
IsArray    : False
Origin     : Win32_LogicalDisk
Qualifiers : {CIMTYPE, MappingStrings, read, write}

Name       : VolumeSerialNumber
Value      :
Type       : String
IsLocal    : True
IsArray    : False
Origin     : Win32_LogicalDisk
Qualifiers : {CIMTYPE, MappingStrings, read}
(...)
```

To automatically see all writeable classes in the ROOT\CIMV2 namespace, simply run this snippet of PowerShell script:

```
$writeableProperties = Get-WmiObject -List -Recurse |
    Select -Expand Properties |
    Where-Object { $_ | Select -Expand Qualifiers |
        Where-Object { $_.Name -eq "Write" } } | Select Origin,Name
```

Like all other WMI-related cmdlets, the Set-WmiInstance cmdlet lets you configure impersonation, authentication, and privilege restrictions. For more information about working with WMI classes, see Recipe 28.1.

See Also

Recipe 28.1, "Access Windows Management Instrumentation Data"

Appendix G, *WMI Reference*

28.3 Invoke a Method on a WMI Class

Problem

You want to invoke a method supported by a WMI class.

Solution

Use the Invoke-WmiMethod cmdlet:

```
PS > Invoke-WmiMethod -Class Win32_Process -Name Create -Args notepad.exe
(notepad starts)

__GENUS          : 2
__CLASS          : __PARAMETERS
__SUPERCLASS     :
__DYNASTY        : __PARAMETERS
__RELPATH        :
__PROPERTY_COUNT : 2
__DERIVATION     : {}
__SERVER         :
```

```
__NAMESPACE    :
__PATH         :
ProcessId      : 3644
ReturnValue    : 0
```

Discussion

As with .NET types, WMI classes describe the functionality and features of a related set of items. For example, the `Win32_Process` class describes the features and behavior of an entity called an operating system process. When WMI returns information about a specific operating system process, that is called an *instance*.

As with static methods on .NET types, many WMI classes offer methods that relate broadly to the entity they try to represent. For example, the `Win32_Process` class defines methods to start processes, stop them, and more. To invoke any of these methods, call the `Invoke-WmiMethod` cmdlet.

While you may already know the method you want to call, PowerShell also offers a way to see the methods exposed by WMI classes on your system. Each WMI class has a `Methods` collection, and reviewing that collection lists all methods supported by that class. The following snippet lists all methods supported by all classes in the `ROOT \CIMV2` namespace:

```
Get-WmiObject -List -Recurse | Select -Expand Methods | Select Origin,Name
```

Like all other WMI-related cmdlets, the `Invoke-WmiMethod` cmdlet lets you configure impersonation, authentication, and privilege restrictions.

In addition to the `Invoke-WmiMethod` cmdlet, the `[WmiClass]` type shortcut also lets you refer to a WMI class and invoke its methods:

```
$processClass = [WmiClass] "Win32_Process"
$processClass.Create("notepad.exe")
```

This method, however, does not easily support customization of impersonation, authentication, or privilege restrictions.

For more information about working with WMI classes, see Recipe 28.1.

See Also

Recipe 28.1, "Access Windows Management Instrumentation Data"

Appendix G, *WMI Reference*

28.4 Program: Determine Properties Available to WMI Filters

When you want to access a specific WMI instance with PowerShell's `[Wmi]` type shortcut, you might at first struggle to determine what properties WMI lets you search on. These properties are called key properties on the class. Example 28-1 gets all the properties you can use in a WMI filter for a given class.

Example 28-1. Get-WmiClassKeyProperty.ps1

```
##############################################################################
##
## Get-WmiClassKeyProperty
##
## From Windows PowerShell Cookbook (O'Reilly)
## by Lee Holmes (http://www.leeholmes.com/guide)
##
##############################################################################

<#

.SYNOPSIS

Get all of the properties that you can use in a WMI filter for a given class.

.EXAMPLE

Get-WmiClassKeyProperty Win32_Process
Handle

#>

param(
    ## The WMI class to examine
    [WmiClass] $WmiClass
)

Set-StrictMode -Version Latest

## WMI classes have properties
foreach($currentProperty in $wmiClass.Properties)
{
    ## WMI properties have qualifiers to explain more about them
    foreach($qualifier in $currentProperty.Qualifiers)
    {
        ## If it has a 'Key' qualifier, then you may use it in a filter
        if($qualifier.Name -eq "Key")
        {
            $currentProperty.Name
        }
    }
}
```

For more information about running scripts, see Recipe 1.1.

See Also

Recipe 1.1, "Run Programs, Scripts, and Existing Tools"

28.5 Program: Search for WMI Classes

Along with WMI's huge scope comes a related problem: finding the WMI class that accomplishes your task. To help you learn what WMI classes are available, Appendix G provides a helpful listing of the most common ones. If you want to dig a little deeper, though, Example 28-2 lets you search for WMI classes by name, description, property name, or property description.

Example 28-2. Search-WmiNamespace.ps1

```
###############################################################################
##
## Search-WmiNamespace
##
## From Windows PowerShell Cookbook (O'Reilly)
## by Lee Holmes (http://www.leeholmes.com/guide)
##
###############################################################################

<#

.SYNOPSIS

Search the WMI classes installed on the system for the provided match text.

.EXAMPLE

Search-WmiNamespace Registry
Searches WMI for any classes or descriptions that mention "Registry"

.EXAMPLE

Search-WmiNamespace Process ClassName,PropertyName
Searches WMI for any classes or properties that mention "Process"

.EXAMPLE

Search-WmiNamespace CPU -Detailed
Searches WMI for any class names, descriptions, or properties that mention
"CPU"

#>

param(
    ## The pattern to search for
    [Parameter(Mandatory = $true)]
    [string] $Pattern,

    ## Switch parameter to look for class names, descriptions, or properties
    [switch] $Detailed,

    ## Switch parameter to look for class names, descriptions, properties, and
    ## property description.
    [switch] $Full,
```

```
    ## Custom match options.
    ## Supports any or all of the following match options:
    ## ClassName, ClassDescription, PropertyName, PropertyDescription
    [string[]] $MatchOptions = ("ClassName","ClassDescription")
)

Set-StrictMode -Off

## Helper function to create a new object that represents
## a Wmi match from this script
function New-WmiMatch
{
    param( $matchType, $className, $propertyName, $line )

    $wmiMatch = New-Object PsObject -Property @{
        MatchType = $matchType;
        ClassName = $className;
        PropertyName = $propertyName;
        Line = $line
    }

    $wmiMatch
}

## If they've specified the -detailed or -full options, update
## the match options to provide them an appropriate amount of detail
if($detailed)
{
    $matchOptions = "ClassName","ClassDescription","PropertyName"
}

if($full)
{
    $matchOptions =
        "ClassName","ClassDescription","PropertyName","PropertyDescription"
}

## Verify that they specified only valid match options
foreach($matchOption in $matchOptions)
{
    $fullMatchOptions =
        "ClassName","ClassDescription","PropertyName","PropertyDescription"

    if($fullMatchOptions -notcontains $matchOption)
    {
        $error = "Cannot convert value {0} to a match option. " +
            "Specify one of the following values and try again. " +
            "The possible values are ""{1}""."
        $ofs = ", "
        throw ($error -f $matchOption, ([string] $fullMatchOptions))
    }
}

## Go through all of the available classes on the computer
```

```
foreach($class in Get-WmiObject -List -Rec)
{
    ## Provide explicit get options, so that we get back descriptions
    ## as well
    $managementOptions = New-Object System.Management.ObjectGetOptions
    $managementOptions.UseAmendedQualifiers = $true
    $managementClass =
        New-Object Management.ManagementClass $class.Name,$managementOptions

    ## If they want us to match on class names, check if their text
    ## matches the class name
    if($matchOptions -contains "ClassName")
    {
        if($managementClass.Name -match $pattern)
        {
            New-WmiMatch "ClassName" `
                $managementClass.Name $null $managementClass.__PATH
        }
    }

    ## If they want us to match on class descriptions, check if their text
    ## matches the class description
    if($matchOptions -contains "ClassDescription")
    {
        $description =
            $managementClass.Qualifiers |
                foreach { if($_.Name -eq "Description") { $_.Value } }
        if($description -match $pattern)
        {
            New-WmiMatch "ClassDescription" `
                $managementClass.Name $null $description
        }
    }

    ## Go through the properties of the class
    foreach($property in $managementClass.Properties)
    {
        ## If they want us to match on property names, check if their text
        ## matches the property name
        if($matchOptions -contains "PropertyName")
        {
            if($property.Name -match $pattern)
            {
                New-WmiMatch "PropertyName" `
                    $managementClass.Name $property.Name $property.Name
            }
        }

        ## If they want us to match on property descriptions, check if
        ## their text matches the property name
        if($matchOptions -contains "PropertyDescription")
        {
            $propertyDescription =
                $property.Qualifiers |
                    foreach { if($_.Name -eq "Description") { $_.Value } }
```

```
        if($propertyDescription -match $pattern)
        {
            New-WmiMatch "PropertyDescription" `
                $managementClass.Name $property.Name $propertyDescription
        }
    }
  }
}
```

For more information about running scripts, see Recipe 1.1.

See Also

Recipe 1.1, "Run Programs, Scripts, and Existing Tools"

Appendix G, *WMI Reference*

28.6 Use .NET to Perform Advanced WMI Tasks

Problem

You want to work with advanced features of WMI, but PowerShell's access (through the [Wmi], [WmiClass], and [WmiSearcher] accelerators) does not directly support them.

Solution

To interact with advanced features of WMI objects, access their methods and properties.

Advanced instance features

To get WMI instances related to a given instance (its *associators*), call the GetRelated() method:

```
$instance = [Wmi] 'Win32_Service.Name="winmgmt"'
$instance.GetRelated()
```

To change advanced scope options, access the Scope.Options property. While the Invoke-WmiMethod cmdlet lets you enable privileges directly through a parameter, this example provides another option:

```
$system = Get-WmiObject Win32_OperatingSystem
$system.Scope.Options.EnablePrivileges = $true
$system.SetDateTime($class.ConvertFromDateTime("01/01/2007"))
```

Advanced class features

To retrieve the WMI properties and qualifiers of a class, access the Properties property:

```
$class = [WmiClass] "Win32_Service"
$class.Properties
```

Advanced query feature

To configure connection options on a query, such as Packet Privacy and Authentication, set the options on the Scope property:

```
$credential = Get-Credential
$query = [WmiSearcher] "SELECT * FROM IISWebServerSetting"
$query.Scope.Path = "\\REMOTE_COMPUTER\Root\MicrosoftIISV2"
$query.Scope.Options.Username = $credential.Username
$query.Scope.Options.Password = $credential.GetNetworkCredential().Password
$query.Scope.Options.Authentication = "PacketPrivacy"
$query.get() | Select-Object AnonymousUserName
```

Discussion

The [Wmi], [WmiClass], and [WmiSearcher] type shortcuts return instances of .NET System.Management.ManagementObject, System.Management.ManagementClass, and System.Management.ManagementObjectSearcher classes, respectively.

As might be expected, the .NET Framework provides comprehensive support for WMI queries, with PowerShell providing an easier-to-use interface to that support. If you need to step outside the support offered directly by PowerShell, these classes in the .NET Framework provide an advanced outlet.

For more information about working with classes from the .NET Framework, see Recipe 3.8.

See Also

Recipe 3.8, "Work with .NET Objects"

28.7 Improve the Performance of Large-Scale WMI Operations

Problem

You want to perform a large-scale WMI operation across many computers, and you want to control how many computers should be managed at a time.

Solution

Use the -ThrottleLimit parameter on the cmdlet, and invoke that cmdlet as a job:

```
$computers = Get-Content computers.txt
Get-WmiObject Win32_OperatingSystem -Computer $computers -ThrottleLimit 10 -AsJob
```

Discussion

One problem with large-scale WMI operations against many computers is that most scripts invoke them sequentially. If your script acts against 10,000 servers, it will usually process the first computer, and then retrieve the results. Next, it will process the second computer, and then retrieve its results. Since WMI operations are traditionally network-bound, your script spends the vast majority of its time simply waiting for results from remote computers.

 A genesis for this feature was a sobering story we heard from one of our large customers. The customer's scripts had to deal with so many computers that the customer would have to start a second script before the first had finished!

The solution to this quandary comes from invoking the commands in parallel. Not entirely in parallel, however, as most machines would buckle under the load of 10,000 active WMI queries. While it is possible to recognize the solution and pitfalls, actually implementing it is something different altogether. Even with the proper skill set, a job manager that supports automatic throttling is usually not high on an administrator's list of priorities when compared to the collection of fires the administrator needs to put out.

Instead, PowerShell's WMI cmdlets handle all of this complexity for you. For more information about PowerShell's job support, see Recipe 1.4.

See Also

Recipe 1.4, "Invoke a Long-Running or Background Command"

28.8 Convert a VBScript WMI Script to PowerShell

Problem

You want to perform a WMI task in PowerShell, but you can find only VBScript examples that demonstrate the solution to the problem.

Solution

To accomplish the task of a script that retrieves data from a computer, use the Get-WmiObject cmdlet:

```
foreach($printer in Get-WmiObject -Computer COMPUTER Win32_Printer)
{
    ## Work with the properties
    $printer.Name
}
```

To accomplish the task of a script that calls methods on an instance, use the [Wmi] or [WmiSearcher] accelerators to retrieve the instances, and then call methods on the instances like you would call any other PowerShell method.

```
$service = [Wmi] 'Win32_Service.Name="winmgmt"'
$service | Invoke-WmiMethod -Name ChangeStartMode -ArgumentList "Manual"
$service | Invoke-WmiMethod -Name ChangeStartMode -ArgumentList "Automatic"
```

To accomplish the task of a script that calls methods on a class, use the Invoke-WmiMethod cmdlet, or use the [WmiClass] accelerator to retrieve the class, and then call methods on the class like you would call any other PowerShell method:

```
Invoke-WmiMethod Win32_Process Create notepad

$class = [WmiClass] "Win32_Process"
$class.Create("Notepad")
```

Discussion

For many years, VBScript has been the preferred language that administrators use to access WMI data. Because of that, the vast majority of scripts available in books and on the Internet come written in VBScript.

These scripts usually take one of three forms: retrieving data and accessing properties, calling methods of an instance, and calling methods of a class.

 Although most WMI scripts on the Internet accomplish unique tasks, PowerShell supports many of the traditional WMI tasks natively. If you want to translate a WMI example to PowerShell, first check that there aren't any PowerShell cmdlets that might accomplish the task directly.

Retrieving data

One of the most common uses of WMI is for data collection and system inventory tasks. A typical VBScript that retrieves data looks like Example 28-3.

Example 28-3. Retrieving printer information from WMI using VBScript

```
strComputer = "."
Set objWMIService = GetObject("winmgmts:" _
    & "{impersonationLevel=impersonate}!\\" & strComputer & "\root\cimv2")

Set colInstalledPrinters = objWMIService.ExecQuery _
    ("Select * from Win32_Printer")

For Each objPrinter in colInstalledPrinters
    Wscript.Echo "Name: " & objPrinter.Name
    Wscript.Echo "Location: " & objPrinter.Location
    Wscript.Echo "Default: " & objPrinter.Default
Next
```

The first three lines prepare a WMI connection to a given computer and namespace. The next two lines of code prepare a WMI query that requests all instances of a class. The For Each block loops over all the instances, and the objPrinter.*Property* statements interact with properties on those instances.

In PowerShell, the `Get-WmiObject` cmdlet takes care of most of that by retrieving all instances of a class from the computer and namespace that you specify. The first five lines of code then become:

```
$installedPrinters = Get-WmiObject Win32_Printer -ComputerName computer
```

If you need to specify a different computer, namespace, or query restriction, the `Get-WmiObject` cmdlets supports those through optional parameters. If you need to specify advanced connection options (such as authentication levels), simply specify those in the `-Impersonation` and `-Authentication` parameters to the cmdlet.

In PowerShell, the `For Each` block becomes:

```
foreach($printer in $installedPrinters)
{
    $printer.Name
    $printer.Location
    $printer.Default
}
```

Notice that we spend the bulk of the PowerShell conversion of this script showing how to access properties. If you don't actually need to work with the properties (and only want to display them for reporting purposes), PowerShell's formatting commands simplify that even further:

```
Get-WmiObject Win32_Printer -ComputerName computer | Format-List Name,Location,Default
```

For more information about working with the `Get-WmiObject` cmdlet, see Recipe 28.1.

Calling methods on an instance

Although data retrieval scripts form the bulk of WMI management examples, another common task is to call methods of an instance that invoke actions.

For example, Example 28-4 changes the startup type of a service.

Example 28-4. Changing the startup type of a service from WMI using VBScript

```
strComputer = "."
Set objWMIService = GetObject("winmgmts:" _
    & "{impersonationLevel=impersonate}!\\" & strComputer & "\root\cimv2")

Set colServiceList = objWMIService.ExecQuery _
    ("Select * from Win32_Service where StartMode = 'Manual'")

For Each objService in colServiceList
    errReturnCode = objService.ChangeStartMode("Disabled")
Next
```

The first three lines prepare a WMI connection to a given computer and namespace. The next two lines of code prepare a WMI query that requests all instances of a class and adds an additional filter (`StartMode = 'Manual'`) to the query. The `For Each` block loops over all the instances, and the `objService.Change(…)` statement calls the `Change()` method on the service.

In PowerShell, the `Get-WmiObject` cmdlet takes care of most of the setup by retrieving all instances of a class from the computer and namespace that you specify. The first five lines of code then become:

```
$services = Get-WmiObject Win32_Service -Filter "StartMode = 'Manual'"
```

If you need to specify a different computer or namespace, the `Get-WmiObject` cmdlet supports those through optional parameters. If you need to specify advanced connection options (such as authentication levels), simply specify those in the `-Impersonation` and `-Authentication` parameters to the cmdlet.

In PowerShell, the `For Each` block becomes:

```
foreach($service in $services)
{
    $service.ChangeStartMode("Disabled")
}
```

For more information about working with the `Get-WmiObject` cmdlet, see Recipe 28.1.

Calling methods on a class

Although less common than calling methods on an instance, it is sometimes helpful to call methods on a WMI class. PowerShell makes this work almost exactly like calling methods on an instance.

For example, a script that creates a process on a remote computer looks like this:

```
strComputer = "COMPUTER"
Set objWMIService = GetObject _
    ("winmgmts:\\" & strComputer & "\root\cimv2:Win32_Process")

objWMIService.Create("notepad.exe")
```

The first three lines prepare a WMI connection to a given computer and namespace. The final line calls the `Create()` method on the class.

In PowerShell, the Invoke-WmiMethod cmdlet lets you easily work with methods on a class. The entire segment of code then becomes:

```
Invoke-WmiMethod "\\COMPUTER\Root\Cimv2:Win32_Process" Create notepad.exe
```

For more information about invoking methods on WMI classes, see Recipe 28.3.

See Also

Recipe 28.1, "Access Windows Management Instrumentation Data"

Recipe 28.3, "Invoke a Method on a WMI Class"

Remoting

29.0 Introduction

PowerShell's support for local and interactive computer automation makes it an incredibly attractive platform for computer management and administration. Its rich, object-flavored perspective takes even the simplest of management tasks to the next level.

In version one, local administration was essentially the limit of where PowerShell applied its unique perspective. While it supported interaction with traditional remoting technologies (SSH, FTP, Telnet, PsExec, and more), its support was no different than that offered by any other shell.

In version two, the PowerShell and Windows Remote Management (WinRM) teams worked together closely to create a combined release known as the *Windows Management Framework*. Designing a rich remoting experience was one of the top focuses of their collaboration. Starting with standard *interactive remoting*, PowerShell lets you easily connect to a remote system and work with it one to one.

If you want to import the commands from that remote system (but still have them run on the remote system), *implicit remoting* often lets you forget you are managing a remote system altogether. Expanding on interactive and implicit remoting, large-scale *fan-out* remoting is a natural next step. Fan-out remoting let you manage many computers at a time in a bulk, command-based approach.

```
PS > Invoke-Command Lee-Desk { Get-Process -n PowerShell } -Cred Lee

Handles  NPM(K)   PM(K)     WS(K) VM(M)   CPU(s)    Id Process   PSComputer
                                                       Name      Name
-------  ------   -----     ----- -----   ------    -- ---------  ---------
    628      17   39084     58908   214     4.26  7540 powers... lee-des...
```

As with the rest of PowerShell, fan-out remoting offers a unique, object-focused treatment that elevates its experience past plain-text-based approaches.

29.1 Find Commands That Support Their Own Remoting

Problem

You want to find commands that let you access remote computers but that don't require PowerShell Remoting.

Solution

Use the `Get-Command` cmdlet to retrieve all cmdlets, and then access the `Parameters` collection to find all commands that expose a `-ComputerName` parameter:

```
PS > Get-Command -CommandType Cmdlet |
    Where-Object { $_.Parameters["ComputerName"] }


CommandType    Name                 Definition
-----------    ----                 ----------
Cmdlet         Clear-EventLog       Clear-EventLog [-LogName]...
Cmdlet         Connect-WSMan        Connect-WSMan [[-Computer...
Cmdlet         Disconnect-WSMan     Disconnect-WSMan [[-Compu...
Cmdlet         Enter-PSSession      Enter-PSSession [-Compute...
Cmdlet         Get-Counter          Get-Counter [[-Counter] <...
Cmdlet         Get-EventLog         Get-EventLog [-LogName] <...
Cmdlet         Get-HotFix           Get-HotFix [[-Id] <String...
Cmdlet         Get-Process          Get-Process [[-Name] <Str...
(...)
```

Alternatively, use the `-Parameter` parameter of the `Get-Help` cmdlet:

```
PS > Get-Help * -Parameter ComputerName

Name                       Category  Synopsis
----                       --------  --------
Get-WinEvent               Cmdlet    Gets events from event logs...
Get-Counter                Cmdlet    Gets performance counter da...
Test-WSMan                 Cmdlet    Tests whether the WinRM ser...
Invoke-WSManAction         Cmdlet    Invokes an action on the ob...
Connect-WSMan              Cmdlet    Connects to the WinRM servi...
Disconnect-WSMan           Cmdlet    Disconnects the client from...
(...)
```

Discussion

While PowerShell Remoting offers great power and consistency, sometimes you might need to invoke a command against a system that does not have PowerShell installed. A simple Remote Desktop session is a common approach, but PowerShell still offers plenty of remote management options that work independently of its core remoting support.

Each command shown by the output of `Get-Command` and `Get-Help` that exposes a `-ComputerName` parameter does so using its own built-in remoting technology. The WMI cmdlets use a WMI-specific form of DCOM-based remoting. The WSMan cmdlets use SOAP-based remoting. Many of the other cmdlets offer RPC-based remoting.

By building on their own existing remoting protocols, these commands integrate easily with environments that have already enabled WMI or event log management, for example. Since these protocols are designed to handle only their specific technology, often they can offer performance benefits as well.

Despite their benefits, commands that offer a -ComputerName parameter can't replace a generalized remoting technology for most purposes. Since each command builds on its own protocol, using that command means managing firewall rules, services, and more. Command-based remoting generally offers limited functionality as well, and something as simple as alternate credentials is rarely supported.

For more information about enabling PowerShell Remoting, see Recipe 29.5.

See Also

Recipe 29.5, "Enable PowerShell Remoting on a Computer"

29.2 Program: Invoke a PowerShell Expression on a Remote Machine

PowerShell version two includes great support for command execution on remote machines through its PowerShell Remoting features. These require that the remote system have PowerShell version two available, though, which might not always be possible. If PowerShell Remoting is not available on a remote machine, many commands support their own remoting. If you want to do more than invoke a specific command, Example 29-2 offers a useful alternative. It uses PsExec (from *http://www.microsoft.com/tech net/sysinternals/utilities/psexec.mspx*) to support the actual remote command execution.

This script offers more power than just remote command execution, however. As Example 29-1 demonstrates, it leverages PowerShell's capability to import and export strongly structured data, so you can work with the command output using many of the same techniques you use to work with command output on the local system. Example 29-1 demonstrates this power by filtering command output on the remote system but sorting it on the local system.

Example 29-1. Invoking a PowerShell expression on a remote machine

```
PS > $command = { Get-Process | Where-Object { $_.Handles -gt 1000 } }
PS > Invoke-RemoteExpression \\LEE-DESK $command | Sort Handles

Handles  NPM(K)  PM(K)  WS(K)  VM(M)  CPU(s)     Id ProcessName
-------  ------  -----  -----  -----  ------     -- -----------
   1025       8   3780   3772     32  134.42    848 csrss
   1306      37  50364  64160    322  409.23   4012 OUTLOOK
```

```
    1813       39  54764  36360    321  340.45  1452 iTunes
    2316      273  29168  41164    218  134.09  1244 svchost
```

Since this strongly structured data comes from objects on another system, PowerShell does not regenerate the functionality of those objects (except in rare cases). For more information about importing and exporting structured data, see Recipe 10.5.

Example 29-2. Invoke-RemoteExpression.ps1

```
##############################################################################
##
## Invoke-RemoteExpression
##
## From Windows PowerShell Cookbook (O'Reilly)
## by Lee Holmes (http://www.leeholmes.com/guide)
##
##############################################################################

<#

.SYNOPSIS

Invoke a PowerShell expression on a remote machine. Requires PsExec from
http://live.sysinternals.com/tools/psexec.exe. If the remote machine
supports PowerShell version two, use PowerShell remoting instead.

.EXAMPLE

Invoke-RemoteExpression \\LEE-DESK { Get-Process }
Retrieves the output of a simple command from a remote machine

.EXAMPLE

(Invoke-RemoteExpression \\LEE-DESK { Get-Date }).AddDays(1)
Invokes a command on a remote machine. Since the command returns one of
PowerShell's primitive types (a DateTime object), you can manipulate
its output as an object afterward.

.EXAMPLE

Invoke-RemoteExpression \\LEE-DESK { Get-Process } | Sort Handles
Invokes a command on a remote machine. The command does not return one of
PowerShell's primitive types, but you can still use PowerShell's filtering
cmdlets to work with its structured output.

#>

param(
    ## The computer on which to invoke the command.
    $ComputerName = "\\$ENV:ComputerName",

    ## The script block to invoke on the remote machine.
    [Parameter(Mandatory = $true)]
    [ScriptBlock] $ScriptBlock,
```

```powershell
    ## The username / password to use in the connection
    $Credential,

    ## Determines if PowerShell should load the user's PowerShell profile
    ## when invoking the command.
    [switch] $NoProfile
)

Set-StrictMode -Version Latest

## Prepare the command line for PsExec. We use the XML output encoding so
## that PowerShell can convert the output back into structured objects.
## PowerShell expects that you pass it some input when being run by PsExec
## this way, so the 'echo .' statement satisfies that appetite.
$commandLine = "echo . | powershell -Output XML "

if($noProfile)
{
    $commandLine += "-NoProfile "
}

## Convert the command into an encoded command for PowerShell
$commandBytes = [System.Text.Encoding]::Unicode.GetBytes($scriptblock)
$encodedCommand = [Convert]::ToBase64String($commandBytes)
$commandLine += "-EncodedCommand $encodedCommand"

## Collect the output and error output
$errorOutput = [IO.Path]::GetTempFileName()

if($Credential)
{
    ## This lets users pass either a username or full credential to our
    ## credential parameter
    $credential = Get-Credential $credential
    $networkCredential = $credential.GetNetworkCredential()
    $username = $networkCredential.Username
    $password = $networkCredential.Password

    $output = psexec $computername /user $username /password $password `
        /accepteula cmd /c $commandLine 2>$errorOutput
}
else
{
    $output = psexec /acceptEula $computername `
        cmd /c $commandLine 2>$errorOutput
}

## Check for any errors
$errorContent = Get-Content $errorOutput
Remove-Item $errorOutput
if($errorContent -match "(Access is denied)|(failure)|(Couldn't)")
{
    $OFS = "`n"
    $errorMessage = "Could not execute remote expression. "
    $errorMessage += "Ensure that your account has administrative " +
```

```
        "privileges on the target machine.`n"
    $errorMessage += ($errorContent -match "psexec.exe :")

    Write-Error $errorMessage
}

## Return the output to the user
$output
```

For more information about running scripts, see Recipe 1.1.

See Also

Recipe 1.1, "Run Programs, Scripts, and Existing Tools"

Recipe 10.5, "Easily Import and Export Your Structured Data"

Recipe 29.1, "Find Commands That Support Their Own Remoting"

29.3 Test Connectivity Between Two Computers

Problem

You want determine the network availability of a computer or between two computers.

Solution

Use the Test-Connection cmdlet to perform a traditional network ping:

```
PS > Test-Connection leeholmes.com

Source    Destination   IPV4Address    IPV6Address
------    -----------   -----------    -----------
LEE-DESK  leeholmes.com 66.186.25.131  {}
LEE-DESK  leeholmes.com 66.186.25.131  {}
LEE-DESK  leeholmes.com 66.186.25.131  {}
LEE-DESK  leeholmes.com 66.186.25.131  {}
```

Alternatively, the *ping.exe* utility continues to work:

```
PS > ping leeholmes.com

Pinging leeholmes.com [66.186.25.131] with 32 bytes of data:
Reply from 66.186.25.131: bytes=32 time=38ms TTL=115
Reply from 66.186.25.131: bytes=32 time=36ms TTL=115
Reply from 66.186.25.131: bytes=32 time=37ms TTL=115
Reply from 66.186.25.131: bytes=32 time=41ms TTL=115

Ping statistics for 66.186.25.131:
    Packets: Sent = 4, Received = 4, Lost = 0 (0% loss),
Approximate round trip times in milli-seconds:
    Minimum = 36ms, Maximum = 41ms, Average = 38ms
```

Discussion

As a command-line shell, PowerShell of course continues to support traditional command-line utilities. *Ping.exe* is one of the most common network diagnostic tools, and it works as expected from PowerShell.

The Test-Connection cmdlet offers the same features as *ping.exe* plus a great deal of additional functionality. Most ping utilities let you verify the connection between the current computer and a target computer, but the Test-Connection cmdlet lets you also specify the *source computer* for the network test.

Perhaps the most obvious benefit of the Test-Connection cmdlet is its object-based output—making filtering, sorting, and analysis immensely easier. For example, a simple script to monitor the average response time of a cluster of domains:

```
$topTen = "google.com","facebook.com","youtube.com","yahoo.com",
    "live.com","wikipedia.org","blogger.com","baidu.com","msn.com",
    "qq.com"

## Test all of the connections, grouping by address
$results = Test-Connection $topTen -ErrorAction SilentlyContinue | Group Address

## Go through each of the addresses
$averages = foreach($group in $results)
{
    ## Figure out the average response time
    $averageResponse = $group.Group |
        Measure-Object -Average ResponseTime | Select -Expand Average

    ## Create a new custom object to output the Address and ResponseTime
    New-Object PsObject -Property @{
        Address = $group.Name;
        ResponseTime = $averageResponse }
}

## Output the results
$averages | Sort ResponseTime | Select Address,ResponseTime
```

That script gives the following output:

```
Address        ResponseTime
-------        ------------
google.com               22
blogger.com            22.5
facebook.com          35.25
yahoo.com              37.5
youtube.com           86.25
wikipedia.org            99
baidu.com            203.25
qq.com               259.25
```

One thing to notice about this script's output is that not all of the top 10 websites are present. A ping request is a simple network-based handshake, but many websites block them to conserve network bandwidth or for perceived security hardening. When the

Test-Connection cmdlet fails to make a connection, it generates the following error message:

```
Test-Connection : Testing connection to computer 'bing.com' failed: Error
due to lack of resources
```

To verify connectivity to these resources, you can use the -Test parameter of the Send-TcpRequest script given in Recipe 12.9:

```
PS > Send-TcpRequest bing.com -Test
True
PS > Send-TcpRequest bing.com -Test -Port 443
True
PS > Send-TcpRequest bing.com -Test -Port 23
False
```

For an effective use of the Test-Connection cmdlet to verify network resources before trying to manage them, see Recipe 29.4.

See Also

Recipe 12.9, "Program: Interact with Internet Protocols"

Recipe 29.4, "Limit Networking Scripts to Hosts That Respond"

29.4 Limit Networking Scripts to Hosts That Respond

Problem

You have a distributed network management task, and want to avoid the delays caused by hosts that are offline or not responding.

Solution

Use the -Quiet parameter of the Test-Connection to filter your computer set to only hosts that respond to a network ping:

```
$computers = "MISSING",$env:ComputerName,"DOWN","localhost"
$skipped = @()

foreach($computer in $computers)
{
    ## If the computer is not responding, record that we skipped it and
    ## continue. We can review this collection after the script completes.
    if(-not (Test-Connection -Quiet $computer -Count 1))
    {
        $skipped += $computer
    }

    ## Perform some batch of networked operations
    Get-WmiObject -Computer $computer Win32_OperatingSystem
}
```

Discussion

One difficulty when writing scripts that manage a large collection of computers is that a handful of them are usually off or nonresponsive. If you don't address this situation, you are likely to run into many errors and delays as your script attempts to repeatedly manage a system that cannot be reached.

In most domains, a network ping is the most reliable way to determine the responsiveness of a computer. The `Test-Connection` cmdlet provides ping support in PowerShell, so the solution builds on that.

For more information about the `Test-Connection` cmdlet, see Recipe 29.3.

See Also

Recipe 29.3, "Test Connectivity Between Two Computers"

29.5 Enable PowerShell Remoting on a Computer

Problem

You want to allow remote management of a computer via PowerShell Remoting.

Solution

Use the `Enable-PsRemoting` cmdlet to enable PowerShell Remoting:

```
PS > Enable-PsRemoting

WinRM Quick Configuration
Running command "Set-WSManQuickConfig" to enable this machine for remote
management through WinRM service.
 This includes:
    1. Starting or restarting (if already started) the WinRM service
    2. Setting the WinRM service type to auto start
    3. Creating a listener to accept requests on any IP address
    4. Enabling firewall exception for WS-Management traffic (for http only).

Do you want to continue?
[Y] Yes  [A] Yes to All  [N] No  [L] No to All  [S] Suspend  [?] Help
(default is "Y"): Y

WinRM has been updated to receive requests.
WinRM service type changed successfully.
WinRM service started.
Configured LocalAccountTokenFilterPolicy to grant administrative rights
remotely to local users.

WinRM has been updated for remote management.
Created a WinRM listener on HTTP://* to accept WS-Man requests to any IP on
```

```
this machine.
WinRM firewall exception enabled.
```

Discussion

With the combined release of PowerShell and WS-Management (WSMan) into the Windows Management Framework, we've heard the occasional question about whether it's possible to install them independently. This concern is usually focused on security.

Security is a natural concern with any technology that supports network connections, and it is something that both teams took very seriously.

As a background, Windows Remote Management (WinRM) has been part of the operating system since Windows Vista and Server 2008. WinRM does not listen to network connections by default, and it must be explicitly activated.

Both PowerShell and WinRM advanced greatly during the release of version two—most notably by working together to support a rich PowerShell-based remoting experience. The Windows Management Framework download (PowerShell + WinRM) simply updates the binaries on supported operating systems to bring them up to the same version already included in Windows 7 and Windows Server 2008 R2. Investigating this concern further, it usually comes down to worries about increased network attack surface through automatically opening a network port to accept incoming connections.

Installing the Windows Management Framework does not enable any networking features automatically. "Secure by Default" is a guiding principle of Windows Management Framework, and of Microsoft as a whole. To help you manage your network exposure, PowerShell Remoting must be explicitly enabled by an administrator of the machine.

PowerShell Remoting does not require any specific configuration to let you connect to a remote computer, but it does require a configuration step to allow connections from remote computers.

Enable remoting on a single local machine

Once you've decided to enable remoting, PowerShell makes this a snap (after informing you of the impact). Simply call `Enable-PsRemoting` from an elevated shell. The solution demonstrates this approach. To bypass any user prompts or confirmation, also specify the -Force flag.

As part of the `Enable-PsRemoting` process, PowerShell connects to the local WS-Management service to create and configure a new endpoint. This is done through a local network connection, so it is impacted by the Windows restrictions on network connections. For example, Windows does not allow network connections to any account that has a blank password. If your administrator account has a blank password, PowerShell will be unable to properly create and configure the WSMan endpoint.

Enable remoting on a remote machine

Remotely enabling PowerShell Remoting offers many unique challenges. Although you can certainly use Remote Desktop to connect to the system (and then essentially enable it locally), Remote Desktop does not lend itself to automation.

Instead, you can leverage another remoting technology that does lend itself to automation: Windows Management Instrumentation (WMI). WMI is enabled on most domain machines, but it offers only a minor facility for remote command execution: the `Create()` method of the `Win32_Process`. For more information about this approach, see Recipe 29.7.

Enable remoting in an enterprise

If you want to enable PowerShell Remoting in an enterprise, Group Policy is the most flexible and scalable option. Through Group Policy settings, you can enable automatic configuration of WinRM endpoints and firewall rules. For more information about this approach, type `Get-Help about_remote_troubleshooting`.

See Also

Recipe 29.7, "Program: Remotely Enable PowerShell Remoting"

29.6 Enable Remote Desktop on a Computer

Problem

You want to enable Remote Desktop on a computer.

Solution

Set the `fDenyTSConnections` property of the remote desktop registry key to `0`:

```
$regKey = "HKLM:\SYSTEM\CurrentControlSet\Control\Terminal Server"
Set-ItemProperty $regKey fDenyTSConnections 0
```

Discussion

Remote Desktop is the de facto interactive management protocol, but can be difficult to enable automatically. Fortunately, its configuration settings come from the Windows Registry, so you can use PowerShell's registry provider to enable it.

To disable Remote Desktop, set the `fDenyTSConnections` property to `1`.

To enable Remote Desktop on a remote computer, use PowerShell Remoting to change the registry properties, or remotely manage the registry settings directly. To see how to manage remote registry settings directly, see Recipe 21.12.

See Also

Recipe 21.12, "Work with the Registry of a Remote Computer"

29.7 Program: Remotely Enable PowerShell Remoting

As mentioned in Recipe 29.5, the Enable-PsRemoting cmdlet uses a local network connection to create and configure its WS-Management endpoint.

Windows places many restrictions on remote commands that attempt to invoke other remote commands—also known as the double-hop problem. If you attempt to call Enable-PsRemoting from a remote system, your account privileges are disabled during the WSMan configuration's second hop.

Scheduled tasks offer one way to solve this problem, as they let you create a task with the full credentials required to interact with network resources. Unfortunately, most machines are not configured to support remote task management. Most are, however, configured to support WMI connections. As a bootstrapping step, we can use the Create() method of the Win32_Process class to launch an instance of PowerShell, and then provide PowerShell with a script to create, launch, and delete a scheduled task that ultimately configures PowerShell Remoting.

The script shown in Example 29-3 automates this cumbersome process.

Example 29-3. Enable-RemotePsRemoting.ps1

```
##############################################################################
##
## Enable-RemotePsRemoting
##
## From Windows PowerShell Cookbook (O'Reilly)
## by Lee Holmes (http://www.leeholmes.com/guide)
##
##############################################################################

<#

.SYNOPSIS

Enables PowerShell Remoting on a remote computer. Requires that the machine
responds to WMI requests and that its operating system is Windows Vista or
later.

.EXAMPLE

Enable-RemotePsRemoting <Computer>

#>

param(
    ## The computer on which to enable remoting
    $Computername,
```

```
    ## The credential to use when connecting
    $Credential = (Get-Credential)
)

Set-StrictMode -Version Latest
$VerbosePreference = "Continue"

$credential = Get-Credential $credential
$username = $credential.Username
$password = $credential.GetNetworkCredential().Password

$script = @"

`$log = Join-Path `$env:TEMP Enable-RemotePsRemoting.output.txt
Remove-Item -Force `$log -ErrorAction SilentlyContinue
Start-Transcript -Path `$log

## Create a task that will run with full network privileges.
## In this task, we call Enable-PsRemoting
schtasks /CREATE /TN 'Enable Remoting' /SC WEEKLY /RL HIGHEST ``
    /RU $username /RP $password ``
    /TR "powershell -noprofile -command Enable-PsRemoting -Force" /F |
    Out-String
schtasks /RUN /TN 'Enable Remoting' | Out-String

`$securePass = ConvertTo-SecureString $password -AsPlainText -Force
`$credential =
    New-Object Management.Automation.PsCredential $username,`$securepass

## Wait for the remoting changes to come into effect
for(`$count = 1; `$count -le 10; `$count++)
{
    `$output = Invoke-Command localhost { 1 } -Cred `$credential ``
        -ErrorAction SilentlyContinue
    if(`$output -eq 1) { break; }

    "Attempt `$count : Not ready yet."
    Sleep 5
}

## Delete the temporary task
schtasks /DELETE /TN 'Enable Remoting' /F | Out-String
Stop-Transcript

"@

$commandBytes = [System.Text.Encoding]::Unicode.GetBytes($script)
$encoded = [Convert]::ToBase64String($commandBytes)

Write-Verbose "Configuring $computername"
$command = "powershell -NoProfile -EncodedCommand $encoded"
$null = Invoke-WmiMethod -Computer $computername -Credential $credential `
    Win32_Process Create -Args $command
```

```
Write-Verbose "Testing connection"
Invoke-Command $computername {
    Get-WmiObject Win32_ComputerSystem } -Credential $credential
```

For more information about running scripts, see Recipe 1.1.

See Also

Recipe 1.1, "Run Programs, Scripts, and Existing Tools"

Recipe 28.1, "Access Windows Management Instrumentation Data"

Recipe 29.5, "Enable PowerShell Remoting on a Computer"

29.8 Configure User Permissions for Remoting

Problem

You want to control the users who are allowed to make remote connections to a machine.

Solution

Create a new Windows group to define which users can connect to the machine, and then use the Set-PsSessionConfiguration cmdlet to add this group to the permission list of the endpoint:

```
PS > net localgroup "PowerShell Remoting Users" /Add
The command completed successfully.

PS > net localgroup "PowerShell Remoting Users" Administrators /Add
The command completed successfully.

PS > Set-PsSessionConfiguration Microsoft.PowerShell -ShowSecurityDescriptorUI
```

Discussion

Like many objects in Windows, the WS-Management endpoint that provides access to PowerShell Remoting has an associated access control list. By default, this access control list provides access only to Administrators of the machine.

As you use PowerShell Remoting more often, you'll likely want more fine-grained control than that—similar to the type of control that you get from the existing Remote Desktop Users group. Enabling this control is a two-step process: first, create the group, and then add the group to the access control list of the endpoint.

For a one-off configuration, the -ShowSecurityDescriptorUI parameter of the Set-PsSessionConfiguration cmdlet lets you manage the access control list as you would manage a file, directory, or computer share.

To automate this process, though, you need to speak the language of security rules directly—a language called *SDDL*: the Security Descriptor Definition Language. This format is not really designed to be consumed by humans, but it is the format exposed by the -SecurityDescriptorSddl parameter of the Set-PSSessionConfiguration cmdlet. Although it is not user-friendly, you can use several classes from the .NET Framework to create a security rule or SDDL string. Example 29-4 demonstrates this approach.

Example 29-4. Automating security configuration of PowerShell Remoting

```
## Get the SID for the "PowerShell Remoting Users" group
$account = New-Object Security.Principal.NTAccount "PowerShell Remoting Users"
$sid = $account.Translate([Security.Principal.SecurityIdentifier]).Value

## Get the security descriptor for the existing configuration
$config = Get-PsSessionConfiguration Microsoft.PowerShell
$existingSddl = $config.SecurityDescriptorSddl

## Create a CommonSecurityDescriptor object out of the existing SDDL
## so that we don't need to manage the string by hand
$arguments = $false,$false,$existingSddl
$mapper = New-Object Security.AccessControl.CommonSecurityDescriptor $arguments

## Create a new access rule that adds the "PowerShell Remoting Users" group
$mapper.DiscretionaryAcl.AddAccess("Allow",$sid,268435456,"None","None")

## Get the new SDDL for that configuration
$newSddl = $mapper.GetSddlForm("All")

## Update the endpoint configuration
Set-PSSessionConfiguration Microsoft.PowerShell -SecurityDescriptorSddl $newSddl
```

For more information about working with the .NET Framework, see Recipe 3.8. For more information about working with SDDL strings, see Recipe 18.16.

See Also

Recipe 3.8, "Work with .NET Objects"

Recipe 18.16, "Manage Security Descriptors in SDDL Form"

29.9 Enable Remoting to Workgroup Computers

Problem

You want to connect to a machine in a workgroup or by IP address.

Solution

Update the TrustedHosts collection on the *wsman:\localhost\client* path:

```
PS > $trustedHosts = Get-Item wsman:\localhost\client\TrustedHosts
PS > $trustedHosts.Value += ",RemoteComputer"
PS > Set-Item wsman:\localhost\client\TrustedHosts $trustedHosts.Value

WinRM Security Configuration.
This command modifies the TrustedHosts list for the WinRM client. The
computers in the TrustedHosts list might not be authenticated. The client
might send credential information to these computers. Are you sure that
you want to modify this list?
[Y] Yes  [N] No  [S] Suspend  [?] Help (default is "Y"): Y

PS > Get-Item wsman:\localhost\client\TrustedHosts


   WSManConfig: Microsoft.WSMan.Management\WSMan::localhost\Client

Name                    Value
----                    -----
TrustedHosts            Lee-Desk,RemoteComputer
```

Discussion

One of the main aspects of client-side security in any remoting technology is being able to trust who you are connecting to. When you are at an Internet café, you can connect to your bank's website in a browser. If you use SSL, you are guaranteed that it's really your bank and not some fake proxy put up by an attacker who's manipulating the network traffic. This class of interception attack is called a "man-in-the-middle attack."

PowerShell Remoting gives the same guarantee. When you connect to a computer inside of a domain, Kerberos authentication secures the connection. Kerberos authentication guarantees the identity of the endpoint—ensuring that no attacker can intercept your connection. When you're outside of a domain, SSL is the only standard way to guarantee this, which is why https is such an important protocol on the Internet.

There are two situations where built-in authentication mechanisms can't protect against man-in-the-middle attacks:

- Connecting to a host by IP (inside a domain or not)
- Using any authentication mechanism except for Kerberos, SSL, or CredSSP

Workgroup remoting (or cross-forest remoting) is an example of this. When you try to make a connection in either of these scenarios, PowerShell gives the error message:

```
PS > Enter-PsSession SomeComputer

Enter-PSSession : Connecting to remote server failed with the following
error message : The WinRM client cannot process the request. If the
authentication scheme is different from Kerberos, or if the client computer
is not joined to a domain, then HTTPS transport must be used or the destination
```

machine must be added to the TrustedHosts configuration setting. Use winrm.cmd to configure TrustedHosts. Note that computers in the TrustedHosts list might not be authenticated. You can get more information about that by running the following command: winrm help config. For more information, see the about_Remote_Troubleshooting Help topic.

While wordy, this error message exactly explains the problem.

Since PowerShell can't guarantee the identity of the remote computer in this situation, it fails safe and generates an error. All remoting protocols run into this problem:

- Remote Desktop: "... cannot verify the identity of the computer you want to connect to ..."
- SSH: "The authenticity of the host '....' can't be established ..."

The other protocols implement the equivalent of "I acknowledge this and want to continue," but PowerShell's experience is unfortunately more complex.

If you want to connect to a machine that PowerShell can't verify, you can update the TrustedHosts configuration setting. Its name is unfortunately vague, however, as it really means, "I trust my network during connections to this machine."

When you configure the TrustedHosts setting, you have three options: an explicit list (as shown in the solution), "<local>" to bypass this message for all computers in the domain or workgroup, or "*" to disable the message altogether.

For more information, type Get-Help about_Remote_Troubleshooting.

29.10 Interactively Manage a Remote Computer

Problem

You want to interactively work with a remote computer as though it were a local PowerShell session.

Solution

Use the Enter-PsSession cmdlet to connect to a remote session and manage it interactively:

```
PS > Enter-PsSession Lee-Desk
[lee-desk]: PS E:\Lee> Get-Process -Name PowerShell

Handles  NPM(K)    PM(K)      WS(K) VM(M)   CPU(s)     Id ProcessName
-------  ------    -----      ----- -----   ------     -- -----------
   2834      14    85500      86256   218 ...22.83   8396 powershell
    421      12    39220      54204   189    7.41   9708 powershell


[lee-desk]: PS E:\Lee> exit
PS >
```

If your current account does not have access to the remote computer, you can use the -Credential parameter to supply alternate credentials:

```
PS > $cred = Get-Credential LEE-DESK\Lee
PS > Enter-PsSession Lee-Desk -Cred $cred
```

Discussion

Like many traditional shells, PowerShell Remoting offers a simple, direct, interactive management experience known simply as *Interactive Remoting.* Just as in your local PowerShell sessions, you type commands and see their output. This remote PowerShell is just as powerful as your local one; all of the filtering, pipelining, and integrated language features continue to work.

Two aspects make an interactive remote session different from a local one, however.

The first thing to note is that your remote PowerShell sessions have no associated desktop or graphical user interface. PowerShell will launch Notepad if you ask it to, but the user interface won't be displayed to anybody.

 When you use your normal technique (i.e., PS > notepad.exe) to launch an application in interactive remoting, PowerShell waits for it to close before returning control to you. This ends up blocking your session, so press Ctrl-C to regain control of your session. If you want to launch a graphical application, use either the Start-Process cmdlet or command-based remoting.

Also, if you launch a program (such as *edit.com* or *ftp.exe*'s interactive mode) that directly interacts with the console window for its user interface, this program will not work as expected. Some applications (such as *ftp.exe*'s interactive mode) detect that they have no console window available and simply exit. Others (such as *edit.com*) hang and cause PowerShell's interactive remoting to become unresponsive as well. To break free from misbehaving applications like this, press Ctrl-C.

The second aspect to interactive remoting is shared by all Windows network technologies that work without explicit credentials: the double-hop problem. Once you've connected to a computer remotely, Windows gives you full access to all local resources as though you were logged into the computer directly. When it comes to *network* resources, however, Windows prevents your user information from being automatically used on another computer. This typically shows up when trying to access either restricted network shares from a remoting system or intranet websites that require implicit authentication. For information about how to launch a remoting session that supports this type of credential forwarding, see Recipe 29.13.

In addition to supplying a computer name to the Enter-PsSession cmdlet, you can also use the New-PsSession cmdlet to connect to a computer. After connecting, you can enter and exit that session at will:

```
PS > $session = New-PsSession Lee-Desk -Cred $cred
PS > Get-PsSession

Id Name          ComputerName    State    ConfigurationName    Availability
-- ----          ------------    -----    -----------------    --------
 1 Session1      lee-desk        Opened   Microsoft.PowerShell ...lable


PS > Enter-PsSession $session
[lee-desk]: PS E:\Lee> Start-Process calc
[lee-desk]: PS E:\Lee> Get-Process -n calc

Handles  NPM(K)    PM(K)      WS(K) VM(M)   CPU(s)     Id ProcessName
-------  ------    -----      ----- -----   ------     -- -----------
     64       5     4172       7272    44     0.06   7148 calc


[lee-desk]: PS E:\Lee> exit
PS > Get-Process -n calc
Get-Process : Cannot find a process with the name "calc". Verify the process
name and call the cmdlet again.

PS > Enter-PsSession $session
[lee-desk]: PS E:\Lee> Get-Process -n calc

Handles  NPM(K)    PM(K)      WS(K) VM(M)   CPU(s)     Id ProcessName
-------  ------    -----      ----- -----   ------     -- -----------
     64       5     4172       7272    44     0.06   7148 calc


[lee-desk]: PS E:\Lee>
```

After creating a session, you can even combine interactive remoting with bulk, command-based *fan-out* remoting. For more information about command-based remoting, see Recipe 29.11.

See Also

Recipe 29.11, "Invoke a Command on a Remote Computer"

Recipe 29.13, "Create Sessions with Full Network Access"

29.11 Invoke a Command on a Remote Computer

Problem

You want to invoke a command on one or many remote computer(s).

Solution

Use the `Invoke-Command` cmdlet:

```
PS > Invoke-Command -Computer Lee-Desk,LEEHOLMES1C23 -Command { Get-PsDrive } |
    Format-Table Name,Used,Free,PSComputerName -Auto
```

```
Name  Used         Free         PSComputerName
----  ----         ----         --------------
Alias                           lee-desk
C     44830642176  105206947840 lee-desk
E     37626998784  61987717120  lee-desk
F     126526734336 37394722816  lee-desk
G     93445226496  6986330112   lee-desk
H     1703936      0            lee-desk
I     349184       18099200     lee-desk
J     40442880     0            lee-desk
C     24018575360  10339061760  leeholmes1c23
D     0                         leeholmes1c23
(...)
```

If your current account does not have access to the remote computer, you can use the `-Credential` parameter to supply alternate credentials:

```
PS > $cred = Get-Credential LEE-DESK\Lee
PS > Invoke-Command Lee-Desk { Get-Process } -Cred $cred
```

Discussion

As shown in Recipe 29.10, PowerShell offers simple interactive remoting to handle situations when you want to quickly explore or manage a single remote system. For many scenarios, though, one-to-one interactive remoting is not realistic. Simple automation (which by definition is noninteractive) is the most basic example, but another key point is large-scale automation.

Running a command (or set of commands) against a large number of machines has always been a challenging task. To address both one-to-one automation as well as large-scale automation, PowerShell introduces *fan-out* remoting: a command-based, batch-oriented approach to system management.

Fan-out remoting integrates all of the core features you've come to expect from your local PowerShell experience: richly structured output, consistency, and most of all, reach. While a good number of PowerShell cmdlets support their own native form of remoting, PowerShell's support provides it to every command—cmdlets as well as console applications.

When you call the `Invoke-Command` cmdlet simply with a computer name and script block, PowerShell automatically connects to that machine, invokes the command, and returns the results:

```
PS > $result = Invoke-Command leeholmes1c23 { Get-PSDrive }
PS > $result | Format-Table Name,Used,Free,Root,PSComputerName -Auto
```

```
Name            Used Free               Root                PSComputerName
----            ---- ----               ----                --------------
A               0                       A:\                 leeholmes1c23
Alias                                                       leeholmes1c23
C               24018575360 10339061760 C:\                 leeholmes1c23
cert                                    \                   leeholmes1c23
D               0                       D:\                 leeholmes1c23
Env                                                         leeholmes1c23
Function                                                    leeholmes1c23
HKCU                                    HKEY_CURRENT_USER   leeholmes1c23
HKLM                                    HKEY_LOCAL_MACHINE  leeholmes1c23
Variable                                                    leeholmes1c23
WSMan                                                       leeholmes1c23
```

So far, this remoting experience looks similar to many other technologies. Notice the **PSComputerName** property, though. PowerShell automatically adds this property to all of your results, which lets you easily work with the output of multiple computers at once. We get to see PowerShell's unique remoting treatment once we start working with results. For example:

```
PS > $result | Sort Name | Where { $_.Root -like "*\*" }

Name            Used (GB)   Free (GB) Provider   Root
----            ---------   --------- --------   ----
A                                                A:\
C               22.37       9.63                 C:\
cert                                             \
D                                                D:\

PS > $result[2].Used
24018575360
PS > $result[2].Used * 4
96074301440
```

Rather than transport plain text like other remoting technologies, PowerShell transports data in a way that preserves a great deal of information about the original command output. Before sending objects to you, PowerShell *serializes* them into a format that can be moved across the network. This format retains the following "primitive" types, and converts all others to their string representation:

Byte	UInt16	TimeSpan	SecureString
SByte	UInt32	DateTime	Boolean
Byte[]	UInt64	ProgressRecord	Guid
Int16	Decimal	Char	Uri
Int32	Single	String	Version
Int64	Double	XmlDocument	

Perhaps most importantly, serialization removes all methods from non-primitive objects. By converting these objects to what are called *property bags*, your scripts can depend on an interface that won't change between PowerShell releases, .NET Framework releases, or operating system releases.

When the objects reach your computer, PowerShell *rehydrates* them. During this process, it creates objects that have their original structure and repopulates the properties. Any properties that were primitive types will again be fully functional: integer properties can be sorted and computed, XML documents can be navigated, and more.

When PowerShell reassembles an object, it prepends `Deserialized` to its type name. When PowerShell displays a deserialized object, it will use any formatting definitions that apply to the full-fidelity object:

```
PS > $result[2] | Get-Member


    TypeName: Deserialized.System.Management.Automation.PSDriveInfo

Name                MemberType    Definition
----                ----------    ----------
ToString            Method        string ToString(), string ToString(stri...
Free                NoteProperty  System.UInt64 Free=10339061760
PSComputerName      NoteProperty  System.String PSComputerName=leeholmes1c23
PSShowComputerName  NoteProperty  System.Boolean PSShowComputerName=True
RunspaceId          NoteProperty  System.Guid RunspaceId=33f45afd-2381-44...
Used                NoteProperty  System.UInt64 Used=24018575360
Credential          Property      Deserialized.System.Management.Automati...
CurrentLocation     Property      System.String {get;set;}
Description         Property      System.String {get;set;}
Name                Property      System.String {get;set;}
Provider            Property      System.String {get;set;}
Root                Property      System.String {get;set;}
```

In addition to supplying a computer name to the `Invoke-Command` cmdlet, you can also use the `New-PsSession` cmdlet to connect to a computer. After connecting, you can invoke commands in that session at will:

```
PS > $session = New-PsSession leeholmes1c23 -Cred $cred
PS > Get-PsSession

Id Name      ComputerName    State    ConfigurationName      Availability
-- ----      ------------    -----    -----------------      ------------
 1 Session1  leeholmes1c23   Opened   Microsoft.PowerShell   ...lable
```

```
PS > Invoke-Command -Session $session { Get-Process -Name PowerShell }

Handles  NPM(K)    PM(K)      WS(K) VM(M)   CPU(s)     Id Process PSCompu
                                                          Name    terName
-------  ------    -----      ----- -----   ------     -- ------- -------
    716      12    48176      65060   201    23.31   4684 power... leeh...
```

After creating a session, you can even combine commands with interactive remoting, as shown in Recipe 29.10.

Using these techniques, you can easily scale your automation across many, many machines. For more information about this technique, see Recipe 29.16.

One of the primary challenges you will run into with fan-out remoting is shared by all of the Windows network technologies that work without explicit credentials: the double-hop problem. Once you've connected to a computer remotely, Windows gives you full access to all local resources as though you were logged into the computer directly. When it comes to *network* resources, however, Windows prevents your user information from being automatically used on another computer. This typically shows up when you try to access restricted network shares from a remoting system or intranet websites that require implicit authentication. For information about how to launch a remoting session that supports this type of credential forwarding, see Recipe 29.13.

See Also

Recipe 29.10, "Interactively Manage a Remote Computer"

Recipe 29.13, "Create Sessions with Full Network Access"

Recipe 29.16, "Invoke a Command on Many Computers"

29.12 Implicitly Invoke Commands from a Remote Computer

Problem

You have commands on a remote computer that you want to invoke as though they were local.

Solution

Use the Import-PsSession cmdlet to import them into the current session:

```
PS > $cred = Get-Credential

PS > $session = New-PSSession -ConfigurationName Microsoft.Exchange `
    -ConnectionUri https://ps.outlook.com/powershell/ -Credential $cred `
    -Authentication Basic -AllowRedirection

PS > Invoke-Command $session { Get-OrganizationalUnit } |
    Select DistinguishedName
```

```
DistinguishedName
-----------------
OU=leeholmes.com,OU=Microsoft Exchange Hosted Organizations,DC=prod,DC=...
OU=Hosted Organization Security Groups,OU=leeholmes.com,OU=Microsoft Ex...


PS > Import-PSSession $session -CommandName Get-OrganizationalUnit

ModuleType Name                        ExportedCommands
---------- ----                        ----------------
Script     tmp_1e510382-9a3d-43a5...   Get-OrganizationalUnit


PS > Get-OrganizationalUnit | Select DistinguishedName

DistinguishedName
-----------------
OU=leeholmes.com,OU=Microsoft Exchange Hosted Organizations,DC=prod,DC=...
OU=Hosted Organization Security Groups,OU=leeholmes.com,OU=Microsoft Ex...
```

Discussion

When you frequently work with commands from a remote system, the mental and conceptual overhead of continually calling the Invoke-Command and going through PowerShell's remoting infrastructure quickly adds up. When you write a script that primarily uses commands from the remote system, the majority of the script ends up being for the remoting infrastructure itself. When pipelining commands to one another, this gets even more obvious:

```
PS > Invoke-Command $session { Get-User } |
    Where-Object { $_.Identity -eq "lee@leeholmes.com" } |
    Invoke-Command $session { Get-Mailbox } |
    Select Identity,OriginatingServer,ExchangeVersion,DistinguishedName


Identity            OriginatingServer  ExchangeVersion  DistinguishedName
--------            -----------------  ---------------  -----------------
lee@leeholmes.com   BL2PRD0103DC006... 0.10 (14.0.100.0)  CN=lee@leeholm...
```

To address these issues, PowerShell Remoting supports the Import-PsSession cmdlet to let you import and seamlessly use commands from a remote session. This is especially helpful, for example, in scenarios such as Hosted Exchange. It's not reasonable to install an entire toolkit of commands just to manage your mailboxes in the cloud.

Once you've imported those commands, PowerShell enables *implicit remoting* on them:

```
PS > Import-PsSession $session -CommandName Get-Mailbox,GetUser

PS > Get-User | Where-Object { $_.Identity -eq "lee@leeholmes.com" } |
    Get-MailBox |
    Select Identity,OriginatingServer,ExchangeVersion,DistinguishedName
```

```
Identity          OriginatingServer  ExchangeVersion  DistinguishedName
--------          -----------------  ---------------  -----------------
lee@leeholmes.com BL2PRD0103DC006... 0.10 (14.0.100.0) CN=lee@leeholm...


PS > Get-Help Get-User -Examples

NAME
    Get-User

SYNOPSIS
    Use the Get-User cmdlet to retrieve all users in the forest that match
     the specified conditions.

    ------------------------- EXAMPLE 1 -------------------------
    This example retrieves information about users in the Marketing OU.

    Get-User -OrganizationalUnit "Marketing"
(...)
```

Expanding on this further, PowerShell even lets you export commands from a session into a module:

```
PS > $commands = "Get-Mailbox","Get-User"
PS > Export-PsSession $session -CommandName $commands -ModuleName ExchangeCommands


    Directory: E:\Lee\WindowsPowerShell\Modules\ExchangeCommands


Mode            LastWriteTime     Length Name
----            -------------     ------ ----
-a---     2/19/2010  11:11 PM     13177 ExchangeCommands.psm1
-a---     2/19/2010  11:11 PM        99 ExchangeCommands.format.ps1xml
-a---     2/19/2010  11:11 PM       605 ExchangeCommands.psd1
```

When you import the module, PowerShell creates new implicit remoting commands for all commands that you exported. When you invoke a command, it recreates the remoting session (if required), and then invokes your command in that new session:

```
Windows PowerShell
Copyright (C) 2009 Microsoft Corporation. All rights reserved.

PS > Import-Module ExchangeCommands
PS > Get-User | Where-Object { $_.Identity -eq "lee@leeholmes.com" } |
    Get-MailBox |
    Select Identity,OriginatingServer,ExchangeVersion,DistinguishedName

Creating a new session for implicit remoting of "Get-User" command...

Identity          OriginatingServer  ExchangeVersion  DistinguishedName
--------          -----------------  ---------------  -----------------
lee@leeholmes.com BL2PRD0103DC006... 0.10 (14.0.100.0) CN=lee@leeholm...
```

For more information about command-based remoting, see Recipe 29.11. For more information about PowerShell modules, see Recipe 1.24.

See Also

Recipe 1.24, "Extend Your Shell with Additional Commands"

Recipe 29.11, "Invoke a Command on a Remote Computer"

29.13 Create Sessions with Full Network Access

Problem

You want to create a PowerShell Remoting session (interactive, fan-out, or implicit) that has full access to network resources.

Solution

Use the -Authentication parameter, and pick CredSSP as the authentication mechanism:

```
PS > Invoke-Command leeholmes1c23 {
    "Hello World"; dir \\lee-desk\c$ } -Authentication CredSSP -Cred Lee

Hello World

    Directory: \\lee-desk\c$


Mode            LastWriteTime     Length Name             PSComputerName
----            -------------     ------ ----             --------------
d----       2/5/2010   12:31 AM          inetpub          leeholmes1c23
d----       7/13/2009   7:37 PM          PerfLogs         leeholmes1c23
d-r--       2/16/2010   3:14 PM          Program Files    leeholmes1c23
(...)
```

Discussion

When connecting to a computer using PowerShell Remoting, you might sometimes see errors running commands that access a network location:

```
PS > Invoke-Command leeholmes1c23 {
    "Hello World"; dir \\lee-desk\c$ } -Cred Lee

Hello World
Cannot find path '\\lee-desk\c$' because it does not exist.
    + CategoryInfo          : ObjectNotFound: (\\lee-desk\c$:String)
    [Get-ChildItem], ItemNotFoundException
    + FullyQualifiedErrorId : PathNotFound,Microsoft.PowerShell.Commands.
    GetChildItemCommand
```

When you remotely connect to a computer in a domain, Windows (and PowerShell Remoting) by default use an authentication mechanism called *Kerberos*. While you have full access to local resources when connected this way, security features of Kerberos prevent the remote computer from being able to use your account information to connect to additional computers.

This reduces the risk of connecting to a remote computer that has been compromised or otherwise has malicious software running on it. Without these protections, the malicious software can act on your behalf across the entire network—an especially dangerous situation if you are connecting with powerful domain credentials.

Although this Kerberos policy can be managed at the domain level by marking the computer "Trusted for Delegation," changing domain-level policies to accomplish ad-hoc management tasks is a cumbersome process.

To solve this problem, PowerShell supports another authentication mechanism called *CredSSP*—the same authentication mechanism used by Remote Desktop and Terminal Services. Because of its security impact, you must explicitly enable support on both the client you are connecting from and the server you are connecting to.

From the client side, specify `-Role Client` to the `Enable-WsManCredSSP` cmdlet. You can specify either specific computer names in the `-DelegateComputer` parameter or "*" to enable the setting for all target computers.

```
PS > Enable-WSManCredSSP -Role Client -DelegateComputer leeholmes1c23

CredSSP Authentication Configuration for WS-Management
CredSSP authentication allows the user credentials on this computer to be
sent to a remote computer. If you use CredSSP authentication for a
connection to a malicious or compromised computer, that computer will have
access to your user name and password. For more information, see the
Enable-WSManCredSSP Help topic.
Do you want to enable CredSSP authentication?
[Y] Yes  [N] No  [S] Suspend  [?] Help (default is "Y"): Y
```

If you want to use CredSSP authentication within a workgroup (instead of a domain), one additional step is required. Authentication within a workgroup uses a protocol called *NTLM*, which doesn't offer the same security guarantees that Kerberos does—specifically, you can't guarantee the identity of the computer you are connecting to. This is the same caution that drives the `TrustedHosts` configuration requirement, as discussed in Recipe 29.9. To enable CredSSP over NTLM connections, open *gpedit.msc*, and then navigate to Computer Configuration → Administrative Templates → System → Credentials Delegation. Enable the "Allow Delegating Fresh Credentials with NTLM-only Server Authentication" setting, and then add `wsman/`*computername* to the list of supported computers. In the previous example, this would be `wsman/lee holmes1c23`. As with the `-DelegateComputer` parameter, you can also specify `wsman/*` to enable the setting for all target computers.

From the server side, specify -Role Server to the Enable-WsManCredSSP cmdlet. You can invoke this cmdlet remotely, if needed:

```
PS > Enable-WsManCredSSP -Role Server

CredSSP Authentication Configuration for WS-Management
CredSSP authentication allows the server to accept user credentials from a
remote computer. If you enable CredSSP authentication on the server, the
server will have access to the user name and password of the client computer
if the client computer sends them. For more information, see the
Enable-WSManCredSSP Help topic.
Do you want to enable CredSSP authentication?
[Y] Yes  [N] No  [S] Suspend  [?] Help (default is "Y"):
```

Ironically, remotely configuring CredSSP runs into the very same issues that CredSSP is designed to solve. To work around these, we can create a scheduled task to run the Enable-WsManCredSSP cmdlet (Example 29-5), as done in Recipe 29.7.

Example 29-5. Enable-RemoteCredSSP.ps1

```
##############################################################################
##
## Enable-RemoteCredSSP
##
## From Windows PowerShell Cookbook (O'Reilly)
## by Lee Holmes (http://www.leeholmes.com/guide)
##
##############################################################################

<#

.SYNOPSIS

Enables CredSSP support on a remote computer. Requires that the machine
have PowerShell Remoting enabled and that its operating system is Windows
Vista or later.

.EXAMPLE

Enable-RemoteCredSSP <Computer>

#>

param(
    ## The computer on which to enable CredSSP
    $Computername,

    ## The credential to use when connecting
    $Credential = (Get-Credential)
)

Set-StrictMode -Version Latest

## Call Get-Credential again, so that the user can type something like
## Enable-RemoteCredSSP -Computer Computer -Cred DOMAIN\user
```

```
$credential = Get-Credential $credential
$username = $credential.Username
$password = $credential.GetNetworkCredential().Password

## Define the script we will use to create the scheduled task
$powerShellCommand =
    "powershell -noprofile -command Enable-WsManCredSSP -Role Server -Force"
$script = @"
schtasks /CREATE /TN 'Enable CredSSP' /SC WEEKLY /RL HIGHEST ``
    /RU $username /RP $password ``
    /TR "$powerShellCommand" /F

schtasks /RUN /TN 'Enable CredSSP'
"@

## Create the task on the remote system to configure CredSSP
$command = [ScriptBlock]::Create($script)
Invoke-Command $computername $command -Cred $credential

## Wait for the remoting changes to come into effect
for($count = 1; $count -le 10; $count++)
{
    $output =
        Invoke-Command $computername { 1 } -Auth CredSSP -Cred $credential
    if($output -eq 1) { break; }

    "Attempt $count : Not ready yet."
    Sleep 5
}

## Clean up
$command = [ScriptBlock]::Create($script)
Invoke-Command $computername {
    schtasks /DELETE /TN 'Enable CredSSP' /F } -Cred $credential

## Verify the output
Invoke-Command $computername {
    Get-WmiObject Win32_ComputerSystem } -Auth CredSSP -Cred $credential
```

After completing these configuration steps, your remote sessions will have unrestricted network access.

See Also

Recipe 29.7, "Program: Remotely Enable PowerShell Remoting"

Recipe 29.9, "Enable Remoting to Workgroup Computers"

29.14 Pass Variables to Remote Sessions

Problem

You want to invoke a command on a remote computer but supply some of its information as a dynamic argument.

Solution

Use the -ArgumentList parameter of the Invoke-Command cmdlet:

```
PS > $cred = Get-Credential

PS > $command = {
    param($cred)

    Invoke-Command leeholmes1c23 {
        "Hello from $($env:Computername)" } -Credential $cred
}

PS > Invoke-Command Remote-Computer $command -ArgumentList $cred -Credential $cred
Hello from LEEHOLMES1C23
```

Discussion

When processing commands on a remote system, you sometimes need dynamic information from the local system—such as the value of a variable or something that changes for each invocation. A perfect example of this is a credential, where hardcoding usernames or passwords is a practice you should strive to avoid.

The solution gives an example of this approach. On a client computer, we request a credential from the user. We make a connection to Remote-Computer using that credential and invoke a command. The command itself makes yet another connection—this time to leeholmes1c23. That final command simply retrieves the computer name of the remote system. Rather than hardcode a username and password (or request them again), it uses the $cred variable passed in by the original call to Invoke-Command.

To support this, the Invoke-Command cmdlet offers the -ArgumentList parameter. Variables supplied to this parameter will be converted into a version safe for remoting, which will then be made available to the commands inside of the -ScriptBlock parameter.

 Arguments that you supply to the -ArgumentList parameter go through a serialization process before being sent to the remote computer. Although their properties closely resemble the original objects, they no longer have methods. For more information about PowerShell serialization, see Recipe 29.11.

As with arguments in other scripts, functions, and script blocks, the script block used in `Invoke-Command` can access arguments directly through the `$args` array, or through a `param()` statement to make the script easier to read. Unlike most `param()` statements, however, these parameter statements must all be positional. Named arguments (e.g., `-ArgumentList "-Cred","$cred"`) are not supported, nor are advanced parameter attributes (such as `[Parameter(Mandatory = $true)]`).

For more information about arguments and `param()` statements, see Recipe 11.11.

See Also

Recipe 11.11, "Access Arguments of a Script, Function, or Script Block"

Recipe 29.11, "Invoke a Command on a Remote Computer"

29.15 Configure Advanced Remoting Options

Problem

You want to configure compression, profiles, proxy authentication, certificate verification, or culture information for a remote session.

Solution

For client-side configuration settings, call the `New-PsSessionOption` cmdlet and provide values for parameters that you want to customize:

```
PS > $options = New-PSSessionOption -Culture "fr-CA"
PS > $sess = New-PsSession Lee-Desk -Cred Lee -SessionOption $options
PS > Invoke-Command $sess { Get-Date | Out-String }

20 février 2010 17:40:16
```

For server-side configuration settings, review the options under *WSMan:\localhost\Shell* and *WSMan:localhost\Service*.

```
Set-Item WSMan:\localhost\shell\MaxShellsPerUser 10
```

Discussion

PowerShell lets you define advanced client connection options through two paths: the `New-PsSessionOption` cmdlet and the `$PSSessionOption` automatic variable.

When you call the `New-PsSession` cmdlet, PowerShell returns an object that holds configuration settings for a remote session. You can customize all of the values through the cmdlet's parameters or set properties on the object that is returned.

Several of the options refer to timeout values: `OperationTimeout`, `Open Timeout`, `CancelTimeout`, and `IdleTimeout`. These parameters are generally not required (for example, even when invoking a long-running command), but they can be used to overcome errors when you encounter extremely slow or congested network conditions.

If you want to configure session options for every new connection, a second alternative is the `$PSSessionOption` automatic variable:

```
PS > $PSSessionOption

MaximumConnectionRedirectionCount : 5
NoCompression                     : False
NoMachineProfile                  : False
ProxyAccessType                   : None
ProxyAuthentication               : Negotiate
ProxyCredential                   :
SkipCACheck                       : False
SkipCNCheck                       : False
SkipRevocationCheck               : False
OperationTimeout                  : 00:03:00
NoEncryption                      : False
UseUTF16                          : False
Culture                           :
UICulture                         :
MaximumReceivedDataSizePerCommand :
MaximumReceivedObjectSize         :
ApplicationArguments              :
OpenTimeout                       : 00:03:00
CancelTimeout                     : 00:01:00
IdleTimeout                       : 00:04:00
```

If you don't provide explicit settings during a connection attempt, PowerShell Remoting looks at the values in this variable for its defaults.

From the server perspective, all configuration sits in the WSMan drive. The most common configuration options come from the *WSMan:\localhost\Shell* path:

```
PS > dir WSMan:\localhost\Shell

    WSManConfig: Microsoft.WSMan.Management\WSMan::localhost\Shell
```

Name	Value
AllowRemoteShellAccess	true
IdleTimeout	180000
MaxConcurrentUsers	5
MaxShellRunTime	2147483647
MaxProcessesPerShell	15
MaxMemoryPerShellMB	150
MaxShellsPerUser	10

See Also

Recipe 29.11, "Invoke a Command on a Remote Computer"

29.16 Invoke a Command on Many Computers

Problem

You want to manage many computers simultaneously.

Solution

Use the -ThrottleLimit and -AsJob parameters to configure how PowerShell scales out your commands:

```
PS > $sessions = $(
    New-PsSession localhost;
    New-PsSession localhost;
    New-PsSession localhost)


PS > $start = Get-Date
PS > Invoke-Command $sessions { Start-Sleep 2; "Test $pid" }
Test 720
Test 6112
Test 4792
PS > (Get-Date) - $start | Select TotalSeconds | Format-Table -Auto

TotalSeconds
------------
    2.09375


PS >
PS > $start = Get-Date
PS > Invoke-Command $sessions { Start-Sleep 2; "Test $pid" } -ThrottleLimit 1
Test 6112
Test 4792
Test 720
PS > (Get-Date) - $start | Select TotalSeconds | Format-Table -Auto

TotalSeconds
------------
      6.25
```

Discussion

One of the largest difficulties in traditional networking scripts comes from managing many computers at once. Remote computer management is typically network-bound, so most scripts spend the majority of their time waiting for the network.

The solution to this is to scale. Rather than manage one computer at a time, you manage several. Not too many, however, as few machines can handle the demands of connecting to hundreds or thousands of remote machines at once.

Despite the benefits, writing a networking script that supports smart automatic throttling is beyond the capability of many and too far down "the big list of things to do" of most. Fortunately, PowerShell Remoting's main focus is to solve these common problems, and throttling is no exception.

By default, PowerShell Remoting connects to 32 computers at a time. After running your command on the first 32 computers in your list, it waits for commands to complete before running your command on additional computers.

To demonstrate this automatic scaling, the solution shows the difference between calling `Invoke-Command` with the default throttle limit and calling it with a throttle limit of one computer.

When working against many computers at a time, you might want to continue using your shell while these long-running tasks process in the background. To support background processing of tasks, the `Invoke-Command` cmdlet offers `-AsJob`, which lets you run your command as a PowerShell Job.

For more information about PowerShell Jobs, see Recipe 1.4.

See Also

Recipe 1.4, "Invoke a Long-Running or Background Command"

Recipe 29.11, "Invoke a Command on a Remote Computer"

29.17 Run a Local Script on a Remote Computer

Problem

You have a local script and want to run it on a remote computer.

Solution

Use the `-FilePath` parameter of the `Invoke-Command` cmdlet:

```
PS > Get-Content .\Get-ProcessByName.ps1
param($name)

Get-Process -Name $name

PS > Invoke-Command -Computername Lee-Desk `
    -FilePath .\Get-ProcessByname.ps1 -ArgumentList PowerShell `
    -Cred Lee
```

```
Handles  NPM(K)    PM(K)      WS(K) VM(M)    CPU(s)     Id Process    PSComputer
                                                           Name        Name
-------  ------    -----      ----- -----    ------     -- ---------   ---------
    628      17    39084      58908   214      4.26   7540 powers...   lee-des...
```

Discussion

For quick one-off actions, the -ScriptBlock parameter of the Invoke-Command cmdlet lets you easily invoke commands against a remote computer:

```
PS > Invoke-Command Lee-Desk { Get-Process -n PowerShell } -Cred Lee
```

```
Handles  NPM(K)    PM(K)      WS(K) VM(M)    CPU(s)     Id Process    PSComputer
                                                           Name        Name
-------  ------    -----      ----- -----    ------     -- ---------   ---------
    628      17    39084      58908   214      4.26   7540 powers...   lee-des...
```

When these commands become more complicated, however, writing them all in a script block becomes cumbersome. You have no syntax highlighting, line numbering, or any of the other creature comforts offered by writing script-based execution.

To let you write scripts against a remote computer instead, PowerShell offers the -FilePath parameter on the Invoke-Command cmdlet. When you use this parameter, PowerShell reads the script from disk and invokes its contents on the remote computer.

In this mode, PowerShell makes no attempt to address dependencies during this process. If your script requires any other scripts, commands, or environmental dependencies, ensure that they are available on the remote computer.

For one option on how to transfer items to a remote computer, see Recipe 29.18.

See Also

Recipe 29.11, "Invoke a Command on a Remote Computer"

Recipe 29.18, "Program: Transfer a File to a Remote Computer"

29.18 Program: Transfer a File to a Remote Computer

When working with remote computers, a common problem is how to bring your local tools and environment to that computer. Using file shares or FTP transfers is a common way to share tools between systems, but these options are not always available.

As a solution, Example 29-6 builds on PowerShell Remoting to transfer the file content over a regular PowerShell Remoting connection.

To do this, it reads the content of the file into an array of bytes. Then, it breaks that array into one-megabyte chunks. It streams each chunk to the remote system, which then recombines the chunks into the destination file. By breaking the file into large chunks, the script optimizes the network efficiency of PowerShell Remoting. By limiting these chunks to one megabyte, it avoids running into any quota issues.

Example 29-6. Send-File.ps1

```
###############################################################################
##
## Send-File
##
## From Windows PowerShell Cookbook (O'Reilly)
## by Lee Holmes (http://www.leeholmes.com/guide)
##
###############################################################################

<#

.SYNOPSIS

Sends a file to a remote session.

.EXAMPLE

PS >$session = New-PsSession leeholmes1c23
PS >Send-File c:\temp\test.exe c:\temp\test.exe $session

#>

param(
    ## The path on the local computer
    [Parameter(Mandatory = $true)]
    $Source,

    ## The target path on the remote computer
    [Parameter(Mandatory = $true)]
    $Destination,

    ## The session that represents the remote computer
    [Parameter(Mandatory = $true)]
    [System.Management.Automation.Runspaces.PSSession] $Session
)

Set-StrictMode -Version Latest

## Get the source file, and then get its content
$sourcePath = (Resolve-Path $source).Path
$sourceBytes = [IO.File]::ReadAllBytes($sourcePath)
$streamChunks = @()

## Now break it into chunks to stream
Write-Progress -Activity "Sending $Source" -Status "Preparing file"
$streamSize = 1MB
for($position = 0; $position -lt $sourceBytes.Length;
    $position += $streamSize)
{
    $remaining = $sourceBytes.Length - $position
    $remaining = [Math]::Min($remaining, $streamSize)

    $nextChunk = New-Object byte[] $remaining
    [Array]::Copy($sourcebytes, $position, $nextChunk, 0, $remaining)
```

```
        $streamChunks += ,$nextChunk
}

$remoteScript = {
    param($destination, $length)

    ## Convert the destination path to a full filesytem path (to support
    ## relative paths)
    $Destination = $executionContext.SessionState.`
        Path.GetUnresolvedProviderPathFromPSPath($Destination)

    ## Create a new array to hold the file content
    $destBytes = New-Object byte[] $length
    $position = 0

    ## Go through the input, and fill in the new array of file content
    foreach($chunk in $input)
    {
        Write-Progress -Activity "Writing $Destination" `
            -Status "Sending file" `
            -PercentComplete ($position / $length * 100)

        [GC]::Collect()
        [Array]::Copy($chunk, 0, $destBytes, $position, $chunk.Length)
        $position += $chunk.Length
    }

    ## Write the content to the new file
    [IO.File]::WriteAllBytes($destination, $destBytes)

    ## Show the result
    Get-Item $destination
    [GC]::Collect()
}

## Stream the chunks into the remote script
$streamChunks | Invoke-Command -Session $session $remoteScript `
    -ArgumentList $destination,$sourceBytes.Length
```

For more information about running scripts, see Recipe 1.1.

See Also

Recipe 1.1, "Run Programs, Scripts, and Existing Tools"

Recipe 29.11, "Invoke a Command on a Remote Computer"

29.19 Determine Whether a Script Is Running on a Remote Computer

Problem

You have a script that needs to know whether it is running on a local or remote computer.

Solution

Review the output of the `$host.Name` property. If it is `ServerRemoteHost`, it is running remotely. If it is anything else, it is running locally.

```
PS > $host.Name
ConsoleHost

PS > Invoke-Command leeholmes1c23 { $host.Name }
ServerRemoteHost
```

Discussion

While your scripts should work no matter whether they are running locally or remotely, you might run into situations where you need to verify which environment your script is being launched under.

The `$host` automatic variable exposes information about the current host, of which PowerShell Remoting is one. When you access this variable in a remoting session, the value is `ServerRemoteHost`. Although the value on the console host is `ConsoleHost`, you should not depend on this as an indicator of a local script. There are many other PowerShell hosts—such as the PowerShell Integrated Scripting Environment (`Windows PowerShell ISE Host`), PowerGUI, PowerShell Plus, and more. Each has a customized host name, but none is `ServerRemoteHost`.

For more information about the `$host` automatic variable, see Recipe 13.9.

See Also

Recipe 13.9, "Access Features of the Host's User Interface"

29.20 Program: Create a Task-Specific Remoting Endpoint

In addition to its main feature of offering full and rich Remoting endpoints, PowerShell lets you configure a session to the other extreme as well. This is through a mechanism known as *restricted runspaces*.

Restricted runspaces let you control which commands you expose to the user, create proxy functions to wrap commands with more secure versions, and remove access to the PowerShell language altogether.

The most typical implementation of a restricted runspace is a developer's task: creating a custom assembly, building an *initial session state*, and more. When you create an initial session state, there are two types of commands: *public* and *private*. The main distinction is that users can call only public commands, while public commands can internally call both public and private commands. This lets you write a public function, for example, that calls many private PowerShell cmdlets to accomplish its task.

For administrators, there is a relatively simple alternative to the developer's approach: creating a custom endpoint that uses a startup script for its configuration tasks.

The implementation of this startup script is still a challenge, though. Which commands should you make public in order to support interactive remoting? Which parameters should you remove from the commands that you do expose?

Fortunately, the developer's API supports a command to answer this exact question. The CreateRestricted() method on the InitialSessionState class creates a minimal and secure startup environment. To create a startup script based on this information, you can examine the commands in the InitialSessionState object and clone that information in your restricted session.

After importing all of the proxy functions, the last step is to configure their proper visibility, disable access to scripts and applications, and then remove access to the PowerShell language.

Once you've built a script that can restrict a PowerShell session, call the Register-PSSessionConfiguration cmdlet to assign it a new endpoint name and configuration:

```
PS > Set-ExecutionPolicy RemoteSigned
PS > Register-PSSessionConfiguration -Name Inventory `
    -StartupScript 'C:\Program Files\Endpoints\Inventory.ps1'

Confirm
Are you sure you want to perform this action?
Performing operation "Register-PSSessionConfiguration" on Target "Name:
Inventory. This will allow administrators to remotely run Windows PowerShell
commands on this computer."
[Y] Yes  [A] Yes to All  [N] No  [L] No to All  [S] Suspend  [?] Help
(default is "Y"): Y


   WSManConfig: Microsoft.WSMan.Management\WSMan::localhost\Plugin

Name                    Type                Keys
----                    ----                ----
Inventory               Container           {Name=Inventory}

Confirm
Are you sure you want to perform this action?
```

```
Performing operation ""Restart-Service"" on Target "Name: WinRM".
[Y] Yes  [A] Yes to All  [N] No  [L] No to All  [S] Suspend  [?] Help
(default is "Y"): Y
```

```
Enter-PSSession -Computer leeholmes1c23 -ConfigurationName Inventory
```

As with the `Microsoft.PowerShell` remoting endpoint, you can configure permissions, quotas, and more. For more information about endpoint configuration, see Recipes 29.8 and 29.15.

Example 29-7 gives an example of a startup script, building an endpoint that exposes only a `Get-Inventory` command.

Example 29-7. Inventory.ps1

```
##############################################################################
##
## Inventory
##
## From Windows PowerShell Cookbook (O'Reilly)
## by Lee Holmes (http://www.leeholmes.com/guide)
##
##############################################################################

<#

.SYNOPSIS

Serves as the configuration script for a custom remoting endpoint that
exposes only the Get-Inventory custom command.

.EXAMPLE

PS >Register-PsSessionConfiguration Inventory `
    -StartupScript 'C:\Program Files\Endpoints\Inventory.ps1'
PS >Enter-PsSession leeholmes1c23 -ConfigurationName Inventory

[leeholmes1c23]: [Inventory] > Get-Command

CommandType     Name                 Definition
-----------     ----                 ----------
Function        Exit-PSSession       [CmdletBinding()]...
Function        Get-Command          [CmdletBinding()]...
Function        Get-FormatData       [CmdletBinding()]...
Function        Get-Help             [CmdletBinding()]...
Function        Get-Inventory        ...
Function        Measure-Object       [CmdletBinding()]...
Function        Out-Default          [CmdletBinding()]...
Function        prompt               ...
Function        Select-Object        [CmdletBinding()]...

[leeholmes1c23]: [Inventory] > Get-Inventory

SystemDirectory : C:\Windows\system32
```

```
Organization    :
BuildNumber     : 6002
RegisteredUser  : Lee Holmes
SerialNumber    : 89580-433-1295803-71477
Version         : 6.0.6002

[leeholmes1c23]: [Inventory] > 1+1
The syntax is not supported by this runspace. This might be because it is
in no-language mode.
    + CategoryInfo          :
    + FullyQualifiedErrorId : ScriptsNotAllowed

[leeholmes1c23]: [Inventory] > Exit-PsSession
PS >

#>

Set-StrictMode -Off

## Create a new function to get inventory
function Get-Inventory
{
    Get-WmiObject Win32_OperatingSystem
}

## Customize the prompt
function Prompt
{
    "[Inventory] > "
}

## Remember which functions we want to expose to the user
$exportedCommands = "Get-Inventory","Prompt"

## The System.Management.Automation.Runspaces.InitialSessionState class
## has a CreateRestricted() method that creates a default locked-down
## secure configuration for a remote session. This configuration only
## supports the bare minimum required for interactive remoting.
$issType = [System.Management.Automation.Runspaces.InitialSessionState]
$iss = $issType::CreateRestricted("RemoteServer")

## Add the commands to a hashtable so that we can access them easily
$issHashtable = @{}
foreach($command in $iss.Commands)
{
    $issHashtable[$command.Name + "-" + $command.CommandType] = $command
}

## Go through all of the functions built into the restricted runspace and add
## them to this session. These are proxy functions to limit the functionality
## of commands that we need (such as Get-Command, Select-Object, etc.).
foreach($function in $iss.Commands |
    Where-Object { $_.CommandType -eq "Function" })
{
    Set-Content "function:\$($function.Name)" -Value $function.Definition
```

```
}

## Go through all of the commands in this session
foreach($command in Get-Command)
{
    ## If it was one of our exported commands, keep it Public
    if($exportedCommands -contains $command.Name) { continue }

    ## If the current command is defined as Private in the initial session
    ## state, mark it as Private here as well.
    $issCommand = $issHashtable[$command.Name + "-" + $command.CommandType]
    if((-not $issCommand) -or ($issCommand.Visibility -ne "Public"))
    {
        $command.Visibility = "Private"
    }
}

## Finally, prevent all access to the PowerShell language
$executionContext.SessionState.Scripts.Clear()
$executionContext.SessionState.Applications.Clear()
$executionContext.SessionState.LanguageMode = "NoLanguage"
```

For more information about running scripts, see Recipe 1.1. For more information about proxy functions, see Recipe 11.23.

See Also

Recipe 1.1, "Run Programs, Scripts, and Existing Tools"

Recipe 11.23, "Program: Enhance or Extend an Existing Cmdlet"

Recipe 29.8, "Configure User Permissions for Remoting"

Transactions

30.0 Introduction

Transactions describe a system's ability to support tentative or multistep changes. When you make changes within the context of a transaction, the system provides four main guarantees:

Isolation

> To observers not participating in the transaction, the commands inside the transaction have not impacted the system.

Atomicity

> Once you decide to finalize (*commit*) a transaction, either all of the changes take effect or none of them do.

Consistency

> Errors caused during a transaction that would cause an inconsistent system state are dealt with in order to bring the system back to a consistent state.

Durability

> Once the system has informed you of the transaction's successful completion, you can be certain that the changes are permanent.

As a real-world example of a transaction, consider a money transfer between two bank accounts. This might happen in two stages: subtract the money from the first account, and then add the money to the second account. In this situation, you have the exact same goals for robustness and correctness:

Isolation

> While the money transfer is taking place (but has not yet completed), the balance of both bank accounts appears unchanged.

Atomicity

> At some point in the process, it's possible that we've subtracted the money from the first account but haven't added it yet to the second account. When we process

the money transfer, it's critical that the system never show this intermediate state. Either all of the changes take effect or none of them do.

Consistency

If an error occurs during the money transfer, the system takes corrective action to ensure that it is not left in an intermediate state. Perhaps it accounts for a lack of funds by adding an overdraft charge or by abandoning the money transfer altogether. It should not, for example, take the funds from one account without depositing them into the second account.

Durability

Once the money transfer completes, you don't have to worry about a system error undoing all or part of it.

Although transactions are normally a developer topic, PowerShell exposes transactions as an end-user concept, opening a great deal of potential for consistent system management.

To start a transaction, call the `Start-Transaction` cmdlet. To use a cmdlet that supports transactions, specify the `-UseTransaction` parameter. Being explicit about this parameter is crucial, as many cmdlets that support transactions can work equally well without one. Because of that, PowerShell lets the cmdlet participate in the transaction only when you supply this parameter.

In Windows Vista and later, PowerShell's registry provider supports transactions as a first-class concept. You can see this in action in Recipe 21.6.

```
PS > Set-Location HKCU:
PS > Start-Transaction

PS > mkdir TempKey -UseTransaction


    Hive: HKEY_CURRENT_USER

SKC  VC Name                        Property
---  -- ----                        --------
  0   0 TempKey                     {}

PS > New-Item TempKey\TempKey2 -UseTransaction


    Hive: HKEY_CURRENT_USER\TempKey

SKC  VC Name                        Property
---  -- ----                        --------
  0   0 TempKey2                    {}

PS > Get-ChildItem TempKey
Get-ChildItem : Cannot find path 'HKEY_CURRENT_USER\TempKey' because it
does not exist.

PS > Complete-Transaction
PS > Get-ChildItem TempKey
```

```
    Hive: HKEY_CURRENT_USER\TempKey

SKC  VC Name                          Property
---  -- ----                          --------
  0   0 TempKey2                       {}
```

Once you have completed the transactional work, call either the Complete-Transac
tion cmdlet to make it final or the Undo-Transaction cmdlet to discard the changes.
While you may now be tempted to experiment with transactions on other providers
(for example, the filesystem), be aware that only the registry provider currently supports
them.

30.1 Safely Experiment with Transactions

Problem

You want to experiment with PowerShell's transactions support but don't want to use
the Registry Provider as your playground.

Solution

Use PowerShell's System.Management.Automation.TransactedString object along with
the Use-Transaction cmdlet to experiment with a string, rather than registry keys:

```
PS > Start-Transaction

Suggestion [1,Transactions]: Once a transaction is started, only commands that
get called with the -UseTransaction flag become part of that transaction.
PS >
PS > $transactedString = New-Object Microsoft.PowerShell.Commands.Management.
TransactedString
PS > $transactedString.Append("Hello ")
PS >
PS > Use-Transaction -UseTransaction { $transactedString.Append("World") }

Suggestion [2,Transactions]: The Use-Transaction cmdlet is intended for
scripting of transaction-enabled .NET objects. Its ScriptBlock should contain
nothing else.
PS >
PS > $transactedString.ToString()
Hello
PS >
PS > Complete-Transaction
PS >
PS > $transactedString.ToString()
Hello World
PS >
```

Discussion

PowerShell's transaction support builds on four core cmdlets: Start-Transaction, Use-Transaction, Complete-Transaction, and Undo-Transaction.

The Start-Transaction begins a transaction, creating a context where changes are visible to commands within the transaction, but not outside of it. For the most part, after starting a transaction, you'll apply commands to that transaction by adding the -Use Transaction parameter to a cmdlet that supports it. For example, when a PowerShell provider supports transactions, all of PowerShell's core cmdlets (Get-ChildItem, Remove-Item, etc.) let you specify the -UseTransaction parameter for actions against that provider.

The Use-Transaction cmdlet is slightly different. Although it still requires the -UseTran saction parameter to apply its script block to the current transaction, its sole purpose is to let you script against .NET objects that support transactions themselves. Since they have no way to supply a -UseTransaction parameter, PowerShell offers this generic cmdlet for any type of transactional .NET scripting.

 Other transaction-enabled cmdlets should not be called within the Use-Transaction script block. You still need to provide the -UseTransaction parameter to the cmdlet being called, and there's a chance that they might cause instability with your PowerShell-wide transactions.

To give users an opportunity to play with something a little less risky than the Windows Registry, PowerShell includes the Microsoft.PowerShell.Commands.Management.Trans actedString class. This class acts like you'd expect any transacted command to act and lets you become familiar with how the rest of PowerShell's transaction cmdlets work together. Since this is a .NET object, it must be called from within the script block of the Use-Transaction cmdlet.

Finally, when you are finished performing tasks for the current transaction, call either the Complete-Transaction or the Undo-Transaction cmdlet. As compared to the solution, here's an example session where the Undo-Transaction cmdlet lets you discard changes made during the transaction:

```
PS > Start-Transaction

Suggestion [1,Transactions]: Once a transaction is started, only commands that
get called with the -UseTransaction flag become part of that transaction.
PS >
PS > $transactedString = New-Object Microsoft.PowerShell.Commands.Management.Tra
nsactedString
PS > $transactedString.Append("Hello ")
PS >
PS > Use-Transaction -UseTransaction { $transactedString.Append("World") }
```

```
Suggestion [2,Transactions]: The Use-Transaction cmdlet is intended for
scripting of transaction-enabled .NET objects. Its ScriptBlock should contain
nothing else.
PS >
PS > $transactedString.ToString()
Hello
PS >
PS > Undo-Transaction
PS >
PS > $transactedString.ToString()
Hello
```

For more information about transactions in the Windows Registry, see Recipe 21.6.

See Also

Recipe 21.6, "Safely Combine Related Registry Modifications"

30.2 Change Error Recovery Behavior in Transactions

Problem

You want to change how PowerShell responds to errors during the execution of a transacted cmdlet.

Solution

Use the -RollbackPreference parameter of the Start-Transaction cmdlet to control what type of error will cause PowerShell to automatically undo your transaction:

```
HKCU:\ >Start-Transaction
HKCU:\ >New-Item Foo -UseTransaction


    Hive: HKEY_CURRENT_USER

SKC  VC Name                        Property
---  -- ----                        --------
  0   0 Foo                         {}

HKCU:\ >Copy IDoNotExist Foo -UseTransaction
Copy-Item : Cannot find path 'HKCU:\IDoNotExist' because it does not exist.

HKCU:\ >Complete-Transaction
Complete-Transaction : Cannot commit transaction. The transaction has been
rolled back or has timed out.

HKCU:\ >Start-Transaction -RollbackPreference TerminatingError


    Hive: HKEY_CURRENT_USER

SKC  VC Name                        Property
---  -- ----                        --------
```

```
    0    0 Foo                           {}

HKCU:\ >Copy IDoNotExist Foo -UseTransaction
Copy-Item : Cannot find path 'HKCU:\IDoNotExist' because it does not exist.

HKCU:\ >Complete-Transaction
HKCU:\ >Get-Item Foo

    Hive: HKEY_CURRENT_USER

SKC  VC Name                        Property
---  -- ----                        --------
    0    0 Foo                           {}
```

Discussion

Errors in scripts are an extremely frequent cause of system inconsistency. If a script incorrectly assumes the existence of a registry key or other system state, this type of error tends to waterfall through the entire script. As the script continues, some of the operations succeed while others fail. When the script completes, you're in the difficult situation of not knowing exactly what portions of the script worked correctly.

Sometimes running the script again will magically make the problems go away. Unfortunately, it's just as common to face a painstaking manual cleanup effort.

Addressing these consistency issues is one of the primary goals of system transactions.

When PowerShell creates a new transaction, it undoes (*rolls back*) your transaction for any error it encounters that is operating in the context of that transaction. When PowerShell rolls back your transaction, the system impact is clear: no part of your transaction was made permanent, so your system is still entirely consistent.

Some situations are simply too volatile to depend on this rigid interpretation of consistency, though, so PowerShell offers the -RollbackPreference parameter on the Start-Transaction to let you configure how it should respond to errors:

Error
 PowerShell rolls back your transaction when any error occurs.

TerminatingError
 PowerShell rolls back your transaction only when a terminating error occurs.

Never
 PowerShell never automatically rolls back your transaction in response to errors.

For more information about PowerShell's error handling and error levels, see Chapter 15.

See Also

Chapter 15, *Tracing and Error Management*

Event Handling

31.0 Introduction

Much of system administration is reactionary: taking some action when a system service shuts down, when files are created or deleted, when changes are made to the Windows registry, or even on a timed interval.

The easiest way to respond to system changes is to simply *poll* for them. If you're waiting for a file to be created, just check for it every once in a while until it shows up. If you're waiting for a process to start, just keep calling the `Get-Process` cmdlet until it's there.

This approach is passable for some events (such as waiting for a process to come or go), but it quickly falls apart when you need to monitor huge portions of the system— such as the entire Registry or filesystem.

An an alternative to polling for system changes, many technologies support automatic notifications—known as *events*. When an application registers for these automatic notifications, it can respond to them as soon as they happen, rather than having to poll for them.

Unfortunately, each technology offers its own method of event notification: .NET defines one approach and WMI defines another. When you have a script that wants to generate its own events, neither technology offers an option.

PowerShell addresses this complexity by introducing a single, consistent set of event-related cmdlets. These cmdlets let you work with all of these different event sources. When an event occurs, you can let PowerShell store the notification for you in its event queue or use an `Action` script block to process it automatically:

```
PS > "Hello" > file.txt
PS > Get-Item file.txt


    Directory: C:\temp
```

```
Mode             LastWriteTime     Length Name
----             -------------     ------ ----
-a---         2/21/2010  12:57 PM      16 file.txt


PS > Get-Process notepad

Handles  NPM(K)    PM(K)      WS(K) VM(M)   CPU(s)     Id ProcessName
-------  ------    -----      ----- -----   ------     -- -----------
     64       3     1140       6196    63     0.06   3240 notepad


PS > Register-WmiEvent Win32_ProcessStopTrace `
    -SourceIdentifier ProcessStopWatcher `
    -Action {
        if($EventArgs.NewEvent.ProcessName -eq "notepad.exe")
        {
            Remove-Item c:\temp\file.txt
        }
    }

PS > Stop-Process -n notepad
PS > Get-Item c:\temp\file.txt
Get-Item : Cannot find path 'C:\temp\file.txt' because it does not exist.
```

By building on PowerShell eventing, you can write scripts to quickly react to an ever-changing system.

31.1 Respond to Automatically Generated Events

Problem

You want to respond automatically to a .NET, WMI, or engine event.

Solution

Use the -Action parameter of the Register-ObjectEvent, Register-WmiEvent, and Register-EngineEvent cmdlets to be notified when an event arrives and have PowerShell invoke the script block you supply:

```
PS > $timer = New-Object Timers.Timer
PS > $timer.Interval = 1000
PS > Register-ObjectEvent $timer Elapsed -SourceIdentifier Timer.Elapsed `
    -Action { $GLOBAL:lastRandom = Get-Random }


Id              Name            State      HasMoreData  Location
--              ----            -----      -----------  --------
2               Timer.Elapsed   NotStarted False


PS > $timer.Enabled = $true
```

```
PS > $lastRandom
836077209
PS > $lastRandom
2030675971
PS > $lastRandom
1617766254
PS > Unregister-Event Timer.Elapsed
```

Discussion

PowerShell's event registration cmdlets give you a consistent way to interact with many different event technologies: .NET events, WMI events, and PowerShell engine events.

By default, when you register for an event, PowerShell adds a new entry to the session-wide event repository called the *event queue*. You can use the Get-Event cmdlet to see events added to this queue, and the Remove-Event cmdlet to remove events from this queue.

In addition to its support for manual processing of events, you can also supply a script block to the -Action parameter of the event registration cmdlets. When you provide a script block to the -Action parameter, PowerShell automatically processes events when they arrive.

However, doing two things at once means multithreading. And multithreading? Thar be dragons! To prevent you from having to deal with multithreading issues, PowerShell tightly controls the execution of these script blocks. When it's time to process an action, it suspends the current script or pipeline, executes the action, and then resumes where it left off. It processes only one action at a time.

```
PS > $timer = New-Object Timers.Timer
PS > $timer.Interval = 1000
PS > Register-ObjectEvent $timer Elapsed -SourceIdentifier Timer.Elapsed `
    -Action { Write-Host "Processing event" }
$timer.Enabled = $true

PS > while($true) { Write-Host "Processing loop"; Sleep 1 }
Processing loop
Processing event
Processing loop
Processing event
Processing loop
Processing event
Processing loop
Processing event
Processing loop
(...)
```

Inside of the -Action scriptblock, PowerShell gives your script access to five automatic variables:

eventSubscriber

> The subscriber (event registration) that generated this event.

event

The details of the event itself: `MessageData`, `TimeGenerated`, etc.

args

The arguments and parameters of the event handler. Most events place the event sender and customized event information as the first two arguments, but this depends on the event handler.

sender

The object that fired the event (if any).

eventArgs

The customized event information that the event defines, if any. For example, the `Timers.Timer` object provides a `TimerElapsedEventArgs` object for this parameter. This object includes a `SignalTime` parameter, which identifies exactly when the timer fired. Likewise, WMI events define an object that places most of the information in the `$eventArgs.NewEvent` property.

In addition to the script block that you supply to the `-Action` parameter, you can also supply any objects you'd like to the `-MessageData` parameter during your event registration. PowerShell associates this data with any event notifications it generates for this event registration.

To prevent your script block from accidentally corrupting the state of scripts that it interrupts, PowerShell places it in a very isolated environment. Primarily, PowerShell gives you access to your event action through its job infrastructure. As with other PowerShell jobs, you can use the `Receive-Job` cmdlet to retrieve any output generated by your event action:

```
PS > $timer = New-Object Timers.Timer
PS > $timer.Interval = 1000
PS > Register-ObjectEvent $timer Elapsed -SourceIdentifier Timer.Elapsed `
    -Action {
        $SCRIPT:triggerCount = 1 + $SCRIPT:triggerCount
        "Processing Event $triggerCount"
    }
$timer.Enabled = $true

Id            Name           State      HasMoreData   Location
--            ----           -----      -----------   --------
1             Timer.Elapsed  NotStarted False

PS > Get-Job 1

Id            Name           State      HasMoreData   Location
--            ----           -----      -----------   --------
1             Timer.Elapsed  Running    True


PS > Receive-Job 1
Processing Event 1
Processing Event 2
```

```
Processing Event 3
(...)
```

For more information about working with PowerShell jobs, see Recipe 1.4.

In addition to exposing your event actions through a job interface, PowerShell also uses a module to ensure that your -Action script block is not impacted by (and does not impact) other scripts running on the system. As with all modules, $GLOBAL variables are shared by the entire session. $SCRIPT variables are shared and persisted for all invocations of the script block. All other variables persist only for the current triggering of your event action. For more information about PowerShell modules, see Recipe 11.7.

For more information about useful .NET and WMI events, see Appendix I.

See Also

Recipe 1.4, "Invoke a Long-Running or Background Command"

Recipe 11.7, "Write Commands That Maintain State"

Appendix I, *Selected Events and Their Uses*

31.2 Create and Respond to Custom Events

Problem

You want to create new events for other scripts to consume or want to respond automatically when they occur.

Solution

Use the New-Event cmdlet to generate a custom event. Use the -Action parameter of the Register-EngineEvent cmdlet to respond to that event automatically.

```
PS > Register-EngineEvent -SourceIdentifier Custom.Event `
    -Action { Write-Host "Received Event" }


PS > $null = New-Event Custom.Event
Received Event
```

Discussion

The New-Event cmdlet lets you create new custom events for other scripts or event registrations to consume. When you call the New-Event cmdlet, PowerShell adds a new entry to the session-wide event repository called the *event queue*. You can use the Get-Event cmdlet to see events added to this queue, or you can use the Register-EngineEvent cmdlet to have PowerShell respond automatically.

One prime use of the New-Event cmdlet is to adapt complex events surfaced through the generic WMI and .NET event cmdlets. By writing task-focused commands to surface this adapted data, you can offer and work with data that is simpler to consume.

To accomplish this goal, use the Register-ObjectEvent or Register-WmiEvent cmdlets to register for one of their events. In the -Action script block, use the New-Event cmdlet to generate a new, more specialized event.

In this scenario, the event registrations that interact with .NET or WMI directly are merely "support" events, and users would not expect to see them when they use the Get-EventSubscriber cmdlet. To hide these event registrations by default, both the Register-ObjectEvent and Register-WmiEvent cmdlets offer a -SupportEvent parameter.

Here is an example of two functions that notify you when a new process starts:

```
## Enable process creation events
function Enable-ProcessCreationEvent
{
    $identifier = "WMI.ProcessCreated"
    $query = "SELECT * FROM __instancecreationevent " +
                "WITHIN 5 " +
                "WHERE targetinstance isa 'win32_process'"
    Register-WmiEvent -Query $query -SourceIdentifier $identifier `
        -SupportEvent -Action {
            [void] (New-Event "PowerShell.ProcessCreated" `
                -Sender $sender -EventArguments $EventArgs.NewEvent.TargetInstance)
        }
}

## Disable process creation events
function Disable-ProcessCreationEvent
{
    Unregister-Event -Force -SourceIdentifier "WMI.ProcessCreated"
}
```

When used in the shell, the experience is much simpler than working with the WMI events directly:

```
PS > Enable-ProcessCreationEvent
PS > calc
PS > Get-Event

ComputerName     :
RunspaceId       : feeda302-4386-4360-81d9-f5455d74950f
EventIdentifier  : 2
Sender           : System.Management.ManagementEventWatcher
SourceEventArgs  :
SourceArgs       : {calc.exe}
SourceIdentifier : PowerShell.ProcessCreated
TimeGenerated    : 2/21/2010 3:15:57 PM
MessageData      :

PS > (Get-Event).SourceArgs
```

```
(...)
Caption               : calc.exe
CommandLine           : "C:\Windows\system32\calc.exe"
CreationClassName     : Win32_Process
CreationDate          : 20100221151553.574124-480
CSCreationClassName   : Win32_ComputerSystem
CSName                : LEEHOLMES1C23
Description           : calc.exe
ExecutablePath        : C:\Windows\system32\calc.exe
(...)

PS > Disable-ProcessCreationEvent
PS > notepad
PS > Get-Event

ComputerName     :
RunspaceId       : feeda302-4386-4360-81d9-f5455d74950f
EventIdentifier  : 2
Sender           : System.Management.ManagementEventWatcher
SourceEventArgs  :
SourceArgs       : {calc.exe}
SourceIdentifier : PowerShell.ProcessCreated
TimeGenerated    : 2/21/2010 3:15:57 PM
MessageData      :
```

In addition to events that you create, engine events also represent events generated by the engine itself. In PowerShell version two, the only defined engine event is `Power Shell.Exiting`, which lets you do some work when the PowerShell session exits. For PowerShell to handle this event, you must use the **exit** keyword to close your session, rather than the X button at the top right of the console window. In the Integrated Scripting Environment, the close button generates this event as well. For an example of this, see Recipe 1.26.

PowerShell treats engine events like any other type of event. You can use the `Register-EngineEvent` cmdlet to automatically react to these events, just as you can use the `Register-ObjectEvent` and `Register-WmiEvent` cmdlets to react to .NET and WMI events, respectively. For information about how to respond to events automatically, see Recipe 31.1.

See Also

Recipe 1.26, "Save State Between Sessions"

Recipe 31.1, "Respond to Automatically Generated Events"

31.3 Create a Temporary Event Subscription

Problem

You want to automatically perform an action when an event arrives but automatically remove the event subscription once that event fires.

Solution

To create an event subscription that automatically removes itself once processed, remove the event subscriber and related job as the final step of the event action. The `Register-TemporaryEvent` command shown in Example 31-1 automates this for you.

Example 31-1. Register-TemporaryEvent.ps1

```
##############################################################################
##
## Register-TemporaryEvent
##
## From Windows PowerShell Cookbook (O'Reilly)
## by Lee Holmes (http://www.leeholmes.com/guide)
##
##############################################################################

<#

.SYNOPSIS

Registers an event action for an object and automatically unregisters
itself afterward.

.EXAMPLE

PS >$timer = New-Object Timers.Timer
PS >Register-TemporaryEvent $timer Disposed { [Console]::Beep(100,100) }
PS >$timer.Dispose()
PS >Get-EventSubscriber
PS >Get-Job

#>

param(
    ## The object that generates the event
    $Object,

    ## The event to subscribe to
    $Event,

    ## The action to invoke when the event arrives
    [ScriptBlock] $Action
)

Set-StrictMode -Version Latest
```

```
$actionText = $action.ToString()
$actionText += @'

$eventSubscriber | Unregister-Event
$eventSubscriber.Action | Remove-Job
'@

$eventAction = [ScriptBlock]::Create($actionText)
$null = Register-ObjectEvent $object $event -Action $eventAction
```

Discussion

When you provide a script block for the -Action parameter of `Register-ObjectEvent`, PowerShell creates an event subscriber to represent that subscription, and it also creates a job that lets you interact with the environment and results of that action. If the event registration is really a "throwaway" registration that you no longer want after the event gets generated, cleaning up afterward is a little complex.

Fortunately, PowerShell automatically populates several variables for event actions, one of the most important being `$eventSubscriber`. This variable represents, perhaps not surprisingly, the event subscriber related to this action. To automatically clean up after the event is generated, pass the event subscriber to the `Unregister-Event` cmdlet, and then pass the action's job (`$eventSubscriber.Action`) to the `Remove-Job` cmdlet.

See Also

Recipe 31.1, "Respond to Automatically Generated Events"

31.4 Forward Events from a Remote Computer

Problem

You have a client connected to a remote machine through PowerShell Remoting, and you want to be notified when an event occurs on that machine.

Solution

Use any of PowerShell's event registration cmdlets to subscribe to the event on the remote machine. Then, use the -`Forward` parameter to tell PowerShell to forward these events when they arrive:

```
PS > Get-Event
PS > $session = New-PsSession leeholmes1c23
PS > Enter-PsSession $session

[leeholmes1c23]: PS C:\> $timer = New-Object Timers.Timer
[leeholmes1c23]: PS C:\> $timer.Interval = 1000
[leeholmes1c23]: PS C:\> $timer.AutoReset = $false
[leeholmes1c23]: PS C:\> Register-ObjectEvent $timer Elapsed `
```

```
      -SourceIdentifier Timer.Elapsed -Forward
[leeholmes1c23]: PS C:\> $timer.Enabled = $true
[leeholmes1c23]: PS C:\> Exit-PsSession

PS >
PS > Get-Event

ComputerName     : leeholmes1c23
RunspaceId       : 053e6232-528a-4626-9b86-c50b8b762440
EventIdentifier  : 1
Sender           : System.Timers.Timer
SourceEventArgs  : System.Management.Automation.ForwardedEventArgs
SourceArgs       : {System.Timers.Timer, System.Timers.ElapsedEventArgs}
SourceIdentifier : Timer.Elapsed
TimeGenerated    : 2/21/2010 11:01:54 PM
MessageData      :
```

Discussion

PowerShell's eventing infrastructure lets you define one of three possible actions when you register for an event:

- Add the event notifications to the event queue.
- Automatically process the event notifications with an -Action script block.
- Forward the event notifications to a client computer.

The -Forward parameter on all of the event registration cmdlets enables this third option. When you are connected to a remote machine that has this type of behavior enabled on an event registration, PowerShell will automatically forward those event notifications to your client machine. Using this technique, you can easily monitor many remote computers for system changes that interest you.

For more information about registering for events, see Recipe 31.1. For more information about PowerShell Remoting, see Chapter 29.

See Also

Chapter 29, *Remoting*

Recipe 31.1, "Respond to Automatically Generated Events"

31.5 Investigate Internal Event Action State

Problem

You want to investigate the internal environment or state of an event subscriber's action.

Solution

Retrieve the event subscriber, and then interact with the `Subscriber.Action` property:

```
PS > $null = Register-EngineEvent -SourceIdentifier Custom.Event `
    -Action {
        "Hello World"

        Write-Error "Got an Error"

        $SCRIPT:privateVariable = 10
    }


PS > $null = New-Event Custom.Event
PS > $subscriber = Get-EventSubscriber Custom.Event
PS > $subscriber.Action | Format-List


Module         : __DynamicModule_f2b39042-e89a-49b1-b460-6211b9895acc
StatusMessage  :
HasMoreData    : True
Location       :
Command        :
                        "Hello World"
                        Write-Error "Got an Error"
                        $SCRIPT:privateVariable = 10

JobStateInfo   : Running
Finished       : System.Threading.ManualResetEvent
InstanceId     : b3fcceae-d878-4c8b-a53e-01873f2cfbea
Id             : 1
Name           : Custom.Event
ChildJobs      : {}
Output         : {Hello World}
Error          : {Got an Error}
Progress       : {}
Verbose        : {}
Debug          : {}
Warning        : {}
State          : Running

PS > $subscriber.Action.Error
Write-Error : Got an Error
At line:4 char:20
+         Write-Error <<<<  "Got an Error"
    + CategoryInfo          : NotSpecified: (:) [Write-Error], WriteError
    Exception
    + FullyQualifiedErrorId : Microsoft.PowerShell.Commands.WriteError
    Exception,Microsoft.PowerShell.Commands.WriteErrorCommand
```

Discussion

When you supply an -Action script block to any of the event registration cmdlets, PowerShell creates a PowerShell job to let you interact with that action. When

---

interacting with this job, you have access to the job's output, errors, progress, verbose output, debug output, and warnings.

For more information about working with PowerShell jobs, see Recipe 1.4.

In addition to the job interface, PowerShell's event system generates a module to isolate your script block from the rest of the system—for the benefit of both you and the system.

When you want to investigate the internal state of your action, PowerShell surfaces this state through the action's `Module` property. By passing the module to the invoke operator, you can invoke commands from within that module:

```
PS > $module = $subscriber.Action.Module
PS > & $module { dir variable:\privateVariable }

Name                           Value
----                           -----
privateVariable                10
```

To make this even easier, you can use the `Enter-Module` script given by Recipe 11.9.

See Also

Recipe 1.4, "Invoke a Long-Running or Background Command"

Recipe 11.9, "Diagnose and Interact with Internal Module State"

Recipe 31.1, "Respond to Automatically Generated Events"

31.6 Use a Script Block as a .NET Delegate or Event Handler

Problem

You want to use a PowerShell script block to directly handle a .NET event or delegate.

Solution

For objects that support a .NET delegate, simply assign the script block to that delegate:

```
$replacer = {
    param($match)

    $chars = $match.Groups[0].Value.ToCharArray()
    [Array]::Reverse($chars)
    $chars -join ''
}

PS > $regex = [Regex] "\w+"
PS > $regex.Replace("Hello World", $replacer)
olleH dlroW
```

To have a script block directly handle a .NET event, call that object's Add_Event() method:

```
$form.Add_Shown( { $form.Activate(); $textbox.Focus() } )
```

Discussion

When working with some .NET developer APIs, you might run into a method that takes a delegate as one of its arguments. Delegates in .NET act as a way to provide custom logic to a .NET method that accepts them. For example, the solution supplies a custom delegate to the regular expression Replace() method to reverse the characters in the match—something not supported by regular expressions at all.

As another example, many array classes support custom delegates for searching, sorting, filtering, and more. In this example, we create a custom sorter to sort an array by the length of its elements:

```
PS > $list = New-Object System.Collections.Generic.List[String]
PS > $list.Add("1")
PS > $list.Add("22")
PS > $list.Add("3333")
PS > $list.Add("444")
PS > $list.Add("5")
PS > $list.Sort( { $args[0].Length - $args[1].Length } )
PS > $list
5
1
22
444
3333
```

Perhaps the most useful delegate per character is the ability to customize the behavior of the .NET Framework when it encounters an invalid certificate in a web network connection. This happens, for example, when you try to connect to a website that has an expired SSL certificate. The .NET Framework lets you override this behavior through a delegate that you supply to the ServerCertificateValidationCallback property in the System.Net.ServicePointManager class. Your delegate should return $true if the certificate should be accepted and $false otherwise. To accept all certificates during a development session, simply run the following statement:

```
[System.Net.ServicePointManager]::ServerCertificateValidationCallback = { $true }
```

In addition to delegates, you can also assign PowerShell script blocks directly to events on .NET objects.

Normally, you'll want to use PowerShell eventing to support this scenario. PowerShell eventing provides a very rich set of cmdlets that let you interact with events from many technologies: .NET, WMI, and the PowerShell engine itself. When you use PowerShell eventing to handle .NET events, PowerShell protects you from the dangers of having multiple script blocks running at once and keeps them from interfering with the rest of your PowerShell session.

However, when you write a self-contained script that uses events to handle events in a WinForms application, directly assigning script blocks to those events can be a much more lightweight development experience. To see an example of this approach, see Recipe 13.10.

For more information about PowerShell's event handling, see Recipe 31.1.

See Also

Recipe 13.10, "Program: Add a Graphical User Interface to Your Script"

Recipe 31.1, "Respond to Automatically Generated Events"

References

PowerShell Language and Environment

Commands and Expressions

PowerShell breaks any line that you enter into its individual units (*tokens*), and then interprets each token in one of two ways: as a command or as an expression. The difference is subtle: expressions support logic and flow control statements (such as if, foreach, and throw), whereas commands do not.

You will often want to control the way that Windows PowerShell interprets your statements, so Table A-1 lists the options available to you.

Table A-1. Windows PowerShell evaluation controls

Statement	Example	Explanation

Precedence control: ( )	```PS > 5 * (1 + 2)```
	```15```
	```PS > (dir).Count```
	```2276```
		Forces the evaluation of a command or expression, similar to the way that parentheses are used to force the order of evaluation in a mathematical expression.

Expression subparse: $( )	```PS > "The answer is (2+2)"```
	```The answer is (2+2)```
	
	```PS > "The answer is $(2+2)"```
	```The answer is 4```
		Forces the evaluation of a command or expression, similar to the way that parentheses are used to force the order of evaluation in a mathematical expression.

	```PS > $value = 10```
	```PS > $result = $(```
	``` if($value -gt 0) { $true }```
	``` else { $false })```
	```PS > $result```
	```True```
		However, a subparse is as powerful as a subprogram and is required only when the subprogram contains logic or flow control statements.
		
		This statement is also used to expand dynamic information inside a string.

List evaluation: @( )	```PS > "Hello".Length```
	```5```
	```PS > @("Hello").Length```
	```1```
		Forces an expression to be evaluated as a list. If it is already a list, it will remain a list.

Statement	Example	Explanation
| | ```
PS > (Get-ChildItem).Count
12
PS > (Get-ChildItem *.txt).Count
PS > @(Get-ChildItem *.txt).Count
1
``` | If it is not, PowerShell temporarily treats it as one. |
| DATA evaluation:<br><br>DATA { } | ```
PS > DATA { 1 + 1 }
2
PS > DATA { $myVariable = "Test" }
Assignment statements are not allowed in
restricted language mode or a Data section.
``` | Evaluates the given script block in the context of the PowerShell data language. The data language supports only data-centric features of the PowerShell language. |

Comments

To create single-line comments, begin a line with the # character. To create a block (or multiline) comment, surround the region with the characters `<#` and `#>`.

```
# This is a regular comment

<# This is a block comment

function MyTest
{
    "This should not be considered a function"
}

$myVariable = 10;

Block comment ends
#>

# This is regular script again
```

Variables

Windows PowerShell provides several ways to define and access variables, as summarized in Table A-2.

Table A-2. Windows PowerShell variable syntaxes

Syntax	Meaning
`$simpleVariable = "Value"`	A simple variable name. The variable name must consist of alphanumeric characters. Variable names are not case-sensitive.
`${arbitrary! @#@#`{var`}iable} = "Value"`	An arbitrary variable name. The variable name must be surrounded by curly braces, but it may contain any characters. Curly braces in the variable name must be escaped with a backtick (`` ` ``).
`${c:\file name.extension}`	Variable "Get and Set Content" syntax. This is similar to the arbitrary variable name syntax. If the name corresponds to a valid PowerShell path, you can get and set the content of the item at that location by reading and writing to the variable.

Syntax	Meaning
[datatype] $variable = *"Value"*	Strongly typed variable. Ensures that the variable may contain only data of the type you declare. PowerShell throws an error if it cannot coerce the data to this type when you assign it.
$SCOPE:variable	Gets or sets the variable at that specific scope. Valid scope names are global (to make a variable available to the entire shell), script (to make a variable available only to the current script or persistent during module commands), local (to make a variable available only to the current scope and subscopes), and private (to make a variable available only to the current scope). The default scope is the *current* scope: global when defined interactively in the shell, script when defined outside any functions or script blocks in a script, and local elsewhere.
New-Item Variable: *variable* -Value *value*	Creates a new variable using the variable provider.
Get-Item Variable: *variable* Get-Variable *variable*	Gets the variable using the variable provider or Get-Variable cmdlet. This lets you access extra information about the variable, such as its options and description.
New-Variable *variable* -Option *option* -Value *value*	Creates a variable using the New-Variable cmdlet. This lets you provide extra information about the variable, such as its options and description.

 Unlike some languages, PowerShell rounds (rather than truncates) numbers when it converts them to the [int] data type:

```
PS > (3/2)
1.5
PS > [int] (3/2)
2
```

To have PowerShell truncate a number, see Chapter 6.

Booleans

Boolean (true or false) variables are most commonly initialized to their literal values of $true and $false. When PowerShell evaluates variables as part of a Boolean expression (for example, an if statement), though, it maps them to a suitable Boolean representation, as listed in Table A-3.

Table A-3. Windows PowerShell Boolean interpretations

Result	Boolean representation
$true	True
$false	False
$null	False
Nonzero number	True
Zero	False

Result	Boolean representation
Nonempty string	True
Empty string	False
Empty array	False
Single-element array	The Boolean representation of its single element
Multi-element array	True
Hashtable (either empty or not)	True

Strings

Windows PowerShell offers several facilities for working with plain-text data.

Literal and Expanding Strings

To define a literal string (one in which no variable or escape expansion occurs), enclose it in single quotes:

```
$myString = 'hello `t $ENV:SystemRoot'
```

$myString gets the actual value of hello `t $ENV:SystemRoot.

To define an expanding string (one in which variable and escape expansion occur), enclose it in double quotes:

```
$myString = "hello `t $ENV:SystemRoot"
```

$myString gets a value similar to hello C:\WINDOWS.

To include a single quote in a single-quoted string or a double quote in a double-quoted string, include two of the quote characters in a row:

```
PS > "Hello ""There""!"
Hello "There"!
PS > 'Hello ''There''!'
Hello 'There'!
```

 To include a complex expression inside an expanding string, use a sub-expression. For example:

```
$prompt = "$(get-location) >"
```

$prompt gets a value similar to c:\temp >.

Accessing the properties of an object requires a subexpression:

```
$output =
    "Current script name is: $($myInvocation.MyCommand.Path)"
```

$output gets a value similar to Current script name is c:\Test-Script.ps1.

Here Strings

To define a *here string* (one that may span multiple lines), place the two characters @" at the beginning and the two characters "@ on their own line at the end.

For example:

```
$myHereString = @"
This text may span multiple lines, and may
contain "quotes."
"@
```

Here strings may be of either the literal (single-quoted) or expanding (double-quoted) variety.

Escape Sequences

Windows PowerShell supports escape sequences inside strings, as listed in Table A-4.

Table A-4. Windows PowerShell escape sequences

Sequence	Meaning
`0	The *null* character. Often used as a record separator.
`a	The *alarm* character. Generates a beep when displayed on the console.
`b	The *backspace* character. The previous character remains in the string but is overwritten when displayed on the console.
`f	A *form feed*. Creates a page break when printed on most printers.
`n	A *newline*.
`r	A *carriage return*. Newlines in PowerShell are indicated entirely by the `n character, so this is rarely required.
`t	A *tab*.
`v	A *vertical tab*.
' ' (two single quotes)	A *single quote*, when in a literal string.
"" (two double quotes)	A *double quote*, when in an expanding string.
`*any other character*	That character, taken literally.

Numbers

PowerShell offers several options for interacting with numbers and numeric data.

Simple Assignment

To define a variable that holds numeric data, simply assign it as you would other variables. PowerShell automatically stores your data in a format that is sufficient to accurately hold it.

```
$myInt = 10
```

$myInt gets the value of 10, as a (32-bit) integer.

```
$myDouble = 3.14
```

$myDouble gets the value of 3.14, as a (53-bit, 9 bits of precision) double.

To explicitly assign a number as a long (64-bit) integer or decimal (96-bit, 96 bits of precision), use the long and decimal suffixes:

```
$myLong = 2147483648L
```

$myLong gets the value of 2147483648, as a long integer.

```
$myDecimal = 0.999D
```

$myDecimal gets the value of 0.999.

PowerShell also supports scientific notation, where e<number> represents multiplying the original number by the <number> power of 10:

```
$myPi = 3141592653e-9
```

$myPi gets the value of 3.141592653.

The data types in PowerShell (integer, long integer, double, and decimal) are built on the .NET data types of the same names.

Administrative Numeric Constants

Since computer administrators rarely get the chance to work with numbers in even powers of 10, PowerShell offers the numeric constants of pb, tb, gb, mb, and kb to represent petabytes (1125899906842624), terabytes (1099511627776), gigabytes (1073741824), megabytes (1048576), and kilobytes (1024), respectively:

```
PS > $downloadTime = (1gb + 250mb) / 120kb
PS > $downloadTime
10871.4666666667
```

Hexadecimal and Other Number Bases

To directly enter a hexadecimal number, use the hexadecimal prefix 0x:

```
$myErrorCode = 0xFE4A
```

`$myErrorCode` gets the integer value 65098.

The PowerShell scripting language does not natively support other number bases, but its support for interaction with the .NET Framework enables conversion to and from binary, octal, decimal, and hexadecimal:

```
$myBinary = [Convert]::ToInt32("101101010101", 2)
```

`$myBinary` gets the integer value of 2901.

```
$myOctal = [Convert]::ToInt32("1234567", 8)
```

`$myOctal` gets the integer value of 342391.

```
$myHexString = [Convert]::ToString(65098, 16)
```

`$myHexString` gets the string value of fe4a.

```
$myBinaryString = [Convert]::ToString(12345, 2)
```

`$myBinaryString` gets the string value of 11000000111001.

 See "Working with the .NET Framework" on page 741 to learn more about using PowerShell to interact with the .NET Framework.

Arrays and Lists

Array Definitions

PowerShell arrays hold lists of data. The @() (*array cast*) syntax tells PowerShell to treat the contents between the parentheses as an array. To create an empty array, type:

```
$myArray = @()
```

To define a nonempty array, use a comma to separate its elements:

```
$mySimpleArray = 1,"Two",3.14
```

Arrays may optionally be only a single element long:

```
$myList = ,"Hello"
```

Or, alternatively (using the array cast syntax):

```
$myList = @("Hello")
```

Elements of an array do not need to be all of the same data type, unless you declare it as a strongly typed array. In the following example, the outer square brackets define a strongly typed variable (as mentioned in "Variables" on page 716), and int[] represents an array of integers:

```
[int[]] $myArray = 1,2,3.14
```

In this mode, PowerShell generates an error if it cannot convert any of the elements in your list to the required data type. In this case, it rounds 3.14 to the integer value of 3:

```
PS > $myArray[2]
3
```

 To ensure that PowerShell treats collections of uncertain length (such as history lists or directory listings) as a list, use the list evaluation syntax @(...) described in "Commands and Expressions" on page 715.

Arrays can also be multidimensional *jagged* arrays (arrays within arrays):

```
$multiDimensional = @(
    (1,2,3,4),
    (5,6,7,8)
)
```

$multiDimensional[0][1] returns 2, coming from row 0, column 1.

$multiDimensional[1][3] returns 8, coming from row 1, column 3.

To define a multidimensional array that is not jagged, create a multidimensional instance of the .NET type. For integers, that would be an array of System.Int32:

```
$multidimensional = New-Object "Int32[,]" 2,4
$multidimensional[0,1] = 2
$multidimensional[1,3] = 8
```

Array Access

To access a specific element in an array, use the [ ] operator. PowerShell numbers your array elements starting at zero. Using $myArray = 1,2,3,4,5,6 as an example:

```
$myArray[0]
```

returns 1, the first element in the array.

```
$myArray[2]
```

returns 3, the third element in the array.

```
$myArray[-1]
```

returns 6, the last element of the array.

```
$myArray[-2]
```

returns 5, the second-to-last element of the array.

You can also access ranges of elements in your array:

```
PS > $myArray[0..2]
1
2
3
```

returns elements 0 through 2, inclusive.

```
PS > $myArray[-1..2]
6
1
2
3
```

returns the final element, wraps around, and returns elements 0 through 2, inclusive. PowerShell wraps around because the first number in the range is positive, and the second number in the range is negative.

```
PS > $myArray[-1..-3]
6
5
4
```

returns the last element of the array through to the third-to-last element in array, in descending order. PowerShell does not wrap around (and therefore scans backward in this case) because both numbers in the range share the same sign.

Array Slicing

You can combine several of the statements in the previous section at once to extract more complex ranges from an array. Use the + sign to separate array ranges from explicit indexes:

```
$myArray[0,2,4]
```

returns the elements at indices 0, 2, and 4.

```
$myArray[0,2+4..5]
```

returns the elements at indices 0, 2, and 4 through 5, inclusive.

```
$myArray[,0+2..3+0,0]
```

returns the elements at indices 0, 2 through 3 inclusive, 0, and 0 again.

 You can use the array slicing syntax to create arrays as well:

```
$myArray = ,0+2..3+0,0
```

Hashtables (Associative Arrays)

Hashtable Definitions

PowerShell *hashtables* (also called *associative arrays*) let you associate keys with values. To define a hashtable, use the syntax:

```
$myHashtable = @{}
```

You can initialize a hashtable with its key/value pairs when you create it. PowerShell assumes that the keys are strings, but the values may be any data type.

```
$myHashtable = @{ Key1 = "Value1"; "Key 2" = 1,2,3; 3.14 = "Pi" }
```

Hashtable Access

To access or modify a specific element in an associative array, you can use either the array-access or property-access syntax:

```
$myHashtable["Key1"]
```

returns "Value1".

```
$myHashtable."Key 2"
```

returns the array 1,2,3.

```
$myHashtable["New Item"] = 5
```

adds "New Item" to the hashtable.

```
$myHashtable."New Item" = 5
```

also adds "New Item" to the hashtable.

XML

PowerShell supports XML as a native data type. To create an XML variable, cast a string to the [xml] type:

```
$myXml = [xml] @"
<AddressBook>
   <Person contactType="Personal">
      <Name>Lee</Name>
      <Phone type="home">555-1212</Phone>
      <Phone type="work">555-1213</Phone>
   </Person>
   <Person contactType="Business">
      <Name>Ariel</Name>
      <Phone>555-1234</Phone>
   </Person>
</AddressBook>
"@
```

PowerShell exposes all child nodes and attributes as properties. When it does this, PowerShell automatically groups children that share the same node type:

```
$myXml.AddressBook
```

returns an object that contains a Person property.

```
$myXml.AddressBook.Person
```

returns a list of Person nodes. Each person node exposes contactType, Name, and Phone as properties.

```
$myXml.AddressBook.Person[0]
```

returns the first **Person** node.

```
$myXml.AddressBook.Person[0].ContactType
```

returns **Personal** as the contact type of the first **Person** node.

Simple Operators

Once you have defined your data, the next step is to work with it.

Arithmetic Operators

The arithmetic operators let you perform mathematical operations on your data, as shown in Table A-5.

 The **System.Math** class in the .NET Framework offers many powerful operations in addition to the native operators supported by PowerShell:

```
PS > [Math]::Pow([Math]::E, [Math]::Pi)
23.1406926327793
```

See "Working with the .NET Framework" on page 741 to learn more about using PowerShell to interact with the .NET Framework.

Table A-5. Windows PowerShell arithmetic operators

Operator	Meaning
+	The *addition operator:* `$leftValue + $rightValue` When used with numbers, returns their sum. When used with strings, returns a new string created by appending the second string to the first. When used with arrays, returns a new array created by appending the second array to the first. When used with hashtables, returns a new hashtable created by merging the two hashtables. Since hashtable keys must be unique, PowerShell returns an error if the second hashtable includes any keys already defined in the first hashtable. When used with any other type, PowerShell uses that type's addition operator (`op_Addition`) if it implements one.
-	The *subtraction operator:* `$leftValue - $rightValue` When used with numbers, returns their difference. This operator does not apply to strings. This operator does not apply to arrays.

Operator	Meaning
	This operator does not apply to hashtables.
	When used with any other type, PowerShell uses that type's subtraction operator (op_Subtraction) if it implements one.
*	The *multiplication operator*:
	`$leftValue * $rightValue`
	When used with numbers, returns their product.
	When used with strings ("=" * 80), returns a new string created by appending the string to itself the number of times you specify.
	When used with arrays (1..3 * 7), returns a new array created by appending the array to itself the number of times you specify.
	This operator does not apply to hashtables.
	When used with any other type, PowerShell uses that type's multiplication operator (op_Multiply) if it implements one.
/	The *division operator*:
	`$leftValue / $rightValue`
	When used with numbers, returns their quotient.
	This operator does not apply to strings.
	This operator does not apply to arrays.
	This operator does not apply to hashtables.
	When used with any other type, PowerShell uses that type's division operator (op_Division) if it implements one.
%	The *modulus operator*:
	`$leftValue % $rightValue`
	When used with numbers, returns the remainder of their division.
	This operator does not apply to strings.
	This operator does not apply to arrays.
	This operator does not apply to hashtables.
	When used with any other type, PowerShell uses that type's modulus operator (op_Modulus) if it implements one.
+=	*Assignment operators*:
-=	`$variable operator= value`
*=	These operators match the simple arithmetic operators (+, -, *, /, and %) but store the result in the variable %= on the lefthand side of the operator. It is a short form for
/=	`$variable = $variable operator value.`
%=	

Logical Operators

The logical operators let you compare Boolean values, as shown in Table A-6.

Table A-6. Windows PowerShell logical operators

Operator	Meaning
-and	*Logical AND*:
	`$leftValue -and $rightValue`
	Returns $true if both lefthand and righthand arguments evaluate to $true. Returns $false otherwise.
	You can combine several -and operators in the same expression:
	`$value1 -and $value2 -and $value3 …`
	PowerShell implements the -and operator as a short-circuit operator and evaluates arguments only if all arguments preceding it evaluate to $true.
-or	*Logical OR*:
	`$leftValue -or $rightValue`
	Returns $true if the lefthand or righthand arguments evaluate to $true. Returns $false otherwise.
	You can combine several -or operators in the same expression:
	`$value1 -or $value2 -or $value3 ...`
	PowerShell implements the -or operator as a short-circuit operator and evaluates arguments only if all arguments preceding it evaluate to $false.
-xor	*Logical exclusive OR*:
	`$leftValue -xor $rightValue`
	Returns $true if either the lefthand or righthand argument evaluates to $true, but not if both do.
	Returns $false otherwise.
-not	*Logical NOT*:
!	`-not $value`
	Returns $true if its righthand (and only) argument evaluates to $false. Returns $false otherwise.

Binary Operators

The binary operators, listed in Table A-7, let you apply the Boolean logical operators bit by bit to the operator's arguments. When comparing bits, a 1 represents $true, whereas a 0 represents $false.

Table A-7. Windows PowerShell binary operators

Operator	Meaning
-band	*Binary AND*:
	`$leftValue -band $rightValue`

Operator	Meaning

Returns a number where bits are set to 1 if the bits of the lefthand and righthand arguments at that position are both 1. All other bits are set to 0.

For example:

```
PS > $boolean1 = "110110110"
PS > $boolean2 = "010010010"
PS > $int1 = [Convert]::ToInt32($boolean1, 2)
PS > $int2 = [Convert]::ToInt32($boolean2, 2)
PS > $result = $int1 -band $int2
PS > [Convert]::ToString($result, 2)
10010010
```

-bor   *Binary OR*:

    $leftValue -bor *$rightValue*

Returns a number where bits are set to 1 if either of the bits of the lefthand and righthand arguments at that position is 1. All other bits are set to 0.

For example:

```
PS > $boolean1 = "110110110"
PS > $boolean2 = "010010010"
PS > $int1 = [Convert]::ToInt32($boolean1, 2)
PS > $int2 = [Convert]::ToInt32($boolean2, 2)
PS > $result = $int1 -bor $int2
PS > [Convert]::ToString($result, 2)
110110110
```

-bxor   *Binary exclusive OR*:

    $leftValue -bxor *$rightValue*

Returns a number where bits are set to 1 if either of the bits of the lefthand and righthand arguments at that position is 1, but not if both are. All other bits are set to 0.

For example:

```
PS > $boolean1 = "110110110"
PS > $boolean2 = "010010010"
PS > $int1 = [Convert]::ToInt32($boolean1, 2)
PS > $int2 = [Convert]::ToInt32($boolean2, 2)
PS > $result = $int1 -bor $int2
PS > [Convert]::ToString($result, 2)
100100100
```

-bnot   *Binary NOT*:

    -bnot *$value*

Returns a number where bits are set to 1 if the bit of the righthand (and only) argument at that position is set to 1. All other bits are set to 0.

For example:

```
PS > $boolean1 = "110110110"
PS > $int1 = [Convert]::ToInt32($boolean1, 2)
PS > $result = -bnot $int1
PS > [Convert]::ToString($result, 2)
11111111111111111111111001001001
```

Other Operators

PowerShell supports several other simple operators, as listed in Table A-8.

Table A-8. Other Windows PowerShell operators

Operator	Meaning
-replace	The *replace operator*:
	`"target" -replace "pattern","replacement"`
	Returns a new string, where the text in `"target"` that matches the regular expression `"pattern"` has been replaced with the replacement text `"replacement"`.
	By default, PowerShell performs a case-insensitive comparison. The -ireplace operator makes this case-insensitivity explicit, whereas the -creplace operator performs a case-sensitive comparison.
	If the regular expression pattern contains named captures or capture groups, the replacement string may reference those as well.
	For example:

	<pre>PS > "Hello World" -replace "(.*) (.*)",'$2 $1'
	World Hello</pre>

	If `"target"` represents an array, the -replace operator operates on each element of that array.
	For more information on the details of regular expressions, see Appendix B.
-f	The *format operator*:
	`"Format String" -f Values`
	Returns a string where the format items in the format string have been replaced with the text equivalent of the values in the value array.
	For example:

	<pre>PS > "{0:n0}" -f 1000000000
	1,000,000,000</pre>

	The format string for the format operator is exactly the format string supported by the .NET String.Format method.
	For more details about the syntax of the format string, see Appendix D.
-as	The *type conversion operator*:
	`$value -as [Type]`
	Returns $value cast to the given .NET type. If this conversion is not possible, PowerShell returns $null.
	For example:

	<pre>PS > 3/2 -as [int]
	2
	PS > $result = "Hello" -as [int]
	PS > $result -eq $null
	True</pre>

-split	The *unary split operator*:
	`-split "Input String"`

Operator	Meaning

Breaks the given input string into an array, using whitespace (\s+) to identify the boundary between elements. It also trims the results.

For example:

```
PS > -split "  Hello    World   "
Hello
World
```

The *binary split operator*:

```
"Input String" -split "delimiter",maximum,options
"Input String" -split { Scriptblock },maximum
```

Breaks the given input string into an array, using the given `delimiter` or `script block` to identify the boundary between elements.

`Delimiter` is interpreted as a regular expression match. `Scriptblock` is called for each character in the input, and a split is introduced when it returns `$true`.

`Maximum` defines the maximum number of elements to be returned, leaving unsplit elements as the last item. This item is optional. Use "0" for unlimited if you want to provide options but not alter the maximum.

`Options` define special behavior to apply to the splitting behavior. The possible enumeration values are:

- `SimpleMatch`: Split on literal strings, rather than regular expressions they may represent.
- `RegexMatch`: Split on regular expressions. This option is the default.
- `CultureInvariant`: Does not use culture-specific capitalization rules when doing a case-insensitive split.
- `IgnorePatternWhitespace`: Ignores spaces and regular expression comments in the split pattern.
- `Multiline`: Allows the ^ and $ characters to match line boundaries, not just the beginning and end of the content.
- `Singleline`: Treats the ^ and $ characters as the beginning and end of the content. This option is the default.
- `IgnoreCase`: Ignores the capitalization of the content when searching for matches.
- `ExplicitCapture`: In a regular expression match, only captures named groups. This option has no impact on the -split operator.

For example:

```
PS > "1a2B3" -split "[a-z]+",0,"IgnoreCase"
1
2
3
```

-join	The *unary join operator*:

```
-join ("item1","item2",...,"item_n")
```

Combines the supplied items into a single string, using no separator. For example:

```
PS > -join ("a","b")
ab
```

Operator	Meaning
	The *binary join operator*:

```
("item1","item2",...,"item_n") -join Delimiter
```

Combines the supplied items into a single string, using `Delimiter` as the separator. For example:

```
PS > ("a","b") -join ", "
a, b
```

Comparison Operators

The PowerShell comparison operators, listed in Table A-9, let you compare expressions against each other. By default, PowerShell's comparison operators are case-insensitive. For all operators where case sensitivity applies, the `-i` prefix makes this case insensitivity explicit, whereas the `-c` prefix performs a case-sensitive comparison.

Table A-9. Windows PowerShell comparison operators

Operator	Meaning
-eq	The *equality operator*:
	`$leftValue -eq $rightValue`
	For all primitive types, returns $true if *$leftValue* and *$rightValue* are equal.
	When used with arrays, returns all elements in *$leftValue* that are equal to *$rightValue*.
	When used with any other type, PowerShell uses that type's Equals() method if it implements one.
-ne	The *negated equality operator*:
	`$leftValue -ne $rightValue`
	For all primitive types, returns $true if*$leftValue* and *$rightValue* are not equal.
	When used with arrays, returns all elements in *$leftValue* that are not equal to*$rightValue*.
	When used with any other type, PowerShell returns the negation of that type's Equals() method if it implements one.
-ge	The *greater-than-or-equal operator*:
	`$leftValue -ge $rightValue`
	For all primitive types, returns $true if *$leftValue* is greater than or equal to *$rightValue*.
	When used with arrays, returns all elements in *$leftValue* that are greater than or equal to *$rightValue*.
	When used with any other type, PowerShell returns the result of that object's Compare() method if it implements one. If the method returns a number greater than or equal to zero, the operator returns $true.
-gt	The *greater-than operator*:
	`$leftValue -gt $rightValue`
	For all primitive types, returns $true if*$leftValue* is greater than *$rightValue*.
	When used with arrays, returns all elements in *$leftValue* that are greater than *$rightValue*.

Operator	Meaning
	When used with any other type, PowerShell returns the result of that object's Compare() method if it implements one. If the method returns a number greater than zero, the operator returns $true.
-lt	The *less-than operator*:
	```$leftValue -lt $rightValue```
	For all primitive types, returns $true if $leftValue is less than $rightValue.
	When used with arrays, returns all elements in $leftValue that are less than $rightValue.
	When used with any other type, PowerShell returns the result of that object's Compare() method if it implements one. If the method returns a number less than zero, the operator returns $true.
-le	The *less-than-or-equal operator*:
	```$leftValue -le $rightValue```
	For all primitive types, returns $true if $leftValue is less than or equal to $rightValue.
	When used with arrays, returns all elements in $leftValue that are less than or equal to $rightValue.
	When used with any other type, PowerShell returns the result of that object's Compare() method if it implements one. If the method returns a number less than or equal to zero, the operator returns $true.
-like	The *like operator*:
	```$leftValue -like Pattern```
	Evaluates the pattern against the target, returning $true if the simple match is successful.
	When used with arrays, returns all elements in $leftValue that match Pattern.
	The -like operator supports the following simple wildcard characters:
	?
	Any single unspecified character
	*
	Zero or more unspecified characters
	[a-b]
	Any character in the range of a–b
	[ab]
	The specified characters a or b
	For example:
	```PS > "Test" -like "[A-Z]e?[tr]"``` ```True```
-notlike	The *negated like operator*:
	Returns $true when the -like operator would return $false.
-match	The *match operator*:
	```"Target" -match Regular Expression```
	Evaluates the regular expression against the target, returning $true if the match is successful. Once complete, PowerShell places the successful matches in the $matches variable.
	When used with arrays, returns all elements in Target that match Regular Expression.

Operator	Meaning
	The $matches variable is a hashtable that maps the individual matches to the text they match. 0 is the entire text of the match, 1 and on contain the text from any unnamed captures in the regular expression, and string values contain the text from any named captures in the regular expression.

For example:

```
PS > "Hello World" -match "(.*) (.*)"
True
PS > $matches[1]
Hello
```

For more information on the details of regular expressions, see Appendix B.

Operator	Meaning
-notmatch	The *negated match operator*:
	Returns $true when the -match operator would return $false.
	The -notmatch operator still populates the $matches variable with the results of match.
-contains	The *contains operator*:
	`$list -contains $value`
	Returns $true if the list specified by *$list* contains the value *$value*, that is, if $item -eq $value returns $true for at least one item in the list.
-notcontains	The *negated contains operator*:
	Returns $true when the -contains operator would return $false.
-is	The *type operator*:
	`$leftValue -is [type]`
	Returns $true if *$value* is (or extends) the specified .NET type.
-isnot	The *negated type operator*:
	Returns $true when the -is operator would return $false.

Conditional Statements

Conditional statements in PowerShell let you change the flow of execution in your script.

if, elseif, and else Statements

```
if(condition)
{
    statement block
}
elseif(condition)
{
    statement block
}
else
{
    statement block
}
```

If *condition* evaluates to $true, PowerShell executes the statement block you provide. Then, it resumes execution at the end of the if/elseif/else statement list. PowerShell requires the enclosing braces around the statement block, even if the statement block contains only one statement.

 See "Simple Operators" on page 725 and "Comparison Operators" on page 731 for a discussion on how PowerShell evaluates expressions as conditions.

If *condition* evaluates to $false, PowerShell evaluates any following (optional) elseif conditions until one matches. If one matches, PowerShell executes the statement block associated with that condition, and then resumes execution at the end of the if/elseif/else statement list.

For example:

```
$textToMatch = Read-Host "Enter some text"
$matchType = Read-Host "Apply Simple or Regex matching?"
$pattern = Read-Host "Match pattern"
if($matchType -eq "Simple")
{
    $textToMatch -like $pattern
}
elseif($matchType -eq "Regex")
{
    $textToMatch -match $pattern
}
else
{
    Write-Host "Match type must be Simple or Regex"
}
```

If none of the conditions evaluate to $true, PowerShell executes the statement block associated with the (optional) else clause, and then resumes execution at the end of the if/elseif/else statement list.

switch Statements

```
switch options expression
{
    comparison value          { statement block }
    -or-
    { comparison expression }  { statement block }
    (...)
    default                    { statement block }
}
```

or:

```
switch options -file filename
{
```

```
      comparison value            { statement block }
      -or
      { comparison expression }    { statement block }
      (...)
      default                      { statement block }
}
```

When PowerShell evaluates a switch statement, it evaluates *expression* against the statements in the switch body. If *expression* is a list of values, PowerShell evaluates each item against the statements in the switch body. If you specify the -file option, PowerShell treats the lines in the file as though they were a list of items in *expression*.

The *comparison value* statements let you match the current input item against the pattern specified by *comparison value*. By default, PowerShell treats this as a case-insensitive exact match, but the options you provide to the switch statement can change this, as shown in Table A-10.

Table A-10. Options supported by PowerShell switch statements

Option	Meaning
-casesensitive	*Case-sensitive match.*
-c	With this option active, PowerShell executes the associated statement block only if the current input item exactly matches the value specified by *comparison value*. If the current input object is a string, the match is case-sensitive.
-exact	*Exact match*
-e	With this option active, PowerShell executes the associated statement block only if the current input item exactly matches the value specified by *comparison value*. This match is case-insensitive. This is the default mode of operation.
-regex	*Regular-expression match*
-r	With this option active, PowerShell executes the associated statement block only if the current input item matches the regular expression specified by *comparison value*. This match is case-insensitive.
-wildcard	*Wildcard match*
-w	With this option active, PowerShell executes the associated statement block only if the current input item matches the wildcard specified by *comparison value*.
	The wildcard match supports the following simple wildcard characters:
	?
	Any single unspecified character
	*
	Zero or more unspecified characters
	[a-b]
	Any character in the range of a–b
	[ab]
	The specified characters a or b
	This match is case-insensitive.

The { *comparison expression* } statements let you process the current input item, which is stored in the $_ variable, in an arbitrary script block. When it processes a { *comparison expression* } statement, PowerShell executes the associated statement block only if { *comparison expression* } evaluates to $true.

PowerShell executes the statement block associated with the (optional) `default` statement if no other statements in the `switch` body match.

When processing a `switch` statement, PowerShell tries to match the current input object against each statement in the `switch` body, falling through to the next statement even after one or more have already matched. To have PowerShell discontinue the current comparison (but retry the switch statement with the next input object), include a `continue` statement as the last statement in the statement block. To have PowerShell exit a `switch` statement completely after it processes a match, include a `break` statement as the last statement in the statement block.

For example:

```
$myPhones = "(555) 555-1212","555-1234"

switch -regex ($myPhones)
{
  { $_.Length -le 8 }  { "Area code was not specified"; break }
  { $_.Length -gt 8 }  { "Area code was specified" }
  "\(((555)\)).*"        { "In the $($matches[1]) area code" }
}
```

produces the output:

```
Area code was specified
In the 555 area code
Area code was not specified
```

 See "Looping Statements" on page 736 for more information about the `break` statement.

By default, PowerShell treats this as a case-insensitive exact match, but the options you provide to the `switch` statement can change this.

Looping Statements

Looping statements in PowerShell let you execute groups of statements multiple times.

for Statement

```
:loop_label for (initialization; condition; increment)
{
```

```
    statement block
}
```

When PowerShell executes a for statement, it first executes the expression given by *initialization*. It next evaluates *condition*. If *condition* evaluates to $true, PowerShell executes the given statement block. It then executes the expression given by *increment*. PowerShell continues to execute the statement block and *increment* statement as long as *condition* evaluates to $true.

For example:

```
for($counter = 0; $counter -lt 10; $counter++)
{
    Write-Host "Processing item $counter"
}
```

The break and continue statements (discussed later in this appendix) can specify the *loop_label* of any enclosing looping statement as their target.

foreach Statement

```
:loop_label foreach (variable in expression)
{
    statement block
}
```

When PowerShell executes a foreach statement, it executes the pipeline given by *expression*—for example, Get-Process | Where-Object {$_.Handles -gt 500} or 1..10. For each item produced by the expression, it assigns that item to the variable specified by *variable* and then executes the given statement block. For example:

```
$handleSum = 0;
foreach($process in Get-Process |
    Where-Object { $_.Handles -gt 500 })
{
    $handleSum += $process.Handles
}
$handleSum
```

The break and continue statements (discussed later in this appendix) can specify the *loop_label* of any enclosing looping statement as their target. In addition to the foreach statement, PowerShell also offers the Foreach-Object cmdlet with similar capabilities. For more information, see Recipe 4.4.

while Statement

```
:loop_label while(condition)
{
    statement block
}
```

When PowerShell executes a while statement, it first evaluates the expression given by *condition*. If this expression evaluates to $true, PowerShell executes the given statement block. PowerShell continues to execute the statement block as long as *condition* evaluates to $true. For example:

```
$command = "";
while($command -notmatch "quit")
{
    $command = Read-Host "Enter your command"
}
```

The break and continue statements (discussed later in this appendix) can specify the *loop_label* of any enclosing looping statement as their target.

do … while Statement/do … until Statement

```
:loop_label do
{
    statement block
} while(condition)
```

or

```
:loop_label do
{
    statement block
} until(condition)
```

When PowerShell executes a do … while or do … until statement, it first executes the given statement block. In a do … while statement, PowerShell continues to execute the statement block as long as *condition* evaluates to $true. In a do … until statement, PowerShell continues to execute the statement as long as *condition* evaluates to $false. For example:

```
$validResponses = "Yes","No"
$response = ""
do
{
    $response = read-host "Yes or No?"
} while($validResponses -notcontains $response)
"Got it."

$response = ""
do
{
    $response = read-host "Yes or No?"
} until($validResponses -contains $response)
"Got it."
```

The break and continue statements (discussed later in this appendix) can specify the *loop_label* of any enclosing looping statement as their target.

Flow Control Statements

PowerShell supports two statements to help you control flow within loops: break and continue.

break

The **break** statement halts execution of the current loop. PowerShell then resumes execution at the end of the current looping statement, as though the looping statement had completed naturally. For example:

```
for($counter = 0; $counter -lt 5; $counter++)
{
    for($counter2 = 0; $counter2 -lt 5; $counter2++)
    {
        if($counter2 -eq 2)
        {
            break
        }

        Write-Host "Processing item $counter,$counter2"
    }
}
```

produces the output:

```
Processing item 0,0
Processing item 0,1
Processing item 1,0
Processing item 1,1
Processing item 2,0
Processing item 2,1
Processing item 3,0
Processing item 3,1
Processing item 4,0
Processing item 4,1
```

If you specify a label with the **break** statement—for example, break outer_loop—PowerShell halts the execution of that loop instead. For example:

```
:outer_loop for($counter = 0; $counter -lt 5; $counter++)
{
    for($counter2 = 0; $counter2 -lt 5; $counter2++)
    {
        if($counter2 -eq 2)
        {
            break outer_loop
        }

        Write-Host "Processing item $counter,$counter2"
    }
}
```

produces the output:

```
Processing item 0,0
Processing item 0,1
```

continue

The `continue` statement skips execution of the rest of the current statement block. PowerShell then continues with the next iteration of the current looping statement, as though the statement block had completed naturally. For example:

```
for($counter = 0; $counter -lt 5; $counter++)
{
    for($counter2 = 0; $counter2 -lt 5; $counter2++)
    {
        if($counter2 -eq 2)
        {
            continue
        }

        Write-Host "Processing item $counter,$counter2"
    }
}
```

produces the output:

```
Processing item 0,0
Processing item 0,1
Processing item 0,3
Processing item 0,4
Processing item 1,0
Processing item 1,1
Processing item 1,3
Processing item 1,4
Processing item 2,0
Processing item 2,1
Processing item 2,3
Processing item 2,4
Processing item 3,0
Processing item 3,1
Processing item 3,3
Processing item 3,4
Processing item 4,0
Processing item 4,1
Processing item 4,3
Processing item 4,4
```

If you specify a label with the `continue` statement—for example, `continue outer_loop`—PowerShell continues with the next iteration of that loop instead.

For example:

```
:outer_loop for($counter = 0; $counter -lt 5; $counter++)
{
    for($counter2 = 0; $counter2 -lt 5; $counter2++)
    {
        if($counter2 -eq 2)
        {
            continue outer_loop
        }
```

```
        Write-Host "Processing item $counter,$counter2"
    }
}
```

produces the output:

```
Processing item 0,0
Processing item 0,1
Processing item 1,0
Processing item 1,1
Processing item 2,0
Processing item 2,1
Processing item 3,0
Processing item 3,1
Processing item 4,0
Processing item 4,1
```

Working with the .NET Framework

One feature that gives PowerShell its incredible reach into both system administration and application development is its capability to leverage Microsoft's enormous and broad .NET Framework.

Work with the .NET Framework in PowerShell comes mainly by way of one of two tasks: calling methods or accessing properties.

Static Methods

To call a static method on a class, type:

```
[ClassName]::MethodName(parameter list)
```

For example:

```
PS > [System.Diagnostics.Process]::GetProcessById(0)
```

gets the process with the ID of 0 and displays the following output:

```
Handles  NPM(K)    PM(K)      WS(K) VM(M)  CPU(s)     Id ProcessName
-------  ------    -----      ----- -----  ------     -- -----------
      0       0        0         16     0                0 Idle
```

Instance Methods

To call a method on an instance of an object, type:

```
$objectReference.MethodName(parameter list)
```

For example:

```
PS > $process = [System.Diagnostics.Process]::GetProcessById(0)
PS > $process.Refresh()
```

This stores the process with ID of 0 into the $process variable. It then calls the Refresh() instance method on that specific process.

Static Properties

To access a static property on a class, type:

```
[ClassName]::PropertyName
```

or:

```
[ClassName]::PropertyName = value
```

For example, the [System.DateTime] class provides a Now static property that returns the current time:

```
PS > [System.DateTime]::Now
Sunday, July 16, 2006 2:07:20 PM
```

Although this is rare, some types let you set the value of some static properties.

Instance Properties

To access an instance property on an object, type:

```
$objectReference.PropertyName
```

or:

```
$objectReference.PropertyName = value
```

For example:

```
PS > $today = [System.DateTime]::Now
PS > $today.DayOfWeek
Sunday
```

This stores the current date in the $today variable. It then calls the DayOfWeek instance property on that specific date.

Learning About Types

The two primary avenues for learning about classes and types are the Get-Member cmdlet and the documentation for the .NET Framework.

The Get-Member cmdlet

To learn what methods and properties a given type supports, pass it through the Get-Member cmdlet, as shown in Table A-11.

Table A-11. Working with the Get-Member cmdlet

Action	Result
[typename] | Get-Member -Static	All the static methods and properties of a given type.
$objectReference | Get-Member -Static	All the static methods and properties provided by the type in $objectReference.

Action	Result
$objectReference | Get-Member	All the instance methods and properties provided by the type in *$objectReference*. If *$objectReference* represents a collection of items, PowerShell returns the instances and properties of the types contained by that collection. To view the instances and properties of a collection itself, use the -InputObject parameter of Get-Member: `Get-Member -InputObject $objectReference`
[typename] | Get-Member	All the instance methods and properties of a System.RuntimeType object that represents this type.

.NET Framework documentation

Another source of information about the classes in the .NET Framework is the documentation itself, available through the search facilities at *http://msdn.microsoft.com*.

Typical documentation for a class first starts with a general overview, and then provides a hyperlink to the members of the class—the list of methods and properties it supports.

 To get to the documentation for the members quickly, search for them more explicitly by adding the term "members" to your MSDN search term:

classname members

The documentation for the members of a class lists their constructors, methods, properties, and more. It uses an S icon to represent the static methods and properties. Click the member name for more information about that member, including the type of object that the member produces.

Type Shortcuts

When you specify a type name, PowerShell lets you use a short form for some of the most common types, as listed in Table A-12.

Table A-12. PowerShell type shortcuts

Type shortcut	Full classname
[Adsi]	[System.DirectoryServices.DirectoryEntry]
[AdsiSearcher]	[System.DirectoryServices.DirectorySearcher]
[Float]	[System.Single]
[Hashtable]	[System.Collections.Hashtable]
[Int]	[System.Int32]
[IPAddress]	[System.Net.IPAddress]
[Long]	[System.Collections.Int64]
[PowerShell]	[System.Management.Automation.PowerShell]

Type shortcut	Full classname
[PSCustomObject]	[System.Management.Automation.PSObject]
[PSModuleInfo]	[System.Management.Automation.PSModuleInfo]
[PSObject]	[System.Management.Automation.PSObject]
[Ref]	[System.Management.Automation.PSReference]
[Regex]	[System.Text.RegularExpressions.Regex]
[Runspace]	[System.Management.Automation.Runspaces.Runspace]
[RunspaceFactory]	[System.Management.Automation.Runspaces.RunspaceFactory]
[ScriptBlock]	[System.Management.Automation.ScriptBlock]
[Switch]	[System.Management.Automation.SwitchParameter]
[Wmi]	[System.Management.ManagementObject]
[WmiClass]	[System.Management.ManagementClass]
[WmiSearcher]	[System.Management.ManagementObjectSearcher]
[Xml]	[System.Xml.XmlDocument]
[*TypeName*]	[System.*TypeName*]

Creating Instances of Types

```
$objectReference = New-Object TypeName parameters
```

Although static methods and properties of a class generate objects, you will often want to create them explicitly yourself. PowerShell's New-Object cmdlet lets you create an instance of the type you specify. The parameter list must match the list of parameters accepted by one of the type's constructors, as documented on MSDN.

For example:

```
$webClient = New-Object Net.WebClient
$webClient.DownloadString("http://search.msn.com")
```

If the type represents a generic type, enclose its type parameters in square brackets:

```
PS > $hashtable = New-Object "System.Collections.Generic.Dictionary[String,Bool]"
PS > $hashtable["Test"] = $true
```

Most common types are available by default. However, many types are available only after you load the library (called the *assembly*) that defines them. The MSDN documentation for a class includes the assembly that defines it.

To load an assembly, use the -AssemblyName parameter of the Add-Type cmdlet:

```
PS > Add-Type -AssemblyName System.Web

PS > [Web.HttpUtility]::UrlEncode("http://www.bing.com")
http%3a%2f%2fwww.bing.com
```

Interacting with COM Objects

PowerShell lets you access methods and properties on COM objects the same way you would interact with objects from the .NET Framework. To interact with a COM object, use its `ProgId` with the `-ComObject` parameter (often shortened to `-Com`) on `New-Object`:

```
PS > $shell = New-Object -Com Shell.Application
PS > $shell.Windows() | Select-Object LocationName,LocationUrl
```

For more information about the COM objects most useful to system administrators, see Appendix H.

Extending Types

PowerShell supports two ways to add your own methods and properties to any type: the `Add-Member` cmdlet and a custom types extension file.

The Add-Member cmdlet

The `Add-Member` cmdlet lets you dynamically add methods, properties, and more to an object. It supports the extensions shown in Table A-13.

Table A-13. Selected member types supported by the Add-Member cmdlet

Member type	Meaning
AliasProperty	A property defined to alias another property:
	`PS > $testObject = [PsObject] "Test"` `PS > $testObject	Add-Member "AliasProperty" Count Length` `PS > $testObject.Count` `4`
CodeProperty	A property defined by a `System.Reflection.MethodInfo`.
	This method must be public, static, return results (nonvoid), and take one parameter of type `PsObject`.
NoteProperty	A property defined by the initial value you provide:
	`PS > $testObject = [PsObject] "Test"` `PS > $testObject	Add-Member NoteProperty Reversed tseT` `PS > $testObject.Reversed` `tseT`
ScriptProperty	A property defined by the script block you provide. In that script block, `$this` refers to the current instance:
	`PS > $testObject = [PsObject] ("Hi" * 100)` `PS > $testObject	Add-Member ScriptProperty IsLong {` ` $this.Length -gt 100` `}` `$testObject.IsLong`  `True`
PropertySet	A property defined as a shortcut to a set of properties. Used in cmdlets such as `Select-Object`:

	`PS > $testObject = [PsObject] [DateTime]::Now`
	`PS > $collection = New-Object ` ` `
	`        Collections.ObjectModel.Collection` `` `1[System.String]`

Member type	Meaning

	```$collection.Add("Month")```
	```$collection.Add("Year")```
	``$testObject
		Add-Member PropertySet MonthYear $collection```
		``$testObject
			select MonthYear```
			
			```Month Year```
			```----- ----```
			``` 3 2010```

CodeMethod	A method defined by a System.Reflection.MethodInfo. This method must be public, static, and take one parameter of type PsObject.

ScriptMethod	A method defined by the script block you provide. In that script block, $this refers to the current instance, and $args refers to the input parameters:
	
	```PS > $testObject = [PsObject] "Hello"```
	``PS > $testObject
		Add-Member ScriptMethod IsLong {```
		``` $this.Length -gt $args[0]```
		``` }```
		```$testObject.IsLong(3)```
		```$testObject.IsLong(100)```
		
		```True```
		```False```

Custom type extension files

While the Add-Member cmdlet lets you customize individual objects, PowerShell also supports configuration files that let you customize all objects of a given type. For example, you might want to add a Reverse() method to all strings or a HelpUrl property (based on the MSDN Url Aliases) to all types.

PowerShell adds several type extensions to the file *types.ps1xml*, in the PowerShell installation directory. This file is useful as a source of examples, but you should not modify it directly. Instead, create a new one and use the Update-TypeData cmdlet to load your customizations. The following command loads *Types.custom.ps1xml* from the same directory as your profile:

```
$typesFile = Join-Path (Split-Path $profile) "Types.Custom.Ps1Xml"
Update-TypeData -PrependPath $typesFile
```

For more information about custom type extensions files, see Recipe 3.17.

Writing Scripts, Reusing Functionality

When you want to start packaging and reusing your commands, the best place to put them is in scripts, functions, and script blocks. A *script* is a text file that contains a sequence of PowerShell commands. A *function* is also a sequence of PowerShell commands but is usually placed within a script to break it into smaller, more easily understood segments. A script block is a function with no name. All three support the same functionality, except for how you define them.

Writing Commands

Writing scripts

To write a script, write your PowerShell commands in a text editor and save the file with a *.ps1* extension.

Writing functions

Functions let you package blocks of closely related commands into a single unit that you can access by name.

```
function SCOPE:name(parameters)
{
    statement block
}
```

or:

```
filter SCOPE:name(parameters)
{
    statement block
}
```

Valid scope names are `global` (to create a function available to the entire shell), `script` (to create a function available only to the current script), `local` (to create a function available only to the current scope and subscopes), and `private` (to create a function available only to the current scope). The default scope is the `local` scope, which follows the same rules as those of default variable scopes.

The content of a function's statement block follows the same rules as the content of a script. Functions support the `$args` array, formal parameters, the `$input` enumerator, cmdlet keywords, pipeline output, and equivalent return semantics.

 A common mistake is to call a function as you would call a method:

```
$result = GetMyResults($item1, $item2)
```

PowerShell treats functions as it treats scripts and other commands, so this should instead be:

```
$result = GetMyResults $item1 $item2
```

The first command passes an array that contains the items `$item1` and `$item2` to the `GetMyResults` function.

A filter is simply a function where the statements are treated as though they are contained within a **process** statement block. For more information about **process** statement blocks, see "Cmdlet keywords in commands" on page 754.

Commands in your script can access only functions that have already been defined. This can often make large scripts difficult to understand when the beginning of the script is composed entirely of helper functions. Structuring a script in the following manner often makes it more clear:

```
function Main
{
    (...)
    HelperFunction
    (...)
}

function HelperFunction
{
    (...)
}

. Main
```

Writing script blocks

```
$objectReference =
{
    statement block
}
```

PowerShell supports script blocks, which act exactly like unnamed functions and scripts. Like both scripts and functions, the content of a script block's statement block follows the same rules as the content of a function or script. Script blocks support the `$args` array, formal parameters, the `$input` enumerator, cmdlet keywords, pipeline output, and equivalent return semantics.

As with both scripts and functions, you can either invoke or dot-source a script block. Since a script block does not have a name, you either invoke it directly (`& { "Hello"}`) or invoke the variable (`& $objectReference`) that contains it.

Running Commands

There are two ways to execute a command (script, function, or script block): by invoking it or by dot-sourcing it.

Invoking

Invoking a command runs the commands inside it. Unless explicitly defined with the GLOBAL scope keyword, variables and functions defined in the script do not persist once the script exits.

By default, a security feature in PowerShell called the Execution Policy prevents scripts from running. When you want to enable scripting in PowerShell, you must change this setting. To understand the different execution policies available to you, type `Get-Help about_signing`. After selecting an execution policy, use the `Set-ExecutionPolicy` cmdlet to configure it:

```
Set-ExecutionPolicy RemoteSigned
```

If the command name has no spaces, simply type its name:

```
c:\temp\Invoke-Commands.ps1 parameter1 parameter2 ...
Invoke-MyFunction parameter1 parameter2 ...
```

You can use either a fully qualified path or a path relative to the current location. If the script is in the current directory, you must explicitly say so:

```
.\Invoke-Commands.ps1 parameter1 parameter2 ...
```

If the command's name has a space (or the command has no name, in the case of a script block), you invoke the command by using the invoke/call operator (&) with the command name as the parameter.

```
& "C:\Script Directory\Invoke-Commands.ps1" parameter1 parameter2 ...
```

Script blocks have no name, so you place the variable holding them after the invocation operator:

```
$scriptBlock = { "Hello World" }
& $scriptBlock parameter1 parameter2 ...
```

If you want to invoke the command within the context of a module, provide a reference to that module as part of the invocation:

```
$module = Get-Module PowerShellCookbook
& $module Invoke-MyFunction parameter1 parameter2 ...
& $module $scriptBlock parameter1 parameter2 ...
```

Dot-sourcing

Dot-sourcing a command runs the commands inside it. Unlike simply invoking a command, variables and functions defined in the script *do* persist after the script exits.

You invoke a script by using the dot operator (.) and providing the command name as the parameter:

```
. "C:\Script Directory\Invoke-Commands.ps1" Parameters
. Invoke-MyFunction parameters
. $scriptBlock parameters
```

When dot-sourcing a script, you can use either a fully qualified path or a path relative to the current location. If the script is in the current directory, you must explicitly say so:

```
. .\Invoke-Commands.ps1 Parameters
```

If you want to dot-source the command within the context of a module, provide a reference to that module as part of the invocation:

```
$module = Get-Module PowerShellCookbook
. $module Invoke-MyFunction parameters
. $module $scriptBlock parameters
```

Parameter splatting

Rather than explicitly providing parameter names and values, you can provide a hashtable that defines them and use the *splatting operator*:

```
$parameters = @{
    Path = "c:\temp"
    Recurse = $true
}

Get-ChildItem @parameters
```

Providing Input to Commands

PowerShell offers several options for processing input to a command.

Argument array

To access the command-line arguments by position, use the argument array that PowerShell places in the $args special variable:

```
$firstArgument = $args[0]
$secondArgument = $args[1]
$argumentCount = $args.Count
```

Formal parameters

To define a command with simple parameter support:

```
param(
    [TypeName] $VariableName = Default,
    ...
)
```

To define one with support for advanced functionality:

```
[CmdletBinding(cmdlet behavior customizations)]
param(
    [Parameter(Mandatory = $true, Position = 1, ...)]
    [Alias("MyParameterAlias")]
    [...]
    [TypeName] $VariableName = Default,
    ...
)
```

Formal parameters let you benefit from some of the many benefits of PowerShell's consistent command-line parsing engine.

PowerShell exposes your parameter names (for example, `$VariableName`) the same way that it exposes parameters in cmdlets. Users need to type only enough of your parameter name to disambiguate it from the rest of the parameters.

If you define a command with simple parameter support, PowerShell attempts to assign the input to your parameters by their position if the user does not type parameter names.

When you add the `[CmdletBinding()]` attribute, `[Parameter()]` attribute, or any of the validation attributes, PowerShell adds support for advanced parameter validation.

Command behavior customizations

The elements of the `[CmdletBinding()]` attribute describe how your script or function interacts with the system.

`SupportsShouldProcess = $true`
> If `$true`, enables the `-WhatIf` and `-Confirm` parameters, which tells the user that your command modifies the system and can be run in one of these experimental modes. When specified, you must also call the `$psCmdlet.ShouldProcess()` method before modifying system state. When not specified, the default is `$false`.

`DefaultParameterSetName = name`
> Defines the default parameter set name of this command. This is used to resolve ambiguities when parameters declare multiple sets of parameters and the user input doesn't supply enough information to pick between available parameter sets. When not specified, the command has no default parameter set name.

`ConfirmImpact = "High"`
> Defines this command as one that should have its confirmation messages (generated by the `$psCmdlet.ShouldProcess()` method) shown by default. More specifically, PowerShell defines three confirmation impacts: `Low`, `Medium`, and `High`. PowerShell generates the cmdlet's confirmation messages automatically whenever the cmdlet's impact level is greater than the preference variable. When not specified, the command's impact is `Medium`.

Parameter attribute customizations

The elements of the `[Parameter()]` attribute mainly define how your parameter behaves in relation to other parameters. All elements are optional.

`Mandatory = $true`
> Defines the parameter as mandatory. If the user doesn't supply a value to this parameter, PowerShell automatically prompts him for it. When not specified, the parameter is optional.

`Position = position`
> Defines the position of this parameter. This applies when the user provides parameter values without specifying the parameter they apply to (e.g., *Argument2* in `Invoke-MyFunction -Param1 Argument1 Argument2`). PowerShell supplies these

values to parameters that have defined a `Position`, from lowest to highest. When not specified, the name of this parameter must be supplied by the user.

ParameterSetName = *name*

Defines this parameter as a member of a set of other related parameters. Parameter behavior for this parameter is then specific to this related set of parameters, and the parameter exists only in the parameter sets that it is defined in. This feature is used, for example, when the user may supply only a Name *or* ID. To include a parameter in two or more specific parameter sets, use two or more `[Parameter()]` attributes. When not specified, this parameter is a member of all parameter sets.

ValueFromPipeline = $true

Declares this parameter as one that directly accepts pipeline input. If the user pipes data into your script or function, PowerShell assigns this input to your parameter in your command's `process {}` block. When not specified, this parameter does not accept pipeline input directly.

ValueFromPipelineByPropertyName = $true

Declares this parameter as one that accepts pipeline input if a property of an incoming object matches its name. If this is true, PowerShell assigns the value of that property to your parameter in your command's `process {}` block. When not specified, this parameter does not accept pipeline input by property name.

ValueFromRemainingArguments = $true

Declares this parameter as one that accepts all remaining input that has not otherwise been assigned to positional or named parameters. Only one parameter can have this element. If no parameter declares support for this capability, PowerShell generates an error for arguments that cannot be assigned.

Parameter validation attributes

In addition to the `[Parameter()]` attribute, PowerShell lets you apply other attributes that add additional behavior or validation constraints to your parameters. All validation attributes are optional.

[Alias("*name*")]

Defines an alternate name for this parameter. This is especially helpful for long parameter names that are descriptive but have a more common colloquial term. When not specified, the parameter can be referred to only by the name you originally declared.

[AllowNull()]

Allows this parameter to receive $null as its value. This is required only for mandatory parameters. When not specified, mandatory parameters cannot receive $null as their value, although optional parameters can.

`[AllowEmptyString()]`
>   Allows this string parameter to receive an empty string as its value. This is required only for mandatory parameters. When not specified, mandatory string parameters cannot receive an empty string as their value, although optional string parameters can. You can apply this to parameters that are not strings, but it has no impact.

`[AllowEmptyCollection()]`
>   Allows this collection parameter to receive an empty collection as its value. This is required only for mandatory parameters. When not specified, mandatory collection parameters cannot receive an empty collection as their value, although optional collection parameters can. You can apply this to parameters that are not collections, but it has no impact.

`[ValidateCount(`*`lower limit, upper limit`*`)]`
>   Restricts the number of elements that can be in a collection supplied to this parameter. When not specified, mandatory parameters have a lower limit of one element. Optional parameters have no restrictions. You can apply this to parameters that are not collections, but it has no impact.

`[ValidateLength(`*`lower limit, upper limit`*`)]`
>   Restricts the length of strings that this parameter can accept. When not specified, mandatory parameters have a lower limit of one character. Optional parameters have no restrictions. You can apply this to parameters that are not strings, but it has no impact.

`[ValidatePattern("`*`regular expression`*`")]`
>   Enforces a pattern that input to this string parameter must match. When not specified, string inputs have no pattern requirements. You can apply this to parameters that are not strings, but it has no impact.

`[ValidateRange(`*`lower limit, upper limit`*`)]`
>   Restricts the upper and lower limit of numerical arguments that this parameter can accept. When not specified, parameters have no range limit. You can apply this to parameters that are not numbers, but it has no impact.

`[ValidateScript( {` *`script block`* `} )]`
>   Ensures that input supplied to this parameter satisfies the condition that you supply in the script block. PowerShell assigns the proposed input to the `$_` variable, and then invokes your script block. If the script block returns `$true` (or anything that can be converted to `$true`, such as nonempty strings), PowerShell considers the validation to have been successful.

`[ValidateSet("`*`First Option`*`", "`*`Second Option`*`", ..., "`*`Last Option`*`")]`
>   Ensures that input supplied to this parameter is equal to one of the options in the set. PowerShell uses its standard meaning of equality during this comparison: the same rules used by the `-eq` operator. If your validation requires nonstandard rules (such as case-sensitive comparison of strings), you can instead write the validation in the body of the script or function.

`[ValidateNotNull()]`

> Ensures that input supplied to this parameter is not null. This is the default be-havior of mandatory parameters, so this is useful only for optional parameters. When applied to string parameters, a `$null` parameter value gets instead converted to an empty string.

`[ValidateNotNullOrEmpty()]`

> Ensures that input supplied to this parameter is not null or empty. This is the default behavior of mandatory parameters, so this is useful only for optional pa-rameters. When applied to string parameters, the input must be a string with a length greater than one. When applied to collection parameters, the collection must have at least one element. When applied to other types of parameters, this attribute is equivalent to the `[ValidateNotNull()]` attribute.

Pipeline input

To access the data being passed to your command via the pipeline, use the input enu-merator that PowerShell places in the `$input` special variable:

```
foreach($element in $input)
{
    "Input was: $element"
}
```

The `$input` variable is a .NET enumerator over the pipeline input. Enumerators support streaming scenarios very efficiently but do not let you access arbitrary elements as you would with an array. If you want to process their elements again, you must call the `Reset()` method on the `$input` enumerator once you reach the end.

If you need to access the pipeline input in an unstructured way, use the following command to convert the input enumerator to an array:

```
$inputArray = @($input)
```

Cmdlet keywords in commands

When pipeline input is a core scenario of your command, you can include statement blocks labeled `begin`, `process`, and `end`:

```
param(...)

begin
{
    ...
}
process
{
    ...
}
end
{
```

```
   ...
}
```

PowerShell executes the `begin` statement when it loads your command, the `process` statement for each item passed down the pipeline, and the `end` statement after all pipeline input has been processed. In the `process` statement block, the `$_` variable represents the current pipeline object.

When you write a command that includes these keywords, all the commands in your script must be contained within the statement blocks.

$MyInvocation automatic variable

The `$MyInvocation` automatic variable contains information about the context under which the script was run, including detailed information about the command (*MyCommand*), the script that defines it (*ScriptName*), and more.

Retrieving Output from Commands

PowerShell provides three primary ways to retrieve output from a command.

Pipeline output

```
any command
```

The return value/output of a script is any data that it generates but does not capture. If a command contains the commands:

```
"Text Output"
5*5
```

then assigning the output of that command to a variable creates an array with the two values Text Output and 25.

Return statement

```
return value
```

The statement:

```
return $false
```

is simply a short form for pipeline output:

```
$false
return
```

Exit statement

```
exit errorlevel
```

The `exit` statement returns an error code from the current command or instance of PowerShell. If called anywhere in a script (inline, in a function, or in a script block), it exits the script. If called outside of a script (for example, a function), it exits PowerShell.

The exit statement sets the $LastExitCode automatic variable to *errorLevel*. In turn, that sets the $? automatic variable to $false if *errorLevel* is not zero.

 Type **Get-Help about_automatic_variables** for more information about automatic variables.

Help Documentation

PowerShell automatically generates help content out of specially tagged comments in your command:

```
<#

.SYNOPSIS
Runs a ...

.EXAMPLE
PS > ...

#>

param(
    ## Help content for the Param1 parameter
    $Param1
)
```

Help-specific comments must be the only comments in a comment block. If PowerShell discovers a nonhelp comment, it discontinues looking for comments in that comment block. If you need to include nonhelp comments in a comment block, place them in a separate block of comments. The following are the most typical help comments used in a comment block:

.SYNOPSIS
> A short summary of the command, ideally a single sentence.

.DESCRIPTION
> A more detailed description of the command.

.PARAMETER *name*
> A description of parameter *name*, with one for each parameter you want to describe. While you can write a .PARAMETER comment for each parameter, PowerShell also supports comments written directly above the parameter. Putting parameter help alongside the actual parameter makes it easier to read and maintain.

.EXAMPLE
> An example of this command in use, with one for each example you want to provide. PowerShell treats the line immediately beneath the .EXAMPLE tag as the example command. If this line doesn't contain any text that looks like a prompt,

PowerShell adds a prompt before it. It treats lines that follow the initial line as additional output and example commentary.

.INPUTS

A short summary of pipeline input(s) supported by this command. For each input type, PowerShell's built-in help follows this convention:

```
System.String
    You can pipe a string that contains a path to Get-ChildItem.
```

.OUTPUTS

A short summary of items generated by this command. For each output type, PowerShell's built-in help follows this convention:

```
System.ServiceProcess.ServiceController
    Get-Service returns objects that represent the services on the computer.
```

.NOTES

Any additional notes or remarks about this command.

.LINK

A link to a related help topic or command, with one .LINK tag per link. If the related help topic is an URL, PowerShell launches that URL when the user supplies the -Online parameter to Get-Help for your command.

Managing Errors

PowerShell supports two classes of errors: *nonterminating* and *terminating*. It collects both types of errors as a list in the $error automatic variable.

Nonterminating Errors

Most errors are *nonterminating errors*, in that they do not halt execution of the current cmdlet, script, function, or pipeline. When a command outputs an error (via PowerShell's error-output facilities), PowerShell writes that error to a stream called the *error output stream*.

You can output a nonterminating error using the Write-Error cmdlet (or the WriteError() API when writing a cmdlet).

The $ErrorActionPreference automatic variable lets you control how PowerShell handles nonterminating errors. It supports the following values, shown in Table A-14.

Table A-14. ErrorActionPreference automatic variable values

Value	Meaning
SilentlyContinue	Do not display errors.
Stop	Treat nonterminating errors as terminating errors.
Continue	Display errors, but continue execution of the current cmdlet, script, function, or pipeline. This is the default.
Inquire	Display a prompt that asks how PowerShell should treat this error.

Most cmdlets let you configure this explicitly by passing one of these values to the ErrorAction parameter.

Terminating Errors

A *terminating error* halts execution of the current cmdlet, script, function, or pipeline. If a command (such as a cmdlet or .NET method call) generates a structured exception (for example, if you provide a method with parameters outside their valid range), PowerShell exposes this as a terminating error. PowerShell also generates a terminating error if it fails to parse an element of your script, function, or pipeline.

You can generate a terminating error in your script using the throw keyword:

```
throw message
```

 In your own scripts and cmdlets, generate terminating errors only when the fundamental intent of the operation is impossible to accomplish. For example, failing to execute a command on a remote server should be considered a nonterminating error, whereas failing to connect to the remote server altogether should be considered a terminating error.

You can intercept terminating errors through the try, catch, and finally statements, as supported by many other programming languages:

```
try
{
    statement block
}
catch [exception type]
{
    error handling block
}
catch [alternate exception type]
{
    alternate error handling block
}
finally
{
    cleanup block
}
```

After a **try** statement, you must provide a **catch** statement, a **finally** statement, or both. If you specify an exception type (which is optional), you may specify more than one **catch** statement to handle exceptions of different types. If you specify an exception type, the **catch** block applies only to terminating errors of that type.

PowerShell also lets you intercept terminating errors if you define a **trap** statement before PowerShell encounters that error:

```
trap [exception type]
{
    statement block
    [continue or break]
}
```

If you specify an exception type, the **trap** statement applies only to terminating errors of that type.

If specified, the **continue** keyword tells PowerShell to continue processing your script, function, or pipeline after the point at which it encountered the terminating error.

If specified, the **break** keyword tells PowerShell to halt processing the rest of your script, function, or pipeline after the point at which it encountered the terminating error. The default mode is **break**, and it applies if you specify neither **break** nor **continue**.

Formatting Output

Pipeline | Formatting Command

When objects reach the end of the output pipeline, PowerShell converts them to text to make them suitable for human consumption. PowerShell supports several options to help you control this formatting process, as listed in Table A-15.

Table A-15. PowerShell formatting commands

Formatting command	Result
Format-Table *Properties*	Formats the properties of the input objects as a table, including only the object properties you specify. If you do not specify a property list, PowerShell picks a default set.
	In addition to supplying object properties, you may also provide advanced formatting statements: ```PS > Get-Process	`\n    Format-Table -Auto Name,`\n @{Label="HexId";\n Expression={ "{0:x}" -f $_.Id}\n Width=4\n Align="Right"\n }``` The advanced formatting statement is a hashtable with the keys Label and Expression (or any short form of them). The value of the expression key should be a script block that returns a result for the current object (represented by the $_ variable). For more information about the Format-Table cmdlet, type **Get-Help Format-Table**.

Formatting command	Result
Format-List Properties	Formats the properties of the input objects as a list, including only the object properties you specify. If you do not specify a property list, PowerShell picks a default set.
	The Format-List cmdlet supports the advanced formatting statements as used by the Format-Table cmdlet.
	The Format-List cmdlet is the one you will use most often to get a detailed summary of an object's properties.
	The command Format-List * returns all properties, but it does not include those that PowerShell hides by default. The command Format-List * -Force returns all properties.
	For more information about the Format-List cmdlet, type **Get-Help Format-List**.
Format-Wide Property	Formats the properties of the input objects in an extremely terse summary view. If you do not specify a property, PowerShell picks a default.
	In addition to supplying object properties, you can also provide advanced formatting statements:
	`` PS > Get-Process	` Format-Wide -Auto ` @{ Expression={ "{0:x}" -f $_.Id } } ```
	The advanced formatting statement is a hashtable with the key Expression (or any short form of it). The value of the expression key should be a script block that returns a result for the current object (represented by the $_ variable).
	For more information about the Format-Wide cmdlet, type **Get-Help Format-Wide**.

Custom Formatting Files

All the formatting defaults in PowerShell (for example, when you do not specify a formatting command, or when you do not specify formatting properties) are driven by the *.Format.Ps1Xml* files in the installation directory in a manner similar to the type extension files mentioned in Recipe 3.17.

To create your own formatting customizations, use these files as a source of examples, but do not modify them directly. Instead, create a new file and use the Update-Format Data cmdlet to load your customizations. The Update-FormatData cmdlet applies your changes to the current instance of PowerShell. If you wish to load them every time you launch PowerShell, call Update-FormatData in your profile script. The following command loads *Format.custom.ps1xml* from the same directory as your profile:

```
$formatFile = Join-Path (Split-Path $profile) "Format.Custom.Ps1Xml"
Update-FormatData -PrependPath $typesFile
```

Capturing Output

There are several ways to capture the output of commands in PowerShell, as listed in Table A-16.

Table A-16. Capturing output in PowerShell

Command	Result
`$variable = Command`	Stores the objects produced by the PowerShell command into `$variable`.
`$variable = Command | Out-String`	Stores the visual representation of the PowerShell command into `$variable`. This is the PowerShell command after it's been converted to human-readable output.
`$variable = NativeCommand`	Stores the (string) output of the native command into `$variable`. PowerShell stores this as a list of strings—one for each line of output from the native command.
`Command -OutVariable variable`	For most commands, stores the objects produced by the PowerShell command into `$variable`. The parameter `-OutVariable` can also be written `-Ov`.
`Command > File`	Redirects the visual representation of the PowerShell (or standard output of a native command) into `File`, overwriting `File` if it exists. Errors are not captured by this redirection.
`Command >> File`	Redirects the visual representation of the PowerShell (or standard output of a native command) into `File`, appending to `File` if it exists. Errors are not captured by this redirection.
`Command 2> File`	Redirects the errors from the PowerShell or native command into `File`, overwriting `File` if it exists.
`Command 2>> File`	Redirects the errors from the PowerShell or native command into `File`, appending to `File` if it exists.
`Command > File 2>&1`	Redirects both the error and standard output streams of the PowerShell or native command into `File`, overwriting `File` if it exists.
`Command >> File 2>&1`	Redirects both the error and standard output streams of the PowerShell or native command into `File`, appending to `File` if it exists.

Common Customization Points

As useful as it is out of the box, PowerShell offers several avenues for customization and personalization.

Console Settings

The Windows PowerShell user interface offers several features to make your shell experience more efficient.

Adjust your window size

In the System menu (right-click the title bar at the top left of the console window), select Properties→Layout. The Window Size options let you control the actual window size (how big the window appears on screen), whereas the Screen Buffer Size options let you control the virtual window size (how much content the window can hold). If the screen buffer size is larger than the actual window size, the console window changes to include scrollbars. Increase the virtual window height to make PowerShell store more output from earlier in your session. If you launch PowerShell from the Start menu, PowerShell launches with some default modifications to the window size.

Make text selection easier

In the System menu, click Options→QuickEdit Mode. QuickEdit mode lets you use the mouse to efficiently copy and paste text into or out of your PowerShell console. If you launch PowerShell from the Start menu, PowerShell launches with QuickEdit mode enabled.

Use hotkeys to operate the shell more efficiently

The Windows PowerShell console supports many hotkeys that help make operating the console more efficient, as shown in Table A-17.

Table A-17. Windows PowerShell hotkeys

Hotkey	Meaning
Windows key-r, and then type **powershell**	Launch Windows PowerShell.
Up arrow	Scan backward through your command history.
Down arrow	Scan forward through your command history.
Page Up	Display the first command in your command history.
Page Down	Display the last command in your command history.
Left arrow	Move cursor one character to the left on your command line.
Right arrow	Move cursor one character to the right on your command line. If at the end of the line, inserts a character from the text of your last command at that position.
Home	Move the cursor to the beginning of the command line.
End	Move the cursor to the end of the command line.
Ctrl-left arrow	Move the cursor one word to the left on your command line.
Ctrl-right arrow	Move the cursor one word to the right on your command line.
Alt-space, e, l	Scroll through the screen buffer.
Alt-space, e, f	Search for text in the screen buffer.
Alt-space, e, k	Select text to be copied from the screen buffer.
Alt-space, e, p	Paste clipboard contents into the Windows PowerShell console.
Alt-space, c	Close the Windows PowerShell console.
Ctrl-c	Cancel the current operation.
Ctrl-break	Forcibly close the Windows PowerShell window.
Ctrl-home	Deletes characters from the beginning of the current command line up to (but not including) the current cursor position.
Ctrl-end	Deletes characters from (and including) the current cursor position to the end of the current command line.
F1	Move cursor one character to the right on your command line. If at the end of the line, inserts a character from the text of your last command at that position.

Hotkey	Meaning
F2	Creates a new command line by copying your last command line up to the character that you type.
F3	Complete the command line with content from your last command line, from the current cursor position to the end.
F4	Deletes characters from your cursor position up to (but not including) the character that you type.
F5	Scan backward through your command history.
F7	Interactively select a command from your command history. Use the arrow keys to scroll through the window that appears. Press the Enter key to execute the command, or use the right arrow key to place the text on your command line instead.
F8	Scan backward through your command history, only displaying matches for commands that match the text you've typed so far on the command line.
F9	Invoke a specific numbered command from your command history. The numbers of these commands correspond to the numbers that the command-history selection window (F7) shows.
Alt-F7	Clear the command history list.

 While useful in their own right, the hotkeys listed in Table A-17 become even more useful when you map them to shorter or more intuitive keystrokes using a hotkey program such as the free AutoHotkey (*http://www.autohotkey.com*).

Profiles

Windows PowerShell automatically runs the four scripts listed in Table A-18 during startup. Each, if present, lets you customize your execution environment. PowerShell runs anything you place in these files as though you had entered it manually at the command line.

Table A-18. Windows PowerShell profiles

Profile purpose	Profile location
Customization of all PowerShell sessions, including PowerShell hosting applications for all users on the system	*InstallationDirectory\profile.ps1*
Customization of *PowerShell.exe* sessions for all users on the system	*InstallationDirectory\Microsoft.PowerShell_profile.ps1*
Customization of all PowerShell sessions, including PowerShell hosting applications	*<My Documents>\WindowsPowerShell\profile.ps1*
Typical customization of *PowerShell.exe* sessions	*<My Documents>\WindowsPowerShell \Microsoft.PowerShell_profile.ps1*

PowerShell makes editing your profile script simple by defining the automatic variable `$profile`. By itself, it points to the "current user, PowerShell.exe" profile. In addition, the `$profile` variable defines additional properties that point to the other profile locations:

```
PS > $profile | Format-List -Force


AllUsersAllHosts        : C:\Windows\System32\WindowsPowerShell\v1.0\
                          profile.ps1
AllUsersCurrentHost     : C:\Windows\System32\WindowsPowerShell\v1.0\
                          Microsoft.PowerShell_profile.ps1
CurrentUserAllHosts     : E:\Lee\WindowsPowerShell\profile.ps1
CurrentUserCurrentHost  : E:\Lee\WindowsPowerShell\Microsoft.PowerShell_
                          profile.ps1
```

To create a new profile, type:

```
New-Item -Type file -Force $profile
```

To edit this profile, type:

```
notepad $profile
```

Prompts

To customize your prompt, add a `prompt` function to your profile. This function returns a string. For example:

```
function Prompt
{
    "PS [$env:COMPUTERNAME] >"
}
```

For more information about customizing your prompt, see also Recipe 1.6.

Tab Completion

You can define a `TabExpansion` function to customize the way that Windows PowerShell completes properties, variables, parameters, and files when you press the Tab key.

Your `TabExpansion` function overrides the one that PowerShell defines by default, though, so you may want to use its definition as a starting point:

```
Get-Content function:\TabExpansion
```

As its arguments, this function receives the entire command line as input, as well as the last word of the command line. If the function returns one or more strings, PowerShell cycles through those strings during tab completion. Otherwise, it uses its built-in logic to tab-complete filenames, directory names, cmdlet names, and variable names.

Regular Expression Reference

Regular expressions play an important role in most text parsing and text matching tasks. They form an important underpinning of the -split and -match operators, the switch statement, the Select-String cmdlet, and more. Tables B-1 through B-9 list commonly used regular expressions.

Table B-1. Character classes: Patterns that represent sets of characters

Character class	Matches

.	Any character except for a newline. If the regular expression uses the SingleLine option, it matches any character.
	
	`PS > "T" -match '.'`
	`True`

[*characters*]	Any character in the brackets. For example: [aeiou].
	
	`PS > "Test" -match '[Tes]'`
	`True`

[^*characters*]	Any character not in the brackets. For example: [^aeiou].
	
	`PS > "Test" -match '[^Tes]'`
	`False`

[*start-end*]	Any character between the characters *start* and *end*, inclusive. You may include multiple character ranges between the brackets. For example, [a-eh-j].
	
	`PS > "Test" -match '[e-t]'`
	`True`

[^*start-end*]	Any character not between any of the character ranges *start* through *end*, inclusive. You may include multiple character ranges between the brackets. For example, [^a-eh-j].
	
	`PS > "Test" -match '[^e-t]'`
	`False`

\p{*character class*}	Any character in the Unicode group or block range specified by {*character class*}.
	
	`PS > "+" -match '\p{Sm}'`
	`True`

\P{*character class*}	Any character not in the Unicode group or block range specified by {*character class*}.

Character class	Matches
| | ```
PS > "+" -match '\P{Sm}'
False
``` |
| \w | Any word character. Note that this is the *Unicode* definition of a word character, which includes digits, as well as many math symbols and various other symbols. |
| | ```
PS > "a" -match '\w'
True
``` |
| \W | Any nonword character. |
| | ```
PS > "!" -match '\W'
True
``` |
| \s | Any whitespace character. |
| | ```
PS > "`t" -match '\s'
True
``` |
| \S | Any nonwhitespace character. |
| | ```
PS > " `t" -match '\S'
False
``` |
| \d | Any decimal digit. |
| | ```
PS > "5" -match '\d'
True
``` |
| \D | Any character that isn't a decimal digit. |
| | ```
PS > "!" -match '\D'
True
``` |

Table B-2. Quantifiers: Expressions that enforce quantity on the preceding expression

Quantifier	Meaning
<none>	One match.
| | ```
PS > "T" -match 'T'
True
``` |
| * | Zero or more matches, matching as much as possible. |
| | ```
PS > "A" -match 'T*'
True
PS > "TTTTT" -match '^T*$'
True

PS > 'ATTT' -match 'AT*'; $Matches[0]
True
ATTT
``` |
| + | One or more matches, matching as much as possible. |
| | ```
PS > "A" -match 'T+'
False
PS > "TTTTT" -match '^T+$'
True

PS > 'ATTT' -match 'AT+'; $Matches[0]
True
ATTT
``` |
| ? | Zero or one matches, matching as much as possible. |

Quantifier	Meaning
	PS > "TTTTT" -match '^T?$' False PS > 'ATTT' -match 'AT?'; $Matches[0] True AT
{n}	Exactly *n* matches. PS > "TTTTT" -match '^T{5}$' True
{n,}	*n* or more matches, matching as much as possible. PS > "TTTTT" -match '^T{4,}$' True
{n,m}	Between *n* and *m* matches (inclusive), matching as much as possible. PS > "TTTTT" -match '^T{4,6}$' True
*?	Zero or more matches, matching as little as possible. PS > "A" -match '^AT*?$' True PS > 'ATTT' -match 'AT*?'; $Matches[0] True A
+?	One or more matches, matching as little as possible. PS > "A" -match '^AT+?$' False PS > 'ATTT' -match 'AT+?'; $Matches[0] True AT
??	Zero or one matches, matching as little as possible. PS > "A" -match '^AT??$' True PS > 'ATTT' -match 'AT??'; $Matches[0] True A
{n}?	Exactly *n* matches. PS > "TTTTT" -match '^T{5}?$' True
{n,}?	*n* or more matches, matching as little as possible. PS > "TTTTT" -match '^T{4,}?$' True
{n,m}?	Between *n* and *m* matches (inclusive), matching as little as possible. PS > "TTTTT" -match '^T{4,6}?$' True

Table B-3. Grouping constructs: Expressions that let you group characters, patterns, and other expressions

Grouping construct	Description
(text)	Captures the text matched inside the parentheses. These captures are named by number (starting at one) based on the order of the opening parenthesis. ``` PS > "Hello" -match '^(.*)llo$'; $matches[1] True He ```
(?<name>)	Captures the text matched inside the parentheses. These captures are named by the name given in *name*. ``` PS > "Hello" -match '^(?<One>.*)llo$'; $matches.One True He ```
(?<name1-name2>)	A balancing group definition. This is an advanced regular expression construct, but lets you match evenly balanced pairs of terms.
(?:)	Noncapturing group. ``` PS > "A1" -match '((A|B)\d)'; $matches True Name Value ---- ----- 2 A 1 A1 0 A1 PS > "A1" -match '((?:A|B)\d)'; $matches True Name Value ---- ----- 1 A1 0 A1 ```
(?imnsx-imnsx:)	Applies or disables the given option for this group. Supported options are: ``` i case-insensitive m multiline n explicit capture s singleline x ignore whitespace PS > "Te`nst" -match '(T e.st)' False PS > "Te`nst" -match '(?sx:T e.st)' True ```
(?=)	Zero-width positive lookahead assertion. Ensures that the given pattern matches to the right, without actually performing the match. ``` PS > "555-1212" -match '(?=...-)(.*)'; $matches[1] True 555-1212 ```
(?!)	Zero-width negative lookahead assertion. Ensures that the given pattern does not match to the right, without actually performing the match.

Grouping construct	Description
	```PS > "friendly" -match '(?!friendly)friend'``` ```False```

(?<=)	Zero-width positive lookbehind assertion. Ensures that the given pattern matches to the left, without actually performing the match.
	```PS > "public int X" -match '^.*(?<=public)int .*$'```
	```True```

(?<!)	Zero-width negative lookbehind assertion. Ensures that the given pattern does not match to the left, without actually performing the match.
	```PS > "private int X" -match '^.*(?<!private)int .*$'```
	```False```

(?>)	Nonbacktracking subexpression. Matches only if this subexpression can be matched completely.
	```PS > "Hello World" -match '(Hello.*)orld'```
	```True```
	```PS > "Hello World" -match '(?>Hello.*)orld'```
	```False```
	
	The nonbacktracking version of the subexpression fails to match, as its complete match would be "Hello World".

Table B-4. Atomic zero-width assertions: Patterns that restrict where a match may occur

Assertion	Restriction

^	The match must occur at the beginning of the string (or line, if the Multiline option is in effect).
	```PS > "Test" -match '^est'```
	```False```

$	The match must occur at the end of the string (or line, if the Multiline option is in effect).
	```PS > "Test" -match 'Tes$'```
	```False```

\A	The match must occur at the beginning of the string.
	```PS > "The`nTest" -match '(?m:^Test)'```
	```True```
	```PS > "The`nTest" -match '(?m:\ATest)'```
	```False```

\Z	The match must occur at the end of the string, or before \n at the end of the string.
	```PS > "The`nTest`n" -match '(?m:The$)'```
	```True```
	```PS > "The`nTest`n" -match '(?m:The\Z)'```
	```False```
	```PS > "The`nTest`n" -match 'Test\Z'```
	```True```

\z	The match must occur at the end of the string.
	```PS > "The`nTest`n" -match 'Test\z'```
	```False```

\G	The match must occur where the previous match ended. Used with System.Text.RegularExpressions.Match.NextMatch().

Assertion	Restriction
\b	The match must occur on a word boundary: the first or last characters in words separated by nonalphanumeric characters.
	`PS > "Testing" -match 'ing\b'` `True`
\B	The match must not occur on a word boundary.
	`PS > "Testing" -match 'ing\B'` `False`

Table B-5. Substitution patterns: Patterns used in a regular expression replace operation

Pattern	Substitution
$*number*	The text matched by group number *number*.
	`PS > "Test" -replace "(.*)st",'$1ar'` `Tear`
${*name*}	The text matched by group named *name*.

	`PS > "Test" -replace "(?<pre>.*)st",'${pre}ar'`
	`Tear`

$$	A literal $.
	`PS > "Test" -replace ".",'$$'` `$$$$`
$&	A copy of the entire match.
	`PS > "Test" -replace "^.*$",'Found: $&'` `Found: Test`
$`	The text of the input string that precedes the match.
	`PS > "Test" -replace "est$",'Te$`'` `TTeT`
$'	The text of the input string that follows the match.
	`PS > "Test" -replace "^Tes",'Res$''` `Restt`
$+	The last group captured.
	`PS > "Testing" -replace "(.*)ing",'$+ed'` `Tested`
$_	The entire input string.
	`PS > "Testing" -replace "(.*)ing",'String: $_'` `String: Testing`

Table B-6. Alternation constructs: Expressions that let you perform either/or logic

Alternation construct	Description

|	Matches any of the terms separated by the vertical bar character.
	
	`PS > "Test" -match '(B|T)est'`
	`True`

`(?(expression)yes|no)`	Matches the *yes term* if expression matches at this point. Otherwise, matches the *no term*. The *no term* is optional.
	
	`PS > "3.14" -match '(?(\d)3.14|Pi)'`
	`True`
	`PS > "Pi" -match '(?(\d)3.14|Pi)'`
	`True`
	`PS > "2.71" -match '(?(\d)3.14|Pi)'`
	`False`

`(?(name)yes|no)`	Matches the *yes term* if the capture group named name has a capture at this point. Otherwise, matches the *no term*. The *no term* is optional.
	
	`PS > "123" -match '(?<one>1)?(?(one)23|234)'`
	`True`
	`PS > "23" -match '(?<one>1)?(?(one)23|234)'`
	`False`
	`PS > "234" -match '(?<one>1)?(?(one)23|234)'`
	`True`

Table B-7. Backreference constructs: Expressions that refer to a capture group within the expression

Backreference construct	Refers to

`\number`	Group number *number* in the expression.
	
	`PS > "|Text|" -match '(.)Text\1'`
	`True`
	`PS > "|Text+" -match '(.)Text\1'`
	`False`

`\k<name>`	The group named *name* in the expression.
	
	`PS > "|Text|" -match '(?<Symbol>.)Text\k<Symbol>'`
	`True`
	`PS > "|Text+" -match '(?<Symbol>.)Text\k<Symbol>'`
	`False`

Table B-8. Other constructs: Other expressions that modify a regular expression

Construct	Description
`(?imnsx-imnsx)`	Applies or disables the given option for the rest of this expression. Supported options are: `i    case-insensitive` `m    multiline` `n    explicit capture` `s    singleline` `x    ignore whitespace` `PS > "Te`nst" -match '(?sx)T e.st'` `True`

Construct	Description
(?#)	Inline comment. This terminates at the first closing parenthesis.
	`PS > "Test" -match '(?# Match 'Test')Test'` `True`
# [to end of line]	Comment form allowed when the regular expression has the `IgnoreWhitespace` option enabled.
	`PS > "Test" -match '(?x)Test # Matches Test'` `True`

Table B-9. Character escapes: Character sequences that represent another character

Escaped character	Match
<ordinary characters>	Characters other than . $ ^ { [(	) * + ? \ match themselves.
\a	A bell (alarm) \u0007.
\b	A backspace \u0008 if in a [ ] character class. In a regular expression, \b denotes a word boundary (between \w and \W characters) except within a [ ] character class, where \b refers to the backspace character. In a replacement pattern, \b always denotes a backspace.
\t	A tab \u0009.
\r	A carriage return \u000D.
\v	A vertical tab \u000B.
\f	A form feed \u000C.
\n	A new line \u000A.
\e	An escape \u001B.
\ddd	An ASCII character as octal (up to three digits). Numbers with no leading zero are treated as backreferences if they have only one digit, or if they correspond to a capturing group number.
\xdd	An ASCII character using hexadecimal representation (exactly two digits).
\cC	An ASCII control character; for example, \cC is control-C.
\udddd	A Unicode character using hexadecimal representation (exactly four digits).
\	When followed by a character that is not recognized as an escaped character, matches that character. For example, * is the literal character *.

XPath Quick Reference

Just as regular expressions are the standard way to interact with plain text, XPath is the standard way to interact with XML. Because of that, XPath is something you are likely to run across in your travels. Several cmdlets support XPath queries: `Select-Xml`, `Get-WinEvent`, and more. Tables C-1 and C-2 give a quick overview of XPath concepts.

For these examples, consider this sample XML:

```
<AddressBook>
  <Person contactType="Personal">
    <Name>Lee</Name>
    <Phone type="home">555-1212</Phone>
    <Phone type="work">555-1213</Phone>
  </Person>
  <Person contactType="Business">
    <Name>Ariel</Name>
    <Phone>555-1234</Phone>
  </Person>
</AddressBook>
```

Table C-1. Navigation and selection

Syntax	Meaning
/	Represents the root of the XML tree.
	For example:
	`PS > $xml	Select-Xml "/"	Select -Expand Node`  `AddressBook` `-----------` `AddressBook`
/Node	Navigates to the node named *Node* from the root of the XML tree.
	For example:
	`PS > $xml	Select-Xml "/AddressBook"	Select -Expand Node`  `Person` `------` `{Lee, Ariel}`

Syntax	Meaning
/Node/*/Node2	Navigates to the noded named *Node2* via *Node*, allowing any single node in between.

For example:

```
PS > $xml | Select-Xml "/AddressBook/*/Name" | Select -Expand Node

#text
-----
Lee
Ariel
```

//Node	Finds all nodes named *Node*, anywhere in the XML tree.

For example:

```
PS > $xml | Select-Xml "//Phone" | Select -Expand Node

type                                    #text
----                                    -----
home                                    555-1212
work                                    555-1213
                                        555-1234
```

..	Retrieves the parent node of the given node.

For example:

```
PS>$xml | Select-Xml "//Phone" | Select -Expand Node

type                                    #text
----                                    -----
home                                    555-1212
work                                    555-1213
                                        555-1234


PS>$xml | Select-Xml "//Phone/.." | Select -Expand Node

contactType        Name              Phone
-----------        ----              -----
Personal           Lee               {Phone, Phone}
Business           Ariel             555-1234
```

@Attribute	Accesses the value of the attribute named *Attribute*.

For example:

```
PS > $xml | Select-Xml "//Phone/@type" | Select -Expand Node

#text
-----
home
work
```

Table C-2. Comparisons

Syntax	Meaning
[ ]	Filtering, similar to the Where-Object cmdlet.

For example:

```
PS > $xml | Select-Xml "//Person[@contactType = 'Personal']" |
    Select -Expand Node

contactType            Name                Phone
-----------            ----                -----
Personal               Lee                 {Phone, Phone}


PS > $xml | Select-Xml "//Person[Name = 'Lee']" | Select -Expand Node

contactType            Name                Phone
-----------            ----                -----
Personal               Lee                 {Phone, Phone}
```

Syntax	Meaning
and	Logical *and*.
or	Logical *or*.
not()	Logical *negation*.
=	*Equality*.
!=	*Inequality*.

.NET String Formatting

String Formatting Syntax

The format string supported by the format (-f) operator is a string that contains format items. Each format item takes the form of:

```
{index[,alignment][:formatString]}
```

index represents the zero-based index of the item in the object array following the format operator.

alignment is optional and represents the alignment of the item. A positive number aligns the item to the right of a field of the specified width. A negative number aligns the item to the left of a field of the specified width.

```
PS > ("{0,6}" -f 4.99), ("{0,6:##.00}" -f 15.9)
  4.99
 15.90
```

formatString is optional and formats the item using that type's specific format string syntax (as laid out in Tables D-1 and D-2).

Standard Numeric Format Strings

Table D-1 lists the standard numeric format strings. All format specifiers may be followed by a number between 0 and 99 to control the precision of the formatting.

Table D-1. Standard numeric format strings

Format specifier	Name	Description	Example
C or c	Currency	A currency amount.	PS > "{0:C}" -f 1.23 $1.23
D or d	Decimal	A decimal amount (for integral types). The precision specifier controls the minimum number of digits in the result.	PS > "{0:D4}" -f 2 0002

Format specifier	Name	Description	Example
E or e	Scientific	Scientific (exponential) notation. The precision specifier controls the number of digits past the decimal point.	`PS > "{0:E3}" -f [Math]::Pi` `3.142E+000`
F or f	Fixedpoint	Fixed point notation. The precision specifier controls the number of digits past the decimal point.	`PS > "{0:F3}" -f [Math]::Pi` `3.142`

G or g	General	The most compact representation (between fixed-point and scientific) of the number. The precision specifier controls the number of significant digits.	`PS > "{0:G3}" -f [Math]::Pi`
			`3.14`
			`PS > "{0:G3}" -f 1mb`
			`1.05E+06`

N or n	Number	The human-readable form of the number, which includes separators between number groups. The precision specifier controls the number of digits past the decimal point.	`PS > "{0:N4}" -f 1mb` `1,048,576.0000`
P or p	Percent	The number (generally between 0 and 1) represented as a percentage. The precision specifier controls the number of digits past the decimal point.	`PS > "{0:P4}" -f 0.67` `67.0000 %`

R or r	Roundtrip	The Single or Double number formatted with a precision that guarantees the string (when parsed) will result in the original number again.	`PS > "{0:R}" -f (1mb/2.0)`
			`524288`
			`PS > "{0:R}" -f (1mb/9.0)`
			`116508.44444444444`

X or x	Hexadecimal	The number converted to a string of hexadecimal digits. The case of the specifier controls the case of the resulting hexadecimal digits. The precision specifier controls the minimum number of digits in the resulting string.	`PS > "{0:X4}" -f 1324` `052C`

Custom Numeric Format Strings

You can use custom numeric strings, listed in Table D-2, to format numbers in ways not supported by the standard format strings.

Table D-2. Custom numeric format strings

Format specifier	Name	Description	Example
0	Zero placeholder	Specifies the precision and width of a number string. Zeroes not matched by digits in the original number are output as zeroes.	`PS > "{0:00.0}" -f 4.12341234` `04.1`
#	Digit placeholder	Specifies the precision and width of a number string. # symbols not matched by digits in the input number are not output.	`PS > "{0:##.#}" -f 4.12341234` `4.1`
.	Decimal point	Determines the location of the decimal.	`PS > "{0:##.#}" -f 4.12341234` `4.1`

Format specifier	Name	Description	Example
,	Thousands separator	When placed between a zero or digit placeholder before the decimal point in a formatting string, adds the separator character between number groups.	PS > "{0:#,#.#}" -f 1234.121234 1,234.1
,	Number scaling	When placed before the literal (or implicit) decimal point in a formatting string, divides the input by 1000. You can apply this format specifier more than once.	PS > "{0:##,,.000}" -f 1048576 1.049
%	Percentage placeholder	Multiplies the input by 100, and inserts the percent sign where shown in the format specifier.	PS > "{0:%##.000}" -f .68 %68.000
E0 E+0 E-0 e0 e+0 e-0	Scientific notation	Displays the input in scientific notation. The number of zeroes that follow the E define the minimum length of the exponent field.	PS > "{0:##.#E000}" -f 2.71828 27.2E-001
'text' "text"	Literal string	Inserts the provided text literally into the output without affecting formatting.	PS > "{0:#.00'##'}" -f 2.71828 2.72##
;	Section separator	Allows for conditional formatting. If your format specifier contains no section separators, the formatting statement applies to all input. If your format specifier contains one separator (creating two sections), the first section applies to positive numbers and zero, and the second section applies to negative numbers. If your format specifier contains two separators (creating three sections), the sections apply to positive numbers, negative numbers, and zero.	PS > "{0:POS;NEG;ZERO}" -f -14 NEG
Other	Other character	Inserts the provided text literally into the output without affecting formatting.	PS > "{0:$## Please}" -f 14 $14 Please

.NET DateTime Formatting

DateTime format strings convert a `DateTime` object to one of several standard formats, as listed in Table E-1.

Table E-1. Standard DateTime format strings

Format specifier	Name	Description	Example
d	Short date	The culture's short date format.	PS > "{0:d}" -f [DateTime] "01/23/4567" 1/23/4567
D	Long date	The culture's long date format.	PS > "{0:D}" -f [DateTime] "01/23/4567" Friday, January 23, 4567
f	Full date/short time	Combines the long date and short time format patterns.	PS > "{0:f}" -f [DateTime] "01/23/4567" Friday, January 23, 4567 12:00 AM
F	Full date/long time	Combines the long date and long time format patterns.	PS > "{0:F}" -f [DateTime] "01/23/4567" Friday, January 23, 4567 12:00:00 AM
g	General date/short time	Combines the short date and short time format patterns.	PS > "{0:g}" -f [DateTime] "01/23/4567" 1/23/4567 12:00 AM
G	General date/long time	Combines the short date and long time format patterns.	PS > "{0:G}" -f [DateTime] "01/23/4567" 1/23/4567 12:00:00 AM
M or m	Month day	The culture's `MonthDay` format.	PS > "{0:M}" -f [DateTime] "01/23/4567" January 23
o	Round-trip date/time	The date formatted with a pattern that guarantees the string (when parsed) will result in the original DateTime again.	PS > "{0:o}" -f [DateTime] "01/23/4567" 4567-01-23T00:00:00.0000000
R or r	RFC1123	The standard RFC1123 format pattern.	PS > "{0:R}" -f [DateTime] "01/23/4567" Fri, 23 Jan 4567 00:00:00 GMT
s	Sortable	Sortable format pattern. Conforms to ISO 8601 and provides output suitable for sorting.	PS > "{0:s}" -f [DateTime] "01/23/4567" 4567-01-23T00:00:00
t	Short time	The culture's `ShortTime` format.	PS > "{0:t}" -f [DateTime] "01/23/4567" 12:00 AM

Format specifier	Name	Description	Example
T	Long time	The culture's LongTime format.	PS > "{0:T}" -f [DateTime] "01/23/4567" 12:00:00 AM
u	Universal sortable	The culture's UniversalSortable DateTime format applied to the UTC equivalent of the input.	PS > "{0:u}" -f [DateTime] "01/23/4567" 4567-01-23 00:00:00Z
U	Universal	The culture's FullDateTime format applied to the UTC equivalent of the input.	PS > "{0:U}" -f [DateTime] "01/23/4567" Friday, January 23, 4567 8:00:00 AM
Y or y	Year month	The culture's YearMonth format.	PS > "{0:Y}" -f [DateTime] "01/23/4567" January, 4567

Custom DateTime Format Strings

You can use the custom DateTime format strings listed in Table E-2 to format dates in ways not supported by the standard format strings.

 Single-character format specifiers are by default interpreted as a standard DateTime formatting string unless they are used with other formatting specifiers. Add the % character before them to have them interpreted as a custom format specifier.

Table E-2. Custom DateTime format strings

Format specifier	Description	Example
d	Day of the month as a number between 1 and 31. Represents single-digit days without a leading zero.	PS > "{0:%d}" -f [DateTime] "01/02/4567" 2
dd	Day of the month as a number between 1 and 31. Represents single-digit days with a leading zero.	PS > "{0:dd}" -f [DateTime] "01/02/4567" 02
ddd	Abbreviated name of the day of week.	PS > "{0:ddd}" -f [DateTime] "01/02/4567" Fri
dddd	Full name of the day of the week.	PS > "{0:dddd}" -f [DateTime] "01/02/4567" Friday
f	Most significant digit of the seconds fraction (milliseconds).	PS > $date = Get-Date PS > $date.Millisecond 93 PS > "{0:%f}" -f $date 0
ff	Two most significant digits of the seconds fraction (milliseconds).	PS > $date = Get-Date PS > $date.Millisecond 93 PS > "{0:ff}" -f $date 09

Format specifier	Description	Example
fff	Three most significant digits of the seconds fraction (milliseconds).	PS > $date = Get-Date PS > $date.Millisecond 93 PS > "{0:fff}" -f $date 093
ffff	Four most significant digits of the seconds fraction (milliseconds).	PS > $date = Get-Date PS > $date.Millisecond 93 PS > "{0:ffff}" -f $date 0937
fffff	Five most significant digits of the seconds fraction (milliseconds).	PS > $date = Get-Date PS > $date.Millisecond 93 PS > "{0:fffff}" -f $date 09375
ffffff	Six most significant digits of the seconds fraction (milliseconds).	PS > $date = Get-Date PS > $date.Millisecond 93 PS > "{0:ffffff}" -f $date 093750
fffffff	Seven most significant digits of the seconds fraction (milliseconds).	PS > $date = Get-Date PS > $date.Millisecond 93 PS > "{0:fffffff}" -f $date 0937500
F FF FFF (...) FFFFFFF	Most significant digit of the seconds fraction (milliseconds). When compared to the lowercase series of 'f' specifiers, displays nothing if the number is zero.	PS > "{0:|F FF FFF FFFF|}" -f [DateTime] "01/02/4567" | |
%g or gg	Era (e.g., A.D.).	PS > "{0:gg}" -f [DateTime] "01/02/4567" A.D.
%h	Hours, as a number between 1 and 12. Single digits do not include a leading zero.	PS > "{0:%h}" -f [DateTime] "01/02/4567 4:00pm" 4
hh	Hours, as a number between 01 and 12. Single digits include a leading zero. Note: This is interpreted as a standard DateTime formatting string unless used with other formatting specifiers.	PS > "{0:hh}" -f [DateTime] "01/02/4567 4:00pm" 04
%H	Hours, as a number between 0 and 23. Single digits do not include a leading zero.	PS > "{0:%H}" -f [DateTime] "01/02/4567 4:00pm" 16
HH	Hours, as a number between 00 and 23. Single digits include a leading zero.	PS > "{0:HH}" -f [DateTime] "01/02/4567 4:00am" 04
K	DateTime.Kind specifier that corresponds to the kind (i.e., Local, Utc, or Unspecified) of input date.	PS > "{0:%K}" -f [DateTime]::Now.ToUniversalTime() Z

Format specifier	Description	Example
m	Minute, as a number between 0 and 59. Single digits do not include a leading zero.	PS > "{0:%m}" -f [DateTime]::Now 7
mm	Minute, as a number between 00 and 59. Single digits include a leading zero.	PS > "{0:mm}" -f [DateTime]::Now 08
M	Month, as a number between 1 and 12. Single digits do not include a leading zero.	PS > "{0:%M}" -f [DateTime] "01/02/4567" 1
MM	Month, as a number between 01 and 12. Single digits include a leading zero.	PS > "{0:MM}" -f [DateTime] "01/02/4567" 01
MMM	Abbreviated month name.	PS > "{0:MMM}" -f [DateTime] "01/02/4567" Jan
MMMM	Full month name.	PS > "{0:MMMM}" -f [DateTime] "01/02/4567" January
s	Seconds, as a number between 0 and 59. Single digits do not include a leading zero.	PS > $date = Get-Date PS > "{0:%s}" -f $date 7
ss	Seconds, as a number between 00 and 59. Single digits include a leading zero.	PS > $date = Get-Date PS > "{0:ss}" -f $date 07
t	First character of the a.m./p.m. designator.	PS > $date = Get-Date PS > "{0:%t}" -f $date P
tt	a.m./p.m. designator.	PS > $date = Get-Date PS > "{0:tt}" -f $date PM
y	Year, in (at most) two digits.	PS > "{0:%y}" -f [DateTime] "01/02/4567" 67
yy	Year, in (at most) two digits.	PS > "{0:yy}" -f [DateTime] "01/02/4567" 67
yyy	Year, in (at most) four digits.	PS > "{0:yyy}" -f [DateTime] "01/02/4567" 4567
yyyy	Year, in (at most) four digits.	PS > "{0:yyyy}" -f [DateTime] "01/02/4567" 4567
yyyyy	Year, in (at most) five digits.	PS > "{0:yyyyy}" -f [DateTime] "01/02/4567" 04567
z	Signed time zone offset from GMT. Does not include a leading zero.	PS > "{0:%z}" -f [DateTime]::Now -8
zz	Signed time zone offset from GMT. Includes a leading zero.	PS > "{0:zz}" -f [DateTime]::Now -08
zzz	Signed time zone offset from GMT, measured in hours and minutes.	PS > "{0:zzz}" -f [DateTime]::Now -08:00

Format specifier	Description	Example
:	Time separator.	PS > "{0:y/m/d h:m:s}" -f [DateTime] "01/02/4567 4:00pm" 67/0/2 4:0:0
/	Date separator.	PS > "{0:y/m/d h:m:s}" -f [DateTime] "01/02/4567 4:00pm" 67/0/2 4:0:0
"text" 'text'	Inserts the provided text literally into the output without affecting formatting.	PS > "{0:'Day: 'dddd}" -f [DateTime]::Now Day: Monday
%c	Syntax allowing for single-character custom formatting specifiers. The % sign is not added to the output.	PS > "{0:%h}" -f [DateTime] "01/02/4567 4:00pm" 4
Other	Inserts the provided text literally into the output without affecting formatting.	PS > "{0:dddd!}" -f [DateTime]::Now Monday!

Selected .NET Classes and Their Uses

Tables F-1 through F-16 provide pointers to types in the .NET Framework that usefully complement the functionality that PowerShell provides. For detailed descriptions and documentation, search *http://msdn.microsoft.com* for the official documentation.

Table F-1. Windows PowerShells

Class	Description
System.Management. Automation.PSObject	Represents a PowerShell object to which you can add notes, properties, and more.

Table F-2. Utility

Class	Description
System.DateTime	Represents an instant in time, typically expressed as a date and time of day.
System.Guid	Represents a globally unique identifier (GUID).
System.Math	Provides constants and static methods for trigonometric, logarithmic, and other common mathematical functions.
System.Random	Represents a pseudorandom number generator, a device that produces a sequence of numbers that meet certain statistical requirements for randomness.
System.Convert	Converts a base data type to another base data type.
System.Environment	Provides information about, and means to manipulate, the current environment and platform.
System.Console	Represents the standard input, output, and error streams for console applications.
System.Text. RegularExpressions.Regex	Represents an immutable regular expression.
System.Diagnostics.Debug	Provides a set of methods and properties that help debug your code.
System.Diagnostics.EventLog	Provides interaction with Windows event logs.

Class	Description
System.Diagnostics.Process	Provides access to local and remote processes and enables you to start and stop local system processes.
System.Diagnostics.Stopwatch	Provides a set of methods and properties that you can use to accurately measure elapsed time.
System.Media.SoundPlayer	Controls playback of a sound from a *.wav* file.

Table F-3. Collections and object utilities

Class	Description
System.Array	Provides methods for creating, manipulating, searching, and sorting arrays, thereby serving as the base class for all arrays in the Common Language Runtime.
System.Enum	Provides the base class for enumerations.
System.String	Represents text as a series of Unicode characters.
System.Text.StringBuilder	Represents a mutable string of characters.
System.Collections. Specialized.OrderedDictionary	Represents a collection of key/value pairs that are accessible by the key or index.
System.Collections.ArrayList	Implements the IList interface using an array whose size is dynamically increased as required.

Table F-4. The .NET Framework

Class	Description
System.AppDomain	Represents an application domain, which is an isolated environment where applications execute.
System.Reflection.Assembly	Defines an Assembly, which is a reusable, versionable, and self-describing building block of a Common Language Runtime application.
System.Type	Represents type declarations: class types, interface types, array types, value types, enumeration types, type parameters, generic type definitions, and open or closed constructed generic types.
System.Threading.Thread	Creates and controls a thread, sets its priority, and gets its status.
System.Runtime.Interop Services.Marshal	Provides a collection of methods for allocating unmanaged memory, copying unmanaged memory blocks, and converting managed to unmanaged types, as well as other miscellaneous methods used when interacting with unmanaged code.
Microsoft.CSharp.CSharp CodeProvider	Provides access to instances of the C# code generator and code compiler.

Table F-5. Registry

Class	Description
Microsoft.Win32.Registry	Provides RegistryKey objects that represent the root keys in the local and remote Windows registry and static methods to access key/value pairs.
Microsoft.Win32.RegistryKey	Represents a key-level node in the Windows registry.

Table F-6. Input and Output

Class	Description
System.IO.Stream	Provides a generic view of a sequence of bytes.
System.IO.BinaryReader	Reads primitive data types as binary values.
System.IO.BinaryWriter	Writes primitive types in binary to a stream.
System.IO.BufferedStream	Adds a buffering layer to read and write operations on another stream.
System.IO.Directory	Exposes static methods for creating, moving, and enumerating through directories and subdirectories.
System.IO.FileInfo	Provides instance methods for the creation, copying, deletion, moving, and opening of files, and aids in the creation of FileStream objects.
System.IO.DirectoryInfo	Exposes instance methods for creating, moving, and enumerating through directories and subdirectories.
System.IO.File	Provides static methods for the creation, copying, deletion, moving, and opening of files, and aids in the creation of FileStream objects.
System.IO.MemoryStream	Creates a stream whose backing store is memory.
System.IO.Path	Performs operations on String instances that contain file or directory path information. These operations are performed in a cross-platform manner.
System.IO.TextReader	Represents a reader that can read a sequential series of characters.
System.IO.StreamReader	Implements a TextReader that reads characters from a byte stream in a particular encoding.
System.IO.TextWriter	Represents a writer that can write a sequential series of characters.
System.IO.StreamWriter	Implements a TextWriter for writing characters to a stream in a particular encoding.
System.IO.StringReader	Implements a TextReader that reads from a string.
System.IO.StringWriter	Implements a TextWriter for writing information to a string.
System.IO.Compression.Deflate Stream	Provides methods and properties used to compress and decompress streams using the Deflate algorithm.
System.IO.Compression.GZipStream	Provides methods and properties used to compress and decompress streams using the GZip algorithm.
System.IO.FileSystemWatcher	Listens to the filesystem change notifications and raises events when a directory or file in a directory changes.

Table F-7. Security

Class	Description
System.Security.Principal.WindowsIdentity	Represents a Windows user.
System.Security.Principal.WindowsPrincipal	Allows code to check the Windows group membership of a Windows user.
System.Security.Principal.WellKnownSidType	Defines a set of commonly used security identifiers (SIDs).
System.Security.Principal.WindowsBuiltInRole	Specifies common roles to be used with IsInRole.
System.Security.SecureString	Represents text that should be kept confidential. The text is encrypted for privacy when being used and deleted from computer memory when no longer needed.
System.Security.Cryptography.TripleDESCryptoServiceProvider	Defines a wrapper object to access the cryptographic service provider (CSP) version of the TripleDES algorithm.
System.Security.Cryptography.PasswordDeriveBytes	Derives a key from a password using an extension of the PBKDF1 algorithm.
System.Security.Cryptography.SHA1	Computes the SHA1 hash for the input data.
System.Security.AccessControl.FileSystemSecurity	Represents the access control and audit security for a file or directory.
System.Security.AccessControl.RegistrySecurity	Represents the Windows access control security for a registry key.

Table F-8. User interface

Class	Description
System.Windows.Forms.Form	Represents a window or dialog box that makes up an application's user interface.
System.Windows.Forms.FlowLayoutPanel	Represents a panel that dynamically lays out its contents.

Table F-9. Image manipulation

Class	Description
System.Drawing.Image	A class that provides functionality for the Bitmap and Metafile classes.
System.Drawing.Bitmap	Encapsulates a GDI+ bitmap, which consists of the pixel data for a graphics image and its attributes. A bitmap is an object used to work with images defined by pixel data.

Table F-10. Networking

Class	Description
System.Uri	Provides an object representation of a uniform resource identifier (URI) and easy access to the parts of the URI.
System.Net.NetworkCredential	Provides credentials for password-based authentication schemes such as basic, digest, Kerberos authentication, and NTLM.
System.Net.Dns	Provides simple domain name resolution functionality.
System.Net.FtpWebRequest	Implements a File Transfer Protocol (FTP) client.
System.Net.HttpWebRequest	Provides an HTTP-specific implementation of the WebRequest class.
System.Net.WebClient	Provides common methods for sending data to and receiving data from a resource identified by a URI.
System.Net.Sockets.TcpClient	Provides client connections for TCP network services.
System.Net.Mail.MailAddress	Represents the address of an electronic mail sender or recipient.
System.Net.Mail.MailMessage	Represents an email message that can be sent using the SmtpClient class.
System.Net.Mail.SmtpClient	Allows applications to send email by using the Simple Mail Transfer Protocol (SMTP).
System.IO.Ports.SerialPort	Represents a serial port resource.
System.Web.HttpUtility	Provides methods for encoding and decoding URLs when processing web requests.

Table F-11. XML

Class	Description
System.Xml.XmlTextWriter	Represents a writer that provides a fast, noncached, forward-only way of generating streams or files containing XML data that conforms to the W3C Extensible Markup Language (XML) 1.0 and the namespaces in XML recommendations.
System.Xml.XmlDocument	Represents an XML document.

Table F-12. Windows Management Instrumentation (WMI)

Class	Description
System.Management.Management Object	Represents a WMI instance.
System.Management.Management Class	Represents a management class. A management class is a WMI class such as Win32_LogicalDisk, which can represent a disk drive, or Win32_Process, which represents a process such as an instance of *Notepad.exe*. The members of this class enable you to access WMI data using a specific WMI class path. For more information, see "Win32 Classes" in the Windows Management Instrumentation documentation in the MSDN Library at *http://msdn.microsoft.com/library*.

Class	Description
System.Management.Management ObjectSearcher	Retrieves a collection of WMI management objects based on a specified query. This class is one of the more commonly used entry points to retrieving management information. For example, it can be used to enumerate all disk drives, network adapters, processes, and many more management objects on a system or to query for all network connections that are up, services that are paused, and so on. When instantiated, an instance of this class takes as input a WMI query represented in an ObjectQuery or its derivatives, and optionally a ManagementScope representing the WMI namespace to execute the query in. It can also take additional advanced options in an EnumerationOptions. When the Get method on this object is invoked, the ManagementObjectSearcher executes the given query in the specified scope and returns a collection of management objects that match the query in a ManagementObjectCollection.
System.Management.Management DateTimeConverter	Provides methods to convert DMTF datetime and time intervals to CLR-compliant DateTime and TimeSpan formats, and vice versa.
System.Management.Management EventWatcher	Subscribes to temporary event notifications based on a specified event query.

Table F-13. Active Directory

Class	Description
System.DirectoryServices. DirectorySearcher	Performs queries against Active Directory.
System.DirectoryServices. DirectoryEntry	The DirectoryEntry class encapsulates a node or object in the Active Directory hierarchy.

Table F-14. Database

Class	Description
System.Data.DataSet	Represents an in-memory cache of data.
System.Data.DataTable	Represents one table of in-memory data.
System.Data.SqlClient.SqlCommand	Represents a Transact-SQL statement or stored procedure to execute against a SQL Server database.
System.Data.SqlClient.Sql Connection	Represents an open connection to a SQL Server database.
System.Data.SqlClient.SqlData Adapter	Represents a set of data commands and a database connection that are used to fill the DataSet and update a SQL Server database.
System.Data.Odbc.OdbcCommand	Represents a SQL statement or stored procedure to execute against a data source.
System.Data.Odbc.OdbcConnection	Represents an open connection to a data source.
System.Data.Odbc.OdbcDataAdapter	Represents a set of data commands and a connection to a data source that are used to fill the DataSet and update the data source.

Table F-15. Message queuing

Class	Description
System.Messaging.MessageQueue	Provides access to a queue on a Message Queuing server.

Table F-16. Transactions

Class	Description
System.Transactions.Transaction	Represents a transaction.

WMI Reference

The Windows Management Instrumentation (WMI) facilities in Windows offer thousands of classes that provide information of interest to administrators. Table G-1 lists the categories and subcategories covered by WMI and can be used to get a general idea of the scope of WMI classes. Table G-2 provides a selected subset of the most useful WMI classes. For more information about a category, search the official WMI documentation at *http://msdn.microsoft.com*.

Table G-1. WMI class categories and subcategories

Category	Subcategory
Computer system hardware	Cooling device, input device, mass storage, motherboard, controller and port, networking device, power, printing, telephony, video, and monitor
Operating system	COM, desktop, drivers, filesystem, job objects, memory and page files, multimedia audio/visual, networking, operating system events, operating system settings, processes, registry, scheduler jobs, security, services, shares, Start menu, storage, users, Windows NT event log, Windows product activation
WMI Service Management	WMI configuration, WMI management
General	Installed applications, performance counter, security descriptor

Table G-2. Selected WMI Classes

Class	Description
Win32_BaseBoard	Represents a baseboard, which is also known as a motherboard or system board.
Win32_BIOS	Represents the attributes of the computer system's basic input/output services (BIOS) that are installed on a computer.
Win32_BootConfiguration	Represents the boot configuration of a Windows system.
Win32_CDROMDrive	Represents a CD-ROM drive on a Windows computer system. Be aware that the name of the drive does not correspond to the logical drive letter assigned to the device.

Class	Description
Win32_ComputerSystem	Represents a computer system in a Windows environment.
Win32_Processor	Represents a device that can interpret a sequence of instructions on a computer running on a Windows operating system. On a multiprocessor computer, one instance of the Win32_Processor class exists for each processor.
Win32_ComputerSystemProduct	Represents a product. This includes software and hardware used on this computer system.
CIM_DataFile	Represents a named collection of data or executable code. Currently, the provider returns files on fixed and mapped logical disks. In the future, only instances of files on local fixed disks will be returned.
Win32_DCOMApplication	Represents the properties of a DCOM application.
Win32_Desktop	Represents the common characteristics of a user's desktop. The properties of this class can be modified by the user to customize the desktop.
Win32_DesktopMonitor	Represents the type of monitor or display device attached to the computer system.
Win32_DeviceMemoryAddress	Represents a device memory address on a Windows system.
Win32_DiskDrive	Represents a physical disk drive as seen by a computer running the Windows operating system. Any interface to a Windows physical disk drive is a descendant (or member) of this class. The features of the disk drive seen through this object correspond to the logical and management characteristics of the drive. In some cases, this may not reflect the actual physical characteristics of the device. Any object based on another logical device would not be a member of this class.
Win32_DiskQuota	Tracks disk space usage for NTFS filesystem volumes. A system administrator can configure Windows to prevent further disk space use and log an event when a user exceeds a specified disk space limit. An administrator can also log an event when a user exceeds a specified disk space warning level. This class is new in Windows XP.
Win32_DMAChannel	Represents a direct memory access (DMA) channel on a Windows computer system. DMA is a method of moving data from a device to memory (or vice versa) without the help of the microprocessor. The system board uses a DMA controller to handle a fixed number of channels, each of which can be used by one (and only one) device at a time.
Win32_Environment	Represents an environment or system environment setting on a Windows computer system. Querying this class returns environment variables found in *HKLM\System\CurrentControlSet\Control\Sessionmanager\Environment* as well as *HKEY_USERS\<user sid>\Environment*.
Win32_Directory	Represents a directory entry on a Windows computer system. A *directory* is a type of file that logically groups data files and provides path information for the grouped files. Win32_Directory does not include directories of network drives.
Win32_Group	Represents data about a group account. A group account allows access privileges to be changed for a list of users (for example, Administrators).

Class	Description
Win32_IDEController	Manages the capabilities of an integrated device electronics (IDE) controller device.
Win32_IRQResource	Represents an interrupt request line (IRQ) number on a Windows computer system. An interrupt request is a signal sent to the CPU by a device or program for time-critical events. IRQ can be hardware- or software-based.
Win32_ScheduledJob	Represents a job created with the AT command. The Win32_Scheduled Job class does not represent a job created with the Scheduled Task Wizard from the Control Panel. You cannot change a task created by WMI in the Scheduled Tasks UI. Windows 2000 and Windows NT 4.0: You can use the Scheduled Tasks UI to modify the task you originally created with WMI. However, although the task is successfully modified, you can no longer access the task using WMI. Each job scheduled against the schedule service is stored persistently (the scheduler can start a job after a reboot) and is executed at the specified time and day of the week or month. If the computer is not active or if the scheduled service is not running at the specified job time, the schedule service runs the specified job on the next day at the specified time. Jobs are scheduled according to Universal Coordinated Time (UTC) with bias offset from Greenwich mean time (GMT), which means that a job can be specified using any time zone. The Win32_ScheduledJob class returns the local time with UTC offset when enumerating an object, and converts to local time when creating new jobs. For example, a job specified to run on a computer in Boston at 10:30 p.m. Monday PST will be scheduled to run locally at 1:30 a.m. Tuesday EST. Note that a client must take into account whether daylight saving time is in operation on the local computer, and if it is, then subtract a bias of 60 minutes from the UTC offset.
Win32_LoadOrderGroup	Represents a group of system services that define execution dependencies. The services must be initiated in the order specified by the Load Order Group, as the services are dependent on one another. These dependent services require the presence of the antecedent services to function correctly. The data in this class is derived by the provider from the registry key *System \CurrentControlSet\Control\ GroupOrderList*.
Win32_LogicalDisk	Represents a data source that resolves to an actual local storage device on a Windows system.
Win32_LogonSession	Describes the logon session or sessions associated with a user logged on to Windows NT or Windows 2000.
Win32_CacheMemory	Represents internal and external cache memory on a computer system.
Win32_LogicalMemoryConfiguration	Represents the layout and availability of memory on a Windows system. Beginning with Windows Vista, this class is no longer available in the operating system. Windows XP and Windows Server 2003: This class is no longer supported. Use the Win32_OperatingSystem class instead.

Class	Description
	Windows 2000: This class is available and supported.
Win32_PhysicalMemoryArray	Represents details about the computer system physical memory. This includes the number of memory devices, memory capacity available, and memory type (for example, system or video memory).
WIN32_NetworkClient	Represents a network client on a Windows system. Any computer system on the network with a client relationship to the system is a descendant (or member) of this class (for example, a computer running Windows 2000 Workstation or Windows 98 that is part of a Windows 2000 domain).
Win32_NetworkLoginProfile	Represents the network login information of a specific user on a Windows system. This includes but is not limited to password status, access privileges, disk quotas, and login directory paths.
Win32_NetworkProtocol	Represents a protocol and its network characteristics on a Win32 computer system.
Win32_NetworkConnection	Represents an active network connection in a Windows environment.
Win32_NetworkAdapter	Represents a network adapter of a computer running on a Windows operating system.
Win32_NetworkAdapter Configuration	Represents the attributes and behaviors of a network adapter. This class includes extra properties and methods that support the management of the TCP/IP and Internetworking Packet Exchange (IPX) protocols that are independent from the network adapter.
Win32_NTDomain	Represents a Windows NT domain.
Win32_NTLogEvent	Used to translate instances from the Windows NT event log. An application must have SeSecurityPrivilege to receive events from the security event log; otherwise, "Access Denied" is returned to the application.
Win32_NTEventlogFile	Represents a logical file or directory of Windows NT events. The file is also known as the event log.
Win32_OnBoardDevice	Represents common adapter devices built into the motherboard (system board).
Win32_OperatingSystem	Represents an operating system installed on a computer running on a Windows operating system. Any operating system that can be installed on a Windows system is a descendant or member of this class. Win32_Opera tingSystem is a singleton class. To get the single instance, use @ for the key.
	Windows Server 2003, Windows XP, Windows 2000, and Windows NT 4.0: If a computer has multiple operating systems installed, this class returns only an instance for the currently active operating system.
Win32_PageFileUsage	Represents the file used for handling virtual memory file swapping on a Win32 system. Information contained within objects instantiated from this class specifies the runtime state of the page file.
Win32_PageFileSetting	Represents the settings of a page file. Information contained within objects instantiated from this class specifies the page file parameters used when the file is created at system startup. The properties in this class can be

Class	Description
	modified and deferred until startup. These settings are different from the runtime state of a page file expressed through the associated class `Win32_PageFileUsage`.
`Win32_DiskPartition`	Represents the capabilities and management capacity of a partitioned area of a physical disk on a Windows system (for example, Disk #0, Partition #1).
`Win32_PortResource`	Represents an I/O port on a Windows computer system.
`Win32_PortConnector`	Represents physical connection ports, such as DB-25 pin male, Centronics, or PS/2.
`Win32_Printer`	Represents a device connected to a computer running on a Microsoft Windows operating system that can produce a printed image or text on paper or another medium.
`Win32_PrinterConfiguration`	Represents the configuration for a printer device. This includes capabilities such as resolution, color, fonts, and orientation.
`Win32_PrintJob`	Represents a print job generated by a Windows application. Any unit of work generated by the Print command of an application that is running on a computer running on a Windows operating system is a descendant or member of this class.
`Win32_Process`	Represents a process on an operating system.
`Win32_Product`	Represents products as they are installed by Windows Installer. A product generally correlates to one installation package. For information about support or requirements for installation of a specific operating system, visit *http://msdn.microsoft.com* and search for "Operating System Availability of WMI Components".
`Win32_QuickFixEngineering`	Represents system-wide Quick Fix Engineering (QFE) or updates that have been applied to the current operating system.
`Win32_QuotaSetting`	Contains setting information for disk quotas on a volume.
`Win32_OSRecoveryConfiguration`	Represents the types of information that will be gathered from memory when the operating system fails. This includes boot failures and system crashes.
`Win32_Registry`	Represents the system registry on a Windows computer system.
`Win32_SCSIController`	Represents a SCSI controller on a Windows system.
`Win32_PerfRawData_PerfNet_Server`	Provides raw data from performance counters that monitor communications using the WINS Server service.
`Win32_Service`	Represents a service on a computer running on a Microsoft Windows operating system. A service application conforms to the interface rules of the Service Control Manager (SCM), and can be started by a user automatically at system start through the Services Control Panel utility or by an application that uses the service functions included in the Windows API. Services can start when there are no users logged on to the computer.
`Win32_Share`	Represents a shared resource on a Windows system. This may be a disk drive, printer, interprocess communication, or other shareable device.

Class	Description
Win32_SoftwareElement	Represents a software element, part of a software feature (a distinct subset of a product, which may contain one or more elements). Each software element is defined in a Win32_SoftwareElement instance, and the association between a feature and its Win32_SoftwareFeature instance is defined in the Win32_SoftwareFeatureSoftware Element s association class. For information about support or requirements for installation on a specific operating system, visit *http://msdn.microsoft .com* and search for "Operating System Availability of WMI Components".
Win32_SoftwareFeature	Represents a distinct subset of a product that consists of one or more software elements. Each software element is defined in a Win32_Software Element instance, and the association between a feature and its Win32_ SoftwareFeature instance is defined in the Win32_Software FeatureSoftwareElement s association class. For information about support or requirements for installation on a specific operating system, visit *http://msdn.microsoft.com* and search for "Operating System Availability of WMI Components".
WIN32_SoundDevice	Represents the properties of a sound device on a Windows computer system.
Win32_StartupCommand	Represents a command that runs automatically when a user logs on to the computer system.
Win32_SystemAccount	Represents a system account. The system account is used by the operating system and services that run under Windows NT. There are many services and processes within Windows NT that need the capability to log on internally, for example, during a Windows NT installation. The system account was designed for that purpose.
Win32_SystemDriver	Represents the system driver for a base service.
Win32_SystemEnclosure	Represents the properties that are associated with a physical system enclosure.
Win32_SystemSlot	Represents physical connection points, including ports, motherboard slots and peripherals, and proprietary connection points.
Win32_TapeDrive	Represents a tape drive on a Windows computer. Tape drives are primarily distinguished by the fact that they can be accessed only sequentially.
Win32_TemperatureProbe	Represents the properties of a temperature sensor (e.g., electronic thermometer).
Win32_TimeZone	Represents the time zone information for a Windows system, which includes changes required for the daylight saving time transition.
Win32_UninterruptiblePowerSupply	Represents the capabilities and management capacity of an uninterruptible power supply (UPS). Beginning with Windows Vista, this class is obsolete and not available, because the UPS service is no longer available. This service worked with serially attached UPS devices, not USB devices.
	Windows Server 2003 and Windows XP: This class is available, but not usable, because the UPS service fails. Windows Server 2003, Windows XP, Windows 2000, and Windows NT 4.0: This class is available and implemented.

Class	Description
Win32_UserAccount	Contains information about a user account on a computer running on a Windows operating system. Because both the Name and Domain are key properties, enumerating Win32_UserAccount on a large network can affect performance negatively. Calling GetObject or querying for a specific instance has less impact.
Win32_VoltageProbe	Represents the properties of a voltage sensor (electronic voltmeter).
Win32_VolumeQuotaSetting	Relates disk quota settings with a specific disk volume. Windows 2000/NT: This class is not available.
Win32_WMISetting	Contains the operational parameters for the WMI service. This class can have only one instance, which always exists for each Windows system and cannot be deleted. Additional instances cannot be created.

Selected COM Objects and Their Uses

As an extensibility and administration interface, many applications expose useful functionality through COM objects. Although PowerShell handles many of these tasks directly, many COM objects still provide significant value.

Table H-1 lists a selection of the COM objects most useful to system administrators.

Table H-1. COM identifiers and descriptions

Identifier	Description
Access.Application	Allows for interaction and automation of Microsoft Access.
Agent.Control	Allows for the control of Microsoft Agent 3D animated characters.
AutoItX3.Control	(non-default) Provides access to Windows Automation via the AutoIt administration tool.
CEnroll.CEnroll	Provides access to certificate enrollment services.
CertificateAuthority.Request	Provides access to a request to a certificate authority.
COMAdmin.COMAdminCatalog	Provides access to and management of the Windows COM+ catalog.
Excel.Application	Allows for interaction and automation of Microsoft Excel.
Excel.Sheet	Allows for interaction with Microsoft Excel worksheets.
HNetCfg.FwMgr	Provides access to the management functionality of the Windows Firewall.
HNetCfg.HNetShare	Provides access to the management functionality of Windows Connection Sharing.
HTMLFile	Allows for interaction and authoring of a new Internet Explorer document.
InfoPath.Application	Allows for interaction and automation of Microsoft InfoPath.
InternetExplorer.Application	Allows for interaction and automation of Microsoft Internet Explorer.
IXSSO.Query	Allows for interaction with Microsoft Index Server.
IXSSO.Util	Provides access to utilities used along with the IXSSO.Query object.
LegitCheckControl.LegitCheck	Provide access to information about Windows Genuine Advantage status on the current computer.
MakeCab.MakeCab	Provides functionality to create and manage cabinet (*.cab*) files.

Identifier	Description
MAPI.Session	Provides access to a Messaging Application Programming Interface (MAPI) session, such as folders, messages, and the address book.
Messenger.MessengerApp	Allows for interaction and automation of Messenger.
Microsoft.FeedsManager	Allows for interaction with the Microsoft RSS feed platform.
Microsoft.ISAdm	Provides management of Microsoft Index Server.
Microsoft.Update.AutoUpdate	Provides management of the auto update schedule for Microsoft Update.
Microsoft.Update.Installer	Allows for installation of updates from Microsoft Update.
Microsoft.Update.Searcher	Provides search functionality for updates from Microsoft Update.
Microsoft.Update.Session	Provides access to local information about Microsoft Update history.
Microsoft.Update.SystemInfo	Provides access to information related to Microsoft Update for the current system.
MMC20.Application	Allows for interaction and automation of Microsoft Management Console (MMC).
MSScriptControl.ScriptControl	Allows for the evaluation and control of WSH scripts.
Msxml2.XSLTemplate	Allows for processing of XSL transforms.
Outlook.Application	Allows for interaction and automation of your email, calendar, contacts, tasks, and more through Microsoft Outlook.
OutlookExpress.MessageList	Allows for interaction and automation of your email through Microsoft Outlook Express.
PowerPoint.Application	Allows for interaction and automation of Microsoft PowerPoint.
Publisher.Application	Allows for interaction and automation of Microsoft Publisher.
RDS.DataSpace	Provides access to proxies of Remote DataSpace business objects.
SAPI.SpVoice	Provides access to the Microsoft Speech API.
Scripting.FileSystemObject	Provides access to the computer's filesystem. Most functionality is available more directly through PowerShell or through PowerShell's support for the .NET Framework.
Scripting.Signer	Provides management of digital signatures on WSH files.
Scriptlet.TypeLib	Allows the dynamic creation of scripting type library (*.tlb*) files.
ScriptPW.Password	Allows for the masked input of plain-text passwords. When possible, you should avoid this, preferring the Read-Host cmdlet with the -AsSecureString parameter.
SharePoint.OpenDocuments	Allows for interaction with Microsoft SharePoint Services.
Shell.Application	Provides access to aspects of the Windows Explorer Shell application, such as managing windows, files and folders, and the current session.
Shell.LocalMachine	Provides access to information about the current machine related to the Windows shell.
Shell.User	Provides access to aspects of the current user's Windows session and profile.
SQLDMO.SQLServer	Provides access to the management functionality of Microsoft SQL Server.
Vim.Application	(non-default) Allows for interaction and automation of the VIM editor.

Identifier	Description
WIA.CommonDialog	Provides access to image capture through the Windows Image Acquisition facilities.
WMPlayer.OCX	Allows for interaction and automation of Windows Media Player.
Word.Application	Allows for interaction and automation of Microsoft Word.
Word.Document	Allows for interaction with Microsoft Word documents.
WScript.Network	Provides access to aspects of a networked Windows environment, such as printers and network drives, as well as computer and domain information.
WScript.Shell	Provides access to aspects of the Windows Shell, such as applications, shortcuts, environment variables, the registry, and the operating environment.
WSHController	Allows the execution of WSH scripts on remote computers.

Selected Events and Their Uses

PowerShell's eventing commands give you access to events from the .NET Framework, as well as events surfaced by Windows Management Instrumentation (WMI). Table I-1 lists a selection of .NET events. Table I-2 lists a selection of WMI events.

Table I-1. Selected .NET events

Type	Event	Description
System.AppDomain	AssemblyLoad	Occurs when an assembly is loaded.
System.AppDomain	TypeResolve	Occurs when the resolution of a type fails.
System.AppDomain	ResourceResolve	Occurs when the resolution of a resource fails because the resource is not a valid linked or embedded resource in the assembly.
System.AppDomain	AssemblyResolve	Occurs when the resolution of an assembly fails.
System.AppDomain	ReflectionOnlyAssemblyResolve	Occurs when the resolution of an assembly fails in the reflection-only context.
System.AppDomain	UnhandledException	Occurs when an exception is not caught.
System.Console	CancelKeyPress	Occurs when the Control modifier key (CTRL) and C console key (C) are pressed simultaneously (CTRL-C).
Microsoft.Win32.SystemEvents	DisplaySettingsChanging	Occurs when the display settings are changing.
Microsoft.Win32.SystemEvents	DisplaySettingsChanged	Occurs when the user changes the display settings.
Microsoft.Win32.SystemEvents	InstalledFontsChanged	Occurs when the user adds fonts to or removes fonts from the system.
Microsoft.Win32.SystemEvents	LowMemory	Occurs when the system is running out of available RAM.

Type	Event	Description
Microsoft.Win32.System Events	PaletteChanged	Occurs when the user switches to an application that uses a different palette.
Microsoft.Win32.System Events	PowerModeChanged	Occurs when the user suspends or resumes the system.
Microsoft.Win32.System Events	SessionEnded	Occurs when the user is logging off or shutting down the system.
Microsoft.Win32.System Events	SessionEnding	Occurs when the user is trying to log off or shut down the system.
Microsoft.Win32.System Events	SessionSwitch	Occurs when the currently logged-in user has changed.
Microsoft.Win32.System Events	TimeChanged	Occurs when the user changes the time on the system clock.
Microsoft.Win32.System Events	UserPreferenceChanged	Occurs when a user preference has changed.
Microsoft.Win32.System Events	UserPreferenceChanging	Occurs when a user preference is changing.
System.Net.WebClient	OpenReadCompleted	Occurs when an asynchronous operation to open a stream containing a resource completes.
System.Net.WebClient	OpenWriteCompleted	Occurs when an asynchronous operation to open a stream to write data to a resource completes.
System.Net.WebClient	DownloadStringCompleted	Occurs when an asynchronous resource-download operation completes.
System.Net.WebClient	DownloadDataCompleted	Occurs when an asynchronous data download operation completes.
System.Net.WebClient	DownloadFileCompleted	Occurs when an asynchronous file download operation completes.
System.Net.WebClient	UploadStringCompleted	Occurs when an asynchronous string-upload operation completes.
System.Net.WebClient	UploadDataCompleted	Occurs when an asynchronous data-upload operation completes.
System.Net.WebClient	UploadFileCompleted	Occurs when an asynchronous file-upload operation completes.
System.Net.WebClient	UploadValuesCompleted	Occurs when an asynchronous upload of a name/value collection completes.
System.Net.WebClient	DownloadProgressChanged	Occurs when an asynchronous download operation successfully transfers some or all of the data.

Type	Event	Description
System.Net.WebClient	UploadProgressChanged	Occurs when an asynchronous upload operation successfully transfers some or all of the data.
System.Net.Sockets.Socket AsyncEventArgs	Completed	The event used to complete an asynchronous operation.
System.Net.Network Information.NetworkChange	NetworkAvailabilityChanged	Occurs when the availability of the network changes.
System.Net.Network Information.NetworkChange	NetworkAddressChanged	Occurs when the IP address of a network interface changes.
System.IO.FileSystem Watcher	Changed	Occurs when a file or directory in the specified path is changed.
System.IO.FileSystem Watcher	Created	Occurs when a file or directory in the specified path is created.
System.IO.FileSystem Watcher	Deleted	Occurs when a file or directory in the specified path is deleted.
System.IO.FileSystem Watcher	Renamed	Occurs when a file or directory in the specified path is renamed.
System.Timers.Timer	Elapsed	Occurs when the interval elapses.
System.Diagnostics. EventLog	EntryWritten	Occurs when an entry is written to an event log on the local computer.
System.Diagnostics.Process	OutputDataReceived	Occurs when an application writes to its redirected StandardOutput stream.
System.Diagnostics.Process	ErrorDataReceived	Occurs when an application writes to its redirected StandardError stream.
System.Diagnostics.Process	Exited	Occurs when a process exits.
System.IO.Ports.SerialPort	ErrorReceived	Represents the method that handles the error event of a SerialPort object.
System.IO.Ports.SerialPort	PinChanged	Represents the method that will handle the serial pin changed event of a SerialPort object.
System.IO.Ports.SerialPort	DataReceived	Represents the method that will handle the data received event of a SerialPort object.
System.Management. Automation.Job	StateChanged	Event fired when the status of the job changes, such as when the job has completed in all runspaces or failed in any one runspace. This event is introduced in Windows PowerShell 2.0.
System.Management. Automation.Debugger	DebuggerStop	Event raised when Windows PowerShell stops execution of the script and enters the debugger as the result of

Type	Event	Description
		encountering a breakpoint or executing a step command. This event is introduced in Windows PowerShell 2.0.
System.Management. Automation.Debugger	BreakpointUpdated	Event raised when the breakpoint is updated, such as when it is enabled or disabled. This event is introduced in Windows PowerShell 2.0.
System.Management. Automation.Runspaces. Runspace	StateChanged	Event that is raised when the state of the runspace changes.
System.Management. Automation.Runspaces. Runspace	AvailabilityChanged	Event that is raised when the availability of the runspace changes, such as when the runspace becomes available and when it is busy. This event is introduced in Windows PowerShell 2.0.
System.Management. Automation.Runspaces. Pipeline	StateChanged	Event raised when the state of the pipeline changes.
System.Management. Automation.PowerShell	InvocationStateChanged	Event raised when the state of the pipeline of the PowerShell object changes. This event is introduced in Windows PowerShell 2.0.
System.Management. Automation. PSDataCollection[T]	DataAdded	Event that is fired after data is added to the collection. This event is introduced in Windows PowerShell 2.0.
System.Management. Automation. PSDataCollection[T]	Completed	Event that is fired when the Complete method is called to indicate that no more data is to be added to the collection. This event is introduced in Windows PowerShell 2.0.
System.Management. Automation.Runspaces. RunspacePool	StateChanged	Event raised when the state of the runspace pool changes. This event is introduced in Windows PowerShell 2.0.
System.Management. Automation.Runspaces. PipelineReader[T]	DataReady	Event fired when data is added to the buffer.
System.Diagnostics. Eventing.Reader. EventLogWatcher	EventRecordWritten	Allows setting a delegate (event handler method) that gets called every time an event is published that matches the criteria specified in the event query for this object.
System.Data.Common. DbConnection	StateChange	Occurs when the state of the event changes.

Type	Event	Description
System.Data.SqlClient.SqlBulkCopy	SqlRowsCopied	Occurs every time that the number of rows specified by the NotifyAfter property have been processed.
System.Data.SqlClient.SqlCommand	StatementCompleted	Occurs when the execution of a Transact-SQL statement completes.
System.Data.SqlClient.SqlConnection	InfoMessage	Occurs when SQL Server returns a warning or informational message.
System.Data.SqlClient.SqlConnection	StateChange	Occurs when the state of the event changes.
System.Data.SqlClient.SqlDataAdapter	RowUpdated	Occurs during Update after a command is executed against the data source. The attempt to update is made, so the event fires.
System.Data.SqlClient.SqlDataAdapter	RowUpdating	Occurs during Update before a command is executed against the data source. The attempt to update is made, so the event fires.
System.Data.SqlClient.SqlDataAdapter	FillError	Returned when an error occurs during a fill operation.
System.Data.SqlClient.SqlDependency	OnChange	Occurs when a notification is received for any of the commands associated with this SqlDependency object.

Table I-2. Selected WMI Events

Event	Description
__InstanceCreationEvent	This event class generically represents the creation of instances in WMI providers, such as Processes, Services, Files, and more.
	A registration for this generic event looks like:
| | ```
$query = "SELECT * FROM __InstanceCreationEvent " +
          "WITHIN 5 " +
          "WHERE targetinstance isa 'Win32_UserAccount'
Register-WmiEvent -Query $query
``` |
| __InstanceDeletionEvent | This event class generically represents the removal of instances in WMI providers, such as Processes, Services, Files, and more. |
| | A registration for this generic event looks like: |
| | ```
$query = "SELECT * FROM __InstanceDeletionEvent " +
          "WITHIN 5 " +
          "WHERE targetinstance isa 'Win32_UserAccount'
Register-WmiEvent -Query $query
``` |
| __InstanceModificationEvent | This event class generically represents the modification of instances in WMI providers, such as Processes, Services, Files, and more. |
| | A registration for this generic event looks like: |

Event	Description

	``
	$query = "SELECT * FROM __InstanceModificationEvent " +
	                "WITHIN 5 " +
	                "WHERE targetinstance isa 'Win32_UserAccount'
	Register-WmiEvent -Query $query
	``

Msft_WmiProvider_OperationEvent	The Msft_WmiProvider_OperationEvent event class is the root definition of all WMI provider events. A provider operation is defined as some execution on behalf of a client via WMI that results in one or more calls to a provider executable. The properties of this class define the identity of the provider associated with the operation being executed and is uniquely associated with instances of the class Msft_Providers. Internally, WMI can contain any number of objects that refer to a particular instance of __Win32Provider since it differentiates each object based on whether the provider supports per user or per locale instantiation and also depending on where the provider is being hosted. Currently TransactionIdentifier is always an empty string.
Win32_ComputerSystemEvent	This event class represents events related to a computer system.
Win32_ComputerShutdownEvent	This event class represents events when a computer has begun the process of shutting down.
Win32_IP4RouteTableEvent	The Win32_IP4RouteTableEvent class represents IP route change events resulting from the addition, removal, or modification of IP routes on the computer system.
RegistryEvent	The registry event classes allow you to subscribe to events that involve changes in hive subtrees, keys, and specific values.
RegistryKeyChangeEvent	The RegistryKeyChangeEvent class represents changes to a specific key. The changes apply only to the key, not its subkeys.
RegistryTreeChangeEvent	The RegistryTreeChangeEvent class represents changes to a key and its subkeys.
RegistryValueChangeEvent	The RegistryValueChangeEvent class represents changes to a single value of a specific key.
Win32_SystemTrace	The SystemTrace class is the base class for all system trace events. System trace events are fired by the kernel logger via the event tracing API.
Win32_ProcessTrace	This event is the base event for process events.
Win32_ProcessStartTrace	The ProcessStartTrace event class indicates a new process has started.
Win32_ProcessStopTrace	The ProcessStopTrace event class indicates a process has terminated.
Win32_ModuleTrace	The ModuleTrace event class is the base event for module events.
Win32_ModuleLoadTrace	The ModuleLoadTrace event class indicates a process has loaded a new module.
Win32_ThreadTrace	The ThreadTrace event class is the base event for thread events.
Win32_ThreadStartTrace	The ThreadStartTrace event class indicates a new thread has started.
Win32_ThreadStopTrace	The ThreadStopTrace event class indicates a thread has terminated.
Win32_PowerManagementEvent	The Win32_PowerManagementEvent class represents power management events resulting from power state changes. These state changes

Event	Description
	are associated with either the Advanced Power Management (APM) or the Advanced Configuration and Power Interface (ACPI) system management protocols.
Win32_DeviceChangeEvent	The Win32_DeviceChangeEvent class represents device change events resulting from the addition, removal, or modification of devices on the computer system. This includes changes in the hardware configuration (docking and undocking), the hardware state, or newly mapped devices (mapping of a network drive). For example, a device has changed when a WM_DEVICECHANGE message is sent.
Win32_SystemConfiguration ChangeEvent	The Win32_SystemConfigurationChangeEvent is an event class that indicates the device list on the system has been refreshed, meaning a device has been added or removed or the configuration changed. This event is fired when the Windows message 'DevMgrRefreshOn<ComputerName>' is sent. The exact change to the device list is not contained in the message, and therefore a device refresh is required in order to obtain the current system settings. Examples of configuration changes affected are IRQ settings, COM ports, and BIOS version, to name a few.
Win32_VolumeChangeEvent	The Win32_VolumeChangeEvent class represents a local drive event resulting from the addition of a drive letter or mounted drive on the computer system (e.g., CD-ROM). Network drives are not currently supported.

Standard PowerShell Verbs

Cmdlets and scripts should be named using a *Verb-Noun* syntax, for example, `Get-ChildItem`. The official guidance is that, with rare exception, cmdlets should use the standard PowerShell verbs. They should avoid any synonyms or concepts that can be mapped to the standard. This allows administrators to quickly understand a set of cmdlets that use a new noun.

To quickly access this list (without the definitions), type **Get-Verb**.

Verbs should be phrased in the present tense, and nouns should be singular. Tables J-1 through J-6 list the different categories of standard PowerShell verbs.

Table J-1. Standard Windows PowerShell common verbs

Verb	Meaning	Synonyms
Add	Adds a resource to a container or attaches an element to another element	Append, Attach, Concatenate, Insert
Clear	Removes all elements from a container	Flush, Erase, Release, Unmark, Unset, Nullify
Close	Removes access to a resource	Shut, Seal
Copy	Copies a resource to another name or container	Duplicate, Clone, Replicate
Enter	Sets a resource as a context	Push, Telnet, Open
Exit	Returns to the context that was present before a new context was entered	Pop, Disconnect
Find	Searches within an unknown context for a desired item	Dig, Discover
Format	Converts an item to a specified structure or layout	Layout, Arrange

Verb	Meaning	Synonyms
Get	Retrieves data	Read, Open, Cat, Type, Dir, Obtain, Dump, Acquire, Examine, Find, Search
Hide	Makes a display not visible	Suppress
Join	Joins a resource	Combine, Unite, Connect, Associate
Lock	Locks a resource	Restrict, Bar
Move	Moves a resource	Transfer, Name, Migrate
New	Creates a new resource	Create, Generate, Build, Make, Allocate
Open	Enables access to a resource	Release, Unseal
Pop	Removes an item from the top of a stack	Remove, Paste
Push	Puts an item onto the top of a stack	Put, Add, Copy
Redo	Repeats an action or reverts the action of an Undo	Repeat, Retry, Revert
Remove	Removes a resource from a container	Delete, Kill
Rename	Gives a resource a new name	Ren, Swap
Reset	Restores a resource to a predefined or original state	Restore, Revert
Select	Creates a subset of data from a larger data set	Pick, Grep, Filter
Search	Finds a resource (or summary information about that resource) in a collection (does not actually retrieve the resource but provides information to be used when retrieving it)	Find, Get, Grep, Select
Set	Places data	Write, Assign, Configure
Show	Retrieves, formats, and displays information	Display, Report
Skip	Bypasses an element in a seek or navigation	Bypass, Jump
Split	Separates data into smaller elements	Divide, Chop, Parse
Step	Moves a process or navigation forward by one unit	Next, Iterate
Switch	Alternates the state of a resource between different alternatives or options	Toggle, Alter, Flip
Unlock	Unlocks a resource	Free, Unrestrict
Use	Applies or associates a resource with a context	With, Having
Watch	Continually monitors an item	Monitor, Poll

Table J-2. Standard Windows PowerShell communication verbs

Verb	Meaning	Synonyms
Connect	Connects a source to a destination	Join, Telnet
Disconnect	Disconnects a source from a destination	Break, Logoff
Read	Acquires information from a nonconnected source	Prompt, Get

Verb	Meaning	Synonyms
Receive	Acquires information from a connected source	Read, Accept, Peek
Send	Writes information to a connected destination	Put, Broadcast, Mail
Write	Writes information to a nonconnected destination	Puts, Print

Table J-3. Standard Windows PowerShell data verbs

Verb	Meaning	Synonyms
Backup	Backs up data	Save, Burn
Checkpoint	Creates a snapshot of the current state of data or its configuration	Diff, StartTransaction
Compare	Compares a resource with another resource	Diff, Bc
Compress	Reduces the size or resource usage of an item	Zip, Squeeze, Archive
Convert	Changes from one representation to another when the cmdlet supports bidirectional conversion or conversion of many data types	Change, Resize, Resample
ConvertFrom	Converts from one primary input to several supported outputs	Export, Output, Out
ConvertTo	Converts from several supported inputs to one primary output	Import, Input, In
Dismount	Detaches a name entity from a location in a namespace	Dismount, Unlink
Edit	Modifies an item in-place	Change, Modify, Alter
Expand	Increases the size or resource usage of an item	Extract, Unzip
Export	Stores the primary input resource into a backing store or interchange format	Extract, Backup
Group	Combines an item with other related items	Merge, Combine, Map
Import	Creates a primary output resource from a backing store or interchange format	Load, Read
Initialize	Prepares a resource for use and initializes it to a default state	Setup, Renew, Rebuild
Limit	Applies constraints to a resource	Quota, Enforce
Merge	Creates a single data instance from multiple data sets	Combine, Join
Mount	Attaches a named entity to a location in a namespace	Attach, Link
Out	Sends data to a terminal location	Print, Format, Send
Publish	Make a resource known or visible to others	Deploy, Release, Install
Restore	Restores a resource to a set of conditions that have been predefined or set by a checkpoint	Repair, Return, Fix
Save	Stores pending changes to a recoverable store	Write, Retain, Submit
Sync	Synchronizes two resources with each other	Push, Update
Unpublish	Removes a resource from public visibility	Uninstall, Revert
Update	Updates or refreshes a resource	Refresh, Renew, Index

Table J-4. Standard Windows PowerShell diagnostic verbs

Verb	Meaning	Synonyms
Debug	Examines a resource, diagnoses operational problems	Attach, Diagnose
Measure	Identifies resources consumed by an operation or retrieves statistics about a resource	Calculate, Determine, Analyze
Ping	Determines whether a resource is active and responsive (in most instances, this should be replaced by the verb Test)	Connect, Debug
Repair	Recovers an item from a damaged or broken state	Fix, Recover, Rebuild
Resolve	Maps a shorthand representation to a more complete one	Expand, Determine
Test	Verify the validity or consistency of a resource	Diagnose, Verify, Analyze
Trace	Follow the activities of the resource	Inspect, Dig

Table J-5. Standard Windows PowerShell life cycle verbs

Verb	Meaning	Synonyms
Approve	Gives approval or permission for an item or resource	Allow, Let
Assert	Declares the state of an item or fact	Verify, Check
Complete	Finalizes a pending operation	Finalize, End
Confirm	Approves or acknowledges a resource or process	Check, Validate
Deny	Disapproves or disallows a resource or process	Fail, Halt
Disable	Configures an item to be unavailable	Halt, Hide
Enable	Configures an item to be available	Allow, Permit
Install	Places a resource in the specified location and optionally initializes it	Setup, Configure
Invoke	Calls or launches an activity that cannot be stopped	Run, Call, Perform
Register	Adds an item to a monitored or publishing resource	Record, Submit, Journal, Subscribe
Request	Submits for consideration or approval	Ask, Query
Restart	Stops an operation and starts it again	Recycle, Hup
Resume	Begins an operation after it has been suspended	Continue
Start	Begins an activity	Launch, Initiate
Stop	Discontinues an activity	Halt, End, Discontinue
Submit	Adds to a list of pending actions or sends for approval	Send, Post
Suspend	Pauses an operation, but does not discontinue it	Pause, Sleep, Break
Uninstall	Removes a resource from the specified location	Remove, Clear, Clean
Unregister	Removes an item from a monitored or publishing resource	Unsubscribe, Erase, Remove
Wait	Pauses until an expected event occurs	Sleep, Pause, Join

Table J-6. Standard Windows PowerShell security verbs

Verb	Meaning	Synonyms
Block	Restricts access to a resource	Prevent, Limit, Deny
Grant	Grants access to a resource	Allow, Enable
Protect	Limits access to a resource	Encrypt, Seal
Revoke	Removes access to a resource	Remove, Disable
Unblock	Removes a restriction of access to a resource	Clear, Allow
Unprotect	Removes restrictions from a protected resource	Decrypt, Decode

Index

Symbols

\# (single-line) comment, 716
\$ (variable name), 8, 94
\$( ) expression subparse, 715
\$? ("dollar hook") Boolean variable, 382
\$args array, 750
\$_ current character, 153
\$_ current object variable, 9
% (modulus) operator, 726
%= (modulus assignment) operator, 726
& (invoke) operator, 20, 261, 710
( ) precedence control, 715
* (multiplication) operator, 726
*= (multiplication assignment) operator, 726
+ (addition) operator, 725
+ (array range) separator, 723
+= (addition assignment) operator, 726
, (unary comma) operator, 116, 186
- (subtraction) operator, 725
-= (subtraction assignment) operator, 726
/ (division) operator, 726
/= (division assignment) operator, 726
0x (hexadecimal) prefix, 720
<# #> (multiline) comment, 716
@ (array cast) syntax, 721
@" "@ here string, 143, 719
@( ) list evaluation, 715
[ ] strongly typed variable or array, 717, 721
` (backtick) escape character, 144, 719
{ } script block, 64
| (pipeline character) pass output, 9

A

Abs() method, 173

accelerator key, 337
Accept script block parameters with local variables, 284
Access a .NET SDK library, 436
Access and manage your console history, 46
Access and scope, control, 100
Access arguments of a script, function, or script block, 276
Access elements of an array, 186
Access environment variables, 95
Access event logs of a remote machine, 565
Access features of the host's user interface, 350
Access information about your command's invocation, 401
Access information in an XML file, 237
Access pipeline input, 295
Access user and machine certificates, 467
Access Windows API functions, 422
Access Windows Management Instrumentation data, 635
Access Windows performance counters, 419
Access, full network, 676
ACL misconfiguration, getting, 506
ACL of a file or directory, set, 508
ACL of a registry key, get, 529
ACL of a registry key, set, 530
ACL of file or directory, get, 506
Active Directory
    computer accounts, 603–605
    containers, 588
    importing users in bulk, 590
    organizational units (OUs), 585–588, 602
    security/distribution groups, 595–602
    Service Interface (ADSI), 13, 581, 583

We'd like to hear your suggestions for improving our indexes. Send email to *index@oreilly.com*.

Z

About the Author

Lee Holmes is a developer on the Microsoft Windows PowerShell team, and he has been an authoritative source of information about PowerShell since its earliest betas. His vast experience with Windows PowerShell lets him integrate both the "how" and the "why" into discussions. Lee's involvement with the PowerShell and administration community (via newsgroups, mailing lists, and blogs) gives him a great deal of insight into the problems faced by all levels of administrators and PowerShell users alike.

Colophon

The animal on the cover of *Windows PowerShell Cookbook*, Second Edition, is a box turtle (*Terrapene carolina carolina*). This box turtle is native to North America, specifically northern parts of the United States and Mexico. The male turtle averages about six inches long and has red eyes; the female is a bit smaller and has yellow eyes. This turtle is omnivorous as a youth but largely herbivorous as an adult. It has a domed shell that is hinged on the bottom and which snaps tightly shut if the turtle is in danger. Box turtles usually stay within the area in which they were born, rarely leaving a 750 foot radius. When mating, male turtles sometimes shove and push one another to win a female's attention. During copulation, it is possible for the male turtle to fall backward, be unable to right himself, and starve to death.

Although box turtles can live for more than 100 years, their habitats are seriously threatened by land development and roads. Turtles need loose, moist soil in which to lay eggs and burrow during their long hibernation season. Experts strongly discourage taking turtles from their native habitats—not only will it disrupt the community's breeding opportunities, but turtles become extremely stressed outside of their known habitats and may perish quickly.

The cover image is from *Dover Pictorial Images*. The cover font is Adobe ITC Garamond. The text font is Linotype Birka; the heading font is Adobe Myriad Condensed; and the code font is LucasFont's TheSansMonoCondensed.

CPSIA information can be obtained at www.ICGtesting.com
Printed in the USA
BVOW061539301111

277288BV00007B/7/P